Early Analytic Philosophy

ALSO AVAILABLE FROM BLOOMSBURY

Ontology and Metaontology, by Francesco Berto and Matteo Plabani
The Bloomsbury Companion to Analytic Philosophy, by Barry Dainton
The History and Philosophy of Science: A Reader, edited by
Daniel J. McKaughan and Holly VandeWall
The Philosophies of America Reader, edited by
Kim Díaz and Mathew A. Foust

Early Analytic Philosophy

An Inclusive Reader with Commentary

Edited by
Kevin Morris and
Consuelo Preti

BLOOMSBURY ACADEMIC
LONDON • NEW YORK • OXFORD • NEW DELHI • SYDNEY

BLOOMSBURY ACADEMIC
Bloomsbury Publishing Plc
50 Bedford Square, London, WC1B 3DP, UK
1385 Broadway, New York, NY 10018, USA
29 Earlsfort Terrace, Dublin 2, Ireland

BLOOMSBURY, BLOOMSBURY ACADEMIC and the Diana logo are trademarks
of Bloomsbury Publishing Plc

First published in Great Britain 2023

Copyright © Kevin Morris and Consuelo Preti, 2023

Kevin Morris and Consuelo Preti have asserted their right under the Copyright,
Designs and Patents Act, 1988, to be identified as Editors of this work.

For legal purposes the Acknowledgements on p. xiii constitute an extension of
this copyright page.

Cover design by Louise Dugdale
Cover image © Richard Horvath/Unsplash

All rights reserved. No part of this publication may be reproduced or transmitted in
any form or by any means, electronic or mechanical, including photocopying,
recording, or any information storage or retrieval system, without prior
permission in writing from the publishers.

Bloomsbury Publishing Plc does not have any control over, or responsibility for,
any third-party websites referred to or in this book. All internet addresses given
in this book were correct at the time of going to press. The author and publisher
regret any inconvenience caused if addresses have changed or sites have ceased
to exist, but can accept no responsibility for any such changes.

A catalogue record for this book is available from the British Library.

A catalog record for this book is available from the Library of Congress.

ISBN: HB: 978-1-3503-2358-2
PB: 978-1-3503-2359-9
ePDF: 978-1-3503-2360-5
eBook: 978-1-3503-2361-2

Typeset by RefineCatch Limited, Bungay, Suffolk
Printed and bound in Great Britain

To find out more about our authors and books visit www.bloomsbury.com
and sign up for our newsletters.

Contents

Preface ix
  How to use *Early Analytic Philosophy* ix
  Comments on the text x
  Acknowledgments xiii

1 Introducing Analytic Philosophy 1

Analytic philosophy: Themes and ideas 1
Further reading 7

2 F. H. Bradley and Monistic Idealism 9

Background and commentary
  Background 9
  Monistic idealism 11
  Critique of relations 11
  Appearance and reality 16
  Concluding remarks 18
  Further reading 19
Readings
  Appearance and Reality (selections from Chs 1–3, 12–14) 20

3 G. E. Moore on Idealism, the Good, and Common Sense 49

Background and commentary
  Background 50
  Critique of monistic idealism 51
  Goodness and the naturalistic fallacy 55
  Common sense and philosophy 56
  Concluding remarks 60
  Further reading 61

vi   **Contents**

Readings
"The Refutation of Idealism" 62
Principia Ethica, Chapter 1 80
"A Defence of Common Sense" 107
"Proof of an External World" 131

4 Gottlob Frege: Logic and the Philosophy of Language 151

Background and commentary
Background 151
Logic and logicism 153
Sinn, Bedeutung, and thoughts 158
Concluding remarks 163
Further reading 164
Readings
"On Sinn and Bedeutung" 165
"The Thought" 185

5 Bertrand Russell on Relations, Descriptions, and Knowledge 207

Background and commentary
Background 208
Monism and relations 210
Names and descriptions 213
Analysis, sense-data, and scientific philosophy 217
Concluding remarks 220
Further reading 221
Readings
Russell on Monism and Relations (selections from *The Principles of Mathematics* and *Our Knowledge of the External World*) 222
"On Denoting" 250
"Knowledge by Acquaintance and Knowledge by Description" 263

6 E. E. Constance Jones on Language and Logic 279

Background and commentary

Contents   vii

Background 279
Developments in logic 280
Jones and Russell: The 1910–11 debate 284
Concluding remarks 289
Further reading 290

Readings
"Mr. Russell's Objections to Frege's Analysis of Propositions" 291
"A New Law of Thought" 300

7   Ludwig Wittgenstein on Language and Philosophy 317

Background and commentary
Background 317
Language, reality, and philosophy in the *Tractatus* 320
After the *Tractatus* 328
Concluding remarks 330
Further reading 331

Readings
Tractatus Logico-Philosophicus (selections) 332

8   Logical Empiricism: Meaning, Metaphysics, and Mathematics 361

Background and commentary
Background 362
Meaning, verification, and the critique of metaphysics 363
Ethical discourse 371
Philosophy of mathematics and logic 373
Concluding remarks 375
Further reading 376

Readings
Schlick, "Meaning and Verification" 377
Carnap, "The Elimination of Metaphysics ..." 402
Ayer, *Language, Truth, and Logic* (selections from Chs 4, 6) 421

viii   Contents

9 Susan Stebbing on Logic, Language, and Analysis 451

Background and commentary
Background 452
Logic and language 454
Language and science 456
Empiricism and analysis 459
Concluding remarks 460
Further reading 460
Readings
A Modern Introduction to Logic (selections from Chs 1, 24) 462
Philosophy and the Physicists (selections from Ch. 3) 481
"Logical Positivism and Analysis" 495

10 W. V. O. Quine on Analyticity and Ontology 521

Background and Commentary
Background 521
Analyticity rejected 523
Ontological commitment 527
Concluding remarks 531
Further reading 532
Readings
"On What There Is" 533
"Two Dogmas of Empiricism" 547

11 Analytic Philosophy Since 1950 569

References 577
Index 585

Preface

How to use *Early Analytic Philosophy*

Contemporary philosophy cannot be properly understood without taking into account the ideas and arguments at the origins of the analytic tradition. Although there is scholarly controversy concerning just what counts as analytic philosophy, its historical origins are relatively well-established in the work of thinkers like Frege, Moore, and Russell, and the context of their ideas. We believe that students should be exposed to this material as part of an undergraduate education in philosophy. On the other hand, much of the work during this period is quite challenging. For example, Moore's dense discussions in "The Refutation of Idealism" and Russell's presentation of the theory of descriptions in "On Denoting" can be challenging for even seasoned scholars. It suffices to say that students need some guidance in grappling with this material.

Early Analytic Philosophy: An Inclusive Reader with Commentary aims to make this central philosophical field more accessible for the student of philosophy. After discussing some main themes in the analytic tradition in Chapter 1, each of the next nine chapters includes readings from a particular thinker or movement in early analytic philosophy. In each case, we provide detailed background information, along with discussion of some of the main ideas in the readings provided and recommendations for further reading. In these "Background and commentary" sections, we have also aimed to draw as many connections between the chapters as possible, given the somewhat diverse topics addressed in the readings. These commentaries are intended to be read along with the readings provided. Students may wish to read the commentaries first, then read the source material, and then return to the commentaries after reading the source material, though other pedagogical strategies are of course available. The final chapter sketches some themes and ideas in analytic philosophy since around 1950 and provides suggestions for further reading. An entire course in early analytic

x   Preface

philosophy can be constructed from the readings provided in this collection, though it is unlikely that all of the readings can be covered in a single semester. We leave it to instructors to choose exactly which readings to include in a course.

The list of references at the end of the book includes those works mentioned or referred to in the "Background and commentary" sections. Although Chapters 2 through 10 each include a list of further reading (in Chapter 11, further readings are in effect included in the main text), these are not typically included in the list of references at the end of the book. Some entries, however, do appear both as recommendations for further reading and are also mentioned or referred to in a "Background and commentary" section, and thus are also included in the list of references at the end of the book. In the "Background and commentary" sections, page references are to the original texts, not to the page numbers of the texts as they appear in the "Readings" sections of this book. Likewise, references and footnotes in the readings have been left as they appeared in the original texts from which the readings were pulled. While this is perhaps imperfect, and may require some work on the part of the reader to track down the references, we do not know of a better strategy aside, perhaps, from removing such references (along with the corresponding footnotes) altogether (in a few places, we have indeed chosen to remove footnotes and any references included in them).

We cite many texts both by original publication date and the volume from which we pulled the reading, if these are different. In both the "Further reading" sections and the list of references at the end of the book, we have distinguished primary from secondary sources. We classify texts as primary or secondary largely based on whether they are cited mainly as stand-alone original works or whether, on the other hand, they are cited mainly as commentary on some other text. This is why, for example, while most of Russell's works are included as primary sources, some are included as secondary sources—in the latter case, because they are mentioned or cited mainly as commentary on some other text or author.

Comments on the text

The readings in Chapters 2 through 10 focus on the development of analytic philosophy from about 1890 to 1950. We are aware that it is impossible to choose readings from this period that will please everyone. Here we will say a few things about our choice of readings and why we have included certain figures and readings rather than others.

First and foremost, this text is intended as a resource and teaching aid for undergraduate students without much previous experience with early analytic philosophy. It is because of this that we have chosen seminal work from, for instance, Frege, Moore, and Russell. This also forced some tough choices; for instance, when deciding on what readings to include in Chapter 8, "Logical Empiricism," we decided to including readings from A. J. Ayer's *Language, Truth, and Logic*. While some scholars find Ayer's work disappointing, we believe that the material from Ayer on empiricist approaches to the philosophy of mathematics and ethics presents an accessible and reasonably clear presentation of ideas that were indeed held by at least some of the logical empiricists. We also provide references to works by other logical empiricists on related topics. We have also chosen, in part for reasons associated with permission fees, to use excerpts from C. K. Ogden and Frank Ramsey's translation of Ludwig Wittgenstein's *Tractatus Logico-Philosophicus*, rather than the translation by David Pears and Brian McGuinness.

While we have aimed to provide students with the major influential works in the development of analytic philosophy up until about 1950, we also believe that it is important for students to be exposed to some lesser-known figures, in part to correct the historical record. To this end, we have included chapters on E. E. Constance Jones and L. Susan Stebbing. We believe, for example, that Jones's work on logic and language, as well as Stebbing's work on analysis and metaphysics, is important enough to be included in this kind of volume. In this sense, we have tried to make our account of early analytic philosophy more inclusive. We understand that we have not filled in all of the gaps, so to speak, and that there are some ways in which this reader could have been more inclusive of figures from diverse backgrounds. We believe, though, that some progress on this front is better than none. A book more specifically dedicated to bringing out the role of lesser-known philosophers from increasingly diverse backgrounds in the tradition would be a somewhat different undertaking—one that we hope others will pursue.

Some will invariably feel that we have neglected certain figures and trends in early analytic philosophy. For example, we say little about the so-called "ordinary language philosophy" that flourished at Oxford in the middle of the 1900s. We also have little to say about important figures like Karl Popper, Wilfrid Sellars, Nelson Goodman, and Hilary Putnam, to name a few. In response to concerns along these lines, we will first note that this book is

Preface

intended as an introduction to early analytic philosophy, not as an introduction to twentieth-century analytic philosophy more generally, and certainly not as an introduction to twentieth-century philosophy as such. It is because of this that while we do mention some points of contact, we do not have much to say about pragmatism, phenomenology, continental philosophy, existentialism, or ordinary language philosophy. A book that covers this material in detail, or parts of it (say, the connections between analytic philosophy and pragmatism, or the "split" between analytic philosophy and continental philosophy and phenomenology[1]), would be very different in orientation than the present volume, with different aims and motivations. We decided, somewhat arbitrarily, that our cut-off would be around 1950. And for this, we viewed Quine as an excellent candidate for the final central chapter of the book, especially given his early engagement with logical empiricism.

In the "Background and commentary" sections, we have tried to provide clear explanations of the relevant arguments and ideas found in the readings. We also believe it is important for students to encounter the material with enough space for discussion and reflection in class and through class assignments. It is partly for this reason that we have only removed content in some select places. Neither of us find the idea of "snippet"-style anthologies very attractive. We believe that students should wrestle with the ideas of these thinkers—the major, influential ideas, but also those that have garnered less attention in subsequent literature. In the "Background and commentary" sections, we have moreover tried to remain as neutral as possible and to avoid deep scholarly disputes. In some cases, of course, neutrality isn't entirely possible—this is probably the case, say, when it comes to explaining the ideas in Wittgenstein's *Tractatus* or the myriad details surrounding logical empiricism. Nonetheless, we have tried our best to present fair discussions of these figures for students.

We have also tried, as much as possible, to retain the original formatting of the readings. Because of this, the formatting of quotations, punctuations, and the like differs somewhat across the readings, as well as across the readings on the one hand and the "Background and commentary" sections on the other hand. Where, for considerations of space, primary source material has been removed, we indicate this as follows: [material removed].

---

[1]For discussion of the connections between the pragmatism of William James, C. S. Peirce and others and the analytic tradition, see Cheryl Misak's *Cambridge Pragmatism* (2016); for discussion of the analytic/continental split, see Michael Friedman's *A Parting of the Ways* (2000).

Acknowledgments

The editors and publisher gratefully acknowledge the permission granted to reproduce the copyright material in this book. Every effort has been made to trace copyright holders and to obtain their permission for the use of copyright material. The publisher apologizes for any errors or omissions in the below list and would be grateful if notified of any corrections that should be incorporated in future reprints or editions of this book.

Chapter 2
Appearance and Reality by F. H. Bradley (selections from Chapters 1–3, 12–14). Clarendon Press, 1893.

Chapter 3
"The Refutation of Idealism" by G. E. Moore. *Mind* 12: 433–53, 1903.

Principia Ethica by G. E. Moore (selections from Chapter 1), Cambridge University Press, 1903.

"A Defence of Common Sense" by G. E. Moore. *Contemporary British Philosophy*, George Allen and Unwin, 1925.

"Proof of an External World" by G.E. Moore. *Proceedings of the British Academy* 25: 273–300, 1939. © 1939 British Academy. Reprinted with permission from The British Academy.

Chapter 4
"On Sinn and Bedeutung" by Gottlob Frege. *The Frege Reader*, (ed. Michael Beaney), Wiley-Blackwell. © 1997 John Wiley and Sons. Permissions cleared through PLSclear.

"The Thought: A Logical Inquiry" by Gottlob Frege. *Mind* 65: 289–311, 1956. © 1956 Oxford University Press. Permissions cleared through Copyright Clearance Center.

Chapter 5
The Principles of Mathematics by Bertrand Russell (selections). Cambridge University Press 1903.

Our Knowledge of the External World by Bertrand Russell (selections). Open Court 1914.

"On Denoting" by Bertrand Russell. *Mind* 14: 479–93, 1905.

"Knowledge by Acquaintance and Knowledge by Description" by Bertrand Russell. *Proceedings of the Aristotelian Society* 11: 108–28, 1910.

xiv **Preface**

Chapter 6
"Mr. Russell's Objections to Frege's Analysis of Propositions" by E. E.C Jones. *Mind* 19: 379–86, 1910.

"A New Law of Thought" by E.E.C. Jones. *Proceedings of the Aristotelian Society* 11: 166–86, 1910–11.

Chapter 7
Tractatus Logico-Philosophicus by Ludwig Wittgenstein, translated by C. K. Ogden. Keegan Paul, Trench, Trubner & Co., 1922.

Chapter 8
"Meaning and Verification" by Moritz Schlick. *The Philosophical Review* 45: 339–69, 1936. © 1936 Cornell University. Reprinted with permission of Duke University Press.

"The Elimination of Metaphysics Through the Logical Analysis of Language" by Rudolf Carnap from *Logical Positivism*, The Free Press 1959. © 1959 by The Free Press. Reprinted with permission of The Free Press, a division of Simon & Schuster, Inc. Permissions cleared through PLSClear.

Language, Truth, and Logic by A. J. Ayer (selections), Dover Press, 1936. Reprinted with permission of Dover.

Chapter 9
A Modern Introduction to Logic by Susan Stebbing (selections from Chapters 1 and 24). Metheun 1930. © Taylor and Francis. Permissions cleared through Copyright Clearance Center.

Philosophy and the Physicists (selections) by Susan Stebbing. Methuen 1937.

"Logical Positivism and Analysis" by Susan Stebbing. *Proceedings of the British Academy* 53–87, 1933.

Chapter 10
"On What There Is" by W. V. O. Quine. *The Review of Metaphysics* 2: 21–38, 1948. © 1948 *The Review of Metaphysics*. Reprinted with permission of *The Review of Metaphysics*.

"Two Dogmas of Empiricism" by W. V. O. Quine. *The Philosophical Review* 60: 20–43, 1951. © Cornell University. Reprinted with permission of Duke University Press.

KEVIN MORRIS

Early Analytic Philosophy was conceived as a result of teaching this material to my students at Tulane University. I would like to thank the students in these courses for the many excellent questions that they asked and which helped to motivate this project. I would also like to thank the five (!) anonymous referees from Bloomsbury Press who provided helpful comments and suggestions, which resulted in a better final product. Two of my students at Tulane, Nicholas Allmaier and Aidan Watson, did an excellent job proofreading early drafts of the manuscript. Chara Kokkiou and Sam Hage helped produce the images, and David Ween helped to transcribe some of the Frege writings.

I would like to thank the philosophy departments at The College of New Jersey, Brown University, Northern Arizona University, and Tulane University for providing me with engaging environments to pursue my philosophical endeavors. I am especially grateful to Tulane University's School of Liberal Arts for providing a book subvention grant that helped to cover permission fees associated with some of the readings.

I am fortunate, even lucky, to have the opportunity to spend my time teaching and writing about philosophy.

I would like to thank the following for personal support and generosity: Allison Morris, Michael Morris, Sonia Morris, and Consuelo Preti. Thanks to everyone!

CONSUELO PRETI

When Kevin (a former student of mine at The College of New Jersey) proposed this reader to me as a joint venture, I was enthusiastic. I have taught versions of courses in analytic philosophy for years and have never been entirely satisfied with any of the available materials that purport to put this material in context. The primary source material is challenging, and the effort to engage undergraduates on some of the more technical and opaque motivations of the early analytic tradition is equally challenging. As an undergraduate, Kevin was exposed to this material for the first time in one of my seminars and the fact that he was motivated, in the progress of his professional career, to pursue further research in the area is a source of great pride and satisfaction for me both as a philosopher and as a teacher. I am most grateful to Kevin for the opportunity to work with him on this volume. I am in addition grateful to the Dean's Office of the School of Humanities and Social Sciences at The College of New Jersey for providing me with a grant that helped to cover permission fees associated with some of the readings.

1

Introducing Analytic Philosophy

Chapter Outline

Analytic philosophy: Themes and ideas	1
Further reading	7

Analytic philosophy: Themes and ideas

If you are a student of contemporary philosophy around 2020, and likely into the future, you probably already have some knowledge of analytic philosophy through exposure to figures in the tradition. At present, so far as we can discern, the majority of philosophers in the English-speaking world, in the majority of philosophy departments, identify as analytic philosophers. But the question "what is analytic philosophy?" is not easy to answer. Any attempt to give a strict definition for someone to count as an analytic philosopher (or for a work to count as a work of analytic philosophy) is unlikely to succeed.[1] One way to understand analytic philosophy—and to attempt to answer the question "what is analytic philosophy?"—is through practice, through engaging with the themes and problems that make up the tradition. This, in effect, is the strategy that we will pursue throughout the following chapters, where we consider the work of various thinkers at

---

[1] See Glock 2008 for various unsuccessful attempts to define analytic philosophy in this way.

Early Analytic Philosophy

the origins of analytic philosophy. Our strategy in this opening chapter, however, will be to present some characteristics and tendencies of analytic philosophers, without pretending that these provide a strict definition, and with the caveat that we can gain a better understanding of the character of analytic philosophy through engagement with the work of those in the tradition.

Analytic philosophy, at the time of this writing, is a tradition in philosophy that has been around for about 120 years and has its roots in the work of philosophers like Bertrand Russell (1872–1970), G. E. Moore (1873–1958), and Gottlob Frege (1848–1925). Despite not sharing a single doctrine or theory—a claim to which we will return—it may be said, first, that analytic philosophers typically favor formal methods in the formulation of issues, distinctions, and arguments in their approach to problems in philosophy. Modern symbolic logic, the kind that appears in most introductory logic courses at present, was developed near the end of the 1800s by Frege in his *Begriffsshrift* (([1879] 1967); translated as *Concept-Script*) and further articulated by Russell, along with Alfred North Whitehead (1861–1947), in their three-volume *Principia Mathematica* (1910, 1912, 1913). Most analytic philosophers take it that the development of modern symbolic logic was an important landmark in the history of human thought and, in some cases, have also believed that a proper appreciation and understanding of modern logic could help to resolve philosophical issues and puzzles. We will see some examples of this in the chapters that follow.

Along with a healthy appreciation of logic and formal methods, analytic philosophers typically value precision and clarity, with logic representing a paradigmatic example. They have also sometimes believed that philosophical puzzles arise, in part, because of lack of clarity in the very way in which philosophical problems are stated. Moore, for instance, wrote in the introduction to *Principia Ethica* ([1903b] 1993):

> It appears to me that in Ethics, as in all other philosophical studies, the difficulties and disagreements ... are mainly due to a very simple cause: namely to the attempt to answer questions, without first discovering precisely what question it is which you desire to answer. (33)

Thus analytic philosophers have often devoted effort to attempting to clarify and articulate philosophical problems, with the hope that improved clarity concerning the problems themselves will make them less difficult to resolve than might otherwise be the case. Some have gone so far as to argue that philosophy consists in the clarification of ideas and language. Ludwig

Wittgenstein (1889–1951), for example, wrote in his *Tractatus Logico-Philosophicus* (1922):

> The object of philosophy is the logical clarification of thoughts.
> Philosophy is not a theory but an activity.
> A philosophical work consists essentially of elucidations.
> The result of philosophy is not a number of "philosophical propositions", but to make propositions clear.
> Philosophy should make clear and delimit sharply the thoughts which otherwise are, as it were, opaque and blurred. (4.112)

Similarly, Russell wrote in "Logical Atomism" ([1924] 1993):

> The business of philosophy . . . is essentially that of logical analysis, followed by logical synthesis . . . The most important part of philosophy consists in criticizing and clarifying notions which are apt to be regarded as fundamental and accepted uncritically. (178)

Yet Wittgenstein's and Russell's views here are not uniformly accepted across the tradition. Contrary to the above remarks, many of those who identify as analytic philosophers have sought to develop theories in metaphysics, ethics, and epistemology, and in doing so have put forward "philosophical propositions." Indeed, contrary to the suggestions in the above passages, Wittgenstein and Russell could themselves be plausibly considered examples of such philosophers!

Analytic philosophers also typically view natural science as a legitimate, paradigmatic source for knowledge about the world, and many (though not all) analytic philosophers are skeptical about the idea, however prominent in the history of philosophy, that philosophy can furnish us with some kind of supra-empirical insight into the nature of reality. Russell put it this way in "Logical Atomism":

> What shall we regard as having the greatest likelihood of being true . . .? It seems to me that science has a much greater likelihood of being true than any philosophy hitherto advanced . . . We shall be wise to build our philosophy upon science. (175–6)

As we will see in later chapters, in some cases analytic philosophers have taken this respect for science and scientific method to raise issues concerning the very nature of philosophical inquiry. They have wondered, for example, what intellectual work is left for philosophy, given the success of the natural sciences. This is an issue that analytic philosophers have taken seriously, and we will see some ways in which analytic philosophers have tried to address

Early Analytic Philosophy

this issue in the following chapters. In some cases, they have proposed that philosophy ought to be in the business of analyzing and clarifying scientific concepts, which can be viewed as a precursor to some contemporary philosophy of science.

It is worth emphasizing that the respect that analytic philosophers typically give to science, while perhaps something that we now take for granted, has not always been the case in philosophy. Plato, for example, apparently thought that the real world lies beyond sense experience and observation, and that it is through philosophical reflection that we can grasp this supra-sensible reality. Similarly, as we will see in Chapter 2, F. H. Bradley (1846–1924) argued in *Appearance and Reality* ([1893] 1969) that the very concepts employed in scientific and ordinary discourse only concern appearance and are, in a sense, incoherent upon rational reflection. Bradley held that philosophy, in contrast, can get us some insight into reality, in so far as this is possible at all. While it would be a mistake to suppose that analytic philosophers dogmatically cling to science and scientific methods for learning about the world—or, similarly, to think that all analytic philosophy is in some manner philosophy of science—many analytic philosophers would reject the idea, found in Plato, Bradley, and others, that philosophical inquiry can somehow reveal truths deeper and more fundamental than the sort of truths discerned through science and observation.

Finally, and related to the previous point, many analytic philosophers hold that it is at least a strike against a position if it radically conflicts with how we ordinarily take the world to be. This stance was defended by Moore in "A Defence of Common Sense" ([1925] 1959) and "Proof of an External World" ([1939] 1993), both of which we will discuss in Chapter 3. This raises various questions, including "what exactly is common sense?" and "why should common sense be afforded this status?" It would also be a mistake to think that a commitment to common sense—to the literal truth of a commonsense view of the world—is uniformly accepted by those who identify as analytic philosophers. Still, it is a definite tendency within the tradition and, at least according to Moore, one that can be supported by rational argument.

In sketching these inclinations among analytic philosophers, it is important to note what we have not included.

First, we have not described analytic philosophy as "linguistic philosophy." It is true that those in the tradition have often thought that clarifying language is important to addressing philosophical problems. It is also true that they have sometimes viewed the analysis of language as a central part of philosophical inquiry. And some have been interested in understanding how we use various words—words like "knowledge," "cause," "mind"—in everyday communication. Nonetheless, it would be a mistake to think of this as generally representative of analytic philosophy. It would be a disservice (and a distortion) of the work of the early analytic philosophers like Russell and Moore to say that they were engaged in "linguistic philosophy." We would rather say that out of their discussions and analyses of language grew substantive projects in epistemology, metaphysics, and ethics. Further, when we look to contemporary analytic philosophy in Chapter 11, it will also be apparent that many more recent philosophers in the tradition cannot be profitably described as concerned primarily with matters related to language. Analytic philosophers do, perhaps, view issues in the philosophy of language as pertinent to issues in epistemology, metaphysics, ethics, and philosophy of science. But this is simply to respect the interconnectedness of these areas of philosophy, and provides no basis for thinking of analytic philosophy as "linguistic philosophy."

Second, we have not characterized analytic philosophy in terms of "analysis." This may seem surprising! After all, one might think that the very label "analytic philosophy" involves a commitment to philosophy as involving "analysis" rather than "synthesis," a kind of "breaking down" as opposed to "bringing together." There are a few things to say here. For one, to characterize analytic philosophy as philosophy-as-analysis would require a substantive account of just what analysis involves (an analysis of "analysis," one might say!), which is itself a matter of much dispute. For example, Russell's so-called "theory of descriptions," which we will discuss in Chapter 5, may in some manner be described as an "analysis" of sentences that include expressions of the form "the F" (such as "the present King of France is bald"). Similarly, Moore's "Proof of an External World" includes what may be regarded as an "analysis" of what is at issue concerning the existence of a world outside of our minds. Now, first, it is just not clear in what sense these projects indeed involve something that can fruitfully be called "analysis." For instance, they do not involve "analysis" in the sense of breaking something down to its most basic constituents. Nor is it clear just how the output of such "analysis" should be understood. For instance, it is not clear to what extent Russell and Moore were "analyzing" what we actually mean by the relevant sentences and expressions, as opposed to presenting a kind of prescriptive formulation of what we ought to mean by them.[2] Further,

---

[2]For an accessible discussion of some of the issues in this vicinity, see Beaney 2017. See also Susan Stebbing's (1885–1943) "Logical Positivism and Analysis" (1933), presented in Chapter 9, as well as her "The Method of Analysis in Metaphysics" (1932).

Early Analytic Philosophy

despite engaging in some form of analysis, some of those at the origins of the analytic tradition—plausibly including Moore and Russell—were clearly engaged in developing big-picture, "synthetic" accounts of how various issues across philosophy fit together. This has continued to be the case, and many contemporary philosophers who identify as analytic are engaged in constructive philosophical projects in metaphysics, epistemology, ethics, and philosophy of science. At least for these reasons, we do not think it is useful to characterize analytic philosophy in terms of something called "analysis." More generally, as above, analytic philosophy cannot be described in terms of a set of shared theories—there is no philosophical theory, idea, or even method that all analytic philosophers agree upon, and we believe that any attempt to answer the question "what is analytic philosophy?" by appealing to some such common theory, idea, or method will likely fail.

Third, we have not described analytic philosophy as "Anglo-American philosophy." From a historical perspective, such a characterization misses the mark. Frege, one of those at the origins of the tradition, was German. Some of the psychologists and mathematicians that influenced Russell's and Moore's earliest work hailed from Germany, Austria, and Italy. The logical empiricist movement in the 1920s and 1930s, which we will discuss in Chapter 8, arose primarily in Austria and Germany. While Wittgenstein worked at Cambridge, he was Austrian and wrote in German. From a more contemporary perspective, it is true that most journals in analytic philosophy are in English. Yet it remains the case that many philosophers working in Germany and Poland, for example, identify as analytic. So, it really cannot be said that analytic philosophy is distinctively "Anglo-American." Rather, both historically and in contemporary thought, analytic philosophy is a global phenomenon.

Finally, in sketching some common characteristics of analytic philosophy and analytic philosophers, we have said nothing about the contrast between analytic philosophy on the one hand and "continental" philosophy on the other hand. Continental philosophy is, like analytic philosophy, a tradition that has taken shape roughly over the last 120 years. As the label suggests, it has taken shape most prominently in continental Europe. Thinkers such as Frederick Nietzsche (1844–1900), Edmund Husserl (1859–1938), Martin Heidegger (1889–1976), Jean-Paul Sartre (1905–80), Simone de Beauvoir (1908–86), Hannah Arendt (1906–75), Gilles Deleuze (1925–95), Jacques Derrida (1920–2004), and Luce Irigaray (b. 1930) are often included as important continental figures. One could, we suppose, engage in a compare-and-contrast project, but we are not sure about how fruitful this would be.

Moreover, figures in the continental tradition, like Husserl, Nietzsche, Sartre, and Arendt, have in some cases influenced those within the analytic tradition; similarly, those in the continental tradition have been influenced by analytic figures like Wittgenstein and W. V. O. Quine (1908–2000). Finally, we are analytic philosophers, and we feel that it would be stepping beyond our proper epistemic bounds to speculate on just what distinguishes the analytic tradition from the continental tradition. In any case, for our purposes here—for the purpose of presenting some typical-though-not-universal characteristics of analytic philosophy and analytic philosophers—it is not necessary to engage with the vexed question concerning the relationship between analytic and continental philosophy.

The reader is encouraged to return to the present material upon completing this book and to reflect on the extent to which the material encountered in the chapters that follow conforms to the outlines of analytic philosophy sketched in the present chapter.

Further reading

Beaney, M. (ed.) (2015), *The Oxford Handbook of the History of Analytic Philosophy*, Oxford: Oxford University Press.

Beaney, M. (2017), *Analytic Philosophy: A Very Short Introduction*, Oxford: Oxford University Press.

Biltzeki, A. and Matar, A. (1998), *The Story of Analytic Philosophy: Plot and Heroes*, New York: Routledge.

Glock, H. (2008), *What is Analytic Philosophy?* Cambridge: Cambridge University Press.

Preston, A. (2007), *Analytic Philosophy: The History of an Illusion*, London: Continuum.

Schwartz, S. (2012), *A Brief History of Analytic Philosophy*, Oxford: Wiley-Blackwell.

Soames, S. (2005), *Philosophical Analysis in the Twentieth Century*, Vol. 1 and 2, Princeton: Princeton University Press.

Stroll, A. (2000), *Twentieth-Century Analytic Philosophy*, New York: Columbia University Press.

2

F. H. Bradley and Monistic Idealism

Chapter Outline

Background and commentary	
Background	9
Monistic idealism	11
Critique of relations	11
Appearance and reality	16
Concluding remarks	18
Further reading	19
Readings	
Appearance and Reality (selections from Chs 1–3, 12–14)	20

Background and commentary

Background

Who was Francis Herbert (F. H.) Bradley (1846–1924)? If you are an undergraduate (or even graduate!) student in philosophy, you may have never heard this name before opening this book. Bradley is not widely read and discussed in contemporary philosophy. Yet in the late 1800s and early 1900s, he was one of the most influential and widely discussed living philosophers. Bradley wrote on ethics (*Ethical Studies* ([1876] 1927)), logic

(*The Principles of Logic* ([1883] 2011)), and metaphysics (*Appearance and Reality* ([1893] 1969)). The selections below focus on his metaphysics and, especially, his critique of the reality of relations. As we will see in later chapters, it was this material that Moore and Russell, two thinkers at the origins of the analytic tradition, most vehemently rejected.

Bradley was born in what is now part of London. His father was an Evangelical preacher and his siblings were similarly inclined to intellectual pursuits. Following his schooling at University College, Oxford, Bradley was awarded a lifetime fellowship in 1870 at Merton College, Oxford. The fellowship included no teaching duties, but (perhaps surprisingly, given our modern sensibilities!) was terminable upon marriage. Bradley did not marry and retained the fellowship until his death. During his lifetime, he experienced several illnesses, which resulted in his living a somewhat solitary life. Thus Collingwood, one of Bradley's colleagues at Oxford, wrote: "Although I lived within a few hundred yards of him for sixteen years, I never to my knowledge set eyes on him" ([1939] 1982: 16). Similarly, Brand Blanshard (1892–1987), who was influenced by Bradley, wrote in his obiturary for Bradley that "few of the thirty or forty teachers of philosophy have ever talked with him . . . to the students of philosophy he was known by writings only" (1925: 5). Nonetheless, Bradley's influence on the philosophical landscape during his lifetime was immense. Blanshard recalled:

> When I came first as an Oxford undergraduate in 1913 . . . the philosophical capital of Britain was undoubtedly Oxford, and in Oxford the great figure of Bradley, rarely seen by anyone, and magnified now to legendary proportions, hovered everywhere over the scene. (1952: 39)

Indeed, while they would go on to offer influential critiques of Bradley's ideas, Russell and Moore were themselves influenced by Bradley. Reflecting on his days as a student, Russell wrote that "I read Bradley at this time [during the 1890s] with avidity, and admired him more than any other recent philosopher" (1944: 10), while Moore prefaced his 1897 dissertation by writing that "it is to Mr. Bradley that I chiefly owe my conception of the fundamental problems of metaphysics" ([1879] 2011: 4).[1] On the other side of the Atlantic, Bradley's work was respected by the American pragmatist William James (1842–1910), among others.[2]

---

[1]For this and further biographical information, see Candlish and Basile 2017.
[2]For example, despite disagreeing with Bradley's monism, James describes *Appearance and Reality* as a "wonderful book" in his *A Pluralistic Universe* ([1909] 1977).

Monistic idealism

Bradley is typically classified as a British Idealist, along with philosophers like Edward Caird (1835–1908), T. H. Green (1836–82), and Harold Joachim (1868–1938), a movement that incorporated elements from German Idealists like Immanuel Kant (1724–1804) and Georg Friedrich Hegel (1770–1831). It was due to the influence of Hegel that Russell sometimes referred to Bradley and his fellow British Idealists collectively as "Hegelians" (Bradley himself rejected the label). Indeed, aside from the specific content of his philosophical treatises, Bradley was influential, in part, for taking seriously ideas from continental Europe and bringing these ideas into English-speaking philosophy.

Bradley's metaphysics can be described as a form of monistic idealism. First, the monistic part. Suppose we ask: Does the world consist of a plurality of separately existing entities standing in relations? Or is the world a unified whole, with each putative separately existing entity a mere abstraction from the whole? Monism, in opposition to atomism or pluralism, holds that the world is a unified whole, that the world does not consist of separately existing entities standing in relations. As we will see, Bradley's case for monism is premised on an overarching rejection of relations as "unreal" and a corresponding rejection of atomism or pluralism as unintelligible or incoherent. Second, the idealism part. Suppose we ask: Does the world consist of nothing but consciousness or sentience—in short, mentality? Or is the world both partly mental and partly physical or material? Or is the world exhaustively physical, with consciousness or sentience somehow derivative from physical reality? Idealism holds that the world consists of consciousness or sentience, and is opposed to dualism, which holds that the world is both partly mental and partly physical, as well as physicalism or materialism, which holds that the world is exhaustively physical or material. Note that monism and idealism are different views. For example, one could be a monist without being an idealist (as with Baruch Spinoza (1623–77)) as well as an idealist without being a monist (as with the British Empiricists George Berkeley (1685–1753) and perhaps David Hume (1711–76)).

Critique of relations

Much of ordinary and scientific discourse uses certain basic concepts— concepts like thing or object, quality or attribute, space, time, cause, self, and so on. These concepts provide the core materials in terms of which we think about and conceptualize ourselves and the world around us. In Book I of

Early Analytic Philosophy

Appearance and Reality, Bradley asks: To what extent can these concepts be said to accurately reflect reality? To what extent, for example, does the distinction between an object and its attributes correspond to a genuine distinction in reality? Bradley's conclusion is that none of these concepts accurately characterizes reality. In this sense, when we think about the world using these concepts, our thought involves some degree of falsification. He announces this position at the start of Chapter 1:

> The fact of illusion and error is in various ways forced early upon the mind; and the ideas, by which we try to understand the universe, may be considered as attempts to set right our failure. In this division of my work I shall criticize some of these, and shall endeavor to show that they have not reached their object. I shall point out that the world, as so understood, contradicts itself; and is therefore appearance, not reality. (9)

While Bradley offers various detailed arguments for this conclusion, his overarching concern is that our basic concepts for thinking about the world all presuppose, in one way or another, relations between distinct entities. For example, the concept of space presupposes a spatial framework involving individual things related by distances. Similarly, the concept of time presupposes a framework involving distinct moments ordered by beforeness and afterness relations. The problem, according to Bradley, is that the very idea of a plurality of items ("terms") standing in relations is incoherent or unintelligible upon reflection. Thus near the end of Chapter 3, Bradley writes:

> The conclusion to which I am brought is that a relational way of thought— any one that moves by the machinery of terms and relations—must give appearance, and not truth. It is a makeshift, a device, a mere practical compromise, most necessary, but in the end most indefensible. (28)

And given that the "relational way of thought" must merely "give appearance," Bradley concludes Chapter 3 as follows:

> The reader, who has followed and grasped the principle of this chapter, will have little need to spend his time upon those which succeed it. He will have seen that our experience, where relational, is not true; and he will have condemned, almost without hearing, the great mass of phenomena. (29)

In other words, the idea of distinct items standing in relations is unintelligible and so cannot accurately characterize reality. And since many of our most basic concepts presuppose a framework of terms standing in relations, these concepts similarly cannot accurately characterize reality.

F. H. Bradley and Monistic Idealism   13

Chapters 1 and 2 of *Appearance and Reality* provide examples of Bradley's critical method, his manner of showing that some concept or concepts are ultimately unintelligible and so must fall short of characterizing reality. Thus in Chapter 1, Bradley argues that the distinction between primary and secondary qualities or properties cannot be taken to capture a distinction in reality; in Chapter 2, he critiques the distinction between a thing or object ("substantive") and its qualities or properties ("adjectives"), as one might distinguish between a lump of sugar as an object and its quality of whiteness. Moreover, the material in Chapter 2 both foreshadows and leads into Bradley's critique of relations in Chapter 3. Bradley's conclusion at the end of Chapter 2 is that the conception of the world as consisting of objects with qualities is intelligible only if relations are intelligible. He then argues in Chapter 3 that the very idea of relations suffers fatal objections.

Before looking at Bradley's critique of relations, it will be useful to briefly reflect on the notion of intelligibility (or lack thereof) presupposed in the previous remarks. Roughly, Bradley's presupposition is that reality must be intelligible or, to put it another way, that reality must be coherent or non-contradictory. Given this, Bradley thinks that we can test whether some concept accurately reflects reality by considering whether that concept is coherent or non-contradictory. In the readings below, Bradley is most explicit about this in Chapter 13 where he writes that "reality is such that it does not contradict itself" (120). While this may seem reasonably straightforward, in practice Bradley understands coherence or intelligibility in a somewhat broad sense. For example, in practice he supposes that a lack of coherence or intelligibility—that some concept is "self-contradictory" or "contradicts itself"—can be established by drawing out an infinite regress. Indeed, articulating just how this notion of intelligibility or coherence should be understood is one of the more difficult aspects of Bradleyian exegesis.

When it comes to his rejection of relations in Chapter 3, Bradley formulates the issue using a distinction between qualities (like the hardness, sweetness, and whiteness of a lump of sugar) on the one hand, and relations on the other. Nonetheless, the critique is clearly intended to be general, to show that the very idea of relations between distinct entities of any ontological category suffers inescapable difficulties. His strategy is to show that each possible way of making sense of this manner of conceptualizing the world fails for one reason or another, from which he concludes that the very idea of entities standing in relations is unintelligible or contradictory. The argument may be understood as consisting in four central claims, as follows:

1 Qualities, and terms more generally, are unintelligible without relations.
2 Qualities, and terms more generally, are unintelligible with relations.
3 Relations without qualities, and terms more generally, are unintelligible.
4 Relations with qualities, and terms more generally, are unintelligible.

Regarding (1), the idea at least seems straightforward: if there are a plurality of terms, there must be relations between them. For example, as distinct, the terms must at least be different from one another. Hence, the world cannot consist only of terms without relations between them. Regarding (2), Bradley first contends that a quality, and a term more generally, cannot be wholly resolved into relations. Consider, for example, the quality of redness. Redness seems to stand in various relations to other qualities. For example, it seems to be more similar to orange than it is to green. However, redness also seems to be something apart from these relations. So, qualities, and terms more generally, need relations, but also cannot be nothing but relations. In response, however, Bradley proposes what is sometimes known as the "fission argument,"[3] claiming that the idea of terms with relations—here, the relations dependent on the terms, and in some manner obtaining in virtue of the nature of the terms—leads to a kind of infinite regress of distinct aspects within the terms. In this way, he supposes that taking relations to depend on terms leads to a kind of complexity within the terms themselves. Given this, he infers that the world cannot consist of self-subsistent qualities or terms, with the relations between the terms somehow dependent on and obtaining in virtue of the qualities or terms. If an "internal relation" is understood as a relation that obtains in virtue of the nature of its terms, (2) can be understood as a case against the intelligibility and so reality of "internal relations."[4]

Regarding (3), Bradley contends that the idea of relations as existing independently of terms "loudly contradicts itself" (27). For example, take the

---

[3] As in Candlish 2007.
[4] Much of the reaction to Bradley's critique of relations has couched the issue in terms of "internal" versus "external" relations. This way of framing the issue raises a number of issues, in part because of lack of clarity in the use of "internal" and "external"; for example, in *Idealism: A Critical Survey* ([1934] 2013), A. C. Ewing (1899–1973) distinguishes an array of different meanings associated with calling a relation "internal" as opposed to "external." What can be said, however, is that contra some of the remarks of Moore and Russell (and others), Bradley did not hold that all relations are "internal" in any straightforward sense. Rather, he rejected all relations as unreal, whether "internal" or "external." For discussion of issues in this vicinity, see Candlish 2007.

F. H. Bradley and Monistic Idealism   15

father of relation, a relation that obtains, for example, between George H. Bush and Jeb Bush, such that George H. Bush is the father of Jeb Bush. Bradley's claim is that the idea of the world as consisting of relations, but nothing standing in the relations, is unintelligible. What would it be, for example, for there to be *father of* relations, but no things standing in this relation? Hence, the world cannot consist of nothing but relations; there must also be something that stands in the relations. Finally, regarding (4), Bradley considers the possibility of combining relations with terms, and in such a way that relations are "more or less independent" from what they relate. Here Bradley offers what is sometimes referred to as the "chain argument,"[5] according to which the proposal leads to an infinite regress, this time a regress of relations between relations and terms. In particular, Bradley claims that if relations are "more or less independent" from what they relate, this requires further relations between a relation and its terms; by parity of reasoning, this requires further relations between the second set of relations and their terms, and so on, and so on. If an "external relation" is one that is "more or less independent" from what it relates, (4) amounts to a case against the intelligibility of "external relations" so understood.[6]

Given his critique of relations, Bradley infers a monistic conclusion. Anticipating this in Chapter 2, he writes:

> we are forced to see, when we reflect, that a relation standing alongside its terms is a delusion. If it is to be real, it must be so somehow at the expense of the terms, or, at least, must be something which appears in them or to which they belong.... everywhere there must be a whole embracing what is related. (18)

Similarly, in the posthumously published "Relations," he writes:

> any relational view involves self-contradiction in its essence. It rests on a form of experience which is more primary and, in a sense, more ultimate.... And thus the relational view, while justified and more than justified in advancing, must fail in the end to reach full reality or truth. (630)

In other words, reality cannot consist of entities standing in relations; rather, reality is one, a kind of all embracing-whole, what Bradley sometimes refers to as a "supra-relational unity" or "the Absolute." As Bradley puts it in Chapter 14 of *Appearance and Reality*, "the Absolute is not many; there are no

---

[5] As in Candlish 2007.
[6] See fn. 4.

16   Early Analytic Philosophy

independent reals. The universe is one in this sense that its differences exist harmoniously within one whole, beyond which there is nothing" (127).

Appearance and reality

Bradley takes the rejection of relations to have far-reaching consequences. Indeed, he takes it to imply that all ordinary and scientific discourse—and, perhaps, any possible discourse or thought—concerns appearance. Because of this, Bradley supposes that all such discourse or thought involves some degree of falsification. For example, any thought that characterizes the world in terms of objects having properties cannot be wholly true. In this respect, Bradley's critique of the "relational way of thought" raises a challenge to the very idea of accurate representation of the world. This position, however, raises a number of questions. For one thing, how is this apparent division of the world into appearance and reality to be understood? Second, what, if anything, can we know about reality, given that our modes for conceptualizing the world provide us with mere appearance? Book II of *Appearance and Reality* is dedicated to trying to answer these questions.

Perhaps most importantly, Bradley denies that appearance is something apart from reality, or the Absolute. In Chapter 12, he provides the following description of such a view, which he rejects:

> the universe, on this view ... falls apart into two regions, we may call them two hemispheres. One of these is the world of experience as knowledge—in every sense without reality. The other is the kingdom of reality—without either knowledge or experience ... [the] Things as they are in themselves and as they do not appear ... we may call this side the Unknowable. (110)

Bradley rejects this position, commonly associated with Kant, as self-contradictory. Perhaps most directly, Bradley recognizes that given the rejection of relations as unreal, reality or the Absolute cannot be something apart from appearance, as this would in turn imply that reality or the Absolute is somehow related to appearance. But this cannot be, given that relations have themselves been rejected. Thus Bradley writes in Chapter 12:

> Everything so far ... has turned out to be appearance. It is that which, taken as it stands, proves inconsistent with itself ... But to deny its existence or to divorce it from reality is out of the question. For it has a positive character which is indubitable fact, and ... it can have no place in which to live except reality. And reality, set on one side and apart from all appearance, would

assuredly be nothing. Hence what is certain is that, in some way, these inseparables are joined. (114–15)

Making sense of this idea of reality as including appearance, despite the harmonious nature of reality and the self-contradictory nature of appearance, is another of the more challenging aspects of Bradleyian exegesis, and the reader is encouraged to reflect on these and related remarks concerning appearance and reality.

What can we know about reality? One of Bradley's answers is that we can know that reality is self-consistent or non-self-contradictory. In Chapter 13, Bradley argues that this can provide substantive, positive knowledge of reality. For example, given the previous contention that "appearance must belong to reality" and cannot be apart from it, Bradley concludes that we can know of reality that "everything, which appears, is somehow real in such a way as to be self-consistent" and that "the character of the real is to possess everything phenomenal in a harmonious form" (123). Bradley moreover contends in Chapter 14 that we can know that reality consists of sentience, that the "matter" of the world is nothing but sentience or consciousness. Given his rejection of atomism and his corresponding embrace of a monistic worldview, the result is that reality or the Absolute is a kind of all-embracing experience.

Bradley's appeal to experience or sentience is also significant because it is through reflecting on what he calls "immediate experience" or "feeling" that we can come to grasp something like the kind of unity that characterizes reality. In Chapter 14, he writes:

in mere feeling or immediate presentation, we have the experience of a whole. This whole contains diversity, and ... is not parted by relations. Such an experience ... serves to suggest to us the general idea of a total experience, where will and thought and feeling may all once more be one. (140–1)

Likewise, in "Relations," Bradley expresses this as follows:

What I fail to understand is the position of those who seek apparently to deny or ignore the very existence of what I call "feeling"—an experience, that is, which, being more than merely simple, holds a many in one, and contains a diversity within a unity which itself is not relational ... To attempt to deny that an emotion is one whole, or to treat its unity as consisting in no more than some relation or relations, I cannot but regard as really monstrous. (633)

Bradley's idea is that immediate experience exhibits a kind of unity similar to that which characterizes reality. The point might be put as follows. Reflect on your current conscious experience. On an atomistic or pluralistic interpretation, the experience consists of, say, an auditory component, a visual component, a tactile component, an emotional component, and so on, and the total experience is nothing but the sum of these components. On a monistic or holistic interpretation, each apparent component of the total experience—the auditory component, the visual component, the tactile component, the emotional component, and so on—cannot be separated without distortion from the total experience (what Bradley would call "false abstraction"). Bradley's claim is that the atomistic interpretation of immediate experience is "monstrous" and that when we reflect on immediate experience, it is the monistic interpretation that is to be preferred. In this respect, Bradley claims, we can gain some grasp of the unity possessed by reality or the Absolute by reflecting on immediate experience or "feeling."

Putting this together, it can be said that for Bradley, appearances (appearances to the contrary, perhaps!) are somehow not distinct from reality; that reality can be known to be self-consistent or non-self-contradictory; that reality is sentience; and that we can have some grasp of the "supra-relational unity" of reality by reflecting on immediate experience. As above, much of Book II of *Appearance and Reality* attempts to make sense of these ideas, and again the reader is encouraged to reflect on the challenges that this kind of position may face.

Concluding remarks

Bradley was one of the most important and influential philosophers in the late 1800s and early 1900s. Yet soon after this, his reputation and influence declined sharply. In the following chapters, we will consider some of the criticisms of Bradley that were developed by Moore, Russell, and others. One question to keep in mind is whether these criticisms were successful or whether, on the other hand, Bradley's decline in reputation and influence was due, perhaps, more to sociological factors and influences than rational ones.

At least part of the reason for Bradley's influence during his lifetime was how ambitious he was a thinker. This is perhaps most evident in *Appearance and Reality*: from a few basic presumptions, he offers a wide-ranging critique of ordinary and scientific concepts as unsuited to characterize reality and concludes that reality must be a kind of harmonious whole consisting of consciousness or sentience. As we will see, however, it was this unbridled ambition in metaphysics, and philosophical inquiry more generally, that many of Bradley's critics would find untenable.

Further reading

Primary sources

Bradley, F. H. (1914), *Essays on Truth and Reality*, Oxford: Clarendon Press.

Bradley, F. H. ([1935] 1969), *Collected Essays*. H. Joachim (ed.), Oxford: Clarendon Press.

Bradley, F. H. ([1935] 1969), "Relations", in H. H. Joachim (ed.), *Collected Essays*. Oxford: Clarendon Press.

Green, T. H. ([1883] 2004), *Prolegomena to Ethics*, Oxford: Clarendon Press.

Joachim, H. H. (1906), *The Nature of Truth*, Oxford: Clarendon Press.

Secondary sources

Basile, P. (1999), *Experience and Relations: An Examination of F. H. Bradley's Conception of Reality*, Berne: Paul Haupt.

Candlish, S. (2007), *The Russell/Bradley Dispute and its Significance for Twentieth-Century Philosophy*, Basingstoke: Palgrave Macmillan.

Candlish, S. and Basile, F. (2017), "Francis Herbert Bradley", *Stanford Encyclopedia of Philosophy*. Available online: https://plato.stanford.edu/archives/spr2017/entries/bradley/

Mander, W. (1994), *An Introduction to Bradley's Metaphysics*, Oxford: Clarendon Press.

Wollheim, R. (1969), *F. H. Bradley*, Harmondsworth: Penguin.

Readings

Bradley, F. H. *Appearance and Reality* (selections from Chs 1–3, 12–14).
Reprinted from Bradley, F. H. (1893), *Appearance and Reality*. Oxford: Clarendon Press.

Book I. Appearance

Chapter I. Primary and Secondary Qualities

The fact of illusion and error is in various ways forced early upon the mind; and the ideas by which we try to understand the universe, may be considered as attempts to set right our failure. In this division of my work I shall criticize some of these, and shall endeavour to show that they have not reached their object. I shall point out that the world, as so understood, contradicts itself; and is therefore appearance, and not reality.

In this chapter I will begin with the proposal to make things intelligible by the distinction between primary and secondary qualities. This view is old, but, I need hardly say, is far from obsolete, nor can it ever disappear. From time to time, without doubt, so long as there are human beings, it will reappear as the most advanced and as the one scientific theory of first principles. And I begin with it, because it is so simple, and in the main so easily disposed of. The primary qualities are those aspects of what we perceive or feel, which, in a word, are spatial; and the residue is secondary. The solution of the world's enigma lies in taking the former as reality, and everything else somehow as derivative, and as more or less justifiable appearance.

The foundation of this view will be known to the reader, but for the sake of clearness I must trace it in outline. We assume that a thing must be self-consistent and self-dependent. It either has a quality or has not got it. And, if it has it, it cannot have it only sometimes, and merely in this or that relation. But such a principle is the condemnation of secondary qualities.

It matters very little how in detail we work with it. A thing is coloured, but not coloured in the same way to every eye; and, except to some eye, it seems not coloured at all. Is it then coloured or not? And the eye—relation to which appears somehow to make the quality—does that itself possess colour? Clearly not so, unless there is another eye which sees it. Nothing therefore is really coloured; colour seems only to belong to what itself is colourless. And the same result holds, again, with cold and heat. A thing may be cold or hot according to different

F. H. Bradley and Monistic Idealism   **21**

parts of my skin; and, without some relation to a skin, it seems without any such quality. And, by a like argument, the skin is proved not itself to own the quality, which is hence possessed by nothing. And sounds, not heard, are hardly real; while what hears them is the ear, itself not audible, nor even always in the enjoyment of sound. With smell and with taste the case seems almost worse; for they are more obviously mixed up with our pleasure and pain. If a thing tastes only in the mouth, is taste its quality? Has it smell where there is no nose? But nose and tongue are smelt or tasted only by another nose or tongue; nor can either again be said to have as a quality what they sometimes enjoy. And the pleasant and disgusting, which we boldly locate in the object, how can they be there? Is a thing delightful or sickening really and in itself? Am even I the constant owner of these wandering adjectives? But I will not weary the reader by insistence on detail. The argument shows everywhere that things have secondary qualities only for an organ; and that the organ itself has these qualities in no other way. They are found to be adjectives, somehow supervening on relations of the extended. The extended only is real. And the facts of what is called subjective sensation, under which we may include dream and delusion of all kinds, may be adduced in support. They go to show that, as we can have the sensation without the object, and the object without the sensation, the one cannot possibly be a quality of the other. The secondary qualities, therefore, are appearance, coming from the reality, which itself has no quality but extension.

This argument has two sides, a negative and a positive. The first denies that secondary qualities are the actual nature of things, the second goes on to make an affirmation about the primary. I will enquire first if the negative assertion is justified. I will not dispute the truth of the principle that, if a thing has a quality, it must have it; but I will ask whether on this basis some defence may not be made. And we may attempt it in this way. All the arguments, we may protest, do but show defect in, or interference with, the organ of perception. The fact that I cannot receive the secondary qualities except under certain conditions, fails to prove that they are not there and existing in the thing. And, supposing that they are there, still the argument proves their absence, and is hence unsound. And sheer delusion and dreams do not overthrow this defence. The qualities are constant in the things themselves; and, if they fail to impart themselves, or impart themselves wrongly, that is always due to something outside their nature. If we could perceive them, they are there.

But this way of defence seems hardly tenable. For, if the qualities impart themselves never except under conditions, how in the end are we to say what they are when unconditioned? Having once begun, and having been compelled, to take their appearance into the account, we cannot afterwards strike it out. It being

22   Early Analytic Philosophy

admitted that the qualities come to us always in a relation, and always as appearing, then certainly we know them only as appearance. And the mere supposition that in themselves they may really be what they are, seems quite meaningless or self-destructive. Further, we may enforce this conclusion by a palpable instance. To hold that one's mistress is charming, ever and in herself, is an article of faith, and beyond reach of question. But, if we turn to common things, the result will be otherwise. We observed that the disgusting and the pleasant may make part of the character of a taste or a smell, while to take these aspects as a constant quality, either of the thing or of the organ, seems more than unjustifiable, and even almost ridiculous. And on the whole we must admit that the defence has broken down. The secondary qualities must be judged to be merely appearance.

But are they the appearance of the primary, and are these the reality? The positive side of the contention was that in the extended we have the essence of the thing; and it is necessary to ask if this conclusion is true. The doctrine is, of course, materialism, and is a very simple creed. What is extended, together with its spatial relations, is substantive fact, and the rest is adjectival. We have not to ask here if this view is scientific, in the sense of being necessarily used for work in some sciences. That has, of course, nothing to do with the question now before us, since we are enquiring solely whether the doctrine is true. And, regarded in this way, perhaps no student would call materialism scientific.

I will indicate briefly the arguments against the sole reality of primary qualities. (a) In the first place, we may ask how, in the nature the extended, the terms stand to the relations which have to hold between them. This is a problem to be handled later (Chapter iv), and I will only remark here that its result is fatal to materialism. And, (b) in the second place, the relation of the primary qualities to the secondary in which class feeling and thought have presumably to be placed seems wholly unintelligible. For nothing is actually removed from existence by being labelled 'appearance'. What appears is there, and must be dealt with; but materialism has no rational way of dealing with appearance. Appearance must belong, and yet cannot belong, to the extended. It neither is able to fall somewhere apart, since there is no other real place; nor ought it, since, if so, the relation would vanish and appearance would cease to be derivative. But, on the other side, if it belongs in any sense to the reality, how can it be shown not to infect that with its own unreal character? Or we may urge that matter must cease to be itself, if qualified essentially by all that is secondary. But, taken otherwise, it has become itself but one out of two elements, and is not the reality.

And, (c) thirdly, the line of reasoning which showed that secondary qualities are not real, has equal force as applied to primary. The extended comes to us

F. H. Bradley and Monistic Idealism   23

only by relation to an organ; and, whether the organ is touch or is sight or muscle-feeling or whatever else it may be makes no difference to the argument. For, in any case, the thing is perceived by us through an affection of our body, and never without that. And our body itself is no exception, for we perceive that, as extended, solely by the action of one part upon another percipient part. That we have no miraculous intuition of our body as spatial reality is perfectly certain. But, if so, the extended thing will have its quality only when perceived by something else; and the percipient something else is again in the same case. Nothing, in short, proves extended except in relation to another thing, which itself does not possess the quality, if you try to take it by itself. And, further, the objection from dream and delusion holds again. That objection urges that error points to a necessary relation of the object to our knowledge, even where error is not admitted. But such a relation would reduce every quality to appearance. We might, indeed, attempt once more here to hold the former line of defence. We might reply that the extended thing is a fact real by itself, and that only its relation to our percipience is variable. But the inevitable conclusion is not so to be averted. If a thing is known to have a quality only under a certain condition, there is no process of reasoning from this which will justify the conclusion that the thing, if unconditioned, is yet the same. This seems quite certain; and, to go further, if we have no other source of information, if the quality in question is non-existent for us except in one relation, then for us to assert its reality away from that relation is more than unwarranted. It is, to speak plainly, an attempt in the end without meaning. And it would seem that, if materialism is to stand, it must somehow get to the existence of primary qualities in a way which avoids their relation to an organ. But since, as we shall hereafter see (Chapter iv), their very essence is relative, even this refuge is closed.

(d) But there is a more obvious argument against the sole reality of spatial qualities; and, if I were writing for the people an attack upon materialism, I should rest great weight on this point. Without secondary quality extension is not conceivable, and no one can bring it, as existing, before his mind if he keeps it quite pure. In short, it is the violent abstraction of one aspect from the rest, and the mere confinement of our attention to a single side of things, a fiction which, forgetting itself, takes a ghost for solid reality. And I will say a few words on this obvious answer to materialism.

That doctrine, of course, holds that the extended can be actual, entirely apart from every other quality. But extension is never so given. If it is visual, it must be coloured; and if it is tactual, or acquired in the various other ways which may fall under the head of the 'muscular sense'—then it is never free from sensations, coming from the skin, or the joints, or the muscles, or, as some would like to add, from a central source. And a man may say what he likes, but he cannot think of extension without thinking at the same time of a 'what' that is extended. And not only is this so, but particular differences, such as 'up and down', 'right and left', are necessary to the terms of the spatial relation. But these differences clearly are not merely spatial. Like the general 'what', they will consist in all cases of secondary quality from a sensation of the kinds I have mentioned above. Some psychologists, indeed, could go further, and could urge that the secondary qualities are original, and the primary derivative; since extension (in their view) is a construction or growth from the wholly non-extended. I could not endorse that, but I can appeal to what is indisputable. Extension cannot be presented, or thought of, except as one with quality that is secondary. It is by itself a mere abstraction, for some purposes necessary, but ridiculous when taken as an existing thing. Yet the materialist, from defect of nature or of education, or probably both, worships without justification this thin product of his untutored fancy.

'Not without justification,' he may reply, 'since in the procedure of science the secondary qualities are explained as results from the primary. Obviously, therefore, these latter are independent and prior.' But this is a very simple error. For suppose that you have shown that, given one element, A, another, b, does in fact follow on it; suppose that you can prove that b comes just the same, whether A is attended by c, or d, or e, or any one of a number of other qualities, you cannot go from this to the result that A exists and works naked. The secondary b can be explained, you urge, as issuing from the primary A, without consideration of aught else. Let it be so; but all that could follow is, that the *special* natures of A's accompaniments are not concerned in the process. There is not only no proof, but there is not even the very smallest presumption, that A could act by itself, or could be a real fact if alone. It is doubtless scientific to disregard certain aspects when we work; but to urge that therefore such aspects are not fact, and that what we use without regard to them is an independent real thing—this is barbarous metaphysics.

We have found then that, if the secondary qualities are appearance, the primary are certainly not able to stand by themselves. This distinction, from which materialism is blindly developed, has been seen to bring us no nearer to the true nature of reality.

Chapter II. Substantive and Adjective

We have seen that the distinction of primary from secondary qualities has not taken us far. Let us, without regard to it, and once more directly turning to what

F. H. Bradley and Monistic Idealism   25

meets us, examine another way of making that intelligible. We find the world's contents grouped into things and their qualities. The substantive and adjective is a time-honoured distinction and arrangement of facts, with a view to understand them and to arrive at reality. I must briefly point out the failure of this method, if regarded as a serious attempt at theory.

We may take the familiar instance of a lump of sugar. This is a thing, and it has properties, adjectives which qualify it. It is, for example, white, and hard, and sweet. The sugar, we say, *is* all that; but what the *is* can really mean seems doubtful. A thing is not any one of its qualities, if you take that quality by itself; if 'sweet' were the same as 'simply sweet', the thing would clearly be not sweet. And, again, in so far as sugar is sweet it is not white or hard; for these properties are all distinct. Nor, again, can the thing be all its properties, if you take them each severally. Sugar is obviously not mere whiteness, mere hardness, and mere sweetness; for its reality lies somehow in its unity. But if, on the other hand, we inquire what there can be in the thing beside its several qualities, we are baffled once more. We can discover no real unity existing outside these qualities, or, again, existing within them.

But it is our emphasis, perhaps, on the aspect of unity which has caused this confusion. Sugar is, of course, not the mere plurality of its different adjectives; but why should it be more than its properties in relation? When 'white', 'hard', 'sweet', and the rest co-exist in a certain way, that is surely the secret of the thing. The qualities are, and are in relation. But here, as before, when we leave phrases we wander among puzzles. 'Sweet', 'white', and 'hard' seem now the subjects about which we are saying something. We certainly do not predicate one of the other; for, if we attempt to identify them, they at once resist. They are in this wholly incompatible, and, so far, quite contrary. Apparently, then, a relation is to be asserted of each. One quality, *A*, is in relation with another quality, *B*. But what are we to understand here by *is*? We do not mean that 'in relation with *B*' is *A*, and yet we assert that *A is* 'in relation with *B*'. In the same way *C* is called 'before *D*', and *E* is spoken of *being* 'to the right of *F*'. We say all this, but from the interpretation, then 'before *D*' is *C*, and 'to the right of *F* is *E*, we recoil in horror. No, we should reply, the relation is not identical with the thing. It is only a sort of attribute which inheres or belongs. The word to use, when we are pressed, should not be *is*, but only *has*. But this reply comes to very little. The whole question is evidently as to the meaning of *has*; and, apart from metaphors not taken seriously, there appears really to be no answer. And we seem unable to clear ourselves from the old dilemma, If you predicate what is different, you ascribe to the subject what it is *not*; and if you predicate what is *not* different, you say nothing at all.

26   Early Analytic Philosophy

Driven forward, we must attempt to modify our statement. We must assert the relation now, not of one term, but of both. *A* and *B* are identical in such a point, and in such another point they differ; or, again, they are so situated in space or in time. And thus we avoid *is*, and keep to *are*. But, seriously, that does not look like the explanation of a difficulty; it looks more like trifling with phrases. For, if you mean that *A* and *B*, taken each severally, even 'have' this relation, you are asserting what is false. But if you mean that *A* and *B* in such a relation are so related, you appear to mean nothing. For here, as before, if the predicate makes no difference, it is idle; but, if it makes the subject other than it is, it is false.

But let us attempt another exit from this bewildering circle. Let us abstain from making the relation an attribute of the related, and let us make it more or less independent. 'There is a relation *C*, in which *A* and *B* stand; and it appears with both of them.' But here again we have made no progress. The relation *C* has been admitted different from *A* and *B*, and no longer is predicated of them. Something, however, seems to be said of this relation *C*, and said, again, of *A* and *B*. And this something is not to be the ascription of one to the other. If so, it would appear to be another relation, *D*, in which *C*, on one side, and, on the other side, *A* and *B*, stand. But such a makeshift leads at once to the infinite process. The new relation *D* can be predicated in no way of *C*, or of *A* and *B*; and hence we must have recourse to a fresh relation, *E*, which comes between *D* and whatever we had before. But this must lead to another, *F*; and so on, indefinitely. Thus the problem is not solved by taking relations as independently real. For, if so, the qualities and their relation fall entirely apart, and then we have said nothing. Or we have to make a new relation between the old relation and the terms; which, when it is made, does not help us. It either itself demands a new relation, and so on without end, or it leaves us where we were, entangled in difficulties.

The attempt to resolve the thing into properties, each a real thing, taken somehow together with independent relations, has proved an obvious failure. And we are forced to see, when we reflect, that a relation standing alongside of its terms is a delusion. If it is to be real, it must be so somehow at the expense of the terms, or, at least, must be something which appears in them or to which they belong. A relation between *A* and *B* implies really a substantial foundation within them. This foundation, if we say that *A* is like to *B*, is the identity *X* which holds these differences together. And so with space and time—everywhere there must be a whole embracing what is related, or there would be no differences and no relation. It seems as if a reality possessed differences, *A* and *B*, incompatible with one another and also with itself. And so in order, without contradiction, to retain its various properties, this whole consents to wear the form of relations between them. And this is why qualities are found to be some incompatible and some compatible. They are all different, and, on the other hand, because belonging to one whole, are all forced to come together. And it is only where they come together distantly by the help of a relation, that they cease to conflict. On the other hand, where a thing fails to set up a relation between its properties, they are contrary at once. Thus colours and smells live together at peace in the reality; for the thing divides itself, and so leaves them merely side by side within itself. But colour collides with colour, because their special identity drives them together. And here again, if the identity becomes relational by help of space, they are outside one another, and are peaceful once more. The 'contrary', in short, consists of differences possessed by that which cannot find the relation which serves to couple them apart. It is marriage attempted without a *modus vivendi*. But where the whole, relaxing its unity, takes the form of an arrangement, there is co-existence with concord.

I have set out the above mainly because of the light which it throws upon the nature of the 'contrary'. It affords no solution of our problem of inherence. It tells us how we are forced to arrange things in a certain manner, but it does not justify that arrangement. The thing avoids contradiction by its disappearance into relations, and by its admission of the adjectives to a standing of their own. But it avoids contradiction by a kind of suicide. It can give no rational account of the relations and the terms which it adopts, and it cannot recover the real unity, without which it is nothing. The whole device is a clear makeshift. It consists in saying to the outside world, 'I am the owner of these my adjectives', and to the properties, 'I am but a relation, which leaves you your liberty'. And to itself and for itself it is the futile pretence to have both characters at once. Such an arrangement may work, but the theoretical problem is not solved.

The immediate unity, in which facts come to us, has been broken up by experience, and later by reflection. The thing with its adjectives is a device for enjoying at once both variety and concord. But the distinctions, once made, fall apart from the thing, and away from one another. And our attempt to understand their relations brought us round merely to a unity, which confesses itself a pretence, or else falls back upon the old undivided substance, which admits of no relations. We shall see the hopelessness of its dilemma more clearly when we have examined how relation stands to quality. But this demands another chapter.

I will, in conclusion, dispose very briefly of a possible suggestion. The distinctions taken in the thing are to be held only, it may be urged, as the ways in which *we* regard it. The thing itself maintains its unity, and the aspects of adjective and substantive are only *our* points of view. Hence they do no injury to the real. But this defence is futile, since the question is how without error we may think of reality. If then your collection of points of view is a defensible way of so thinking, by all means apply it to the thing, and make an end of our puzzle. Otherwise the thing, without the points of view, appears to have no character at all, and they, without the thing, to possess no reality—even if they could be made compatible among themselves, the one with the other. In short, this distinction, drawn between the fact and our manner of regarding it, only serves to double the original confusion. There will now be an inconsistency in my mind as well as in the thing; and, far from helping, the one will but aggravate the other.

Chapter III. Relation and Quality

It must have become evident that the problem, discussed in the last chapter, really turns on the respective natures of quality and relation. And the reader may have anticipated the conclusion we are now to reach. The arrangement of given facts into relations and qualities may be necessary in practice, but it is theoretically unintelligible. The reality, so characterized, is not true reality, but is appearance.

And it can hardly be maintained that this character calls for no understanding—that it is a unique way of being which the reality possesses, and which we have got merely to receive. For it most evidently has ceased to be something quite immediate. It contains aspects now distinguished and taken as differences, and which tend, so far as we see, to a further separation. And, if the reality really has a way of uniting these in harmony, that way assuredly is not manifest at first sight. On our own side those distinctions which even consciously we make may possibly in some way give the truth about reality. But, so long as we fail to justify them and to make them intelligible to ourselves, we are bound, so far, to set them down as mere appearance.

The object of this chapter is to show that the very essence of these ideas is infected and contradicts itself. Our conclusion briefly will be this. Relation presupposes quality, and quality relation. Each can be something neither together with, nor apart from, the other; and the vicious circle in which they turn is not the truth about reality.

1. Qualities are nothing without relations. In trying to exhibit the truth of this statement, I will lay no weight on a considerable mass of evidence. This, furnished by psychology, would attempt to show how qualities are variable by changes of relation. The differences we perceive in many cases seem to have been so created. But I will not appeal to such an argument, since I do not see that it could prove wholly the non-existence of original and independent qualities. And the line of proof through the necessity of contrast for perception has, in my opinion, been carried beyond logical limits. Hence, though these considerations

F. H. Bradley and Monistic Idealism   29

have without doubt an important bearing on our problem, I prefer here to disregard them. And I do not think that they are necessary.

We may proceed better to our conclusion in the following way. You can never, we may argue, find qualities without relations. Whenever you take them so, they are made so, and continue so, by an operation which itself implies relation. Their plurality gets for us all its meaning through relations; and to suppose it otherwise in reality is wholly indefensible. I will draw this out in greater detail.

To find qualities without relations is surely impossible. In the field of consciousness, even when we abstract from the relations of identity and difference, they are never independent. One is together with, and related to, one other, at the least—in fact, always to more than one. Nor will an appeal to a lower and undistinguished state of mind, where in one feeling are many aspects, assist us in any way. I admit the existence of such states without any relation, but I wholly deny there the presence of qualities. For if these felt aspects, while merely felt, are to be called qualities proper, they are so only for the observation of an outside observer. And then for him they are given *as* aspects—that is, together with relations. In short, if you go back to mere unbroken feeling, you have no relations and no qualities. But if you come to what is distinct, you get relations at once.

I presume we shall be answered in this way. Even though, we shall be told, qualities proper cannot be discovered apart from relations, that is no real disproof of their separate existence. For we are well able to distinguish them and to consider them by themselves. And for this perception certainly an operation of our minds is required. So far, therefore, as you say, what is different must be distinct, and, in consequence, related. But this relation does not really belong to the reality. The relation has existence only for us, and as a way of our getting to know. But the distinction, for all that, is based upon differences in the actual; and these remain when our relations have fallen away or have been removed.

But such an answer depends on the separation of product from process, and this separation seems indefensible. The qualities, as distinct, are always made so by an action which is admitted to imply relation. They are made so, and, what is more, they are emphatically kept so. And you cannot ever get your product standing apart from its process. Will you say, the process is not essential? But that is a conclusion to be proved, and it is monstrous to assume it. Will you try to prove it by analogy? It is possible for many purposes to accept and employ the existence of processes and relations which do not affect specially the inner nature of objects. But the very possibility of so distinguishing in the end between

30   Early Analytic Philosophy

inner and outer, and of setting up the inner as absolutely independent of all relation, is here in question. Mental operations such as comparison, which presuppose in the compared qualities already existing, could in no case prove that these qualities depend on no relations at all. But I cannot believe that this is a matter to be decided by analogy, for the whole case is briefly this. There is an operation which, removing one part of what is given, presents the other part in abstraction. This result is never to be found anywhere apart from a persisting abstraction. And, if we have no further information, I can find no excuse for setting up the result as being fact without the process. The burden lies wholly on the assertor, and he fails entirely to support it. The argument that in perception one quality must be given first and before others, and therefore cannot be relative, is hardly worth mentioning. What is more natural than for qualities always to have come to us in some conjunction, and never alone?

We may go further. Not only is the ignoring of the process a thing quite indefensible—even if it blundered into truth—but there is evidence that it gives falsehood. For the result bears internally the character of the process. The manyness of the qualities cannot, in short, be reconciled with their simplicity. Their plurality depends on relation, and, without that relation, they are not distinct. But, if not distinct, then not different, and therefore not qualities.

I am not urging that quality without difference is in every sense impossible. For all I know, creatures may exist whose life consists, for themselves, in one unbroken simple feeling; and the arguments urged against such a possibility in my judgment come short. And, if you want to call this feeling a quality, by all means gratify your desire. But then remember that the whole point is quite irrelevant. For no one is contending whether the universe is or is not a quality in this sense; but the question is entirely as to qualities. And a universe confined to one feeling would not only not be qualities, but it would fail even to be one quality, as different from others and as distinct from relations. Our question is really whether relation is essential to differences.

We have seen that in fact the two are never found apart. We have seen that the separation by abstraction is no proof of real separateness. And now we have to urge, in short, that any separateness implies separation, and so relation, and is therefore, when made absolute, a self-discrepancy. For consider, the qualities A and B are to be different from each other; and, if so, that difference must fall somewhere. If it falls, in any degree or to any extent, outside A or B, we have relation at once. But, on the other hand, how can difference and otherness fall inside? If we have in A any such otherness, then inside A we must distinguish its own quality and its otherness. And, if so, then the unsolved problem breaks out inside each quality, and separates each into two qualities in

F. H. Bradley and Monistic Idealism   31

relation. In brief, diversity without relation seems a word without meaning. And it is no answer to urge that plurality proper is not in question here. I am convinced of the opposite, but by all means, if you will, let us confine ourselves to distinctness and difference. I rest my argument upon this, that if there are no differences, there are no qualities, since all must fall into one. But, if there is any difference, then that implies a relation. Without a relation it has no meaning; it is a mere word, and not a thought; and no one would take it for a thought if he did not, in spite of his protests, import relation into it. And this is the point on which all seems to turn, Is it possible to think of qualities without thinking of distinct characters? Is it possible to think of these without some relation between them, either explicit, or else unconsciously supplied by the mind that tries only to apprehend? Have qualities without relation any meaning for thought? For myself, I am sure that they have none.

And I find a confirmation in the issue of the most thorough attempt to build a system on this ground. There it is not too much to say that all the content of the universe becomes something very like an impossible illusion. The Reals are secluded and simple, simple beyond belief if they never suspect that they are not so. But our fruitful life, on the other hand, seems due to their persistence in imaginary recovery from unimaginable perversion. And they remain guiltless of all real share in these ambiguous connections, which seem to make the world. They are above it, and fixed like stars in the firmament—if there only were a firmament.

2. We have found that qualities, taken without relations, have no intelligible meaning. Unfortunately, taken together with them, they are equally unintelligible. They cannot, in the first place, be wholly resolved into the relations. You may urge, indeed, that without distinction no difference is left; but, for all that, the differences will not disappear into the distinction. They must come to it, more or less, and they cannot wholly be made by it. I still insist that for thought what is not relative is nothing. But I urge, on the other hand, that nothings cannot be related, and that to turn qualities in relation into mere relations is impossible. Since the fact seems constituted by both, you may urge, if you please, that either one of them constitutes it. But if you mean that the other is not wanted, and that relations can somehow make the terms upon which they seem to stand, then, for my mind, your meaning is quite unintelligible. So far as I can see, relations must depend upon terms, just as much as terms upon relations. And the partial failure, now manifest, of the Dialectic Method seems connected with some misapprehension on this point.

Hence the qualities must be, and must *also* be related. But there is hence a diversity which falls inside each quality. It has a double character, as both

32 Early Analytic Philosophy

supporting and as being made by the relation. It may be taken as at once condition and result, and the question is as to how it can combine this variety. For it must combine the diversity, and yet it fails to do so. A is both made, and is not made, what it is by relation; and these different aspects are not each the other, nor again is either A. If we call its diverse aspects a and α, then A is partly each of these. As a it is the difference on which distinction is based, while as α it is the distinctness that results from connection. A is really both somehow together as A (a–α). But (as we saw in Chapter ii.) *without* the use of a relation it is impossible to predicate this variety of A. And, on the other hand, with an internal relation A's unity disappears, and its contents are dissipated in an endless process of distinction. A at first becomes a in relation with α, but these terms themselves fall hopelessly asunder. We have got, against our will, not a mere aspect, but a new quality a, which itself stands in a relation; and hence (as we saw before with A) its content must be manifold. As going into the relation it itself is a^2, and as resulting from the relation it itself is a^2. And it combines, and yet cannot combine, these adjectives. We, in brief, are led by a principle of fission which conducts us to no end. Every quality in relation has, in consequence, a diversity within its own nature, and this diversity cannot immediately be asserted of the quality. Hence the quality must exchange its unity for an internal relation. But, thus set free, the diverse aspects, because each something in relation, must each be something also beyond. This diversity is fatal to the internal unity of each; and it demands a new relation, and so on without limit. In short, qualities in a relation have turned out as unintelligible as were qualities without one. The problem from both sides has baffled us.

3. We may briefly reach the same dilemma from the side of relations. They are nothing intelligible, either with or without their qualities. In the first place, a relation without terms seems mere verbiage; and terms appear, therefore, to be something beyond their relation. At least, for myself, a relation which somehow precipitates terms which were not there before, or a relation which can get on somehow without terms, and with no differences beyond the mere ends of a line of connection, is really a phrase without meaning. It is, to my mind, a false abstraction, and a thing which loudly contradicts itself; and I fear that I am obliged to leave the matter so. As I am left without information, and can discover with my own ears no trace of harmony, I am forced to conclude to a partial deafness in others. And hence a relation, we must say, without qualities is nothing.

But how the relation can stand to the qualities is, on the other side, unintelligible. If it is nothing to the qualities, then they are not related at all; and, if so, as we saw, they have ceased to be qualities, and their relation is a

F. H. Bradley and Monistic Idealism   **33**

nonentity. But if it is to be something to them, then clearly we now shall require a *new* connecting relation. For the relation hardly can be the mere adjective of one or both of its terms; or, at least, as such it seems indefensible. [footnote removed] And, being something itself, if it does not itself bear a relation to the terms, in what intelligible way will it succeed in being anything to them? But here again we are hurried off into the eddy of a hopeless process, since we are forced to go on finding new relations without end. The links are united by a link, and this bond of union is a link which also has two ends; and these require each a fresh link to connect them with the old. The problem is to find how the relation can stand to its qualities; and this problem is insoluble. If you take the connection as a solid thing, you have got to show, and you cannot show, how the other solids are joined to it. And, if you so, as we saw, they have ceased to be qualities, and their relation is a nonentity. But if it is to be something to them, then clearly we now shall require a new connecting relation. For the relation hardly can be the mere adjective of one or both of its terms; or, at least, as such it seems indefensible. And, being something itself, if it does not itself bear a relation to the terms, in what intelligible way will it succeed in being anything to them? But here again we are hurried off into the eddy of a hopeless process, since we are forced to go on finding new relations without end. The links are united by a link, and this bond of union is a link which also has two ends; and these require each a fresh link to connect them with the old. The problem is to find how the relation can stand to its qualities; and this problem is insoluble. If you take the connection as a solid thing, you have got to show, and you cannot show, how the other solids are joined to it. And, if you take it as a kind of medium or unsubstantial atmosphere, it is a connection no longer. You find, in this case, that the whole question of the relation of the qualities (for they certainly in some way *are* related) arises now outside it, in precisely the same form as before. The original relation, in short, has become a nonentity, but, in becoming this, it has removed no element of the problem.

I will bring this chapter to an end. It would be easy, and yet profitless, to spin out its argument with ramifications and refinements. And for me to attempt to anticipate the reader's objections would probably be useless. I have stated the case, and I must leave it. The conclusion to which I am brought is that a relational way of thought—any one that moves by the machinery of terms and relations—must give appearance, and not truth. It is a makeshift, a device, a mere practical compromise, most necessary, but in the end most indefensible. We have to take reality as many, and to take it as one, and to avoid contradiction. We want to divide it, or to take it, when we please, as indivisible; to go as far as we desire in either of these directions, and to stop when that suits us. And we succeed,

34   **Early Analytic Philosophy**

but succeed merely by shutting the eye, which if left open would condemn us; or by a perpetual oscillation and a shifting of the ground, so as to turn our back upon the aspect we desire to ignore. But when these inconsistencies are forced together, as in metaphysics they must be, the result is an open and staring discrepancy. And we cannot attribute this to reality; while, if we try to take it on ourselves, we have changed one evil for two. Our intellect, then, has been condemned to confusion and bankruptcy, and the reality has been left outside uncomprehended. Or rather, what is worse, it has been stripped bare of all distinction and quality. It is left naked and without a character, and we are covered with confusion.

The reader who has followed and has grasped the principle of this chapter, will have little need to spend his time upon those which succeed it. He will have seen that our experience, where relational, is not true; and he will have condemned, almost without a hearing, the great mass of phenomena. I feel, however, called on next to deal very briefly with Space and Time.

Chapter XII. Things in Themselves

We have found, so far, that we have not been able to arrive at reality. The various ways, in which things have been taken up, have all failed to give more than mere appearance. Whatever we have tried has turned out something which, on investigation, has been proved to contradict itself. But that which does not attain to internal unity, has clearly stopped short of genuine reality. And, on the other hand, to sit down contented is impossible, unless, that is we are resolved to put up with mere confusion. For to transcend what is given is clearly obligatory, if we are to think at all and to have any views whatever. But, the deliverance of the moment once left behind, we have succeeded in meeting with nothing that holds together. Every view has been seen only to furnish appearance, and the reality has escaped. It has baffled us so constantly, so persistently retreated, that in the end we are forced to set it down as unattainable. It seems to have been discovered to reside in another world than ours.

We have here reached a familiar way of regarding the universe, a doctrine held with very different degrees of comprehension. The universe, upon this view (whether it understands itself or not), falls apart into two regions, we may call them two hemispheres. One of these is the world of experience and knowledge— in every sense without reality. The other is the kingdom of reality—without either knowledge or experience. Or we have on one side phenomena, in other words, things as they are to us, and ourselves so far as we are anything to ourselves; while on the other side are Things as they are in themselves and as they do not

F. H. Bradley and Monistic Idealism 35

appear; or, if we please, we may call this side the Unknowable. And our attitude towards such a divided universe varies a good deal. We may be thankful to be rid of that which is not relative to our affairs, and which cannot in any way concern us; and we may be glad that the worthless is thrown over the wall. Or we may regret that Reality is too good to be known, and from the midst of our own confusion may revere the other side in its inaccessible grandeur. We may even naively felicitate ourselves on total estrangement, and rejoice that at last utter ignorance has removed every scruple which impeded religion. Where we know nothing we can have no possible objection to worship. [footnote removed]

This view is popular, and to some extent is even plausible. It is natural to feel that the best and the highest is unknowable, in the sense of being something which our knowledge cannot master. And this is probably all that for most minds the doctrine signifies. But of course this is *not* what it says, nor what it means, when it has any definite meaning. For it does not teach that our knowledge of reality is imperfect; it asserts that it does not exist, and that we have no knowledge at all, however imperfect. There is a hard and fast line, with our apprehension on the one side and the Thing on the other side, and the two hopelessly apart. This is the doctrine, and its plausibility vanishes before criticism.

Its absurdity may be shown in several ways. The Unknowable must, of course, be prepared either to deserve its name or not. But, if it actually were not knowable, we could not know that such a thing even existed. It would be much as if we said, 'Since all my faculties are totally confined to my garden, I cannot tell if the roses next door are in flower.' And this seems inconsistent. And we may push the line of attack which we mentioned in the last chapter. If the theory really were true, then it must be impossible. There is no reconciling our knowledge of its truth with that general condition which exists if it is true. But I propose to adopt another way of criticism, which perhaps may be plainer.

I will first make a remark as to the plurality involved in Things in themselves. If this is *meant*, then within their secluded world we have a long series of problems. Their diversity and their relations bring us back to those very difficulties which we were endeavouring to avoid. And it seems clear that, if we wish to be consistent, the plural must be dropped. Hence in future we shall confine ourselves to the Thing in itself.

We have got this reality on one side and our appearances on the other, and we are naturally led to enquire about their connection. Are they related, the one to the other, or not? If they are related, and if in any way the appearances are made the adjectives of reality, then the Thing has become qualified by them. It is qualified, but on what principle? That is what we do not know. We have in effect every unsolved problem which vexed us before; and we have, besides,

36   Early Analytic Philosophy

this whole confusion now predicated of the Thing, no longer, therefore, something by itself. But this perplexed attribution was precisely that which the doctrine intended to avoid. We must therefore deny any relation of our appearances to the Thing. But, if so, other troubles vex us. Either our Thing has qualities, or it has not. If it has them, then within itself the same puzzles break out which we intended to leave behind—to make a prey of phenomena and to rest contented with *their* ruin. So we must correct ourselves and assert that the Thing is unqualified. But, if so, we are destroyed with no less certainty. For a Thing without qualities is clearly not real. It is mere Being, or mere Nothing, according as you take it simply for what it is, or consider also that which it *means* to be. Such an abstraction is palpably of no use to us.

And, if we regard the situation from the side of phenomena, it is not more encouraging. We must take appearances in connection with reality, or not. In the former case, they are not rendered one whit less confused. They offer precisely the old jungle in which no way could be found, and which is not cleared by mere attribution to a Thing in itself. But, if we deny the connection of phenomena with the Real, our condition is not improved. Either we possess now two realms of confusion and disorder, existing side by side, or the one above the other. And, in this case, the 'other world' of the Thing in itself only serves to reduplicate all that troubles us here. Or, on the other hand, if we suppose the Thing to be unqualified, it still gives us no assistance. Everything in our concrete world remains the same, and the separate existence somewhere of this wretched abstraction serves us only as a poor and irrelevant excuse for neglecting our own concerns.

And I will allow myself to dwell on this last feature of the case. The appearances after all, being what we experience, must be what matters for us. They are surely the one thing which, from the nature of the case, can possess human value. Surely, the moment we understand what we mean by our words, the Thing in itself becomes utterly worthless and devoid of all interest. And we discover a state of mind which would be ridiculous to a degree, if it had not unfortunately a serious side. It is contended that contradictions in phenomena are something quite in order, so long as the Thing in itself is not touched. That is to say that everything, which we know and can experience, does not matter, however distracted its case, and that this purely irrelevant ghost is the ark of salvation to be preserved at all costs. But how it can be anything to us whether something outside our knowledge contradicts itself or not—is simply unintelligible. What is too visible is our own readiness to sacrifice everything which possesses any possible claim on us. And what is to be inferred is our confusion, and our domination by a theory which lives only in the world of misunderstanding.

We have seen that the doctrine of a Thing in itself is absurd. A reality of this sort is assuredly not something unverifiable. It has on the contrary a nature which is fully transparent, as a false and empty abstraction, whose generation is plain. We found that reality was not the appearances, and that result must hold good; but, on the other hand, reality is certainly not something else which is unable to appear. For that is sheer self-contradiction, which is plausible only so long as we do not realise its meaning. The assertion of a reality falling outside knowledge, is quite nonsensical.

And so this attempt to shelve our problems, this proposal to take no pains about what are *only* phenomena, has broken down. It was a vain notion to set up an idol apart, to dream that facts for that reason had ceased to be facts, and had somehow become *only* something else. And this false idea is an illusion which we should attempt to clear out of our minds once for all. We shall have hereafter to enquire into the nature of appearance; but for the present we may keep a fast hold upon this, that appearances exist. That is absolutely certain, and to deny it is nonsense. And whatever exists must belong to reality. That is also quite certain, and its denial once more is self-contradictory. Our appearances no doubt may be a beggarly show, and their nature to an unknown extent may be something which, as it is, is not true of reality. That is one thing, and it is quite another thing to speak as if these facts had no actual existence, or as if there could be anything but reality to which they might belong. And I must venture to repeat that such an idea would be sheer nonsense. What appears, for that sole reason, most indubitably *is*; and there is no possibility of conjuring its being away from it. And, though we ask no question at present as to the exact nature of reality, we may be certain that it cannot be less than appearances; we may be sure that the least of these in some way contributes to make it what it is. And the whole result of this Book may be summed up in a few words. Everything so far, which we have seen, has turned out to be appearance. It is that which, taken as it stands, proves inconsistent with itself, and for this reason cannot be true of the real. But to deny its existence or to divorce it from reality is out of the question. For it has a positive character which is indubitable fact, and, however much this fact maybe pronounced appearance, it can have no place in which to live except reality. And reality, set on one side and apart from all appearance, would assuredly be nothing. Hence what is certain is that, in some way, these inseparables are joined. This is the positive result which has emerged from our discussion. Our failure so far lies in this, that we have not found the way in which

38   **Early Analytic Philosophy**

appearances can belong to reality. And to this further task we must now address ourselves, with however little hope of more than partial satisfaction.

Book II. Reality.

Chapter XIII. The General Nature of Reality

The result of our First Book has been mainly negative. We have taken up a number of ways of regarding reality and we have found that they all are vitiated by self-discrepancy. The reality can accept not one of these predicates, at least in the character in which so far they have come. We certainly ended with a reflection which promised something positive. Whatever is rejected as appearance is, for that very reason, no mere nonentity. It cannot bodily be shelved and merely got rid of, and, therefore, since it must fall somewhere, it must belong to reality. To take it as existing somehow and somewhere in the unreal, would surely be quite meaningless. For reality must own and cannot be less than appearance, and that is the one positive result which, so far, we have reached. But as to the character which, otherwise, the real possesses, we at present know nothing; and a further knowledge is what we must aim at through the remainder of our search. The present Book, to some extent, falls into two divisions. The first of these deals mainly with the general character of reality, and with the defence of this against a number of objections. Then from this basis, in the second place, I shall go on to consider mainly some special features. But I must admit that I have kept to no strict principle of division. I have really observed no rule of progress, except to get forward in the best way that I can.

At the beginning of our inquiry into the nature of the real we encounter, of course, a general doubt or denial. To know the truth, we shall be told, is impossible, or is, at all events, wholly impracticable. We cannot have positive knowledge about first principles; and, if we could possess it, we should not know when actually we had got it. What is denied is, in short, the existence of a criterion. I shall, later on, in Chapter xxvii, have to deal more fully with the objections of a thorough-going scepticism, and I will here confine myself to what seems requisite for the present.

Is there an absolute criterion? This question, to my mind, is answered by a second question: How otherwise should we be able to say anything at all about appearance? For through the last Book, the reader will remember, we were for the most part criticising. We were judging phenomena and were condemning them, and throughout we proceeded as if the self-contradictory could not be real. But this was surely to have and to apply an absolute criterion. For consider:

F. H. Bradley and Monistic Idealism 39

you can scarcely propose to be quite passive when presented with statements about reality. You can hardly take the position of admitting any and every nonsense to be truth, truth absolute and entire, at least so far as you know. For, if you think at all so as to discriminate between truth and falsehood, you will find that you cannot accept open self-contradiction. Hence to think is to judge, and to judge is to criticise, and to criticise is to use a criterion of reality. And surely to doubt this would be mere blindness or confused self-deception. But, if so, it is clear that, in rejecting the inconsistent as appearance, we are applying a positive knowledge of the ultimate nature of things. Ultimate reality is such that it does not contradict itself; here is an absolute criterion. And it is proved absolute by the fact that, either in endeavouring to deny it, or even in attempting to doubt it, we tacitly assume its validity.

One of these essays in delusion may be noticed briefly in passing. We may be told that our criterion has been developed by experience, and that therefore at least it may not be absolute. But why anything should be weaker for having been developed is, in the first place, not obvious. And, in the second place, the whole doubt, when understood, destroys itself. For the alleged origin of our criterion is delivered to us by knowledge which rests throughout on its application as an absolute test. And what can be more irrational than to try to prove that a principle is doubtful, when the proof through every step rests on its unconditional truth? It would, of course, not be irrational to take one's stand on this criterion, to use it to produce a conclusion hostile to itself, and to urge that therefore our whole knowledge is self-destructive, since it essentially drives us to what we cannot accept. But this is not the result which our supposed objector has in view, or would welcome. He makes no attempt to show in general that a psychological growth is in any way hostile to metaphysical validity. And he is not prepared to give up his own psychological knowledge, which knowledge plainly is ruined if the criterion is *not* absolute. The doubt is seen, when we reflect, to be founded on that which it endeavours to question. And it has but blindly borne witness to the absolute certainty of our knowledge about reality.

Thus we possess a criterion, and our criterion is supreme. I do not mean to deny that we might have several standards, giving us sundry pieces of information about the nature of things. But, be that as it may, we still have an over-ruling test of truth, and the various standards (if they exist) are certainly subordinate. This at once becomes evident, for we cannot refuse to bring such standards together, and to ask if they agree. Or, at least, if a doubt is suggested as to their consistency, each with itself and with the rest, we are compelled, so to speak, to assume jurisdiction. And if they were guilty of self-contradiction, when examined or compared, we should condemn them as appearance. But

40   Early Analytic Philosophy

we could not do that if they were not subject all to one tribunal. And hence, as we find nothing not subordinate to the test of self-consistency, we are forced to set that down as supreme and absolute.

But it may be said that this supplies us with no real information. If we think, then certainly we are not allowed to be inconsistent, and it is admitted that this test is unconditional and absolute. But it will be urged that, for knowledge about any matter, we require something more than a bare negation. The ultimate reality (we are agreed) does not permit self-contradiction, but a prohibition or an absence (we shall be told) by itself does not amount to positive knowledge. The denial of inconsistency, therefore, does not predicate any positive quality. But such an objection is untenable. It may go so far as to assert that a bare denial is possible, that we may reject a predicate though we stand on no positive basis, and though there is nothing special which serves to reject. This error has been refuted in my *Principles of Logic* (Book I, Chapter iii.), and I do not propose to discuss it here. I will pass to another sense in which the objection may seem more plausible. The criterion, it may be urged, in itself is doubtless positive; but, for our knowledge and in effect, is merely negative. And it gives us therefore no information at all about reality, for, although knowledge is there, it cannot be brought out. The criterion is a basis, which serves as the foundation of denial; but, since this basis cannot be exposed, we are but able to stand on it and unable to see it. And it hence, in effect, tells us nothing, though there are assertions which it does not allow us to venture on. This objection, when stated in such a form, may seem plausible, and there is a sense in which I am prepared to admit that it is valid. If by the nature of reality we understand its full nature, I am not contending that this in a complete form is knowable. But that is very far from being the point here at issue. For the objection denies that we have a standard which gives *any* positive knowledge, *any* information, complete or incomplete, about the genuine reality. And this denial assuredly is mistaken.

The objection admits that we know what reality *does*, but it refuses to allow us any understanding of what reality is. The standard (it is agreed) both exists and possesses a positive character, and it is agreed that this character rejects inconsistency. It is admitted that we know this, and the point at issue is whether such knowledge supplies any positive information. And to my mind this question seems not hard to answer. For I cannot see how, when I observe a thing at work, I am to stand there and to insist that I know nothing of its nature. I fail to perceive how a function is nothing at all, or how it does not positively qualify that to which I attribute it. To know only so much, I admit, may very possibly be useless; it may leave us without the information which we desire most to obtain; but, for all that, it is not total ignorance.

F. H. Bradley and Monistic Idealism 41

Our standard denies inconsistency, and therefore asserts consistency. If we can be sure that the inconsistent is unreal, we must, logically, be just as sure that the reality is consistent. The question is solely as to the meaning to be given to consistency. We have now seen that it is not the bare exclusion of discord, for that is merely our abstraction, and is otherwise nothing. And our result, so far, is this. Reality is known to possess a positive character, but this character is at present determined only as that which excludes contradiction.

But we may make a further advance. We saw (in the preceding chapter) that all appearance must belong to reality. For what appears is, and whatever is cannot fall outside the real. And we may now combine this result with the conclusion just reached. We may say that everything, which appears, is somehow real in such a way as to be self-consistent. The character of the real is to possess everything phenomenal in a harmonious form.

I will repeat the same truth in other words. Reality is one in this sense that it has a positive nature exclusive of discord, a nature which must hold throughout everything that is to be real. Its diversity can be diverse only so far as not to clash, and what seems otherwise anywhere cannot be real. And, from the other side, everything which appears must be real. Appearance must belong to reality, and it must therefore be concordant and other than it seems. The bewildering mass of phenomenal diversity must hence somehow be at unity and self-consistent; for it cannot be elsewhere than in reality, and reality excludes discord. Or again we may put it so: the real is individual. It is one in the sense that its positive character embraces all differences in an inclusive harmony. And this knowledge, poor as it may be, is certainly more than bare negation or simple ignorance. So far as it goes, it gives us positive news about absolute reality.

Let us try to carry this conclusion a step farther on. We know that the real is one; but its oneness, so far, is ambiguous. Is it one system, possessing diversity as an adjective; or is its consistency, on the other hand, an attribute of independent realities? We have to ask, in short, if a plurality of reals is possible, and if these can merely co-exist so as not to be discrepant? Such a plurality would mean a number of beings not dependent on each other. On the one hand they would possess somehow the phenomenal diversity, for that possession, we have seen, is essential. And, on the other hand, they would be free from external disturbance and from inner discrepancy. After the enquiries of our First Book the possibility of such reals hardly calls for discussion. For the internal states of each give rise to hopeless difficulties. And, in the second place, the plurality of the reals cannot be reconciled with their independence. I will briefly resume the arguments which force us to this latter result.

Early Analytic Philosophy

If the Many are supposed to be without internal quality, each would forthwith become nothing, and we must therefore take each as being internally somewhat. And, if they are to be plural, they must be a diversity somehow co-existing together. Any attempt again to take their togetherness as unessential seems to end in the unmeaning. We have no knowledge of a plural diversity, nor can we attach any sense to it, if we do not have it somehow as one. And, if we abstract from this unity, we have also therewith abstracted from the plurality, and are left with mere being.

Can we then have a plurality of independent reals which merely co-exist? No, for absolute independence and co-existence are incompatible. Absolute independence is an idea which consists merely in one-sided abstraction. It is made by an attempted division of the aspect of several existence from the aspect of relatedness; and these aspects, whether in fact or thought, are really indivisible.

If we take the diversity of our reals to be such as we discover in feeling and at a stage where relations do not exist, that diversity is never found except as one integral character of an undivided whole. And if we forcibly abstract from that unity, then together with feeling we have destroyed the diversity of feeling. We are left not with plurality, but with mere being, or, if you prefer it, with nothing. Co-existence in feeling is hence an instance and a proof not of self-sufficiency, but of dependence, and beside this it would add a further difficulty. If the nature of our reals is the diversity found at a stage below relations, how are we to dispose of the mass of relational appearance? For that exists, and existing it must somehow qualify the world, a world the reality of which is discovered only at a level other than its own. Such a position would seem not easy to justify.

Thus a mode of togetherness such as we can verify in feeling destroys the independence of our reals. And they will fare no better if we seek to find their co-existence elsewhere. For any other verifiable way of togetherness must involve relations, and they are fatal to self-sufficiency. Relations, we saw, are a development of and from the felt totality. They inadequately express, and they still imply in the background that unity apart from which the diversity is nothing. Relations are unmeaning except within and on the basis of a substantial whole, and related terms, if made absolute, are forthwith destroyed. Plurality and relatedness are but features and aspects of a unity.

If the relations in which the reals somehow stand are viewed as essential, that, as soon as we understand it, involves at once the internal relativity of the reals. And any attempt to maintain the relations as merely external must fail. For if, wrongly and for argument's sake, we admit processes and arrangements which do not qualify their terms, yet such arrangements, if admitted, are at any rate not ultimate. The terms would be prior and independent only with regard to *these* arrangements, and they would remain relative otherwise, and vitally dependent on some whole. And severed from this unity, the terms perish by the very stroke which aims to set them up as absolute.

The reals therefore cannot be self-existent, and, if self-existent, yet taken as the world they would end in inconsistency. For the relations, because they exist, must somehow qualify the world. The relations then must externally qualify the sole and self-contained reality, and that seems self-contradictory or meaningless. [footnote removed] And if it is urged that a plurality of independent beings may be unintelligible, but that after all some unintelligible facts must be affirmed—the answer is obvious. An unintelligible fact may be admitted so far as, first, it is a fact, and so far as, secondly, it has a meaning which does not contradict itself internally or make self-discrepant our view of the world. But the alleged independence of the reals is no fact, but a theoretical construction; and, so far as it has a meaning, that meaning contradicts itself, and issues in chaos. A reality of this kind may safely be taken as unreal. We cannot therefore maintain a plurality save as dependent on the relations in which it stands. Or if desiring to avoid relations we fall back on the diversity given in feeling, the result is the same. The plurality then sinks to become merely an integral aspect in a single substantial unity, and the reals have vanished.

Chapter XIV. The General Nature of Reality (continued)

Our result so far is this. Everything phenomenal is somehow real; and the absolute must at least be as rich as the relative. And, further, the Absolute is not many; there are no independent reals. The universe is one in this sense that its differences exist harmoniously within one whole, beyond which there is nothing. Hence the Absolute is, so far, an individual and a system, but, if we stop here, it remains but formal and abstract. Can we then, the question is, say anything about the concrete nature of the system?

Certainly, I think, this is possible. When we ask as to the matter which fills up the empty outline, we can reply in one word, that this matter is experience. And experience means something much the same as given and present fact. We perceive, on reflection, that to be real, or even barely to exist, must be to fall within sentience. Sentient experience, in short, is reality, and what is not this is not real. We may say, in other words, that there is no being or fact outside of that which is commonly called psychical existence. Feeling, thought,

Early Analytic Philosophy

and volition (any groups under which we class psychical phenomena) are all the material of existence, and there is no other material, actual or even possible. This result in its general form seems evident at once; and, however serious a step we now seem to have taken, there would be no advantage at this point in discussing it at length. For the test in the main lies ready to our hand, and the decision rests on the manner in which it is applied. I will state the case briefly thus. Find any piece of existence, take up anything that any one could possibly call a fact, or could in any sense assert to have being, and then judge if it does not consist in sentient experience. Try to discover any sense in which you can still continue to speak of it, when all perception and feeling have been removed; or point out any fragment of its matter, any aspect of its being, which is not derived from and is not still relative to this source. When the experiment is made strictly, I can myself conceive of nothing else than the experienced. Anything, in no sense felt or perceived, becomes to me quite unmeaning. And as I cannot try to think of it without realising either that I am not thinking at all, or that I am thinking of it against my will as being experienced, I am driven to the conclusion that for me experience is the same as reality. The fact that falls elsewhere seems, in my mind, to be a mere word and a failure, or else an attempt at self-contradiction. It is a vicious abstraction whose existence is meaningless nonsense, and is therefore not possible.

This conclusion is open, of course, to grave objection, and must in its consequences give rise to serious difficulties. I will not attempt to anticipate the discussion of these, but before passing on, will try to obviate a dangerous mistake. For, in asserting that the real is nothing but experience, I may be understood to endorse a common error. I may be taken first to divide the percipient subject from the universe; and then, resting on that subject, as on a thing actual by itself, I may be supposed to urge that it cannot transcend its own states [footnote removed]. Such an argument would lead to impossible results, and would stand on a foundation of faulty abstraction. To set up the subject as real independently of the whole, and to make the whole into experience in the sense of an adjective of that subject, seems to me indefensible. And when I contend that reality must be sentient, my conclusion almost consists in the denial of this fundamental error. For if, seeking for reality, we go to experience, what we certainly do *not* find is a subject or an object, or indeed any other thing whatever, standing separate and on its own bottom. What we discover rather is a whole in which distinctions can be made, but in which divisions do not exist. And this is the point on which I insist, and it is the very ground on which I stand, when I urge that reality is sentient experience. I mean that to be real is to be indissolubly one thing with sentience. It is to be something which comes as a feature and aspect within one whole of

F. H. Bradley and Monistic Idealism   45

feeling, something which, except as an integral element of such sentience, has no meaning at all. And what I repudiate is the separation of feeling from the felt, or of the desired from desire, or of what is thought from thinking, or the division—I might add—of anything from anything else. Nothing is ever so presented as real by itself, or can be argued so to exist without demonstrable fallacy. And in asserting that the reality is experience, I rest throughout on this foundation. You cannot find fact unless in unity with sentience, and one cannot in the end be divided from the other, either actually or in idea. But to be utterly indivisible from feeling or perception, to be an integral element in a whole which is experienced, this surely is itself to *be* experience. Being and reality are, in brief, one thing with sentience; they can neither be opposed to, nor even in the end distinguished from it.

I am well aware that this statement stands in need of explanation and defence. This will, I hope, be supplied by succeeding chapters, and I think it better for the present to attempt to go forward. Our conclusion, so far, will be this, that the Absolute is one system, and that its contents are nothing but sentient experience. It will hence be a single and all-inclusive experience, which embraces every partial diversity in concord. For it cannot be less than appearance, and hence no feeling or thought, of any kind, can fall outside its limits. And if it is more than any feeling or thought which we know, it must still remain more of the same nature. It cannot pass into another region beyond what falls under the general head of sentience. For to assert that possibility would be in the end to use words without a meaning. We can entertain no such suggestion except as self-contradictory, and as therefore impossible.

This conclusion will, I trust, at the end of my work bring more conviction to the reader; for we shall find that it is the one view which will harmonise all facts. And the objections brought against it, when it and they are once properly defined, will prove untenable. But our general result is at present seriously defective; and we must now attempt to indicate and remedy its failure in principle.

[material removed]

And hence, for the present at least, we must believe that reality satisfies our whole being. Our main wants—for truth and life, and for beauty and goodness— must all find satisfaction. And we have seen that this consummation must somehow be experience, and be individual. Every element of the universe, sensation, feeling, thought and will, must be included within one comprehensive sentience. And the question which now occurs is whether really we have a positive idea of such sentience. Do we at all know what we mean when we say that it is actual?

Fully to realise the existence of the Absolute is for finite beings impossible. In order thus to know we should have to be, and then *we* should not exist. This

46   Early Analytic Philosophy

result is certain, and all attempts to avoid it are illusory. But then the whole question turns on the sense in which we are to understand 'knowing'. What is impossible is to construct absolute life in its detail, to have the specific experience in which it consists. But to gain an idea of its main features—an idea true so far as it goes, though abstract and incomplete—is a different endeavour. And it is a task, so far as I see, in which we may succeed. For these main features, to some extent, are within our own experience; and again the idea of their combination is, in the abstract, quite intelligible. And surely no more than this is wanted for a knowledge of the Absolute. It is a knowledge which of course differs enormously from the fact. But it is true, for all that, while it respects its own limits; and it seems fully attainable by the finite intellect.

I will end this chapter by briefly mentioning the sources of such knowledge. First, in mere feeling, or immediate presentation, we have the experience of a whole (Chapters ix, xix, xxvi, xxvii). This whole contains diversity, and, on the other hand, is not parted by relations. Such an experience, we must admit, is most imperfect and unstable, and its inconsistencies lead us at once to transcend it. Indeed, we hardly possess it as more than that which we are in the act of losing. But it serves to suggest to us the general idea of a total experience, where will and thought and feeling may all once more be one. Further, this same unity, felt below distinctions, shows itself later in a kind of hostility against them. We find it in the efforts made both by theory and practice, each to complete itself and so to pass into the other. And, again, the relational form, as we saw, pointed everywhere to a unity. It implies a substantial totality beyond relations and above them, a whole endeavouring without success to realise itself in their detail. Further, the ideas of goodness, and of the beautiful, suggest in different ways the same result. They more or less involve the experience of a whole beyond relations though full of diversity. Now, if we gather (as we can) such considerations into one, they will assuredly supply us with a positive idea. We gain from them the knowledge of a unity which transcends and yet contains every manifold appearance. They supply not an experience but an abstract idea, an idea which we make by uniting given elements. And the mode of union, once more in the abstract, is actually given. Thus we know what is meant by an experience, which embraces all divisions, and yet somehow possesses the direct nature of feeling. We can form the general idea of an absolute experience in which phenomenal distinctions are merged, a whole become immediate at a higher stage without losing any richness. Our complete inability to understand this concrete unity in detail is no good ground for our declining to entertain it. Such a ground would be irrational, and its principle could hardly everywhere be adhered to. But if we can realise at all the general features of the Absolute, if we can see that somehow they come together in a way known vaguely and in the abstract, our result is certain. Our conclusion, so far as it goes, is real knowledge of the Absolute, positive knowledge built on experience, and inevitable when we try to think consistently. We shall realise its nature more clearly when we have confronted it with a series of objections and difficulties. If our result will hold against them all, we shall be able to urge that in reason we are bound to think it true.

3

G. E. Moore on Idealism, Goodness, and Common Sense

Chapter Outline

Background and commentary

Background	50
Critique of monistic idealism	51
Goodness and the naturalistic fallacy	55
Common sense and philosophy	56
Concluding remarks	60
Further reading	61

Readings

"The Refutation of Idealism"	62
Principia Ethica (Ch. 1).	80
"A Defence of Common Sense"	107
"Proof of an External World"	131

Background and commentary

Background

Who was George Edward (G. E.) Moore (1873–1958)? If you are an undergraduate (and especially graduate!) student in philosophy, there is a good chance you have heard this name before, as Moore's ideas continue to be widely discussed in ethics and epistemology.[1] Moore is usually regarded as one of the founders of the analytic tradition and was one of the most influential philosophers in Britain during the years preceding and following the First World War. Though his very early work exhibits an inclination toward Bradley's monistic idealism, he soon went on to develop influential critiques of both monism and idealism. Moore is also known for his contributions to ethics and, especially, his contention that a wide swath of ethical theories can be rejected on the basis of committing the so-called "naturalistic fallacy," as well as the central place that he gives to commonsense beliefs in philosophical inquiry. Aside from his impact on academic philosophy, Moore's ethical writings influenced members of the Bloomsbury Group, a collection of British intellectuals that included E. M. Forster (1879–1970), J. M. Keynes (1883–1946), and Virginia Woolf (1882–1941), among others.

Moore was born in London into a comfortable middle-class family. After completing his initial schooling at Dulwich College, a boy's school in London, Moore matriculated in 1892 at Trinity College, Cambridge, to study classics with no greater ambition than to become a classics teacher at a school like Dulwich. However, Moore met Russell near the end of his first year at Cambridge, and Russell suggested to Moore that he study philosophy in addition to classics (Russell himself had added philosophy to his own studies in mathematics). J. M. E. McTaggart (1866–1925), a young fellow at Trinity, was also influential in spurring Moore's interest in philosophy and played an important role in Moore's initial adoption of the idealist views. In 1894, Moore was elected to the Cambridge Apostles, a select society that met weekly in semi-secrecy to discuss topics in philosophy, classics, poetry, and literature. After completing his studies in 1896, Moore twice attempted to secure a fellowship at Trinity College (as Russell had in 1895 and as McTaggart had in 1891), which would allow him to continue his studies in

---

[1]See, for example, Horgan and Timmons 2006 and Nuccetelli and Seay 2009.

philosophy. The first version of the dissertation that Moore submitted for this purpose in 1897, "The Metaphysical Basis of Ethics," was unsuccessful, but he revised and resubmitted it in 1898, and was awarded a Trinity Prize Fellowship. This included room, board, a modest stipend, and no teaching duties. When the fellowship ended in 1904, Moore remained active in philosophy though was not officially affiliated with Cambridge again until 1911 (an inheritance permitted him to pursue his philosophical endeavors without a regular salary). He returned to Trinity College as a lecturer in 1911 and was awarded a professorship in 1925, a position he retained until his retirement in 1939. He married Dorothy Ely (1892–1977) in 1916, with whom he had two sons.[2]

Critique of monistic idealism

The study of philosophy at Cambridge in the late nineteenth century was a blend of what was known as "mental science" (psychology, logic, and metaphysics) which, in conjunction with the study of ethics, was known as "moral science." Before the formal methods that contemporary philosophers now take for granted, "logic" and "psychology" roughly comprised the study of the mind and its ways of knowing, with varying standards of rigor. By this characterization, Bradley, Hegel, and Kant all were psychologists and logicians. It was during this time that the study of the foundations of mathematics, the application of formal methods to deductive reasoning, and the shift to empirical methods in psychology all began to be characterized by an anti-psychologist and objectivist turn. This, in short, was the idea that knowledge, thought, and perception could be characterized and understood in terms of relations between minds and mind-independent, objective entities.

For Moore, the move towards an anti-psychologist and objectivist approach to thought and perception was brewing in his 1897 dissertation. In this work, Moore attempted to stitch together a view of the nature of ethics which was composed of (1) criticisms of Kant's notion of free will as fundamental to the study of ethics; (2) criticisms of Henry Sidgwick's (1823–1900) utilitarian and intuitionist ethics as an improvement on Kant's but still too empirically based; and (3) his own attempt to account for the metaphysical character of the object of ethical judgment. For Moore, this required an account of how an ethical judgment could be normative (tell us what should or ought to be the

---

[2]For this and further biographical information, see Baldwin 1990, Baldwin and Preti 2011, and Moore 1942a.

Early Analytic Philosophy

case), while still being a judgment, something both graspable by the mind but not subjective in nature. Moore's proposal was a firmly "realist" distinction between an act of judgment and an object of judgment: the object of judgment—what the judgment is about—is not a mental entity like the act of judging, but is rather some entity that exists independently of the judgment. This was the foundation of a realist or mind-independent approach to thought, content, logic, knowledge, and metaphysics. Once Moore made the distinction between what is being thought (the object of thought) from the act of thought the cornerstone of his formulation of the nature of judgment— and, more specifically, of the nature of ethical judgment—Russell saw the implications for his own view of mathematical judgment and the foundations of mathematics, and he prefaced *The Principles of Mathematics* (1903) by remarking that "on fundamental questions of philosophy, my position, in all its chief features, is derived from Mr. G. E. Moore" (xviii).[3]

While Moore's distinction between the act of judging and its object can be discerned in his 1897 dissertation, it is exhibited most explicitly in two papers, "The Nature of Judgement" (1899), which was drawn largely from his 1898 dissertation, along with "The Refutation of Idealism" ([1903a] 1993), which is presented below. Despite differing in details, the common theme that runs through these papers is a distinction between mental acts, like believing, perceiving, and knowing, and the objects of those acts, what they are about. Thus in "The Nature of Judgement," Moore argues for a distinction between thinking and the object of thought and, in particular, argues that the objects of thought—what Moore calls "propositions," which in turn are composed of what he calls "concepts"—exist independently of our thinking them. Thus he writes:

> A proposition is composed not of words, nor yet of thoughts, but of concepts. Concepts are possible objects of thought ... It is indifferent to their nature whether anyone thinks them or not. They are incapable of change; and the relation into which they enter with the knowing subject implies no action or reaction. It is a unique relation which can begin or cease with a change in the subject; but the concept is neither cause nor effect of such a change. (179)

For example,

> When I say "The chimera has three heads," the chimera is not an idea in my mind, nor any part of such idea. What I mean to assert is nothing about my mental states, but a specific connexion of concepts. If the judgment is false,

---

[3]For further discussion, see Preti 2019.

that is not because my ideas do not correspond to reality, but because such a conjunction of concepts is not to be found among existents. (179)

The idea that what is thought is distinct from and does not depend on being thought has anti-idealist import, on the assumption that the idealist contends that everything that exists depends for its existence on a mind. It also has anti-monist import, as it supposes that there is at least one relation that obtains between distinct items, namely the relation between a thinker and what is thought, which also contravenes the idealist contention that when an individual has some item of knowledge, the individual and that item of knowledge form a kind of inseparable unity, such that being known by the individual is part of the very nature of that which is known.

Moore further develops his case against monism and idealism in "The Refutation of Idealism." In this paper, Moore focuses on the idealist formula that "*esse* is *percipi*"—that to be is to be experienced or perceived. According to Moore, this thesis is central to any argument for any idealist metaphysic. Moore's strategy is not to show that idealism so understood is false, but rather that it is unsupported, on the grounds that the "*esse* is *percipi*" formula is itself either unsupported or false. After an extended initial discussion aimed at clarifying the terms of the debate—a common theme in Moore's work—he eventually concludes that there are two routes that an idealist may take to attempt to justify the thesis that *esse* is *percipi*. First, the idealist may deny that there is any distinction between being and being experienced or perceived. Moore has little patience with this; thus, concerning an experience of yellow, he takes it as plain that the "experience is, after all, something distinct from yellow" (32). Second, the idealist may contend that what is experienced and the experience itself may form an "inseparable unity," what he calls an "organic unity." This is something like the kind of unity that Bradley held to be characteristic of reality itself, such that each seemingly independently existing thing is but an abstraction from the whole. Moore charges, however, that the relevant notion of an organic unity is self-contradictory, a charge that he repeats in Chapter 1 of *Principia Ethica*. Moore's idea seems to be that the very notion of an organic unity entails the absurd conclusion that any such "organic whole" is identical to any of its parts; hence, the notion should be rejected as self-contradictory; and, given this, cannot provide a basis for supposing that *esse* is *percipi*. Hence, there is no reason to think that to be is to be experienced. Moore's rejection of a certain notion of an organic unity is plainly anti-monistic; in effect, Moore claims that the very idea of a unified whole characteristic of monism is incoherent. The reader is encouraged to reflect on Moore's case against this notion of an organic unity and to consider what someone like Bradley might say in response.

54   Early Analytic Philosophy

At this point, Moore proposes to "make a complete break in my argument" (34), and in the remainder of the article he develops an account of experience or perception. Moore's core claim, reminiscent of "The Nature of Judgement," is that in any experience or perception, it is necessary to distinguish between the object of the experience and the experience itself. He argues for this by noting, first, that a sensation, experience, or perception of blue differs from that of green; he then notes that a sensation of blue and a sensation of green are both sensations, experiences, or perceptions. Given this, he reasons that both such sensations have a common constituent, which Moore here calls "consciousness." Hence, in every sensation, experience, or perception, it is necessary to distinguish between "consciousness," the respect in which all sensations, experiences, or perceptions are alike, and the respect in which sensations, experiences, and perceptions differ, which Moore calls the "object" of the sensation. That is:

> We have then in every sensation two distinct elements, one which I call consciousness, and another which I call the object of consciousness. This must be so if the sensation of blue and the sensation of green, though different in one respect, are alike in another: blue is one object of sensation and green is another, and consciousness, which both sensations have in common, is different from either (35)

Moore takes this to have anti-idealist import, writing:

> There is ... no question of how we are to 'get outside the circle of our own ideas and sensations'. Merely to have a sensation is already to *be* outside that circle. It is to know something which is truly and really not a part of my experience, as anything which I can ever know. (42)

In other words, in any experience, what is experienced is distinct from and can exist without the experience of it, which contravenes the *esse* is *percipi* formula that, according to Moore, is at the center of any argument for idealism. For example, according to Moore, in an experience of blue, the blue that is the object of the experience can exist without the experience of it.

Moore did not stop thinking about monism and idealism; "External and Internal Relations" (1919–20) offers an extended critique of monistic ideas, and as we will see below, there are anti-idealist elements in "Proof of an External World" ([1939] 1993). Nonetheless, by the time these papers were published, monism and idealism were far less prevalent in English-speaking philosophy—and less prevalent, in part, due to the influence of "The Nature of Judgment" and "The Refutation of Idealism."

Goodness and the naturalistic fallacy

Principia Ethica grew out of a series of lectures on ethics that Moore gave in 1898. Moore takes as his starting point that the central task of ethical inquiry is to consider the definition of good, that this is "the most fundamental question in all Ethics" (57). As Moore attempts to make clear, in this context "definition" does not concern the meaning of a word in the sense that one might discover the "definition" of a word in a dictionary. Rather, Moore has in mind what might be called the "metaphysical definition," the quality or property to which the expression "goodness" or "good" refers and in this sense means. Moore seems to further assume that such definitions are inherently compositional—that in the relevant sense of "definition," a definition of goodness will specify the constituents of the quality or property of goodness. However, Moore announces that goodness cannot be defined in this sense:

> If I am asked, 'What is good?' my answer is that good is good, and that is the end of the matter. Or if I am asked, 'How is good to be defined?' my answer is that it cannot be defined ... if I am right, then nobody can foist upon us such an axiom as that 'Pleasure is the only good' or that 'The good is the desired' on the pretence that this is 'the very meaning of the word.' (58)

He explains:

> [Good] is not composed of any parts, which we can substitute for it in our minds when we are thinking of it. We might think just as clearly and correctly about a horse, if we thought of all its parts and their arrangement instead of thinking of the whole ... but there is nothing whatsoever which we could so substitute for good; and that is what I mean, when I say that good is indefinable. (60)

Among Moore's best-known positions is his criticism of what he calls the "naturalistic fallacy" in ethics—the supposition that good is definable, as one might claim that yellow is definable rather than simple:

> If anyone were to say ... that pleasure *means* the sensation of red ... we should be entitled to laugh at him and to distrust his future statements about pleasure. Well, that would be the same fallacy which I have called the naturalistic fallacy. (64–5)

For example, one might suppose that goodness can be defined in terms of a "natural property" like pleasure or what is desirable. This cannot be, however, as goodness is simple.

Why we should think that goodness is simple in the way that Moore contends? Moore proposes that if goodness were not simple, then either (a) it is complex or (b) "good" means nothing and thus "there is no such

Early Analytic Philosophy

subject as Ethics" (66). Regarding (a), Moore offers what is known as the "open question argument." The argument, in effect, claims that for any "natural property" P, given that something has P, it is always a substantive further question whether that something is also good. For example, suppose we attempt to define goodness as that which we desire to desire. Compare:

1 Granted that x is what we desire to desire, is x good?
2 Granted that x is what we desire to desire, is x what we desire to desire?

Moore observes that while (2) is trivial, (1) is not, which he takes to show that good cannot be defined in terms of what we desire to desire—or, generalizing, in terms of any such property. Moore further contends that "good" clearly means something. For example, the question "Is pleasure good?" is meaningful and substantive, which it seemingly could not be if "good" were meaningless. If goodness cannot be defined in any such terms, how can we know whether something is good? Moore's answer is that knowledge of goodness is grounded in a kind of special intellectual, and seemingly non-empirical, intuition.

As we will see Chapter 8, some philosophers have charged that in arguing that goodness is a simple property, Moore ignores at least one further option—that while the word "good" is meaningful, it does not mean or refer to a property at all and instead has a kind of non-descriptive meaning. On this line of thought, the linguistic function of "good" is not to mean or refer to a property, but rather to serve a very different, non-descriptive function, such as to express approval.

Common sense and philosophy

Common sense played a role in Moore's philosophical method from the very beginning.[4] For instance, in "The Refutation of Idealism," Moore points out the various ways in which idealism seems to contravene ordinary beliefs about the world. Given this, Moore supposes that the burden of proof is on the idealist; and as we saw, he claims that this burden cannot be discharged. Nonetheless, the importance of commonsense beliefs became increasingly explicit later in Moore's career, culminating in "A Defence of Common Sense" ([1925] 1993) and "Proof of an External World."

---

[4]Both Sidgwick and McTaggart were influences on Moore's adoption of the point of view of common sense in philosophical method. See Baldwin and Preti 2011 for discussion.

Moore begins "A Defence of Common Sense" by listing a series of propositions that he claims to know with certainty, including "truisms" like "there exists at present a living human body, which is *my* body," "there have, at every moment since its birth, been large numbers of other living human bodies," "ever since it [my body] was born, it has been either in contact with or not far from the surface of the earth," and "I have, at different times since my body was born, had many different experiences" (107). He claims, moreover, that each of us has known propositions about our bodies and ourselves corresponding to those that he claims to know about his body and his self. For Moore, this amounts to a description of a commonsense picture of the world. Moore emphasizes that in stating these propositions, he is using words in their ordinary sense. For example, that "The earth has existed for many years past" is "the very type of an unambiguous expression, the meaning of which we all understand." In this context, he seems to be addressing those philosophers—idealists and skeptics, perhaps—who might respond to his initial list of propositions by supposing that whether these propositions are known depends on what we mean by "body," "human," "experience," "earth," and so on. Moore has little patience with this type of maneuver.

At this point, Moore proceeds to reject idealism. Specifically, he takes an idealist to deny that we know the relevant propositions on the grounds that such propositions—in particular, those that concern mind-independent bodies—are false. In response, Moore argues that such a philosopher faces a kind of incoherence. Essentially, his point is that all such philosophers use words like "we," but in doing so, they presuppose the commonsense picture, which involves humans with physical bodies. Moore here introduces what is sometimes referred to as the "reversal argument": he contends that whereas an idealist would wish to reject at least some aspects of the commonsense view of the world on the basis of an idealist metaphysic, our knowledge of the propositions that constitute the commonsense view is more secure than our knowledge of the premises that might be used to derive an idealist conclusion. Hence, rather than reject common sense on the basis of idealism, we may as well just reject idealism on the basis of its apparent conflict with common sense.

Moore then turns his attention to skepticism. According to the skeptic, while perhaps the propositions that form the commonsense picture are true, we cannot know at least some of these propositions, especially those that concern the existence of physical things. Moore charges that such skepticism proves "self-contradictory". In effect, Moore supposes that when the skeptic claims that no human beings have ever known the propositions of common sense, the skeptic is implicitly claiming to know that there are human beings. In this case, however, the skeptic is implicitly claiming to know the propositions of common sense, since the skeptic supposes that there are human beings. The reader is encouraged to reflect on Moore's reasoning here and to consider how a skeptic or an idealist might respond.

Despite differences in style and presentation, realism is a constant theme in Moore's work: "metaphysical" realism, consisting in a commitment to mind-independent objects, along with "epistemological" realism, consisting in a commitment to our knowledge of a mind-independent reality. These themes continue in "A Proof of an External World.". Moore begins by discussing Kant's lamenting the lack of a satisfactory proof of "things outside of us." Moore's aim is to provide such a proof. However, in his characteristic fashion, Moore thinks that it is first important to clarify what it at issue—just what it means to offer a proof of "things outside of us" or an "external world." Moore articulates this by developing a distinction between "things to be met with in space" and "things presented in space." The former includes things like rocks, mountains, soap-bubbles, hands, and shadows, while the latter include after-images, pains, and hallucinations. Things that are presented in space but not to be met with in space are in a sense private. According to Moore, it is absurd, for example, to suppose that two people have numerically the same pain or after-image. In this sense, things that are merely presented in space are "mind-dependent" and not "external to our minds." Moore here seems to be rejecting his earlier view in "The Refutation of Idealism," according to which all objects of experience exist independently of our experiencing them. In the present context, Moore is conceding that pains, after-images, and so on, as objects of experience, are mind-dependent entities. In contrast, regarding things to be met with in space, Moore writes:

> there is no absurdity in supposing with regard to any one of them which is, at a given time, perceived, both (1) that it might have existed at that very time, without being perceived; (2) that it might have existed at another time, without being perceived at that other time; and (3) that during the whole period of its existence, it need not have been perceived at any time. (155)

For example,

> If I say of anything which I am perceiving, 'That is a soap-bubble', I am, it seems to me, certainly implying that there would be no contradiction in

G. E. Moore on Idealism, Goodness, and Common Sense 59

asserting that it existed before I perceived it and that it will continue to exist, even if I cease to perceive it ... a thing would not be a soap-bubble unless its existence at any given time were logically independent of my perception of it at that time; unless that is to say, from the proposition, with regard to a particular time, that it existed at that time, it never follows that I perceived it at that time. (164)

Hence, while some objects of experience are mind-dependent, others are not, in that such things can exist independently of our experiencing or perceiving them.

Given this way of setting up the dialectic—in effect, Moore's analysis of what is at issue concerning the external world—to show that there are "things outside of us" and in this sense an "external world," it suffices to show that there are at least some things to be met with in space. At this point, Moore offers his proof. He writes:

I can prove now ... that two hands exist. How? By holding up my two hands, and saying, as I make a certain gesture with the right hand, 'Here is one hand', and adding, as I make a certain gesture with the left, 'and here is another'. And if, by doing this, I have proved ipso facto the existence of external things, you will all see that I can also do it now in numbers of other ways: there is no need to multiply examples. (166)

The argument can be put as follows:

1 Here is one hand.
2 Here is another hand.
3 Hence, there are hands.
4 Hence, there are things to be met with in space.
5 Hence, there is an external world, a world outside of our minds.

Moore goes on to defend this proof, noting, for example, that the premises are known to be true and that the subsequent steps in the argument follow from the premises.

Moore's proof continues to be discussed in contemporary philosophy.[5] One interpretative question concerns just who Moore is targeting with the proof. Is he aiming to refute the skeptic, who denies that we know that there is an external world, or is he aiming to refute the idealist, who denies that there is an external, mind-independent world? While many have adopted the

---

[5]See, for example, Coliva 2004, Lycan 2001, Pryor 2000 and 2004, and Wright 2002.

Early Analytic Philosophy

former interpretation, Moore himself seems to have understood the proof as targeting the idealist. For example, Moore concedes near the end of "Proof of an External World" that his proof does not refute the skeptic who claims that we cannot know that we are dreaming, and he reiterated this point several years later in a volume dedicated to his work.[6] Further, the argument may have some success against idealism: the idealist accepts (1) and (2), and so to deny the conclusion (5), the idealist will have to either deny that hands are things to be met with in space or deny Moore's analysis of what is at issue concerning a proof of an external world. In contrast, while not a matter of universal consensus, the proof seems to be largely ineffective against the skeptic, since the skeptic will deny that Moore knows (1) and (2).[7]

Concluding remarks

Throughout his career, Moore embraced both metaphysical and epistemological realism: he held that when we have a thought, the object of that thought is not an idea in our minds in any straightforward sense; that there is an external physical world that exists apart from our experience of it; and that we can know many things about this external world. Moore believed that these commitments could be rationally defended and that views that attempt to contravene them face an array of difficulties.

We will conclude this chapter by remarking on the profound differences in orientation towards the aims and ambitions of philosophy between Moore on the one hand and Bradley on the other. For Bradley, just about everything is up for grabs and if philosophical inquiry should reveal common sense and scientific concepts to be incoherent and at best to figure in partial truths, well, that's the conclusion that ought to be accepted. In contrast, while Moore did develop substantive positions in metaphysics, epistemology, and ethics, it suffices to say that his aims were far more modest than Bradley and that for Moore, a wholesale rejection of the subject matter of common sense and science as "unreal" is far beyond the proper bounds of philosophical inquiry. As we will see in later chapters, while certainly disagreeing in the details, Moore's modesty concerning the aims of philosophy would prove influential in the development of the analytic tradition.

---

[6] See Moore 1942b.
[7] For further discussion of the interpretation of Moore's proof, see Morris and Preti 2015.

Further reading

Primary sources

Moore, G. E. ([1897] 2011), *The Metaphysical Basis of Ethics*, in C. Preti and T. Baldwin (eds), *G. E. Moore: Early Philosophical Writings*, Cambridge: Cambridge University Press.

Moore, G. E. (1899), "The Nature of Judgement", *Mind* 8: 176–93.

Moore, G. E. (1919–20), "External and Internal Relations", *Proceedings of the Aristotelean Society* 20: 40–62.

Moore, G. E. (1942a), "Autobiography", in P. A. Schilpp (ed.), *The Philosophy of G. E. Moore*, Illinois: Open Court.

Secondary sources

Baldwin, T. (1992), *G. E. Moore*, London: Routledge.

Baldwin. T. (2010), "George Edward Moore", *Stanford Encyclopedia of Philosophy*. Available online: https://plato.stanford.edu/entries/moore/

Klemke, E. D. (2000), *A Defense of Realism: Reflections on the Metaphysics of G. E. Moore*, New York: Humanities Books.

Levy, P. (1979), *G. E. Moore and the Cambridge Apostles*, London: Weidenfeld and Nicolson.

Morris, K. and Preti, C. (2015), "How to Read Moore's 'Proof of an External World'", *Journal for the History of Analytical Philosophy* 4: 1–16.

Preti, C. (2022), *The Metaphysical Basis of Ethics: G. E. Moore and the Origins of Analytical Philosophy*, Basingstoke: Palgrave Macmillan.

Early Analytic Philosophy

62

Readings

Moore, G. E. "The Refutation of Idealism".
Reprinted from Moore, G. E. (1903), "The Refutation of Idealism",
Mind **12: 433–53.**

Modern Idealism, if it asserts any general conclusion about the universe at all, asserts that it is *spiritual.* There are two points about this assertion to which I wish to call attention. These points are that, whatever be its exact meaning, it is certainly meant to assert (1) that the universe is very different indeed from what it seems, and (2) that it has quite a large number of properties which it does not seem to have. Chairs and tables and mountains *seem* to be very different from us; but, when the whole universe is declared to be spiritual, it is certainly meant to assert that they are far more like us than we think. The idealist means to assert that they are *in some sense* neither lifeless nor unconscious, as they certainly seem to be; and I do not think his language is so grossly deceptive, but that we may assume him to believe that they really are very different indeed from what they seem. And secondly when he declares that they are *spiritual,* he means to include in that term quite a large number of different properties. When the whole universe is declared to be spiritual, it is meant not only that it is in some sense *conscious,* but that it has what we recognise in ourselves as the *higher* forms of consciousness. That it is intelligent; that it is purposeful; that it is not mechanical; all these different things are commonly asserted of it. In general, it may be said, this phrase 'reality is spiritual' excites and expresses the belief that the *whole* universe possesses *all the qualities* the possession of which is held to make us so superior to things which seem to be inanimate: at least, if it does not possess exactly those which we possess, it possesses not one only, but several others, which, by the same ethical standard, would be judged equal to or better than our own. When we say it is *spiritual* we mean to say that it has quite a number of excellent qualities, different from any which we commonly attribute either to stars or planets or to cups and saucers.

Now why I mention these two points is that when engaged in the intricacies of philosophic discussion, we are apt to overlook the vastness of the difference between this idealistic view and the ordinary view of the world, and to overlook the number of *different* propositions which the idealist must prove. It is, I think, owing to the vastness of this difference and owing to the number of different excellencies which Idealists attribute to the universe, that it seems such an interesting and important question whether Idealism be true or not. But, when we begin to argue about it, I think we are apt to forget what a vast number of

G. E. Moore on Idealism, Goodness, and Common Sense 63

arguments this interesting question must involve: we are apt to assume, that if one or two points be made on either side, the whole case is won. I say this lest it should be thought that any of the arguments which will be advanced in this paper would be sufficient to disprove, or any refutation of them sufficient to prove, the truly interesting and important proposition that reality is spiritual. For my own part I wish it to be clearly understood that I do not suppose that anything I shall say has the smallest tendency to prove that reality is not spiritual: I do not believe it possible to refute a single one of the many important propositions contained in the assertion that it is so. Reality may be spiritual, for all I know; and I devoutly hope it is. But I take 'Idealism' to be a wide term and to include not only this interesting conclusion, but a number of arguments which are supposed to be, if not sufficient, at least *necessary*, to prove it. Indeed I take it that modern Idealists are chiefly distinguished by certain arguments which they have in common. That reality is spiritual has, I believe, been the tenet of many theologians; and yet, for believing that alone, they should hardly be called Idealists. There are besides, I believe, many persons, not improperly called Idealists, who hold certain characteristic propositions, without venturing to think them quite sufficient to prove so grand a conclusion. It is, therefore, only with Idealistic *arguments* that I am concerned; and if any Idealist holds that *no* argument is necessary to prove that reality is spiritual, I shall certainly not have refuted him. I shall, however, attack at least one argument, which, to the best of my belief, is considered necessary to their position by *all* Idealists. And I wish to point out a certain advantage which this procedure gives me – an advantage which justifies the assertion that, if my arguments are sound, they will have refuted Idealism. If I can refute a single proposition which is a necessary and essential step in all Idealistic arguments, then, no matter how good the rest of these arguments may be, I shall have proved that Idealists have *no reason whatever* for their conclusion.

Suppose we have a chain of argument which takes the form: Since A is B, and B is C, and C is D, it follows A is D. In such an argument, though 'B is C' and 'C is D' may both be perfectly true, yet if 'A is B' be false, we have no more reason for asserting A is D than if all three were false. It does not, indeed, follow that A is D is false; nor does it follow that no other arguments would prove it to be true. But it does follow that, so far as this argument goes, it is the barest supposition, without the least bit of evidence. I propose to attack a proposition which seems to me to stand in this relation to the conclusion 'Reality is spiritual'. I do not propose to dispute that 'Reality is spiritual'; I do not deny that there may be reasons for thinking that it is: but I do propose to show that one reason upon which, to the best of my judgment, all other arguments ever used by Idealists depend is *false*. These other arguments may, for all I shall say, be eminently

64   **Early Analytic Philosophy**

ingenious and true; they are very many and various, and different Idealists use the most different arguments to prove the same most important conclusions. Some of these *may* be sufficient to prove that B is C and C is D; but if, as I shall try to show, their 'A is B' is false, the conclusion A is D remains a pleasant supposition. I do not deny that to suggest pleasant and plausible suppositions may be the proper function of philosophy: but I am assuming that the name Idealism can only be properly applied where there is a certain amount of argument, intended to be cogent.

The subject of this paper is, therefore, quite uninteresting. Even if I prove my point, I shall have proved nothing about the Universe in general. Upon the important question whether Reality is or is not spiritual my argument will not have the remotest bearing. I shall only attempt to arrive at the truth about a matter, which is in itself quite trivial and insignificant, and from which, so far as I can see and certainly so far as I shall say, no conclusions can be drawn about any of the subjects about which we most want to know. The only importance I can claim for the subject I shall investigate is that it seems to me to be a matter upon which not Idealists only, but all philosophers and psychologists also, have been in error, and from their erroneous view of which they have inferred (validly or invalidly) their most striking and interesting conclusions. And that it has even this importance I cannot hope to prove. If it has this importance, it will indeed follow that all the most striking results of philosophy – Sensationalism, Agnosticism and Idealism alike – have, for all that has hitherto been urged in their favour, no more foundation than the supposition that a chimera lives in the moon. It will follow that, unless new reasons never urged hitherto can be found, all the most important philosophic doctrines have as little claim to assent as the most superstitious beliefs of the lowest savages. Upon the question what we have *reason* to believe in the most interesting matters, I do, therefore, think that my results will have an important bearing; but I cannot too clearly insist that upon the question whether these beliefs are true they will have none whatever.

The trivial proposition which I propose to dispute is this: that *esse* is *percipi*. This is a very ambiguous proposition, but, in some sense or other, it has been very widely held. That it is, in some sense, essential to Idealism, I must for the present merely assume. What I propose to show is that, in all the senses ever given to it, it is false.

But, first of all, it may be useful to point out briefly in what relation I conceive it to stand to Idealistic arguments. That wherever you can truly predicate *esse* you can truly predicate *percipi*, in some sense or other, is, I take it, a necessary step in all arguments, properly to be called Idealistic, and, what is more, in all

G. E. Moore on Idealism, Goodness, and Common Sense   65

arguments hitherto offered for the Idealistic conclusion. If *esse* is *percipi*, this is at once equivalent to saying that whatever is is experienced; and this, again, is equivalent, in a sense, to saying that whatever is is something mental. But this is not the sense in which the Idealist *conclusion* must maintain that Reality is *mental*. The Idealist *conclusion* is that *esse* is *percipere*; and hence, whether *esse* be *percipi* or not, a further and different discussion is needed to show whether or not it is also *percipere*. And again, even if *esse* be *percipere*, we need a vast quantity of further argument to show that what has *esse* has also those higher mental qualities which are denoted by spiritual. This is why I said that the question I should discuss, namely, whether or not *esse* is *percipi*, must be utterly insufficient either to prove or to disprove that reality is spiritual. But, on the other hand, I believe that every argument ever used to show that reality is spiritual has inferred this (validly or invalidly) from '*esse* is *percipere*' as one of its premisses; and that this again has never been pretended to be proved except by use of the premiss that *esse* is *percipi*. The type of argument used for the latter purpose is familiar enough. It is said that since whatever is, is experienced, and since some things are which are not experienced by the individual, these must at least form part of some experience. Or again that, since an object necessarily implies a subject, and since the whole world must be an object, we must conceive it to belong to some subject or subjects, in the same sense in which whatever is the object of our experience belongs to us. Or again, that, since thought enters into the essence of all reality, we must conceive behind it, in it, or as its essence, a spirit akin to ours, who think: that 'spirit greets spirit' in its object. Into the validity of these inferences I do not propose to enter: they obviously require a great deal of discussion. I only desire to point out that, however correct they may be, yet if *esse* is not *percipi*, they leave us as far from a proof that reality is spiritual, as if they were all false too.

But now: Is *esse percipi*? There are three very ambiguous terms in this proposition, and I must begin by distinguishing the different things that may be meant by some of them.

And first with regard to *percipi*. This term need not trouble us long at present. It was, perhaps, originally used to mean 'sensation' only; but I am not going to be so unfair to modern Idealists – the only Idealists to whom the term should now be applied without qualification – as to hold that, if they say *esse* is *percipi*, they mean by *percipi* sensation only. On the contrary I quite agree with them that, if *esse* be *percipi* at all, *percipi* must be understood to include not sensation only, but that other type of mental fact, which is called 'thought': and, whether *esse* be *percipi* or not, I consider it to be the main service of the philosophic school, to which modern Idealists belong, that they have insisted on distinguishing

Early Analytic Philosophy

'sensation' and 'thought' and on emphasising the importance of the latter. Against Sensationalism and Empiricism they have maintained the true view. But the distinction between sensation and thought need not detain us here. For, in whatever respects they differ, they have at least this in common, that they are both forms of consciousness or, to use a term that seems to be more in fashion just now, they are both ways of experiencing. Accordingly, whatever *esse* is *percipi* may mean, it does *at least* assert that whatever is, is *experienced*. And since what I wish to maintain is, that even this is untrue, the question whether it be experienced by way of sensation or thought or both is for my purpose quite irrelevant. If it be not experienced at all, it cannot be either an object of thought or an object of sense. It is only if being involves 'experience' that the question, whether it involves sensation or thought or both, becomes important. I beg, therefore, that *percipi* may be understood, in what follows, to refer merely to what is *common* to sensation and thought. A very recent article states the meaning of *esse* is *percipi* with all desirable clearness in so far as *percipi* is concerned. 'I will undertake to show,' says Mr. Taylor [in *International Journal of Ethics*, October 1902], 'that what makes [any piece of fact] real can be nothing but its presence as an inseparable aspect of a *sentient experience*.' I am glad to think that Mr. Taylor has been in time to supply me with so definite a statement that this is the ultimate premiss of Idealism. My paper will at least refute Mr. Taylor's Idealism, if it refutes anything at all: for I *shall* undertake to show that what makes a thing real cannot possibly be its presence as an inseparable aspect of a sentient experience.

But Mr. Taylor's statement, though clear, I think, with regard to the meaning of *percipi*, is highly ambiguous in other respects. I will leave it for the present to consider the next ambiguity in the statement: *Esse* is *percipi*. What does the copula mean? What can be meant by saying that esse *is* percipi? There are just three meanings, one or other of which such a statement *must* have, if it is to be true: and of these there is only one which it can have, if it is to be important. (1) The statement may be meant to assert that the word 'esse' is used to signify nothing either more or less than the word 'percipi': that the two words are precise synonyms: that they are merely different names for one and the same thing: that what is meant by *esse* is absolutely identical with what is meant by *percipi*. I think I need not prove that the principle *esse* is *percipi* is *not* thus intended merely to define a word; nor yet that, if it were, it would be an extremely bad definition. But if it does *not* mean this, only two alternatives remain. The second is (2) that what is meant by *esse*, though not absolutely identical with what is meant by *percipi*, yet *includes* the latter as a *part* of its meaning. If this were the meaning of '*esse* is *percipi*', then to say that a thing was real would not

G. E. Moore on Idealism, Goodness, and Common Sense

be the same thing as to say that it was experienced. That it was *real* would mean that it was experienced and *something else besides*: 'being experienced' would be *analytically essential* to reality, but would not be the whole meaning of the term. From the fact that a thing was real we should be able to infer, by the law of contradiction, that it was experienced; since the latter would be *part* of what is meant by the former. But, on the other hand, from the fact that a thing was experienced we should *not* be able to infer that it was real; since it would not follow from the fact that it had one of the attributes essential to reality, that it also had the other or others. Now, if we understand *esse* is *percipi* in this second sense, we must distinguish *three* different things which it asserts. First of all, it gives a definition of the word 'reality': asserting that that word stands for a complex whole, of which what is meant by '*percipi*' forms a part. And secondly it asserts that 'being experienced' forms a part of a certain whole. Both these propositions may be true, and at all events I do not wish to dispute them. I do not, indeed, think that the word 'reality' is commonly used to include 'percipi'; but I do not wish to argue about the meaning of words. And that many things which are experienced are also something else – that to be experienced forms part of certain wholes, is, of course, indisputable. But what I wish to point out is that neither of these propositions is of any importance, unless we add to them a *third*. That 'real' is a convenient name for a union of attributes which *sometimes* occurs, it could not be worth any one's while to assert: no inferences of any importance could be drawn from such an assertion. Our principle could only mean that when a thing happens to have *percipi* as well as the other qualities included under *esse*, it has *percipi*: and we should never be able to *infer* that it was experienced, except from a proposition which already asserted that it was both experienced and something else. Accordingly, if the assertion that *percipi* forms part of the whole meant by reality is to have any importance, it must mean that the whole is organic, at least in this sense, that the other constituent or constituents of it *cannot* occur without *percipi*, even if *percipi* can occur without them. Let us call these other constituents x. The proposition that *esse* includes *percipi*, and that therefore from *esse percipi* can be inferred, can only be important if it is meant to assert that *percipi* can be inferred from x. The only importance of the question whether the whole *esse* includes the part *percipi* rests therefore on the question whether the part x is necessarily connected with the part *percipi*. And this is (3) the third possible meaning of the assertion *esse* is *percipi*: and, as we now see, the only important one. *Esse* is *percipi* asserts that wherever you have x you also have *percipi*: that whatever has the property x also has the property that it is *experienced*. And this being so, it will be convenient if, for the future, I may be allowed to use the term '*esse*' to

Early Analytic Philosophy

denote *x alone*. I do not wish thereby to beg the question whether what we commonly mean by the word 'real' does or does not include *percipi* as well as *x*. I am quite content that my definition of *'esse'* to denote *x*, should be regarded merely as an arbitrary verbal definition. Whether it is so or not, the only question of interest is whether from *x percipi* can be inferred, and I should prefer to be able to express this in the form: can *percipi* be inferred from *esse*? Only let it be understood that when I say *esse*, that term will not for the future *include percipi*: it denotes only that *x*, which Idealists, perhaps rightly, include *along with percipi* under *their* term *esse*. That there is such an *x* they must admit on pain of making the proposition an *absolute* tautology; and that from this *x percipi* can be inferred they must admit, on pain of making it a perfectly barren analytic proposition. Whether *x* alone should or should not be called *esse* is not worth a dispute: what is worth dispute is whether *percipi* is necessarily connected with *x*.

We have therefore discovered the ambiguity of the copula in *esse* is *percipi*, so far as to see that this principle asserts two distinct terms to be so related, that whatever has the *one*, which I call *esse*, has also the property that it is experienced. It asserts a necessary connexion between *esse* on the one hand and *percipi* on the other; these two words denoting each a distinct term, and *esse* denoting a term in which that denoted by *percipi* is not included. We have, then, in *esse* is *percipi*, a *necessary synthetic* proposition which I have undertaken to refute. And I may say at once that, understood as such, it cannot be refuted. If the Idealist chooses to assert that it is merely a self-evident truth, I have only to say that it does not appear to me to be so. But I believe that no Idealist ever has maintained it to be so. Although this – that two distinct terms are necessarily related – is the only sense which *'esse* is *percipi'* can have if it is to be true and important, it *can* have another sense, if it is to be an important falsehood. I believe that Idealists all hold this important falsehood., They do not perceive that *Esse* is *percipi* must, if true, be *merely* a self-evident synthetic truth: they either identify with it or give as a reason for it another proposition which must be false because it is self-contradictory. Unless they did so, they would have to admit that it was a perfectly unfounded assumption; and if they recognised that it was *unfounded*, I do not think they would maintain its truth to be evident. *Esse* is *percipi*, in the sense I have found for it, *may* indeed be true; I cannot refute it: but if this sense were clearly apprehended, no one, I think, would *believe* that it was true.

Idealists, we have seen, must assert that whatever is experienced, is *necessarily* so. And this doctrine they commonly express by saying that 'the object of experience is inconceivable apart from the subject'. I have hitherto been concerned with pointing out what meaning this assertion must have, if it

G. E. Moore on Idealism, Goodness, and Common Sense   69

is to be an important truth. I now propose to show that it may have an important meaning, which must be false, because it is self-contradictory.

It is a well-known fact in the history of philosophy that *necessary* truths in general, but especially those of which it is said that the opposite is inconceivable, have been commonly supposed to be *analytic*, in the sense that the proposition denying them was self-contradictory. It was, in this way, commonly supposed, before Kant, that many truths could be proved by the law of contradiction alone. This is, therefore, a mistake which it is plainly easy for the best philosophers to make. Even since Kant many have continued to assert it; but I am aware that among those Idealists, who most properly deserve the name, it has become more fashionable to assert that truths are *both* analytic and synthetic. Now with many of their reasons for asserting this I am not concerned: it is possible that in some connexions the assertion may bear a useful and true sense. But if we understand 'analytic' in the sense just defined, namely, what is proved by the law of contradiction *alone*, it is plain that, if 'synthetic' means what is *not* proved by this alone, no truth can be both analytic and synthetic. Now it seems to me that those who do maintain truths to be both, do nevertheless maintain that they are so in this as well as in other senses. It is, indeed, extremely unlikely that so essential a part of the historical meaning of 'analytic' and 'synthetic' should have been entirely discarded, especially since we find no express recognition that it is discarded. In that case it is fair to suppose that modern Idealists have been influenced by the view that certain truths can be proved by the law of contradiction alone. I admit they also expressly declare that they can *not*: but this is by no means sufficient to prove that they do not also think they are; since it is very easy to hold two mutually contradictory opinions. What I suggest then is that Idealists hold the particular doctrine in question, concerning the relation of subject and object in experience, because they think it is an analytic truth in this restricted sense that it is proved by the law of contradiction alone.

I am suggesting that the Idealist maintains that object and subject are necessarily connected, mainly because he fails to see that they are *distinct*, that they are *two*, at all. When he thinks of 'yellow' and when he thinks of the 'sensation of yellow', he fails to see that there is anything whatever in the latter which is not in the former. This, being so, to deny that yellow can ever *be* apart from the sensation of yellow is merely to deny that yellow can ever be other than it is; since yellow and the sensation of yellow are absolutely identical. To assert that yellow is necessarily an object of experience is to assert that yellow is necessarily yellow – a purely identical proposition, and therefore proved by the law of contradiction alone. Of course, the proposition also implies that experience is, after all, something distinct from yellow – else there would be no reason for insisting that

70   Early Analytic Philosophy

yellow is a sensation: and that the argument thus both affirms and denies that yellow and sensation of yellow are distinct, is what sufficiently refutes it. But this contradiction can easily be overlooked, because though we are convinced, in other connexions, that 'experience' does mean something and something most important, yet we are never distinctly aware *what* it means, and thus in every particular case we do not notice its presence. The facts present themselves as a kind of antinomy: (1) Experience *is* something unique and different from anything else; (2) Experience of green is entirely indistinguishable from green; two propositions which cannot both be true. Idealists, holding both, can only take refuge in arguing from the one in some connexions and from the other in others.

But I am well aware that there are many Idealists who would repel it as an utterly unfounded charge that they fail to distinguish between a sensation or idea and what I will call its object. And there are, I admit, many who not only imply, as we all do, that green is distinct from the sensation of green, but expressly insist upon the distinction as an important part of their system. They would perhaps only assert that the two form an inseparable unity. But I wish to point out that many, who use this phrase, and who do admit the distinction, are not thereby absolved from the charge that they deny it. For there is a certain doctrine, very prevalent among philosophers nowadays, which by a very simple reduction may be seen to assert that two distinct things both are and are not distinct. A distinction is asserted; but it is *also* asserted that the things distinguished form an 'organic unity'. But, forming such a unity, it is held, each would not be what it is apart from *its relation to the other*. Hence to consider either by itself is to make an *illegitimate abstraction*. The recognition that there are 'organic unities' and 'illegitimate abstractions' in this sense is regarded as one of the chief conquests of modern philosophy. But what is the sense attached to these terms? An abstraction is illegitimate, when and only when we attempt to assert of *a part* – of something abstracted – that which is true only of the *whole* to which it belongs: and it may perhaps be useful to point out that this should not be done. But the application actually made of this principle, and what perhaps would be expressly acknowledged as its meaning, is something much the reverse of useful. The principle is used to assert that certain abstractions are *in all cases* illegitimate; that whenever you try to assert *anything whatever* of that which is *part* of an organic whole, what you assert can only be true of the whole. And this principle, so far from being a useful truth, is necessarily false. For if the whole can, nay *must*, be substituted for the part in all propositions and for all purposes, this can only be because the whole is absolutely identical with the part. When, therefore, we are told that green and the sensation of green are certainly distinct but yet are not separable, or that it is an illegitimate abstraction

G. E. Moore on Idealism, Goodness, and Common Sense   71

to consider the one apart from the other, what these provisos are used to assert is, that though the two things are distinct yet you not only can but must treat them as if they were not. Many philosophers, therefore, when they admit a distinction, yet (following the lead of Hegel) boldly assert their right, in a slightly more obscure form of words, *also* to deny it. The principle of organic unities, like that of combined analysis and synthesis, is mainly used to defend the practice of holding *both* of two contradictory propositions, wherever this may seem convenient. In this, as in other matters, Hegel's main service to philosophy has consisted in giving a name to and erecting into a principle, a type of fallacy to which experience had shown philosophers, along with the rest of mankind, to be addicted. No wonder that he has followers and admirers.

I have shown then, so far, that when the Idealist asserts the important principle '*Esse* is *percipi*' he must, if it is to be true, mean by this that: Whatever is experienced also *must* be experienced. And I have also shown that he *may* identify with, or give as a reason for, this proposition, one which must be false, because it is self-contradictory. But at this point I propose to make a complete break in my argument. '*Esse* is *percipi*', we have seen, asserts of two terms, as distinct from one another as 'green' and 'sweet', that whatever has the one has also the other: it asserts that 'being' and 'being experienced' are necessarily connected: that whatever *is* is *also* experienced. And this, I admit, cannot be directly refuted. But I believe it to be false; and I have asserted that anybody who saw that '*esse* and *percipi*' *were* as distinct as 'green' and 'sweet' would be no more ready to believe that whatever *is* is *also* experienced, than to believe that whatever is green is also sweet. I have asserted that no one would believe that '*esse* is *percipi*' if they saw how different *esse* is from *percipi*: but this I shall not try to prove. I have asserted that all who do believe that '*esse* is *percipi*' identify with it or take as a reason for it a self-contradictory proposition: but this I shall not try to prove. I shall only try to show that certain propositions which I assert to be believed, are false. That they are believed, and that without this belief '*esse* is *percipi*' would not be believed either, I must leave without a proof.

I pass, then, from the uninteresting question 'Is *esse percipi*?' to the still more uninteresting and apparently irrelevant question 'What is a sensation or idea?'

We all know that the sensation of blue differs from that of green. But it is plain that if both are *sensations* they also have some point in common. What is it that they have in common? And how is this common element related to the points in which they differ?

I will call the common element 'consciousness' without yet attempting to say what the thing I so call *is*. We have then in every sensation two distinct

72   Early Analytic Philosophy

terms, (1) 'consciousness', in respect of which all sensations are alike; and (2) something else, in respect of which one sensation differs from another. It will be convenient if I may be allowed to call this second term the 'object' of a sensation: this also without yet attempting to say what I mean by the word.

We have then in every sensation two distinct elements, one which I call consciousness, and another which I call the object of consciousness. This must be so if the sensation of blue and the sensation of green, though different in one respect, are alike in another: blue is one object of sensation and green is another, and consciousness, which both sensations have in common, is different from either.

But, further, sometimes the sensation of blue exists in my mind and sometimes it does not; and knowing, as we now do, that the sensation of blue includes two different elements, namely consciousness and blue, the question arises whether, when the sensation of blue exists, it is the consciousness which exists, or the blue which exists, or both. And one point at least is plain: namely that these three alternatives are all different from one another. So that, if any one tells us that to say 'Blue exists' is the *same* thing as to say that 'Both blue and consciousness exist', he makes a mistake and a self-contradictory mistake.

But another point is also plain, namely, that when the sensation exists, the consciousness, at least, certainly does exist; for when I say that the sensations of blue and of green both exist, I certainly mean that what is common to both and in virtue of which both are called sensations, exists in each case. The only alternative left, then, is that *either* both exist *or* the consciousness exists alone. If, therefore, any one tells us that the existence of blue is the same thing as the existence of the sensation of blue he makes a mistake and a self-contradictory mistake, for he asserts *either* that blue is the same thing as blue together with consciousness, *or* that it is the same thing as consciousness alone.

Accordingly to identify either 'blue' or any other of what I have called '*objects*' of sensation, with the corresponding sensation is in every case, a self-contradictory error. It is to identify a part either with the whole of which it is a part or else with the other part of the same whole. If we are told that the assertion 'Blue exists' is *meaningless* unless we mean by it that 'The sensation of blue exists', we are told what is certainly false and self-contradictory. If we are told that the existence of blue is inconceivable apart from the existence of the sensation, the speaker *probably* means to convey to us, by this ambiguous expression, what is a self-contradictory error. For we can and must conceive the existence of blue as something quite distinct from the existence of the sensation. We can and must conceive that blue might exist and yet the sensation of blue not exist. For my own part I not only conceive this, but conceive it to be

G. E. Moore on Idealism, Goodness, and Common Sense

true. Either therefore this terrific assertion of inconceivability means what is false and self-contradictory or else it means only that *as a matter of fact* blue never can exist unless the sensation of it exists also.

And at this point I need not conceal my opinion that no philosopher has ever yet succeeded in avoiding this self-contradictory error: that the most striking results both of Idealism and of Agnosticism are only obtained by identifying blue with the sensation of blue: that *esse* is held to be *percipi.* solely because *what is experienced* is held to be identical with *the experience of it.* That Berkeley and Mill committed this error will, perhaps, be granted: that modern Idealists make it will, I hope, appear more probable later. But that my opinion is plausible, I will now offer two pieces of evidence. The first is that language offers us no means of referring to such objects as 'blue' and 'green' and 'sweet', except by calling them sensations: it is an obvious violation of language to call them 'things' or 'objects' or 'terms'. And similarly we have no natural means of referring to such objects as 'causality' or 'likeness' or 'identity', except by calling them 'ideas' or 'notions' or 'conceptions'. But it is hardly likely that if philosophers had clearly distinguished in the past between a sensation or idea and what I have called its object, there should have been no separate name for the latter. They have always used the same name for these two different 'things' (if I may call them so); and hence there is some probability that they have supposed these 'things' *not* to be two and different, but one and the same. And, secondly, there is a very good reason why they should have supposed so, in the fact that when we refer to introspection and try to discover what the sensation of blue is, it is very easy to suppose that we have before us only a single term. The term 'blue' is easy enough to distinguish, but the other element which I have called 'consciousness' – that which sensation of blue has in common with sensation of green – is extremely difficult to fix. That many people fail to distinguish it at all is sufficiently shown by the fact that there are materialists. And, in general, that which makes the sensation of blue a mental fact seems to escape us; it seems, if I may use a metaphor, to be transparent – we look through it and see nothing but the blue; we may be convinced that there *is something*, but *what* it is no philosopher, I think, has yet clearly recognised.

But this was a digression. The point I had established so far was that in every sensation or idea we must distinguish two elements, (1) the 'object', or that in which one differs from another; and (2) 'consciousness', or that which all have in common – that which makes them sensations or mental facts. This being so, it followed that when a sensation or idea exists, we have to choose between the alternatives that either object alone or consciousness alone or both exist; and I showed that of these alternatives one, namely that the object only exists, is

74   Early Analytic Philosophy

excluded by the fact that what we mean to assert is certainly the existence of a mental fact. There remains the question: Do both exist? Or does the consciousness alone? And to this question one answer has hitherto been given universally: That both exist.

This answer follows from the analysis hitherto accepted of the relation of what I have called 'object' to 'consciousness' in any sensation or idea. It is held that what I call the object is merely the 'content' of a sensation or idea. It is held that in each case we can distinguish two elements and two only, (1) the fact that there is feeling or experience; and (2) *what* is felt or experienced; the sensation or idea, it is said, forms a whole, in which we must distinguish two 'inseparable aspects', 'content' and 'existence'. I shall try to show that this analysis is false; and for that purpose I must ask what may seem an extraordinary question: namely what is meant by saying that one thing is 'content' of another? It is not usual to ask this question; the term is used as if everybody must understand it. But since I am going to maintain that 'blue' is *not* the content of the sensation of blue; and, what is more important, that, even if it were, this analysis would leave out the most important element in the sensation of blue, it is necessary that I should try to explain precisely what it is that I shall deny.

What then is meant by saying that one thing is the 'content' of another? First of all I wish to point out that 'blue' is rightly and properly said to be part of the content of a blue flower. If, therefore, we also assert that it is part of the content of the sensation of blue, we assert that it has to the other parts (if any) of this whole the same relation which it has to the other parts of a blue flower – and we assert only this: we cannot mean to assert that it has to the sensation of blue any relation which it does not have to the blue flower. And we have seen that the sensation of blue contains at least one other element beside blue – namely, what I call 'consciousness', which makes it a sensation. So far then as we assert that blue is the content of the sensation, we assert that it has to this 'consciousness' the same relation which it has to the other parts of a blue flower: we do assert this, and we assert no more than this. Into the question what exactly the relation is between blue and a blue flower in virtue of which we call the former part of its 'content' I do not propose to enter. It is sufficient for my purpose to point out that it is the general relation most commonly meant when we talk of a thing and its qualities; and that this relation is such that to say the thing exists implies that the qualities also exist. The *content* of the thing is *what* we assert to exist, when we assert *that* the thing exists.

When, therefore, blue is said to be part of the content of the 'sensation of blue', the latter is treated as if it were a whole constituted in exactly the same way as any other 'thing'. The 'sensation of blue', on this view, differs from a blue

G. E. Moore on Idealism, Goodness, and Common Sense

bead or a blue beard, in exactly the same way in which the two latter differ from one another: the blue bead differs from the blue beard, in that while the former contains glass, the latter contains hair; and the 'sensation of blue' differs from both in that, instead of glass or hair, it contains consciousness. The relation of the blue to the consciousness is conceived to be exactly the same as that of the blue to the glass or hair: it is in all three cases the *quality* of a *thing*.

But I said just now that the sensation of blue was analysed into 'content' and 'existence', and that blue was said to be the content of the idea of blue. There is an ambiguity in this and a possible error, which I must note in passing. The term 'content' may be used in two senses. If we use 'content' as equivalent to what Mr. Bradley calls the '*what*' – if we mean by it the *whole* of what is said to exist, when the thing is said to exist, then blue is certainly not *the* content of the sensation of blue: part of the *content* of the sensation is, in this sense of the term, that other element which I have called consciousness. The analysis of this sensation into the 'content' 'blue', on the one hand, and mere existence on the other, is therefore certainly false; in it we have again the self-contradictory identification of 'Blue exists' with 'The sensation of blue exists'. But there is another sense in which 'blue' might properly be said to be *the* content of the sensation – namely, the sense in which 'content', like εἶδος is opposed to 'substance' or 'matter'. For the element 'consciousness', being common to all sensations, may be and certainly is regarded as in some sense their 'substance', and by the 'content' of each is only meant that in respect of which one differs from another. In this sense then 'blue' might be said to be *the* content of the sensation; but, in that case, the analysis into 'content' and 'existence' is, at least, misleading, since under 'existence' must be included 'what exists' in the sensation other than blue.

We have it, then, as a universally received opinion that blue is related to the sensation or idea of blue, as its *content*, and that this view, if it is to be true, must mean that blue is part of *what* is said to exist when we say that the sensation exists. To say that the sensation exists is to say both that blue exists and that 'consciousness', whether we call it the substance of which blue is *the* content or call it another part of the content, exists too. Any sensation or idea is a '*thing*', and what I have called its object is the quality of this thing. Such a 'thing' is what we think of when we think of a *mental image*. A mental image is conceived as if it were related to that of which it is the image (if there be any such thing) in exactly the same way as the image in a looking-glass is related to that of which it is the reflexion; in both cases there is identity of content, and the image in the looking-glass differs from that in the mind solely in respect of the fact that in the one case the other constituent of the image is 'glass' and in

76   Early Analytic Philosophy

the other case it is consciousness. If the image is of blue, it is not conceived that this 'content' has any relation to the consciousness but what it has to the glass; it is conceived *merely* to be its *content*. And owing to the fact that sensations and ideas are all considered to be *wholes* of this description – things in the mind – the question: What do we know? is considered to be identical with the question: What reason have we for supposing that there are things outside the mind *corresponding* to these that are inside it?

What I wish to point out is (1) that we have no reason for supposing that there are such things as mental images at all – for supposing that blue *is* part of the content of the sensation of blue, and (2) that even if there are mental images, no mental image and no sensation or idea is *merely* a thing of this kind: that 'blue', even if it is part of the content of the image or sensation or idea of blue, is always *also* related to it in quite another way, and that this other relation, omitted in the traditional analysis, is the *only* one which makes the sensation of blue a mental fact at all.

The true analysis of a sensation or idea is as follows. The element that is common to them all, and which I have called 'consciousness', really *is* consciousness. A sensation is, in reality, a case of 'knowing' or 'being aware of' or 'experiencing' something. When we know that the sensation of blue exists, the fact we know is that there exists an awareness of blue. And this awareness is not merely, as we have hitherto seen it must be, itself something distinct and unique, utterly different from blue: it also has a perfectly distinct and unique relation to blue, a relation which is *not* that of thing or substance to content, nor of one part of content to another part of content. This relation is just that which we mean in every case by 'knowing'. To have in your mind 'knowledge' of blue, is *not* to have in your mind a 'thing' or 'image' of which blue is the content. To be aware of the sensation of blue is *not* to be aware of a mental image – of a 'thing', of which 'blue' and some other element are constituent parts in the same sense in which blue and glass are constituents of a blue bead. It is to be aware of an awareness of blue; awareness being used, in both cases, in exactly the same sense. This element, we have seen, is certainly neglected by the 'content' theory: that theory entirely fails to express the fact that there is, in the sensation of blue, this unique relation between blue and the other constituent. And what I contend is that this omission is *not* mere negligence of expression, but is due to the fact that though philosophers have recognised that *something* distinct is meant by consciousness, they have never yet had a clear conception of *what* that something is. They have not been able to hold *it* and *blue* before their minds and to compare them, in the same way in which they can compare *blue* and *green*. And this for the reason I gave above: namely that the moment

G. E. Moore on Idealism, Goodness, and Common Sense   77

we try to fix our attention upon consciousness and to see *what*, distinctly, it is, it seems to vanish: it seems as if we had before us a mere emptiness. When we try to introspect the sensation of blue, all we can see is the blue: the other element is as if it were diaphanous. Yet it can be distinguished if we look attentively enough, and if we know that there is something to look for. My main object in this paragraph has been to try to make the reader *see* it: but I fear I shall have succeeded very ill.

It being the case, then, that the sensation of blue includes in its analysis, beside blue, *both* a unique element 'awareness' *and* a unique relation of this element to blue, I can make plain what I meant by asserting, as two distinct propositions, (1) that blue is probably not part of the content of the sensation at all, and (2) that, even if it were, the sensation would nevertheless not be the sensation *of* blue, if blue had only this relation to it. The first hypothesis may now be expressed by saying that, if it were true, then, when the sensation of blue exists, there exists a *blue awareness*: offence may be taken at the expression, but yet it expresses just what should be and is meant by saying that blue is, in this case, a *content* of consciousness or experience. Whether or not, when I have the sensation of blue, my consciousness or awareness is thus blue, my introspection does not enable me to decide with certainty: I only see no reason for thinking that it is. But whether it is or not, the point is unimportant, for introspection *does* enable me to decide that something else is also true: namely that I am aware *of* blue, and by this I mean, that my awareness has to blue a quite different and distinct relation. It is possible; I admit, that my awareness is blue *as well* as being *of* blue: but what I am quite sure of is that it is of blue; that it has to blue the simple and unique relation the existence of which alone justifies us in distinguishing knowledge of a thing from the thing known, and indeed in distinguishing mind from matter. And this result I may express by saying that what is called the *content* of a sensation is in very truth what I originally called it – the sensation's *object*.

But, if all this be true, what follows?

Idealists admit that some things really exist of which they are not aware: there are some things, they hold, which are not inseparable aspects of *their* experience, even if they be inseparable aspects of some experience. They further hold that some of the things of which they are sometimes aware do really exist, even when they are not aware of them: they hold for instance that they are sometimes aware of other minds, which continue to exist even when they are not aware of them. They are, therefore, sometimes aware of something which is *not* an inseparable aspect of their own experience. They do *know some* things which are *not* a mere part or content of their experience. And what my

Early Analytic Philosophy

analysis of sensation has been designed to show is, that whenever I have a mere sensation or idea, the fact is that I am then aware of something which is equally and in the same sense *not* an inseparable aspect of my experience. The awareness which I have maintained to be included in sensation is the very same unique fact which constitutes every kind of knowledge: 'blue' is as much an object, and as little a mere content, of my experience, when I experience it, as the most exalted and independent real thing of which I am ever aware. There is, therefore, no question of how we are to 'get outside the circle of our own ideas and sensations'. Merely to have a sensation is already to *be* outside that circle. It is to know something which is as truly and really *not* a part of *my* experience, as anything which I can ever know.

Now I think I am not mistaken in asserting that the reason why Idealists suppose that everything which *is* must be an inseparable aspect of some experience, is that they suppose some things, at least, to be inseparable aspects of *their* experience. And there is certainly nothing which they are so firmly convinced to be an inseparable aspect of their experience as what they call the *content* of their ideas and sensations. If, therefore, *this* turns out in every case, whether it be also the content or not, to be at least *not* an inseparable aspect of the experience of it, it will be readily admitted that nothing else which we experience ever is such an inseparable aspect. But if we never experience anything but what is not an inseparable aspect of *that* experience, how can we infer that anything whatever, let alone *everything*, is an inseparable aspect of *any* experience? How utterly unfounded is the assumption that '*esse* is *percipi*' appears in the clearest light.

But further I think it may be seen that if the object of an Idealist's sensation were, as he supposes, *not* the object but merely the content of that sensation, if, that is to say, it really were an inseparable aspect of his experience, each Idealist could never be aware either of himself or of any other real thing. For the relation of a sensation to its object is certainly the same as that of any other instance of experience to its object; and this, I think, is generally admitted even by Idealists: they state as readily that *what* is judged or thought or perceived is the *content* of that judgment or thought or perception, as that blue is the content of the sensation of blue. But, if so, then, when any Idealist thinks he is *aware* of himself or of any one else, this cannot really be the case. The fact is, on his own theory, that himself and that other person are in reality mere *contents* of an awareness, which is aware *of* nothing whatever. All that can be said is that there is an awareness in him, *with* a certain content: it can never be true that there is in him a consciousness *of* anything. And similarly he is never aware either of the fact that he exists or that reality is spiritual. The real fact, which he describes in

G. E. Moore on Idealism, Goodness, and Common Sense 79

those terms, is that his existence and the spirituality of reality are *contents* of an awareness, which is aware of nothing – certainly not, then, of its own content.

And further if everything, of which he thinks he is aware, is in reality merely a content of his own experience he has certainly no *reason* for holding that anything does exist except himself: it will, of course, be possible that other persons do exist; solipsism will not be necessarily true; but he cannot possibly infer from anything he holds that it is not true. That he himself exists will of course follow from his premiss that many things are contents of his experience. But since everything, of which he thinks himself aware, is. in reality merely an inseparable aspect of that awareness; this premiss allows no inference that any of these contents, far less any other consciousness, exists at all except as an inseparable aspect of his awareness, that is, as part of himself.

Such, and not those which he takes to, follow from it, are the consequences which *do* follow from the Idealist's supposition that the object of an experience is in reality merely a content or inseparable aspect of that experience. If, on the other hand, we clearly recognise the nature of that peculiar relation which I have called 'awareness of anything'; if we see that this is involved equally in the analysis of every experience – from the merest sensation to the most developed perception or reflexion, and that *this* is in fact the only essential element in an experience – the only thing that is both common and peculiar to all experiences – the only thing which gives us reason to call any fact mental; if, further, we recognise that this awareness is and must be in all cases of such a nature that its object, when we are aware of it, is precisely what it would be, if we were not aware: then it becomes plain that the existence of a table in space is related to my experience of *it* in precisely the same way as the existence of my own experience is related to my experience of *that*. Of both we are merely aware: if we are aware that the one exists, we are aware in precisely the same sense that the other exists; and, if it is true that my experience can exist, even when I do not happen to be aware of its existence, we have exactly the same reason for supposing that the table can do so also. When, therefore, Berkeley, supposed that the only thing of which I am directly aware is my own sensations and ideas, he supposed what was false; and when Kant supposed that the objectivity of things in space *consisted* in the fact that they were 'Vorstellungen' having to one another different relations from those which the same 'Vorstellungen' have to one another in subjective experience, he supposed what was equally false. I am as directly aware of the existence of material things in space as of my own sensations; and *what* I am aware of with regard to each is exactly the same – namely that in one case the material thing, and in the other case my sensation does really exist. The question requiring to be asked about material things is thus not: What reason have we for supposing that

Early Analytic Philosophy

anything exists *corresponding* to our sensations? but: What reason have we for supposing that material things do *not* exist, since *their* existence has precisely the same evidence as that of our sensations? That either exist *may* be false; but if it is a reason for doubting the existence of matter, that it is an inseparable aspect of our experience, the same reasoning will prove conclusively that our experience does not exist either, since that must also be an inseparable aspect of our experience of *it*. The only *reasonable* alternative to the admission that matter exists *as well as* spirit, is absolute Scepticism – that, as likely as not *nothing* exists at all. All other suppositions – the Agnostic's, that something, at all events, does exist, as much as the Idealist's, that spirit does – are, if we have no reason for believing in matter, as baseless as the grossest superstitions.

Moore, G. E. *Principia Ethica* (Ch. 1).
Reprinted from Moore, G. E. (1903), *Principia Ethica*, Cambridge: Cambridge University Press.

Chapter 1. The Subject-Matter of Ethics.

1. It is very easy to point out some among our every-day judgments, with the truth of which Ethics is undoubtedly concerned. Whenever we say, 'So and so is a good man,' or 'That fellow is a villain'; whenever we ask 'What ought I to do?' or 'Is it wrong for me to do like this?'; whenever we hazard such remarks as 'Temperance is a virtue and drunkenness a vice'–it is undoubtedly the business of Ethics to discuss such questions and such statements; to argue what is the true answer when we ask what it is right to do, and to give reasons for thinking that our statements about the character of persons or the morality of actions are true or false. In the vast majority of cases, where we make statements involving any of the terms 'virtue,' 'vice,' 'duty,' 'right,' 'ought,' 'good,' 'bad,' we are making ethical judgments; and if we wish to discuss their truth, we shall be discussing a point of Ethics.

So much as this is not disputed; but it falls very far short of defining the province of Ethics. That province may indeed be defined as the whole truth about that which is at the same time common to all such judgments and peculiar to them. But we have still to ask the question: What is it that is thus common and peculiar? And this is a question to which very different answers have been given by ethical philosophers of acknowledged reputation, and none of them, perhaps, completely satisfactory.

G. E. Moore on Idealism, Goodness, and Common Sense   81

2. If we take such examples as those given above, we shall not be far wrong in saying that they are all of them concerned with the question of 'conduct'–with the question, what, in the conduct of us, human beings, is good, and what is bad, what is right, and what is wrong. For when we say that a man is good, we commonly mean that he acts rightly; when we say that drunkenness is a vice, we commonly mean that to get drunk is a wrong or wicked action. And this discussion of human conduct is, in fact, that with which the name 'Ethics' is most intimately associated. It is so associated by derivation; and conduct is undoubtedly by far the commonest and most generally interesting object of ethical judgments.

Accordingly, we find that many ethical philosophers are disposed to accept as an adequate definition of 'Ethics' the statement that it deals with the question what is good or bad in human conduct. They hold that its enquiries are properly confined to 'conduct' or to 'practice'; they hold that the name 'practical philosophy' covers all the matter with which it has to do. Now, without discussing the proper meaning of the word (for verbal questions are properly left to the writers of dictionaries and other persons interested in literature; philosophy, as we shall see, has no concern with them), I may say that I intend to use 'Ethics' to cover more than this–a usage, for which there is, I think, quite sufficient authority. I am using it to cover an enquiry for which, at all events, there is no other word: the general enquiry into what is good.

Ethics is undoubtedly concerned with the question what good conduct is; but, being concerned with this, it obviously does not start at the beginning, unless it is prepared to tell us what is good as well as what is conduct. For 'good conduct' is a complex notion: all conduct is not good; for some is certainly bad and some may be indifferent. And on the other hand, other things, beside conduct, may be good; and if they are so, then, 'good' denotes some property, that is common to them and conduct; and if we examine good conduct alone of all good things, then we shall be in danger of mistaking for this property, some property which is not shared by those other things: and thus we shall have made a mistake about Ethics even in this limited sense; for we shall not know what good conduct really is. This is a mistake which many writers have actually made, from limiting their enquiry to conduct. And hence I shall try to avoid it by considering first what is good in general; hoping, that if we can arrive at any certainty about this, it will be much easier to settle the question of good conduct; for we all know pretty well what 'conduct' is. This, then, is our first question: What is good? and What is bad? and to the discussion of this question (or these questions) I give the name Ethics, since that science must, at all events, include it.

3. But this is a question which may have many meanings. If, for example, each of us were to say 'I am doing good now' or 'I had a good dinner yesterday,' these

Early Analytic Philosophy

statements would each of them be some sort of answer to our question, although perhaps a false one. So, too, when A asks B what school he ought to send his son to, B's answer will certainly be an ethical judgment. And similarly all distribution of praise or blame to any personage or thing that has existed, now exists, or will exist, does give some answer to the question 'What is good?' In all such cases some particular thing is judged to be good or bad: the question 'What?' is answered by 'This.' But this is not the sense in which a scientific Ethics asks the question. Not one, of all the many million answers of this kind, which must be true, can form a part of an ethical system; although that science must contain reasons and principles sufficient for deciding on the truth of all of them. there are far too many persons, things and events in the world, past, present, or to come, for a discussion of their individual merits to be embraced in any science. Ethics, therefore, does not deal at all with facts of this nature, facts that are unique, individual, absolutely particular; facts with which such studies as history, geography, astronomy are compelled, in part at least, to deal. And, for this reason, it is not the business of the ethical philosopher to give personal advice or exhortation.

4. But there is another meaning which may be given to the question 'What is good?' 'Books are good' would be an answer to it, though an answer obviously false; for some books are very bad indeed. And ethical judgments of this kind do indeed belong to Ethics; though I shall not deal with many of them. Such is the judgment 'Pleasure is good'–a judgment, of which Ethics should discuss the truth, although it is not nearly as important as that other judgment, with which we shall be much occupied presently–'Pleasure *alone* is good.' It is judgments of this sort, which are made in such books on Ethics as contain a list of 'virtues'–in Aristotle's 'Ethics' for example. But it is judgments of precisely the same kind, which form the substance of what is commonly supposed to be a study different from Ethics, and one much less respectable–the study of Casuistry. We may be told that Casuistry differs from Ethics in that it is much more detailed and particular, Ethics much more general. But it is most important to notice that Casuistry does not deal with anything that is absolutely particular–particular in the only sense in which it a perfectly precise line can be drawn between it and what is general. It is not particular in the sense just noticed, the sense in which this book is a particular book, and A's friend's advice particular advice. Casuistry may indeed be *more* particular and Ethics *more* general; but that means they differ only in degree and not in kind. And this is universally true of 'particular' and 'general,' when used in this common, but inaccurate, sense. So far as Ethics allows itself to give lists of virtues or even to name constituents of the Ideal, it is indistinguishable from Casuistry. Both alike deal with what is general, in the sense in which physics and chemistry deal with what is general. Just as chemistry aims at discovering what

G. E. Moore on Idealism, Goodness, and Common Sense   83

are the properties of oxygen, *wherever it occurs*, and not only of this or that particular specimen of oxygen; so Casuistry aims at discovering what actions are good, *whenever they occur*. In this respect Ethics and Casuistry alike are to be classed with such sciences as physics, chemistry, and physiology, in their absolute distinction from those of which history and geography are instances. And it is to be noted that, owing to their detailed nature, casuistical investigations are actually nearer to physics and to chemistry than are the investigations usually assigned to Ethics. For just as physics cannot rest content with the discovery that light is propagated by waves of ether, but must go on to discover the particular nature of the ether-waves corresponding to each several colour; so Casuistry, not content with the general law that charity is a virtue must attempt to discover the relative merits of every different form of charity. Casuistry forms, therefore, part of the ideal of ethical science: Ethics cannot be complete without it. The defects of Casuistry are not defects of principle; no objection can be taken to its aim and object. It has failed only because it is far too difficult a subject to be treated adequately in our present state of knowledge. The casuist has been unable to distinguish, in the cases which he treats, those elements upon which their value depends. Hence he often thinks two cases to be alike in respect of value, when in reality they are alike only in some other respect. It is to mistakes of this kind that the pernicious influence of such investigations has been due. For Casuistry is the goal of ethical investigation. It cannot be safely attempted at the beginning of our studies, but only at the end.

5. But our question 'What is good?' may still have another meaning. We may, in the third place, mean to ask, not what thing or things are good, but how 'good' is to be defined. This is an enquiry which belongs only to Ethics, not to Casuistry; and this is the enquiry which will occupy us first.

It is an enquiry to which most special attention should be directed; since this question, how 'good' is to be defined, is the most fundamental question in all Ethics. That which is meant by 'good' is, in fact, except its converse 'bad,' the *only* simple object of thought which is peculiar to Ethics. Its definition is, therefore, the most essential point in the definition of Ethics; and moreover a mistake with regard to it entails a far larger number of erroneous ethical judgments than any other. Unless this first question be fully understood, and its true answer clearly recognised, the rest of Ethics is as good as useless from the point of view of systematic knowledge. True ethical judgments, of the two kinds last dealt with, may indeed be made by those who do not know the answer to this question as well as by those who do; and it goes without saying that the two classes of people may live equally good lives. But it is extremely unlikely that the *most general* ethical judgments will be equally valid, in the absence of

84   Early Analytic Philosophy

a true answer to this question; I shall presently try to shew that the gravest errors have been largely due to beliefs in a false answer. And, in any case, it is impossible that, till the answer to this question be known, any one should know *what is the evidence* for any ethical judgment whatsoever. But the main object of Ethics, as a systematic science, is to give correct *reasons* for thinking that this or that is good; and, unless this question be answered, such reasons cannot be given. Even, therefore, apart from the fact that a false answer leads to false conclusions, the present enquiry is a most necessary and important part of the science of Ethics.

6. What, then, is good? How is good to be defined? Now it may be thought that this is a verbal question. A definition does indeed often mean the expressing of one word's meaning in other words. But this is not the sort of definition I am asking for. Such a definition can never be of ultimate importance to any study except lexicography. If I wanted that kind of definition I should have to consider in the first place how people generally used the word 'good'; but my business is not with its proper usage, as established by custom. I should, indeed, be foolish if I tried to use it for something which it did not usually denote: if, for instance, I were to announce that, whenever I used the word 'good,' I must be understood to be thinking of that object which is usually denoted by the word 'table.' I shall, therefore, use the word in the sense in which I think it is ordinarily used; but at the same time I am not anxious to discuss whether I am right in thinking it is so used. My business is solely with that object or idea, which I hold, rightly or wrongly, that the word is generally used to stand for. What I want to discover is the nature of that object or idea, and about this I am extremely anxious to arrive at an agreement.

But if we understand the question in this sense, my answer to it may seem a very disappointing one. If I am asked, 'What is good?' my answer is that good is good, and that is the end of the matter. Or if I am asked 'How is good to be defined?' my answer is that it cannot be defined, and that is all I have to say about it. But disappointing as these answers may appear, they are of the very last importance. To readers who are familiar with philosophic terminology, I can express their importance by saying that they amount to this: That propositions about the good are all of them synthetic and never analytic; and that is plainly no trivial matter. And the same thing may be expressed more popularly, by saying that, if I am right, then nobody can foist upon us such an axiom as that 'Pleasure is the only good' or that 'The good is the desired' on the pretence that this is 'the very meaning of the word.'

7. Let us, then, consider this position. My point is that 'good' is a simple notion, just as 'yellow' is a simple notion; that, just as you cannot, by any manner of means, explain to anyone who does not already know it, what yellow is, so

G. E. Moore on Idealism, Goodness, and Common Sense   **85**

you cannot explain what good is. Definitions of the kind that I was asking for, definitions which describe the real nature of the object or notion denoted by a word, and which do not merely tell us what the word is used to mean, are only possible when the object or notion in question is something complex. You can give a definition of a horse, because a horse has many different properties and qualities, all of which you can enumerate. But when you have enumerated them all, when you have reduced a horse to his simplest terms, you can no longer define those terms. They are simply something which you think of or perceive, and to anyone who cannot think of or perceive them, you can never, by any definition, make their nature known. It may perhaps be objected to this that we are able to describe to others, objects which they have never seen or thought of. We can, for instance, make a man understand what a chimaera is, although he has never heard of one or seen one. You can tell him that it is an animal with a lioness's head and body, with a goat's head growing from the middle of its back, and with a snake in place of its tail. But here the object which you are describing is a complex object; it is entirely composed of parts, with which we are all perfectly familiar–a snake, a goat, a lioness; and we know, too, the manner in which those parts are to be put together, because we know what is meant by the middle of a lioness's back, and where her tail is wont to grow. And so it is with all objects not previously known, which we are able to define: they are all complex; all composed of parts, which may themselves, in the first instance, be capable of similar definition, but which must in the end be reducible to simplest parts, which can no longer be defined. But yellow and good, we say, are not complex: they are notions of that simple kind, out of which definitions are composed and with which the power of further defining ceases.

8. When we say, as Webster says, 'The definition of horse is "A hoofed quadruped of the genus Equus,"' we may, in fact, mean three different things. (1) We may mean merely 'When I say "horse," you are to understand that I am talking about a hoofed quadruped of the genus Equus.' This might be called the arbitrary verbal definition: and I do not mean that good is indefinable in that sense. (2) We may mean, as Webster ought to mean: 'When most English people say "horse," they mean a hoofed quadruped of the genus Equus.' This may be called the verbal definition proper, and I do not say that good is indefinable in this sense either; for it is certainly possible to discover how people use a word: otherwise, we could never have known that 'good' may be translated by 'gut' in German and by 'bon' in French. But (3) we may, when we define horse, mean something much more important. We may mean that a certain object, which we all of us know, is composed in a certain manner: that it has four legs, a head, a heart, a liver, etc., etc., all of them arranged in definite relations to one another. It

86 **Early Analytic Philosophy**

is in this sense that I deny good to be definable. I say that it is not composed of any parts, which we can substitute for it in our minds when we are thinking of it. We might think just as clearly and correctly about a horse, if we thought of all its parts and their arrangement instead of thinking of the whole: we could, I say, think how a horse differed from a donkey just as well, just as truly, in this way, as now we do, only not so easily; but there is nothing whatsoever which we could substitute for good; and that is what I mean, when I say that good is indefinable.

9. But I am afraid I have still not removed the chief difficulty which may prevent acceptance of the proposition that good is indefinable. I do not mean to say that *the* good, that which is good, is thus indefinable; if I did think so, I should not be writing on Ethics, for my main object is to help towards discovering that definition. It is just because I think there will be less risk of error in our search for a definition of 'the good,' that I am now insisting that *good* is indefinable. I must try to explain the difference between these two. I suppose it may be granted that 'good' is an adjective. Well, 'the good,' 'that which is good,' must therefore be the substantive to which the adjective 'good' will apply: it must be the whole of that to which the adjective will apply, and the adjective must *always* truly apply to it. But if it is that to which the adjective will apply, it must be something different from that adjective itself; and the whole of that something different, whatever it is, will be our definition of *the* good. Now it may be that this something will have other adjectives, beside 'good,' that will apply to it. It may be full of pleasure, for example; it may be intelligent; and if those two adjectives are really part of its definition, then it will certainly be true, that pleasure and intelligence are good. And many people appear to think that, if we say 'Pleasure and intelligence are good,' or if we say 'Only pleasure and intelligence are good,' we are defining 'good.' Well, I cannot deny that propositions of this nature may sometimes be called definitions; I do not know well enough how the word is generally used to decide upon this point. I only wish it to be understood that that is not what I mean when I say there is no possible definition of good, and that I shall not mean this if I use the word again. I do most fully believe that some true proposition of the form 'Intelligence is good and intelligence alone is good' can be found; if none could be found, our definition of *the* good would be impossible. As it is, I believe *the* good to be definable; and yet I still say that good itself is indefinable.

10. 'Good,' then, if we mean by it that quality which we assert to belong to a thing, when we say that the thing is good, is incapable of any definition, in the most important sense of that word. The most important sense of 'definition' is that in which a definition states what are the parts which invariably compose a certain whole; and in this sense 'good' has no definition because it is simple and

G. E. Moore on Idealism, Goodness, and Common Sense 87

has no parts. It is one of those innumerable objects of thought which are themselves incapable of definition, because they are the ultimate terms of reference to which whatever *is* capable of definition must be defined. That there must be an indefinite number of such terms is obvious, on reflection; since we cannot define anything except by an analysis, which, when carried as far as it will go, refers us to something, which is simply different from anything else, and which by that ultimate difference explains the peculiarity of the whole which we are defining: for every whole contains some parts which are common to other wholes also. There is, therefore, no intrinsic difficulty in the contention that 'good' denotes a simple and indefinable quality. There are many other instances of such qualities.

Consider yellow, for example. We may try to define it, by describing its physical equivalent; we may state what kind of light-vibrations must stimulate the normal eye, in order that we may perceive it. But a moment's reflection is sufficient to shew that those light-vibrations are not themselves what we mean by yellow. *They* are not what we perceive. Indeed, we should never have been able to discover their existence, unless we had first been struck by the patent difference of quality between the different colours. The most we can be entitled to say of those vibrations is that they are what corresponds in space to the yellow which we actually perceive.

Yet a mistake of this simple kind has commonly been made about 'good.' It may be true that all things which are good are *also* something else, just as it is true that all things which are yellow produce a certain kind of vibration in the light. And it is a fact, that Ethics aims at discovering what are those other properties belonging to all things which are good. But far too many philosophers have thought that when they named those other properties they were actually defining good; that these properties, in fact, were simply not 'other,' but absolutely and entirely the same with goodness. This view I propose to call the 'naturalistic fallacy' and of it I shall now endeavour to dispose.

11. Let us consider what it is such philosophers say. And first it is to be noticed that they do not agree among themselves. They not only say that they are right as to what good is, but they endeavour to prove that other people who say that it is something else, are wrong. One, for instance, will affirm that good is pleasure, another, perhaps, that good is that which is desired; and each of these will argue eagerly to prove that other people who say that it is something else, are wrong. One, for instance, will affirm that good is pleasure, another, perhaps, that good is that which is desired; and each of these will argue eagerly to prove that the other is wrong. But how is that possible? One of them says that good is nothing but the object of desire, and at the same time tries to prove

Early Analytic Philosophy

that it is not pleasure. But from his first assertion, that good just means the object of desire, one of two things must follow as regards his proof:

(1) He may be trying to prove that the object of desire is not pleasure. But, if this be all, where is his Ethics? The position he is maintaining is merely a psychological one. Desire is something which occurs in our minds, and pleasure is something else which so occurs; and our would-be ethical philosopher is merely holding that the latter is not the object of the former. But what has that to do with the question in dispute? His opponent held the ethical proposition that pleasure was the good, and although he should prove a million times over the psychological proposition that pleasure is not the object of desire, he is no nearer proving his opponent to be wrong. The position is like this. One man says a triangle is a circle: another replies, 'A triangle is a straight line, and I will prove to you that I am right: *for*' (this is the only argument) 'a straight line is not a circle.' 'That is quite true,' the other may reply; 'but nevertheless a triangle is a circle, and you have said nothing whatever to prove the contrary. What is proved is that one of us is wrong, for we agree that a triangle cannot be both a straight line and a circle: but which is wrong, there can be no earthly means of proving, since you define triangle as straight line and I define it as circle.'—Well, that is one alternative which any naturalistic Ethics has to face; if good is *defined* as something else, then it is impossible either to prove that any other definition is wrong or even to deny such definition.

(2) The other alternative will scarcely be more welcome. It is that the discussion is after all a verbal one. When A says 'Good means pleasant' and B says 'Good means desired,' they may merely wish to assert that most people have used the word for what is pleasant and for what is desired respectively. And this is quite an interesting subject for discussion: only it is not a whit more an ethical discussion than the last was. Nor do I think that any exponent of naturalistic Ethics would be willing to allow that this was all he meant. They are all so anxious to persuade us that what they call the good is what we really ought to do. 'Do, pray, act so, because the word "good" is generally used to denote actions of this nature': such, on this view, would be the substance of their teaching. And in so far as they tell us how we ought to act, their teaching is truly ethical, as they mean it to be. But how perfectly absurd is the reason they would give for it! 'You are to do this, because most people use a certain word to denote conduct such as this.' 'You are to say the thing which is not, because most people call it lying.' That is an argument just as good!—My dear sirs, what we want to know from you as ethical teachers, is not how people use a word; it is not even, what kind of actions they approve, which the use of this word 'good' may certainly imply: what we want to know is simply what *is* good. We may indeed

G. E. Moore on Idealism, Goodness, and Common Sense 89

agree that what most people do think good, is actually so; we shall at all events be glad to know their opinions: but when we say that their opinions about what *is* good, we do mean what we say; we do not care whether they call that thing 'horse' or 'table' or 'chair,' 'gut' or 'bon' or 'ἀγαθός'; we want to know what it is that they so call. When they say 'Pleasure is good,' we cannot believe that they merely mean 'Pleasure is pleasure' and nothing more than that.

12. Suppose a man says 'I am pleased'; and suppose it is not a lie or a mistake but the truth. Well, if it is true, what does that mean? It means that his mind, a certain definite mind, distinguished by certain definite marks from all others has at this moment a certain definite feeling called pleasure. 'Pleased' *means* nothing but having pleasure, and though we may be more pleased or less pleased, and even, we may admit for the present, have one or another kind of pleasure; yet in so far as it is pleasure we have, whether there be more or less of it, and whether it be of one kind or another, what we have is one definite thing, absolutely indefinable, some one thing that is the same in all the various degrees and in all the various kinds of it that there may be. We may be able to say how it is related to other things: that, for example, it is in the mind, that it causes desire, that we are conscious of it, etc., etc. We can, I say, describe its relations to other things, but define it we can *not*. And if anybody tried to define pleasure for us as being any other natural object; if anybody were to say, for instance, that pleasure *means* the sensation of red, and were to proceed to deduce from that that pleasure is a colour, we should be entitled to laugh at him and to distrust his future statements about pleasure. Well, that would be the same fallacy which I have called the naturalistic fallacy. That 'pleased' does not mean 'having the sensation of red,' or anything else whatever, does not prevent us from understanding what it does mean. It is enough for us to know that 'pleased' does mean 'having the sensation of pleasure,' and though pleasure is absolutely indefinable, though pleasure is pleasure and nothing else whatever, yet we feel no difficulty in saying that we are pleased. The reason is, of course, that when I say 'I am pleased,' I do *not* mean that 'I' am the same thing as 'having pleasure.' And similarly no difficulty need be found in my saying that 'pleasure is good' and yet not meaning that 'pleasure' is the same thing as 'good,' that pleasure *means* good, and that good *means* pleasure. If I were to imagine that when I said 'I am pleased,' I meant that I was exactly the same thing as 'pleased,' I should not indeed call that a naturalistic fallacy, although it would be the same fallacy as I have called naturalistic with reference to Ethics. The reason of this is obvious enough. When a man confuses two natural objects with one another, defining the one by the other, if for instance, he confuses himself, who is one natural object, with 'pleased' or with 'pleasure' which are others, then there is no reason

90   Early Analytic Philosophy

to call the fallacy naturalistic. But if he confuses 'good', which is not in the same sense a natural object, with any natural object whatever, then there is a reason for calling that a naturalistic fallacy; its being made with regard to 'good' marks it as something quite specific, and this specific mistake deserves a name because it is so common. As for the reasons why good is not to be considered a natural object, they may be reserved for discussion in another place. But, for the present, it is sufficient to notice this: Even if it were a natural object, that would not alter the nature of the fallacy nor diminish its importance one whit. All that I have said about it would remain quite equally true: only the name which I have called it would not be so appropriate as I think it is. And I do not care about the name: what I do care about is the fallacy. It does not matter what we call it, provided we recognise it when we meet with it. It is to be met with in almost every book on Ethics; and yet it is not recognised: and that is why it is necessary to multiply illustrations of it, and convenient to give it a name. It is a very simple fallacy indeed. When we say that an orange is yellow, we do not think our statement binds us to hold that 'orange' means nothing else than 'yellow', or that nothing can be yellow but an orange. Supposing the orange is also sweet! Does that bind us to say that 'sweet' is exactly the same thing as 'yellow', that 'sweet' must be defined as 'yellow'? And supposing it be recognised that 'yellow' just means 'yellow' and nothing else whatever, does that make it any more difficult to hold that oranges are yellow? Most certainly it does not: on the contrary, it would be absolutely meaningless to say that oranges were yellow unless yellow did in the end mean just 'yellow' and nothing else whatever–unless it was absolutely indefinable. We should not get any very clear notion about things, which are yellow–we should not get very far with our science, if we were bound to hold that everything which was yellow, *meant* exactly the same thing as yellow. We should find we had to hold that an orange was exactly the same thing as a stool, a piece of paper, a lemon, anything you like. We could prove any number of absurdities; but should we be the nearer to the truth? Why, then, should it be different with 'good'? Why, if good is good and indefinable, should I be held to deny that pleasure is good? Is there any difficulty in holding both to be true at once? On the contrary, there is no meaning in saying that pleasure is good, unless good is something different from pleasure. It is absolutely useless, so far as Ethics is concerned, to prove, as Mr Spencer tries to do, that increase of pleasure coincides with increase of life, unless good *means* something different from either life or pleasure. He might just as well try to prove that an orange is yellow by shewing that it is always wrapped up in paper.

13. In fact, if it is not the case that 'good' denotes something simple and indefinable, only two alternatives are possible: either it is a complex, a given

G. E. Moore on Idealism, Goodness, and Common Sense 91

whole, about the correct analysis of which there could be disagreement; or else it means nothing at all, and there is no such subject as Ethics. In general, however, ethical philosophers have attempted to define good, without recognising what such an attempt must mean. They actually use arguments which involve one or both of the absurdities considered in §11. We are, therefore, justified in concluding that the attempt to define good is chiefly due to want of clearness as to the possible nature of definition. There are, in fact, only two serious alternatives to be considered, in order to establish the conclusion that 'good' does denote a simple and indefinable notion. It might possibly denote a complex, as 'horse' does; or it might have no meaning at all. Neither of these possibilities has, however, been clearly conceived and seriously maintained, as such, by those who presume to define good; and both may be dismissed by a simple appeal to facts.

(1) The hypothesis that disagreement about the meaning of good is disagreement with regard to the correct analysis of a given whole, may be most plainly seen to be incorrect by consideration of the fact that, whatever definition may be offered, it may always, be asked, with significance, of the complex so defined, whether it is itself good. To take, for instance, one of the more plausible, because one of the more complicated of such proposed definitions, it may easily be thought, at first sight, that to be good may mean to be that which we desire to desire. Thus if we apply this definition to a particular instance and say 'When we think that A is good, we are thinking that A is one of the things which we desire to desire,' our proposition may seem quite plausible. But, if we carry the investigation further, and ask ourselves 'Is it good to desire to desire A?' it is apparent, on a little reflection, that this question is itself as intelligible, as the original question, 'Is A good?'–that we are, in fact, now asking for exactly the same information about the desire to desire A, for which we formerly asked with regard to A itself. But it is also apparent that the meaning of this second question cannot be correctly analysed into 'Is the desire to desire A one of the things which we desire to desire?': we have not before our minds anything so complicated as the question 'Do we desire to desire to desire to desire A?' Moreover any one can easily convince himself by inspection that the predicate of this proposition–'good'–is positively different from notion of 'desiring to desire' which enters into its subject: 'That we should desire to desire A is good' is *not* merely equivalent to 'That A should be good is good.' It may indeed be true that what we desire to desire is always good; perhaps, even the converse may be true: but it is very doubtful whether this is the case, and the mere fact that we understand very well what is meant by doubting it, shews clearly that we have to different notions before our mind.

92   Early Analytic Philosophy

(2) And the same consideration is sufficient to dismiss the hypothesis that 'good' has no meaning whatsoever. It is very natural to make the mistake of supposing that what is universally true is of such a nature that its negation would be self-contradictory: the importance which has been assigned to analytic propositions in the history of philosophy shews how easy such a mistake is. And thus it is very easy to conclude that what seems to be a universal ethical principle is in fact an identical proposition; that, if, for example, whatever is called 'good' seems to be pleasant, the proposition 'Pleasure is the good' does not assert a connection between two different notions, but involves only one, that of pleasure, which is easily recognised as a distinct entity. But whoever will attentively consider with himself what is actually before his mind when he asks the question 'Is pleasure (or whatever it may be) after all good?' can easily satisfy himself that he is not merely wondering whether pleasure is pleasant. And if he will try this experiment with each suggested definition in succession, he may become expert enough to recognise that in every case he has before his mind a unique object, with regard to the connection of which with any other object, a distinct question may be asked. Every one does in fact understand the question 'Is this good?' When he thinks of it, his state of mind is different from what it would be, were he asked 'Is this pleasant, or desired, or approved?' It has a distinct meaning for him, even though he may not recognise in what respect it is distinct. Whenever he thinks of 'intrinsic value,' or 'intrinsic worth,' or says that a thing 'ought to exist,' he has before his mind the unique object–the unique property of things–that I mean by 'good.' Everybody is constantly aware of this notion, although he may never become aware at all that it is different from other notions of which he is also aware. But, for correct ethical reasoning, it is extremely important that he should become aware of this fact; and as soon as the nature of the problem is closely understood, there should be little difficulty in advancing so far in analysis.

14. 'Good,' then, is indefinable; and yet, so far as I know, there is only one ethical writer, Prof. Henry Sidgwick, who has clearly recognised and stated this fact. We shall see, indeed, how far many of the most reputed ethical systems fall short of drawing the conclusions which follow from such a recognition. At present I will only quote from one instance, which will serve to illustrate the meaning and importance of this principle that 'good' is indefinable, or, as Prof. Sidgwick says, an 'unanalysable notion.' It is an instance to which Prof. Sidgwick himself refers in a note on the passage, in which he argues that 'ought' is unanalyzable [in *Methods of Ethics*, Bk. 1, Chap. iii, §1 (6th edition)].

'Bentham,' says Sidgwick, 'explains that his fundamental principle "states the greatest happiness of all those whose interest is in question as being the right and proper end of human action"'; and yet 'his language in other passages

G. E. Moore on Idealism, Goodness, and Common Sense

93

of the same chapter would seem to imply' that he *means* by the word 'right' 'conducive to the general happiness.' Prof. Sidgwick sees that, if you take these two statements together, you get the absurd result that 'greatest happiness is the end of human action, which is conducive to the general happiness'; and so absurd does it seem to him to call this result, as Bentham calls it, 'the fundamental principle of a moral system,' that he suggests that Bentham cannot have meant it. Yet Prof. Sidgwick himself states elsewhere [*Methods of Ethics*, Bk. 1, Chap. iii, §1] that Psychological Hedonism is 'not seldom confounded with Egoistic Hedonism'; and that confusion, as we shall see, rests chiefly on that same fallacy, the naturalistic fallacy, which is implied in Bentham's statements. Prof. Sidgwick admits therefore that this fallacy is sometimes committed, absurd as it is; and I am inclined to think that Bentham may really have been one of those who committed it. Mill, as we shall see, certainly did commit it. In any case, whether Bentham committed it or not, his doctrine, as above quoted, will serve as a very good illustration of this fallacy, and of the importance of the contrary proposition that good is indefinable.

Let us consider this doctrine. Bentham seems to imply, so Prof. Sidgwick says, that the word 'right' *means* 'conducive to general happiness.' Now this, by itself, need not necessarily involve the naturalistic fallacy. For the word 'right' is very commonly appropriated to actions which lead to the attainment of what is good; which are regarded as *means* to the ideal and not as ends-in-themselves. This use of 'right', as denoting what is good as a means, whether or not it also be good as an end, is indeed the use to which I shall confine the word. Had Bentham been using 'right' in this sense, it might be perfectly consistent for him to *define* right as 'conducive to the general happiness' *provided only* (and note this proviso) he had already proved, or laid down as an axiom, that general happiness was *the* good, or (what is equivalent to this) that general happiness alone was good. For in that case he would have already defined *the* good as general happiness (a position perfectly consistent, we have seen, with the contention that 'good' is indefinable), and, since right was to be defined as 'conducive to *the* good,' it would actually *mean* 'conducive to general happiness.' But this method of escape from the charge of having committed the naturalistic fallacy has been closed by Bentham himself. For his fundamental principle is, we see, that the greatest happiness of all concerned is the *right* and proper *end* of human action. He applies the word 'right,' therefore, to the end, as such, not only to the means which are conducive to it; and that being so, right can no longer be defined as 'conducive to the general happiness,' without involving the fallacy in question. For now it is obvious that the definition of right as conducive to general happiness can be used by him in support of the fundamental principle

Early Analytic Philosophy

that general happiness is the right end; instead of being itself derived from that principle. If right, by definition, means conducive to general happiness, then it is obvious that general happiness is the right end. It is not necessary now first to prove or assert that general happiness is the right end, before right is defined as conducive to general happiness—a perfectly valid procedure; but on the contrary the definition of right as conducive to general happiness proves general happiness to be the right end—a perfectly invalid procedure, since in this case the statement that 'general happiness is the right end of human action' is not an ethical principle at all, but either, as we have seen, a proposition about the meaning of words, or else a proposition about the *nature* of general happiness, not about its rightness or its goodness.

Now, I do not wish the importance I assign to this fallacy to be misunderstood. The discovery of it does not at all refute Bentham's contention that greatest happiness is the proper end of human action, if that be understood as an ethical proposition, as he undoubtedly intended it. That principle may be true all the same; we shall consider whether it is so in the succeeding chapters. Bentham might have maintained it, as Prof. Sidgwick does, even if the fallacy had been pointed out to him. What I am maintaining is that the *reasons* which he actually gives for his ethical proposition are fallacious ones so far as they consist in a definition of right. What I suggest is that he did not perceive them to be fallacious; that, if he had done so, he would have been led to seek for other reasons in support of his Utilitarianism; and that, had he sought for other reasons, he *might* have found none which he thought to be sufficient. In that case he would have changed his whole system—a most important consequence. It is undoubtedly also possible that he would have thought other reasons to be sufficient, and in that case his ethical system, in its main results, would still have stood. But, even in this latter case, his use of the fallacy would be a serious objection to him as an ethical philosopher. For it is the business of Ethics, I must insist, not only to obtain true results, but also to find valid reasons for them. The direct object of Ethics is knowledge and not practice; and any one who uses the naturalistic fallacy has certainly not fulfilled this first object, however correct his practical principles may be.

My objections to Naturalism are then, in the first place, that it offers no reason at all, far less any valid reason, for any ethical principle whatever; and in this it already fails to satisfy the requirements of Ethics, as a scientific study. But in the second place I contend that, though it gives a reason for no ethical principle, it is the *cause* of the acceptance of false principles—it deludes the mind into accepting ethical principles, which are false; and in this it is contrary to every aim of Ethics. It is easy to see that if we start with a definition of right

G. E. Moore on Idealism, Goodness, and Common Sense   95

conduct as conduct conducive to general happiness; then, knowing that right conduct is universally conduct conducive to the good, we very easily arrive at the result that the good is general happiness. If, on the other hand, we once recognise that we must start our Ethics without a definition, we shall be much more apt to look about us, before we adopt any ethical principle whatever, and the more we look about us, the less likely we are to adopt a false one. It may be replied to this: Yes, but we shall look about us just as much, before we settle on our definition, and are therefore just as likely to be right. But I will try to shew that this is not the case. If we start with the conviction that a definition of good can be found, we start with the conviction that the good *can mean* nothing else than some one property of things, and our only business will then be to discover what that property is. But if we recognise that, so far as the meaning of good goes, anything whatever may be good, we start with a much more open mind. Moreover, apart from the fact that, when we think we have a definition, we cannot logically defend our ethical principles in any way whatever, we shall also be much less apt to defend them well, even if illogically. For we shall start with the conviction that good must mean so and so, and shall therefore be inclined either to misunderstand our opponent's arguments or to cut them short with the reply, 'This is not an open question: the very meaning of the word decides it; no one can think otherwise except through confusion.'

15. Our first conclusion as to the subject-matter of Ethics is, then, that there is a simple, indefinable, unanalysable object of thought by reference to which it must be defined. By what name we call this unique object is a matter of indifference, so long as we clearly recognise what it is and that it does differ from other objects. The words which are commonly taken as the signs of ethical judgments all do refer to it; and they are expressions of ethical judgments solely because they do so refer. But they may refer to it in two different ways, which it is very important to distinguish, if we are to have a complete definition of the range of ethical judgments. Before I proceeded to argue that there was such an indefinable notion involved in ethical notions, I stated (§4) that it was necessary for Ethics to enumerate all true universal judgments, asserting that such and such a thing was good, whenever it occurred. But, although all such judgments do refer to that unique notion which I have called 'good,' they do not all refer to it in the same way. They may either assert that this unique property does always attach to the thing in question, or else they may assert only that the thing in question is *a cause or necessary condition* for the existence of other things to which this unique property does attach. The nature of these two species of universal ethical judgments is extremely different; and a great part of the difficulties, which are met with in ordinary ethical speculation, are due to the

Early Analytic Philosophy

failure to distinguish them clearly. Their difference has, indeed, received expression in ordinary language by the contrast between the terms 'good as means' and 'good in itself,' 'value as a means' and 'intrinsic value.' But those terms are apt to be applied correctly only in the more obvious instances; and this seems to be due to the fact that the distinction between the conceptions which they denote has not been made a separate object of investigation. This distinction may be briefly pointed out as follows.

16. Whenever we judge that a thing is 'good as a means,' we are making a judgment with regard to its causal relations: we judge *both* that it will have a particular kind of effect, *and* that that effect will be good in itself. But to find causal judgments that are universally true is notoriously a matter of extreme difficulty. The late date at which most of the physical sciences became exact, and the comparative fewness of the laws which they have succeeded in establishing even now, are sufficient proofs of this difficulty. With regard, then, to what are the most frequent objects of ethical judgments, namely actions, it is obvious that we cannot be satisfied that any of our universal causal judgments are true, even in the sense in which scientific laws are so. We cannot even discover hypothetical laws of the form 'Exactly this action will always, under these conditions, produce exactly that effect.' But for a correct ethical judgment with regard to the effects of certain actions we require more than this in two respects. (1) We require to know that a given action will produce a certain effect, *under whatever circumstances it occurs.* But this is certainly impossible. It is certain that in different circumstances the same action may produce effects that are utterly different in all respects upon which the value of the effects depends. Hence we can never be entitled to more than a *generalization*–to a proposition of the form 'This result *generally* follows this kind of action'; and even this generalisation will only be true, if the circumstances under which the action occurs are generally the same. This is in fact the case, to a great extent, within any one particular age and state of society. But, when we take other ages into account, in many most important cases the normal circumstances of a given kind of action will be so different, that the generalisation which is true for one will not be true for another. With regard then to ethical judgments which assert that a certain kind of action is good as a means to a certain kind of effect, none will be *universally* true; and many, though *generally* true at one period, will be generally false at others. But (2) we require to know not only that *one* good effect will be produced, but that, among all subsequent events affected by the action in question, the balance of good will be greater than if any other possible action had been performed. In other words, to judge that an action is generally a means to good is to judge not only that it generally does *some* good, but that

it generally does the greatest good of which the circumstances admit. In this respect ethical judgments about the effects of action involve a difficulty and a complication far greater than that involved in the establishment of scientific laws. For the latter we need only consider a single effect; for the former it is essential to consider not only this, but the effects of that effect, and so on as far as our view into the future can reach. It is, indeed, obvious that our view can never reach far enough for us to be certain that any action will produce the best possible effects. We must be content, if the greatest possible balance of good seems to be produced within a limited period. But it is important to notice that the whole series of effects within a period of considerable length is actually taken account of in our common judgments that an action is good as a means; and that hence this additional complication, which makes ethical generalisations so far more difficult to establish than scientific laws, is one which is involved in actual ethical discussions, and is of practical importance. The commonest rules of conduct involve such considerations as the balancing of future bad health against immediate gains; and even if we can never settle with any certainty how we shall secure the greatest possible total of good, we try at least to assure ourselves that probable future evils will not be greater than the immediate good.

17. There are, then, judgments which state that certain kinds of things have good effects; and such judgments, for the reasons just given, have the important characteristics (1) that they are unlikely to be true, if they state that the kind of thing in question *always* has good effects, and (2) that, even if they only state that it *generally* has good effects, many of them will only be true of certain periods in the world's history. On the other hand there are judgments which state that certain kinds of things are themselves good; and these differ from the last in that, if true at all, they are all of them universally true. It is, therefore, extremely important to distinguish these two kinds of possible judgments. Both may be expressed in the same language: in both cases we commonly say 'Such and such a thing is good.' But in the one case 'good' will mean 'good as means,' i.e. merely that the thing is a means to good—will have good effects: in the other case it will mean 'good as end'—we shall be judging that the thing itself has the property which, in the first case, we asserted only to belong to its effects. It is plain that these are very different assertions to make about a thing; it is plain that either or both of them may be made, both truly and falsely, about all manner of things; and it is certain that unless we are clear as to which of the two we mean to assert, we shall have a very poor chance of deciding rightly whether our assertion is true or false. It is precisely this clearness as to the meaning of the question asked which has hitherto been almost entirely lacking in ethical

Early Analytic Philosophy

speculation. Ethics has always been predominantly concerned with the investigation of a limited class of actions. With regard to these we may ask *both* how far they are good in themselves *and* how far they have a general tendency to produce good results. And the arguments brought forward in ethical discussion have always been of both classes–both such as would prove the conduct in question to be good in itself and such as would prove it to be good as a means. But that these are the only questions which any ethical discussion can have to settle, and that to settle the one is *not* the same thing as to settle the other–these two fundamental facts have in general escaped the notice of ethical philosophers. Ethical questions are commonly asked in an ambiguous form. It is asked 'What is a man's duty under these circumstances?' or 'Is it right to act this way?' or 'What ought we to aim at securing?' But all these questions are capable of further analysis; a correct answer to any of them involves both judgments of what is good in itself and causal judgments. This is implied even by those who maintain that we have a direct and immediate judgment of absolute rights and duties. Such a judgment can only mean that the course of action in question is *the* best thing to do; that, by acting so, every good that *can* be secured will have been secured. Now we are not concerned with the question whether such a judgment will ever be true. The question is: What does it imply, if it is true? And the only possible answer is that, whether true or false, it implies both a proposition as to the degree of goodness of the action in question, as compared with other things, and a number of causal propositions. For it cannot be denied that the action will have consequences: and to deny that the consequences matter is to make a judgment of their intrinsic value, as compared with the action itself. In asserting that the action is *the* best thing to do, we assert that it together with its consequences presents a greater sum of intrinsic value than any possible alternative. And this condition may be realised by any of the three cases:–(*a*) If the action itself has greater intrinsic value than any alternative, whereas both its consequences and those of the alternatives are absolutely devoid either of intrinsic merit or intrinsic demerit; or (*b*) if, though its consequences are intrinsically bad, the balance of intrinsic value is greater than would be produced by any alternative; or (*c*) if, its consequences being intrinsically good, the degree of value belonging to them and it conjointly is greater than that of any alternative series. In short, to assert that a certain line of conduct is, at a given time, absolutely right or obligatory, is obviously to assert that more good or less evil will exist in the world, if it be adopted than if anything else be done instead. But this implies a judgment as to the value both of its own consequences and of those of any possible alternative. And that an action will have such and such consequences involves a number of causal judgments.

G. E. Moore on Idealism, Goodness, and Common Sense   99

Similarly, in answering the question 'What ought we to aim at securing?' causal judgments are again involved, but in a somewhat different way. We are liable to forget, because it is so obvious, that this question can never be answered correctly except by naming something which *can* be secured. Not everything can be secured; and, even if we judge that nothing which cannot be obtained would be of equal value with that which can, the possibility of the latter, as well as its value, is essential to its being a proper end of action. Accordingly neither our judgments as to what actions we ought to perform, nor even our judgments as to the ends which they ought to produce, are pure judgments of intrinsic value. With regard to the former, an action which is absolutely obligatory *may* have no intrinsic value whatsoever; that it is perfectly virtuous may mean merely that it causes the best possible effects. And with regard to the latter, these best possible results which justify our action can, in any case, have only so much of intrinsic value as the laws of nature allow us to secure; and they in their turn *may* have no intrinsic value whatsoever, but may merely be a means to the attainment (in a still further future) of something that has such value. Whenever, therefore, we ask 'What ought we to do?' or 'What ought we to try to get?' we are asking questions which involve a correct answer to two others, completely different in kind from one another. We must know *both* what degree of intrinsic value different things have, *and* how these different things may be obtained. But the vast majority of questions which have actually been discussed in Ethics–*all* practical questions, indeed–involve this double knowledge; and they have been discussed without any clear separation of the two distinct questions involved. A great part of the vast disagreements prevalent in Ethics is to be attributed to this failure in analysis. By the use of conceptions which involve both that of intrinsic value and that of causal relation, as if they involved intrinsic value only, two different errors have been rendered almost universal. Either it is assumed that nothing has intrinsic value which is not possible, or else it is assumed that what is necessary must have intrinsic value. Hence the primary and peculiar business of Ethics, the determination of what things have intrinsic value and in what degrees, has received no adequate treatment at all. And on the other hand a *thorough* discussion of means has been also largely neglected, owing to an obscure perception of the truth that it is perfectly irrelevant to the question of intrinsic values. But however this may be, and however strongly any particular reader may be convinced that some one of the mutually contradictory systems which hold the field has a given correct answer either to the question what has intrinsic value, or to the question what we ought to do, or to both, it must at least be admitted that the questions what is best in itself and what will bring about the best possible, are utterly distinct; that both belong to the actual subject-matter of

Early Analytic Philosophy

Ethics; and that the more clearly distinct questions are distinguished, the better is our chance of answering both correctly.

18. There remains one point which must not be omitted in a complete description of the kind of questions which Ethics has to answer. The main division of these questions is, as I have said, into two; the question what things are good in themselves, and the question to what other things these are related as effects. The first of these, which is the primary ethical question and is presupposed by the other, includes a correct comparison of the various things which have intrinsic value (if there are many such) in respect of the degree of value which they have; and such comparison involves a difficulty of principle which has greatly aided the confusion of intrinsic value with mere 'goodness as a means.' It has been pointed out that one difference between a judgment which asserts that a thing is good in itself, and a judgment which asserts that it is a means to good, consists in the fact that the first, if true of one instance of the thing in question, is necessarily true of all; whereas a thing which has good effects under some circumstances may have bad ones under others. Now it is certainly true that all judgments of intrinsic value are in this sense universal; but the principle which I have now to enunciate may easily make it appear as if they were not so but resembled the judgment of means in being merely general. There is, as will presently be maintained, a vast number of different things, each of which has intrinsic value; there are also very many which are positively bad; and there is a still larger class of things, which appear to be indifferent. But a thing belonging to any of these three classes may occur as part of a whole, which includes among its other parts other things belonging both to the same and to the other two classes; and these wholes, as such, may also have intrinsic value. The paradox, to which it is necessary to call attention, is that *the value of such a whole bears no regular proportion to the sum of the values of its parts.* It is certain that a good thing may exist in such a relation to another good thing that the value of the whole thus formed is immensely greater than the sum of the values of the two good things. It is certain that a whole formed of a good thing and an indifferent thing may have immensely greater value than that good thing itself possesses. It is certain that two bad things or a bad thing and an indifferent thing may form a whole much worse than the sum of badness of its parts. And it seems as if indifferent things may also be the sole constituents of a whole which has great value, either positive or negative. Whether the addition of a bad thing to a good whole may increase the positive value of the whole, or the addition of a bad thing to a bad may produce a whole having a positive value, may seem more doubtful; but it is, at least, possible, and this possibility must be taken into account in our ethical investigations. However we may decide

particular questions, the principle is clear. *The value of a whole must not be assumed to be the same as the sum of the values of its parts.*

A single instance will suffice to illustrate the kind of relation in question. It seems to be true that to be conscious of a beautiful object is of great intrinsic value; whereas the same object, if no one be conscious of it, has certainly comparatively little value, and it is commonly held to have none at all. But the consciousness of a beautiful object is certainly a whole of some sort in which we can distinguish as parts the object on the one hand and the being conscious on the other. Now this latter factor occurs as part of a different whole, whenever we are conscious of anything; and it would seem that some of these wholes have at all events very little value, and may even be indifferent or positively bad. Yet we cannot always attribute the slightness of their value to any positive demerit in the object which differentiates them from the consciousness of beauty; the object itself may approach as near as possible to absolute neutrality. Since, therefore, mere consciousness does not always confer great value upon the whole of which it forms a part, we cannot attribute the great superiority of the consciousness of a beautiful thing over the beautiful thing itself to the mere addition of the value of consciousness to that of the beautiful thing. Whatever the intrinsic value of consciousness may be, it does not give to the whole of which it forms a part a value proportional to the sum of its value and that of its object. If this be so, we have here an instance of a whole possessing a different intrinsic value from the sum of that of its parts; and whether it be so or not, what is meant by such a difference is illustrated by this case.

19. There are, then, wholes which possess the property that their value is different from the sum of the values of their parts, and the relations which subsist between such parts and the whole of which they form a part have not hitherto been distinctly recognised or received a separate name. Two points are especially worthy of notice. (1) It is plain that the existence of any such part is a necessary condition for the existence of that good which is constituted by the whole. And exactly the same language will also express the relation between a means and the good thing which is its effect. But yet there is a most important difference between the two cases, constituted by the fact that the part is, whereas the means is not, a part of the good thing for the existence of which its existence is a necessary condition. The necessity by which, if the good in question is to exist, the means to it must exist is merely a natural or causal necessity. If the laws of nature were different, exactly the same good might exist, although what is now a necessary condition of its existence did not exist. The existence of the means has no intrinsic value; and its utter annihilation would leave the value of that which it is now necessary to secure entirely

Early Analytic Philosophy

unchanged. But in the case of a part of such a whole as we are now considering, it is otherwise. In this case the good in question cannot conceivably exist, unless the part exist also. The necessity which connects the two is quite independent of natural law. What is asserted to have intrinsic value is the existence of the whole; and the existence of the whole includes the existence of its part. Suppose the part removed, and what remains is *not* what was asserted to have intrinsic value; but if we suppose a means removed, what remains is just what *was* asserted to have intrinsic value. And yet (2) the existence of the part may *itself* have no more intrinsic value than that of the means. It is this fact which constitutes the paradox of the relation which we are discussing. It has just been said that what has intrinsic value is the existence of the whole, and that this includes the existence of the part; and from this it would seem a natural inference that the existence of the part has intrinsic value. But the inference would be as false as if we were to conclude that, because the number of two stones was two, each of the stones was also two. The part of a valuable whole retains exactly the same value when it is, as when it is not, a part of that whole. If it had value under other circumstances, its value is not any greater, when it is part of a far more valuable whole; and if it had no value by itself, it has none still, however great be that of the whole of which it now forms a part. We are not then justified in asserting that one and the same thing is under some circumstances intrinsically good, and under others not so; as we are justified in asserting of a means that it sometimes does and sometimes does not produce good results. And yet we are justified in asserting that it is far more desirable that a certain thing should exist under some circumstances than under others; namely when other things will exist in such relations to it as to form a more valuable whole. *It* will not have more intrinsic value under those circumstances than under others; it will not necessarily even be a means to the existence of things having more intrinsic value; but it will, like a means, be a necessary condition for the existence of that which *has* greater intrinsic value, although, unlike a means, it will itself form a part of the more valuable existent.

20. I have said that the peculiar relation between part and whole which I have just been trying to define is one which has received no separate name. It would, however, be useful that it should have one; and there is a name, which might well be appropriated to it, if only it could be divorced from its present unfortunate usage. Philosophers, especially those who profess to have derived great benefit from the writings of Hegel, have latterly made much use of the terms 'organic whole,' 'organic unity,' 'organic relation.' The reason why these terms might well be appropriated to the use suggested is that the peculiar relation of parts to whole, just defined, is one of the properties which distinguishes the wholes to

which they are actually applied with the greatest frequency. And the reason why it is desirable that they should be divorced from their present usage is that, as at present used, they have no distinct sense and, on the contrary, both imply and propagate errors of confusion.

To say that a thing is an 'organic whole' is generally understood to imply that its parts are related to one another and to itself as means to end; it is also understood to imply that they have a property described in some such phrase as that they have 'no meaning or significance apart from the whole'; and finally such a whole is also treated as if it had the property to which I am proposing that the name should be confined. But those who use the term give us, in general, no hint as to how they suppose these three properties to be related to one another. It seems generally to be assumed that they are identical; and always, at least, that they are necessarily connected with one another. That they are not identical I have already tried to shew; to suppose them so is to neglect the very distinctions pointed out in the last paragraph; and the usage might well be discontinued merely because it encourages such neglect. But a still more cogent reason for its discontinuance is that, so far from being necessarily connected, the second is a property which can attach to nothing, being a self-contradictory conception; whereas the first, if we insist on its most important sense, applies to many cases, to which we have no reason to think that the third applies also, and the third certainly applies to many to which the first does not apply.

21. These relations between the three properties just distinguished may be illustrated by references to a whole of the kind from which the name 'organic' was derived–a whole which is an organism in the scientific sense–namely the human body.

(1) There exists between many parts of our body (though not between all) a relation which has been familiarised by the fable, attributed to Menenius Agrippa, concerning the belly and its members. We can find it in parts such that the continued existence of one is a necessary condition for the continued existence of the other; while the continued existence of this latter is also a necessary condition for the continued existence of the former. This amounts to no more than saying that in the body we have instances of two things, both enduring for some time, which have a relation of mutual causal dependence on one another–a relation of 'reciprocity.' Frequently no more than this is meant by saying that the parts of the body form an 'organic unity,' or that they are mutually means and ends to one another. And we certainly have here a striking characteristic of living things. But it would be extremely rash to assert that this relation of mutual causal dependence was only exhibited by living things and hence was sufficient to define their peculiarity. And it is obvious that of two things which have this relation of mutual

104 Early Analytic Philosophy

dependence, neither may have intrinsic value, or one may have it and the other lack it. They are not necessarily 'ends' to one another in any sense except that in which 'end' means 'effect.' And moreover it is plain that in this sense the whole cannot be an end to any of its parts. We are apt to talk of 'the whole' in contrast to one of its parts, when in fact we mean only *the rest* of the parts. But strictly the whole must include all its parts and no part can be a cause of the whole, because it cannot be a cause of itself. It is plain, therefore, that this relation of mutual causal dependence implies nothing with regard to the value of either of the objects which have it; and that, even if both of them happen also to have value, this relation between them is one which cannot hold between part and whole.

But (2) it may also be the case that our body as a whole has a value greater than the sum of values of its parts; and this may be what is meant when it is said that the parts are means to the whole. It is obvious that if we ask the question 'Why *should* the parts be such as they are?' a proper answer may be 'Because the whole they form has so much value.' But it is equally obvious that the relation which we thus assert to exist between part and whole is quite different from that which we assert to exist between part and part when we say 'This part exists, because that one could not exist without it.' In the latter case we assert the two parts to be causally connected; but, in the former, part and whole cannot be causally connected and the relation which we assert to exist between them may exist even though the parts are not causally connected either. All the parts of a picture do not have that relation of mutual causal dependence, which certain parts of the body have, and yet the existence of those which do not have it may be absolutely essential to the value of the whole. The two relations are quite distinct in kind, and we cannot infer the existence of the one from that of the other. It can, therefore, serve no useful purpose to include them both under the same name; and if we are to say that a whole is organic because its parts are (in this sense) 'means' to the whole, we must *not* say that it is organic because its parts are causally dependent on one another.

22. But finally (3) the sense which has been most prominent in recent uses of the term 'organic whole' is one whereby it asserts the parts of such a whole have a property which the parts of no whole can possibly have. It is supposed that just as the whole would not be what it is but for the existence of the parts, so the parts would not be what they are but for the existence of the whole; and this is understood to mean not merely that any particular part could not exist unless the others existed too (which is the case where relation (1) exists between the parts), but actually that the part is no distinct object of thought—that the whole, of which it is a part, is in turn a part of it. That this supposition is self-contradictory a very little reflection should be sufficient to shew. We may admit, indeed, that when a

particular thing is a part of a whole, it does possess a predicate which it would not otherwise possess–namely that it is a part of the whole. But what cannot be admitted is that this predicate alters the nature or enters into the definition of the thing which has it. When we think of the part *itself*, we mean just *that which* we assert, in this case, to *have* the predicate that it is part of the whole; and the mere assertion that *it* is a part of the whole involves that it should itself be distinct from that which we assert of it. Otherwise we contradict ourselves since we assert that, not *it*, but something else–namely it together with that which we assert of it–has the predicate which we assert of it. In short, it is obvious that no part contains analytically the whole to which it belongs, or any other parts of that whole. The relation of part to whole is *not* the same as that of whole to part; and the very definition of the latter is that it does contain analytically that which it is said to be its part. And yet this very self-contradictory doctrine is the chief mark which shews the influence of Hegel upon modern philosophy–an influence which pervades almost the whole of orthodox philosophy. This is what is generally implied by the cry against falsification by abstraction: that a whole is always a part of its part! 'If you want to know the truth about a part,' we are told, 'you must consider *not* that part, but something else–namely the whole: *nothing* is true of the part, but only of the whole.' Yet plainly it must be true of the part at least that it is part of the whole; and it is obvious that when we say it is, we do *not* mean merely that the whole is a part of itself. This doctrine, therefore, that a part can have 'no meaning or significance apart from its whole' must be utterly rejected. It implies itself that the statement 'This is a part of that whole' has a meaning; and in order that this may have one, both subject and predicate must have a distinct meaning. And it is easy to see how this false doctrine has arisen by confusion with the two relations (1) and (2) which may really be properties of wholes.

(*a*) The *existence* of a part may be connected by a natural or causal necessity with the existence of the other parts of its whole; and further what is a part of a whole and what has ceased to be such a part, although differing intrinsically from one another, may be called by one and the same name. Thus, to take a typical example, if an arm be cut off from the human body, we still call it an arm. Yet an arm, when it is a part of the body, undoubtedly differs from a dead arm; and hence we may easily be led to say 'The arm which is a part of the body would not be what it is, if it were not such a part,' and to think that the contradiction thus expressed is in reality a characteristic of things. But, in fact, the dead arm never was a part of the body; it is only *partially* identical with the living arm. Those parts of it which are identical with parts of the living arm are exactly the same, whether they belong to the body or not; and in them we have an undeniable instance of one and the same thing at one time forming a part,

Early Analytic Philosophy

and at another not forming a part of the presumed 'organic whole.' On the other hand those properties which are possessed by the living, and *not* by the dead arm, do not exist in a changed form in the latter: they simply do not exist there *at all*. By a causal necessity their existence depends on their having that relation to the other parts of the body which we express by saying that they form part of it. Yet, most certainly, *if* they ever did not form part of the body, they *would* be exactly what they are when they do. That they differ intrinsically from the properties of the dead arm and that they form part of the body are propositions not analytically related to one another. There is no contradiction in supposing them to retain such intrinsic differences and yet not to form part of the body.

But (*b*) when we are told that a living arm has no *meaning* or *significance* apart from the body to which it belongs, a different fallacy is also suggested. 'To have meaning or significance' is commonly used in the sense of 'to have importance'; and this again means 'to have value either as a means or as an end.' Now it is quite possible that even a living arm, apart from its body, would have no intrinsic value whatever; although the whole of which it is a part has great intrinsic value owing to its presence. Thus we may easily come to say that, *as* a part of the body, it has great value, whereas *by itself* it would have none; and thus that its whole 'meaning' lies in its relation to the body. But in fact the value in question obviously does not belong to *it* at all. To have value merely as a part is equivalent to having no value at all, but merely being a part of that which has it. Owing, however, to neglect of this distinction, the assertion that a part has value, *as a part*, which it would not otherwise have, easily leads to the assumption that it is also different, as a part, from what it would otherwise be; for it is, in fact, true that two things which have a different value must also differ in other respects. Hence the assumption that one and the same thing, because it is a part of a more valuable whole at one time than at another, therefore has more intrinsic value at one time than at another, has encouraged the self-contradictory belief that one and the same thing may be two different things, and that only in one of its forms is it truly what it is.

For these reasons, I shall, where it seems convenient, take the liberty to use the term 'organic' with a special sense. I shall use it to denote the fact that a whole has an intrinsic value different in amount from the sum of the values of its parts. I shall use it to denote this and only this. The term will not imply any causal relation whatever between the parts of the whole in question. And it will not imply either, that the parts are inconceivable except as parts of that whole, or that, when they form parts of such a whole, they have a value different from that which they would have if they did not. Understood in this special and perfectly definite sense the relation of an organic whole to its parts is one of the most important which Ethics has to recognise. A chief part of that science should be occupied in comparing the relative values of various goods; and the grossest errors will be committed in such comparison if it be assumed that wherever two things form a whole, the value of that whole is merely the sum of the values of those two things. With this question of 'organic wholes,' then, we complete the enumeration of the kind of problems, with which it is the business of Ethics to deal.

23. In this chapter I have endeavoured to enforce the following conclusions. (1) The peculiarity of Ethics is not that it investigates assertions about human conduct, but that it investigates assertions about the property of things which is denoted by the term 'good,' and the converse property denoted by the term 'bad.' It must, in order to establish its conclusions, investigate the truth of *all* such assertions, *except* those which assert the relation of this property only to a single existent (1–4). (2) This property, by reference to which the subject-matter of Ethics must be defined, is itself simple and indefinable (5–14). And (3) all assertions about its relation to other things are of two, and only two, kinds: they either assert in what degree things themselves possess this property, or else they assert causal relations between other things and those which possess it (15–17). Finally, (4) in considering the different degrees in which things themselves possess this property, we have to take account of the fact that a whole may possess it in a degree different from that which is obtained by summing the degrees in which its parts possess it (18–22).

Moore, G. E. "A Defence of Common Sense".
Reprinted from Moore, G. E. (1925), "A Defence of Common Sense", in J. H. Muirhead (ed.), *Contemporary British Philosophy*, London: Allen and Unwin.

In what follows I have merely tried to state, one by one, some of the most important points in which my philosophical position differs from positions which have been taken up by *some* other philosophers. It may be that the points which I have had room to mention are not really the most important, and possibly some of them may be points as to which no philosopher has ever really differed from me. But, to the best of my belief, each is a point as to which many have really differed; although (in most cases, at all events) each is also a point as to which many have agreed with me.

I. The first point is a point which embraces a great many other points. And it is one which I cannot state as clearly as I wish to state it, except at some length.

108   Early Analytic Philosophy

The method I am going to use for stating it is this. I am going to begin by enunciating, under the heading (1), a whole long list of propositions, which may seem, at first sight, such obvious truisms as not to be worth stating: they are, in fact, a set of propositions, every one of which (in my own opinion) I *know*, with certainty, to be true. I shall, next, under the heading (2), state a single proposition which makes an assertion about a whole set of *classes* of propositions – each class being defined, as the class consisting of all propositions which resemble *one* of the propositions in (1) in a certain respect. (2), therefore, is a proposition which could not be stated, until the list of propositions in (1), or some similar list, had already been given. (2) is itself a proposition which may seem such an obvious truism as not to be worth stating: and it is also a proposition which (in my own opinion) I *know*, with certainty, to be true. But, nevertheless, it is, to the best of my belief, a proposition with regard to which many philosophers have, for different reasons, differed from me; even if they have not directly denied (2) itself, they have held views incompatible with it. My first point, then, may be said to be that (2), together with all its implications, some of which I shall expressly mention, is true.

(1) I begin, then, with my list of truisms, every one of which (in my own opinion) I *know*, with certainty, to be true. The propositions to be included in this list are the following:

There exists at present a living human body, which is *my* body. This body was born at a certain time in the past, and has existed continuously ever since, though not without undergoing changes; it was, for instance, much smaller when it was born, and for some time afterwards, than it is now. Ever since it was born, it has been either in contact with or not far from the surface of the earth; and, at every moment since it was born, there have also existed many other things, having shape and size in three dimensions (in the same familiar sense in which it has), from which it has been *at various distances* (in the familiar sense in which it is now at a distance both from that mantelpiece and from that bookcase, and at a greater distance from the bookcase than it is from the mantelpiece); also there have (very often, at all events) existed some other things of this kind with which it was in *contact* (in the familiar sense in which it is now in contact with the pen I am holding in my right hand and with some of the clothes I am wearing). Among the things which have, in this sense, formed part of its environment (i.e. have been either in contact with it, or at *some* distance from it, however *great*) there have, at every moment since its birth, been large numbers of other living human bodies, each of which has, like it, (*a*) at some time been born, (*b*) continued to exist from some time after birth, (*c*) been, at every moment of its life after birth,

G. E. Moore on Idealism, Goodness, and Common Sense   109

either in contact with or not far from the surface of the earth; and many of these bodies have already died and ceased to exist. But the earth had existed also for many years before my body was born; and for many of these years, also, large numbers of human bodies had, at every moment, been alive upon it; and many of these bodies had died and ceased to exist before it was born. Finally (to come to a different class of propositions), I am a human being, and I have, at different times since my body was born, had many different experiences, of each of many different kinds: e.g. I have often perceived both my own body and other things which formed part of its environment, including other human bodies; I have not only perceived things of this kind, but have also observed facts about them, such as, for instance, the fact which I am now observing, that that mantelpiece is at present nearer to my body than that bookcase; I have been aware of other facts, which I was not at the time observing, such as, for instance, the fact, of which I am now aware, that my body existed yesterday and was then also for some time nearer to that mantelpiece than to that bookcase; I have had expectations with regard to the future, and many beliefs of other kinds, both true and false; I have thought of imaginary things and persons and incidents, in the reality of which I did not believe; I have had dreams; and I have had feelings of many different kinds. And, just as my body has been the body of a human being, namely myself, who has, during his lifetime, had many experiences of each of these (and other) different kinds; so, in the case of very many of the other human bodies which have lived upon the earth, each has been the body of a different human being, who has, during the lifetime of that body, had many different experiences of each of these (and other) different kinds.

(2) I now come to the single truism which, as will be seen, could not be stated except by reference to the whole list of truisms, just given in (1). This truism also (in my own opinion) I *know*, with certainty to be true; and it is as follows:

In the case of *very many* (I do not say *all*) of the human beings belonging to the class (which includes myself) defined in the following way, i.e. as human beings who have had human bodies, that were born and lived for some time upon the earth, and who have, during the lifetime of those bodies, had many different experiences of each of the kinds mentioned in (1), it is true that each has frequently, during the life of his body, known, with regard to *himself* or *his* body, and with regard to some time earlier than any of the times at which I wrote down the propositions in (1), a proposition *corresponding* to each of the propositions in (1), in the sense that it asserts with regard to *himself* or *his* body and the earlier time in question (namely, in each case, the time at which he knew it), just what the corresponding proposition in (1) asserts with regard to *me* or *my* body and the time at which I wrote that proposition down.

110   Early Analytic Philosophy

In other words what (2) asserts is only (what seems an obvious enough truism) that each of *us* (meaning by 'us', very many human beings of the class defined) has frequently *known*, with regard to *himself* or *his* body and the time at which he knew it, everything which, in writing down my list of propositions in (1), I was claiming to know about myself or *my* body and the time at which I wrote that proposition down, i.e. just as *I* knew (when I wrote it down) 'There exists at present a living human body which is my body', so each of us has frequently known with regard to himself and some other time the different but corresponding proposition, which *he* could *then* have properly expressed by, 'There exists *at present* a human body which is *my* body'; just as *I* know 'Many human bodies other than mine have before now lived on the earth', so each of us has frequently known the different but corresponding proposition 'Many human bodies other than *mine* have before *now* lived on the earth'; just as *I* know 'Many human beings other than myself have before now perceived, and dreamed, and felt', so each of us has frequently known the different but corresponding proposition 'Many human beings other than *myself* have before *now* perceived, and dreamed, and felt'; and so on, in the case of *each* of the propositions enumerated in (1).

I hope there is no difficulty in understanding, so far, what this proposition (2) asserts. I have tried to make clear by examples what I mean by 'propositions *corresponding* to each of the propositions in (1)'. And what (2) asserts is merely that each of us has frequently known to be true a proposition *corresponding* (in that sense) to each of the propositions in (1) – a *different* corresponding proposition, of course, at each of the times at which he knew such a proposition to be true.

But there remain two points, which, in view of the way in which some philosophers have used the English language, ought, I think, to be expressly mentioned, if I am to make quite clear exactly how much I am asserting in asserting (2).

The first point is this. Some philosophers seem to have thought it legitimate to use the word 'true' in such a sense that a proposition which is partially false may nevertheless also be true; and some of these, therefore, would perhaps *say* that propositions like those enumerated in (1) are, in their view, true, when all the time they believe that every such proposition is partially false. I wish, therefore, to make it quite plain that I am not using 'true' in any such sense. I am using it in such a sense (and I think this is the ordinary usage) that if a proposition is partially false, it follows that it is *not* true, though, of course, it may be *partially* true. I am maintaining, in short, that all the propositions in (1), and also many propositions corresponding to each of these, are *wholly* true; I am asserting this

G. E. Moore on Idealism, Goodness, and Common Sense 111

in asserting (2). And hence any philosopher, who does in fact believe, with regard to any or all of these classes of propositions, that every proposition of the class in question is partially false, is, in fact, disagreeing with me and holding a view incompatible with (2), even though he may think himself justified in *saying* that he believes some propositions belonging to all of these classes to be 'true'.

And the second point is this. Some philosophers seem to have thought it legitimate to use such expressions as, e.g., 'The earth has existed for many years past', as if they expressed something which they really believed, when in fact they believe that every proposition, which such an expression would *ordinarily* be understood to express, is, at least partially, false; and all they really believe is that there is some *other* set of propositions, related in a certain way to those which such expressions do actually express, which, unlike these, really are true. That is to say, they use the expression 'The earth has existed for many years past' to express, not what it would ordinarily be understood to express, but the proposition that some proposition, related to this in a certain way, is true; when all the time they believe that the proposition, which this expression would ordinarily be understood to express, is, at least partially, false. I wish, therefore, to make it quite plain that I was not using the expressions I used in (1) in any such subtle sense. I meant by each of them precisely what every reader, in reading them, will have understood me to mean. And any philosopher, therefore, who holds that any of these expressions, if understood in this popular manner, expresses a proposition which embodies some popular error, is disagreeing with me and holding a view incompatible with (2), even though he may hold that there is some *other*, true, proposition which the expression in question might be legitimately used to express.

In what I have just said, I have assumed that there is some meaning which is *the* ordinary or popular meaning of such expressions as 'The earth has existed for many years past'. And this, I am afraid, is an assumption which some philosophers are capable of disputing. They seem to think that the question 'Do you believe that the earth has existed for many years past?' is not a plain question, such as should be met either by a plain 'Yes' or 'No', or by a plain 'I can't make up my mind', but is the sort of question which can be properly met by: 'It all depends on what you mean by "the earth" and "exists" and "years": if you mean so and so, and so and so, and so and so, then I do; but if you mean so and so, and so and so, and so and so, or so and so, and so and so, and so and so, or so and so, and so and so, and so and so, then I don't, or at least I think it is extremely doubtful'. It seems to me that such a view is as profoundly mistaken as any view can be. Such an expression as 'The earth has existed for many years past' is the very type of an unambiguous expression, the meaning of which we

Early Analytic Philosophy

all understand. Anyone who takes a contrary view must, I suppose, be confusing the question whether we understand its meaning (which we all certainly do) with the entirely different question whether we *know what it means*, in the sense that we are able to give *a correct analysis* of its meaning. The question what is the correct analysis of *the* proposition meant *on any occasion* (for, of course, as I insisted in defining (2), a different proposition is meant at every different time at which the expression is used) by 'The earth has existed for many years past' is, it seems to me, a profoundly difficult question, and one to which, as I shall presently urge, no one knows the answer. But to hold that we do not know what, in certain respects, is the analysis of what we understand by such an expression, is an entirely different thing from holding that we do not understand the expression. It is obvious that we cannot even raise the question how what we do understand by it is to be analysed, unless we do understand it. So soon, therefore, as we know that a person who uses such an expression is using it in its ordinary sense, we understand his meaning. So that in explaining that I was using the expressions used in (1) in their ordinary sense (those of them which have an ordinary sense, which is not the case with quite all of them), I have done all that is required to make my meaning clear.

But now, assuming that the expressions which I have used to express (2) are understood, I think, as I have said, that many philosophers have really held views incompatible with (2). And the philosophers who have done so may, I think, be divided into two main groups. A. What (2) asserts is, with regard to a whole set of *classes* of propositions, that we have, each of us, frequently *known* to be true propositions belonging to *each* of these classes. And one way of holding a view incompatible with this proposition is, of course, to hold, with regard to one or more of the classes in question, that no propositions of that class *are* true – that all of them are, at least partially, false; since if, in the case of any one of these classes, *no* propositions of that class *are* true, it is obvious that nobody can have *known* any propositions of that class to be true, and therefore that *we* cannot have known to be true propositions belonging to *each* of these classes. And my first group of philosophers consists of philosophers who have held views incompatible with (2) for this reason. They have held, with regard to one or more of the classes in question, simply that no propositions of that class *are* true. Some of them have held this with regard to *all* the classes in question; some only with regard to *some* of them. But, of course, whichever of these two views they have held, they have been holding a view inconsistent with (2). B. Some philosophers, on the other hand, have not ventured to assert, with regard to any of the classes in (2), that no propositions of that class are true, but what they have asserted is that, in the case of some of these classes,

G. E. Moore on Idealism, Goodness, and Common Sense 113

no human being has ever *known*, with certainty, that any propositions of the class in question are true. That is to say, they differ profoundly from philosophers of group A, in that they hold that propositions of *all* these classes *may* be true; but nevertheless they hold a view incompatible with (2) since they hold, with regard to some of these classes, that none of us has ever *known* a proposition of the class in question to be true.

A. I said that some philosophers, belonging to this group, have held that no propositions belonging to *any* of the classes in (2) are wholly true, while others have only held this with regard to *some* of the classes in (2). And I think the chief division of this kind has been the following. Some of the propositions in (1) (and, therefore, of course, all propositions belonging to the corresponding classes in (2)) are propositions which cannot be true, unless some *material things* have existed and have stood *in spatial relations* to one another: that is to say, they are propositions which, *in a certain sense*, imply *the reality of material things*, and *the reality of Space*. E.g. the proposition that my body has existed for many years past, and has, at every moment during that time been either in contact with or not far from the earth, is a proposition which implies both the *reality of material things* (provided you use 'material things' in such a sense that to deny the reality of material things implies that no proposition which asserts that human bodies have existed, or that the earth has existed, is wholly true) and also the *reality of Space* (provided, again, that you use 'Space' in such a sense that to deny the reality of Space implies that no proposition which asserts that anything has ever been in contact with or at a distance from another, in the familiar senses pointed out in (1), is wholly true). But others among the propositions in (1) (and, therefore, propositions belonging to the corresponding classes in (2)), do not (at least obviously) imply either the reality of material things or the reality of Space: e.g. the propositions that I have often had dreams, and have had many different feelings at different times. It is true that propositions of this second class do imply one thing which is also implied by all propositions of the first, namely that (*in a certain sense*) *Time is real*, and imply also one thing not implied by propositions of the first class, namely that (*in a certain sense*) *at least one Self is real*. But I think there are some philosophers, who, while denying that (in the senses in question) either material things or Space are real, have been willing to admit that Selves and Time are real, in the sense required. Other philosophers, on the other hand, have used the expression 'Time is not real', to express some view that they held; and some, at least, of these have, I think, meant by this expression something which is incompatible with the truth of *any* of the propositions in (1) – they have meant, namely, that *every* proposition of the sort that is expressed by the use of 'now' or 'at present', e.g., 'I am now

114   Early Analytic Philosophy

both seeing and hearing' or 'There exists at present a living human body', or by the use of a past tense, e.g. 'I *have* had many experiences in the past', or 'The earth *has* existed for many years', are, at least partially, false.

All the four expressions I have just introduced, namely, 'Material things are not real', 'Space is not real', 'Time is not real', 'The Self is not real', are, I think, unlike the expressions I used in (1), really ambiguous. And it may be that, in the case of each of them, some philosopher has used the expression in question to express some view he held which was not incompatible with (2). With such philosophers, if there are any, I am not, of course, at present concerned. But it seems to me that the most natural and proper usage of each of these expressions is a usage in which it *does* express a view incompatible with (2); and, in the case of each of them, some philosophers have, I think, really used the expression in question to express such a view. All such philosophers have, therefore, been holding a view incompatible with (2).

All such views, whether incompatible with *all* of the propositions in (1), or only with *some* of them, seems to me to be quite certainly false; and I think the following points are specially deserving of notice with regard to them:

(*a*) If *any* of the classes of propositions in (2) is such that no proposition of that class is true, then no philosopher has ever existed, and therefore none can ever have held with regard to any such class, that no proposition belonging to it is true. In other words, the proposition that some propositions belonging to each of these classes are true is a proposition which has the peculiarity, that, if any philosopher has ever denied it, it follows from the fact that he has denied it, that he must have been wrong in denying it. For when I speak of 'philosophers' I mean, of course (as we all do), exclusively philosophers who have been human beings, with human bodies that have lived upon the earth, and who have at different times had many different experiences. If, therefore, there have been any philosophers, there have been human beings of this class; and if there have been human beings of this class, all the rest of what is asserted in (1) is certainly true too. Any view, therefore, incompatible with the proposition that many propositions corresponding to each of the propositions in (1) are true, can only be true, on the hypothesis that no philosopher has ever held any such view. It follows, therefore, that, in considering whether this proposition is true, I cannot consistently regard the fact that many philosophers, whom I respect, have, to the best of my belief, held views incompatible with it, as having any weight at all against it. Since, if I know that they have held such views, I am, *ipso facto*, knowing that they were mistaken; and, if I have no reason to believe that the proposition in question is true, I have still less reason to believe that they have held views incompatible with it; since I am more certain that they have existed

G. E. Moore on Idealism, Goodness, and Common Sense 115

and held *some* views, i.e. that the proposition in question is true, than that they have held any views incompatible with it.

(*b*) It is, of course, the case that all philosophers who have held such views have repeatedly, even in their philosophical works, expressed other views inconsistent with them: i.e., no philosopher has ever been able to hold such views consistently. One way in which they have betrayed this inconsistency, is by alluding to the existence of other philosophers. Another way is by alluding to the existence of the human race, and in particular by using 'we' in the sense in which I have already constantly used it, in which any philosopher who asserts that 'we' do so and so, e.g., that '*we* sometimes believe propositions that are not true', is asserting not only that he himself has done the thing in question, but that *very many other human beings, who have had bodies and lived upon the earth*, have done the same. The fact is, of course, that all philosophers have belonged to the class of human beings which exists only if (2) be true: that is to say, to the class of human beings who have frequently *known* propositions corresponding to each of the propositions in (1). In holding views incompatible with the proposition that propositions of all these classes are true, they have, therefore, been holding views inconsistent with propositions which they themselves knew to be true; and it was, therefore, only to be expected that they should sometimes betray their knowledge of such propositions. The strange thing is that philosophers should have been able to hold sincerely, as part of their philosophical creed, propositions inconsistent with what they themselves *knew* to be true; and yet, so far as I can make out, this has really frequency happened. My position, therefore, on this first point, differs from that of philosophers belonging to this group A, not in that I hold anything which they don't hold, but only in that I don't hold, as part of my philosophical creed, things which they do! hold as part of theirs – that is to say, propositions inconsistent with some which they and I both hold in common. But this difference seems to me to be an important one.

(*c*) Some of these philosophers have brought forward, in favour of their position, arguments designed to show, in the case of some or all of the propositions in (1), that no propositions of that type can possibly be wholly true, because every such proposition entails both of two incompatible propositions. And I admit, of course, that if any of the propositions in (1) did entail both of two incompatible propositions it could not be true. But it seems to me I have an absolutely conclusive argument to show that none of them does entail both of two incompatible propositions. Namely this: All of the propositions in (1) are true; no true proposition entails both of two incompatible propositions; therefore, none of the propositions in (1) entails both of two incompatible propositions.

116   Early Analytic Philosophy

(*d*) Although, as I have urged, no philosopher who has held with regard to any of these types of propositions that no propositions of that type are true, has failed to hold also other views inconsistent with his view in this respect, yet I do not think that the view, with regard to any or all of these types, that no proposition belonging to them is true, is *in itself* a self-contradictory view, i.e. entails both of two incompatible propositions. On the contrary, it seems to me quite clear that it *might* have been the case that Time was not real, material things not real, Space not real, selves not real. And in favour of my view that none of these things, which might have been the case, *is* in fact the case, I have, I think, no better argument than simply this – namely, that all the propositions in (1) are, in fact, true.

B. This view, which is usually considered a much more modest view than A, has, I think, the defect that, unlike A, it really is self-contradictory, i.e. entails both of two mutually incompatible propositions.

Most philosophers who have held this view, have held, I think, that though each of us knows propositions corresponding to *some* of the propositions in (1), namely to those which merely assert that *I* myself have had in the past experiences of certain kinds at many different times, yet none of us knows *for certain* any propositions either of the type (a) which assert the existence of *material things* or of the type (b) which assert the existence of *other* selves, beside myself, and that they also have had experiences. They admit that we do in fact *believe* propositions of both these types, and that they *may* be true: some would even say that we know them to be highly probable; but they deny that we ever know them, *for certain*, to be true. Some of them have spoken of such beliefs as 'beliefs of Common Sense', expressing thereby their conviction that beliefs of this kind are very commonly entertained by mankind: but they are convinced that these things are, in all cases, only *believed*, not known for certain; and some have expressed this by saying that they are matters of Faith, not of Knowledge.

Now the remarkable thing which those who take this view have not, I think, in general duly appreciated, is that, in each case, the philosopher who takes it is making an assertion about 'us' – that is to say, not merely about himself, but about *many other human beings as well*. When he says 'No human being has ever known of the existence of other human beings', he is saying: 'There have been many other human beings beside myself, and none of them (including myself) has ever known of the existence of other human beings'. If he says: "These beliefs are beliefs of Common Sense, but they are not matters of *knowledge*," he is saying: 'There have been many other human beings, beside myself, who have shared these beliefs, but neither I nor any of the rest has ever known them to be true'. In other words, he asserts with confidence that these beliefs *are* beliefs of Common Sense, and seems often to fail to notice that, *if* they are, they must be true; since the proposition that they are beliefs of Common Sense is one which logically entails propositions both of type (*a*) and of type (*b*); it logically entails the proposition that many human beings, beside the philosopher himself, have had human bodies, which lived upon the earth, and have had various experiences, including beliefs of this kind. This is why this position, as contrasted with positions of group A, seems to me to be self-contradictory. Its difference from A consists in the fact that it is making a proposition about *human knowledge* in general, and therefore is actually asserting the existence of many human beings, whereas philosophers of group A in stating their position are not doing this: they are only contradicting *other* things which they hold. It is true that a philosopher who says 'There have existed many human beings beside myself, and none of us has ever known of the existence of any human beings beside himself', is only contradicting himself if what he holds is 'There have *certainly* existed many human beings beside myself' or, in other words, '*I* know that there have existed other human beings beside myself'. But this, it seems to me, is what such philosophers have in fact been generally doing. They seem to me constantly to betray the fact that they regard the proposition that those beliefs are beliefs of Common Sense, or the proposition that they themselves are not the only members of the human race, as not merely true, but *certainly* true; and *certainly* true it cannot be, unless one member, at least, of the human race, namely themselves, has *known* the very things which that member is declaring that no human being has ever known.

Nevertheless, my position that I *know*, with certainty, to be true all of the propositions in (1), is certainly not a position, the denial of which entails both of two incompatible propositions. If I do *know* all these propositions to be true, then, I think, it is quite certain that other human beings also have known corresponding propositions: that is to say (2) also *is* true, and *I* know it to be true. But do I really *know* all the propositions in (1) to be true? Isn't it possible that I merely believe them? Or know them to be highly probable? In answer to this question, I think I have nothing better to say than that it seems to me that I *do* know them, with certainty. It is, indeed, obvious that, in the case of most of them, I do not know them *directly*: that is to say, I only know them because, in the past, I have known to be true *other* propositions which were evidence for them. If, for instance, I do know that the earth had existed for many years before I was born, I certainly only know this because I have known other things in the past which were evidence for it. And I certainly do not know exactly what the evidence was. Yet all this seems to me to be no good reason for doubting that I

118   Early Analytic Philosophy

do know it. We are all, I think, in this strange position that we do *know* many things, with regard to which we *know* further that we must have had evidence for them, and yet we do not know *how* we know them, i.e., we do not know what the evidence was. If there is any 'we', and if we know that there is, this must be so: for that there is a 'we' is one of the things in question. And that I do know that there is a 'we', that is to say, that many other human beings, with human bodies, have lived upon the earth, it seems to me that I do know, for certain.

If this first point in my philosophical position, namely my belief in (2), is to be given any name, which has actually been used by philosophers in classifying the positions of other philosophers, it would have, I think, to be expressed by saying that I am one of those philosophers who have held that the 'Common Sense view of the world' is, in certain fundamental features, *wholly* true. But it must be remembered that, according to me, *all* philosophers, without exception, have agreed with me in holding this: and that the real difference, which is commonly expressed in this way, is only a difference between those philosophers, who have *also* held views inconsistent with these features in 'the Common Sense view of the world', and those who have not.

The features in question (namely, propositions of any of the classes defined in defining (2)) are all of them features, which have this peculiar property – namely, that *if we know that they are features in the 'Common Sense view of the world', it follows that they are true*: it is self-contradictory to maintain that we know them to be features in the Common Sense view, and that yet they are not true; since to say that we know this, is to say that they are true. And many of them also have the further peculiar property that, *if they are features in the Common Sense view of the world (whether 'we' know this or not), it follows that they are true*, since to say that there is a "Common Sense view of the world," is to say that they are true. The phrases 'Common Sense view of the world' or 'Common Sense beliefs' (as used by philosophers) are, of course, extraordinarily vague; and, for all I know, there may be many propositions which may be properly called features in 'the Common Sense view of the world' or 'Common Sense beliefs', which are not true, and which deserve to be mentioned with the contempt with which some philosophers speak of 'Common Sense beliefs'. But to speak with contempt of those 'Common Sense beliefs' which I have mentioned is quite certainly the height of absurdity. And there are, of course, enormous numbers of other features in 'the Common Sense view of the world' which, if these are true, are quite certainly true too: e.g., that there have lived upon the surface of the earth not only human beings, but also many different species of plants and animals, etc., etc.

G. E. Moore on Idealism, Goodness, and Common Sense

II. What seems to me the next in importance of the points in which my philosophical position differs from positions held by *some* other philosophers, is one which I will express in the following way. I hold, namely, that there is no good reason to suppose either (A) that *every* physical fact is *logically* dependent upon some mental fact or (B) that *every* physical fact is *causally* dependent upon some mental fact. In saying this, I am not, of course, saying that there *are* any physical facts which are wholly independent (i.e., both logically and causally) of mental facts: I do, in fact, believe that there are; but that is not what I am asserting. I am only asserting that there is *no good reason* to suppose the contrary; by which I mean, of course, that none of the human beings, who have had human bodies that lived upon the earth, have, during the lifetime of their bodies, had any good reason to suppose the contrary. Many philosophers have, I think, not only believed either that *every* physical fact is *logically* dependent upon some mental fact ('physical fact' and 'mental fact' being understood in the sense in which I am using these terms) or that *every* physical fact is *causally* dependent upon some mental fact, or both, but also that they themselves had good reason for these beliefs. In this respect, therefore, I differ from them.

In the case of the term 'physical fact', I can only explain how I am using it by giving examples. I mean by 'physical facts', facts *like* the following: 'That mantelpiece is at present nearer to this body than that bookcase is', 'The earth has existed for many years past', 'The moon has at every moment for many years past been nearer to the earth than to the sun', 'That mantelpiece is of a light colour'. But, when I say 'facts *like* these', I mean, of course, facts like them *in a certain respect*; and what this respect is I cannot define. The term 'physical fact' is, however, in common use; and I think that I am using it in its ordinary sense. Moreover, there is no need for a definition to make my point clear; since among the examples I have given there are some with regard to which I hold that there is no reason to suppose *them* (i.e., these particular physical facts) either logically or causally dependent upon any mental fact.

'Mental fact', on the other hand, is a much more unusual expression, and I am using it in a specially limited sense, which, though I think it is a natural one, does need to be explained. There may be many other senses in which the term can be properly used, but I am only concerned with this one; and hence it is essential that I should explain what it is.

There may, possibly, I hold, be 'mental facts' of three different kinds. It is only with regard to the first kind that am sure that there are facts of that kind; but if there we any facts of either of the other two kinds, they would 'mental facts' in my limited sense, and therefore I must plain what is meant by the hypothesis that there are facts those two kinds.

Early Analytic Philosophy

(*a*) My first kind is this. I am conscious now; and also 11 seeing something now. These two facts are both of the mental facts of my first kind; and my first kind consists exclusively of facts which resemble one or other of the two *in a certain respect.*

(α) The fact that I am conscious now is obviously, in certain sense, a fact, with regard to a particular individual and a particular time, to the effect that that individual is conscious at that time. And every fact which resembles this in that respect is to be included in my first kind of men fact. Thus the fact that I was also conscious at many different times yesterday is not itself a fact of this kind: but it tails that there *are* (or, as we should commonly say, because the times in question are past times, 'were') many other facts of this kind, namely each of the facts, which, at each of times in question, I could have properly expressed by 'I conscious *now*'. *Any* fact which is, in this sense, a fact regard to an individual and a time (whether the individual be myself or another, and whether the time be past or pr ent), to the effect that that individual is conscious at that time, is to be included in my first kind of mental fact: and I call such facts, facts of class (α).

(β) The second example I gave, namely the fact that I am seeing something now, is obviously related to the fact that I am conscious now in a peculiar manner. It not only *entails* the fact that I am conscious now (for from the fact that I am seeing something it *follows* that I am conscious: I *could* not have been seeing anything, unless I had been conscious, though I might quite well have been conscious without seeing anything) but it also is a fact, with regard to a *specific way* (or mode) of being conscious, to the effect that I am conscious in that way: in the same sense in which the proposition (with regard to any particular thing) 'This is red' both entails the proposition (with regard to the same thing) 'This is coloured', and is also a proposition, with regard to a specific way of being coloured, to the effect that that thing is coloured in that way. And any fact which is related in this peculiar manner to any fact of class (α), is also to be included in my first kind of mental fact, and is to be called a fact of class (β). Thus the fact that I am hearing now is, like the fact that I am seeing now, a fact of class (β); and so is any fact, with regard to myself and a past time, which could at that time have been properly expressed by 'I am dreaming now', 'I am imagining now', 'I am at present aware of the fact that . . .', etc., etc. In short, any fact, which is a fact with regard to a particular individual (myself or another), a particular time (past or present), and *any particular kind of experience*, to the effect that that individual is having at that time an experience of that particular kind, is a fact of class (β): and only such facts are facts of class (β).

My first kind of mental facts consists exclusively of facts of classes (α) and (β), and consists of *all* facts of either of these kinds.

G. E. Moore on Idealism, Goodness, and Common Sense 121

(b) That there are many facts of classes (α) and (β) seems to me perfectly certain. But many philosophers seem to me to have held a certain view with regard to the *analysis* of facts of class (a), which is such that, if it were true, there would be facts of another kind, which I should wish also to call 'mental facts'. I don't feel at all sure that this analysis is true; but it seems to me that it *may* be true; and since we can understand what is meant by the supposition that it is true, we can also understand what is meant by the supposition that there are 'mental facts' of this second kind.

Many philosophers have, I think, held the following view as to the analysis of what each of us knows, when he knows (at any time) 'I am conscious now'. They have held, namely, that there is a certain intrinsic property (with which we are all of us familiar and which might be called that of 'being an experience') which is such that, at any time at which any man knows 'I am conscious now', he is knowing, with regard to that property and himself and the time in question, 'There is occurring now an event which has this property (i.e., "is an experience") and which is an experience of *mine*', and such that this fact is what he expresses by 'I am conscious now'. And if this view is true, there must be many facts of each of three kinds, each of which I should wish to call 'mental facts'; *viz.* (1) facts with regard to some event, which has this supposed intrinsic property, and to some time, to the effect that that event is occurring at that time, (2) facts with regard to this supposed intrinsic property and some time, to the effect that *some* event which has that property is occurring at that time, and (3) facts with regard to some property, which is a *specific way* of having the supposed intrinsic property (in the sense above explained in which 'being red' is a specific way of 'being coloured') and some time, to the effect that some event which has that specific property is occurring at that time. Of course, there not only are not, but *cannot* be, facts of any of these kinds, unless there is an intrinsic property related to what each of us (on any occasion) expresses by 'I am conscious now', in the manner defined above; and I feel very doubtful whether there is any such property; in other words, although I know for certain both that I have had many experiences, and that I have had experiences of many different kinds, I feel very doubtful whether to say the first is the same thing as to say that there have been many events, each of which was an experience and experience of mine, and whether to say the second is the same thing as to say that there have been many events, each of which was an experience of mine, and each of which also had a different property, which was a specific way of being an experience. The proposition that I have had experiences does not necessarily entail the proposition that there have been any events which were experiences; and I cannot satisfy myself that I am acquainted with any events of the supposed kind. But yet it seems to me possible that the proposed

Early Analytic Philosophy

analysis of 'I am conscious now' is correct: that I am really acquainted with events of the supposed kind, though I cannot see that I am. And *if* I am, then I should wish to call the three kinds of facts defined above 'mental facts'. Of course, if there are 'experiences' in the sense defined, it would be possible (as many have held) that there can be no experiences which are not some individual's experiences; and in that case any fact of any of these three kinds would be logically dependent on, though not necessarily identical with, some fact of class (α) or class (β). But it seems to me also a possibility that, if there are 'experiences', there might be experiences which did not belong to any individual; and, in that case, there would be 'mental facts' which were neither identical with nor logically dependent on any fact of class (α) or class (β).

(*c*) Finally some philosophers have, so far as I can make out, held that there are or may be facts which are facts with regard to some individual, to the effect that he is conscious, or is conscious in some specific way, but which differ from facts of classes (α) and (β), in the important respect that they are not facts *with regard to any time*: they have conceived the possibility that there may be one or more individuals, who are *timelessly* conscious, and timelessly conscious in specific modes. And others, again, have, I think, conceived the hypothesis that the intrinsic property defined in (*b*) may be one which does not belong only to *events*, but may also belong to one or more wholes, which do *not* occur at any time: in other words, that there may be one or more *timeless* experiences, which might or might not be the experiences of some individual. It seems to me very doubtful whether any of these hypotheses are even possibly true; but I cannot see for certain that they are not possible: and, if they are possible, then I should wish to give the name 'mental fact' to any fact (if there were any) of any of the five following kinds, *viz.* (1) to any fact which is the fact, with regard to any individual, that he is *timelessly* conscious, (2) to any fact which is the fact, with regard to any individual, that he is *timelessly* conscious in any specific way, (3) to any fact which is the fact with regard to a *timeless* experience that it exists, (4) to any fact which is the fact with regard to the supposed intrinsic property 'being an experience', that something timelessly exists which has that property, and (5) to any fact which is the fact, with regard to any property, which is a specific mode of this supposed intrinsic property, that something timelessly exists which has that property.

I have, then, defined three different kinds of facts, each of which is such that, if there *were* any facts of that kind (as there certainly *are*, in the case of the first kind), the facts in question *would be* 'mental facts' in my sense; and to complete the definition of the limited sense in which I am using 'mental facts', I have only to add that I wish also to apply the name to one *fourth* class of facts: namely to

G. E. Moore on Idealism, Goodness, and Common Sense   123

any fact, which is the fact, with regard to any of these three kinds of facts, or any kinds included in them, *that there are facts of the kind in question*; i.e. not only will each individual fact of class (α) be, in my sense, a 'mental fact', but also the general fact 'that there are facts of class (α)', will itself be a 'mental fact'; and similarly in all other cases: e.g. not only will the fact that I am now perceiving (which is a fact of class (β)) be a 'mental fact', but also the general fact that *there are* facts, with regard to individuals and times, to the effect that the individual in question is perceiving at the time in question, will be a 'mental fact'.

A. Understanding "physical fact" and "mental fact" in the senses just explained, I hold, then, that there is no good reason to suppose that *every* physical fact is *logically* dependent upon some mental fact. And I use the phrase, with regard to two facts, F_1 and F_2, 'F_1 is *logically dependent* on F_2', wherever and only where F_1 *entails* F_2, either in the sense in which the proposition 'I am seeing now' *entails* the proposition 'I am conscious now', or the proposition (with regard to any particular thing) 'This is red' entails the proposition (with regard to the same thing) 'This is coloured', or else in the more strictly logical sense in which (for instance) the conjunctive proposition 'All men are mortal, and Mr. Baldwin is a man' entails the proposition 'Mr. Baldwin is mortal'. To say, then, of two facts, F_1 and F_2, that F_1 is *not* logically dependent upon F_2, is only to say that F_1 *might* have been a fact, even if there had been no such fact as F_2; or that the conjunctive proposition 'F_1 is a fact, but there is no such fact as F_2' is a proposition which is not self-contradictory, i.e., does not entail both of two mutually incompatible propositions.

I hold, then, that, in the case of *some* physical facts, there is no good reason to suppose that there is some mental fact, such that the physical fact in question could not have been a fact unless the mental fact in question had also been one. And my position is perfectly definite, since I hold that this is the case with all the four physical facts, which I have given as examples of physical facts. For example, there is no good reason to suppose that there is any mental fact whatever, such that the fact that that mantelpiece is at present nearer to my body than that bookcase could not have been a fact, unless the mental fact in question had also been a fact; and, similarly, in all the other three cases.

In holding this I am certainly differing from some philosophers. I am, for instance, differing from Berkeley, who held that that mantelpiece, that bookcase, and my body are, all of them, either 'ideas' or 'constituted by ideas', and that no 'idea' can possibly exist without being perceived. He held, that is, that this physical fact is logically dependent upon a mental fact of my fourth class: namely a fact which is the fact that there is at least one fact, which is a fact with regard to an individual and the present time, to the effect that that individual is now

Early Analytic Philosophy

perceiving something. He does not say that this physical fact is logically dependent upon any fact which is a fact of any of my first three classes, e.g., on any fact which is the fact, with regard to a particular individual and the present time, that *that* individual is now perceiving something: what he does say is that the physical fact couldn't have been a fact, unless it had been a fact that there was *some* mental fact of this sort. And it seems to me that many philosophers, who would perhaps disagree either with Berkeley's assumption that my body is an 'idea' or 'constituted by ideas', or with his assumption that 'ideas' cannot exist without being perceived, or with both, nevertheless would agree with him in thinking that this physical fact is logically dependent upon *some* 'mental fact': e.g., they might say that it could not have been a fact, unless there had been, at some time or other, or, were timelessly, *some* 'experience'. Many, indeed, so far as I can make out, have held that *every* fact is logically dependent on every other fact. And, of course, they have held in the case of their opinions, as Berkeley did in the case of his, that they had good reasons for them.

B. I also hold that there is no good reason to suppose that *every* physical fact is *causally* dependent upon some mental fact. By saying that F_1 is *causally* dependent on F_2, I mean only that F_1 *wouldn't* have been a fact unless F_2 had been; *not* (which is what "logically dependent" asserts) that F_1 *couldn't conceivably* have been a fact, unless F_2 had been. And I can illustrate my meaning by reference to the example which I have just given. The fact that that mantelpiece is at present nearer to my body than that bookcase, is (as I have just explained) so far as I can see, not *logically* dependent upon any mental fact; it *might* have been a fact, even if there had been no mental facts. But it certainly is *causally* dependent on many mental facts: my body *would* not have been here unless I had been conscious in various ways in the past; and the mantelpiece and the bookcase certainly *would* not have existed, unless other men had been conscious too.

But with regard to two of the facts, which I gave as instances of physical facts, namely the fact that the earth has existed for many years past, and the fact that the moon has for many years past been nearer to the earth than to the sun, I hold that there is no good reason to suppose that these are *causally* dependent upon any mental fact. So far as I can see, there is no reason to suppose that there is any mental fact of which it could be truly said: unless this fact had been a fact, the earth would not have existed for many years past. And in holding this, again, I think I differ from some philosophers. I differ, for instance, from those who have held that all material things were created by God, and that they had good reasons for supposing this.

III. I have just explained that I differ from those philosophers who have held that there is good reason to suppose that all material things were created by

G. E. Moore on Idealism, Goodness, and Common Sense   125

God. And it is, I think, an important point in my position, which should be mentioned, that I differ also from all philosophers who have held that there is good reason to suppose that there is a God at all, whether or not they have held it likely that he created all material things.

And similarly, whereas some philosophers have held that there is good reason to suppose that we, human beings, shall continue to exist and to be conscious after the death of our bodies, I hold that there is no good reason to suppose this.

IV. I now come to a point of a very different order.

As I have explained under I., I am not at all sceptical as to the *truth* of such propositions as 'The earth has existed for many years past'. 'Many human bodies have each lived for many years upon it', i.e., propositions which assert the existence of material things: on the contrary, I hold that we all know, with certainty, many such propositions to be true. But I am very sceptical as to what, in certain respects, the correct *analysis* of such propositions is. And this is a matter as to which I think I differ from many philosophers. Many seem to hold that there is no doubt at all as to their *analysis*, nor, therefore, as to the analysis of the proposition 'Material things have existed', in certain respects in which I hold that the analysis of the propositions in question is extremely doubtful; and some of them, as we have seen, while holding that there is no doubt as to their *analysis*, seem to have doubted whether any such propositions are *true*. I, on the other hand, while holding that there is no doubt whatever that many such propositions are wholly true, hold also that no philosopher, hitherto, has succeeded in suggesting an analysis of them, as regards certain important points, which comes anywhere near to being certainly true.

It seems to me quite evident that the question how propositions of the type I have just given are to be analysed, depends on the question how propositions of another and simpler type are to be analysed. I know, at present, that I am perceiving a human hand, a pen, a sheet of paper, etc.; and it seems to me that I cannot know how the proposition 'Material things exist' is to be analysed, until I know how, in certain respects, these simpler propositions are to be analysed. But even these are not simple enough. It seems to me quite evident that my knowledge that I am now perceiving a human hand is a deduction from a pair of propositions simpler still – propositions which I can only express in the form 'I am perceiving *this*' and '*This* is a human hand'. It is the analysis of propositions of the latter kind which seems to me to present such great difficulties, while nevertheless the whole question as to the *nature* of material things obviously depends upon their analysis. It seems to me a surprising thing that so few philosophers, while saying a great deal as to what material things *are* and as to

Early Analytic Philosophy

what it is to perceive them, have attempted to give a clear account as to what precisely they suppose themselves to *know* (or to *judge*, in case they have held that we don't *know* any such propositions to be true, or even that no such propositions *are* true) when they know or judge such things as 'This is a hand', 'That is the sun', 'This is a dog', etc., etc., etc.

Two things only seem to me to be quite certain about the analysis of such propositions (and even with regard to these I am afraid some philosophers would differ from me) namely that whenever I know, or judge, such a proposition to be true, (1) there is always some *sense-datum* about which the proposition in question is a proposition – some sense-datum which is *a* subject (and, in a certain sense, the principal or ultimate subject) of the proposition in question, and (2) that, nevertheless, *what* I am knowing or judging to be true about this sense-datum is not (in general) that it is *itself* a hand, or a dog, or the sun, etc. etc., as the case may be.

Some philosophers have I think doubted whether there are any such things as other philosophers have meant by 'sense-data' or 'sensa'. And I think it is quite possible that some philosophers (including myself, in the past) have used these terms in senses such that it is really doubtful whether there are any such things. But there is no doubt at all that there are sense-data, in the sense in which I am now using that term. I am at present seeing a great number of them, and feeling others. And in order to point out to the reader what sort of things I mean by sense-data, I need only ask him to look at his own right hand. If he does this he will be able to pick out something (and, unless he is seeing double, *only* one thing) with regard to which he will see that it is, at first sight, a natural view to take that that thing is identical, not, indeed, with his whole right hand, but with that part of its surface which he is actually seeing, but will also (on a little reflection) be able to see that it is doubtful whether it can be identical with the part of the surface of his hand in question. Things *of the sort* (in a certain respect) of which this thing is, which he sees in looking at his hand, and with regard to which he can understand how some philosophers should have supposed it to be the part of the surface of his hand which he is seeing, while others have supposed that it can't be, are what I mean by 'sense-data'. I therefore define the term in such a way that it is an open question whether the sense-datum which I now see in looking at my hand and which is a sense-datum of my hand is or is not identical with that part of its surface which I am now actually seeing.

That what I know, with regard to this sense-datum, when I know 'This is a human hand', is not that it is *itself* a human hand, seems to me certain because I know that my hand has many parts (e.g., its other side, and the bones inside it), which are quite certainly *not* parts of this sense-datum.

G. E. Moore on Idealism, Goodness, and Common Sense   127

I think it certain, therefore, that the analysis of the proposition 'This is a human hand' is, roughly at least, of the form 'There is a thing, and only one thing, of which it is true both that it is a human hand and that *this surface* is a part of its surface'. In other words, to put my view in terms of the phrase 'theory of representative perception', I hold it to be quite certain that I do not *directly* perceive *my hand*; and that when I am said (as I may be correctly said) to 'perceive' it, that I 'perceive' it means that I perceive (in a different and more fundamental sense) something which is (in a suitable sense) *representative* of it, namely, a certain part of its surface.

This is all that I hold to be *certain* about the analysis of the proposition 'This is a human hand'. We have seen that it includes in its analysis a proposition of the form 'This is part of the surface of a human hand' (where 'This', of course, has a different meaning from that which it has in the original proposition which has now been analysed). But this proposition also is undoubtedly a proposition about the sense-datum, which I am seeing, which is a sense-datum *of* my hand. And hence the further question arises: *What*, when I know '*This* is *part of the surface of* a human hand', am I knowing about the sense-datum in question? Am I, in this case, really knowing about the sense-datum in question that it *itself* is part of the surface of a human hand? Or, just as we found in the case of 'This is a human hand', that what I was knowing about the sense-datum was certainly not that it *itself* was a human hand, so, is it perhaps the case, with this new proposition, that even here I am not knowing, with regard to the sense-datum, that it is *itself* part of the surface of a hand? And, if so, what is it that I am knowing about the sense-datum itself?

This is the question to which, as it seems to me, no philosopher has hitherto suggested an answer which comes anywhere near to being *certainly* true.

There seem to me to be three, and only three, alternative types of answer possible; and to any answer yet suggested, of any of these types, there seem to me to be very grave objections.

(1) Of the first type, there is but one answer: namely, that in this case what I am knowing really is that the sense-datum *itself* is part of the surface of a human hand. In other words that, though I don't perceive *my hand* directly, I do *directly* perceive part of its surface; that the sense-datum itself is this part of its surface and not merely something which (in a sense yet to be determined) 'represents' this part of its surface; and that hence the sense in which I 'perceive' this part of the surface of my hand, is not in its turn a sense which needs to be defined by reference to yet a third more ultimate sense of "perceive," which is the only one in which perception is direct, namely that in which I perceive the sense-datum.

128   Early Analytic Philosophy

If this view is true (as I think it may just possibly be), it seems to me certain that we must abandon a view which has been held to be certainly true by most philosophers, namely the view that our sense-data always really have the qualities which they sensibly appear to us to have. For I know that if another man were looking through a microscope at the same surface which I am seeing with the naked eye, the sense-datum which he saw would sensibly appear to him to have qualities very different from and incompatible with those which my sense-datum sensibly appears to me to have: and yet, if my sense-datum is identical with the surface we are both of us seeing, his must be identical with it also. My sense-datum can, therefore, be identical with this surface only on condition that it is identical with his sense-datum; and, since his sense-datum sensibly appears to him to have qualities incompatible with those which mine sensibly appears to me to have, his sense-datum can be identical with mine only on condition that the sense-datum in question either has not got the qualities which it sensibly appears to me to have, or has not got those which it sensibly appears to him to have.

I do not, however, think that this is a fatal objection to this first type of view. A far more serious objection seems to me to be that, when we see a thing double (have what is called 'a double image' of it), we certainly have *two* sense-data each of which is *of* the surface seen, and which cannot therefore both be identical with it; and that yet it seems as if, if any sense-datum is ever identical with the surface of which it is a sense-datum, each of these so-called 'images' must be so. It looks, therefore, as if every sense-datum is, after all, only 'representative' of the surface, of which it is a sense-datum.

(2) But, if so, what relation has it to the surface in question?

This second type of view is one which holds that when I know 'This is part of the surface of a human hand', what I am knowing with regard to the sense-datum which is *of* that surface, is, *not* that it is *itself* part of the surface of a human hand, but something of the following kind. There is, it says, *some* relation, R, such that what I am knowing with regard to the sense-datum is either 'There is one thing and only one thing, of which it is true both that it is a part of the surface of a human hand, and that it has R to this sense-datum', or else 'There are a set of things, of which it is true both that that set, taken collectively, are part of the surface of a human hand, and also that each member of the set has R to this sense-datum, and that nothing which is not a member of the set has R to it'.

Obviously, in the case of this second type, many different views are possible, differing according to the view they take as to what the relation R is. But there is only one of them, which seems to me to have any plausibility; namely that which holds that R is an ultimate and unanalysable relation, which might be expressed by saying that "*xRy*" means the same as '*y* is an appearance or manifestation of *x*'. I.e. the analysis which this answer would give of 'This is part of the surface of a human hand' would be 'There is one and only one thing of which it is true both that it is part of the surface of a human hand, and that this sense-datum is an appearance or manifestation of it'.

To this view also there seem to me to be very grave objections, chiefly drawn from a consideration of the questions how we can possibly *know* with regard to any of our sense-data that there is one thing and one thing only which has to them such a supposed ultimate relation; and how, if we do, we can possibly know anything further about such things, e.g. of what size or shape they are.

(3) The third type of answer, which seems to me to be the only possible alternative if (1) and (2) are rejected, is the type of answer which J. S. Mill seems to have been implying to be the true one when he said that material things are 'permanent possibilities of sensation'. He seems to have thought that when I know such a fact as 'This is part of the surface of a human hand', what I am knowing with regard to the sense-datum which is the principal subject of that fact, is not that it is itself part of the surface of a human hand, nor yet, with regard to any relation, that *the* thing which has to it that relation is part of the surface of a human hand, but a whole set of hypothetical facts each of which is a fact of the form 'If *these* conditions had been fulfilled, I should have been perceiving a sense-datum intrinsically related to *this* sense-datum in *this* way', 'If *these* (other) conditions had been fulfilled, I should have been perceiving a sense-datum intrinsically related to this sense-datum in *this* (other) way', etc., etc.

With regard to this third type of view as to the analysis of propositions of the kind; we are considering, it seems to me, again, just *possible* that it is a true one; but to hold (as Mill himself and others seem to have held) that it is *certainly*, or nearly certainly, true, seems to me as great a mistake, as to hold with regard either to (1) or to (2), that they are certainly, or nearly certainly, true. There seem to me to be very grave objections to it; in particular the three, (*a*) that though, in general, when I know such a fact as 'This is a hand', I certainly do know some hypothetical facts of the form 'If *these* conditions had been fulfilled, I should have been perceiving a sense-datum of *this* kind, which would have been a sense-datum of the same surface of which *this* is a sense-datum', it seems doubtful whether any conditions with regard to which I know this are not themselves conditions of the form 'If this and that *material thing* had been in those positions and conditions . . .', (*b*) that it seems again very doubtful whether

130 Early Analytic Philosophy

there is any intrinsic relation, such that my knowledge that (under *these* conditions) I should have been perceiving a sense-datum of *this* kind, which would have been a sense-datum of the same surface of which *this* is a sense-datum, is equivalent to a knowledge, with regard to that relation, that I should, under those conditions, have been perceiving a sense-datum related by it to *this* sense-datum, and (*c*) that, if it were true, the sense in which a material surface is 'round' or 'square', would necessarily be utterly different from that in which our sense-data sensibly appear to us to be 'round' or 'square'.

V. Just as I hold that the proposition 'There are and have been material things' is quite certainly true, but that the question how this proposition is to be analysed is one to which no answer that has been hitherto given is anywhere near certainly true; so I hold that the proposition 'There are and have been many Selves' is quite certainly true, but that here again all the analyses of this proposition that have been suggested by philosophers are highly doubtful.

That I am now perceiving many different sense-data, and that I have at many times in the past perceived many different sense-data, I know for certain – that is to say, I know that there are mental facts of class (β), connected in a way which it is proper to express by saying that they are all of them facts about *me*; but how this kind of connection is to be analysed, I do not know for certain, nor do I think that any other philosopher knows with any approach to certainty. Just as in the case of the proposition 'This is part of the surface of a human hand', there are several extremely different views as to its analysis, each of which seems to me *possible*, but none nearly certain, so also in the case of the proposition 'This, that and that sense-datum are all at present being perceived by *me*', and still more so in the case of the proposition '*I* am now perceiving this sense-datum, and *I* have in the past perceived sense-data of these other kinds'. Of the *truth* of these propositions there seems to me to be no doubt, but as to what is the correct analysis of them there seems to me to be the gravest doubt – the true analysis may, for instance, *possibly* be quite as paradoxical as is the third view given under IV as to the analysis of 'This is part of the surface of a human hand'; but whether it *is* as paradoxical as this seems to me to be quite as doubtful as in that case. Many philosophers, on the other hand, seem to me to have assumed that there is little or no doubt as to the correct analysis of such propositions; and many of these, just reversing my position, have also held that the propositions themselves are not true.

G. E. Moore on Idealism, Goodness, and Common Sense 131

Moore, G. E. "Proof of an External World".
Reprinted from Moore, G. E. (1939), "Proof of an External World", *Proceedings of the British Academy* 25: 273–300.

In the Preface to the second edition of Kant's *Critique of Pure Reason* some words occur, which, in Professor Kemp Smith's translation, are rendered as follows:

> It still remains a scandal to philosophy . . . that the existence of things outside of us . . . must be accepted merely on *faith,* and that, if anyone thinks good to doubt their existence, we are unable to counter his doubts by any satisfactory proof. [B xxxix, note: Kemp Smith, p.34; footnote removed]

It seems clear from these words that Kant thought it a matter of some importance to give a proof of 'the existence of things outside of us' or perhaps rather (for it seems to me possible that the force of the German words is better rendered in this way) of 'the existence of *the* things outside of us'; for had he not thought it important that a proof should be given, he would scarcely have called it a 'scandal' that no proof had been given. And it seems clear also that he thought that the giving of such a proof was a task which fell properly within the province of philosophy; for, if it did not, the fact that no proof had been given could not possibly be a scandal to *philosophy*.

Now, even if Kant was mistaken in both of these two opinions, there seems to me to be no doubt whatever that it is a matter of some importance and also a matter which falls properly within the province of philosophy, to discuss the question what sort of proof, if any, can be given of 'the existence of things outside of us'. And to discuss this question was my object when I began to write the present lecture. But I may say at once that, as you will find, I have only, at most, succeeded in saying a very small part of what ought to be said about it.

The words 'it . . . remains a scandal to philosophy . . . that we are unable . . .' would, taken strictly, imply that, at the moment at which he wrote them, Kant himself was unable to produce a satisfactory proof of the point in question. But I think it is unquestionable that Kant himself did not think that he personally was at the time unable to produce such a proof. On the contrary, in the immediately preceding sentence, he has declared that he has, in the second edition of his *Critique,* to which he is now writing the Preface, given a 'rigorous proof' of this very thing; and has added that he believes this proof of his to be 'the only possible proof'. It is true that in this preceding sentence he does not describe the proof which he has given as a proof of 'the existence of things outside of us' or of 'the existence of the things outside of us', but describes it instead as a proof of 'the objective reality of outer intuition'. But the context leaves no doubt

Early Analytic Philosophy

that he is using these two phrases, 'the objective reality of outer intuition' and 'the existence of things (or 'the things') outside of us', in such a way that whatever is a proof of the first is also necessarily a proof of the second. We must, therefore, suppose that when he speaks as if *we* are unable to give a satisfactory proof, he does not mean to say that he himself, as well as others, is *at the moment* unable; but rather that, until he discovered the proof which he has given, both he himself and everybody else *were* unable. Of course, if he is right in thinking that he has given a satisfactory proof, the state of things which he describes came to an end as soon as his proof was published. As soon as that happened, anyone who read it was able to give a satisfactory proof by simply repeating that which Kant had given, and the 'scandal' to philosophy had been removed once, for all.

If, therefore, it were certain that the proof of the point in question given by Kant in the second edition is a satisfactory proof, it would be certain that at least one satisfactory proof can be given; and all that would remain of the question which I said I proposed to discuss would be, firstly, the question as to what *sort* of a proof this of Kant's is, and secondly the question whether (contrary to Kant's own opinion) there may not perhaps be other proofs, of the same or of a different sort, which are also satisfactory. But I think it is by no means certain that Kant's proof is satisfactory. I think it is by no means certain that he did succeed in removing once for all the state of affairs which he considered to be a scandal to philosophy. And I think, therefore, that the question whether it is possible to give *any* satisfactory proof of the point in question still deserves discussion.

But what is the point in question? I think it must be owned that the expression 'things outside of us' is rather an odd expression, and an expression the meaning of which is certainly not perfectly clear. It would have sounded less odd if, instead of 'things outside of us' I had said 'external things', and perhaps also the meaning of this expression would have seemed to be clearer; and I think we make the meaning of 'external things' clearer still if we explain that this phrase has been regularly used by philosophers as short for 'things external to *our minds*'. The fact is that there has been a long philosophical tradition, in accordance with which the three expressions 'external things', 'things external to *us*', and 'things external to *our minds*' have been used as equivalent to one another, and have, each of them, been used as if they needed no explanation. The origin of this usage I do not know. It occurs already in Descartes; and since he uses the expressions as if they needed no explanation, they had presumably been used with the same meaning before. Of the three, it seems to me that the expression 'external to *our minds*' is the clearest, since it at least makes clear that what is meant is not 'external to *our bodies*'; whereas both the other expressions might

G. E. Moore on Idealism, Goodness, and Common Sense

be taken to mean this: and indeed there has been a good deal of confusion, even among philosophers, as to the relation of the two conceptions 'external things' and 'things external to *our bodies*'. But even the expression 'things external to our minds' seems to me to be far from perfectly clear; and if I am to make really clear what I mean by 'proof of the existence of things outside of us', I cannot do it by merely saying that by 'outside of us' I mean 'external to our minds'.

There is a passage *(Kritik der reinen Vernunft,* A373) in which Kant himself says that the expression 'outside of us' 'carries with it an unavoidable ambiguity'. He says that 'sometimes it means something which exists *as a thing in itself* distinct from us, and sometimes something which merely belongs to external *appearance'*; he calls things which are 'outside of us' in the first of these two senses 'objects which might be called external in the transcendental sense', and things which are so in the second *'empirically external* objects'; and he says finally that, in order to remove all uncertainty as to the latter conception, he will distinguish empirically external objects from objects which might be called 'external' in the transcendental sense, 'by calling them outright things which are *to be met with in space'.*

I think that this last phrase of Kant's 'things which are to be met with in space', does indicate fairly clearly what sort of things it is with regard to which I wish to inquire what sort of proof, if any, can be given that there are any things of that sort. My body, the bodies of other men, the bodies of animals, plants of all sorts, stones, mountains, the sun, the moon, stars, and planets, houses and other buildings, manufactured articles of all sorts – chairs, tables, pieces of paper, etc., are all of them 'things which are to be met with in space'. In short, all things of the sort that philosophers have been used to call 'physical objects', 'material things', or 'bodies' obviously come under this head. But the phrase 'things that are to be met with in space' can be naturally understood as applying also in cases where the names 'physical object', 'material thing', or 'body' can hardly be applied. For instance, shadows are sometimes to be met with in space, although they could hardly be properly called 'physical objects', 'material things', or 'bodies'; and although in one usage of the term 'thing' it would not be proper to call a shadow a 'thing', yet the phrase 'things which are to be met with in space' can be naturally understood as synonymous with 'whatever can be met with in space', and this is an expression which can quite properly be understood to include shadows. I wish the phrase 'things which are to be met with in space' to be understood in this wide sense; so that if a proof can be found that there ever have been as many as two different shadows it will follow at once that there have been at least two 'things which were to be met with in space', and this proof will be as good a proof of the point in question as would be a proof that there have been at least two 'physical objects' of no matter what sort.

Early Analytic Philosophy

The phrase 'things which are to be met with in space' can, therefore, be naturally understood as having a very wide meaning – a meaning even wider than that of 'physical object' or 'body', wide as is the meaning of these latter expressions. But wide as is its meaning, it is not, in one respect, so wide as that of another phrase which Kant uses as if it were equivalent to this one; and a comparison between the two will, I think, serve to make still clearer what sort of things it is with regard to which I wish to ask what proof, if any, can be given that there are such things.

The other phrase which Kant uses as if it were equivalent to 'things which are to be met with in space' is used by him in the sentence immediately preceding that previously quoted in which he declares that the expression 'things outside of us' 'carries with it an unavoidable ambiguity' (A373). In this preceding sentence he says that an 'empirical object' 'is called *external,* if it is presented *(vorgestellt) in space'.* He treats, therefore, the phrase 'presented in space' as if it were equivalent to 'to be met with in space'. But it is easy to find examples of 'things', of which it can hardly be denied that they are 'presented in space', but of which it could, quite naturally, be emphatically denied that they are 'to be met with in space'. Consider, for instance, the following description of one set of circumstances under which what some psychologists have called a 'negative after-image' and others a 'negative after-sensation' can be obtained. 'If, after looking steadfastly at a white patch on a black ground, the eye be turned to a white ground, a grey patch is seen for some little time' [Foster's *Text-book of Physiology,* rv, iii, 3, p.1266; quoted in Stout's *Manual of Psychology,* 3rd edition, p.280; endnotes removed]. Upon reading these words recently, I took the trouble to cut out of a piece of white paper a four-pointed star, to place it on a black ground, to 'look steadfastly' at it, and then to turn my eyes to a white sheet of paper: and I did find that I saw a grey patch for some little time – I not only saw a grey patch, but I saw it *on* the white ground, and also this grey patch was of roughly the same shape as the white four-pointed star at which I had 'looked steadfastly' just before – it also was a four-pointed star. I repeated this simple experiment successfully several times. Now each of those grey four-pointed stars, one of which I saw in each experiment, was what is called an 'after-image' or 'after-sensation'; and can anybody deny that each of these after-images can be quite properly said to have been 'presented in space'? I saw each of them on a real white background, and, if so, each of them was 'presented' on a real white background. But though they were 'presented in space' everybody, I think, would feel that it was gravely misleading to say that they were 'to be met with in space'. The white star at which I 'looked steadfastly', the black ground on which I saw it, and the white ground on which I saw the after-images, were, of

G. E. Moore on Idealism, Goodness, and Common Sense

course, 'to be met with in space': they were, in fact, 'physical objects' or surfaces of physical objects. But one important difference between them, on the one hand, and the grey after-images, on the other, can be quite naturally expressed by saying that the latter were *not* 'to be met with in space'. And one reason why this is so is, I think, plain. To say that so and so was at a given time 'to be met with in space' naturally suggests that there are conditions such that *anyone* who fulfilled them might, conceivably, have 'perceived' the 'thing' in question – might have seen it, if it was a visible object, have felt it, if it was a tangible one, have heard it, if it was a sound, have smelt it, if it was a smell. When I say that the white four-pointed paper star, at which I looked steadfastly, was a 'physical object' and was 'to be met with in space', I am implying that *anyone,* who had been in the room at the time, and who had normal eyesight and a normal sense of touch, might have seen and felt it. But, in the case of those grey after-images which I saw, it is not conceivable that anyone besides myself should have seen any one of them. It is, of course, quite conceivable that other people, if they had been in the room with me at the time, and had carried out the same experiment which I carried out, would have seen grey after-images *very like* one of those which I saw: there is no absurdity in supposing even that they might have seen after-images *exactly* like one of those which I saw. But there is an absurdity in supposing that any one of the after-images which I saw could also have been seen by anyone else: in supposing that two different people can ever see the *very same* after-image. One reason, then, why we should say that none of those grey after-images which I saw was 'to be met with in space', although each of them was certainly 'presented in space' to me, is simply that none of them could conceivably have been seen by anyone else. It is natural so to understand the phrase 'to be met with in space', that to say of anything which a man perceived that it was to be met with in space is to say that it might have been perceived by *others* as well as by the man in question.

Negative after-images of the kind described are, therefore, one example of 'things' which, though they must be allowed to be 'presented in space', are nevertheless *not* 'to be met with in space', and are *not* 'external to our minds' in the sense with which we shall be concerned. And two other important examples may be given.

The first is this. It is well known that people sometimes see things double, an occurrence which has also been described by psychologists by saying that they have a 'double image', or two 'images', of some object at which they are looking. In such cases it would certainly be quite natural to say that each of the two 'images' is 'presented in space': they are seen, one in one place, and the other in another, in just the same sense in which each of those grey after-images

Early Analytic Philosophy

which I saw was seen at a particular place on the white background at which I was looking. But it would be utterly unnatural to say that, when I have a double image, each of the two images is 'to be met with in space'. On the contrary it is quite certain that *both* of them are not 'to be met with in space'. If both were, it would follow that somebody else might see the *very same* two images which I see; and, though there is no absurdity in supposing that another person might see a pair of images exactly similar to a pair which I see, there is an absurdity in supposing that anyone else might see the *same identical pair*. In every case, then, in which anyone sees anything double, we have an example of at least one 'thing' which, though 'presented in space' is certainly not 'to be met with in space'.

And the second important example is this. Bodily pains can, in general, be quite properly said to be 'presented in space'. When I have a toothache, I feel it *in* a particular region of my jaw or *in* a particular tooth; when I make a cut on my finger smart by putting iodine on it, I feel the pain in a particular place in my finger; and a man whose leg has been amputated may feel a pain *in* a place where his foot might have been if he had not lost it. It is certainly perfectly natural to understand the phrase 'presented in space' in such a way that if, in the sense illustrated, a pain is felt *in* a particular place, that pain is 'presented in space'. And yet of pains it would be quite unnatural to say that they are 'to be met with in space', for the same reason as in the case of after-images or double images. It is quite conceivable that another person should feel a pain exactly like one which I feel, but there is an absurdity in supposing that he could feel *numerically the same* pain which I feel. And pains are in fact a typical example of the sort of 'things' of which philosophers say that they are *not* 'external' to our minds, but 'within' them. Of any pain which *I* feel they would say that it is necessarily *not* external to my mind but *in* it.

And finally it is, I think, worth while to mention one other class of 'things', which are certainly not 'external' objects and certainly not 'to be met with in space', in the sense with which I am concerned, but which yet some philosophers would be inclined to say are 'presented in space', though they are not 'presented in space' in quite the same sense in which pains, double images, and negative after-images of the sort I described are so. If you look at an electric light and then close your eyes, it sometimes happens that you see, for some little time, against the dark background which you usually see when your eyes are shut, a bright patch similar in shape to the light at which you have just been looking. Such a bright patch, if you see one, is another example of what some psychologists have called 'after-images' and others 'after-sensations'; but, unlike the negative after-images of which I spoke before, it is seen when your eyes are

G. E. Moore on Idealism, Goodness, and Common Sense   137

shut. Of such an after-image, seen with closed eyes, some philosophers might be inclined to say that this image too was 'presented in space', although it is certainly not 'to be met with in space'. They would be inclined to say that it is 'presented in space', because it certainly is presented as at some little distance from the person who is seeing it: and how can a thing be presented as at some little distance from me, without being 'presented in space'? Yet there is an important difference between such after-images, seen with closed eyes, and after-images of the sort I previously described – a difference which might lead other philosophers to deny that these after-images, seen with closed eyes, are 'presented in space' at all. It is a difference which can be expressed by saying that when your eyes are shut, you are not seeing any part of *physical* space at all – of the space which is referred to when we talk of 'things which are to be met with in *space*'. An after-image seen with closed eyes certainly is presented in *a* space, but it may be questioned whether it is proper to say that it is presented in *space*.

It is clear, then, I think, that by no means everything which can naturally be said to be 'presented in space' can also be naturally said to be 'a thing which is to be met with in space'. Some of the 'things', which are presented in space, are very emphatically *not* to be met with in space: or, to use another phrase, which may be used to convey the same notion, they are emphatically *not* 'physical realities' at all. The conception 'presented in space' is therefore, in one respect, much wider than the conception 'to be met with in space': many 'things' fall under the first conception which do not fall under the second – many after-images, one at least of the pair of 'images' seen whenever anyone sees double, and most bodily pains, are 'presented in space', though none of them are to be met with in space. From the fact that a 'thing' is presented in space, it by no means follows that it is to be met with in space. But just as the first conception is, in one respect, wider than the second, so, in another, the second is wider than the first. For there are many 'things' to be met with in space, of which it is not true that they are presented in space. From the fact that a 'thing' is to be met with in space, it by no means follows that it is presented in space. I have taken 'to be met with in space' to imply, as I think it naturally may, that a 'thing' *might be* perceived; but from the fact that a thing *might be* perceived, it does not follow that it *is* perceived; and if it is not actually perceived, then it will not be presented in space. It is characteristic of the sorts of 'things', including shadows, which I have described as 'to be met with in space', that there is no absurdity in supposing with regard to any one of them which *is*, at a given time, perceived, both (1) that it might have existed at that very time, without being perceived; (2) that it might have existed at another time, without being perceived at that other time; and (3)

Early Analytic Philosophy

that during the whole period of its existence, it need not have been perceived at any time at all. There is, therefore, no absurdity in supposing that many things, which were at one time to be met with in space, never were 'presented' at any time at all, and that many things which *are* to be met with in space now, are not now 'presented' and also never were and never will be. To use a Kantian phrase, the conception of 'things which are to be met with in space', embraces not only objects of actual experience, but also objects of *possible* experience; and from the fact that a thing is or was an object of *possible* experience, it by no means follows that it either was or is or will be 'presented' at all.

I hope that what I have now said may have served to make clear enough what sorts of 'things' I was originally referring to as 'things outside us' or 'things external to our minds'. I said that I thought that Kant's phrase 'things that are to be met with in space' indicated fairly clearly the sorts of 'things' in question; and I have tried to make the range clearer still, by pointing out that this phrase only serves the purpose, if (a) you understand it in a sense, in which many 'things', e.g., after-images, double images, bodily pains, which might be said to be 'presented in space', are nevertheless *not* to be reckoned as 'things that are to be met with in space', and (b) you realise clearly that there is no contradiction in supposing that there have been and are 'to be met with in space' things which never have been, are not now, and never will be perceived, nor in supposing that among those of them which have at some time been perceived many existed at times at which they were not being perceived. I think it will now be clear to everyone that, since I do not reckon as 'external things' after-images, double images, and bodily pains, I also should not reckon as 'external things', any of the 'images' which we often 'see with the mind's eye' when we are awake, nor any of those which we see when we are asleep and dreaming; and also that I was so using the expression 'external' that from the fact that a man was at a given time having a visual hallucination, it will follow that he was seeing at that time something which was *not* 'external' to his mind, and from the fact that he was at a given time having an auditory hallucination, it will follow that he was at the time hearing a sound which was *not* 'external' to his mind. But I certainly have not made my use of these phrases, 'external to our minds' and 'to be met with in space', so clear that in the case of every kind of 'thing' which might be suggested, you would be able to tell at once whether I should or should not reckon it as 'external to our minds' and 'to be met with in space'. For instance, I have said nothing which makes it quite clear whether a reflection which I see in a looking-glass is or is not to be regarded as 'a thing that is to be met with in space' and 'external to our minds', nor have I said anything which makes it quite clear whether the sky is or is not to be so regarded. In the case of the sky,

G. E. Moore on Idealism, Goodness, and Common Sense

everyone, I think, would feel that it was quite inappropriate to talk of it as 'a thing that is to be met with in space'; and most people, I think, would feel a strong reluctance to affirm, without qualification, that reflections which people see in looking-glasses are 'to be met with in space'. And yet neither the sky nor reflections seen in mirrors are in the same position as bodily pains or after-images in the respect which I have emphasised as a reason for saying of these latter that they are *not* to be met with in space – namely that there is an absurdity in supposing that *the very same* pain which I feel could be felt by someone else or that *the very same* after-image which I see could be seen by someone else. In the case of reflections in mirrors we should quite naturally, in certain circumstances, use language which implies that another person may see the same reflection which we see. We might quite naturally say to a friend: 'Do you see that reddish reflection in the water there? I can't make out what it's a reflection of', just as we might say, pointing to a distant hill-side: 'Do you see that white speck on the hill over there? I can't make out what it is'. And in the case of the sky, it is quite obviously *not* absurd to say that other people see it as well as I.

It must, therefore, be admitted that I have not made my use of the phrase 'things to be met with in space', nor therefore that of 'external to our minds', which the former was used to explain, so clear that in the case of every kind of 'thing' which may be mentioned, there will be no doubt whatever as to whether things of that kind are or are not 'to be met with in space' or 'external to our minds'. But this lack of a dear-cut definition of the expression 'things that are to be met with in space', does not, so far as I can see, matter for my present purpose. For my present purpose it is, I think, sufficient if I make clear, in the case of many kinds of things, that I am so using the phrase 'things that are to be met with in space', that, in the case of each of these kinds, from the proposition that there are things of that kind it *follows* that there are things to be met with in space. And I have, in fact, given a list (though by no means an exhaustive one) of kinds of things which are related to my use of the expression 'things that are to be met with in space' in this way. I mentioned among others the bodies of men and of animals, plants, stars, houses, chairs, and shadows; and I want now to emphasise that I am so using 'things to be met with in space' that, in the case of each of these kinds of 'things', from the proposition that there are 'things' of that kind it *follows* that there are things to be met with in space: e.g., from the proposition that there are plants or that plants exist it *follows* that there are things to be met with in space, from the proposition that shadows exist, *it follows* that there are things to be met with in space, and so on, in the case of all the kinds of 'things' which I mentioned in my first list. That

Early Analytic Philosophy

this should be clear is sufficient for my purpose, because, if it is clear, then it will also be clear that, as I implied before, if you have proved that two plants exist, or that a plant and a dog exist, or that a dog and a shadow exist, etc., etc., you will *ipso facto* have proved that there are things to be met with in space: you will not require *also* to give a separate proof that from the proposition that there are plants it *does* follow that there are things to be met with in space.

Now with regard to the expression 'things that are to be met with in space' I think it will readily be believed that I may be using it in a sense such that no proof is required that from 'plants exist' there follows 'there are things to be met with in space'; but with regard to the phrase 'things external to our minds' I think the case is different. People may be inclined to say: 'I can see quite clearly that from the proposition "At least two dogs exist at the present moment" there *follows* the proposition "At least two things are to be met with in space at the present moment", so that if you can prove that there are two dogs in existence at the present moment you will *ipso facto* have proved that two things at least are to be met with in space at the present moment. I can see that you do not also require a separate proof that from "Two dogs exist" "Two things are to be met with in space" *does* follow; it is quite obvious that there couldn't be a dog which wasn't to be met with in space. But it is not by any means so clear to me that if you can prove that there are two dogs or two shadows, you will *ipso facto* have proved that there are two things *external to our minds*. Isn't it possible that a dog, though it certainly must be "to be met with in space", might *not* be an external object – an object external to our minds? Isn't a separate proof required that anything that is to be met with in space must be external to our minds? Of course, if you are using "external" as a mere synonym for "to be met with in space", no proof will be required that dogs are external objects: in that case, if you can prove that two dogs exist, you will *ipso facto* have proved that there are some external things. But I find it difficult to believe that you, or anybody else, do really use "external" as a mere synonym for "to be met with in space"; and if you don't, isn't some proof required that whatever is to be met with in space must be external to our minds?'

Now Kant, as we saw, asserts that the phrases 'outside of us' or 'external' are in fact used in two very different senses; and with regard to one of these two senses, that which he calls the 'transcendental' sense, and which he tries to explain by saying that it is a sense in which 'external' means 'existing *as a thing in itself* distinct from us', it is notorious that he himself held that things which are to be met with in space are *not* 'external' in that sense. There is, therefore, according to him, *a* sense of 'external', a sense in which the word has been commonly used by philosophers – such that, if 'external' be used in that

G. E. Moore on Idealism, Goodness, and Common Sense   141

sense, then from the proposition 'Two dogs exist' it will *not* follow that there are some external things. What this supposed sense is I do not think that Kant himself ever succeeded in explaining clearly; nor do I know of any reason for supposing that philosophers ever have used 'external' in a sense, such that in *that* sense things that are to be met with in space are *not* external. But how about the other sense, in which, according to Kant, the word 'external' has been commonly used – that which he calls 'empirically external'? How is this conception related to the conception 'to be met with in space'? It may be noticed that, in the passages which I quoted (A373), Kant himself does not tell us at all clearly what he takes to be the proper answer to this question. He only makes the rather odd statement that, in order to remove all uncertainty as to the conception 'empirically external', he will distinguish objects to which it applies from those which might be called 'external' in the transcendental sense, by 'calling them outright things which are *to be met with in space*'. These odd words certainly suggest, as one possible interpretation of them, that in Kant's opinion the conception 'empirically external' is *identical* with the conception 'to be met with in space' – that he does think that 'external', when used in this second sense, is a mere synonym for 'to be met with in space'. But, if this is his meaning, I do find it very difficult to believe that he is right. Have philosophers, in fact, ever used 'external' as a mere synonym for 'to be met with in space'? Does he himself do so?

I do not think they have, nor that he does himself; and, in order to explain how they have used it, and how the two conceptions 'external to our minds' and 'to be met with in space' are related to one another, I think it is important expressly to call attention to a fact which hitherto I have only referred to incidentally: namely the fact that those who talk of certain things as 'external to' our minds, do, in general, as we should naturally expect, talk of other 'things', with which they wish to contrast the first, as 'in' our minds. It has, of course, been often pointed out that when 'in' is thus used, followed by 'my mind', 'your mind', 'his mind', etc., 'in' is being used metaphorically. And there are some metaphorical uses of 'in', followed by such expressions, which occur in common speech, and which we all understand quite well. For instance, we all understand such expressions as 'I had you in mind, when I made that arrangement' or 'I had you in mind, when I said that there are some people who can't bear to touch a spider'. In these cases 'I was thinking of you' can be used to mean the same as 'I had you in mind'. But it is quite certain that this particular metaphorical use of 'in' is not the one in which philosophers are using it when they contrast what is 'in' my mind with what is 'external' to it. On the contrary, in their use of 'external', you will be external to my mind even at a moment when I have you in mind. If

Early Analytic Philosophy

we want to discover what this peculiar metaphorical use of '*in* my mind' is, which is such that nothing, which is, in the sense we are now concerned with, 'external' to my mind, can ever be 'in' it, we need, I think, to consider instances of the sort of 'things' which they would say are 'in' my mind in this special sense. I have already mentioned three such instances, which are, I think, sufficient for my present purpose: any bodily pain which I feel, any after-image which I see with my eyes shut, and any image which I 'see' when I am asleep and dreaming, are typical examples of the sort of 'thing' of which philosophers have spoken as '*in* my mind'. And there is no doubt, I think, that when they have spoken of such things as my body, a sheet of paper, a star – in short 'physical objects' generally – as 'external', they have meant to emphasize some important difference which they feel to exist between such things as these and such 'things' as a pain, an after-image seen with closed eyes, and a dream-image. But *what* difference? What difference do they feel to exist between a bodily pain which I feel or an after-image which I see with closed eyes, on the one hand, and my body itself, on the other – what difference which leads them to say that whereas the bodily pain and the after-image are 'in' my mind, my body itself is *not* 'in' my mind – not even when I am feeling it and seeing it or thinking of it? I have already said that one difference which there is between the two, is that my body is to be met with in space, whereas the bodily pain and the after-image are not. But I think it would be quite wrong to say that this is *the* difference which has led philosophers to speak of the two latter as 'in' my mind, and of my body as *not* 'in' my mind.

The question what the difference is which has led them to speak in this way, is not, I think, at all an easy question to answer; but I am going to try to give, in brief outline, what I *think* is a right answer.

It should, I think, be noted, first of all, that the use of the word 'mind', which is being adopted when it is said that any bodily pains which I feel are 'in my mind', is one which is not quite in accordance with any usage common in ordinary speech, although we are very familiar with it in philosophy. Nobody, I think, would say that bodily pains which I feel are 'in my mind', unless he was also prepared to say that it is *with* my mind that I feel bodily pains; and to say this latter is, I think, not quite in accordance with common non-philosophic usage. It is natural enough to say that it is with my mind that I remember, and think, and imagine, and feel *mental* pains – e.g., disappointment, but not, I think, quite so natural to say that it is with my mind that I feel *bodily* pains, e.g., a severe headache; and perhaps even less natural to say that it is with my mind that I see and hear and smell and taste. There is, however, a well-established philosophical usage according to which seeing, hearing, smelling, tasting, and having a bodily pain are just as much *mental* occurrences or processes as are

G. E. Moore on Idealism, Goodness, and Common Sense   143

remembering, or thinking, or imagining. This usage was, I think, adopted by philosophers, because they saw a real resemblance between such statements as 'I saw a cat', 'I heard a clap of thunder', 'I smelt a strong smell of onions', 'My finger smarted horribly', on the one hand, and such statements as 'I remembered having seen him', 'I was thinking out a plan of action', 'I pictured the scene to myself', 'I felt bitterly disappointed', on the other – a resemblance which puts all these statements in one class together, as contrasted with other statements in which 'I' or 'my' is used, such as, e.g., 'I was less than four feet high', 'I was lying on my back', 'My hair was very long'. What is the resemblance in question? It is a resemblance which might be expressed by saying that all the first eight statements are the sort of statements which furnish data for psychology, while the three latter are not. It is also a resemblance which may be expressed, in a way now common among philosophers, by saying that in the case of all the first eight statements, if we make the statement more specific by adding a date, we get a statement such that, if it is true, then it *follows* that I was 'having an experience' at the date in question, whereas this does not hold for the three last statements. For instance, if it is true that I saw a cat between 12 noon and 5 minutes past, today, it *follows* that I was 'having some experience' between 12 noon and 5 minutes past, today; whereas from the proposition that I was less than four feet high in December 1877, it does not *follow* that I had any experiences in December 1877. But this philosophic use of 'having an experience' is one which itself needs explanation, since it is not identical with any use of the expression that is established in common speech. An explanation, however, which is, I think, adequate for the purpose, can be given by saying that a philosopher, who was following this usage, would say that I was at a given time 'having an experience' if and only if either (1) I was conscious at the time or (2) I was dreaming at the time or (3) something else was true of me at the time, which resembled what is true of me when I am conscious and when I am dreaming, in a certain very obvious respect in which what is true of me when I am dreaming resembles what is true of me when I am conscious, and in which what would be true of me, if at any time, for instance, I had a vision, would resemble both. This explanation is, of course, in some degree vague; but I think it is clear enough for our purpose. It amounts to saying that, in this philosophic usage of 'having an experience', it would be said of me that I was, at a given time, having *no* experience, if I was at the time neither conscious nor dreaming nor having a vision nor *anything else of the sort;* and, of course, this is vague in so far as it has not been specified what else would be *of the sort:* this is left to be gathered from the instances given. But I think this is sufficient: often at night when I am asleep, I am neither conscious nor dreaming nor having a vision nor

144   Early Analytic Philosophy

anything else of the sort – that is to say, I am having no experiences. If this explanation of this philosophic usage of 'having an experience' is clear enough, then I think that what has been meant by saying that any pain which I feel or any after-image which I see with my eyes closed is '*in* my mind', can be explained by saying that what is meant is neither more nor less than that there would be a contradiction in supposing *that very same pain* or *that very same after-image* to have existed at a time at which I was having no experience; or, in other words, that from the proposition, with regard to any time, that *that* pain or *that* after-image existed at that time, it *follows* that I was having some experience at the time in question. And if so, then we can say that the felt difference between bodily pains which I feel and after-images which I see, on the one hand, and my body on the other, which has led philosophers to say that any such pain or after-image is '*in* my mind', whereas my body *never* is but is always 'outside of or 'external to' my mind, is just this, that whereas there is a contradiction in supposing a pain which I feel or an after-image which I see to exist at a time when I am having no experience, there is no contradiction in supposing my body to exist at a time when I am having no experience; and we can even say, I think, that just this and nothing more is what they have meant by these puzzling and misleading phrases 'in my mind' and 'external to my mind'.

But now, if to say of anything, e.g., my body, that it is external to *my* mind, means merely that from a proposition to the effect that it existed at a specified time, there in no case follows the further proposition that *I* was having an experience at the time in question, then to say of anything that it is external to *our* minds, will mean similarly that from a proposition to the effect that it existed at a specified time, it in no case follows that any of us were having experiences at the time in question. And if by *our* minds be meant, as is, I think, usually meant, the minds of human beings living on the earth, then it will follow that any pains which animals may feel, any after-images they may see, any experiences they may have, though not external to *their* minds, yet are external to *ours*. And this at once makes plain how different is the conception 'external to our minds' from the conception 'to be met with in space'; for, of course, pains which animals feel or after-images which they see are no more to be met with in space than are pains which *we* feel or after-images which *we* see. From the proposition that there are external objects – objects that are not in any of *our* minds, it does *not* follow that there are things to be met with in space; and hence 'external to our minds' is not a mere synonym for 'to be met with in space': that is to say, 'external to our minds' and 'to be met with in space' are two different conceptions. And the true relation between these conceptions seems to me to be this. We have already seen that there are ever so many kinds of 'things', such

G. E. Moore on Idealism, Goodness, and Common Sense   145

that, in the case of each of these kinds, from the proposition that there is at least one thing of that kind there *follows* the proposition that there is at least one thing to be met with in space: e.g., this follows from 'There is at least one star', from 'There is at least one human body', from 'There is at least one shadow', etc. And I think we can say that of every kind of thing of which this is true, it is also true that from the proposition that there is at least one 'thing' of that kind there *follows* the proposition that there is at least one thing external to our minds: e.g., from 'There is at least one star' there follows not only 'There is at least one thing to be met with in space' but also 'There is at least one external thing', and similarly in all other cases. My reason for saying this is as follows. Consider any kind of thing, such that anything of that kind, if there is anything of it, must be 'to be met with in space': e.g., consider the kind 'soap-bubble'. If I say of anything which I am perceiving, 'That is a soap-bubble', I am, it seems to me, certainly implying that there would be no contradiction in asserting that it existed before I perceived it and that it will continue to exist, even if I cease to perceive it. This seems to me to be part of what is meant by saying that it is a real soap-bubble, as distinguished, for instance, from an hallucination of a soap-bubble. Of course, it by no means follows, that if it really is a soap-bubble, it did in fact exist before I perceived it or will continue to exist after I cease to perceive it: soap-bubbles are an example of a kind of 'physical object' and 'thing to be met with in space', in the case of which it is notorious that particular specimens of the kind often do exist only so long as they are perceived by a particular person. But a thing which I perceive would not be a soap-bubble unless its existence at any given time were *logically independent* of my perception of it at that time; unless that is to say, from the proposition, with regard to a particular time, that it existed at that time, it *never* follows that I perceived it at that time. But, if it is true that it would not be a soap-bubble, unless it *could* have existed at any given time without being perceived by me at that time, it is certainly also true that it would not be a soap-bubble, unless it *could* have existed at any given time, without its being true that I was having any experience of any kind at the time in question: it would not be a soap-bubble, unless, whatever time you take, from the proposition that it existed at that time it does *not* follow that I was having any experience at that time. That is to say, from the proposition with regard to anything which I am perceiving that it is a soap-bubble, there *follows* the proposition that it is external to *my* mind. But if, when I say that anything which I perceive is a soap-bubble, I am implying that it is external to *my* mind, I am, I think, certainly also implying that it is also external to all other minds: I am implying that it is not a thing of a sort such that things of that sort *can* only exist at a time when somebody is having an experience. I think, therefore, that from

146   Early Analytic Philosophy

any proposition of the form 'There's a soap-bubble!' there does really *follow* the proposition 'There's an external object!' 'There's an object external to *all* our minds!' And, if this is true of the kind 'soap-bubble', it is certainly also true of any other kind (including the kind 'unicorn') which is such that, if there are any things of that kind, it follows that there are *some* things to be met with in space.

I think, therefore, that in the case of all kinds of 'things', which are such that if there is a pair of things, both of which are of one of these kinds, or a pair of things one of which is of one of them and one of them of another, then it will follow at once that there are some things to be met with in space, it is true also that if I can prove that there are a pair of things, one of which is of one of these kinds and another of another, or a pair both of which are of one of them, then I shall have proved *ipso facto* that there are at least two 'things outside of us'. That is to say, if I can prove that there exist now both a sheet of paper and a human hand, I shall have proved that there are now 'things outside of us'; if I can prove that there exist now both a shoe and sock, I shall have proved that there are now 'things outside of us', etc.; and similarly I shall have proved it, if I can prove that there exist now two sheets of paper, or two human hands, or two shoes, or two socks, etc. Obviously, then, there are thousands of different things such that, if, at any time, I can prove any one of them, I shall have proved the existence of things outside of us. Cannot I prove any of these things?

It seems to me that, so far from its being true, as Kant declares to be his opinion, that there is only one possible proof of the existence of things outside of us, namely the one which he has given, I can now give a large number of different proofs, each of which is a perfectly rigorous proof; and that at many other times I have been in a position to give many others. I can prove now, for instance, that two human hands exist. How? By holding up my two hands, and saying, as I make a certain gesture with the right hand, 'Here is one hand', and adding, as I make a certain gesture with the left, 'and here is another'. And if, by doing this, I have proved *ipso facto* the existence of external things, you will all see that I can also do it now in numbers of other ways: there is no need to multiply examples.

But did I prove just now that two human hands were then in existence? I do want to insist that I did; that the proof which I gave was a perfectly rigorous one; and that it is perhaps impossible to give a better or more rigorous proof of anything whatever. Of course, it would not have been a proof unless three conditions were satisfied; namely (1) unless the premiss which I adduced as proof of the conclusion was different from the conclusion I adduced it to prove; (2) unless the premiss which I adduced was something which I *knew* to be the case, and not merely something which I believed but which was by no means certain, or something which, though in fact true, I did not know to be so; and (3)

G. E. Moore on Idealism, Goodness, and Common Sense   147

unless the conclusion did really follow from the premiss. But all these three conditions were in fact satisfied by my proof. (1) The premiss which I adduced in proof was quite certainly different from the conclusion, for the conclusion was merely 'Two human hands exist at this moment'; but the premiss was something far more specific than this – something which I expressed by showing you my hands, making certain gestures, and saying the words 'Here is one hand, and here is another'. It is quite obvious that the two were different, because it is quite obvious that the conclusion might have been true, even if the premiss had been false. In asserting the premiss I was asserting much more than I was asserting in asserting the conclusion. (2) I certainly did at the moment *know* that which I expressed by the combination of certain gestures with saying the words 'There is one hand and here is another'. I *knew* that there was one hand in the place indicated by combining a certain gesture with my first utterance of 'here' and that there was another in the different place indicated by combining a certain gesture with my second utterance of 'here'. How absurd it would be to suggest that I did not know it, but only believed it, and that perhaps it was not the case! You might as well suggest that I do not know that I am now standing up and talking – that perhaps after all I'm not, and that it's not quite certain that I am! And finally (3) it is quite certain that the conclusion did follow from the premiss. This is as certain as it is that if there is one hand here and another here *now*, then it follows that there are two hands in existence *now*.

My proof, then, of the existence of things outside of us did satisfy three of the conditions necessary for a rigorous proof. Are there any other conditions necessary for a rigorous proof, such that perhaps it did not satisfy one of them? Perhaps there may be; I do not know; but I do want to emphasise that, so far as I can see, we all of us do constantly take proofs of this sort as absolutely conclusive proofs of certain conclusions – as finally settling certain questions, as to which we were previously in doubt. Suppose, for instance, it were a question whether there were as many as three misprints on a certain page in a certain book. A says there are, B is inclined to doubt it. How could A prove that he is right? Surely he *could* prove it by taking the book, turning to the page, and pointing to three separate places on it, saying 'There's one misprint here, another here, and another here': surely that is a method by which it *might* be proved! Of course, A would not have proved, by doing this, that there were at least three misprints on the page in question, unless it was certain that there was a misprint in each of the places to which he pointed. But to say that he *might* prove it in this way, is to say that it *might* be certain that there was. And if such a thing as that could ever be certain, then assuredly it was certain just now that there was one hand in one of the two places I indicated and another in the other.

Early Analytic Philosophy

I did, then, just now, give a proof that there were *then* external objects; and obviously, if I did, I could *then* have given many other proofs of the same sort that there were external objects *then,* and could now give many proofs of the same sort that there are external objects *now.*

But, if what I am asked to do is to prove that external objects have existed *in the past,* then I can give many different proofs of this also, but proofs which are in important respects of a different sort from those just given. And I want to emphasise that, when Kant says it is a scandal not to be able to give a proof of the existence of external objects, a proof of their existence in the past would certainly *help* to remove the scandal of which he is speaking. He says that, if it occurs to anyone to question their existence, we ought to be able to confront him with a satisfactory proof. But by a person who questions their existence, he certainly means not merely a person who questions whether any exist at the moment of speaking, but a person who questions whether any have *ever* existed; and a proof that some have existed in the past would certainly therefore be relevant to *part* of what such a person is questioning. How then can I prove that there have been external objects in the past? Here is one proof. I can say: 'I held up two hands above this desk not very long ago; therefore two hands existed not very long ago; therefore at least two external objects have existed at some time in the past, QED'. This is a perfectly good proof, provided I *know* what is asserted in the premiss. But I *do* know that I held up two hands above this desk not very long ago. As a matter of fact, in this case you all know it too. There's no doubt whatever that I did. Therefore I have given a perfectly conclusive proof that external objects have existed in the past; and you will all see at once that, if this is a conclusive proof, I could have given many others of the same sort, and could now give many others. But it is also quite obvious that this sort of proof differs in important respects from the sort of proof I gave just now that there were two hands existing *then.*

I have, then, given two conclusive proofs of the existence of external objects. The first was a proof that two human hands existed at the time when I gave the proof; the second was a proof that two human hands had existed at a time previous to that at which I gave the proof. These proofs were of a different sort in important respects. And I pointed out that I could have given, then, many other conclusive proofs of both sorts. It is also obvious that I could give many others of both sorts now. So that, if these are the sort of proof that is wanted, nothing is easier than to prove the existence of external objects.

But now I am perfectly well aware that, in spite of all that I have said, many philosophers will still feel that I have not given any satisfactory proof of the point in question. And I want briefly, in conclusion, to say something as to why this dissatisfaction with my proofs should be felt.

G. E. Moore on Idealism, Goodness, and Common Sense   149

One reason why, is, I think, this. Some people understand 'proof of an external world' as including a proof of things which I haven't attempted to prove and haven't proved. It is not quite easy to say *what* it is that they want proved – *what* it is that is such that unless they got a proof of it, they would not say that they had a proof of the existence of external things; but I can make an approach to explaining what they want by saying that if I had proved the propositions which I used as *premisses* in my two proofs, then they would perhaps admit that I had proved the existence of external things, but, in the absence of such a proof (which, of course, I have neither given nor attempted to give), they will say that I have not given what they mean by a proof of the existence of external things. In other words, they want a proof of what I assert *now* when I hold up my hands and say 'Here's one hand and here's another'; and, in the other case, they want a proof of what I assert *now* when I say 'I did hold up two hands above this desk just now'. Of course, what they really want is not merely a proof of these two propositions, but something like a general statement as to how *any* propositions of this sort may be proved. This, of course, I haven't given; and I do not believe it can be given: if this is what is meant by proof of the existence of external things, I do not believe that any proof of the existence of external things is possible. Of course, in some cases what might be called a proof of propositions which seem like these can be got. If one of you suspected that one of my hands was artificial he might be said to get a proof of my proposition 'Here's one hand, and here's another', by coming up and examining the suspected hand close up, perhaps touching and pressing it, and so establishing that it really was a human hand. But I do not believe that any proof is possible in nearly all cases. How am I to prove now that 'Here's one hand, and here's another'? I do not believe I can do it. In order to do it, I should need to prove for one thing, as Descartes pointed out, that I am not now dreaming. But how can I prove that I am not? I have, no doubt, conclusive reasons for asserting that I am not now dreaming; I have conclusive evidence that I am awake: but that is a very different thing from being able to prove it. I could not tell you what all my evidence is; and I should require to do this at least, in order to give you a proof.

But another reason why some people would feel dissatisfied with my proofs is, I think, not merely that they want a proof of something which I haven't proved, but that they think that, if I cannot give such extra proofs, then the proofs that I have given are not conclusive proofs at all. And this, I think, is a definite mistake. They would say: 'If you cannot prove your premiss that here is one hand and here is another, then you do not know it. But you yourself have admitted that, if you did not know it, then your proof was not conclusive. Therefore your proof was not, as you say it was, a conclusive proof'. This view

150 Early Analytic Philosophy

that, if I cannot prove such things as these, I do not know them, is, I think, the view that Kant was expressing in the sentence which I quoted at the beginning of this lecture, when he implies that so long as we have no proof of the existence of external things, their existence must be accepted merely on *faith*. He means to say, I think, that if I cannot prove that there is a hand here, I must accept it merely as a matter of faith – I cannot know it. Such a view, though it has been very common among philosophers, can, I think, be shown to be wrong – though shown only by the use of premisses which are not known to be true, unless we do know of the existence of external things. I can know things, which I cannot prove; and among things which I certainly did know, even if (as I think) I could not prove them, were the premisses of my two proofs. I should say, therefore, that those, if any, who are dissatisfied with these proofs merely on the ground that I did not know their premisses, have no good reason for their dissatisfaction.

4

Gottlob Frege: Logic and the Philosophy of Language

Chapter Outline

Background and commentary
Background	151
Logic and logicism	153
Sinn, Bedeutung, and thoughts	158
Concluding remarks	163
Further reading	164

Readings
"On Sinn and Bedeutung"	165
"The Thought: A Logical Inquiry"	185

Background and commentary

Background

Who was Gottlob Frege (1848–1925)? While contemporary students of philosophy may have heard this name before opening this book, Frege was not especially prominent during his own lifetime. Indeed, English translations of Frege's work were not widely available until well into the twentieth century. However, he is now typically regarded as one of the

152   Early Analytic Philosophy

founders of the analytic tradition; some have gone so far as to call Frege (rightly or wrongly!) "the first analytic philosopher."[1] Despite being trained as a mathematician, Frege's interests in the foundations of mathematics led him to produce groundbreaking work in logic and the philosophy of language. Russell came across Frege's work in 1900 and famously corresponded with him about the paradox that sank Frege's attempt to reduce mathematics to pure logic. In 1911, Wittgenstein discovered Frege's work, went to meet with him, and took Frege's advice to go to Cambridge to study with Russell. Frege also was known to and influenced Rudolf Carnap (1891–1970) as well as Edmund Husserl (1859–1938).

Frege published three books, *Begriffschrift, eine der arithmetischen nachgebildete Formelsprache des reinen Denkens* (([1879] 1967), translated as *Concept-Script: A formal language of pure thought, modeled upon that of arithmetic)*; *Die Grundlagen der Arithmetic* (([1884] 1980), translated as *The Foundations of Arithmetic)*; and *Grundgesetze der Arithmetik*, Vol. 1 and 2 (([1892, 1903] 2013), translated as *Basic Laws of Arithmetic)*, as well as various articles. While the readings below focus on Frege's philosophy of language, we will also offer some remarks on Frege's important logical investigations.

Frege was born in Germany to parents who founded and operated a girls' school. In 1869, he began attending the University of Jena, where he stayed for two semesters before moving on to the University of Göttingen. This move seems to have been suggested to Frege by his mentor at Jena, Ernst Abbe (1840–1905), himself a physicist and mathematician and, starting in 1866, a research director and later partner at the profitable Zeiss Optical Works in Jena. During this time, Frege took courses in mathematics, physics, and philosophy. He was awarded a doctorate degree from Göttingen in 1873. In 1874, perhaps with the help of Abbe, Frege returned to Jena as a lecturer. While the position was without pay, Frege received a stipend from Abbe's Zeiss Optical Works. In 1879, Frege was promoted to professor at Jena, where he would remain until his retirement in 1918.

Carnap attended Frege's lectures from 1910 to 1914. He wrote of Frege's 1910 lectures:

---

[1]Sluga 1980; for related remarks, see Dummett 1973. Aside from questions about the historical credentials of this claim, we believe that it relies on a narrow conception of analytic philosophy as concerned with logic and language. We rather more modestly maintain that Frege was among the first wave of analytic philosophers.

Gottlob Frege: Logic and the Philosophy of Language   153

Frege looked old beyond his years. He was of small stature, rather shy, extremely introverted. He seldom looked at the audience. Ordinarily we only saw his back, while he drew the strange diagrams of his symbolism on the blackboard and explained them. Never did a student ask a question or make a remark ... The possibility of a discussion seemed to be out of the question. (1963: 5)

Frege's work was not very well received during his lifetime, to his disappointment. He suffered in his personal life as well. While he married Margarete Lieseburg (1856–1905) in 1887, she passed away in 1905. For the next dozen or so years, Frege wrote little. Frege adopted a son, Alfred, in 1908, and would later entrust Alfred with his unpublished letters and writings. Upon giving his work to Alfred, Frege wrote: "I believe there are things here which will one day be prized much more highly than they are now" and that "even if all is not gold, there is gold in them" (1979: ix). Near the end of his life, Frege adopted right-wing and, indeed, anti-Semitic views about the place of Jewish people in German society.[2]

Logic and logicism

Frege's *Begriffschrift* is now regarded as one of the most important works in the history of logic and perhaps the most important logical work since Aristotle (385–323 BC). Aristotle's logic was based on the analysis of so-called "categorical" statements or propositions: statements of the form All Fs are Gs (All dogs are animals), No Fs are Gs (No dogs are cats), Some Fs are Gs (Some cats are rabid), and Some Fs are not Gs (Some cats are not rabid). Aristotle's logic systematized arguments consisting of these and related types of statements, and moreover supposed that such statements should be understood as having a subject-predicate form (they attribute a predicate to a subject). Among Frege's insights was that the subject-predicate form was not the only kind of logical form, so that some statements instead must be understood as expressing relations between two or more things. Moreover, Frege maintained that categorical statements should be understood in quantificational terms, as statements about quantities of things. For instance, he supposed that a sentence like "All dogs are animals" should be analyzed as follows: for anything at all, if it is a dog, then it is an animal.

Although the symbolism used in modern logic textbooks is different from that employed by Frege, his *Begriffschrift* pioneered many of the

---

[2]Mendelson 1996. For this and further biographical information, see Beaney 1997, Jacquette 2019, and Zalta 2019.

154   Early Analytic Philosophy

significant elements of contemporary logic. It can be said that the ideas of modern logic are primarily due to Frege, while the symbolism used to express these ideas is due largely to Russell and Whitehead in their three-volume *Principia Mathematica*, which itself was influenced by the work of the Italian mathematician and logician Guiseppe Peano (1858–1932). Frege's achievement consisted, in part, in constructing a logical language that could represent both sentential or propositional logic (the logical behavior of words like "… and …", "not …", and "if … then …") as well as predicate or quantificational logic (the logical behavior of words like "all" and "some", and the occurrence of predicates across statements and arguments). In part because of this, Frege's logical language could represent mathematical sentences like "Every number has some successor" in a way that previous logical languages could not, and was thus more suitable for the analysis of mathematical discourse.

Frege believed that ordinary language often obscures thought, but that his logical language—his "concept-script"—could be useful for clarifying thought and its expression. Regarding the analysis of mathematical thought, which provided the impetus for Frege's logical investigations, he thus wrote that "I found the inadequacy of language an obstacle … This deficiency led me to the idea of the present *Begriffsschrift*" ([1879] 1967: 5–6). Frege also viewed his logical language as having some use for philosophy:

> If it is a task of philosophy to break the domination of the word over the human spirit by uncovering deceptions about the relations of concepts which arise almost inevitably from common linguistic usage, and by freeing thought from that with which it is infected only by the nature of the linguistic means of expression, then my *Begriffsschrift* can become a useful tool for the philosopher, if it is further developed for these purposes. ([1879] 1967: 7)

In other words, Frege viewed his logical language—essentially, a version of the predicate logic now taught in elementary symbolic logic—as providing a tool for clarifying thoughts and inferences, perhaps most especially in the context of mathematical and philosophical discourse.

Another important insight of Frege's was his criticism of psychologistic accounts of logic and mathematics, according to which truths of logic and mathematics could somehow be understood as deriving from truths about human psychology. Against this, Frege argued that logic and mathematics must be understood as autonomous disciplines with distinctive, mind-independent, and objective subject matter. The task of logic, as Frege put it, is to discover the "laws of truth" ([1918–19] 1956: 289).

Gottlob Frege: Logic and the Philosophy of Language   155

In his books *Die Grundlagen der Arithmetik (The Foundations of Arithmetic)*, published in 1884, *and Grundgesetze der Arithmetik (Basic Laws of Arithmetic)*, published in 1893, Frege employed his "concept-script" in the service of the ambitious project now known as "logicism"—the project of showing that mathematics (especially arithmetic) is nothing but logic: first, that mathematical concepts can be defined solely in terms of logical concepts; second, that the truths of mathematics can be derived from the truths of logic. Despite the importance of Frege's developments in logic, the logicist project is typically regarded as a failure due in part to what is commonly referred to as "Russell's paradox," which, along with Kurt Gödel's (1906–78) later demonstration of the incompleteness of arithmetic, showed that the logicist project was fundamentally flawed. Some of the main ideas here are as follows.

Logicism can be described as the attempt to show that mathematics is nothing but logic and set theory, along with the supposition that set theory is itself a branch of logic. One way to understand Russell's paradox, and why it seems to undermine logicism, is that it shows that set theory is not pure logic. Setting aside various details, the idea is this. First, Frege's various attempts to define mathematical concepts in logical terms appeal to the notion of a set or class of things, and suppose that any predicate or concept determines a set or class. The latter supposition, that any predicate or concept determines a set, is premised on the idea that any such restriction would go beyond "pure logic" and would instead enter the domain of metaphysics. Russell's paradox shows, however, that there must be restrictions on "set formation" on what predicates or concepts determine a set, since without some such restriction, the very notion of a set or class leads to a contradiction.

A set or class is essentially a collection of things. A set may be specified, first, simply by listing its members, as the set of the three most famous ancient Greek philosophers might be represented as {Socrates, Plato, Aristotle}. A set can also be specified by providing a condition for membership in the set, as the set of the three most famous Greek philosophers might be represented as {x: x is among the three most famous ancient Greek philosophers}, or as the set of natural numbers might be represented as {x: x is a natural number}. In this sense, the predicate "x is a natural number" determines a set, namely the set consisting of the natural numbers. Similarly, on the assumption that every predicate or concept determines a set or class of things, predicates like "x red or located in New Orleans, Louisiana," "x is a set or cat," "x is a cat and has rabies," "x is taller than Michael Jordan but shorter than the tallest human" each determine a set or collection of things.

156   Early Analytic Philosophy

Frege's attempts to define mathematical concepts in logical terms appeal to the notion of a set in various ways. For example, Frege proposed that the number of Fs = the number of Gs just in case the set of Fs can be put into a one-to-one correspondence with the set of Gs. Given this, Frege proposed that a particular number, such as the number two, could then be defined as a set of "equinumerous"—that is, same-numbered—sets. That is, the number two could be defined as the set of all two-membered sets. Being a two-membered set can then be defined in logical terms. In particular, using the symbolism of modern predicate logic, Frege held that a two-membered set can be defined as a set R such that $(\exists x)(\exists y)[(x \in R \wedge y \in R) \wedge x \neq y \wedge; (\forall z)(z \in R \rightarrow (z = x \vee z = y))]$. In other words, for R to be a two-membered set is for there to be some x and some distinct y such that x and y are members of R and nothing else is a member of R. Given all this, the idea is that for any number n, n can be defined in logical terms, as a set of equinumerous sets.

This just scratches the surface of Frege's project, but even at this stage we can see that it uses the notion of a set. The problem revealed by Russell's paradox is that without some restriction on what predicates or concepts determine a set, the notion of a set or class leads to a contradiction. To understand Russell's paradox, note, first, that many sets are not members of themselves. For example, take the set of all cats. This set is not a member of itself, since the set of all cats consists of cats, and the set of all cats is a set, not a cat. That is, the predicate "x is a cat" determines a set or class of things, namely the set of all cats. But the set of all cats is not among the things to which "x is a cat" applies, and hence is not included in itself. The set of all cats is thus not a self-member. Second, however, some sets are members of themselves. Take the set of all non-cats, the set consisting of everything that is not a cat. This set is a member of itself, since it consists of everything that is not a cat, and the set of everything that is not a cat is a set, and not a cat. That is, the predicate "x is a non-cat" determines a set or class of things, and the set of all non-cats is included in this set, since "x is a non-cat" applies to the set of all non-cats. Hence, the set of all non-cats is a self-member.

So, some predicates or concepts determine a set, and the set they determine is a self-member, while other predicates or concepts determine a set, and the set they determine is not a self-member. Given this, Russell (roughly) asked: What about the set of all sets that are not members of themselves? Call this set "R." Is R a self-member or not a self-member? When we consider the members of R, do we find R among them? The problem is that both an affirmative and a negative answer appear to lead to a contradiction. First, suppose that R is a

Gottlob Frege: Logic and the Philosophy of Language   157

member of itself. However, R is the set of all sets that are not members of themselves; hence, if R is a member of R, then R is not a member of R. Hence, R is both a self-member and not a self-member—a contradiction. Second, suppose that R is not a member of itself. However, R is the set of all sets that are not members of themselves; hence, if R is not a member of R, then R is a member of R. Hence, R is not a self-member but also a self-member—again, a contradiction. Since both options lead to a contradiction, it seems that we must deny that any predicate or concept determines a set.

Russell wrote to Frege about the paradox in 1902 as the second volume of Frege's *Grundgesetze* was in press. In response, Frege added an appendix discussing certain aspects of the paradox. Frege wondered: "May I always speak of the extension of a concept, of a class? And if not, are the exceptions to be recognized? ... These are questions arise from Mr. Russell's communication" ([1892, 1903] 2013: 253). Moreover, Frege recognized the seriousness of the problem, lamenting that "hardly anything more unwelcome can befall a scientific writer than to have one of the foundations of his edifice shaken after the work is finished" ([1892, 1903] 2013: 253). Russell would later remark on Frege's reaction to the contradiction:

> As I think about acts of integrity and grace, I realise that there is nothing in my knowledge to compare to Frege's dedication to truth. His entire life's work was on the verge of completion, much of his work had been ignored to the benefit of men infinitely less capable, his second volume was about to be published, and upon finding that his fundamental assumption was in error, he responded with intellectual pleasure, clearly submerging any feelings of disappointment. It was almost superhuman, and a telling indication of that of which men are capable if their dedication is to creative work and knowledge instead of cruder efforts to dominate and be known. (1992: 237)

Russell's paradox thus seems to show that some restrictions need to be placed on what predicates or concepts determine a set or class of things. Such restrictions need to be robust enough to entail that there is no set of all sets that are not members of themselves, but weak enough to permit for those sets needed for mathematics. There are various strategies that have been employed in this context, including some developed by Russell himself.[3] However, it is plausible the restrictions needed to rule against Russell's

---

[3]Russell's solution, the so-called "Theory of Types" raises a number of challenging issues. One question is whether the ideas at work in the Theory of Types are themselves properly regarded as part of pure logic. For an accessible discussion of Russell's Theory of Types and some of the issues that it encounters, see Ayer 1972; see also Irvine and Deutsch 2016 and Griffin, N. 1992.

Early Analytic Philosophy

contradictory set, while nonetheless permitting for those sets needed for mathematics, cannot be regarded as pure logic. Essentially, the logicist project of reducing mathematics to logic requires set theory, but Russell's paradox shows that set theory is not pure logic.

Sinn, Bedeutung, and thoughts

Frege's contributions to the philosophy of language are numerous. However, his most influential and widely read articles are the two presented below, "Über Sinn und Bedeutung" (([1892] 1970), translated as "On Sinn and Bedeutung" or "On Sense and Reference"[4]) and "Der Gedanke" (([1918–19] 1956), translated as "The Thought: A Logical Inquiry"). Whereas "On Sinn and Bedeutung" develops Frege's influential distinction between the sense of an expression and its reference, "The Thought" pursues the idea, present in "On Sinn and Bedeutung" and implicit in his logical works, that what he calls "thoughts" are objective, mind-independent entities, which can be grasped by more than one person. At least in this respect, Frege can be viewed as developing a kind of anti-psychologistic account of thought similar to Moore's anti-psychologism developed in "The Nature of Judgement" and discussed in Chapter 3. The similarity should not be overstated, however. In "The Nature of Judgement," Moore seems to take concepts, as the constituents of propositions, to make up the world; for Frege, on the other hand, while senses are conceived as mind-independent entities in "On Sinn and Bedeutung" and "The Thought," the world itself is made up not of senses, but rather of objects to which expressions refer in virtue of their senses. In this respect, while senses are, again, intended to be mind-independent, they function more as intermediaries between language and the world rather than as constituents of the world.

Frege's project in "On Sinn and Bedeutung" can be approached by asking, in general, what we mean when we speak of the "meaning" of an expression. Frege claims that there are at least three things that we might have in mind. First, we can speak of the meaning of an expression as its "Bedeutung" or reference, what it stands for or denotes. For instance, we can think of the

---

[4]In translating the title of "Über Sinn und Bedeutung," "Sinn" is often translated as "Sense" while "Bedeutung" is translated as "Reference." We have chosen to include a translation below that leaves "Sinn" and "Bedeutung" untranslated in the German (in part simply due to issues surrounding permission fees associated with reproducing the material). We will not here engage with difficult issues concerning, for instance, the propriety of translating "Sinn" as "sense" and "Bedeutung" as "reference."

meaning of "Socrates" simply as the man to which the expression "Socrates" refers. Second, we can speak of the meaning of an expression as what Frege calls its "Sinn" or sense and what can at least roughly be thought of as the descriptive content of the expression. For instance, we can think of "Socrates" as meaning something like what could similarly be expressed by "the snub-nosed philosopher of antiquity," at least roughly in that language users associate some such descriptive meaning with "Socrates." Third, we can speak of the meaning of an expression as the subjective idea associated with the expression by an individual language user. For instance, we can think of the meaning of the word "Socrates" in terms of the specific images and memories that a particular language user associates with "Socrates." Frege argues that reference, sense, and subjective idea each need to be recognized and that each is distinct from the others.

Frege motivates the need to recognize the "Sinn" or sense of an expression, as apart from its "Bedeutung" or reference, based on two related issues. The first is introduced at the very start of "On Sinn and Bedeutung" and concerns the question of how an identity statement (for example, "Samuel Clemens = Mark Twain" or "the Evening Star = the Morning Star") can be both meaningful and significant. For suppose the meaning of an expression just is its reference—for example, that the meaning of "Socrates" is nothing more nor less than the man, the object, to which "Socrates" refers. In that case, if an expression "a" stands for the same object as an expression "b"—that is, if "a" and "b" have the same reference and thus "a = b" is true—it seems that "a = b" must mean the same as "a = a". However, Frege observes that while statements of the form "a = a" are analytic and *a priori*, statements of the form "a = b" "often contain very valuable extensions of our knowledge and cannot always be established *a priori*" (56). For instance, it was a genuine astronomical discovery that the Evening Star = the Morning Star, something that could not be known independently of experience. At least in this sense, what Frege calls the "cognitive value" of "the Evening Star = the Evening Star" differs from that of "the Evening Star = the Morning Star". Frege proposes to account for this difference by appealing to the notion of "Sinn" or sense. In particular, Frege proposes that even if "the Evening Star" and "the Morning Star" have the same "Bedeutung" or reference, they differ in "Sinn" or sense— they present the object to which they refer differently—which is why "the Evening Star = the Morning Star" cannot be known *a priori* but rather requires empirical investigation. Roughly, while "the Evening Star" and "the Morning Star" refer to the same object, they have different descriptive content and in this way present that object differently.

Early Analytic Philosophy

Frege's second motivation for introducing the notion of sense is a bit less straightforward. To understand this motivation, it is important to make explicit a certain "compositionality" principle that Frege endorsed. Specifically, Frege held that whole sentences have a reference, either the True or the False, and moreover that the reference of a whole sentence to the True or the False is determined by the reference of its constituent expressions. Generally, setting aside Frege's view of truth-values as objects,[5] the idea is that whether a sentence is true or false is determined by the reference of the expressions in that sentence. This entails that replacing an expression e in a sentence S with an expression e' that refers to the same object as e cannot change the truth value of S. This is intuitive: for example, given that "Mark Twain wrote *Huckleberry Finn*" is true, and given that "Mark Twain" and "Samuel Clemens" refer to the same object, a particular man, it follows that "Samuel Clemens wrote *Huckleberry Finn*" must also be true. Frege realized, however, that in certain contexts, this compositionality principle seems to break down. Take, for example, the sentence "Beyoncé Knowles believes that Mark Twain wrote *Huckleberry Finn*," and suppose that this sentence is true. Now, "Mark Twain" and "Samuel Clemens" have the same "Bedeutung" or reference, they refer to or stand for the same man. However, substituting "Samuel Clemens" for "Mark Twain" in the above sentence can, at least in principle, result in a false sentence: even if "Beyoncé Knowles believes that Mark Twain wrote *Huckleberry Finn*" is true, "Beyoncé Knowles believes that Samuel Clemens wrote *Huckleberry Finn*" may yet be false—this may be the case, for example, if Beyoncé doesn't know that Samuel Clemens = Mark Twain. But this contravenes the above compositionality principle, since it seems to suppose that substituting expressions with the same reference can result in a change of the truth value of a sentence. This generally seems to be the case for what are now referred to as "propositional attitude contexts"—in the context of sentences of the form x knows that S, x believes that S, x wishes that S, and so on. In these contexts, it seems that replacing co-referential expressions within the context of S does not guarantee a resulting sentence with the same truth-value as the original.

Frege's response, in short, is to claim that in these contexts, expressions do not have their usual reference—for example, that in the context of "Beyoncé Knowles believes that Mark Twain wrote *Huckleberry Finn*," "Mark Twain" does not have its usual reference, a particular man. Rather, Frege claimed

---

[5]For more on Frege's view of truth-values as objects, see his "On Function and Concept" ([1891] 1997) and "On Concept and Object" ([1892] 1997).

that in this context, the reference of "Mark Twain" is not the man himself, but rather the usual sense of the name "Mark Twain"—what Frege calls the "indirect reference" of "Mark Twain." This motivates the need to accept that an expression like "Mark Twain" has a sense, a cognitive value, apart from its reference. Given this story, in the context of "Beyoncé Knowles believes that Mark Twain wrote *Huckleberry Finn*" and "Beyoncé Knowles believes that Samuel Clemens wrote *Huckleberry Finn*," "Mark Twain" and "Samuel Clemens" are not, in fact, co-referential expressions, since the "Sinn" or sense of "Mark Twain" is not the same as the sense of "Samuel Clemens." In this way, Frege uses the distinction between sense and reference to maintain the above compositionality principle in the face of apparent counterexamples.

Frege offers a number of proposals concerning the relationship between sense, reference, and subjective idea. For one, Frege insists that sense cannot be understood as a subjective idea in someone's mind. Rather, he proposes that senses are objective in that they can be "grasped" by more than one mind, and at least in this respect are similar to Moore's "concepts" in "The Nature of Judgement." Intuitively, this is the idea that two speakers can mean the same thing by an expression beyond just using that expression to refer to the same object. For example, aside from simply using "Socrates" to refer to the same man, two or more speakers may think of Socrates under the description "the snub-nosed philosopher of antiquity." Similarly, Frege writes:

> The same sense is not always connected, even in the same man, with the same idea. The idea is subjective: one man's idea is not that of another. There result, as a matter of course, a variety of differences in the ideas associated with the same sense. A painter, a horseman, and a zoologist will probable connect different ideas with the name 'Bucephalus.' This constitutes an essential distinction between the idea and the sign's sense, which may be the common property of many and therefore is not a part or a mode of the individual mind. (59)

Second, Frege proposes that sense determines reference—that what an expression refers to is determined by its sense. For example, that "Socrates" refers to a particular man is determined by its sense, roughly in that "Socrates" refers to whatever uniquely satisfies the descriptive content given by the sense. This entails that if two speakers associate the same sense with an expression, the expression will refer to the same object. However, it allows that two speakers may refer to the same object with an expression despite associating different senses with that expression. For example, two speakers may refer to the same man with the expression "Socrates" even though one

162   Early Analytic Philosophy

speaker thinks of Socrates as the snub-nosed philosopher of antiquity while the other speaker thinks of Socrates as the philosopher of antiquity who drank hemlock, given that the same man meets both of these descriptive conditions. Third, Frege holds that an expression can have a sense but not have a reference. Frege provides the examples "the celestial body most distant from Earth" and "the least rapidly converging series" as expressions that may have a sense, but lack a reference (58). The reader is encouraged to reflect on these and the other roles that Frege assigns to sense and to ask whether the considerations that Frege uses to motivate the sense/reference distinction support his myriad claims about sense and its relation to reference.

"The Thought" was one of Frege's last articles and was intended to be a chapter in a logic textbook; Frege also completed two further articles intended for this purpose, "Negation" ([1918] 1997) and "Compound Thoughts" ([1923] 1963). Yet despite being written more than twenty-five years after "On Sinn and Bedeutung," "The Thought" continues with several similar themes. One of these is Frege's "realism" about sense: the idea that senses—as meanings of words and sentences, in one sense of "meaning"—are objective, mind-independent entities that can be grasped by multiple language users. Indeed, Frege argues in "The Thought" that a "third realm must be recognized" for what he calls "thoughts," which are the senses of whole sentences (302). His case for this conclusion is essentially that thoughts can be understood as occupying neither the inner world of subjective ideas nor the outer world of physical objects. In "The Thought," Frege appeals to mathematical examples. Thus he writes:

> Thus the thought ... which we expressed in the Pythagorean theorem is timelessly true, true independently of whether anyone takes it to be true. It needs no bearer. It is not true for the first time when it is discovered, but is like a planet which, already before anyone has seen it, has been in interaction with other planets. (302)

Similarly:

> If the thought I express in the Pythagorean theorem can be recognized by others just as much as by me then it does not belong to the content of my consciousness, I am not its bearer; yet I can, nevertheless, recognize it to be true. (301)

Frege is especially at pains to argue against "psychological" or "subjective" conceptions of sense or meaning, arguing that they lead to a number of implausible conclusions. For example, in "The Thought," he writes:

Gottlob Frege: Logic and the Philosophy of Language   **163**

However, if it is not the same thought at all which is taken to be the content of the Pythagorean theorem by me and by another person, one should not really say "the Pythagorean theorem" but "my Pythagorean theorem", "his Pythagorean theorem" and these would be different ... Then my thought can be the content of my consciousness and his thought the content of his. Could the sense of my Pythagorean theorem be true while that of his was false? ... Then truth would be restricted to the content of my consciousness and it would remain doubtful whether anything at all comparable occurred in the consciousness of others. (301)

While offering various arguments against this kind of idea, Frege's strategy is essentially to point out how counterintuitive it seems to think, say, that the Pythagoreon theorem—or, indeed, the truths of science and everyday life— are in fact truths about individual minds as opposed to truths about a mind-independent, objective reality. The reader is encouraged to reflect on these discussions and to consider whether the intuitive idea, for instance, that different language users can mean the same thing by an expression or sentence, or that science and mathematics are concerned with a mind-independent realities, mandates positing senses and thoughts as mind-independent entities occupying what Frege describes as a "third realm."

Concluding remarks

Frege's contributions to logic, the foundations of mathematics, and the philosophy of language are unparalleled. Further, while certainly differing in the details, like Moore in his early work, Frege championed an anti-psychologistic conception of thought, with thoughts consisting of mind-independent entities that could be grasped by more than one person.

Aside from the content of Frege's views in logic and the philosophy of language, Russell saw in Frege a new kind of method for doing philosophy, an approach focused, in part, on the careful analysis of language and meaning, and Russell credited Frege with providing the "first complete example" of the "logico-analytic method in philosophy." Russell described this method as "something perfectly definite, capable of embodiment in maxims, and adequate, in all branches of philosophy, to yield whatever objective scientific knowledge it is possible to obtain" ([1914] 2009: xv). In the next chapter, we will see some examples of this method and how Russell applied it to various philosophical issues.

Further reading

Primary sources

Frege, G. ([1884] 1980), *The Foundations of Arithmetic*, Chicago: Northwestern University Press.

Frege, G. ([1891] 1997), "On Function and Concept", in M. Beaney (ed.), *The Frege Reader*, Oxford: Blackwell Publishing.

Frege, G. ([1893, 1903] 2013), *Basic Laws of Arithmetic*, Vol. 1 and 2, Oxford: Oxford University Press.

Frege, G. (1893] 1997), "On Concept and Object", in M. Beaney (ed.), *The Frege Reader*, Oxford: Blackwell Publishing.

Secondary sources

Beaney, M. (1997), "Introduction", in M. Beaney (ed.), *The Frege Reader*, Oxford: Blackwell Publishing.

Dummett, M. (1973), *Frege: Philosophy of Language*, London: Duckworth.

Heck, R. and May, R. (2006), "Frege's Contribution to the Philosophy of Language", in E. Lepore and B. Smith (eds), *The Oxford Handbook of Philosophy of Language*, Oxford: Oxford University Press.

Irvine, A. and Deutsch, H. (2016), "Russell's Paradox", *Stanford Encyclopedia of Philosophy*. Available online: https://plato.stanford.edu/entries/russell-paradox/

Sluga, H. (1980), *Gottlob Frege*, London: Routledge and Keegan Paul.

Zalta, E. (2019), "Gottlob Frege", *Stanford Encyclopedia of Philosophy*. Avaiable online: https://plato.stanford.edu/entries/frege/

Gottlob Frege: Logic and the Philosophy of Language · 165

Readings

Frege, G. "On *Sinn* and *Bedeutung*".
Reprinted from Frege, G. (1997), "On *Sinn* and *Bedeutung*", in M. Beaney (ed.), *The Frege Reader*, Oxford: Blackwell (pp. 151–71). Originally published in German as "Über Sinn und Bedeutung," in *Zeitshcrift für Philosophie and philosophische Kritik* (1892, vol. 100), pp. 25–50.

Equality[1] gives rise to challenging questions which are not altogether easy to answer. Is it a relation? A relation between objects, or between names or signs of objects? In my *Begriffsschrift* I assumed the latter.[2] The reasons which seem to favour this are the following: $a = a$ and $a = b$ are obviously statements of differing cognitive value [*Erkenntniswert*]; $a = a$ holds *a priori* and, according to Kant, is to be labelled analytic, while statements of the form $a = b$ often contain very valuable extensions of our knowledge and cannot always be established *a priori*. The discovery that the rising sun is not new every morning, but always the same, was one of the most fertile astronomical discoveries. Even today the reidentification of a small planet or a comet is not always a   matter of course. Now if we were to regard equality as a relation between that which the names '*a*' and '*b*' designate [*bedeuten*], it would seem that $a = b$ could not differ from $a = a$, i.e. provided $a = b$ is true. A relation would thereby be expressed of a thing to itself, and indeed one in which each thing stands to itself but to no other thing. What we apparently want to state by $a = b$ is that the signs or names '*a*' and '*b*' designate [*beteuten*] the same thing, so that those signs themselves would be under discussion; a relation between them would be asserted. But this relation would hold between the names or signs only in so far as they named or designated something. It would be mediated by the connection of each of the two signs with the same designated thing. But this is arbitrary. Nobody can be forbidden to use any arbitrarily producible event or object as a sign for something. In that case the sentence $a = b$ would no longer be concerned with the subject matter, but only with its mode of designation; we would express no proper knowledge by its means. But in many cases this is just what we want to do. If

---

[1] I use this word in the sense of identity [*Identität*] and understand '$a = b$' to have the sense of 'a is the same as b' or 'a and b coincide'.

[2] See esp. *BS*, §8 (pp. 64-5 above). [Editor's note: as explained in the Preface, references and footnotes in the original texts have been retained unaltered. Thus in this context, "pp. 64-65 above" refers to pp. 64-65 in the source text from which "On Sinn and Bedeutung" was pulled, as given above. In the present case, some of these references and footnotes were added by previous editors; these also remain in the text unaltered.]

the sign 'a' is distinguished from the sign 'b' only as an object (here, by means of its shape), not as a sign (i.e. not by the manner in which it designates something), the cognitive value of a = a becomes essentially equal to that of a = b, provided a = b is true. A difference can arise only if the difference between the signs corresponds to a difference in the mode of presentation [*Art des Gegebenseins*] of the thing designated. Let a, b, c be the lines connecting the vertices of a triangle with the midpoints of the opposite sides. The point of intersection of a and b is then the same as the point of intersection of b and c. So we have different designations for the same point, and these names ('point of intersection of a and b', 'point of intersection of b and c') likewise indicate the mode of presentation; and hence the statement contains actual knowledge.[3]

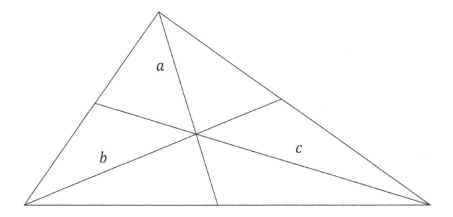

It is natural, now, to think of there being connected with a sign (name, combination of words, written mark), besides which the sign designates, which may be called the *Bedeutung* of the sign, also what I should like to call the *sense* of the sign, wherein the mode of presentation is contained. In our example, accordingly, the *Bedeutung* of the expressions 'the point of intersection of a and b' and 'the point of intersection of b and c' would be the same, but not their sense. The *Bedeutung* of the 'Evening Star' would be the same as that of 'Morning Star', but not the sense.

It is clear from the context that by sign and name I have here understood any designation figuring as a proper name, which thus has as its *Bedeutung* a

---

[3] A diagram is added here to illustrate Frege's example. Compare this (rather simpler example) with the geometrical example Frege gave in *BS* in motivating his earlier distinction between 'content' and 'mode of determination of content' (see pp. 64-5 above). On the relationship between Frege's earlier and later views, see the Introduction, pp. 21-2 above.

Gottlob Frege: Logic and the Philosophy of Language 167

definite object (this word taken in the widest range), but not a concept or a relation, which shall be discussed further in another article.[4] The designation of a single object can also consist of several words or other signs. For brevity, let every such designation be called a proper name.

The sense of a proper name is grasped by everybody who is sufficiently familiar with the language or totality of designations to which it belongs;[5] but this serves to illuminate only a single aspect of the *Bedeutung*, supposing it to have one. Comprehensive knowledge of the *Bedeutung* would require us to be able to say immediately whether any given sense attaches to it. To such knowledge we never attain.

The regular connection between a sign, its sense and its *Bedeutung* is of such a kind that to the sign there corresponds a definite sense and to that in turn a definite *Bedeutung*, while to a given *Bedeutung* (an object) there does not belong only a single sign. The same sense has different expressions in different languages or even in the same language. To be sure, exceptions to this regular behaviour occur. To every expression belonging to a complete totality of signs, there should certainly correspond a definite sense; but natural languages often do not satisfy this condition, and one must be content if the same word has the same sense in the same context. It may perhaps be granted that every grammatically well-formed expression figuring as a proper name always has a sense. But this is not to say that to the sense there also corresponds a *Bedeutung*. The words 'the celestial body most distant from the Earth' have a sense, but it is very doubtful if they also have a *Bedeutung*. The expression 'the least rapidly convergent series' has a sense, but demonstrably there is no *Bedeutung*, since for every given convergent series, another convergent, but less rapidly convergent, series can be found. In grasping a sense, one is not thereby assured of a *Bedeutung*.

If words are used in the ordinary way, what one intends to speak of is their *Bedeutung*. It can also happen, however, that one wishes to talk about the words themselves or their sense. This happens, for instance, when the words of another are quoted. One's own words then first designate [*bedeuten*] words

---

[4] See 'On Concept and Object', pp. 181-93 below.

[5] In the case of an actual proper name such as 'Aristotle' opinions as to the sense may differ. It might, for instance, be taken to be the following: the pupil of Plato and teacher of Alexander the Great. Anybody who does this will attach another sense to the sentence 'Aristotle was born in Stagira' than will someone who takes as the sense of the name: the teacher of Alexander the Great who was born in Stagira. So long as the *Bedeutung* remains the same, such as variations of sense may be tolerated, although they are to be avoided in the theoretical structure of a demonstrative science and ought not to occur in a perfect language.

Early Analytic Philosophy

of the other speaker, and only the latter have their usual *Bedeutung*. We then have signs of signs. In writing, the words are in this case enclosed in quotation marks. Accordingly, a word standing between quotation marks must not be taken as having its ordinary *Bedeutung*.

In order to speak of the sense of an expression 'A' one may simply use the phrase 'the sense of the expression "A"'. In indirect speech one talks about the sense, e.g., of another person's remarks. It is quite clear that in this way of speaking words do not have their customary *Bedeutung* but designate [*bedeuten*] what is usually their sense. In order to have a short expression, we will say: in indirect speech, words are used *indirectly* or have their *indirect Bedeutung*. We distinguish accordingly the *customary* from the *indirect Bedeutung* of a word; and its *customary* sense from its *indirect* sense. The indirect *Bedeutung* of a word is accordingly its customary sense. Such exceptions must always be borne in mind if the mode of connection between sign, sense and *Bedeutung* in particular cases is to be correctly understood.

The *Bedeutung* and sense of a sign are to be distinguished from the associated idea [*Vorstellung*]. If the *Bedeutung* of a sign is an object perceivable by the senses, my idea of it is an internal image, arising from memories of sense impressions which I have had and acts, both internal and external, which I have performed.[6] Such an idea is often imbued with feeling; the clarity of its separate parts varies and oscillates. The same sense is not always connected, even in the same man, with the same idea. The idea is subjective: one man's idea is not that of another. There result, as a matter of course, a variety of differences in the ideas associated with the same sense. A painter, a horseman, and a zoologist will probably connect different ideas with the name 'Bucephalus'. This constitutes an essential distinction between the idea and the sign's sense, which may be the common property of many people, and so is not a part or a model of the individual mind. For one can hardly deny that mankind has a common store of thoughts which is transmitted from one generation to another.[7]

In the light of this, one need have no scruples in speaking simply of *the* sense, whereas in the case of an idea one must, strictly speaking, add whom it belongs to and at what time. It might perhaps be said: just as one man connects

---

[6]We may include with ideas intuitions [*Anschauungen*]: here, sense impressions and acts themselves take the place of the traces which they have left in the mind. The distinction is unimportant for our purpose, especially since memories of sense impressions and acts always go along with such impressions and acts themselves to complete the perceptual image [*Anschauungsbild*]. One may on the other hand understand intuition as including any object in so far as it is sensibly perceptible or spatial.
[7]Hence it is inadvisable to use the word 'idea' to designate something so basically different.

Gottlob Frege: Logic and the Philosophy of Language 169

this idea, and another that idea, with the same word, so also one man can associate this sense and another that sense. But there still remains a difference in the mode of connection. They are not prevented from grasping the same sense; but they cannot have the same idea. *Si duo idem faciunt, non est idem.* If two persons picture the same thing, each still has his own idea. It is indeed sometimes possible to establish differences in the ideas, or even in the sensations, of different men; but an exact comparison is not possible, because we cannot have both ideas together in the same consciousness.

The *Bedeutung* of a proper name is the object itself which we designate by using it; the idea which we have in that case is wholly subjective; in between lies the sense, which is indeed no longer subjective like the idea, but is yet not the object itself. The following analogy will perhaps clarify these relationships. Somebody observes the Moon through a telescope. I compare the Moon itself to the *Bedeutung*; it is the object of the observation, mediated by the real image projected by the object glass in the interior of the telescope, and by the retinal image of the observer. The former I compare to the sense, the latter is like the idea or intuition [*Anschauung*]. The optical image in the telescope is indeed one-sided and dependent upon the standpoint of observation; but it is still objective, inasmuch as it can be used by several observers. At any rate it could be arranged for several to use it simultaneously. But each one would have his own retinal image. On account of the diverse shapes of the observers' eyes, even a geometrical congruence could hardly be achieved, and an actual coincidence would be out of the question. This analogy might be developed still further, by assuming A's retinal image made visible to B; or A might also see his own retinal image in a mirror. In this way we might perhaps show how an idea can itself be taken as an object, but as such is not for the observer what it directly is for the person having the idea. But to pursue this would take us too far afield.

We can now recognize three levels of difference between words, expressions, or whole sentences. The difference may concern at most the ideas, or the sense but not the *Bedeutung*, or, finally, the *Bedeutung* as well. With respect to the first level, it is to be noted that, on account of the uncertain connection of ideas with words, a difference may hold for one person, which another does not find. The difference between a translation and the original text should properly not overstep the first level. To the possible differences here belong also the colouring and shading which poetic eloquence seeks to give to the sense. Such colouring and shading are not objective, and must be evoked by each hearer or reader according to the hints of the poet or the speaker. Without some affinity in human ideas art would certainly be impossible; but it can never be exactly determined how far the intentions of the poet are realized.

170   Early Analytic Philosophy

In what follows there will be no further discussion of ideas and intuitions; they have been mentioned here only to ensure that the idea aroused in the hearer by a word shall not be confused with its sense or its *Bedeutung*.

To make short and exact expressions possible, let the following phraseology be established:

A proper name (word, sign, combination of signs, expression) *expresses* its sense, *stands for* [*bedeutet*] or *designates* [*bezeichnet*] its *Bedeutung*. By employing a sign we express its sense and designate its *Bedeutung*.

Idealists or sceptics will perhaps long since have objected: 'you talk, without further ado, of the Moon as an object; but how do you know that the name "the Moon" has any *Bedeutung*? How do you know that anything whatsoever has a *Bedeutung*?' I reply that when we say 'the Moon', we do not intend to speak of our idea of the Moon, nor are we satisfied with the sense alone, but we presuppose a *Bedeutung*. To assume that in the sentence 'The Moon is smaller than the Earth' the idea of the Moon is in question, would be flatly to misunderstand the sense. If this is what the speaker wanted, he would use the phrase 'my idea of the Moon'. Now we can of course be mistaken in the presupposition, and such mistakes have indeed occurred. But the question whether the presupposition is perhaps always mistaken need not be answered here; in order to justify speaking of the *Bedeutung* of a sign, it is enough, at first, to point out our intention in speaking or thinking. (We must then add the reservation: provided such a *Bedeutung* exists.)

So far we have considered the sense and *Bedeutung* only of such expressions, words, or signs as we have called proper names. We now inquire concerning the sense and *Bedeutung* of an entire assertoric sentence. Such a sentence contains a thought.[8] Is this thought, now, to be regarded as its sense or its *Bedeutung*? Let us assume for the time being that the sentence has a *Bedeutung*. If we now replace one word of the sentence by another having the same *Bedeutung*, but a difference sense, this can have no effect upon the *Bedeutung* of the sentence. Yet we can see that in such a case the thought changes; since, e.g., the thought in the sentence 'The Morning Star is a body illuminated by the Sun' differs from that in the sentence 'The Evening Star is a body illuminated by the Sun'. Anybody who did not know that the Evening Star is the Morning Star might hold the one thought to be true, the other false. The thought, accordingly, cannot be the *Bedeutung* of the sentence, but must rather

---

[8] By a thought I understand not the subjective performance of thinking but its objective content, which is capable of being the common property of several thinkers.

Gottlob Frege: Logic and the Philosophy of Language **171**

be considered as its sense. What is the position now with regard to the *Bedeutung*? Have we a right even to inquire about it? Is it possible that a sentence as a whole has only a sense, but no *Bedeutung*? At any rate, one might expect that such sentences occur, just as there are parts of sentences having sense but no *Bedeutung*. And sentences which contain proper names without *Bedeutung* will be of this kind. The sentence 'Odysseus was set ashore at Ithaca while sound asleep' obviously has a sense. But since it is doubtful whether the name 'Odysseys', occurring therein, has a *Bedeutung*, it is also doubtful whether the whole sentence does. Yet it is certain, nevertheless, that anyone who seriously took the sentence to be true or false would ascribe to the name 'Odysseus' a *Bedeutung*, not merely a sense; for it is of the *Bedeutung* of the name that the predicate is affirmed or denied. Whoever does not admit the name has a *Bedeutung* can neither apply nor withhold the predicate. But in that case it would be superfluous to advance to the *Bedeutung* of the name; one could be satisfied with the sense, if one wanted to go no further than the thought, it would be needles to bother with the *Bedeutung* of a part of the sentence; only the sense, not the *Bedeutung*, of the part is relevant to the sense of the whole sentence. The thought remains the same whether 'Odysseus' has a *Bedeutung* or not. The fact that we concern ourselves at all about the *Bedeutung* of a part of the sentence indicates that we generally recognize and expect a *Bedeutung* for the sentence itself. The thought loses value for us as soon as we recognize that the *Bedeutung* of one of its parts is missing. We are therefore justified in not being satisfied with the sense of a sentence, and in inquiring also as to its *Bedeutung*. But now why do we want every proper name to have not only a sense but also a *Bedeutung*? Why is the thought not enough for us? Because, and to the extent that, we are concerned with its truth-value. This is not always the case. In hearing an epic poem, for instance, apart from the euphony of the language we are interested only in the sense of the sentences and the images and feelings thereby aroused. The question of truth would cause us to abandon aesthetic delight for an attitude of scientific investigation. Hence it is a matter of no concern to us whether the name 'Odysseys', for instance, has a *Bedeutung*, so long as we accept the poem as a work of art.[9] It is the striving for truth that drives us always to advance from the sense to the *Bedeutung*.

---

[9]It would be desirable to have a special term for signs intended to have only sense. If we name them say, representations [*Bilder*], the words of the actors on the stage would be representations; indeed the actor himself would be a representation.

We have seen that the *Bedeutung* of a sentence may always be sought, whenever the *Bedeutung* of its components is involved; and that this is the case when and only when we are inquiring after the truth-value.

We are therefore driven into accepting the *truth-value* of a sentence as constituting its *Bedeutung*. By the truth-value of a sentence I understand the circumstance that it is true or false. There are no further truth-values. For brevity I call the one the True, the other the False. Every assertoric sentence concerned with the *Bedeutung* of its words is therefore to be regarded as a proper name, and its *Bedeutung*, if it has one, is either the True or the False. These two objects are recognized, if only implicitly by everybody who judges something to be true – and so even by a sceptic. The designation of the truth-values as objects may appear to be an arbitrary fancy or perhaps a mere play upon words, from which no profound consequences could be drawn. What I am calling an object can be more exactly discussed only in connection with concept and relation. I will reserve this for another article.[10] But so much should already be clear, that in every judgment,[11] no matter how trivial, the step from the level of thoughts to the level of *Bedeutung* (the objective) has already been taken.

One might be tempted to regard the relation of the thought to the True not as that of sense to *Bedeutung*, but rather as that of subject to predicate. One can, indeed, say: 'The thought that 5 is a prime number is true'. But closer examination shows that nothing more has been said than in the simple sentence '5 is a prime number'. The truth claim arises in each case from the form of the assertoric sentence, and when the latter lacks its usual force, e.g., in the mouth of an actor upon the stage, even the sentence 'The thought that 5 is a prime number is true' contains only a thought, and indeed the same thought as the simple '5 is a prime number'. It follows that the relation of the thought to the True may not be compared with that of subject to predicate. Subject and predicate (understood in the logical sense) are just elements of thought; they stand on the same level for knowledge. By combining subject and predicate, one reaches only a thought, never passes from a sense to its *Bedeutung*, never from a thought to its truth-value. One moves at the same level but never advances from one level to the next. A truth-value cannot be a part of a thought, any more than, say, the Sun can, for it is not a sense but an object.

If our supposition that the *Bedeutung* of a sentence is its truth-value is correct, the latter must remain unchanged when a part of the sentence is

---

[10]See 'On Concept and Object', pp. 181-93 below.
[11]A judgement for me is not the mere grasping of a thought, but the admission [*Anerkennung*] of its truth.

Gottlob Frege: Logic and the Philosophy of Language   **173**

replaced by an expression with the same *Bedeutung*. And this is in fact the case. Leibniz gives the definition: '*Eadem sunt, quae sibi mutuo substituti possunt, salva veritate*'.[12] If we are dealing with sentences for which the *Bedeutung* of their component parts is at all relevant, then what feature except the truth-value can be found that belongs to such sentences quite generally and remains unchanged by substitutions of the kind just mentioned?

If now the truth-value of a sentence is its *Bedeutung*, then on the one hand all true sentences have the same *Bedeutung* and so, on the other hand, do all false sentences. From this we see that in the *Bedeutung* of the sentence all that is specific is obliterated. We can never be concerned only with the *Bedeutung* of a sentence; but again the mere thought alone yields no knowledge, but only the thought together with its *Bedeutung*, i.e. its truth-value. Judgements can be regarded as advances from a thought to a truth-value. Naturally this cannot be a definition. Judgement is something quite peculiar and incomparable. One might also say that judgements are distinctions of parts within truth-values. Such distinction occurs by a return to the thought. To every sense attaching to a truth-value would correspond its own manner of analysis. However, I have here used the word 'part' in a special sense. I have in fact transferred the relation between the parts and the whole of the sentence to its *Bedeutung*, by calling the *Bedeutung* of a word part of the *Bedeutung* of the sentence, if the word itself is a part of the sentence. This way of speaking can certainly be attacked, because the whole *Bedeutung* and one part of it do not suffice to determine the remainder, and because the word 'part' is already used of bodies in another sense. A special term would need to be invented.

The supposition that the truth-value of a sentence is its *Bedeutung* shall now be put to further test. We have found that the truth-value of a sentence remains unchanged when an expression in it is replaced by another with the same *Bedeutung*:[13] but we have not yet considered the case in which the expression to be replaced is itself a sentence. Now if our view is correct, the truth-value of a sentence containing another as part must remain unchanged when the part is replaced by another sentence having the same truth-value. Exceptions are to be expected when the whole sentence or its part is direct or indirect quotation; for in such cases, as we have seen, the words to not have their customary *Bedeutung*. In direct quotation, a sentence designates [*bedeutet*] another sentence, and in indirect speech a thought.

---

[12]"Those things are the same which can be substituted for one another without loss of truth." This is just the same Leibnizian principle that Frege took as his definition of identity in §65 of the *Foundations* (the difference in formulation is trivial); see p. 112 above.

[13]"Wenn wir darin einen Ausdruck durch einen gleichbedeutenden ersetzen".

174   Early Analytic Philosophy

We are thus led to consider subordinate sentences or clauses. These occur as parts of a sentence complex, which is, from the logical standpoint, likewise a sentence – a main sentence. But here we meet the question whether it is also true of the subordinate sentence that its *Bedeutung* is a truth-value. Of indirect speech we already know the opposite. Grammarians view subordinate clauses as representatives of parts of sentences and divide them accordingly into noun clauses, adjective clauses, adverbial clauses. This might generate the supposition that the *Bedeutung* of a subordinate clause was not a truth-value but rather of the same kind as the *Bedeutung* of a noun or adjective or adverb – in short, of a part of a sentence, whose sense was not a thought but only a part of a thought. Only a more thorough investigation can clarify the issue. In so doing, we shall not follow the grammatical categories strictly, but rather group together what is logically of the same kind. Let us first search for cases in which the sense of the subordinate clause, as we have just supposed, is not an independent thought.

The case of an abstract noun clause,[14] introduced by 'that', includes the case of indirect speech, in which we have seen the words to have their indirect *Bedeutung*, coincident with what is customarily their sense. In this case, then, the subordinate clause has for its *Bedeutung* a thought, not a truth-value, and for its sense not a thought, but the sense of the words 'the thought . . .', which is only a part of the thought in the entire complex sentence. This happens after 'say', 'hear', 'be of the opinion', 'be convinced', 'conclude', and similar words.[15] There is a different, and indeed somewhat complicated, situation after words like 'recognize', 'know', 'fancy',[16] which are to be considered later.

That in the case of the first kind the *Bedeutung* of the subordinate clause is in fact the thought can also be recognized by seeing that it is indifferent to the truth of the whole whether the subordinate clause is true or false. Let us compare, for instance, the two sentences 'Copernicus believed that the planetary orbits are circles' and 'Copernicus believed that the apparent motion of the Sun is produced by the real motion of the Earth'. One subordinate clause can be substitutued for the other without harm to the truth. The main clause and the subordinate clause together have as their sense only a single thought, and the truth of the whole includes neither the truth nor the untruth of the subordinate

---

[14]Frege probably means clauses grammatically replaceable by an abstract noun-phrase; e.g. 'Smith denies *that dragons exist*' = 'Smith denies *the existence of dragons*'; or again, in this context, after 'denies', 'that Brown is wise' is replaceable by 'the wisdom of Brown'. (*Tr.*)

[15]In 'A lied that he had seen B', the subordinate clause designates [*bedeutet*] a thought, of which it is being said, firstly, that A asserted it as true, and secondly, that A was convinced of its falsity.

[16]The German words here are 'erkennen', 'wissen' and 'wähnen'. The last means 'to imagine', but with the implication of doing so *wrongly*.

Gottlob Frege: Logic and the Philosophy of Language 175

clause. In such cases it is not permissible to replace one expression in the subordinate clause by another having the same customary *Bedeutung*, but only by one having the same indirect *Bedeutung*, i.e. the same customary sense. Somebody might conclude: the *Bedeutung* of a sentence is not its truth-value, for in that case it could always be replaced by another sentence of the same truth-value. But this proves too much; one might just as well claim that the *Bedeutung* of 'Morning Star' is not Venus, since one may not always say 'Venus' in place of 'Morning Star'. One has the right to conclude only that the *Bedeutung* of a sentence is not *always* its truth value, and that 'Morning Star' does not always stand for [*bedeutet*] the planet venus, viz. when the word has its indirect *Bedeutung*. An exception of such a kind occurs in the subordinate clause just considered, which has a thought as its *Bedeutung*.

If one says 'It seems that . . .' one means [*meint*] 'It seems to me that . . .' or 'I think that . . .'. We therefore have the same case again. The situation is similar in the case of expressions such as 'to be pleased', 'to regret', 'to approve', 'to blame', 'to hope', 'to fear'. If, toward the end of the battle of Waterloo,[17] Wellington was glad that the Prussians were coming, the basis for his joy was a conviction. Had he been deceived, he would have been no less pleased so long as his illusion lasted; and before he became so convinced he could not have been pleased that the Prussians were coming – even though in fact they might have been already approaching.

Just as a conviction or a belief is the ground of a feeling, it can, as in inference, also be the ground of a conviction. In the sentence 'Columbus inferred from the roundness of the Earth that he could reach India by travelling towards the west', we have as the *Bedeutungen* of the parts two thoughts, that the earth is round, and that Columbus by travelling to the west could reach India. All that is relevant here is that Columbus was convinced of both, and that the one conviction was a ground for the other. Whether the Earth is really round and Columbus could really reach India be travelling west, as he thought, is immaterial to the truth of our sentence; but it is not immaterial whether we replace 'the Earth' by 'the planet which is accompanied by a moon whose diameter is greater than the fourth part of its own'. Here also we have the indirect Bedeutung of the words.

Adverbial final clauses beginning 'in order that' also belong here; for obviously the purpose is a thought; therefore: indirect *Bedeutung* for the words, subjective mood.

A subordinate clause with 'that' after 'command', 'ask', 'forbid', would appear in direct speech as an imperative. Such a sentence has no *Bedeutung* but only

---

[17]Frege uses the Prussian name for the battle 'Belle-Alliance'. (*Tr.*)

176   Early Analytic Philosophy

a sense. A command, a request, are indeed not thoughts, but they stand on the same level as thoughts. Hence in subordinate clauses depending upon 'command', 'ask', etc., words have a truth-value but a command, a request, and so forth.

The case is similar for the dependent question in phrases such as 'doubt whether', 'not to know what'. It is easy to see that here also the words are to be taken to have their indirect *Bedeutung*. Dependent clauses expressing questions beginning with 'who', 'what', 'where', 'when', 'how', 'by what means', etc., seem at times to approximate very closely to adverbial clauses in which words have their customary *Bedeutung*. These cases are distinguished linguistically [in German] by the mood of the verb. With the subjunctive, we have a dependent question and the words have their indirect *Bedeutung*, so that a proper name cannot in general be replaced by another name of the same object.

In the cases so far considered the words of the subordinate clauses had their indirect *Bedeutung*, and this made it clear that the *Bedeutung* of the subordinate clause itself was indirect, i.e. not a truth-value but a thought, a command, a request, a question. The subordinate clause could be regarded as a noun, indeed one could say: as a proper name of that thought, that command, etc., which it represented in the context of the sentence structure.

We now come to other subordinate clauses in which the words do have their customary *Bedeutung* without however a thought occurring as sense and a truth-value as *Bedeutung*. How this is possible is best made clear by examples.

'Whoever discovered the elliptic form of the planetary orbits died in misery.'

If the sense of the subordinate clause were here a thought, it would have to be possible to express it also in a separate sentence. But it does not work, because the grammatical subject 'whoever' has no independent sense and only mediates the relation with the consequent clause 'died in misery'. For this reason the sense of the subordinate clause is not a complete thought, and its *Bedeutung* is Kepler, not a truth-value. One might object that the sense of the whole does contain a thought as part, viz. that there was somebody who first discovered the elliptic form of the planetary orbits; for whoever takes the whole to be true cannot deny this part. This is undoubtedly so; but only because otherwise the dependent clause 'whoever discovered the elliptic form of the planetary orbits' would have no *Bedeutung*. If anything is asserted there is always an obvious presupposition that the simple of compound proper names used have a *Bedeutung*. If therefore one asserts 'Kepler died in misery', there is a presupposition that the name 'Kepler' designates something; but it does not follow that the sense of the sentence 'Kepler died in misery' contains the

Gottlob Frege: Logic and the Philosophy of Language   177

thought that the name 'Kepler' designates something. If this were the case the negation would have run not

'Kepler died in misery',

but

'Kepler did not die in misery, or the name "Kepler" is *Bedeutungslos*'.

That the name 'Kepler' designates something is just as much a presupposition for the assertion

'Kepler died in misery'

as for the contrary assertion. Now languages have the fault of containing expressions which fail to designate an object (although their grammatical form seems to qualify them for that purpose) because the truth of some sentence is a prerequisite. Thus it depends on the truth of the sentence

'There was someone who discovered the elliptic form of the planetary orbits'

whether the subordinate clause

'whoever discovered the elliptic form of the planetary orbits'

really designates an object, or only seems to do so while in fact is *Bedeutungslos*. And thus it may appear as if our subordinate clause contained as a part of its sense the thought that there was somebody who discovered the elliptic form of the planetary orbits. If this were right, the negation would run:

'Either whoever discovered the elliptic form of the planetary orbits did not die in misery or there was nobody who discovered the elliptic form of the planetary orbits'.

This arises from an imperfection of language, from which even the symbolic language of mathematical analysis is not altogether free; even there combinations of symbols can occur that seem to stand for [*bedeuten*] something but (at least so far) are *Bedeutungslos*, e.g. divergent infinite series. This can be avoided, e.g., by means of the special stipulation that divergent infinite series shall stand for [*bedeuten*] the number 0.[18] A logically perfect language (*Begriffsschrift*) should satisfy the conditions that every expression grammatically well constructed as a proper name out of signs-already introduced shall in fact

---

[18]Cf. *GG*, I, §11; see Appendix 2 below.

178 Early Analytic Philosophy

designate an object, and that no new sign shall be introduced as a proper name without being secured a *Bedeutung*. The logic books contain warnings against logical mistakes arising from the ambiguity of expressions. I regard as no less pertinent a warning against apparent proper names that have no *Bedeutung*. The history of mathematics supplies errors which have arisen in this way. This lends itself to demagogic abuse as easily as ambiguity – perhaps more easily. 'The will of the people' can serve as an example; for it is easy to establish that there is at any rate no generally accepted *Bedeutung* for this expression. It is therefore by no means important to eliminate the source of these mistakes, at least in science, once and for all. Then such objections as the one discussed above would become impossible, because it could never depend upon the truth of a thought whether a proper name had a *Bedeutung*.

With the consideration of these noun clauses may be coupled that of types of adjectives and adverbial clauses which are logically in close relation to them.

Adjective clauses also serve to construct compound proper names, though, unlike noun clauses, they are not sufficient by themselves for this purpose. These adjective clauses are to be regarded as equivalent to adjectives. Instead of 'the square root of 4 which is smaller than 0', one can also say 'the negative square root of 4'. We have here the case of a compound proper name constructed from the expression for a concept with the help of a singular definite article. This is at any rate permissible if the concept applies to one and only one single object.[19] Expressions for concepts can be so constructed that marks[20] of a concept are given by adjective clauses as, in our example, by the clause 'which is smaller than 0'. It is evident that such an adjective clause cannot have a thought as sense or a truth-value as *Bedeutung*, any more than a noun clause could. Its sense, which can also in many cases be expressed by a single adjective, is only a part of a thought. Here, as in the case of the noun clause, there is no independent subject and therefore no possibility of reproducing the sense of the subordinate clause in an independent sentence.

Places, instants, stretches of time, logically considered, are objects; hence the linguistic designation of a definite place, a definite instant, or a stretch of time is to be regarded as a proper name. Now adverbial clauses of place and time can be used to construct such a proper name in much the same way as we have seen

---

[19]In accordance with what was said above, an expression of the kind in question must actually always be assured of a *Bedeutung*, by means of a special stipulation, e.g. by the convention that 0 shall count as its *Bedeutung* when the concept applies to no object or to more than one. [See fn. 11 above. (fn. 19 in transcription)]

[20]For the notion of a 'mark' ('Merkmal'), see *GL*, §53 (pp. 102-3 above); *CO*, pp. 189-90 below.

Gottlob Frege: Logic and the Philosophy of Language   179

noun and adjective clauses can. In the same way, expressions for concepts that apply to places, etc., can be constructed. It is to be noted here also that the sense of these subordinate clauses cannot be reproduced in an independent sentence, since an essential component, viz. the determination of place or time, is missing and is just indicated by a relative pronoun or a conjunction.[21]

In conditional clauses, also, there most often recognizably occurs an indefinite indicator, with a correlative indicator in the dependent clause. (We have already seen this occur in noun, adjective, and adverbial clauses.) In so far as each indicator relates to the other, both clauses together form a connected whole, which as a rule expresses only a single thought. In the sentence

'If a number is less than 1 and greater than 0, its square is less than 1 and greater than 0'

the component in question is 'a number' in the antecedent clause and 'its' in the consequent clause. It is by means of this very indefiniteness that the sense acquires the generality expected of a law. It is this which is responsible for the fact that the antecedent clause alone has no complete thought as its sense and in combination with the consequent clause expresses one and only one thought, whose parts are no longer thoughts. It is, in general, incorrect to say that in the hypothetical judgement two judgements are put in reciprocal relationship. If this or something similar is said, the word judgement is used in the same sense as I have connected with the word 'thought', so that I would use the formulation: 'A hypothetical thought establishes a reciprocal relationship between two thoughts'. This could be true only if an indefinite indicator is absent;[22] but in such a case there would also be no generality.

---

[21]In the case of these sentences, various interpretations are easily possible. The sense of the sentence 'After Schleswig-Holstein was separated from Denmark, Prussia and Austria quarelled' can also be rendered in the form 'After the separation of Schleswig-Holstein from Denmark, Prussia and Austria quarrelled'. In this version, it is surely sufficiently clear that the sense is not to be taken as having as a part the thought that Schleswig-Holstein was once separated from Denmark, but that this is the necessary presupposition in order for the expression 'after the separation of Schleswig-Holstein from Denmark' to have a *Bedeutung* at all. To be sure, our sentence can also be interpreted as saying that Schleswig-Holstein was once separated from Denmark. We then have a case which is to be considered later. In order to understand the difference more clearly, let us project ourselves into the mind of a Chinese who, having little knowledge of European history, believes it to be false that Shleswig-Holstein was ever separated from Denmark. He will take out sentence, in the first version, to be neither true nor false but will deny it to have any *Bedeutung*, on the ground that its subordinate clause lacks a *Bedeutung*. This clause would only apparently determine a time. If he interpreted our sentence in the second way, however, he would find a thought expressed in it which he would take to be false, beside a part which would be *bedeutungslos* for him.

[22]At times there is no linguistically explicit indicator and one must be read off from the entire context.

Early Analytic Philosophy

If an instant of time is to be indefinitely indicated in both the antecedent and the consequent clause, this is often achieved merely by using the present tense of the verb, which in such a case however does not indicate the temporal present. This grammatical form is then the indefinite indicator in the main and subordinate clauses. An example of this is: 'When the Sun is in the tropic of Cancer, the longest day in the northern hemisphere occurs'. Here, also, it is impossible to express the sense of the subordinate clause in a full sentence, because this sense is not a complete thought. If we say 'The Sun is in the tropic of Cancer', this would refer to our present time[23] and thereby change the sense. Neither is the sense of the main clause a thought; only the whole, composed of main and subordinate clauses, has such a sense. It may be added that several common components may be indefinitely indicated in the antecedent and consequent clauses.

It is clear that noun clauses with 'who' or 'what' and adverbial clauses with 'where', 'when', 'wherever', 'whenever' are often to be interpreted as having the sense of antecedent clauses, e.g. 'Who touches pitch, defiles himself'.

Adjective clauses can also take the place of conditional clauses. Thus the sense of the sentence previously used can be given in the form 'The square of a number which is less that 1 and greater than 0 is less than 1 and greater than 0'.

The situation is quite different if the common component of the two clauses is designated by a proper name. In the sentence:

'Napoleon, who recognized the danger to his right flank, himself led his guards against the enemy position'

two thoughts are expressed:

(1) Napoleon recognized the danger to his right flank;
(2) Napoleon himself led his guards against the enemy position.

When and where this happened is to be fixed only by the context, but is nevertheless to be taken as definitely determined thereby. If the entire sentence is uttered as an assertion, we thereby simultaneously assert both component sentences. If one of the parts is false, the whole is false. Here we have the case that the subordinate clause by itself has a complete thought as sense (if we complete it by indication of place and time). The *Bedeutung* of the subordinate clause is accordingly a truth-value. We can therefore expect that it may be replaced, without harm to the truth-value of the whole, by a sentence having the same truth-value. This is indeed the case; but it is to be noted that for purely

---

[23]'auf unsere Gegenwart beziehen'.

Gottlob Frege: Logic and the Philosophy of Language 181

grammatical reasons, its subject must be 'Napoleon', for only then can it be brought into the form of an adjective clause attaching to 'Napoleon'. But if the demand that it be expressed in this form is waived, and the connection shown by 'and', this restriction disappears.

Subsidiary clauses beginning with 'although' also express complete thoughts. This conjunction actually has no sense and does not change the sense of the clause but only illuminates it in a peculiar fashion.[24] We could indeed replace the concessive clause without harm to the truth of the whole by another of the same truth-value; but the light in which the clause is placed by the conjunction might then easily appear unsuitable, as if a song with a sad subject were to be sung in a lively fashion.

In the last cases the truth of the whole included the truth of the component clauses. The case is different if an antecedent clause expresses a complete thought by containing, in place of an indefinite indicator, a proper name or something which is to be regarded as equivalent. In the sentence

'If the Sun has already risen, the sky is very cloudy'

the time is the present, that is to say, definite. And the place is also to be thought of as definite. Here it can be said that a relation between the truth-values of antecedent and consequent clauses has been asserted, viz. that the case does not occur in which the antecedent stands for [*bedeute*] the True and the consequent for the False. Accordingly, our sentence is true if the Sun has not yet risen, whether the sky is very cloudy or not, and also if the Sun has risen and the sky is very cloudy. Since only truth-values are here in question, each component clause can be replaced by another of the same truth-value without changing the truth-value of the whole. To be sure, the light in which the subject then appears would usually be unsuitable; the thought might easily seem distorted; but this has nothing to do with its truth-value. One must always observe that there are overtones of subsidiary thoughts, which are however not explicitly expressed and therefore should not be reckoned in the sense. Hence, also, no account need be taken of their truth-values.[25]

The simplest cases have now been discussed. Let us review what we have learned.

The subordinate clause usually has for its sense not a thought, but only a part of one, and consequently no truth-value as *Bedeutung*. The reason for this is either

---

[24]Similarly in the case of 'but', 'yet'.

[25]The thought of our sentence might also be expressed thus: 'Either the Sun has not risen yet or the sky is very cloudy' which shows how this kind of sentence connection is to be understood.

182 **Early Analytic Philosophy**

that the words in the subordinate clause have their indirect *Bedeutung*, so that the *Bedeutung*, not the sense, of the subordinate clause is a thought; or else that, on account of the presence of an indefinite indicator, the subordinate clause is incomplete and expresses a thought only when combined with the main clause. It may happen, however, that the sense of the subsidiary clause is a complete thought, in which case it can be replaced by another of the same truth-value without harm to the truth of the whole – provided there are no grammatical obstacles.

An examination of all the subordinate clauses which one may encounter will soon provide some which do not fit well into these categories. The reason, so far as I can see, is that these subordinate clauses have no such simple sense. Almost always, it seems, we connect with the main thoughts expressed by us subsidiary thoughts which, although not expressed, are associated with our words, in accordance with psychological laws, by the hearer. And since the subsidiary thought appears to be connected with our words on its own account, almost like the main thought itself, we want it also to be expressed. The sense of the sentence is thereby enriched, and it may well happen that we have more simple thoughts than clauses. In many cases the sentence must be understood in this way. In others it may be doubtful whether the subsidiary thought belongs to the sense of the sentence or only accompanies it.[26] One might perhaps find that the sentence

'Napoleon, who recognized the danger to his right flank, himself led his guards against the enemy position'

expresses not only the two thoughts shown above, but also the thought that the knowledge of the danger was the reason why he led the guards against the enemy position. One may in fact doubt whether this thought is just slightly suggested or really expressed. Let the question be considered whether our sentence is false if Napoleon's decision had already been made before he recognized the danger. If our sentence could be true in spite of this, the subsidiary thought should not be understood as part of the sense. One would probably decide in favor of this. The alternative would make for a quite complicated situation: we would have more simple thoughts than clauses. If the sentence

'Napoleon recognized the danger to his right flank'

were now to be replaced by another having the same truth-value, e.g.

'Napoleon was already more than 45 years old',

---

[26]This may be important for the questions whether an assertion is a lie, or an oath a perjury.

Gottlob Frege: Logic and the Philosophy of Language   183

not only would our first thought be changed, but also our third one. Hence the truth-value of the latter might change – viz. if his age was not the reason for the decision to lead the guards against the enemy. This shows why clauses of equal truth-value cannot always be substituted for one another in such cases. The clause expresses more through its connection with another than it does in isolation.

Let us now consider cases where this regularly happens. In the sentence

'Bebel fancies [*wähnt*][27] that the return of Alsace-Lorraine would appease France's desire for revenge'

two thoughts are expressed, which are not however shown by means of antecedent and consequent clauses, viz.

(1) Bebel believes that the return of Alsace-Lorraine would appease France's desire for revenge;
(2) The return of Alsace-Lorraine would not appease France's desire for revenge.

In the expression of the first thought, the words of the subordinate clause have their indirect *Bedeutung*, while the same words have their customary *Bedeutung* in the expression of the second thought. This shows that the subordinate clause in our original complex sentence is to be taken twice over, with different *Bedeutungen*, of which one is a thought, the other a truth-value. Since the truth-value is not the whole *Bedeutung* of the subordinate clause, we cannot simply replace the latter by another of equal truth-value. Similar considerations apply to expressions such as 'know', 'recognize', 'it is well known'.[28]

By means of a subordinate causal clause and the associated main clause we express several thoughts, which however do not correspond separately to the original clauses. In the sentence 'Because ice is less dense than water, it floats on water' we have

(1) Ice is less dense than water;
(2) If anything is less dense than water, it floats on water;
(3) Ice floats on water.

The third thought, however, need not be explicitly introduced, since it is contained in the remaining two. On the other hand, neither the first and third nor

---

[27]See fn. 9 above (fn. 17 in transcription).
[28]'wissen', 'erkennen', 'es ist bekannt'.

Early Analytic Philosophy

the second and third combined would furnish the sense of our sentence. It can now be seen that our subordinate clause

'because ice is less dense than water'

expresses our first thought, as well as a part of our second. This is how it comes to pass that our subsidiary clause cannot be simply replaced by another of equal truth-value; for this would alter our second thought and thereby might well alter its truth-value.

The situation is similar in the sentence

'If iron were less dense than water, it would float on water'.

Here we have the two thoughts that iron is not less dense than water, and that something floats on water if it is less dense than water. The subsidiary clause again expresses one thought and a part of the other.

If we interpret the sentence already considered,

'After Schleswig-Holstein was separated from Denmark, Prussia and Austria quarrelled',

in such a way that it expresses the thought that Schleswig-Holstein was once separated from Denmark, we have first this thought, and secondly the thought that, at a time more closely determined by the subordinate clause, Prussia and Austria quarrelled. Here also the subordinate clause expresses not only one thought but also a part of another. Therefore it may not in general be replaced by another of the same truth-value.

It is hard to exhaust all the possibilities given by language; but I hope to have brought to light at least the essential reasons why a subordinate clause may not always be replaced by another of equal truth-value without harm to the truth of the whole sentence structure. These reasons arise:

(1) When the subordinate clause does not stand for [*bedeutet*] a truth-value, inasmuch as it expresses only a part of a thought;

(2) when the subordinate clause does not stand for [*bedeutet*] a truth-value, but is not restricted to so doing, inasmuch as its sense includes one thought and part of another.

The first case arises:

(a) for words having indirect *Bedeutung*,

(b) if a part of the sentence is only an indefinite indicator instead of a proper name.

In the second case, the subsidiary clause may have to be taken twice over, viz. once in its customary *Bedeutung*, and the other time in its indirect *Bedeutung*; or the sense of a part of the subordinate clause may likewise be a component of another thought, which, taken together with the thought directly expressed by the subordinate clause, makes up the sense of the whole sentence.

It follows with sufficient probability from the foregoing that the cases where a subordinate clause is not replaceable by another of the same value cannot be brought in disproof of our view that a truth-value is the *Bedeutung* of a sentence that has a thought as its sense.

Let us return to our starting point.

If we found '$a = a$' and '$a = b$' to have different cognitive values, the explanation is that for the purpose of acquiring knowledge, the sense of the sentence, viz., the thought expressed by it, is no less relevant that its *Bedeutung*, i.e. its truth-value. If now $a = b$, then indeed the *Bedeutung* of 'b' is the same as that of 'a', and hence the truth-value of '$a = b$' is the same as that of '$a = a$'. In spite of this, the sense of 'b' may differ from the sense of 'a', and thereby the thought expressed by '$a = b$' will differ from that expressed by '$a = a$'. In that case the two sentences do not have the same cognitive value. If we understand by 'judgement' the advance from the thought to its truth-value, as in the present paper, we can also say that the judgements are different.

Frege, G. "The Thought: A Logical Inquiry".
Reprinted from Frege, G. (1956), "The Thought: A Logical Inquiry", *Mind* 65: 289–311. Originally published in German as "Der Gedanke," in *Beträge zur Philosophe des deutschen Idealismus* (1918–1919), pp. 58–77.

The word "true" indicates the aim of logic as does "beautiful" that of aesthetics or "good" that of ethics. All sciences have truth as their goal; but logic is also concerned with it in a quite different way from this. It has much the same relation to truth as physics has to weight or heat. To discover truths is the task of all sciences; it falls to logic to discern the laws of truth. The word "law" is used in two senses. When we speak of laws of morals or the state we mean regulations which ought to be obeyed but with which actual happenings are not always in conformity. Laws of nature are the generalization of natural occurrences with which the occurrences are always in accordance. It is rather in this sense that I speak of laws of truth. This is, to be sure, not a matter of what happens so

186 Early Analytic Philosophy

much as of what is. Rules for asserting, thinking, judging, inferring, follow from the laws of truth. And thus one can very well speak of laws of thought too. But there is an imminent danger here of mixing different things up. Perhaps the expression "law of thought" is interpreted by analogy with "law of nature" and the generalization of thinking as a mental occurrence is meant by it. A law of thought in this sense would be a psychological law. And so one might come to believe that logic deals with the mental process of thinking and the psychological laws in accordance with which it takes place. This would be a misunderstanding of the task of logic, for truth has not been given the place which is its due here. Error and superstition have causes just as much as genuine knowledge. The assertion both of what is false and of what is true takes place in accordance with psychological laws. A derivation from these and an explanation of a mental process that terminates in an assertion can never take the place of a proof of what is asserted. Could not logical laws also have played a part in this mental process? I do not want to dispute this, but when it is a question of truth possibility is not enough. For it is also possible that something not logical played a part in the process and deflected it from the truth. We can only decide this after we have discerned the laws of truth; but then we will probably be able to do without the derivation and explanation of the mental process if it is important to us to decide whether the assertion in which the process terminates is justified. In order to avoid this misunderstanding and to prevent the blurring of the boundary between psychology and logic, I assign to logic the task of discovering the laws of truth, not of assertion or thought. The meaning of the word "true" is explained by the laws of truth.

But first I shall attempt to outline roughly what I want to call true in this connexion. In this way other uses of our word may be excluded. It is not to be used here in the sense of "genuine" or "veracious", nor, as it sometimes occurs in the treatment of questions of art, when, for example, truth in art is discussed, when truth is set up as the goal of art, when the truth of a work of art or true feeling is spoken of. The word "true" is put in front of another word in order to show that this word is to be understood in its proper, unadulterated sense. This use too lies off the path followed here; that kind of truth is meant whose recognition is the goal of science.

Grammatically the word "true" appears as an adjective. Hence the desire arises to delimit more closely the sphere in which truth can be affirmed, in which truth comes into the question at all. One finds truth affirmed of pictures, ideas, statements, and thoughts. It is striking that visible and audible things occur here alongside things which cannot be perceived with the senses. This hints that shifts of meaning have taken place. Indeed! Is a picture, then, as a mere visible

Gottlob Frege: Logic and the Philosophy of Language   **187**

and tangible thing, really true, and a stone, a leaf, not true? Obviously one would not call a picture true unless there were an intention behind it. A picture must represent something. Furthermore, an idea is not called true in itself but only with respect to an intention that it should correspond to something. It might be supposed from this that truth consists in the correspondence of a picture with what it depicts. Correspondence is a relation. This is contradicted, however, by the use of the word "true", which is not a relation-word and contains no reference to anything else to which something must correspond. If I do not know that a picture is meant to represent Cologne Cathedral then I do not know with what to compare the picture to decide on its truth. A correspondence, moreover, can only be perfect if the corresponding things coincide and are, therefore, not distinct things at all. It is said to be possible to establish the authenticity of a banknote by comparing it stereoscopically with an authentic one. But it would be ridiculous to try to compare a gold piece with a twenty-mark note stereoscopically. It would only be possible to compare an idea with a thing if the thing were an idea too. And then, if the first did correspond perfectly with the second, they would coincide. But this is not at all what is wanted when truth is defined as the correspondence of an idea with something real. For it is absolutely essential that the reality be distinct from the idea. But then there can be no complete correspondence, no complete truth. So nothing at all would be true: for what is only half true is untrue. Truth cannot tolerate a more or less. But yet? Can it not be laid down that truth exists when there is correspondence in a certain respect? But in which? For what would we then have to do to decide whether something were true? We should have to inquire whether it were true that an idea and a reality, perhaps, corresponded in the laid-down respect. And then we should be confronted by a question of the same kind and the game could begin again. So the attempt to explain truth as correspondence collapses. And every other attempt to define truth collapses too. For in a definition certain characteristics would have to be stated. And in application to any particular case the question would always arise whether it were true that the characteristics were present. So one goes round in a circle. Consequently, it is probable that the content of the word "true" is unique and indefinable.

When one ascribes truth to a picture one does not really want to ascribe a property which belongs to this picture altogether independently of other things, but one always has something quite different in mind and one wants to say that that picture corresponds in some way to this thing. "My idea corresponds to Cologne Cathedral" is a sentence and the question now arises of the truth of this sentence. So what is improperly called the truth of pictures and ideas is reduced to the truth of sentences. What does one call a sentence? A series of

Early Analytic Philosophy

sounds; but only when it has a sense, by which is not meant that every series of sounds that has sense is a sentence. And when we call a sentence true we really mean its sense is. From which it follows that it is for the sense of a sentence that the question of truth arises in general. Now is the sense of a sentence an idea? In any case being true does not consist in the correspondence of this sense with something else, for otherwise the question of truth would reiterate itself to infinity.

Without wishing to give a definition, I call a thought something for which the question of truth arises. So I ascribe what is false to a thought just as much as what is true.[1] So I can say: the thought is the sense of the sentence without wishing to say as well that the sense of every sentence is a thought. The thought, in itself immaterial, clothes itself in the material garment of a sentence and thereby becomes comprehensible to us. We say a sentence expresses a thought.

A thought is something immaterial and everything material and perceptible is excluded from this sphere of that for which the question of truth arises. Truth is not a quality that corresponds with a particular kind of sense-impression. So it is sharply distinguished from the qualities which we denote by the words "red", "bitter", "lilac-smelling". But do we not see that the sun has risen and do we not then also see that this is true? That the sun has risen is not an object which emits rays that reach my eyes, it is not a visible thing like the sun itself. That the sun has risen is seen to be true on the basis of sense impressions. But being true is not a material, perceptible property. For being magnetic is also recognized on the basis of sense-impressions of something, though this property corresponds as little as truth with a particular kind of sense-impressions. So far these properties agree. However, we need sense-impressions in order to recognize a body as magnetic. On the other hand, when I find that it is true that I do not smell anything at this moment, I do not do so on the basis of sense-impressions.

It may nevertheless be thought that we cannot recognize a property of a thing without at the same time realizing the thought that this thing has this

---

[1] In a similar way it has perhaps been said 'a judgment is something which is either true or false'. In fact I use the word 'thought' in approximately the sense which 'judgment' has in the writings of logicians. I hope it will become clear in what follows why I choose 'thought'. Such an explanation has been objected to on the ground that in it a distinction is drawn between true and false judgments which of all possible distinctions among judgments has perhaps the least significance. I cannot see that it is a logical deficiency that a distinction is given with the explanation. As far as significance is concerned, it should not by any means be judged as trifling if, as I have said, the word 'true' indicates the aim of logic.

Gottlob Frege: Logic and the Philosophy of Language   **189**

property to be true. So with every property of a thing is joined a property of a thought, namely, that of truth. It is also worthy of notice that the sentence "I smell the scent of violets" has just the same content as the sentence "it is true that I smell the scent of violets". So it seems, then, that nothing is added to the thought by my ascribing to it the property of truth. And yet is it not a great result when the scientist after much hesitation and careful inquiry, can finally say "what I supposed is true"? The meaning of the word "true" seems to be altogether unique. May we not be dealing here with something which cannot, in the ordinary sense, be called a quality at all? In spite of this doubt I want first to express myself in accordance with ordinary usage, as if truth were a quality, until something more to the point is found.

In order to work out more precisely what I want to call thought, I shall distinguish various kinds of sentences.[2] One does not want to deny sense to an imperative sentence, but this sense is not such that the question of truth could arise for it. Therefore I shall not call the sense of an imperative sentence a thought. Sentences expressing desires or requests are ruled out in the same way. Only those sentences in which we communicate or state something come into the question. But I do not count among these exclamations in which one vents one's feelings, groaning, sighing, laughing, unless it has been decided by some agreement that they are to communicate something. But how about interrogative sentences? In a word-question we utter an incomplete sentence which only obtains a true sense through the completion for which we ask. Word-questions are accordingly left out of consideration here. Sentence-questions are a different matter. We expect to hear "yes" or "no". The answer "yes" means the same as an indicative sentence, for in it the thought that was already completely contained in the interrogative sentence is laid down as true. So a sentence-question can be formed from every indicative sentence. An exclamation cannot be regarded as a communication on this account, since no corresponding sentence-question can be formed. An interrogative sentence and an indicative one contain the same thought; but the indicative contains something else as well, namely, the assertion. The interrogative sentence contains something more too, namely a request. Therefore two things must be distinguished in an indicative sentence: the content, which it has in common with the corresponding sentence-question, and the assertion. The former is the

---

[2]I am not using the word 'sentence' here in a purely grammatical sense where it also includes subordinate clauses. An isolated subordinate clause does not always have a sense about which the question of truth can arise, whereas the complex sentence to which it belongs has such a sense.

Early Analytic Philosophy

thought, or at least contains the thought. So it is possible to express the thought without laying it down as true. Both are so closely joined in an indicative sentence that it is easy to overlook their separability. Consequently we may distinguish:

(1) the apprehension of a thought–thinking,
(2) the recognition of the truth of a thought–judgment,[3]
(3) the manifestation of this judgment–assertion.

We perform the first act when we form a sentence-question. An advance in science usually takes place in this way, first a thought is apprehended, such as can perhaps be expressed in a sentence-question, and, after appropriate investigations, this thought is finally recognized to be true. We declare the recognition of truth in the form of an indicative sentence. We do not have to use the word "true" for this. And even when we do use it the real assertive force lies, not in it, but in the form of the indicative sentence and where this loses its assertive force the word "true" cannot put it back again. This happens when we do not speak seriously. As stage thunder is only apparent thunder and a stage fight only an apparent fight, so stage assertion is only apparent assertion. It is only acting, only fancy. In his part the actor asserts nothing, nor does he lie, even if he says something of whose falsehood he is convinced. In poetry we have the case of thoughts being expressed without being actually put forward as true in spite of the form of the indicative sentence, although it may be suggested to the hearer to make an assenting judgment himself. Therefore it must still always be asked, about what is presented in the form of an indicative sentence whether it really contains an assertion. And this question must be answered in the negative if the requisite seriousness is lacking. It is irrelevant whether the word "true" is used here. This explains why it is that nothing seems to be added to a thought by attributing to it the property of truth.

An indicative sentence often contains, as well as a thought and the assertion, a third component over which the assertion does not extend. This is often said to act on the feelings, the mood of the hearer or to arouse his imagination.

---

[3]It seems to me that thought and judgment have not hitherto been adequately distinguished. Perhaps language is misleading. For we have no particular clause in the indicative sentence which corresponds to the assertion, that something is being asserted lies rather in the form of the indicative. We have the advantage in German that main and subordinate clauses are distinguished by the word-order. In this connexion it is noticeable that a subordinate clause can also contain an assertion and that often neither main nor subordinate clause express a complete thought by themselves but only the complex sentence does.

Gottlob Frege: Logic and the Philosophy of Language   191

Words like "alas" and "thank God" belong here. Such constituents of sentences are more noticeably prominent in poetry, but are seldom wholly absent from prose. They occur more rarely in mathematical, physical, or chemical than in historical expositions. What are called the humanities are more closely connected with poetry and are therefore less scientific than the exact sciences which are drier the more exact they are, for exact science is directed toward truth and only the truth. Therefore all constituents of sentences to which the assertive force does not reach do not belong to scientific exposition but they are sometimes hard to avoid, even for one who sees the danger connected with them. Where the main thing is to approach what cannot be grasped in thought by means of guesswork these components have their justification. The more exactly scientific an exposition is the less will the nationality of its author be discernible and the easier will it be to translate. On the other hand, the constituents of language, to which I want to call attention here, make the translation of poetry very difficult, even make a complete translation almost always impossible, for it is in precisely that in which poetic value largely consists that languages differ most.

It makes no difference to the thought whether I use the word "horse" or "steed" or "cart-horse" or "mare". The assertive force does not extend over that in which these words differ. What is called mood, fragrance, illumination in a poem, what is portrayed by cadence and rhythm, does not belong to the thought.

Much of language serves the purpose of aiding the hearer's understanding, for instance the stressing of part of a sentence by accentuation or word-order. One should remember words like "still" and "already" too. With the sentence "Alfred has still not come" one really says "Alfred has not come" and, at the same time, hints that his arrival is expected, but it is only hinted. It cannot be said that, since Alfred's arrival is not expected, the sense of the sentence is therefore false. The word "but" differs from "and" in that with it one intimates that what follows is in contrast with what would be expected from what preceded it. Such suggestions in speech make no difference to the thought. A sentence can be transformed by changing the verb from active to passive and making the object the subject at the same time. In the same way the dative may be changed into the nominative while "give" is replaced by "receive". Naturally such transformations are not indifferent in every respect; but they do not touch the thought, they do not touch what is true or false. If the inadmissibility of such transformations were generally admitted then all deeper logical investigation would be hindered. It is just as important to neglect distinctions that do not touch the heart of the matter as to make distinctions which concern what is essential. But what is essential depends on one's purpose. To a mind concerned

Early Analytic Philosophy

with what is beautiful in language what is indifferent to the logician can appear as just what is important.

Thus the contents of a sentence often go beyond the thoughts expressed by it. But the opposite often happens too, that the mere wording, which can be grasped by writing or the gramophone does not suffice for the expression of the thought. The present tense is used in two ways: first, in order to give a date, second, in order to eliminate any temporal restriction where timelessness or eternity is part of the thought. Think, for instance, of the laws of mathematics. Which of the two cases occurs is not expressed but must be guessed. If a time indication is needed by the present tense one must know when the sentence was uttered to apprehend the thought correctly. Therefore the time of utterance is part of the expression of the thought. If someone wants to say the same today as he expressed yesterday using the word "today", he must replace this word with "yesterday". Although the thought is the same its verbal expression must be different so that the sense, which would otherwise be affected by the differing times of utterance, is readjusted. The case is the same with words like "here" and "there". In all such cases the mere wording, as it is given in writing, is not the complete expression of the thought, but the knowledge of certain accompanying conditions of utterance, which are used as means of expressing the thought, are needed for its correct apprehension. The pointing of fingers, hand movements, glances may belong here too. The same utterance containing the word "I" will express different thoughts in the mouths of different men, of which some may be true, others false.

The occurrence of the word "I" in a sentence gives rise to some questions.

Consider the following case. Dr. Gustav Lauben says, "I have been wounded". Leo Peter hears this and remarks some days later, "Dr. Gustav Lauben has been wounded". Does this sentence express the same thought as the one Dr. Lauben uttered himself? Suppose that Rudolph Lingens were present when Dr. Lauben spoke and now hears what is related by Leo Peter. If the same thought is uttered by Dr. Lauben and Leo Peter then Rudolph Lingens, who is fully master of the language and remembers what Dr. Lauben has said in his presence, must now know at once from Leo Peter's report that the same thing is under discussion. But knowledge of the language is a separate thing when it is a matter of proper names. It may well be the case that only a few people associate a particular thought with the sentence "Dr. Lauben has been wounded". In this case one needs for complete understanding a knowledge of the expression "Dr. Lauben". Now if both Leo Peter and Rudolph Lingens understand by "Dr. Lauben" the doctor who lives as the only doctor in a house known to both of them, then they both understand the sentence

Gottlob Frege: Logic and the Philosophy of Language 193

"Dr. Gustav Lauben has been wounded" in the same way, they associate the same thought with it. But it is also possible that Rudolph Lingens does not know Dr. Lauben personally and does not know that he is the very Dr. Lauben who recently said "I have been wounded". In this case Rudolph Lingens cannot know that the same thing is in question. I say, therefore, in this case: the thought which Leo Peter expresses is not the same as that which Dr. Lauben uttered.

Suppose further that Herbert Garner knows that Dr. Gustav Lauben was born on 13th September, 1875 in N.N. and this is not true of anyone else; against this, suppose that he does not know where Dr. Lauben now lives nor indeed anything about him. On the other hand, suppose Leo Peter does not know that Dr. Lauben was born on 13th September 1875, in N.N. Then as far as the proper name "Dr. Gustav Lauben" is concerned, Herbert Garner and Leo Peter do not speak the same language, since, although they do in fact refer to the same man with this name, they do not know that they do so. Therefore Herbert Garner does not associate the same thought with the sentence "Dr. Gustav Lauben has been wounded" as Leo Peter wants to express with it. To avoid the drawback of Herbert Garner's and Leo Peter's not speaking the same language, I am assuming that Leo Peter uses the proper name "Dr. Lauben" and Herbert Garner, on the other hand, uses the proper name "Gustav Lauben". Now it is possible that Herbert Garner takes the sense of the sentence "Dr. Lauben has been wounded" to be true while, misled by false information, taking the sense of the sentence "Gustav Lauben has been wounded" to be false. Under the assumptions given these thoughts are therefore different.

Accordingly, with a proper name, it depends on how whatever it refers to is presented. This can happen in different ways and every such way corresponds with a particular sense of a sentence containing a proper name. The different thoughts which thus result from the same sentence correspond in their truth-value, of course; that is to say, if one is true then all are true, and if one is false then all are false. Nevertheless their distinctness must be recognized. So it must really be demanded that a single way in which whatever is referred to is presented be associated with every proper name. It is often unimportant that this demand should be fulfilled but not always.

Now everyone is presented to himself in a particular and primitive way, in which he is presented to no-one else. So, when Dr. Lauben thinks that he has been wounded, he will probably take as a basis this primitive way in which he is presented to himself. And only Dr. Lauben himself can grasp thoughts determined in this way. But now he may want to communicate with others. He cannot communicate a thought which he alone can grasp. Therefore, if he now

Early Analytic Philosophy

says "I have been wounded", he must use the "I" in a sense which can be grasped by others, perhaps in the sense of "he who is speaking to you at this moment", by doing which he makes the associated conditions of his utterance serve for the expression of his thought.[4]

Yet there is a doubt. Is it at all the same thought which first that man expresses and now this one?

A person who is still untouched by philosophy knows first of all things which he can see and touch, in short, perceive with the senses, such as trees, stones and houses, and he is convinced that another person equally can see and touch the same tree and the same stone which he himself sees and touches. Obviously no thought belongs to these things. Now can he, nevertheless, stand in the same relation to a person as to a tree?

Even an unphilosophical person soon finds it necessary to recognize an inner world distinct from the outer world, a world of sense-impressions, of creations of his imagination, of sensations, of feelings and moods, a world of inclinations, wishes and decisions. For brevity I want to collect all these, with the exception of decisions, under the word "idea".

Now do thoughts belong to this inner world? Are they ideas? They are obviously not decisions. How are ideas distinct from the things of the outer world? First:

Ideas cannot be seen or touched, cannot be smelled, nor tasted, nor heard.

I go for a walk with a companion. I see a green field, I have a visual impression of the green as well. I have it but I do not see it.

Secondly: ideas are had. One has sensations, feelings, moods, inclinations, wishes. An idea which someone has belongs to the content of his consciousness.

The field and the frogs in it, the sun which shines on them·are there no matter whether I look at them or not, but the sense impression I have of green exists only because of me, I am its bearer. It seems absurd to us that a pain, a mood, a wish should rove about the world without a bearer, independently. An experience is impossible without an experient. The inner world presupposes the person whose inner world it is.

---

[4]I am not in the happy position here of a mineralogist who shows his hearers a mountain crystal. I cannot put a thought in the hands of my readers with the request that they should minutely examine it from all sides. I have to content myself with presenting the reader with a thought, in itself immaterial, dressed in sensible linguistic form. The metaphorical aspect of language presents difficulties. The sensible always breaks in and makes expression metaphorical and so improper. So a battle with language takes place and I am compelled to occupy myself with language although it is not my proper concern here. I hope I have succeeded in making clear to my readers what I want to call a thought.

Gottlob Frege: Logic and the Philosophy of Language 195

Thirdly: ideas need a bearer. Things of the outer world are however independent. My companion and I are convinced that we both see the same field; but each of us has a particular sense-impression of green. I notice a strawberry among the green strawberry leaves. My companion does not notice it, he is colour-blind. The colour impression, which he receives from the strawberry, is not noticeably different from the one he receives from the leaf. Now does my companion see the green leaf as red, or does he see the red berry as green, or does he see both as of one colour with which I am not acquainted at all? These are unanswerable, indeed really nonsensical, questions. For when the word "red" does not state a property of things but is supposed to characterize sense-impressions belonging to my consciousness, it is only applicable within the sphere of my consciousness. For it is impossible to compare my sense-impression with that of someone else. For that it would be necessary to bring together in one consciousness a sense-impression, belonging to one consciousness, with a sense-impression belonging to another consciousness. Now even if it were possible to make an idea disappear from one consciousness and, at the same time, to make an idea appear in another consciousness, the question whether it were the same idea in both would still remain unanswerable. It is so much of the essence of each of my ideas to be the content of my consciousness, that every idea of another person is, just as such, distinct from mine. But might it not be possible that my ideas, the entire content of my consciousness might be at the same time the content of a more embracing, perhaps divine, consciousness? Only if I were myself part of the divine consciousness. But then would they really be my ideas, would I be their bearer? This oversteps the limits of human understanding to such an extent that one must leave its possibility out of account. In any case it is impossible for us as men to compare another person's ideas with our own. I pick the strawberry, I hold it between my fingers. Now my companion sees it too, this very same strawberry; but each of us has his own idea. No other person has my idea but many people can see the same thing. No other person has my pain. Someone can have sympathy for me but still my pain always belongs to me and his sympathy to him. He does not have my pain and I do not have his sympathy.

Fourthly: every idea has only one bearer; no two men have the same idea.

For otherwise it would exist independently of this person and independently of that one. Is that lime-tree my idea? By using the expression "that lime-tree" in this question I have really already anticipated the answer, for with this expression I want to refer to what I see and to what other people can also look at and touch. There are now two possibilities. If my intention is realized when I refer to something with the expression "that lime-tree" then the thought

Early Analytic Philosophy

expressed in the sentence "that lime-tree is my idea" must obviously be negated. But if my intention is not realized, if I only think I see without really seeing, if on that account the designation "that lime-tree" is empty, then I have gone astray into the sphere of fiction without knowing it or wanting to. In that case neither the content of the sentence "that lime-tree is my idea" nor the content of the sentence "that lime-tree is not my idea" is true, for in both cases I have a statement which lack an object. So then one can only refuse to answer the question for the reason that the content of the sentence "that lime-tree is my idea" is a piece of fiction. I have, naturally, got an idea then, but I am not referring to this with the words "that lime-tree". Now someone may really want to refer to one of his ideas with the words "that lime-tree". He would then be the bearer of that to which he wants to refer with those words, but then he would not see that lime-tree and no one else would see it or be its bearer.

I now return to the question: is a thought an idea? If the thought I express in the Pythagorean theorem can be recognized by others just as much as by me then it does not belong to the content of my consciousness, I am not its bearer; yet I can, nevertheless, recognize it to be true. However, if it is not the same thought at all which is taken to be the content of the Pythagorean theorem by me and by another person, one should not really say "the Pythagorean theorem" but "my Pythagorean theorem", "his Pythagorean theorem" and these would be different; for the sense belongs necessarily to the sentence. Then my thought can be the content of my consciousness and his thought the content of his. Could the sense of my Pythagorean theorem be true while that of his was false? I said that the word "red" was applicable only in the sphere of my consciousness if it did not state a property of things but was supposed to characterize one of my sense-impressions. Therefore the words "true" and "false", as I understand them, could also be applicable only in the sphere of my consciousness, if they were not supposed to be concerned with something of which I was not the bearer, but were somehow appointed to characterize the content of my consciousness. Then truth would be restricted to the content of my consciousness and it would remain doubtful whether anything at all comparable occurred in the consciousness of others.

If every thought requires a bearer, to the contents of whose consciousness it belongs, then it would be a thought of this bearer only and there would be no science common to many, on which many could work. But I, perhaps, have my science, namely, a whole of thought whose bearer I am and another person has his. Each of us occupies himself with the contents of his own consciousness. No contradiction between the two sciences would then be possible and it would really be idle to dispute about truth, as idle, indeed almost ludicrous, as it would

Gottlob Frege: Logic and the Philosophy of Language   **197**

be for two people to dispute whether a hundred-mark note were genuine, where each meant the one he himself had in his pocket and understood the word "genuine" in his own particular sense. If someone takes thoughts to be ideas, what he then recognizes to be true is, on his own view, the content of his consciousness and does not properly concern other people at all. If he were to hear from me the opinion that a thought is not an idea he could not dispute it, for, indeed, it would not now concern him.

So the result seems to be: thoughts are neither things of the outer world nor ideas.

A third realm must be recognized. What belongs to this corresponds with ideas, in that it cannot be perceived by the senses, but with things, in that it needs no bearer to the contents of whose consciousness to belong. Thus the thought, for example, which we expressed in the Pythagorean theorem is timelessly true, true independently of whether anyone takes it to be true. It needs no bearer. It is not true for the first time when it is discovered, but is like a planet which, already before anyone has seen it, has been in interaction with other planets.[5]

But I think I hear an unusual objection. I have assumed several times that the same thing that I see can also be observed by other people. But how could this be the case, if everything were only a dream? If I only dreamed I was walking in the company of another person, if I only dreamed that my companion saw the green field as I did, if it were all only a play performed on the stage of my consciousness, it would be doubtful whether there were things of the outer world at all. Perhaps the realm of things is empty and I see no things and no men, but have only ideas of which I myself am the bearer. An idea, being something which can as little exist independently of me as my feeling of fatigue, cannot be a man, cannot look at the same field together with me, cannot see the strawberry I am holding. It is quite incredible that I should really have only my inner world instead of the whole environment, in which I am supposed to move and to act. And yet it is an inevitable consequence of the thesis that only what is my idea can be the object of my awareness. What would follow from this thesis if it were true? Would there then be other men? It would certainly be possible but I should know nothing of it. For a man cannot be my idea, consequently, if our thesis were true, he also cannot be an object of my awareness. And so the ground would be removed from under any process of

---

[5]One sees a thing, one has an idea, one apprehends or thinks a thought. When one apprehends or thinks a thought one does not create it but only comes to stand in a certain relation, which is different from seeing a thing or having an idea, to what already existed beforehand.

thought in which I might assume that something was an object for another person as for myself, for even if this were to happen I should know nothing of it. It would be impossible for me to distinguish that of which I was the bearer from that of which I was not. In judging something not to be my idea I would make it the object of my thinking and, therefore, my idea. On this view, is there a green field? Perhaps, but it would not be visible to me. For if a field is not my idea, it cannot, according to our thesis, be an object of my awareness. But if it is my idea it is invisible, for ideas are not visible. I can indeed have the idea of a green field, but this is not green for there are no green ideas. Does a shell weighing a hundred kilogrammes exist, according to this view? Perhaps, but I could know nothing of it. If a shell is not my idea then, according to our thesis, it cannot be an object of my awareness, of my thinking. But if a shell were my idea, it would have no weight. I can have an idea of a heavy shell. This then contains the idea of weight as a part-idea. But this part-idea is not a property of the whole idea any more than Germany is a property of Europe. So it follows:

Either the thesis that only what is my idea can be the object of my awareness is false, or all my knowledge and perception is limited to the range of my ideas, to the stage of my consciousness. In this case I should have only an inner world and I should know nothing of other people.

It is strange how, upon such reflections, the opposites collapse into each other. There is, let us suppose, a physiologist of the senses. As is proper for a scholarly scientist, he is, first of all, far from supposing the things he is convinced he sees and touches to be his ideas. On the contrary, he believes that in sense impressions he has the surest proof of things which are wholly independent of his feeling, imagining, thinking, which have no need of his consciousness. So little does he consider nerve-fibres and ganglion-cells to be the content of his consciousness that he is, on the contrary, rather inclined to regard his consciousness as dependent on nerve-fibres and ganglion-cells. He establishes that light-rays, refracted in the eye, strike the visual nerve-endings and bring about a change, a stimulus, there. Some of it is transmitted through nerve-fibres and ganglion-cells. Further processes in the nervous system are perhaps involved, colour-impressions arise and these perhaps join themselves to what we call the idea of a tree. Physical, chemical and physiological occurrences insert themselves between the tree and my idea. These are immediately connected with my consciousness but, so it seems, are only occurrences in my nervous system and every spectator of the tree has his particular occurrences in his particular nervous system. Now the light-rays, before they enter my eye, may be reflected by a mirror and be spread further as if they came from a place behind the mirror. The effects on the visual nerves and all that follows will now

Gottlob Frege: Logic and the Philosophy of Language 199

take place just as they would if the light-rays had come from a tree behind the mirror and had been transmitted undisturbed to the eve. So an idea of a tree will finally occur even though such a tree does not exist at all. An idea, to which nothing at all corresponds, can also arise through the bending of light, with the mediation of the eye and the nervous system. But the stimulation of the visual nerves need not even happen through light. If lightning strikes near us we believe we see flames, even though we cannot see the lightning itself. In this case the visual nerve is perhaps stimulated by electric currents which originate in our body in consequence of the flash of lightning. If the visual nerve is stimulated by this means, just as it would be stimulated by light-rays coming from flames, then we believe we see flames. It just depends on the stimulation of the visual nerve, it is indifferent how that itself comes about.

One can go a step further still. This stimulation of the visual nerve is not actually immediately given, but is only a hypothesis. We believe that a thing, independent of us, stimulates a nerve and by this means produces a sense-impression, but, strictly speaking, we experience only the end of this process which projects into our consciousness. Could not this sense-impression, this sensation, which we attribute to a nerve-stimulation. have other causes also. as the same nerve-stimulation can arise in different ways? If we call what happens in our consciousness idea, then we really experience only ideas but not their causes. And if the scientist wants to avoid all mere hypothesis, then only ideas are left for him, everything resolves into ideas, the light-rays, nerve-fibres and ganglion-cells from which he started. So he finally undermines the foundations of his own construction. Is everything an idea? Does everything need a bearer without which it could have no stability? I have considered myself as the bearer of my ideas, but am I not an idea myself? It seems to me as if I were lying in a deck-chair, as if I could see the toes of a pair of waxed boots, the front part of a pair of trousers, a waistcoat, buttons, part of a jacket, in particular sleeves, two hands, the hair of a beard, the blurred outline of a nose. Am I myself this entire association of visual impressions, this total idea? It also seems to me as if I see a I chair over there. It is an idea. I am not actually much different from this myself, for am I not myself just an association of sense-impressions, an idea? But where then is the bearer of these ideas? How do I come to single out one of these ideas and set it up as the bearer of the rest? Why must it be the idea which I choose to call "I"? Could I not just as well choose the one that I am tempted to call a chair? Why, after all, have a bearer for ideas at all? But this would always be something essentially different from merely borne ideas, something independent, needing no extraneous bearer. If everything is idea, then there is no bearer of ideas. And so now, once again, I experience a change

200 Early Analytic Philosophy

into the opposite. If there is no bearer of ideas then there are also no ideas, for ideas need a bearer without which they cannot exist. If there is no ruler, there are also no subjects. The dependence, which I found myself induced to confer on the experience as opposed to the experient, is abolished if there is no more bearer. What I called ideas are then independent objects. Every reason is wanting for granting an exceptional position to that object which I call "I".

But is that possible? Can there be an experience without someone to experience it? What would this whole play be without an onlooker? Can there be a pain without someone who has it? Being experienced is necessarily connected with pain, and someone experiencing is necessarily connected with being experienced. But there is something which is not my idea and yet which can be the object of my awareness, of my thinking, I am myself of this nature. Or can I be part of the content of my consciousness while another part is, perhaps, an idea of the moon? Does this perhaps take place when I judge that I am looking at the moon? Then this first part would have a consciousness and part of the content of this consciousness would be I myself once more. And so on. Yet it is surely inconceivable that I should be boxed into myself in this way to infinity, for then there would not be only one I but infinitely many. I am not my own idea and if I assert something about myself, *e.g.* that I do not feel any pain at this moment, then my judgment concerns something which is not a content of my consciousness, is not my idea, that is me myself. Therefore that about which I state something is not necessarily my idea. But, someone perhaps objects, if I think I have no pain at the moment, does not the word 'I' nevertheless correspond with something in the content of my consciousness and is that not an idea? That may be. A certain idea in my consciousness may be associated with the idea of the word 'I'. But then it is an idea among other ideas and I am its bearer as I am the bearer of the other ideas. I have an idea of myself but I am not identical with this idea. What is a content of my consciousness, my idea, should be sharply distinguished from what is an object of my thought. Therefore the thesis that only what belongs to the content of my consciousness can be the object of my awareness, of my thought, is false.

Now the way is clear for me to recognize another person as well as to be an independent bearer of ideas. I have an idea of him but I do not confuse it with him himself. And if I state something about my brother I do not state it about the idea that I have of my brother.

The invalid who has a pain is the bearer of this pain, but the doctor in attendance who reflects on the cause of this pain is not the bearer of the pain. He does not imagine he can relieve the pain by anaesthetizing himself. An idea in the doctor's mind may very well correspond to the pain of the invalid but that

Gottlob Frege: Logic and the Philosophy of Language　201

is not the pain and not what the doctor is trying to remove. The doctor might consult another doctor. Then one must distinguish: first, the pain whose bearer is the invalid, second, the first doctor's idea of this pain, third, the second doctor's idea of this pain. This idea does indeed belong to the content of the second doctor's consciousness, but it is not the object of his reflection, it is rather an aid to reflection, as a drawing can be such an aid perhaps. Both doctors have the invalid's pain, which they do not bear, as their common object of thought. It can be seen from this that not only a thing but also an idea can be the common object of thought of people who do not have the idea.

So, it seems to me, the matter becomes intelligible. If man could not think and could not take something of which he was not the bearer as the object of his thought he would have an inner world but no outer world. But may this not be based on a mistake? I am convinced that the idea I associate with the words 'my brother' corresponds to something that is not my idea and about which I can say something. But may I not be making a mistake about this? Such mistakes do happen. We then, against our will, lapse into fiction. Indeed! By the step with which I secure an environment for myself I expose myself to the risk of error. And here I come up against a further distinction between my inner and outer worlds. I cannot doubt that I have a visual impression of green but it is not so certain that I see a lime-leaf. So, contrary to widespread views, we find certainty in the inner world while doubt never altogether leaves us in our excursions into the outer world. It is difficult in many cases, nevertheless, to distinguish probability from certainty here, so we can presume to judge about things in the outer world. And we must presume this even at the risk of error if we do not want to succumb to far greater dangers.

In consequence of these last considerations I lay down the following: not everything that can be the object of my understanding is an idea. I, as a bearer of ideas, am not myself an idea. Nothing now stands in the way of recognizing other people to be bearers of ideas as I am myself. And, once given the possibility, the probability is very great, so great that it is in my opinion no longer distinguishable from certainty. Would there be a science of history otherwise? Would not every precept of duty, every law otherwise come to nothing? What would be left of religion? The natural sciences too could only be assessed as fables like astrology and alchemy. Thus the reflections I have carried on, assuming that there are other people besides myself who can take the same thing as the object of their consideration, of their thinking, remain essentially unimpaired in force.

Not everything is an idea. Thus I can also recognize the thought, which other people can grasp just as much as I, as being independent of me. I can recognize

Early Analytic Philosophy

a science in which many people can be engaged in research. We are not bearers of thoughts as we are bearers of our ideas. We do not have a thought as we have, say, a sense-impression, but we also do not see a thought as we see, say, a star. So it is advisable to choose a special expression and the word 'apprehend' offers itself for the purpose. A particular mental capacity, the power of thought, must correspond to the apprehension of thought.[6] In thinking we do not produce thoughts but we apprehend them. For what I have called thought stands in the closest relation to truth. What I recognize as true I judge to be true quite independently of my recognition of its truth and of my thinking about it. That someone thinks it has nothing to do with the truth of a thought. 'Facts, facts. facts' cries the scientist if he wants to emphasise the necessity of a firm foundation for science. What is a fact? A fact is a thought that is true. But the scientist will surely not recognise something which depends on men's varying states of mind to be the firm foundation of science. The work of science does not consist of creation but of the discovery of true thoughts. The astronomer can apply a mathematical truth in the investigation of long past events which took place when on earth at least no one had yet recognized that truth. He can do this because the truth of a thought is timeless. Therefore that truth cannot have come into existence with its discovery.

Not everything is an idea. Otherwise psychology would contain all the sciences within it or at least it would be the highest judge over all the sciences. Otherwise psychology would rule over logic and mathematics. But nothing would be a greater misunderstanding of mathematics than its subordination to psychology. Neither logic nor mathematics has the task of investigating minds and the contents of consciousness whose bearer is a single person. Perhaps their task could be represented rather as the investigation of the mind, of the mind not of minds.

The apprehension of a thought presupposes someone who apprehends it, who thinks. He is the bearer of the thinking but not of the thought. Although the thought does not belong to the contents of the thinker's consciousness yet something in his consciousness must be aimed at the thought. But this should not be confused with the thought itself. Similarly Algol itself is different from the idea someone has of Algol.

---

[6]The expression 'apprehend' is as metaphorical as 'content of consciousness'. The nature of language does not permit anything else. What I hold in my hand can certainly be regarded as the content of my hand but is all the same the content of my hand in quite a different way from the bones and muscles of which it is made and their tensions, and is much more extraneous to it than they are.

Gottlob Frege: Logic and the Philosophy of Language   203

The thought belongs neither to my inner world as an idea nor yet to the outer world of material, perceptible things.

This consequence, however cogently it may follow from the exposition, will nevertheless not perhaps be accepted without opposition. It will, I think, seem impossible to some people to obtain information about something not belonging to the inner world except by sense-perception. Sense-perception indeed is often thought to be the most certain, even to be the sole, source of knowledge about everything that does not belong to the inner world. But with what right? For sense-impressions are necessary constituents of sense-perceptions and are part of the inner world. In any case two men do not have the same, though they may have similar, sense-impressions. These alone do not disclose the outer world to us. Perhaps there is a being that has only sense-impressions without seeing or touching things. To have visual impressions is not to see things. How does it happen that I see the tree just there where I do see it? Obviously it depends on the visual impressions I have and on the particular type which occur because I see with two eyes. A particular image arises, physically speaking, on each of the two retinas. Another person sees the tree in the same place. He also has two retinal images but they differ from mine. We must assume that these retinal images correspond to our impressions. Consequently we have visual impressions, not only not the same, but markedly different from each other. And yet we move about in the same outer world. Having visual impressions is certainly necessary for seeing things but not sufficient. What must still be added is non-sensible. And yet this is just what opens up the outer world for us; for without this nonsensible something everyone would remain shut up in his inner world. So since the answer lies in the non-sensible, perhaps something non-sensible could also lead us out of the inner world and enable us to grasp thoughts where no sense-impressions were involved. Outside one's inner world one would have to distinguish the proper outer world of sensible, perceptible things from the realm of the nonsensibly perceptible. We should need something non-sensible for the recognition of both realms but for the sensible perception of things we should need sense-impressions as well and these belong entirely to the inner world. So that in which the distinction between the way in which a thing and a thought is given mainly consists is something which is attributable, not to both realms, but to the inner world. Thus I cannot find this distinction to be so great that on its account it would be impossible for a thought to be given that did not belong to the inner world.

The thought, admittedly, is not something which it is usual to call real. The world of the real is a world in which this acts on that, changes it and again experiences reactions itself and is changed by them. All this is a process in time.

Early Analytic Philosophy

We will hardly recognize what is timeless and unchangeable as real. Now is the thought changeable or is it timeless? The thought we express by the Pythagorean theorem is surely timeless, eternal, unchangeable. But are there not thoughts which are true today but false in six months time? The thought, for example, that the tree there is covered with green leaves, will surely be false in six months time. No, for it is not the same thought at all. The words 'this tree is covered with green leaves' are not sufficient by themselves for the utterance, the time of utterance is involved as well. Without the time-indication this gives we have no complete thought, i.e. no thought at all. Only a sentence supplemented by a time-indication and complete in every respect expresses a thought. But this, if it is true, is true not only today or tomorrow but timelessly. Thus the present tense in 'is true' does not refer to the speaker's present but is, if the expression be permitted, a tense of timelessness. If we use the mere form of the indicative sentence, avoiding the word 'true', two things must be distinguished, the expression of the thought and the assertion. The time-indication that may be contained in the sentence belongs only to the expression of the thought, while the truth, whose recognition lies in the form of the indicative sentence, is timeless. Yet the same words, on account of the variability of language with time, take on another sense, express another thought; this change, however, concerns only the linguistic aspect of the matter.

And yet! What value could there be for us in the eternally unchangeable which could neither undergo effects nor have effect on us? Something entirely and in every respect inactive would be unreal and non-existent for us. Even the timeless, if it is to be anything for us, must somehow be implicated with the temporal. What would a thought be for me that was never apprehended by me? But by apprehending a thought I come into a relation to it and it to me. It is possible that the same thought that is thought by me today was not thought by me yesterday. In this way the strict timelessness is of course annulled. But one is inclined to distinguish between essential and inessential properties and to regard something as timeless if the changes it undergoes involve only its inessential properties. A property of a thought will be called inessential which consists in, or follows from the fact that, it is apprehended by a thinker.

How does a thought act? By being apprehended and taken to be true. This is a process in the inner world of a thinker which can have further consequences in this inner world and which, encroaching on the sphere of the will, can also make itself noticeable in the outer world. If, for example, I grasp the thought which we express by the theorem of Pythagoras, the consequence may be that I recognise it to be true and, further, that I apply it, making a decision which brings about the acceleration of masses. Thus our actions are usually prepared

Gottlob Frege: Logic and the Philosophy of Language 205

by thinking and judgment. And so thought can have an indirect influence on the motion of masses. The influence of one person on another is brought about for the most part by thoughts. One communicates a thought. How does this happen? One brings about changes in the common outside world which, perceived by another person, are supposed to induce him to apprehend a thought and take it to be true. Could the great events of world history have come about without the communication of thoughts? And yet we are inclined to regard thoughts as unreal because they appear to be without influence on events, while thinking, judging, stating, understanding and the like are facts of human life. How much more real a hammer appears compared with a thought. How different the process of handing over a hammer is from the communication of a thought. The hammer passes from one control to another, it is gripped, it undergoes pressure and on account of this its density, the disposition of its parts, is changed in places. There is nothing of all this with a thought. It does not leave the control of the communicator by being communicated. for after all a person has no control over it. When a thought is apprehended, it at first only brings about changes in the inner world of the apprehender, yet it remains untouched in its true essence, since the changes it undergoes involve only inessential properties. There is lacking here something we observe throughout the order of nature: reciprocal action. Thoughts are by no means unreal but their reality is of quite a different kind from that of things. And their effect is brought about by an act of the thinker without which they would be ineffective, at least as far as we can see. And yet the thinker does not create them but must take them as they are. They can be true without being apprehended by a thinker and are not wholly unreal even then, at least if they could be apprehended and by this means be brought into operation.

5

Bertrand Russell on Relations, Descriptions, and Knowledge

Chapter Outline

Background and commentary

Background	208
Monism and relations	210
Names and descriptions	213
Analysis, sense-data, and scientific philosophy	217
Concluding remarks	220
Further reading	221

Readings

Russell on Monism and Relations (selections from *The Principles of Mathematics* and *Our Knowledge of the External World*)	222
"On Denoting"	250
"Knowledge by Acquaintance and Knowledge by Description"	263

Background and commentary

Background

Who was Bertrand Russell (1872–1970)? Unlike most of the other philosophers discussed in this book, you may have heard this name outside of an academic setting. During his lifetime (and to some extent into the present day), Russell was well-known and widely read not only within academic philosophy, but also among the general public. He was one of the most prolific writers of the twentieth century, writing myriad books, pamphlets, articles, essays, and commentaries. Among Russell's more important academic books are *The Principles of Mathematics* (1903), *Principia Mathematica* (1910, 1912, and 1913; with A. N. Whitehead), and *Our Knowledge of the External World* ([1914] 2009), while his popular writings—often focusing on political, social, and ethical issues—include *Political Ideals* (1917), *Why I am Not a Christian* (1927a), and *Marriage and Morals* (1929), along with several autobiographical works.

Russell is typically regarded as a founder of the analytic tradition. He produced important work in logic, philosophy of language, the theory of knowledge, and on the very nature of philosophical inquiry. Aside from his own work, Russell played an important role in bringing the work of Frege, Wittgenstein, and others to a broader audience than would have otherwise been the case, and moreover seriously engaged with the work of William James, among others.[1] While employed as an academic philosopher, Russell was actively engaged in a range of social and political issues, including pacifist and anti-nuclear proliferation movements. As a result of his participation in these movements, he was imprisoned on multiple occasions. Russell provided the following description of his core motivations:

> Three passions, simple but overwhelmingly strong, have governed my life: the longing for love, the search for knowledge, and unbearable pity for the suffering of mankind. These passions, like great winds, have blown me hither and thither, in a wayward course, over a great ocean of anguish, reaching to the very verge of despair. ([1951] 1967: 3)

---

[1]For discussion of the interaction between Russell and James, see Misak 2016. Despite disagreeing on various issues, most centrally the theory of truth, Russell and James shared a deep personal respect for each other. Moreover, despite these disagreements, Russell and James both rejected the monistic idealism of Bradley.

Russell was born into a liberal aristocratic family in Britain. He was raised largely by his grandmother—his mother died when he was two and his father died when he was four—and was educated by tutors until he was sixteen. He later described this time as solitary but not unhappy. From an early age, Russell manifested an intense interest in mathematical studies, writing that his first encounter with Euclid's *Elements* when he was eleven was "as dazzling as first love" ([1951] 1967: 36). When he was eighteen, he entered Trinity College, Cambridge as a mathematics student. In his first year at Cambridge, Russell met Whitehead, who was about ten years his senior, with whom he would later collaborate in writing *Principia Mathematica*. Upon receiving a degree in mathematics in 1893, Russell began seriously studying philosophy. In 1895, he earned a Trinity Prize Fellowship for a dissertation that would later be published as *An Essay on the Foundations of Geometry* (1897). In part due to the influence of McTaggart, Russell adhered to broadly Hegelian and Bradleyian ideas until around 1898, at which point—influenced by Moore—he rejected the monistic doctrines that he had previously adopted. Russell was appointed as lecturer at Cambridge in 1899, a position he retained until 1916, at which point his lectureship was revoked due to his opposition to the First World War. After a series of lectureships in the United States (interrupted in 1940, when he was deemed morally unfit to teach at City College, New York), Russell returned to Trinity in 1944. He was awarded the Nobel Prize for literature in 1950.

Russell married Alys Pearsall Smith (1867–1951) in 1894. Russell reported that it was during a bike ride in 1902 that he realized he no longer loved Alys ([1951] 1967: 222), but they remained married until 1921, at which point he married Dora Black (1894–1986), with whom he had two children. Together with Dora, Russell opened a school that he hoped would better adhere to his educational ideals than the alternatives available in Britain at the time. Russell and Dora divorced in 1935; Russell then married Patricia Helen Spence in 1936 (1910–2004), to whom he would remain married until 1952, at which point he sought a divorce and married Edith Finch (1900–78). Russell and Edith remained married until Russell's death in 1970. Much more could be, and has been, written about Russell's somewhat tumultuous personal life.[2]

---

[2]For these and further biographical details, see Ayer 1972, Griffin 1991, Irvine 2019, and Monk 1996 and 2001.

Monism and relations

Russell began his philosophical career under the influence of broadly Hegelian ideas and, especially, Bradley's monism. Russell wrote in *My Philosophical Development* (1959):

> I was at this time [1894–1898] a full-fledged Hegelian, and I aimed at constructing a complete dialectic of the sciences, which should end up with the proof that all reality is mental. I accepted the Hegelian view that none of the sciences is quite true, since all depend upon some abstraction, and every abstraction leads, sooner or later, to contradiction. (42)

From about 1895 to 1898, Russell's intellectual work centered on a dialectic of the sciences as well as an account of the foundations of mathematics. His idealist commitments, however, made it difficult for him to work out his ideas without running into a series of antinomies and contradictions that were not soluble by the Hegelian dialectical method.[3] In late 1898, however, Moore shared with Russell the views he had argued for in his own Trinity Prize dissertation, which dispensed with the metaphysics of monism and idealism, and defended an anti-psychologistic form of realism about the objects of thought (see Chapter 3). Russell here found the impetus he had been missing. He abandoned the monistic metaphysics of Bradley, turning instead to a critique of monism that focused largely on the nature of relations. Russell regarded the issue of relations as perhaps the most important issue in philosophy, writing in "Logical Atomism" ([1924] 1993):

> The subject of relations is difficult, and I am far from claiming to be now clear about it. The question of relations is one of the most important that arise in philosophy, as most other issues turn on it; monism and pluralism; the question whether anything is wholly true except the whole of truth, or wholly real except the whole of reality; idealism and realism, in some of their forms; perhaps the very existence of philosophy as a subject distinct from science and possessing a method of its own. (169)

Russell's views about relations are extensive and far-ranging. In the selections presented below, he offers three core considerations against monism and in favor of a conception of the world as consisting of separately existing entities standing in relations.

First, recall Bradley's "chain argument" from *Appearance and Reality*, according to which relations cannot be treated as "more or less independent"

---

[3]See Griffin 1991 and Preti 2022.

from what they relate, on the grounds that this would require new relations between a relation and what it relates, leading to an infinite regress (see Chapter 2). As Russell puts it in *The Principles of Mathematics*, on this point Bradley's case is "an argument against the reality of relations [based] upon the endless regress arising from the fact that a relation which relates two terms must be related to them" (99). Russell responds, in part, by distinguishing two sorts of regresses. He concedes that there is a regress involved in taking relations to be independent from what they relate, but doubts that it "forms any logical difficulty" (99). In particular, he supposes that while taking relations to be independent from what they relate implies an infinite number of propositions, it does not require an infinite number of relations between relations and what they relate. In Russell's view, this is a benign, unobjectionable sort of regress, at least in part because any proposition implies an infinite number of further propositions.

Second, Russell argues that there are decisive reasons why relations must be accepted as real. In *The Principles of Mathematics* and elsewhere, he couches the issue in terms of whether every proposition "can be reduced to one of the subject-predicate type" (95). He puts this as follows in *Our Knowledge of the External World*:

> The belief or unconscious conviction that all propositions are of the subject-predicate form—in other words, that every fact consists in some thing having some quality—has rendered most philosophers incapable of giving any account of the world of science and daily life ... Traditional logic, since it holds that all propositions have the subject-predicate form, is unable to admit the reality of relations: all relations, it maintains, must be reduced to properties of the apparently related terms. (45)

In the attempt to reduce apparently relational statements to subject-predicate statements, Russell considers two strategies: first, the "monadistic view," which treats a relational statement "aRb" as equivalent to two subject-predicate statements "aF" and "bH" (where "a" and "b" are names of the entities alleged to stand in the relation and "F" and "H" represent properties of the objects named by "a" and "b"); second, the "monistic view," which treats a relational statement "aRb" as equivalent to a statement "(ab)F," where "F" represents a property of the whole designated by "(ab)." Russell claims that neither of these views can successfully deal with asymmetrical relations, relations (like the *father of* relation and the *beforeness* relation) such that if a stands in R to b, b doesn't stand in R to a. Regarding the monistic view, which Russell attributes to Bradley, the essential problem is that where R is an asymmetrical relation between a and b, it will be necessary to distinguish between the whole (ab)

Early Analytic Philosophy

and the whole (ba), but this can only be accomplished by admitting a further one-directional relation between a and b. Russell writes:

> In order to distinguish a whole (ab) from a whole (ba), as we must do if we are to explain asymmetry, we shall be forced back from the whole to the part and their relation. For (ab) and (ba) consist of precisely the same parts, and differ in no respect whatever save the sense of the relation between a and b. "a is greater than b" and "b is greater than a" are propositions containing precisely the same constituents ... their difference lies solely in the fact that greater is, in the first case, a relation of a to b, in the second, a relation of b to a. Thus the distinction of senses ... is one which the monistic theory of relations is wholly unable to explain. (1903: 225)

The outcome of this, according to Russell, is that at least some relations, namely those that hold in one direction only, must be accepted as real. While this line of thought has been influential, it is worth marking that Bradley remained unconvinced. In "Relations," he responded as follows:

> the objection seems to assume not only that all monism is based on the fact of 'simple inherence', but that it also implies that in this experience we are to find ultimate and absolute reality.
> Now, so far as my monism is concerned, I take the opposite view. Simple inherence, if relational, is to my mind self-contradictory.
> And if I am told that in any case Monism, if it is to stand, must be able to explain, and to exhibit more or less in detail, the positive 'how' of the universe — that again is what I would deny ... some general feature of the world left unexplained can serve to refute a general view only so far as it can be shown that, if that view were true, this particular feature should be explicable. (650)

Bradley can be read as saying two things. First, he is denying the "absolute reality" of subject-predicate statements or propositions themselves. Second, he is claiming that if his monism is correct, one should not expect an account of asymmetrical relations in the way that Russell evidently supposes. Indeed, according to Bradley, if his monism is correct, we should reject all relations, asymmetrical relations included.

Third and finally, Russell points out the strange consequences that seem to follow from the rejection of relations as unreal and a monistic conception of reality. He puts it this way in *Our Knowledge of the External World*:

> The universe, it tells us, is an "organic unity", like an animal or a perfect work of art. By this it means, roughly, that all the different parts fit together and cooperate, and are what they are because of their place in the whole ... If it is true, every part of the universe is a microcosm, a miniature reflection of the

Bertrand Russell on Relations, Descriptions, and Knowledge 213

whole. If we knew ourselves thoroughly, according to this doctrine, we should know everything. Common sense would naturally object that there are people—say in China—with whom our relations are so indirect and trivial that we cannot infer anything important as to them from any fact about ourselves. If there are living beings on Mars or in more distant parts of the universe, the same argument becomes even stronger. (19)

One could read Russell as urging that, given these strange consequences, the burden of proof is on the monist; given the previous considerations, he thinks that this is a burden that the monist cannot discharge. Given the strange consequences that seem to follow from monism, Russell suggests that it is more reasonable to suspect an error in any argument against relations and for monism than to accept any such conception of the world.

While the topic of relations was a central part of the philosophical landscape in the first part of the twentieth century, it has received less attention in recent years.[4] This, in part, is due to the perception that Russell and Moore were decisive victors in the debate with Bradley—that Russell, in particular, conclusively showed that relations must be accepted as real and that arguments for a monistic metaphysic premised on concerns about relations were unsuccessful.[5] Nonetheless, the reader is encouraged to reflect on this material and to consider just how effective Russell's responses to Bradley are and how Bradley might respond to them.

Names and descriptions

An important consequence for both Russell's own work and the history of analytic philosophy was Russell's championing the importance of modern logic for philosophy. Russell argued, particularly in his early work, that ordinary language is in various ways imperfect, and that these imperfections can lead to unnecessary philosophical puzzles.

An example of this, and one that impressed Russell, concerns the word "is." The word "is" evidently can be used in three distinct ways. First, "is" can be used to express predication, as in "Socrates is a man." Second, "is" can be used to express identity, as in "Mark Twain is Samuel Clemens." Third, "is" can be used to express existence, as in "Socrates is" or "the snub-nosed philosopher is." Russell went so far as to say that it is a "disgrace to the human race" (!) that a single word could be used in such different ways, and believed that this

---

[4]For exceptions, see Heil 2015 and Della Rocca 2020.
[5]See Candlish 2007 for discussion.

214 **Early Analytic Philosophy**

"disgrace" was in part responsible for various confusions in philosophy (1919: 172). He believed, however, that this disgrace could be remedied by modern logic, in which each sense of "is" is given a distinct symbolic representation:

1 "is" of predication: "Ms" (e.g., "Socrates is a man," with "s" representing the name "Socrates" and "M" representing "man").

2 "is" of identity: "t = c" (e.g., "Mark Twain is Samuel Clemens," with "t" representing the name "Mark Twain," "c" representing the name "Samuel Clemens," and "=" representing identity).

3 "is" of existence: "($\exists$x) x = s" (e.g., "There is some x such that x = Socrates"); "($\exists$x)Nx" (e.g., "there is some x such that x is a snub-nosed philosopher," with "N" representing the predicate "snub-nosed philosopher").

With these distinct representations, there is less risk of confusing the different senses of "is."

A further example of how logical analysis can be of real philosophical import is captured by Russell's so-called "theory of descriptions," developed most famously in his "On Denoting." As Russell writes at the outset, in his view "the difficulties concerning denoting are ... all the result of a wrong analysis of propositions whose verbal expressions contain denoting phrases" (480). What is the "wrong analysis" that Russell aims to reject? Take a statement like "the present King of France is bald," which involves the definite description "the present King of France." What is the meaning of "the present King of France"? On the view that Russell wishes to reject, in this context and elsewhere, "the present King of France" just means a particular man and in this respect functions like a proper name. On this conception, "the present King of France is bald" is a subject-predicate statement that attributes the property of baldness to a particular individual, the individual named or meant by "the present King of France." As Russell points out, and as we will sketch below, this analysis leads to various seemingly unsavory consequences. In response, Russell proposes that "the present King of France is bald" is not a subject-predicate statement at all, but is rather a quantified statement (a statement about the quantity of things to which one or more predicate applies) which, when spelled out, is equivalent to the conjunction of the following:

1 There is a present King of France
2 There is only one present King of France
3 It is bald

In other words, on Russell's analysis, "the present King of France is bald" says that something, and only one thing, is presently King of France, and that thing is bald. Using the techniques of modern symbolic logic, which Russell helped to develop, "the present King of France is bald" could be symbolized as "$(\exists x)$ $[(Kx \wedge (\forall y)(Ky \rightarrow y = x) \wedge Bx)]$"—there is some x such that x is presently King of France, any y that is presently King of France is x, and x is bald.

Russell writes that this account "gives a reduction of all propositions in which denoting phrases occur to forms in which no such phrases occur" (482); that on this account, an expression like "the present King of France" "has no meaning, because in any proposition in which it occurs the proposition, fully expressed, does not contain the phrase, which has been broken up" (488). The import of this is that while statements in which definite descriptions occur can be evaluated as true or false—"the present King of France is bald" will be true just in case one and only one thing is presently King of France, and it is bald—the meaning of "the present King of France" is not a particular object and statements in which "the present King of France" occurs are not, in general, properly analyzed as having a subject-predicate form. Rather, as above, they are quantified statements, statements about the quantity of things to which predicates like "present King of France" and "bald" apply.

Russell argues that this account, unlike the competing accounts due to the Austrian philosopher Alexius Meinong[6] (1853–1920) and Frege, provides a satisfying solution to various puzzles surrounding definite descriptions. One of these is the so-called puzzle of non-being or "negative existentials"—the puzzle of how we can meaningfully deny the existence of something. Take "the present King of France doesn't exist." Now, suppose, against Russell, that the meaning of "the present King of France" is a particular object. Further, suppose, as seems to be the case, that "the present King of France doesn't exist" is meaningful. In this case, however, the very meaningfulness of "the present King of France doesn't exist" seems to entail that the present King of France does in some manner exist, namely as the object meant by "the present King of France." In contrast, on Russell's analysis, no such puzzles seem to arise: "the present King of France doesn't exist" is true just in case either nothing is presently King of France or more than one thing is presently King of France; and so "the present King of France doesn't exist" will be straightforwardly true, since nothing is presently King of France. Crucially, none of this presupposes that in order for "the present King of France doesn't exist" to be meaningful, there must in some manner exist a present King of France. As we will see in Chapter 10, Russell's analysis would prove influential

---

[6]See, for example, "The Theory of Objects" ([1904] 1960).

216   Early Analytic Philosophy

for those, like Quine, who have a preference for "desert landscapes"—ontological and metaphysical outlooks that aim to dispense with extravagant and unnecessary entities.

At the start of "On Denoting," Russell identifies definite descriptions by their form: a definite description, Russell says, is an expression of the form "the F," where "F" is some predicate expression (479). However, Russell goes on to suggest that what we typically regard as proper names—expressions like "Socrates," "Aristotle," "Barack Obama," "Donald Trump"—are in fact "disguised descriptions." What this means is that, according to Russell, expressions like these are in fact equivalent to definite descriptions, and thus that statements in which they occur should be given the same analysis. Take "Socrates" and the statement "Socrates drank hemlock." We might think that this is a subject-predicate statement—a statement that attributes the property of drinking hemlock to the object named or meant by "Socrates." On Russell's view, this is a mistake: according to Russell, rather than mean a particular object, "Socrates" really means the same as some descriptive phrase, like "the snub-nosed philosopher." In terms of the techniqes of modern logic, when it comes to putting "Socrates drank hemlock" into symbolic notation, for Russell it would be incorrect to represent this as "Hs," with "s" representing the name "Socrates" and "H" representing the predicate "drank hemlock." Rather, it should be symbolized in the same manner as a sentence like "the snub-nosed philosopher drank hemlock," as a quantified statement like "$(\exists x)[(Sx \wedge (\forall y)(Sy \to y = x) \wedge Hx)]$" ("there is some x such that x is a snub-nosed philosopher, any y that is a snub-nosed philosopher is the same as x, and x drank hemlock").

Why think that ordinary names are "disguised descriptions"? One idea goes like this. For just about any ordinary name, it seems perfectly meaningful to use that name in a "negative existential"—statements like "Socrates didn't exist" or "Lady Gaga doesn't exist" are perfectly meaningful (though, as it happens, false). However, for the same reasons as with definite descriptions, this would lead to certain puzzles if the very meaning of "Socrates" or "Lady Gaga" were a particular object, the object meant by the expression. For example, if the very meaning of "Lady Gaga" is a certain person—or, as Russell would put it, if "Lady Gaga doesn't exist" has a subject-predicate form—it would seem that some such person must in some manner exist in order for "Lady Gaga doesn't exist" to even be meaningful. Russell's solution, again, is to suppose that ordinary names like "Lady Gaga" are really shorthand for definite descriptions, and thus that negative existentials involving them ought to be given the same analysis as negative existentials involving the corresponding descriptions.

Russell's account of definite descriptions, and denoting phrases more generally, raises a number of questions. For one thing, Russell's criticisms of alternative positions have been challenged. Indeed, his critique in "On Denoting" of Frege's views has been referred to as "one of the most mysterious passages in twentieth-century philosophy."[7] Further, as we will see in Chapter 6, Russell's contemporary E. E. Constance Jones (1848–1922) questioned how exactly his "theory of descriptions" resolves the various puzzles that he considers in "On Denoting." More generally, as we will see in Chapter 11, Russell's views on names and descriptions, as well as those of Frege, continue to be the subject of lively intellectual debate.

Analysis, sense-data, and scientific philosophy

Russell's "On Denoting" is important as an example of the kind of analysis that Russell (and others) thought could be used to make genuine philosophical progress. It is also important, however, for understanding the extensive role that Russell's theory of descriptions played in much of his subsequent philosophy and, indeed, his conception of philosophy itself.

In some ways, Russell was motivated by epistemological concerns, concerns about what we can and cannot know, from the very start of his philosophical career. Nonetheless, these concerns became especially explicit starting around 1910, as it was around this time that Russell began to seriously engage with the traditional, broadly Cartesian question of what, based on what is available to us in experience, we can and cannot know about the external world. In "Knowledge by Acquaintance and Knowledge by Description" (1910), and elsewhere, Russell in part employs the theory of descriptions in addressing this question.[8] Russell's central distinction in this paper is between two ways in which one can know a thing, one of which he claims is prior to and more fundamental than the other. This is the distinction between knowing a thing by being acquainted with it and knowing a thing as that which satisfies a certain description. Regarding acquaintance, Russell writes:

---

[7] In Miller 2007.

[8] Misak reports that Russell acquired the distinction between knowledge by acquaintance and knowledge by description from William James, though he developed it in a different way (2016: 98); see also Proops 2014 for discussion of the similarities and differences between Russell's and James's account of this distinction.

Early Analytic Philosophy

> I say that I am acquainted with an object when I have a direct cognitive relation to that object, i.e., when I am directly aware of the object itself. When I speak of a cognitive relation here, I do not mean the sort of relation which constitutes judgment, but the sort which constitutes presentation ... to say that S has acquaintance with O is essentially the same thing as to say that O is presented to S. (108)

Given this conception of acquaintance, it turns out that we are not acquainted with all that much. First, and most prominently, Russell maintains that we are acquainted with what he calls "sense-data": things like patches of color in our visual field or momentary sounds in our auditory field, along with tactile, olfactory, and gustatory sensations. He explains such "sensible objects" in *Our Knowledge of the External World* as follows:

> When I speak of a "sensible object," it must be understood that I do not mean such a thing as a table, which is both visible and tangible, can be seen by many people at once, and is more or less permanent. What I mean is just that patch of colour which is momentarily seen when we look at the table, or just that particular hardness which is felt when we press it, or just that particular sound which is heard when we rap it. (83)

Second, he maintains that we are probably acquainted with a self, a view that he would later question. Finally, he maintains that we are acquainted with at least some universals, what he calls "concepts."

It is crucial to notice what is not included in this list. Most pertinently, it does not include ordinary physical objects, things like desks, chairs, trees, flowers—or, indeed, any physical bodies. Nor does the list include other minds; while perhaps I can be acquainted with the contents of my mind, I cannot, it seems, be acquainted with the mind of anybody other than myself. Rather, according to Russell, our knowledge of all such things is via description: we know a chair, for example, not by being acquainted with some such object, but rather as "the F," where "F" is some descriptive expression. This raises the question: what sort of descriptions do we know physical objects under? If I know a chair as "the F," what is the meaning of "F"? Russell's answer is that all knowledge by description is premised on knowledge by acquaintance. He puts this as follows:

> The fundamental epistemological principle in the analysis of propositions containing descriptions is this: every proposition which we can understand must be composed wholly of constituents with which we are acquainted. (117)

> All propositions intelligible to us, whether or not they primarily concern things only known to us by description, are composed wholly of constituents with which we are acquainted, for a constituent with which we are not acquainted is unintelligible to us. (128)

In effect, on Russell's view, talk of physical objects, things like chairs, trees, and so on—things known via description—must be analyzable into talk of objects of acquaintance, things like sense-data and universals. So, when we say something like "the chair is in the hallway," what we are really saying can be understood in terms of some complex description that only makes reference to objects with which we are acquainted—again, things like sense-data and universals.

In various places—including *Our Knowledge of the External World* and *The Philosophy of Logical Atomism* ([1918] 2009) as well as *The Analysis of Mind* (1921) and *The Analysis of Matter* (1927b)—Russell aimed to show that in fact our talk about the physical world, whether in everyday life or within natural science, could indeed be constructed from objects of acquaintance. His motivation for this project was largely epistemological. In some places Russell emphasized the idea of verification, which as we will see in Chapter 8 played a related role in the logical empiricist movement that included Carnap and A. J. Ayer (1910–89). Thus he wrote in *Our Knowledge of the External World*:

> I think it may be laid down quite generally that, in so far as physics or common sense is verifiable, it must be capable of interpretation in terms of actual sense-data alone. The reason for this is simple. Verification consists always in the occurrence of an expected sense-datum. Astronomers tell us there will be an eclipse of the moon. We look at the moon, and find the earth's shadow biting into it, that is to say, we see an appearance quite different from that of the usual full moon. Now if an expected sense datum constitutes a verification, what was asserted must have been about sense-data; or, at any rate, if part of what was asserted was not about sense-data, then only the other part has been verified. (88–9)

Russell was similarly motivated by broadly Cartesian concerns about our knowledge of things beyond immediate acquaintance. In particular, Russell reasoned that if our talk of some sort of object, say a chair or a tree, could not be constructed from objects of acquaintance—and in this sense would have to remain as a hypothetical or merely inferred entity—we could always have doubts about the existence of that sort of object. Russell regarded this as an application of Occam's razor, writing that:

Entities are not to be multiplied without necessity. In other words, in dealing with any subject-matter, find out what entities are undeniably involved, and state everything in terms of these entities. Very often the resulting statement is more complicated and difficult than one which, like common sense and most philosophy, assumes hypothetical entities whose existence there is no good reason to believe in. ([1914] 2009: 112)

Indeed, Russell regarded it as "the supreme maxim of scientific philosophy" that one should always prefer constructions from objects of acquaintance to hypothetical or inferred entities—that "wherever possible, substitute constructions out of known entities for inferences to unknown entities" ([1924] 1993: 161)—and in doing so, he reasoned, one "avoids the risk of introducing fictitious metaphysical entities" ([1914] 2009: 134).

Russell's attempt, in effect, to construct the world out of objects of acquaintance is extremely ambitious and raises a host of philosophical issues. The reader is encouraged to reflect on both Russell's motivations for this project and its chances for success, along with the details of the various examples that Russell discusses in "Knowledge by Acquaintance and Knowledge by Description." We will return to some related issues in Chapter 8, where we will discuss the logical empiricist movement.

Concluding remarks

Russell sometimes recommended a piecemeal approach to philosophy according to which philosophers ought to focus on specific philosophical issues rather than engage in the kind of grand, speculative theorizing of the sort characteristic of Bradley and others. Nonetheless, Russell himself was a systematic, big-picture thinker, bringing together views on philosophy of language, epistemology, and metaphysics to develop a comprehensive position concerning the very nature and point of philosophical inquiry. Indeed, in the history of analytic philosophy, Russell stands out as one of the most systematic, big-picture thinkers.

Russell viewed himself as reacting against Bradley's monistic idealism. Such a view, Russell believed, is unable to provide a viable account of mathematics, science, and the truths of everyday life. For Russell, philosophy and philosophers should not aim to dispute the findings of the sciences, or aim to show that the sciences at best deliver partial truths, but should rather aim to provide an account of them under which they might provide us with genuine truths about the world around us, truths that we can claim to know. In this respect, like Moore, Russell thought that the aims of philosophy ought to be more modest than others may have thought. Moreover, as we will see in later chapters, the kind of method that Russell recommended for philosophy, exhibited in the readings below, would prove influential, particularly for the logical empiricist movement that we will explore in Chapter 8.

Further reading

Primary sources

Russell, B. ([1918] 2009), *The Philosophy of Logical Atomism*, New York: Routledge.

Russell, B. (1919), *Introduction to Mathematical Philosophy*, London: George Allen and Unwin.

Russell, B. (1967, 1968, 1969), *The Autobiography of Bertrand Russell*, Vols 1, 2, and 3, London: George Allen and Unwin (Vols 1 and 2); New York: Simon and Schuster (Vol. 3).

Secondary sources

Candlish, S. (2007), *The Russell/Bradley Dispute and its Significance for Twentieth-Century Philosophy*, Basingstoke: Palgrave Macmillan.

Griffin, N. (1991), *Russell's Idealist Apprenticeship*, Oxford: Clarendon.

Hylton, P. (1990), *Russell, Idealism, and the Emergence of Analytic Philosophy*, New York: Oxford University Press.

Neale, S. (1990), *Descriptions*, Cambridge, MA: The MIT Press.

Pears, D. (1967), *Bertrand Russell and the British Tradition in Philosophy*, London: Collins.

Potter, M. (2020), *The Rise of Analytic Philosophy, 1879–1930*, New York: Routledge.

Preti, C. (Forthcoming, "Yours Fraternally: Russell and Moore", in K. Klement (ed.), *The Oxford Handbook of Bertrand Russell*, Oxford: Oxford University Press.

222 Early Analytic Philosophy

Readings

Russell on Monism and Relations (selections from *The Principles of Mathematics* and *Our Knowledge of the External World*).
Russell, B. *The Principles of Mathematics* (selections).
Reprinted from Russell, B. (1903), *The Principles of Mathematics*, Cambridge: Cambridge University Press.

Selections from Chapter 4, "Proper Names, Adjectives, and Verbs"

53. It may be asked whether everything that, in the logical sense we are concerned with, is a verb, expresses a relation or not. It seems plain that, if we were right in holding that "Socrates is human" is a proposition having only one term, the *is* in this proposition cannot express a relation in the ordinary sense. In fact, subject-predicate propositions are distinguished by just this non-relational character. Nevertheless, a relation between Socrates and humanity is certainly *implied*, and it is very difficult to conceive the proposition as expressing no relation at all. We may perhaps say that it is a relation, although it is distinguished from other relations in that it does not permit itself to be regarded as an assertion concerning either of its terms indifferently, but only as an assertion concerning the referent. A similar remark may apply to the proposition "*A* is," which holds of every term without exception. The *is* here is quite different from the *is* in "Socrates is human"; it may be regarded as complex, and as really predicating Being of *A*. In this way, the true logical verb in a proposition may be always regarded as asserting a relation. But it is so hard to know exactly what is meant by *relation* that the whole question is in danger of becoming purely verbal.

54. The twofold nature of the verb, as actual verb and as verbal noun, may be expressed, if all verbs are held to be relations, as the difference between a relation in itself and a relation actually relating. Consider, for example, the proposition "*A* differs from *B*." The constituents of this proposition, if we analyze it, appear to be only *A*, difference, *B*. Yet these constituents, thus placed side by side, do not reconstitute the proposition. The difference which occurs in the proposition actually relates *A* and *B*, whereas the difference after analysis is a notion which has no connection with *A* and *B*. It may be said that we ought, in the analysis, to mention the relations which difference has to *A* and *B*, relations which are expressed by *is* and *from* when we say "*A* is different from *B*." These

Bertrand Russell on Relations, Descriptions, and Knowledge   223

relations consist in the fact that A is referent and B relatum with respect to difference. But "A, referent, difference, relatum, B" is still merely a list of terms, not a proposition. A proposition, in fact, is essentially a unity, and when analysis has destroyed the unity, no enumeration of constituents will restore the proposition. The verb, when used as a verb, embodies the unity of the proposition, and is thus distinguishable from the verb considered as a term, though I do not know how to give a clear account of the precise nature of the distinction.

55. It may be doubted whether the general concept *difference* occurs at all in the proposition "A differs from B," or whether there is not rather a specific difference of A and B, and another specific difference of C and D, which are respectively affirmed in "A differs from B" and "C differs from D." In this way, *difference* becomes a class-concept of which there are as many instances as there are pairs of different terms; and the instances may be said, in Platonic phrase, to partake of the nature of difference. As this point is quite vital in the theory of relations, it may be well to dwell upon it. And first of all, I must point out that in "A differs from B" I intend to consider the bare numerical difference in virtue of which they are two, not difference in this or that respect.

Let us first try the hypothesis that a difference is *a* complex notion, compounded of difference together with some special quality distinguishing a particular difference from every other particular difference. So far as the relation of difference itself is concerned, we are to suppose that no distinction can be made between different cases; but there are to be different associated qualities in different cases. But since cases are distinguished by their terms, the quality must be primarily associated with the terms, not with difference. If the quality be not a relation, it can have no special connection with the difference of A and B, which it was to render distinguishable from bare difference, and if it fails in this it becomes irrelevant. On the other hand, if it be a new relation between A and B, over and above difference, we shall have to hold that any two terms have two relations, difference and a specific difference, the latter not holding between any other pair of terms. This view is a combination of two others, of which the first holds that the abstract general relation of difference itself holds between A and B, while the second holds that when two terms differ they have, corresponding to this fact, a specific relation of difference, unique and unanalyzable and not shared by any other pair of terms. Either of these views may be held with either the denial or the affirmation of the other. Let us see what is to be said for and against them.

Against the notion of specific differences, it may be urged that, if differences differ, their differences from each other must also differ, and thus we are led into

224   Early Analytic Philosophy

an endless process. Those who object to endless processes will see in this a proof that differences do not differ. But in the present work, it will be maintained that there are no contradictions peculiar to the notion of infinity, and that an endless process is not to be objected to unless it arises in the analysis of the actual meaning of a proposition. In the present case, the process is one of implications, not one of analysis; it must therefore be regarded as harmless.

Against the notion that the abstract relation of difference holds between A and B, we have the argument derived from the analysis of "A differs from B," which gave rise to the present discussion. It is to be observed that the hypothesis which combines the general and the specific difference must suppose that there are two distinct propositions, the one affirming the general, the other the specific difference. Thus if there cannot be a general difference between A and B, this mediating hypothesis is also impossible. And we saw that the attempt to avoid the failure of analysis by including in the meaning of "A differs from B" the relations of difference to A and B was vain. This attempt, in fact, leads to an endless process of the inadmissible kind; for we shall have to include the relations of the said relations to A and B and difference, and so on, and in this continually increasing complexity we are supposed to be only analyzing the *meaning* of our original proposition. This argument establishes a point of very great importance, namely, that when a relation holds between two terms, the relations of the relation to the terms, and of these relations to the relation and the terms, and so on *ad infinitum*, though all implied by the proposition affirming the original relation, form no part of the *meaning* of this proposition.

But the above argument does not suffice to prove that the relation of A to B cannot be abstract difference: it remains tenable that, as was suggested to begin with, the true solution lies in regarding every proposition as having a kind of unity which analysis cannot preserve, and which is lost even though it be mentioned by analysis as an element in the proposition. This view has doubtless its own difficulties, but the view that no two pairs of terms can have the same relation both contains difficulties of its own and fails to solve the difficulty for the sake of which it was invented. For, even if the difference of A and B be absolutely peculiar to A and B, still the three terms A, B, difference of A from B, do not reconstitute the proposition "A differs from B," any more than A and B and difference did. And it seems plain that, even if differences did differ, they would still have to have something in common. But the most general way in which two terms can have something in common is by both having a given relation to a given term. Hence if no two pairs of terms can have the same relation, it follows that no two terms can have anything in common, and hence

Bertrand Russell on Relations, Descriptions, and Knowledge

different differences will not be in any definable sense *instances* of difference.[1] I conclude, then, that the relation affirmed between *A* and *B* in the proposition "*A* differs from *B*" is the general relation of difference, and is precisely and numerically the same as the relation affirmed between *C* and *D* in "*C* differs from *D*." And this doctrine must be held, for the same reasons, to be true of all other relations; relations do not have instances, but are strictly the same in all propositions in which they occur.

We may now sum up the main points elicited in our discussion of the verb. The verb, we saw, is a concept which, like the adjective, may occur in a proposition without being one of the terms of the proposition, though it may also be made into a logical subject. One verb, and one only, must occur as verb in every proposition; but every proposition, by turning its verb into a verbal noun, can be changed into a single logical subject, of a kind which I shall call in future a propositional concept. Every verb, in the logical sense of the word, may be regarded as a relation; when it occurs as verb, it actually relates, but when it occurs as verbal noun it is the bare relation considered independently of the terms which it relates. Verbs do not, like adjectives, have instances, but are identical in all the cases of their occurrence. Owing to the way in which the verb actually relates the terms of a proposition, every proposition has a unity which renders it distinct from the sum of its constituents. All these points lead to logical problems, which, in a treatise on logic, would deserve to be fully and thoroughly discussed.
[material removed]

Selections from Chapter 9, "Relations"

94. Next after subject-predicate propositions come two types of propositions which appear equally simple. These are the propositions in which a relation is asserted between two terms, and those in which two terms are said to be two. The latter class of propositions will be considered hereafter; the former must be considered at once. It has often been held that every proposition can be reduced to one of the subject-predicate type, but this view we shall, throughout the present work, find abundant reason for rejecting. It might be held, however, that all propositions not of the subject-predicate type, and not asserting numbers,

---

[1] The above argument appears to prove that Mr Moore's theory of universals with numerically diverse instances in his paper on Identity (*Proceedings of the Aristotelian Society*, 1900–1901) must not be applied to all concepts. The relation of an instance to its universal, at any rate, must be actually and numerically the same in all cases where it occurs.

226   Early Analytic Philosophy

could be reduced to propositions containing two terms and a relation. This opinion would be more difficult to refute, but this too, we shall find, has no good grounds in its favour.[2] We may therefore allow that there are relations having more than two terms; but as these are more complex, it will be well to consider first such as have two terms only.

A relation between two terms is a concept which occurs in a proposition in which there are two terms not occurring as concepts,[3] and in which the interchange of the two terms gives a different proposition. This last mark is required to distinguish a relational proposition from one of the type "*a* and *b* are two," which is identical with "*b* and *a* are two." A relational proposition may be symbolized by *aRb*, where *R* is the relation and *a* and *b* are the terms; and *aRb* will then always, provided *a* and *b* are not identical, denote a different proposition from *bRa*. That is to say, it is characteristic of a relation of two terms that it proceeds, so to speak, *from* one *to* the other. This is what may be called the *sense* of the relation, and is, as we shall find, the source of order and series. It must be held as an axiom that *aRb* implies and is implied by a relational proposition *bR'a*, in which the relation *R'* proceeds from *b* to *a*, and may or may not be the same relation as *R*. But even when *aRb* implies and is implied by *bRa*, it must be strictly maintained that these are different propositions. We may distinguish the term *from* which the relation proceeds as the *referent*, and the term *to* which it proceeds as the *relatum*. The sense of a relation is a fundamental notion, which is not capable of definition. The relation which holds between *b* and *a* whenever *R* holds between *a* and *b* will be called the *converse* of *R*, and will be denoted (following Schröder) by ˘*R*. The relation of *R* to ˘*R* is the relation of oppositeness, or difference of sense; and this must not be defined (as would seem at first sight legitimate) by the above mutual implication in any single case, but only by the fact of its holding for all cases in which the given relation occurs. The grounds for this view are derived from certain propositions in which terms are related to themselves not-symmetrically, *i.e.* by a relation whose converse is not identical with itself. These propositions must now be examined.

95. There is a certain temptation to affirm that no term can be related to itself; and there is a still stronger temptation to affirm that, if a term can be related to itself, the relation must be symmetrical, *i.e.* identical with its converse. But both these temptations must be resisted. In the first place, if no term were related to itself, we should never be able to assert self-identity, since this is

---

[2]See *inf.*, Part IV, Chap. xxv, §200. [Editor's note: as marked in the Preface, references and footnotes in the original texts have been retained unaltered.]

[3]This description, as we saw above (§48), excludes the pseudo-relation of subject to predicate.

plainly a relation. But since there is such a notion as identity, and since it seems undeniable that every term is identical with itself, we must allow that a term may be related to itself. Identity, however, is still a symmetrical relation, and may be admitted without any great qualms. The matter becomes far worse when we have to admit not-symmetrical relations of terms to themselves. Nevertheless the following propositions seem undeniable; Being is, or has being; 1 is one, or has unity; concept is conceptual; term is a term; class-concept is a class-concept. All these are of one of the three equivalent types which we distinguished at the beginning of Chapter v, which may be called respectively subject-predicate propositions, propositions asserting the relation of predication, and propositions asserting membership of a class. What we have to consider is, then, the fact that a predicate may be predicable of itself. It is necessary, for our present purpose, to take our propositions in the second form (Socrates has humanity), since the subject-predicate form is not in the above sense relational. We may take, as the type of such propositions, "unity has unity." Now it is certainly undeniable that the relation of predication is asymmetrical, since subjects cannot in general be predicated of their predicates. Thus "unity has unity" asserts one relation of unity to itself, and implies another, namely the converse relation: unity has to itself both the relation of subject to predicate, and the relation of predicate to subject. Now if the referent and the relatum are identical, it is plain that the relatum has to the referent the same relation as the referent has to the relatum. Hence if the converse of a relation in a particular case were defined by mutual implication in that particular case, it would appear that, in the present case, our relation has two converses, since two different relations of relatum to referent are implied by "unity has unity." We must therefore define the converse of a relation by the fact that aRb implies and is implied by $b\breve{R}a$ whatever a and b may be, and whether or not the relation R holds between them. That is to say, a and b are here essentially variables, and if we give them any constant value, we may find that aRb implies and is implied by $bR'a$, where R' is some relation other than $\breve{R}$.

Thus three points must be noted with regard to relations of two terms: (1) they all have sense, so that, provided a and b are not identical, we can distinguish aRb from bRa; (2) they all have a converse, i.e. a relation $\breve{R}$ such that aRb implies and is implied by $b\breve{R}a$, whatever a and b may be; (3) some relations hold between a term and itself, and such relations are not necessarily symmetrical, i.e. there may be two different relations, which are each other's converses, and which both hold between a term and itself.

96. For the general theory of relations, especially in its mathematical developments, certain axioms relating classes and relations are of great

Early Analytic Philosophy

importance. It is to be held that to have a given relation to a given term is a predicate, so that all terms having this relation to this term form a class. It is to be held further that to have a given relation at all is a predicate, so that all referents with respect to a given relation form a class. It follows, by considering the converse relation, that all relata also form a class. These two classes I shall call respectively the *domain* and the *converse domain* of the relation; the logical sum of the two I shall call the *field* of the relation.

The axiom that all referents with respect to a given relation form a class seems, however, to require some limitation, and that on account of the contradiction mentioned at the end of Chapter vi. This contradiction may be stated as follows. We saw that some predicates can be predicated of themselves. Consider now those of which this is not the case. These are the referents (and also the relata) in what seems like a complex relation, namely the combination of non-predicability with identity. But there is no predicate which attaches to all of them and to no other terms. For this predicate will either be predicable or not predicable of itself. If it is predicable of itself, it is one of those referents by relation to which it was defined, and therefore, in virtue of their definition, it is not predicable of itself. Conversely, if it is not predicable of itself, then again it is one of the said referents, of all of which (by hypothesis) it is predicable, and therefore again it is predicable of itself. This is a contradiction, which shows that all the referents considered have no exclusive common predicate, and therefore, if defining predicates are essential to classes, do not form a class.

The matter may be put otherwise. In defining the would-be class of predicates, all those not predicable of themselves have been used up. The common predicate of all these predicates cannot be one of them, since for each of them there is at least one predicate (namely itself) of which it is not predicable. But again, the supposed common predicate cannot be any other predicate, for if it were, it would be predicable of itself, *i.e.* it would be a member of the supposed class of predicates, since these were defined as those of which it is predicable. Thus no predicate is left over which could attach to all the predicates considered.

It follows from the above that not every definable collection of terms forms a class defined by a common predicate. This fact must be borne in mind, and we must endeavour to discover what properties a collection must have in order to form such a class. The exact point established by the above contradiction may be stated as follows: A proposition apparently containing only one variable may not be equivalent to any proposition asserting that the variable in question has a certain predicate. It remains an open question whether every class must have a defining predicate.

Bertrand Russell on Relations, Descriptions, and Knowledge

That all terms having a given relation to a given term form a class defined by an exclusive common predicate results from the doctrine of Chapter vii, that the proposition *aRb* can be analyzed into the subject *a* and the assertion *Rb*. To be a term of which *Rb* can be asserted appears to be plainly a predicate. But it does not follow, I think, that to be a term of which, for some value of *y*, *Ry* can be asserted, is a predicate. The doctrine of propositional functions requires, however, that all terms having the latter property should form a class. This class I shall call the *domain* of the relation *R* as well as the class of referents. The domain of the converse relation will be also called the converse domain, as well as the class of relata. The two domains together will be called the *field* of the relation—a notion chiefly important as regards series. Thus if paternity be the relation, fathers form its domain, children its converse domain, and fathers and children together its field.

It may be doubted whether a proposition *aRb* can be regarded as asserting *aR* of *b*, or whether only ˇ*Ra* can be asserted of *b*. In other words, is a relational proposition only an assertion concerning the referent, or also an assertion concerning the relatum? If we take the latter view, we shall have, connected with (say) "*a* is greater than *b*," four assertions, namely "is greater than *b*," "*a* is greater than," "is less than *a*" and "*b* is less than." I am inclined myself to adopt this view, but I know of no argument on either side.

97. We can form the logical sum and product of two relations or of a class of relations exactly as in the case of classes, except that here we have to deal with double variability. In addition to these ways of combination, we have also the relative product, which is in general non-commutative, and therefore requires that the number of factors should be finite. If *R*, *S* be two relations, to say that their relative product *RS* holds between two terms *x*, *z* is to say that there is a term *y* to which *x* has the relation *R*, and which itself has the relation *S* to *z*. Thus brother-in-law is the relative product of wife and brother or of sister and husband: father-in-law is the relative product of wife and father, whereas the relative product of father and wife is mother or step-mother.

98. There is a temptation to regard a relation as definable in extension as a class of couples. This has the formal advantage that it avoids the necessity for the primitive proposition asserting that every couple has a relation holding between no other pair of terms. But it is necessary to give sense to the couple, to distinguish the referent from the relatum: thus a couple becomes essentially distinct from a class of two terms, and must itself be introduced as a primitive idea. It would seem, viewing the matter philosophically, that sense can only be derived from some relational proposition, and that the assertion that *a* is referent and *b* relatum already involves a purely relational proposition in which *a* and *b* are

terms, though the relation asserted is only the general one of referent to relatum. There are, in fact, concepts such as *greater*, which occur otherwise than as terms in propositions having two terms (§§48, 54); and no doctrine of couples can evade such propositions. It seems therefore more correct to take an intensional view of relations, and to identify them rather with class-concepts than with classes. This procedure is formally more convenient, and seems also nearer to the logical facts. Throughout Mathematics there is the same rather curious relation of intensional and extensional points of view: the symbols other than variable terms (*i.e.* the variable class-concepts and relations) stand for intensions, while the actual objects dealt with are always extensions. Thus in the calculus of relations, it is classes of couples that are relevant, but the symbolism deals with them by means of relations. This is precisely similar to the state of things explained in relation to classes, and it seems unnecessary to repeat the explanations at length.

99. Mr Bradley, in *Appearance and Reality*, Chapter iii, has based an argument against the reality of relations upon the endless regress arising from the fact that a relation which relates two terms must be related to each of them. The endless regress is undeniable, if relational propositions are taken to be ultimate, but it is very doubtful whether it forms any logical difficulty. We have already had occasion (§55) to distinguish two kinds of regress, the one proceeding merely to perpetually new implied propositions, the other in the meaning of a proposition itself; of these two kinds, we agreed that the former, since the solution of the problem of infinity, has ceased to be objectionable, while the latter remains inadmissible. We have to inquire which kind of regress occurs in the present instance. It may be urged that it is part of the very meaning of a relational proposition that the relation involved should have to the terms the relation expressed in saying that it relates them, and that this is what makes the distinction, which we formerly (§54) left unexplained, between a relating relation and a relation in itself. It may be urged, however, against this view, that the assertion of a relation between the relation and the terms, though implied, is no part of the original proposition, and that a relating relation is distinguished from a relation in itself by the indefinable element of assertion which distinguishes a proposition from a concept. Against this it might be retorted that, in the concept "difference of a and b," difference relates a and b just as much as in the proposition "a and b differ"; but to this it may be rejoined that we found the difference of a and b, except in so far as some specific point of difference may be in question, to be indistinguishable from bare difference. Thus it seems impossible to prove that the endless regress involved is of the objectionable kind. We may distinguish, I think, between "a exceeds b" and "a is greater than b," though it would be absurd to deny that people usually

mean the same thing by these two propositions. On the principle, from which I can see no escape, that every genuine word must have some meaning, the *is* and *than* must form part of "*a* is greater than *b*," which thus contains more than two terms and a relation. The *is* seems to state that *a* has to *greater* the relation of referent, while the *than* states similarly that *b* has to *greater* the relation of relatum. But "*a* exceeds *b*" may be held to express solely the relation of *a* to *b*, without including any of the implications of further relations. Hence we shall have to conclude that a relational proposition *aRb* does not include in its *meaning* any relation of *a* or *b* to *R*, and that the endless regress, though undeniable, is logically quite harmless. With these remarks, we may leave the further theory of relations to later Parts of the present work.

Selections from Chapter 26, "Asymmetrical Relations"

208. We have now seen that all order depends upon transitive asymmetrical relations. As such relations are of a kind which traditional logic is unwilling to admit, and as the refusal to admit them is one of the main sources of the contradictions which the Critical Philosophy has found in mathematics, it will be desirable, before proceeding further, to make an excursion into pure logic, and to set forth the grounds which make the admission of such relations necessary. At a later stage (in Part VI, Chap. li), I shall endeavour to answer the general objections of philosophers to relations; for the present, I am concerned only with asymmetrical relations.

Relations may be divided into four classes, according as they do or do not possess either of two attributes, transitiveness,[4] and symmetry. Relations such that xRy always implies yRx are called *symmetrical*; relations such that xRy, yRz together always imply xRz are called *transitive*. Relations which do not possess the first property I shall call *not symmetrical*; relations which do possess the opposite property, *i.e.* for which xRy always excludes yRx, I shall call *asymmetrical*. Relations which do not possess the second property I shall call *not transitive*; those which possess the property that xRy, yRz always exclude xRz I shall call *intransitive*. All these cases may be illustrated from human relationships. The relation *brother or sister* is symmetrical, and is transitive if we allow that a man may be his own brother, and a woman her own sister. The

---

[4]This term appears to have been first used in the present sense by De Morgan; see *Camb. Phil. Trans.* ix, p. 104; x, p. 346. The term is now in general use.

232 Early Analytic Philosophy

relation *brother* is not symmetrical, but is transitive. *Half-brother or half-sister* is symmetrical but not transitive. *Spouse* is symmetrical but intransitive; *descendant* is asymmetrical but transitive. *Half-brother* is not symmetrical and not transitive; if third marriages were forbidden, it would be intransitive. *Son-in-law* is asymmetrical and not transitive; if second marriages were forbidden, it would be intransitive. *Brother-in-law* is not symmetrical and not transitive. Finally, *father* is both asymmetrical and intransitive. Of not-transitive but not intransitive relations there is, so far as I know, only one *important* instance, namely diversity; of not-symmetrical but not asymmetrical relations there seems to be similarly only one important instance, namely *implication*. In other cases, of the kind that usually occur, relations are either transitive or intransitive, and either symmetrical or asymmetrical.

209. Relations which are both symmetrical and transitive are formally of the nature of equality. Any term of the field of such a relation has the relation in question to itself, though it may not have the relation to any other term. For denoting the relation by the sign of equality, if a be of the field of the relation, there is some term b such that $a = b$. If a and b be identical, then $a = a$. But if not, then, since the relation is symmetrical, $b = a$; since it is transitive, and we have $a = b$, $b = a$, it follows that $a = a$. The property of a relation which insures that it holds between a term and itself is called by Peano *reflexiveness*, and he has shown, contrary to what was previously believed, that this property cannot be inferred from symmetry and transitiveness. For neither of these properties asserts that there is a b such that $a = b$, but only what follows in case there is such a b; and if there is no such b, then the proof of $a = a$ fails.[5] This property of reflexiveness, however, introduces some difficulty. There is only one relation of which it is true without limitation, and that is identity. In all other cases, it holds only of the terms of a certain class. Quantitative equality, for example, is only reflexive as applied to quantities; of other terms, it is absurd to assert that they have quantitative equality with themselves. Logical equality, again, is only reflexive for classes, or propositions, or relations. Simultaneity is only reflexive for events, and so on. Thus, with any given symmetrical transitive relation, other than identity, we can only assert reflexiveness within a certain class: and of this class, apart from the principle of abstraction (already mentioned in Part III, Chap. xix, and shortly to be discussed at length), there need be no definition except as the extension of the transitive symmetrical relation in question. And when the

---

[5]See *e.g. Revue de Mathématiques*, T. vii, p. 22; *Notations de Logique Mathématique*, Turin, 1894, p. 45, *F*. 1901, p. 193.

Bertrand Russell on Relations, Descriptions, and Knowledge   233

class is so defined, reflexiveness within that class, as we have seen, follows from transitiveness and symmetry.

210. By introducing what I have called the principle of abstraction,[6] a somewhat better account of reflexiveness becomes possible. Peano has defined[7] a process which he calls definition by abstraction, of which, as he shows, frequent use is made in Mathematics. This process is as follows: when there is any relation which is transitive, symmetrical and (within its field) reflexive, then, if this relation holds between u and v, we define a new entity $\varphi(u)$, which is to be identical with $\varphi(v)$. Thus our relation is analyzed into sameness of relation to the new term $\varphi(u)$ or $\varphi(v)$. Now the legitimacy of this process, as set forth by Peano, requires an axiom, namely the axiom that, if there is any instance of the relation in question, then there is such an entity as $\varphi(u)$ or $\varphi(v)$. This axiom is my principle of abstraction, which, precisely stated, is as follows: "Every transitive symmetrical relation, of which there is at least one instance, is analyzable into joint possession of a new relation to a new term, the new relation being such that no term can have this relation to more than one term, but that its converse does not have this property." This principle amounts, in common language, to the assertion that transitive symmetrical relations arise from a common property, with the addition that this property stands, to the terms which have it, in a relation in which nothing else stands to those terms. It gives the precise statement of the principle, often applied by philosophers, that symmetrical transitive relations always spring from identity of content. Identity of content is, however, an extremely vague phrase, to which the above proposition gives, in the present case, a precise signification, but one which in no way answers the purpose of the phrase, which is, apparently, the reduction of relations to adjectives of the related terms.

It is now possible to give a clearer account of the reflexive property. Let R be our symmetrical relation, and let S be the asymmetrical relation which two terms having the relation R must have to some third term. Then the proposition xRy is equivalent to this: "There is some term a such that xSa and ySa." Hence it follows that, if x belongs to what we have called the domain of S, $i.e.$ if there is any term a such that xSa, then xRx; for xRx is merely xSa and xSa. It does not of course follow that there is any other term y such that xRy, and thus Peano's objections to the usual proof of reflexiveness are valid. But by means of the

---

[6]An axiom virtually identical with this principle, but not stated with the necessary precision, and not demonstrated, will be found in De Morgan, *Camb. Phil. Trans.* Vol. x, p. 345.
[7]*Notations de Logique Mathématique*, p. 45.

234   Early Analytic Philosophy

analysis of symmetrical transitive relations, we obtain the proof of the reflexive property, together with the exact limitation to which it is subject.

211. We can now see the reason for excluding from our accounts of the methods of generating series a seventh method, which some readers may have expected to find. This is the method in which position is merely relative—a method which, in Chap. xix, §154, we rejected as regards quantity. As the whole philosophy of space and time is bound up with the question as to the legitimacy of this method, which is in fact the question as to absolute and relative position, it may be well to give an account of it here, and to show how the principle of abstraction leads to the absolute theory of position.

If we consider such a series as that of events, and if we refuse to allow absolute time, we shall have to admit three fundamental relations among events, namely, simultaneity, priority, and posteriority. Such a theory may be formally stated as follows: Let there be a class of terms, such that any two, x and y, have either an asymmetrical transitive relation P, or the converse relation $\check{}P$, or a symmetrical transitive relation R. Also let xRy, yPz imply xPz, and let xPy, yRz imply xPz. Then all the terms can be arranged in a series, in which, however, there may be many terms which have the same place in the series. This place, according to the relational theory of position, is nothing but the transitive symmetrical relation R to a number of other terms. But it follows from the principle of abstraction that there is some relation S, such that, if xRy, there is some one entity t for which xSt, ySt. We shall then find that the different entities t, corresponding to different groups of our original terms, also form a series, but one in which any two different terms have an asymmetrical relation (formally, the product $\check{}SRS$). These terms t will then be the absolute positions of our x's and y's, and our supposed seventh method of generating series is reduced to the fundamental second method. Thus there will be no series having only relative position, but in all series it is the positions themselves that constitute the series.[8]

212. We are now in a position to meet the philosophic dislike of relations. The whole account of order given above, and the present argument concerning abstraction, will be necessarily objected to by those philosophers—and they are, I fear, the major part—who hold that no relations can possess absolute and metaphysical validity. It is not my intention here to enter upon the general question, but merely to exhibit the objections to any analysis of asymmetrical relations.

It is a common opinion—often held unconsciously, and employed in argument, even by those who do not explicitly advocate it—that all propositions,

---

[8]A formal treatment of relative position is given by Schröder, *Sur une extension de l'idée d'ordre*, *Congrès*, Vol. iii, p. 235.

Bertrand Russell on Relations, Descriptions, and Knowledge   235

ultimately, consist of a subject and a predicate. When this opinion is confronted by a relational proposition, it has two ways of dealing with it, of which the one may be called monadistic, the other monistic. Given, say, the proposition aRb, where R is some relation, the monadistic view will analyse this into two propositions, which we may call ar_1 and br_2, which give to a and b respectively adjectives supposed to be together equivalent to R. The monistic view, on the contrary, regards the relation as a property of the whole composed of a and b, and as thus equivalent to a proposition which we may denote by $(ab)r$. Of these views, the first is represented by Leibniz and (on the whole) by Lotze, the second by Spinoza and Mr Bradley. Let us examine these views successively, as applied to asymmetrical relations; and for the sake of definiteness, let us take the relations of greater and less.

213. The monadistic view is stated with admirable lucidity by Leibniz in the following passage:[9] "The ratio or proportion between two lines L and M may be conceived three several ways; as a ratio of the greater L to the lesser M; as a ratio of the lesser M to the greater L; and lastly, as something abstracted from both, that is, as the ratio between L and M, without considering which is the antecedent, or which the consequent; which the subject, and which the object, ... In the first way of considering them, L the greater, in the second M the lesser, is the subject of that accident which philosophers call *relation*. But which of them will be the subject, in the third way of considering them? It cannot be said that both of them, L and M together, are the subject of such an accident; for if so, we should have an accident in two subjects, with one leg in one, and the other in the other; which is contrary to the notion of accidents. Therefore we must say that this relation, in this third way of considering it, is indeed *out of* the subjects; but being neither a substance nor an accident, it must be a mere ideal thing, the consideration of which is nevertheless useful."

214. The third of the above ways of considering the relation of greater and less is, roughly speaking, that which the monists advocate, holding, as they do, that the whole composed of L and M is one subject, so that their way of considering ratio does not compel us, as Leibniz supposed, to place it among bipeds. For the present our concern is only with the first two ways. In the first way of considering the matter, we have "L is (greater than M)," the words in brackets being considered as an adjective of L. But when we examine this adjective it is at once evident that it is complex: it consists, at least, of the parts *greater* and M, and both these parts are essential. To say that L is greater does

---

[9]*Phil. Werke*, Gerhardt's ed., Vol. vii, p. 401.

236　Early Analytic Philosophy

not at all convey our meaning, and it is highly probable that M is also greater. The supposed adjective of L involves some reference to M; but what can be meant by a reference the theory leaves unintelligible. An adjective involving a reference to M is plainly an adjective which is relative to M, and this is merely a cumbrous way of describing a relation. Or, to put the matter otherwise, if L has an adjective corresponding to the fact that it is greater than M, this adjective is logically subsequent to, and is merely derived from, the direct relation of L to M. Apart from M, nothing appears in the analysis of L to differentiate it from M; and yet, on the theory of relations in question, L should differ intrinsically from M. Thus we should be forced, in all cases of asymmetrical relations, to admit a specific difference between the related terms, although no analysis of either singly will reveal any relevant property which it possesses and the other lacks. For the monadistic theory of relations, this constitutes a contradiction; and it is a contradiction which condemns the theory from which it springs.[10]

Let us examine further the application of the monadistic theory to quantitative relations. The proposition "A is greater than B" is to be analyzable into two propositions, one giving an adjective to A, the other giving one to B. The advocate of the opinion in question will probably hold that A and B are quantities, not magnitudes, and will say that the adjectives required are the magnitudes of A and B. But then he will have to admit a relation between the magnitudes, which will be as asymmetrical as the relation which the magnitudes were to explain. Hence the magnitudes will need new adjectives, and so on *ad infinitum*; and the infinite process will have to be completed before any *meaning* can be assigned to our original proposition. This kind of infinite process is undoubtedly objectionable, since its sole object is to explain the meaning of a certain proposition, and yet none of its steps bring it any nearer to that meaning.[11] Thus we cannot take the magnitudes of A and B as the required adjectives. But further, if we take any adjectives whatever except such as have each a reference to the other term, we shall not be able, even formally, to give any account of the relation, without assuming just such a relation between the adjectives. For the

---

[10]See a paper on "The Relations of Number and Quantity," *Mind*, N.S. No. 23. This paper was written while I still adhered to the monadistic theory of relations: the contradiction in question, therefore, was regarded as inevitable. The following passage from Kant raises the same point: "Die rechte Hand ist der linken ähnlich und gleich, und wenn man blos auf eine derselben allein sieht, auf die Proportion der Lage der Theile unter einander und auf die Grösse des Ganzen, so muss eine vollständige Beschreibung der einen in allen Stücken auch von der andern gelten." (*Von dem ersten Grunde des Unterschiedes der Gegenden im Raume*, ed. Hart. Vol. ii, p. 389.)

[11]Where an infinite process of this kind is required we are necessarily dealing with a proposition which is an infinite unity, in the sense of Part II, Chap. xvii.

Bertrand Russell on Relations, Descriptions, and Knowledge **237**

mere fact that the adjectives are different will yield only a symmetrical relation. Thus if our two terms have different colours we find that A has to B the relation of differing in colour, a relation which no amount of careful handling will render asymmetrical. Or if we were to recur to magnitudes, we could merely say that A and B differ in magnitude, which gives us no indication as to which is the greater. Thus the adjectives of A and B must be, as in Leibniz's analysis, adjectives having a reference each to the other term. The adjective of A must be "greater than B," and that of B must be "less than A." Thus A and B differ, since they have different adjectives—B is not greater than B, and A is not less than A—but the adjectives are extrinsic, in the sense that A's adjective has reference to B, and B's to A. Hence the attempted analysis of the relation fails, and we are forced to admit what the theory was designed to avoid, a so-called "external" relation, *i.e.* one implying no complexity in either of the related terms.

The same result may be proved of asymmetrical relations generally, since it depends solely upon the fact that both identity and diversity are symmetrical. Let a and b have an asymmetrical relation R, so that aRb and $b\bar{R}a$. Let the supposed adjectives (which, as we have seen, must each have a reference to the other term) be denoted by β and α respectively. Thus our terms become $a\beta$ and $b\alpha$. α involves a reference to a, and β to b; and α and β differ, since the relation is asymmetrical. But a and b have no intrinsic differences corresponding to the relation R, and prior to it; or, if they have, the points of difference must themselves have a relation analogous to R, so that nothing is gained. Either α or β expresses a difference between a and b, but one which, since either α or β involves reference to a term other than that whose adjective it is, so far from being prior to R, is in fact the relation R itself. And since α and β both presuppose R, the difference between α and β cannot be used to supply an intrinsic difference between a and b. Thus we have again a difference without a prior point of difference. This shows that some asymmetrical relations must be ultimate, and that at least one such ultimate asymmetrical relation must be a component in any asymmetrical relation that may be suggested.

It is easy to criticize the monadistic theory from a general standpoint, by developing the contradictions which spring from the relations of the terms to the adjectives into which our first relation has been analyzed. These considerations, which have no special connection with asymmetry, belong to general philosophy, and have been urged by advocates of the monistic theory. Thus Mr Bradley says of the monadistic theory:[12] "We, in brief, are led by a

---

[12]*Appearance and Reality*, 1st edition, p. 31.

238   Early Analytic Philosophy

principle of fission which conducts us to no end. Every quality in relation has, in consequence, a diversity within its own nature, and this diversity cannot immediately be asserted of the quality. Hence the quality must exchange its unity for an internal relation. But, thus set free, the diverse aspects, because each something in relation, must each be something also beyond. This diversity is fatal to the internal unity of each; and it demands a new relation, and so on without limit." It remains to be seen whether the monistic theory, in avoiding this difficulty, does not become subject to others quite as serious.

215. The monistic theory holds that every relational proposition aRb is to be resolved into a proposition concerning the whole which a and b compose—a proposition which we may denote by $(ab)r$. This view, like the other, may be examined with special reference to asymmetrical relations, or from the standpoint of general philosophy. We are told, by those who advocate this opinion, that the whole contains diversity within itself, that it synthesizes differences, and that it performs other similar feats. For my part, I am unable to attach any precise significance to these phrases. But let us do our best.

The proposition "a is greater than b," we are told, does not really say anything about either a or b, but about the two together. Denoting the whole which they compose by (ab) it says, we will suppose, "(ab) contains diversity of magnitude." Now to this statement—neglecting for the present all general arguments—there is a special objection in the case of asymmetry, (ab) is symmetrical with regard to a and b, and thus the property of the whole will be exactly the same in the case where a is greater than b as in the case where b is greater than a. Leibniz, who did not accept the monistic theory, and had therefore no reason to render it plausible, clearly perceived this fact, as appears from the above quotation. For, in his third way of regarding ratio, we do not consider which is the antecedent, which the consequent; and it is indeed sufficiently evident that, in the whole (ab) as such, there is neither antecedent nor consequent. In order to distinguish a whole (ab) from a whole (ba), as we must do if we are to explain asymmetry, we shall be forced back from the whole to the parts and their relation. For (ab) and (ba) consist of precisely the same parts, and differ in no respect whatever save the sense of the relation between a and b. "a is greater than b" and "b is greater than a" are propositions containing precisely the same constituents, and giving rise therefore to precisely the same whole; their difference lies solely in the fact that *greater* is, in the first case, a relation of a to b, in the second, a relation of b to a. Thus the distinction of sense, *i.e.* the distinction between an asymmetrical relation and its converse, is one which the monistic theory of relations is wholly unable to explain.

Bertrand Russell on Relations, Descriptions, and Knowledge

Arguments of a more general nature might be multiplied almost indefinitely, but the following argument seems peculiarly relevant. The relation of whole and part is itself an asymmetrical relation, and the whole—as monists are peculiarly fond of telling us—is distinct from all its parts, both severally and collectively. Hence when we say "*a* is part of *b*," we really mean, if the monistic theory be correct, to assert something of the whole composed of *a* and *b*, which is not to be confounded with *b*. If the proposition concerning this new whole be not one of whole and part there will be no true judgments of whole and part, and it will therefore be false to say that a relation between the parts is really an adjective of the whole. If the new proposition is one of whole and part, it will require a new one for its meaning, and so on. If, as a desperate measure, the monist asserts that the whole composed of *a* and *b* is not distinct from *b*, he is compelled to admit that a whole is the sum (in the sense of Symbolic Logic) of its parts, which, besides being an abandonment of his whole position, renders it inevitable that the whole should be symmetrical as regards its parts—a view which we have already seen to be fatal. And hence we find monists driven to the view that the only true whole, the Absolute, has no parts at all, and that no propositions in regard to it or anything else are quite true—a view which, in the mere statement, unavoidably contradicts itself. And surely an opinion which holds all propositions to be in the end self-contradictory is sufficiently condemned by the fact that, if it be accepted, it also must be self-contradictory.

216. We have now seen that asymmetrical relations are unintelligible on both the usual theories of relation.[13] Hence, since such relations are involved in Number, Quantity, Order, Space, Time, and Motion, we can hardly hope for a satisfactory philosophy of Mathematics so long as we adhere to the view that no relation can be "purely external." As soon, however, as we adopt a different theory, the logical puzzles, which have hitherto obstructed philosophers, are seen to be artificial. Among the terms commonly regarded as relational, those that are symmetrical and transitive—such as equality and simultaneity—*are* capable of reduction to what has been vaguely called identity of content, but this in turn must be analyzed into sameness of relation to some other term. For the so-called properties of a term are, in fact, only other terms to which it stands in some relation; and a common property of two terms is a term to which both stand in the same relation.

The present long digression into the realm of logic is necessitated by the fundamental importance of order, and by the total impossibility of explaining

---

[13]The grounds of these theories will be examined from a more general point of view in Part VI, Chap. li.

240   **Early Analytic Philosophy**

order without abandoning the most cherished and widespread of philosophic dogmas. Everything depends, where order is concerned, upon asymmetry and difference of sense, but these two concepts are unintelligible to the traditional logic. In the next chapter we shall have to examine the connection of difference of sense with what appears in Mathematics as difference of sign. In this examination, though some pure logic will still be requisite, we shall approach again to mathematical topics; and these will occupy us wholly throughout the succeeding chapters of this Part.

Russell, B. *Our Knowledge of the External World*. (selections)
Reprinted from Russell, B. (1914), *Our Knowledge of the External World*, Chicago: Open Court.

Selections from Chapter 1, "Current Tendencies"

[material removed]

Twenty years ago, the classical tradition, having vanquished the opposing tradition of the English empiricists, held almost unquestioned sway in all Anglo-Saxon universities. At the present day, though it is losing ground, many of the most prominent teachers still adhere to it. In academic France, in spite of M. Bergson, it is far stronger than all its opponents combined; and in Germany it has many vigorous advocates. Nevertheless, it represents on the whole a decaying force, and it has failed to adapt itself to the temper of the age. Its advocates are, in the main, those whose extra-philosophical knowledge is literary, rather than those who have felt the inspiration of science. There are, apart from reasoned arguments, certain general intellectual forces against it— the same general forces which are breaking down the other great syntheses of the past, and making our age one of bewildered groping where our ancestors walked in the clear daylight of unquestioning certainty.

The original impulse out of which the classical tradition developed was the naïve faith of the Greek philosophers in the omnipotence of reasoning. The discovery of geometry had intoxicated them, and its *a priori* deductive method appeared capable of universal application. They would prove, for instance, that all reality is one, that there is no such thing as change, that the world of sense is a world of mere illusion; and the strangeness of their results gave them no qualms because they believed in the correctness of their reasoning. Thus it came to be thought that by mere thinking the most surprising and important truths concerning the whole of reality could be established with a certainty

Bertrand Russell on Relations, Descriptions, and Knowledge   **241**

which no contrary observations could shake. As the vital impulse of the early philosophers died away, its place was taken by authority and tradition, reinforced, in the Middle Ages and almost to our own day, by systematic theology. Modern philosophy, from Descartes onwards, though not bound by authority like that of the Middle Ages, still accepted more or less uncritically the Aristotelian logic. Moreover, it still believed, except in Great Britain, that *a priori* reasoning could reveal otherwise undiscoverable secrets about the universe, and could prove reality to be quite different from what, to direct observation, it appears to be. It is this belief, rather than any particular tenets resulting from it, that I regard as the distinguishing characteristic of the classical tradition, and as hitherto the main obstacle to a scientific attitude in philosophy.

The nature of the philosophy embodied in the classical tradition may be made clearer by taking a particular exponent as an illustration. For this purpose, let us consider for a moment the doctrines of Mr Bradley, who is probably the most distinguished living representative of this school. Mr. Bradley's *Appearance and Reality* is a book consisting of two parts, the first called *Appearance*, the second *Reality*. The first part examines and condemns almost all that makes up our everyday world: things and qualities, relations, space and time, change, causation, activity, the self. All these, though in some sense facts which qualify reality, are not real as they appear. What is real is one single, indivisible, timeless whole, called the Absolute, which is in some sense spiritual, but does not consist of souls, or of thought and will as we know them. And all this is established by abstract logical reasoning professing to find self-contradictions in the categories condemned as mere appearance, and to leave no tenable alternative to the kind of Absolute which is finally affirmed to be real.

One brief example may suffice to illustrate Mr Bradley's method. The world appears to be full of many things with various relations to each other—right and left, before and after, father and son, and so on. But relations, according to Mr Bradley, are found on examination to be self-contradictory and therefore impossible. He first argues that, if there are relations, there must be qualities between which they hold. This part of his argument need not detain us. He then proceeds:

"But how the relation can stand to the qualities is, on the other side, unintelligible. If it is nothing to the qualities, then they are not related at all; and, if so, as we saw, they have ceased to be qualities, and their relation is a nonentity. But if it is to be something to them, then clearly we shall require a *new* connecting relation. For the relation hardly can be the mere adjective of one or both of its terms; or, at least, as such it seems indefensible. And, being something itself, if it does not itself bear a relation to the terms, in what intelligible way will it succeed in being anything to them? But here again we are

242   Early Analytic Philosophy

hurried off into the eddy of a hopeless process, since we are forced to go on finding new relations without end. The links are united by a link, and this bond of union is a link which also has two ends; and these require each a fresh link to connect them with the old. The problem is to find how the relation can stand to its qualities, and this problem is insoluble."[1]

I do not propose to examine this argument in detail, or to show the exact points where, in my opinion, it is fallacious. I have quoted it only as an example of method. Most people will admit, I think, that it is calculated to produce bewilderment rather than conviction, because there is more likelihood of error in a very subtle, abstract, and difficult argument than in so patent a fact as the interrelatedness of the things in the world. To the early Greeks, to whom geometry was practically the only known science, it was possible to follow reasoning with assent even when it led to the strangest conclusions. But to us, with our methods of experiment and observation, our knowledge of the long history of *a priori* errors refuted by empirical science, it has become natural to suspect a fallacy in any deduction of which the conclusion appears to contradict patent facts. It is easy to carry such suspicion too far, and it is very desirable, if possible, actually to discover the exact nature of the error when it exists. But there is no doubt that what we may call the empirical outlook has become part of most educated people's habit of mind; and it is this, rather than any definite argument, that has diminished the hold of the classical tradition upon students of philosophy and the instructed public generally.

The function of logic in philosophy, as I shall try to show at a later stage, is all-important; but I do not think its function is that which it has in the classical tradition. In that tradition, logic becomes constructive through negation. Where a number of alternatives seem, at first sight, to be equally possible, logic is made to condemn all of them except one, and that one is then pronounced to be realised in the actual world. Thus the world is constructed by means of logic, with little or no appeal to concrete experience. The true function of logic is, in my opinion, exactly the opposite of this. As applied to matters of experience, it is analytic rather than constructive; taken *a priori*, it shows the possibility of hitherto unsuspected alternatives more often than the impossibility of alternatives which seemed *prima facie* possible. Thus, while it liberates imagination as to what the world *may* be, it refuses to legislate as to what the world *is*. This change, which has been brought about by an internal revolution in logic, has swept away the ambitious constructions of traditional metaphysics, even for those whose faith in

---

[1] *Appearance and Reality*, pp. 32–3.

Bertrand Russell on Relations, Descriptions, and Knowledge

logic is greatest; while to the many who regard logic as a chimera the paradoxical systems to which it has given rise do not seem worthy even of refutation. Thus on all sides these systems have ceased to attract, and even the philosophical world tends more and more to pass them by.

One or two of the favourite doctrines of the school we are considering may be mentioned to illustrate the nature of its claims. The universe, it tells us, is an "organic unity," like an animal or a perfect work of art. By this it means, roughly speaking, that all the different parts fit together and co-operate, and are what they are because of their place in the whole. This belief is sometimes advanced dogmatically, while at other times it is defended by certain logical arguments. If it is true, every part of the universe is a microcosm, a miniature reflection of the whole. If we knew ourselves thoroughly, according to this doctrine, we should know everything. Common sense would naturally object that there are people— say in China—with whom our relations are so indirect and trivial that we cannot infer anything important as to them from any fact about ourselves. If there are living beings in Mars or in more distant parts of the universe, the same argument becomes even stronger. But further, perhaps the whole contents of the space and time in which we live form only one of many universes, each seeming to itself complete. And thus the conception of the necessary unity of all that is resolves itself into the poverty of imagination, and a freer logic emancipates us from the strait-waistcoated benevolent institution which idealism palms off as the totality of being.

Another very important doctrine held by most, though not all, of the school we are examining is the doctrine that all reality is what is called "mental" or "spiritual," or that, at any rate, all reality is dependent for its existence upon what is mental. This view is often particularised into the form which states that the relation of knower and known is fundamental, and that nothing can exist unless it either knows or is known. Here again the same legislative function is ascribed to *a priori* argumentation: it is thought that there are contradictions in an unknown reality. Again, if I am not mistaken, the argument is fallacious, and a better logic will show that no limits can be set to the extent and nature of the unknown. And when I speak of the unknown, I do not mean merely what we personally do not know, but what is not known to any mind. Here as elsewhere, while the older logic shut out possibilities and imprisoned imagination within the walls of the familiar, the newer logic shows rather what may happen, and refuses to decide as to what *must* happen.

The classical tradition in philosophy is the last surviving child of two very diverse parents: the Greek belief in reason, and the mediæval belief in the tidiness of the universe. To the schoolmen, who lived amid wars, massacres,

Early Analytic Philosophy

and pestilences, nothing appeared so delightful as safety and order. In their idealising dreams, it was safety and order that they sought: the universe of Thomas Aquinas or Dante is as small and neat as a Dutch interior. To us, to whom safety has become monotony, to whom the primeval savageries of nature are so remote as to become a mere pleasing condiment to our ordered routine, the world of dreams is very different from what it was amid the wars of Guelf and Ghibelline. Hence William James's protest against what he calls the "block universe" of the classical tradition; hence Nietzsche's worship of force; hence the verbal bloodthirstiness of many quiet literary men. The barbaric substratum of human nature, unsatisfied in action, finds an outlet in imagination. In philosophy, as elsewhere, this tendency is visible; and it is this, rather than formal argument, that has thrust aside the classical tradition for a philosophy which fancies itself more virile and more vital.

[material removed]

Selections from Chapter 2, "Logic as the Essence of Philosophy"

[material removed]

In every proposition and in every inference there is, besides the particular subject-matter concerned, a certain *form*, a way in which the constituents of the proposition or inference are put together. If I say, "Socrates is mortal," "Jones is angry," "The sun is hot," there is something in common in these three cases, something indicated by the word "is." What is in common is the *form* of the proposition, not an actual constituent. If I say a number of things about Socrates— that he was an Athenian, that he married Xantippe, that he drank the hemlock— there is a common constituent, namely Socrates, in all the propositions I enunciate, but they have diverse forms. If, on the other hand, I take any one of these propositions and replace its constituents, one at a time, by other constituents, the form remains constant, but no constituent remains. Take (say) the series of propositions, "Socrates drank the hemlock," "Coleridge drank the hemlock," "Coleridge drank opium," "Coleridge ate opium." The form remains unchanged throughout this series, but all the constituents are altered. Thus form is not another constituent, but is the way the constituents are put together. It is forms, in this sense, that are the proper object of philosophical logic.

It is obvious that the knowledge of logical forms is something quite different from knowledge of existing things. The form of "Socrates drank the hemlock" is not an existing thing like Socrates or the hemlock, nor does it even have that close relation to existing things that drinking has. It is something altogether more

Bertrand Russell on Relations, Descriptions, and Knowledge   245

abstract and remote. We might understand all the separate words of a sentence without understanding the sentence: if a sentence is long and complicated, this is apt to happen. In such a case we have knowledge of the constituents, but not of the form. We may also have knowledge of the form without having knowledge of the constituents. If I say, "Rorarius drank the hemlock," those among you who have never heard of Rorarius (supposing there are any) will understand the form, without having knowledge of all the constituents. In order to understand a sentence, it is necessary to have knowledge both of the constituents and of the particular instance of the form. It is in this way that a sentence conveys information, since it tells us that certain known objects are related according to a certain known form. Thus some kind of knowledge of logical forms, though with most people it is not explicit, is involved in all understanding of discourse. It is the business of philosophical logic to extract this knowledge from its concrete integuments, and to render it explicit and pure.

In all inference, form alone is essential: the particular subject-matter is irrelevant except as securing the truth of the premisses. This is one reason for the great importance of logical form. When I say, "Socrates was a man, all men are mortal, therefore Socrates was mortal," the connection of premisses and conclusion does not in any way depend upon its being Socrates and man and mortality that I am mentioning. The general form of the inference may be expressed in some such words as, "If a thing has a certain property, and whatever has this property has a certain other property, then the thing in question also has that other property." Here no particular things or properties are mentioned: the proposition is absolutely general. All inferences, when stated fully, are instances of propositions having this kind of generality. If they seem to depend upon the subject-matter otherwise than as regards the truth of the premisses, that is because the premisses have not been all explicitly stated. In logic, it is a waste of time to deal with inferences concerning particular cases: we deal throughout with completely general and purely formal implications, leaving it to other sciences to discover when the hypotheses are verified and when they are not.

But the forms of propositions giving rise to inferences are not the simplest forms: they are always hypothetical, stating that if one proposition is true, then so is another. Before considering inference, therefore, logic must consider those simpler forms which inference presupposes. Here the traditional logic failed completely: it believed that there was only one form of simple proposition (*i.e.* of proposition not stating a relation between two or more other propositions), namely, the form which ascribes a predicate to a subject. This is the appropriate form in assigning the qualities of a given thing—we may say "this thing is round, and red, and so on." Grammar favours this form, but philosophically it is so far

Early Analytic Philosophy

from universal that it is not even very common. If we say "this thing is bigger than that," we are not assigning a mere quality of "this," but a relation of "this" and "that." We might express the same fact by saying "that thing is smaller than this," where grammatically the subject is changed. Thus propositions stating that two things have a certain relation have a different form from subject-predicate propositions, and the failure to perceive this difference or to allow for it has been the source of many errors in traditional metaphysics.

The belief or unconscious conviction that all propositions are of the subject-predicate form—in other words, that every fact consists in some thing having some quality—has rendered most philosophers incapable of giving any account of the world of science and daily life. If they had been honestly anxious to give such an account, they would probably have discovered their error very quickly; but most of them were less anxious to understand the world of science and daily life, than to convict it of unreality in the interests of a super-sensible "real" world. Belief in the unreality of the world of sense arises with irresistible force in certain moods—moods which, I imagine, have some simple physiological basis, but are none the less powerfully persuasive. The conviction born of these moods is the source of most mysticism and of most metaphysics. When the emotional intensity of such a mood subsides, a man who is in the habit of reasoning will search for logical reasons in favour of the belief which he finds in himself. But since the belief already exists, he will be very hospitable to any reason that suggests itself. The paradoxes apparently proved by his logic are really the paradoxes of mysticism, and are the goal which he feels his logic must reach if it is to be in accordance with insight. It is in this way that logic has been pursued by those of the great philosophers who were mystics—notably Plato, Spinoza, and Hegel. But since they usually took for granted the supposed insight of the mystic emotion, their logical doctrines were presented with a certain dryness, and were believed by their disciples to be quite independent of the sudden illumination from which they sprang. Nevertheless their origin clung to them, and they remained—to borrow a useful word from Mr Santayana—"malicious" in regard to the world of science and common sense. It is only so that we can account for the complacency with which philosophers have accepted the inconsistency of their doctrines with all the common and scientific facts which seem best established and most worthy of belief.

The logic of mysticism shows, as is natural, the defects which are inherent in anything malicious. While the mystic mood is dominant, the need of logic is not felt; as the mood fades, the impulse to logic reasserts itself, but with a desire to retain the vanishing insight, or at least to prove that it *was* insight, and that what seems to contradict it is illusion. The logic which thus arises is not quite disinterested or candid, and is inspired by a certain hatred of the daily world to which it is to be applied. Such an attitude naturally does not tend to the best results. Everyone knows that to read an author simply in order to refute him is not the way to understand him; and to read the book of Nature with a conviction that it is all illusion is just as unlikely to lead to understanding. If our logic is to find the common world intelligible, it must not be hostile, but must be inspired by a genuine acceptance such as is not usually to be found among metaphysicians.

Traditional logic, since it holds that all propositions have the subject-predicate form, is unable to admit the reality of relations: all relations, it maintains, must be reduced to properties of the apparently related terms. There are many ways of refuting this opinion; one of the easiest is derived from the consideration of what are called "asymmetrical" relations. In order to explain this, I will first explain two independent ways of classifying relations.

Some relations, when they hold between A and B, also hold between B and A. Such, for example, is the relation "brother or sister." If A is a brother or sister of B, then B is a brother or sister of A. Such again is any kind of similarity, say similarity of colour. Any kind of dissimilarity is also of this kind: if the colour of A is unlike the colour of B, then the colour of B is unlike the colour of A. Relations of this sort are called *symmetrical*. Thus a relation is symmetrical if, whenever it holds between A and B, it also holds between B and A.

All relations that are not symmetrical are called *non-symmetrical*. Thus "brother" is non-symmetrical, because, if A is a brother of B, it may happen that B is a *sister* of A.

A relation is called *asymmetrical* when, if it holds between A and B, it *never* holds between B and A. Thus husband, father, grandfather, etc., are asymmetrical relations. So are *before, after, greater, above, to the right of*, etc. All the relations that give rise to series are of this kind.

Classification into symmetrical, asymmetrical, and merely non-symmetrical relations is the first of the two classifications we had to consider. The second is into transitive, intransitive, and merely non-transitive relations, which are defined as follows.

A relation is said to be *transitive*, if, whenever it holds between A and B and also between B and C, it holds between A and C. Thus *before, after, greater, above* are transitive. All relations giving rise to series are transitive, but so are many others. The transitive relations just mentioned were asymmetrical, but many transitive relations are symmetrical—for instance, equality in any respect, exact identity of colour, being equally numerous (as applied to collections), and so on.

248   **Early Analytic Philosophy**

A relation is said to be *non-transitive* whenever it is not transitive. Thus "brother" is non-transitive, because a brother of one's brother may be oneself. All kinds of dissimilarity are non-transitive.

A relation is said to be *intransitive* when, if A has the relation to B, and B to C, A never has it to C. Thus "father" is intransitive. So is such a relation as "one inch taller" or "one year later."

Let us now, in the light of this classification, return to the question whether all relations can be reduced to predications.

In the case of symmetrical relations—*i.e.* relations which, if they hold between A and B, also hold between B and A—some kind of plausibility can be given to this doctrine. A symmetrical relation which is transitive, such as equality, can be regarded as expressing possession of some common property, while one which is not transitive, such as inequality, can be regarded as expressing possession of different properties. But when we come to asymmetrical relations, such as before and after, greater and less, etc., the attempt to reduce them to properties becomes obviously impossible. When, for example, two things are merely known to be unequal, without our knowing which is greater, we may say that the inequality results from their having different magnitudes, because inequality is a symmetrical relation; but to say that when one thing is *greater* than another, and not merely unequal to it, that means that they have different magnitudes, is formally incapable of explaining the facts. For if the other thing had been greater than the one, the magnitudes would also have been different, though the fact to be explained would not have been the same. Thus mere *difference* of magnitude is not *all* that is involved, since, if it were, there would be no difference between one thing being greater than another, and the other being greater than the one. We shall have to say that the one magnitude is *greater* than the other, and thus we shall have failed to get rid of the relation "greater." In short, both possession of the same property and possession of different properties are *symmetrical* relations, and therefore cannot account for the existence of *asymmetrical* relations.

Asymmetrical relations are involved in all series—in space and time, greater and less, whole and part, and many others of the most important characteristics of the actual world. All these aspects, therefore, the logic which reduces everything to subjects and predicates is compelled to condemn as error and mere appearance. To those whose logic is not malicious, such a wholesale condemnation appears impossible. And in fact there is no reason except prejudice, so far as I can discover, for denying the reality of relations. When once their reality is admitted, all *logical* grounds for supposing the world of sense to be illusory disappear. If this is to be supposed, it must be frankly and simply on the ground of mystic insight

Bertrand Russell on Relations, Descriptions, and Knowledge

unsupported by argument. It is impossible to argue against what professes to be insight, so long as it does not argue in its own favour. As logicians, therefore, we may admit the possibility of the mystic's world, while yet, so long as we do not have his insight, we must continue to study the everyday world with which we are familiar. But when he contends that our world is impossible, then our logic is ready to repel his attack. And the first step in creating the logic which is to perform this service is the recognition of the reality of relations.

Relations which have two terms are only one kind of relations. A relation may have three terms, or four, or any number. Relations of two terms, being the simplest, have received more attention than the others, and have generally been alone considered by philosophers, both those who accepted and those who denied the reality of relations. But other relations have their importance, and are indispensable in the solution of certain problems. Jealousy, for example, is a relation between three people. Professor Royce mentions the relation "giving": when A gives B to C, that is a relation of three terms.[2] When a man says to his wife: "My dear, I wish you could induce Angelina to accept Edwin," his wish constitutes a relation between four people, himself, his wife, Angelina, and Edwin. Thus such relations are by no means recondite or rare. But in order to explain exactly how they differ from relations of two terms, we must embark upon a classification of the logical forms of facts, which is the first business of logic, and the business in which the traditional logic has been most deficient.

The existing world consists of many things with many qualities and relations. A complete description of the existing world would require not only a catalogue of the things, but also a mention of all their qualities and relations. We should have to know not only this, that, and the other thing, but also which was red, which yellow, which was earlier than which, which was between which two others, and so on. When I speak of a "fact," I do not mean one of the simple things in the world; I mean that a certain thing has a certain quality, or that certain things have a certain relation. Thus, for example, I should not call Napoleon a fact, but I should call it a fact that he was ambitious, or that he married Josephine. Now a fact, in this sense, is never simple, but always has two or more constituents. When it simply assigns a quality to a thing, it has only two constituents, the thing and the quality. When it consists of a relation between two things, it has three constituents, the things and the relation. When it consists of a relation between three things, it has four constituents, and so on. The constituents of facts, in the sense in which we are using the word "fact,"

---

[2] *Encyclopædia of the Philosophical Sciences*, vol. i. p. 97.

Early Analytic Philosophy

are not other facts, but are things and qualities or relations. When we say that there are relations of more than two terms, we mean that there are single facts consisting of a single relation and more than two things. I do not mean that one relation of two terms may hold between A and B, and also between A and C, as, for example, a man is the son of his father and also the son of his mother. This constitutes two distinct facts: if we choose to treat it as one fact, it is a fact which has facts for its constituents. But the facts I am speaking of have no facts among their constituents, but only things and relations. For example, when A is jealous of B on account of C, there is only one fact, involving three people; there are not two instances of jealousy, but only one. It is in such cases that I speak of a relation of three terms, where the simplest possible fact in which the relation occurs is one involving three things in addition to the relation. And the same applies to relations of four terms or five or any other number. All such relations must be admitted in our inventory of the logical forms of facts: two facts involving the same number of things have the same form, and two which involve different numbers of things have different forms.

[material removed]

Russell, B. "On Denoting".
Reprinted from Russell, B. (1905), "On Denoting", *Mind* 14: 479–93.

By a "denoting phrase" I mean a phrase such as any one of the following: a man, some man, any man, every man, all men, the present King of England, the present King of France, the centre of mass of the Solar System at the first instant of the twentieth century, the revolution of the earth round the sun, the revolution of the sun round the earth. Thus a phrase is denoting solely in virtue of its *form*. We may distinguish three cases: (1) A phrase map be denoting, and yet not denote anything; *e.g.*, "the present King of France". (2) A phrase may denote one definite object; *e.g.*, "the present King of England" denotes a certain man. (3) A phrase may denote ambiguously; *e.g.*, "a man" denotes not many men, but an ambiguous man. The interpretation of such phrases is a matter of considerable difficulty; indeed, it is very hard to frame any theory not susceptible of formal refutation. All the difficulties with which I am acquainted are met, so far as I can discover, by the theory which I am about to explain.

The subject of denoting is of very great importance, not only in logic and mathematics, but also in theory of knowledge. For example, we know that the centre of mass of the Solar System at a definite instant is some definite point, and we can affirm a number of propositions about it; but we have no immediate

Bertrand Russell on Relations, Descriptions, and Knowledge   251

acquaintance with this point, which is only known to us by description. The distinction between *acquaintance* and *knowledge about* is the distinction between the things we have presentations of, and the things we only reach by means of denoting phrases. It often happens that we know that a certain phrase denotes unambiguously, although we have no acquaintance with what it denotes; this occurs in the above case of the centre of mass. In perception we have acquaintance with the objects of perception, and in thought we have acquaintance with objects of a more abstract logical character; but we do not necessarily have acquaintance with the objects denoted by phrases composed of words with whose meanings we are acquainted. To take a very important instance: There seems no reason to believe that we are ever acquainted with other people's minds, seeing that these are not directly perceived; hence what we know about them is obtained through denoting. All thinking has to start from acquaintance; but it succeeds in thinking about many things with which we have no acquaintance.

The course of my argument will be as follows. I shall begin by stating the theory I intend to advocate;[1] I shall then discuss the theories of Frege and Meinong, showing why neither of them satisfies me; then I shall give the grounds in favour of my theory; and finally I shall briefly indicate the philosophical consequences of my theory.

My theory, briefly, is as follows. I take the notion of the *variable* as fundamental; I use "$C(x)$" to mean a proposition[2] in which x is a constituent, where x, the variable, is essentially and wholly undetermined. Then we can consider the two notions "$C(x)$ is always true" and "$C(x)$ is sometimes true".[3] Then everything and nothing and something (which are the most primitive of denoting phrases) are to be interpreted as follows:–

C (everything) means "$C(x)$ is always true";
C (nothing) means "'$C(x)$ is false' is always true";
C (something) means "It is false that '$C(x)$ is false' is always true".[4]

Here the notion "$C(x)$ is always true" is taken as ultimate and indefinable, and the others are defined by means of it. *Everything, nothing*, and *something*, are

---

[1] I have discussed this subject in *Principles of Mathematics*, chapter v., and §476. The theory there advocated is very nearly the same as Frege's, and is quite different from the theory to be advocated in what follows. [Editor's note: as marked in the Preface, references and footnotes in the original texts have been retained unaltered.]

[2] More exactly, a propositional function.

[3] The second of these can be defined by means of the first, if we take it to mean, "It is not true that 'C (x) is false' is always true."

[4] I shall sometimes use, instead of this complicated phrase, the phrase "$C(x)$ is not always false," or "$C(x)$ is sometimes true," supposed defined to mean the same as the complicated phrase.

Early Analytic Philosophy

not assumed to have any meaning in isolation, but a meaning is assigned to *every* proposition in which they occur. This is the principle of the theory of denoting I wish to advocate: that denoting phrases never have any meaning in themselves, but that every proposition in whose verbal expression they occur has a meaning. The difficulties concerning denoting are, I believe, all the result of a wrong analysis of propositions whose verbal expressions contain denoting phrases. The proper analysis, if I am not mistaken, may be further set forth as follows.

Suppose now we wish to interpret the proposition, "I met a man". If this is true, I met some definite man; but that is not what I affirm. What I affirm is, according to the theory I advocate:–

"'I met x, and x is human' is not always false".

Generally, defining the class of men as the class of objects having the predicate *human*, we say that:–

"C (a man)" means "'$C(x)$ and x is human' is not always false".

This leaves "a man," by itself, wholly destitute of meaning, but gives a meaning to every proposition in whose verbal expression "a man" occurs.

Consider next the proposition "all men are mortal". This proposition[5] is really hypothetical and states that *if* anything is a man, it is mortal. That is, it states that if x is a man, x is mortal, whatever x may be. Hence, substituting 'x is human' for 'x is a man,' we find:–

"All men are mortal" means "'If x is human, x is mortal' is always true".

This is what is expressed in symbolic logic by saying that "all men are mortal" means "'x is human' implies 'x is mortal' for all values of x". More generally, we say:–

"C (all men)" means "'If x is human, then $C(x)$ is true' is always true".

Similarly

"C (no men)" means "'If x is human, then $C(x)$ is false' is always true".
"C (some men)" will mean the same as "C (a man),"[6] and "C (a man)" means
   "It is false that '$C(x)$ and x is human' is always false".
"C (every man)" will mean the same as "C (all men)".

---

[5] As has been ably argued in Mr. Bradley's *Logic*, book i., chap. Ii.
[6] Psychologically "C (a man)" hs a suggestion of *only* one, and "C (some men)" has a suggestion of more *than* one; but we may neglect these suggestions in a preliminary sketch.

Bertrand Russell on Relations, Descriptions, and Knowledge 253

It remains to interpret phrases containing *the*. These are by far the most interesting and difficult of denoting phrases. Take as an instance "the father of Charles II. was executed". This asserts that there was an *x* who was the father of Charles II. and was executed. Now *the*, when it is strictly used, involves uniqueness; we do, it is true, speak of "*the* son of So-and-so" even when So-and-so has several sons, but it would be more correct to say "*a* son of So-and-so". Thus for our purposes we take *the* as involving uniqueness. Thus when we say "*x* was *the* father of Charles II." we not only assert that *x* had a certain relation to Charles II., but also that nothing else had this relation. The relation in question, without the assumption of uniqueness, and without any denoting phrases, is expressed by "*x* begat Charles II." To get an equivalent of "*x* was the father of Charles II.," we must add, "If *y* is other than *x*, *y* did not beget Charles II.," or, what is equivalent, "If *y* begat Charles II., *y* is identical with *x*." Hence "*x* is the father of Charles II." becomes "*x* begat Charles II.; and 'if *y* begat Charles II., *y* is identical with *x*' is always true of *y*."

Thus "the father of Charles II. was executed" becomes:–

"It is not always false of *x* that *x* begat Charles II. and that x was executed and that 'if *y* begat Charles II., *y* is identical with *x*' is always true of *y*."

This may seem a somewhat incredible interpretation; but I am not at present giving reasons, I am merely *stating* the theory.

To interpret "C (the father of Charles II.)," where C stands for any statement about him, we have only to substitute C(*x*) for "*x* was executed" in the above. Observe that, according to the above interpretation, whatever statement C may be, "C (the father of Charles II.)" implies:–

"It is not always false of *x* that 'if *y* begat Charles II., *y* is identical with *x*' is always true of *y*," which is what is expressed in common language by "Charles II. had one father and no more". Consequently if this condition fails, every proposition of the form "C (the father of Charles II.)" is false. Thus *e.g.* every proposition of the form "C (the present King of France)" is false. This is a great advantage in the present theory. I shall show later that it is not contrary to the law of contradiction, as might be at first supposed.

The above gives a reduction of all propositions in which denoting phrases occur to forms in which no such phrases occur. Why it is imperative to effect such a reduction, the subsequent discussion will endeavour to show.

The evidence for the above theory is derived from the difficulties which seem unavoidable if we regard denoting phrases as standing for genuine constituents of the propositions in whose verbal expressions they occur. Of the possible

254   Early Analytic Philosophy

theories which admit such constituents the simplest is that of Meinong.[7] This theory regards any grammatically correct denoting phrase as standing for an *object*. Thus "the present King of France," "the round square," etc., are supposed to be genuine objects. It is admitted that such objects do not subsist, but nevertheless they are supposed to be objects. This is in itself a difficult view; but the chief objection is that such objects, admittedly, are apt to infringe the law of contradiction. It is contended, for example, that the existent present King of France exists, and also does not exist; that the round square is round, and also not round; etc. But this is intolerable; and if any theory can be found to avoid this result, it is surely to be preferred.

The above breach of the law of contradiction is avoided by Frege's theory. He distinguishes, in a denoting phrase, two elements, which we may call the *meaning* and the *denotation*.[8] Thus "the centre of mass of the Solar System at the beginning of the twentieth century" is highly complex in meaning, but its denotation is a certain point, which is simple. The Solar System, the twentieth century, etc., are constituents of the *meaning*; but the *denotation* has no constituents at all.[9] One advantage of this distinction is that it shows why it is often worth while to assert identity. If we say "Scott is the author of *Waverley*," we assert an identity of denotation with a difference of meaning. I shall, however, not repeat the grounds in favour of this theory, as I have urged its claims elsewhere (*loc. cit.*), and am now concerned to dispute those claims.

One of the first difficulties that confront us, when we adopt the view that denoting phrases *express* a meaning and *denote* a denotation,[10] concerns the cases in which the denotation appears to be absent. If we say "the King of England is bald," that is, it would seem, not a statement about the complex *meaning* "the King of England," but about the actual man denoted by the meaning. But now consider "the King of France is bald". By parity of form, this also ought to be about the denotation of the phrase "the King of France". But this phrase, though it has a *meaning* provided "the King of England" has a meaning, has

---

[7]See *Untersuchungen sur Gegenstandstheorie under Psychologie*, Leipzig, 1904, the first three articles (by Meinong, Ameseder and Mally, respectively).

[8]See his "Ueber Sinn und Bedeutung," *Zeitschrift für Phil. And Phil. Kritik*, vol. 100.

[9]Frege distingnishes the two elements of meaning and denotation everywhere, and not only in complex denoting phrases. Thus it is the *meanings* of the constituents of a denoting complex that enter into its *meaning*, not their *denotation*. In the proposition "Mont Blanc is over 1,000 metres high," it is, according to him, the meaning of "Mont Blanc," not the actual mountain, that is a constituent of the *meaning* of the proposition.

[10]In this theory, we shall say that the denoting phrase *expresses* a meaning; and we shall say both of the phrase and of the meaning that they *denote* a denotation. In the other theory, which I advocate, there is no *meaning*, and only sometimes a *denotation*.

certainly no denotation, at least in any obvious sense. Hence one would suppose that "the King of France is bald" ought to be nonsense; but it is not nonsense, since it is plainly false. Or again consider such a proposition as the following: "If *u* is a class which has only one member, then that one member is a member of *u*," or, as we may state it, "If *u* is a unit class, *the u* is a *u*". This proposition ought to be *always* true, since the conclusion is true whenever the hypothesis is true. But "the *u*" is a denoting phrase, and it is the denotation, not the meaning, that is said to be a *u*. Now if *u* is *not* a unit class, "the *u*" seems to denote nothing; hence our proposition would seem to become nonsense as soon as *u* is not a unit class.

Now it is plain that such propositions do *not* become nonsense merely because their hypotheses are false. The King in "The Tempest" might say, "If Ferdinand is not drowned, Ferdinand is my only son". Now "my only son" is a denoting phrase, which, on the face of it, has a denotation when, and only when, I have exactly one son. But the above statement would nevertheless have remained true if Ferdinand had been in fact drowned. Thus we must either provide a denotation in cases in which it is at first sight absent, or we must abandon the view that the denotation is what is concerned in propositions which contain denoting phrases. The latter is the course that I advocate. The former course may be taken, as by Meinong, by admitting objects which do not subsist, and denying that they obey the law of contradiction; this, however, is to be avoided if possible. Another way of taking the same course (so far as our present alternative is concerned) is adopted by Frege, who provides by definition some purely conventional denotation for the cases in which otherwise there would be none. Thus "the King of France," is to denote the null-class; "the only son of Mr. So-and-so" (who has a fine family of ten), is to denote the class of all his sons; and so on. But this procedure, though it may not lead to actual logical error, is plainly artificial, and does not give an exact analysis of the matter. Thus if we allow that denoting phrases, in general, have the two sides of meaning and denotation, the cases where there seems to be no denotation cause difficulties both on the assumption that there really is a denotation and on the assumption that there really is none.

A logical theory may be tested by its capacity for dealing with puzzles, and it is a wholesome plan, in thinking about logic, to stock the mind with as many puzzles as possible, since these serve much the same purpose as is served by experiments in physical science. I shall therefore state three puzzles which a theory as to denoting ought to be able to solve; and I shall show later that my theory solves them.

(1) If *a* is identical with *b*, whatever is true of the one is true of the other, and either may be substituted for the other in any proposition without altering the

Early Analytic Philosophy

truth or falsehood of that proposition. Now George IV. wished to know whether Scott was the author of *Waverley*; and in fact Scott was the author of *Waverley*. Hence we may substitute *Scott* for *the author of " Waverley*," and thereby prove that George IV. wished to know whether Scott was Scott. Yet an interest in the law of identity can hardly be attributed to the first gentleman of Europe.

(2) By the law of excluded middle, either "A is B" or "A is not B" must be true. Hence either "the present King of France is bald" or "the present King of France is not bald" must be true. Yet if we enumerated the things that are bald, and then the things that are not bald, we should not find the present King of France in either list. Hegelians, who love a synthesis, will probably conclude that he wears a wig.

(3) Consider the proposition "A differs from B". If this is true, there is a difference between A and B, which fact may be expressed in the form "the difference between A and B subsists". But if it is false that A differs from B, then there is no difference between A and B, which fact may be expressed in the form "the difference between A and B does not subsist". But how can a non-entity be the subject of a proposition? "I think, therefore I am" is no more evident than "I am the subject of a proposition, therefore I am," provided "I am" is taken to assert subsistence or being,[11] not existence. Hence, it would appear, it must always be self-contradictory to deny the being of anything; but we have seen, in connexion with Meinong, that to admit being also sometimes leads to contradictions. Thus if A and B do not differ, to suppose either that there is, or that there is not, such an object as "the difference between A and B" seems equally impossible.

The relation of the meaning to the denotation involves certain rather curious difficulties, which seem in themselves sufficient to prove that the theory which leads to such difficulties must be wrong.

When we wish to speak about the *meaning* of a denoting phrase, as opposed to its *denotation*, the natural mode of doing so is by inverted commas. Thus we say:–

The centre of mass of the Solar System is a point, not a denoting complex;
"The centre of mass of the Solar System" is a denoting complex, not a point.

Or again,

The first line of Gray's Elegy states a proposition.
"The first line of Gray's Elegy" does not state a proposition. Thus taking any denoting phrase, say C, we wish to consider the relation between C and

---

[11] I use these as synonyms.

Bertrand Russell on Relations, Descriptions, and Knowledge

"C," where the difference of the two is of the kind exemplified in the above two instances.

We say, to begin with, that when C occurs it is the *denotation* that we are speaking about; but when "C" occurs, it is the *meaning*. Now the relation of meaning and denotation is not merely linguistic through the phrase: there must be a logical relation involved, which we express by saying that the meaning denotes the denotation. But the difficulty which confronts us is that we cannot succeed in *both* preserving the connexion of meaning and denotation and preventing them from being one and the same; also that the meaning cannot be got at except by means of denoting phrases. This happens as follows.

The one phrase C was to have both meaning and denotation. But if we speak of "the meaning of C," that gives us the meaning (if any) of the denotation. "The meaning of the first line of Gray's Elegy" is the same as "The meaning of 'The curfew tolls the knell of parting day,'" and is not the same as "The meaning of 'the first line of Gray's Elegy'." Thus in order to get the meaning we want, we must speak not of "the meaning of C," but of "the meaning of 'C,'" which is the same as "C" by itself. Similarly "the denotation of C" does not mean the denotation we want, but means something which, if it denotes at all, denotes what is denoted by the denotation we want. For example, let "C" be "the denoting complex occurring in the second of the above instances." Then

C = "the first line of Gray's Elegy," and

the denotation of C = The curfew tolls the knell of parting day. But what we *meant* to have as the denotation was "the first line of Gray's Elegy." Thus we have failed to get what we wanted.

The difficulty in speaking of the meaning of a denoting complex may be stated thus; The moment we put the complex in a proposition, the proposition is about the denotation; and if we make a proposition in which the subject is "the meaning of C," then the subject is the meaning (if any) of the denotation, which was not intended. This leads us to say that, when we distinguish meaning and denotation, we must be dealing with the meaning: the meaning has denotation and is a complex, and there is not something other than the meaning, which can be called the complex, and be said to *have* both meaning and denotation. The right phrase, on the view in question, is that some meanings have denotations.

But this only makes our difficulty in speaking of meanings more evident. For suppose C is our complex; then we are to say that C *is* the meaning of the complex. Nevertheless, whenever C occurs without inverted commas, what is

258　Early Analytic Philosophy

said is not true of the meaning, but only of the denotation, as when we say: The centre of mass of the Solar System is a point. Thus to speak of C itself, *i.e.,* to make *a* proposition about the meaning, our subject must not be C, but something which denotes C. Thus "C," which is what we use when we want to speak of the meaning, must be not the meaning, but something which denotes the meaning. And C must not be a constituent of this complex (as it is of "the meaning of C"); for if C occurs in the complex, it will be its denotation, not its meaning, that will occur, and there is no backward road from denotations to meanings, because every object can be denoted by an infinite number of different denoting phrases.

Thus it would seem that "C" and C are different entities, such that "C" denotes C; but this cannot be an explanation, because the relation of "C" to C remains wholly mysterious; and where are we to find the denoting complex "C" which is to denote C? Moreover, when C occurs in a proposition, it is not *only* the denotation that occurs (as we shall see in the next paragraph); yet, on the view in question, C is only the denotation, the meaning being wholly relegated to "C". This is an inextricable tangle, and seems to prove that the whole distinction of meaning and denotation has been wrongly conceived.

That the meaning is relevant when a denoting phrase occurs in a proposition is formally proved by the puzzle about the author of *Waverley.* The proposition "Scott was the author of *Waverley*" has a property not possessed by "Scott was Scott," namely the property that George IV. wished to know whether it was true. Thus the two are not identical propositions; hence the meaning of "the author of *Waverley*" must be relevant as well as the denotation, if we adhere to the point of view to which this distinction belongs. Yet, as we have just seen, so long as we adhere to this point of view, we are compelled to hold that only the denotation can be relevant. Thus the point of view in question must be abandoned.

It remains to show how all the puzzles we have been considering are solved by the theory explained at the beginning of this article.

According to the view which I advocate, a denoting phrase is essentially *part* of a sentence, and does not, like most single words, have any significance on its own account. If I say "Scott was a man," that is a statement of the form "*x* was a man," and it has "Scott" for its subject. But if I say "the author of *Waverley* was a man," that is not a statement of the form "*x* was a man," and does not have "the author of *Waverley*" for its subject. Abbreviating the statement made at the beginning of this article, we may put, in place of "the author of *Waverley* was a man," the following: "One and only one entity wrote *Waverley*, and that one was a man". (This is not so strictly what is meant as what was said earlier; but it is easier to follow.) And speaking generally, suppose we wish to say that the author of *Waverley* had the property φ, what we wish to say is equivalent to "One and only one entity wrote *Waverley*, and that one had the property φ".

The explanation of *denotation* is now, as follows. Every proposition in which "the author of *Waverley*" occurs being explained as above, the proposition "Scott was the author of *Waverley*" (*i.e.* "Scott was identical with the author of *Waverley*") becomes "One and only one entity wrote *Waverley*, and Scott was identical with that one"; or, reverting to the wholly explicit form: "It is not always false of *x* that *x* wrote *Waverley*, that it is always true of *y* that if *y* wrote *Waverley* *y* is identical with *x*, and that Scott is identical with *x*". Thus if "C" is a denoting phrase, it may happen that there is one entity *x* (there cannot be more than one) for which the proposition "*x* is identical with C" is true, this proposition being interpreted as above. We may then say that the entity *x* is the denotation of the phrase "C". Thus Scott is the denotation of "the author of *Waverley*". The "C" in inverted commas will be merely the *phrase*, not anything that can be called the *meaning*. The phrase *per se* has no meaning, because in any proposition in which it occurs the proposition, fully expressed, does not contain the phrase, which has been broken up.

The puzzle about George IV.'s curiosity is now seen to have a very simple solution. The proposition "Scott was the author of *Waverley*," which was written out in its unabbreviated form in the preceding paragraph, does not contain any constituent "the author of *Waverley*" for which we could substitute "Scott". This does not interfere with the truth of inferences resulting from making what is *verbally* the substitution of "Scott" for "the author of *Waverley*," so long as "the author of *Waverley*" has what I call a primary occurrence in the proposition considered. The difference of primary and secondary occurrences of denoting phrases is as follows:–

When we say: "George IV. wished to know whether so-and-so," or when we say "So-and-so is surprising" or "So-and-so is true," etc., the "so-and-so" must be a proposition. Suppose now that "so-and-so" contains a denoting phrase. We may either eliminate this denoting phrase from the subordinate proposition "so-and-so," or from the whole proposition in which "so-and-so" is a mere constituent. Different propositions result according to which we do. I have heard of a touchy owner of a yacht to whom a guest, on first seeing it, remarked, "I thought your yacht was larger than it is"; and the owner replied, "No, my yacht is not larger than it is". What the guest meant was, "The size that I thought your yacht was is greater than the size your yacht is"; the meaning attributed to him is, "I thought the size of your yacht was greater than the size of your yacht". To return to George IV. and *Waverley*, when we say, "George IV. wished to know whether Scott was the author of *Waverley*," we normally mean "George IV. wished to know whether one and only one man wrote *Waverley* and Scott was that man"; but we *may* also mean: "One and only one man wrote *Waverley*, and George IV. wished to know whether Scott was that man." In the latter, "the author of *Waverley*" has a *primary* occurrence; in the former, a *secondary*. The latter might be expressed by "George IV. wished to know, concerning the man who in fact wrote *Waverley*, whether he was Scott." This would be true, for example, if George IV. had seen Scott at a distance, and had asked "Is that Scott?" A *secondary* occurrence of a denoting phrase may be defined as one in which the phrase occurs in a proposition p which is a mere constituent of the proposition we are considering, and the substitution for the denoting phrase is to be effected in p, not in the whole proposition concerned. The ambiguity as between primary and secondary occurrences is hard to avoid in language; but it does no harm if we are on our guard against it. In symbolic logic it is of course easily avoided.

The distinction of primary and secondary occurrences also enables us to deal with the question whether the present King of France is bald or not bald, and generally with the logical status of denoting phrases that denote nothing. If "C" is a denoting phrase, say "the term having the property F," then

> "C has the property φ" means "one and only one term has the property F, and that one has the property φ".[12]

If now the property F belongs to no terms, or to several, it follows that "C has the property φ" is false for *all* values of φ. Thus "the present King of France is bald" is certainly false; and "the present King of France is not bald" is false if it means

> "There is an entity which is now King of France and is not bald,"

but is true if it means

> "It is false that there is an entity which is now King of France and is bald."

That is, "the King of France is not bald" is false if the occurrence of "the King of France" is primary, and true if it is secondary. Thus all propositions in which "the King of France" has a primary occurrence are false; the denials of such propositions are true, but in them "the King of France" has a secondary occurrence. Thus we escape the conclusion that the King of France has a wig.

We can now see also how to deny that there is such an object as the difference between A and B in the case when A and B do not differ. If A and B do differ, there is one and only one entity x such that "x is the difference between A and B" is a true proposition; if A and B do not differ, there is no such entity x.

---

[12]This is the abbreviated, not the stricter, interpretation.

Bertrand Russell on Relations, Descriptions, and Knowledge   261

Thus according to the meaning of denotation lately explained, "the difference between A and B" has a denotation when A and B differ, but not otherwise. This difference applies to true and false propositions generally. If "a R b" stands for "a has the relation R to b," then when a R b is true, there is such an entity as the relation R between a and b; when a R b is false, there is no such entity. Thus out of any proposition we can make a denoting phrase, which denotes an entity if the proposition is true, but does not denote an entity if the proposition is false. *E.g.,* it is true (at least we will suppose so) that the earth revolves round the sun, and false that the sun revolves round the earth; hence "the revolution of the earth round the sun" denotes an entity, while "the revolution of the sun round the earth" does not denote an entity.[13]

The whole realm of non-entities, such as "the round square," "the even prime other than 2," "Apollo," "Hamlet," etc., can now be satisfactorily dealt with. All these are denoting phrases which do not denote anything. A proposition about Apollo means what we get by substituting what the classical dictionary tells us is meant by Apollo, say "the sun-god". All propositions in which Apollo occurs are to be interpreted by the above rules for denoting phrases. If "Apollo" has a primary occurrence, the proposition containing the occurrence is false; if the occurrence is secondary, the proposition may be true. So again "the round square is round" means "there is one and only one entity x which is round and square, and that entity is round," which is a false proposition, not, as Meinong maintains, a true one. "The most perfect Being has all perfections; existence is a perfection; therefore the most perfect Being exists" becomes:–

"There is one and only one entity x which is most perfect; that one has all perfections; existence is a perfection; therefore that one exists". As a proof, this fails for want of a proof of the premiss "there is one and only one entity x which is most perfect".[14]

Mr. MacColl (Mind, N.S., No. 54, and again No. 55, p. 401) regards individuals as of two sorts, real and unreal; hence he defines the null-class as the class consisting of all unreal individuals. This assumes that such phrases as "the present King of France," which do not denote a real individual, do, nevertheless, denote an individual, but an unreal one. This is essentially Meinong's theory, which we have seen reason to reject because it conflicts with the law of

---

[13] The propositions from which such entities are derived are not identical either with these entities or with the propositions that these entities have being.

[14] The argument can be made to prove validly that all members of the class of most perfect Beings exist; it can also be proved formally that this class cannot have *more* than one member; but, taking the definition of perfection as possession of all positive predicates, it can be proved almost equally formally that the class does not have even one member.

Early Analytic Philosophy

contradiction. With our theory of denoting, we are able to hold that there are no unreal individuals; so that the null-classis the class containing no members, not the class containing as members all unreal individuals.

It is important to observe the effect of our theory on the interpretation of definitions which proceed by means of denoting phrases. Most mathematical definitions are of this sort: for example, "$m - n$ means the number which, added to m, gives m". Thus $m - n$ is defined as meaning the same as a certain denoting phrase; but we agreed that denoting phrases have no meaning in isolation. Thus what the definition really ought to be is: "Any proposition containing $m - n$ is to mean the proposition which results from substituting for '$m - n$' 'the number which, added to n, gives m'". The resulting proposition is interpreted according to the rules already given for interpreting propositions whose verbal expression contains a denoting phrase. In the case where m and n are such that there is one and only one number x which, added to n, gives m, there is a number x which can be substituted for $m - n$ in any proposition containing $m - n$ without altering the truth or falsehood of the proposition. But in other cases, all propositions in which "$m - n$" has a primary occurrence are false.

The usefulness of *identity* is explained by the above theory. No one outside a logic book ever wishes to say "x is x," and yet assertions of identity are often made in such forms as "Scott was the author of *Waverley*" or "thou art the man". The meaning of such propositions cannot be stated without the notion of identity, although they are not simply statements that Scott is identical with another term, the author of *Waverley*, or that thou art identical with another term, the man. The shortest statement of "Scott is the author of *Waverley*" seems to be: "Scott wrote *Waverley*; and it is always true of y that if y wrote *Waverley*, y is identical with Scott". It is in this way that identity enters into "Scott is the author of *Waverley*"; and it is owing to such uses that identity is worth affirming.

One interesting result of the above theory of denoting is this: when there is anything with which we do not have immediate acquaintance, but only definition by denoting phrases, then the propositions in which this thing is introduced by means of a denoting phrase do not really contain this thing as a constituent, but contain instead the constituents expressed by the several words of the denoting phrase. Thus in every proposition that we can apprehend (*i.e.* not only in those whose truth or falsehood we can judge of, but in all that we can think about), all the constituents are really entities with which we have immediate acquaintance. Now such things as matter (in the sense in which matter occurs in physics) and the minds of other people are known to us only by denoting phrases, *i.e.*, we are not *acquainted* with them, but we know them as what has such and such properties. Hence, although we can form propositional functions $C(x)$ which must hold of such and such a material particle, or of So-and-so's mind, yet we are not acquainted with the propositions which affirm these things that we know must be true, because we cannot apprehend the actual entities concerned. What we know is "So-and-so has a mind which has such and such properties" but we do not know "A has such and such properties," where A *is* the mind in question. In such a case, we know the properties of a thing without having acquaintance with the thing itself, and without, consequently, knowing any single proposition of which the thing itself is a constituent.

Of the many other consequences of the view I have been advocating, I will say nothing. I will only beg the reader not to make up his mind against the view—as he might be tempted to do, on account of its apparently excessive complication—until he has attempted to construct a theory of his own on the subject of denotation. This attempt, I believe, will convince him that, whatever the true theory may be, it cannot have such a simplicity as one might have expected beforehand.

Russell, B. "Knowledge by Acquaintance and Knowledge by Description".
Reprinted from Russell, B. (1910), "Knowledge by Acquaintance and Knowledge by Description", *Proceedings of the Aristotelian Society* 11: 108–28.

The object of the following, paper is to consider what it is that we know in cases where we know propositions about "the so-and-so" without knowing who or what the so-and-so is. For example, I know that the candidate who gets most votes will be elected, though I do not know who is the candidate who will get most votes. The problem I wish to consider is: What do we know in these cases, where the subject is merely described? I have considered this problem elsewhere from a purely logical point of view; but in what follows I wish to consider the question in relation to theory of knowledge as well as in relation to logic, and in view of the above-mentioned logical discussions, I shall in this paper make the logical portion as brief as possible.

In order to make clear the antithesis between "acquaintance" and "description," I shall first of all try to explain what I mean by "acquaintance." I say that I am *acquainted* with an object when I have a direct cognitive relation to that object, i.e. when I am directly aware of the object itself. When I speak of a cognitive relation here, I do not mean the sort of relation which constitutes

Early Analytic Philosophy

judgment, but the sort which constitutes presentation. In fact, I think the relation of subject and object which I call acquaintance is simply the converse of the relation of object and subject which constitutes presentation. That is, to say that S has acquaintance with O is essentially the same thing as to say that O is presented to S. But the associations and natural extensions of the word *acquaintance* are different from those of the word *presentation*. To begin with, as in most cognitive words, it is natural to say that I am acquainted with an object even at moments when it is not actually before my mind, provided it has been before my mind, and will be again whenever occasion arises. This is the same sense in which I am said to know that 2+2 = 4 even when I am thinking of something else. In the second place, the word *acquaintance* is designed to emphasize, more than the word *presentation*, the relational character of the fact with which we are concerned. There is, to my mind, a danger that, in speaking of presentation is, we may so emphasize the object as to lose sight of the subject. The result of this is either to lead to the view that there is no subject, whence we arrive at materialism; or to lead to the view that what is presented is part of the subject, whence we arrive at idealism, and should arrive at solipsism but for the most desperate contortions. Now I wish to preserve the dualism of subject and object in my terminology, because this dualism seems to me a fundamental fact concerning cognition. Hence I prefer the word *acquaintance* because it emphasizes the need of a subject which is acquainted.

When we ask what are the kinds of objects with which we are acquainted, the first and most obvious example is *sense-data*. When I see a colour or hear a noise, I have direct acquaintance with the colour or the noise. The sense-datum with which I am acquainted in these cases is generally, if not always, complex. This is particularly obvious in the case of sight. I do not mean, of course, merely that the supposed physical object is complex, but that the direct sensible object is complex and contains parts with spatial relations. Whether it is possible to be aware of a complex without being aware of its constituents is not an easy question, but on the whole it would seem that there is no reason why it should not be possible. This question arises in an acute form in connection with self-consciousness, which we must now briefly consider.

In introspection, we seem to be immediately aware of varying complexes, consisting of objects in various cognitive and conative relations to ourselves. When I see the sun it often happens that I am aware of my seeing the sun, in addition to being aware of the sun; and when I desire food, it. often happens that I am aware of my desire for food. But it is hard to discover any state of mind in which I am aware of myself alone, as opposed to a complex of which I am a constituent. The question of the nature of self-consciousness is too large, and

Bertrand Russell on Relations, Descriptions, and Knowledge   265

too slightly connected with our subject, to be argued at length here. It is, however, very difficult to account for plain facts if we assume that we do not have acquaintance with ourselves. It is plain that we are not only *acquainted* with the complex "Self-acquainted-with-A," but we also *know* the proposition "I am acquainted with A." Now here the complex has been analysed, and if "I" does not stand for something which is a direct object of acquaintance, we shall have to suppose that "I" is something known by description. If we wished to maintain the view that there is no acquaintance with Self, we might argue as follows: We are acquainted with *acquaintance*, and we know that it is a relation. Also we are acquainted with a complex in which we perceive that acquaintance is the relating relation. Hence we know that this complex must have a constituent which is that which is acquainted, *i.e.* must have a subject-term as well as an object-term. This subject-term we define as "I." Thus "I" means " the subject-term in awarenesses of which *I* am aware." But as a definition this cannot be regarded as a happy effort. It would seem necessary, therefore, to suppose that I am acquainted with myself, and that "I," therefore, requires no definition, being merely the proper name of a certain object. Thus self-consciousness cannot be regarded as throwing light on the question whether we can know a complex without knowing its constituents. This question, however, is not important for our present purposes, and I shall therefore not discuss it further.

The awarenesses we have considered so far have all been awarenesses of particular existents, and might all in a large sense be called sense-data. For, from the point of view of theory of knowledge, introspective knowledge is exactly on a level with knowledge derived from sight or hearing. But, in addition to awareness of the above kind of objects, which may be called awareness of *particulars*, we have also what may be called awareness of *universals*. Awareness of universals is called *conceiving*, and a universal of which we are aware is called a *concept*. Not only are we aware of particular yellows, but if we have seen a sufficient number of yellows and have sufficient intelligence, we are aware of the universal *yellow*; this universal is the subject in such judgments as "yellow differs from blue" or "yellow resembles blue less than green does." And the universal yellow is the predicate in such judgments as "this is yellow," where "this" is a particular sense-datum. And universal relations, too, are objects of awarenesses; up and down, before and after, resemblance, desire, awareness itself, and so on, would seem to be all of them objects of which we can be aware.

In regard to relations, it might be urged that we are never aware of the universal relation itself, but only of complexes in which it is a constituent. For example, it may be said that we do not know directly such a relation as *before*, though we understand such a proposition as "this is before that," and may be

266   **Early Analytic Philosophy**

directly aware of such a complex as "this being, before that." This view, however, is difficult to reconcile with the fact that we often know propositions in which the relation is the subject, or in which the relata are not definite given objects, but "anything." For example, we know that if one thing is before another, and the other before a third, then the first is before the third; and here the things concerned are not definite things, but "anything." It is hard to see how we could know such a fact about "before" unless we were acquainted with "before," and not merely with actual particular cases of one given object being before another given object. And more directly: A judgment such as "this is before that," where this judgment is derived from awareness of a complex, constitutes an analysis, and we should not understand the analysis if we were not acquainted with the meaning of the terms employed. Thus we must suppose that we are acquainted with the meaning of " before," and not merely with instances of it.

There are thus two sorts of objects of which we are aware, namely, particulars and universals. Among particulars I include all existents, and all complexes of which one or more constituents are existents, such as this-before-that, this-above-that, the-yellowness-of-this. Among universals I include all objects of which no particular is a constituent. Thus the disjunction "universal-particular" is exhaustive. We might also call it the disjunction "abstract-concrete." It is not quite parallel with the opposition" concept-percept," because things remembered or imagined belong with particulars, but can hardly be called percepts. (On the other hand, universals with which we are acquainted may be identified with concepts.)

It will be seen that among the objects with which we are acquainted are not included physical objects (as opposed to sense-data), nor other people's minds. These things are known to us by what I call "knowledge by description," which we must now consider.

By a "description" I mean any phrase of the form "a so-and-so" or "the so-and-so." A phrase of the form "a so-and-so" I shall call an "ambiguous" description; a phrase of the form "the so-and-so" (in the singular) I shall call a "definite" description. Thus "a man" is an ambiguous description, and "the man with the iron mask" is a definite description. There are various problems connected with ambiguous descriptions, but I pass them by, since they do not directly concern the matter I wish to discuss. What I wish to discuss is the nature of our knowledge concerning objects in cases where we know that there is an object answering to a definite description, though we are not *acquainted* with any such object. This is a matter which is concerned exclusively with *definite* descriptions. I shall, therefore, in the sequel, speak simply of "descriptions" when I mean "definite descriptions." Thus a description will mean any phrase of the form "the so-and-so" in the singular.

I shall say that an object is "known by description" when we know that it is "*the* so-and-so," *i.e.* when we know that there is one object, and no more, having a certain property; and it will generally be implied that we do not have knowledge of the same object by acquaintance. We know that the man with the iron mask existed, and many propositions are known about him; but we do not know who he was. We know that the candidate who gets most votes will be elected, and in this case we are very likely also acquainted (in the only sense in which one can be acquainted with some one else) with the man who is, in fact, the candidate who will get most votes, but we do not know which of the candidates he is, *i.e.* we do not know any proposition of the form "A is the candidate who will get most votes" where A is one of the candidates by name. We shall say that we have "*merely* descriptive knowledge" of the so-and-so when, although we know that the so-and-so exists, and although we may possibly be acquainted with the object which is, in fact, the so-and-so, yet we do not know any proposition "*a* is the so-and-so," where *a* is something with which we are acquainted.

When we say "the so-and-so exists," we mean that there is just one object which is the so-and-so. The proposition "*a* is the so-and-so" means that *a* has the property so-and-so, and nothing else has. "Sir Joseph Larmor is the Unionist candidate" means "Sir Joseph Larmor is a Unionist candidate, and no one else is." "The Unionist candidate exists" means "some one is a Unionist candidate, and no one else is." Thus, when we are acquainted with an object which is the so-and-so, we know that the so-and-so exists, but we may know that the so-and-so exists when we are not acquainted with any object which we know to be the so-and-so, and even when we are not acquainted with any object which in fact, is the so-and-so.

Common words, even proper names, are usually really descriptions. That is to say, the thought in the mind of a person using a proper name correctly can generally only be expressed explicitly if we replace the proper name by a description. Moreover, the description required to express the thought will vary for different people, or for the same person at different times. The only thing constant (so long as the name is rightly used) is the object to which the name applies. But so long as this remains constant, the particular description involved usually makes no difference to the truth or falsehood of the proposition in which the name appears.

Let us take some illustrations. Suppose some statement made about Bismarck. Assuming that there is such a thing as direct acquaintance with oneself, Bismarck himself might have used his name directly to designate the particular person with whom he was acquainted. In this case, if he made a

Early Analytic Philosophy

judgment about himself, he himself might be a constituent of the judgment. Here the proper name has the direct use which it always wishes to have, as simply standing for a certain object, and not for a description of the object. But if a person who knew Bismarck made a judgment about him, the case is different. What this person was acquainted with were certain sense-data which he connected (rightly, we will suppose) with Bismarck's body. His body as a physical object, and still more his mind, were only known as the body and the mind connected with these sense-data. That is, they were known by description. It is, of course, very much a matter of chance which characteristics of a man's appearance will come into a friend's mind when he thinks of him; thus the description actually in the friend's mind is accidental. The essential point is that he knows that the various descriptions all apply to the same entity, in spite of not being acquainted with the entity in question.

When we, who did not know Bismarck, make a judgment about him, the description in our minds will probably be some more or less vague mass of historical knowledge – far more, in most cases, than is required to identify him. But, for the sake of illustration, let us assume that we think of him as "the first Chancellor of the German Empire." Here all the words are abstract except "German." The word "German" will again have different meanings for different people. To some it will recall travels in Germany, to some the look of Germany on the map, and so on. But if we are to obtain a description which we know to be applicable, we shall be compelled, at some point, to bring in a reference to a particular with which we are acquainted. Such reference is involved in any mention of past, present, and future (as opposed to definite dates), or of here and there, or of what others have told us. Thus it would seem that, in some way or other, a description known to be applicable to a particular must involve some reference to a particular with which we are acquainted, if our knowledge about the thing described is not to be merely what follows logically from the description. For example, "the most long-lived of men" is a description which must apply to some man, but we can make no judgments concerning this man which involve knowledge about him beyond what the description gives. If, however, we say, "the first Chancellor of the German Empire was an astute diplomatist," we can only be assured of the truth of our judgment in virtue of something with which we are acquainted – usually a testimony heard or read. Considered psychologically, apart from the information we convey to others, apart from the fact about the actual Bismarck, which gives importance to our judgment, the thought we really have contains the one or more particulars involved, and otherwise consists wholly of concepts. All names of places – London, England, Europe, the earth, the Solar System – similarly involve, when

Bertrand Russell on Relations, Descriptions, and Knowledge 269

used, descriptions which start from some one or more particulars with which we are acquainted. I suspect that even the Universe, as considered by metaphysics, involves such a connection with particulars. In logic, on the contrary, where we are concerned not merely with what does exist, but with whatever might or could exist or be, no reference to actual particulars is involved.

It would seem that, when we make a statement about something only known by description, we often *intend* to make our statement, not in the form involving the description, but about the actual thing described. That is to say, when we say anything about Bismarck, we should like, if we could, to make the judgment which Bismarck alone can make, namely, the judgment of which he himself is a constituent. In this we are necessarily defeated, since the actual Bismarck is unknown to us. But we know that there is an object B called Bismarck, and that B was an astute diplomatist. We can thus *describe* the proposition we should like to affirm, namely, "B was an astute diplomatist," where B is the object which was Bismarck. What enables us to communicate in spite of the varying descriptions we employ is that we know there is a true proposition concerning the actual Bismarck, and that however we may vary the description (so long as the description is correct), the proposition described is still the same. This proposition, which is described and is known to be true, is what interests us; but we are not acquainted with the proposition itself, and do not know it, though we know it is true.

It will be seen that there are various stages in the removal from acquaintance with particulars: there is Bismarck to people who knew him, Bismarck to those who only know of him through history, the man with the iron mask, the longest-lived of men. These are progressively further removed from acquaintance with particulars, and there is a similar hierarchy in the region of universals. Many universals, like many particulars, are only known to us by description. But here, as in the case of particulars, knowledge concerning what is known by description is ultimately reducible to knowledge concerning what is known by acquaintance.

The fundamental epistemological principle in the analysis of propositions containing descriptions is this: *Every proposition which we can understand must be composed wholly of constituents with which we are acquainted.* From what has been said already, it will be plain why I advocate this principle, and how I propose to meet the case of propositions which at first sight contravene it. Let us begin with the reasons for supposing the principle true.

The chief reason for supposing the principle true is that it seems scarcely possible to believe that we can make a judgment or entertain a supposition without knowing what it is that we are judging or supposing about. If we make a judgment about (say) Julius Caesar, it is plain that the actual person who was

270   Early Analytic Philosophy

Julius Caesar is not a constituent of the judgment. But before going further, it may be well to explain what I mean when I say that this or that is a constituent of a judgement, or of a proposition which we understand. To begin with judgments: a judgment, as an occurrence, I take to be a relation of a mind to several entities, namely, the entities which compose what is judged. If, *e.g.*, I judge that A loves B, the judgment as an event consists in the existence, at a certain moment, of a specific four-term relation, called *judging*, between me and A and love and B. That is to say, at the time when I judge, there is a certain complex whose terms are myself and A and love and B, and whose relating relation is *judging*. (The relation *love* enters as one of the terms of the relation, not as a relating, relation.) My reasons for this view have been set forth elsewhere, [footnote removed] and I shall not repeat them here. Assuming this view of judgment, the constituents of the judgment are simply the constituents of the complex which is the judgment. Thus, in the above case, the constituents are myself and A and love and B and judging. But myself and judging are constituents shared by all my judgments; thus the *distinctive* constituents of the particular judgment in question are A and love and B. Coming now to what is meant by "understanding a proposition," I should say that there is another relation possible between me and A and love and B, which is called my *supposing* that A loves B. When we can suppose that A loves B, we "understand the proposition" A *loves* B. Thus we often understand a proposition in cases where we have not enough knowledge to make a judgment. Supposing, like judging, is a many-term relation, of which a mind is one term. The other terms of the relation are called the constituents of the proposition supposed. Thus the principle which I enunciated may be restated as follows: *Whenever a relation of supposing or judging occurs, the terms to which the supposing or judging mind is related by the relation of supposing or judging must be terms with which the mind in question is acquainted.* This is merely to say that we cannot make a judgment or a supposition without knowing what it is that we are making our judgment or supposition about. It seems to me that the truth of this principle is evident as soon as the principle is understood; I shall, therefore, in what follows, assume the principle, and use it as a guide in analysing judgments that contain descriptions.

Returning now to Julius Caesar, I assume that it will be admitted that he himself is not a constituent of any judgment which I can make. But at this point it is necessary to examine the view that judgments are composed of something called "ideas," and that it is the "idea" of Julius Caesar that is a constituent of my judgment. I believe the plausibility of this view rests upon a failure to form a right theory of descriptions. We may mean by my "idea" of Julius Caesar the

Bertrand Russell on Relations, Descriptions, and Knowledge 271

things that I know about him, *e.g.*, that he conquered Gaul, was assassinated on the Ides of March, and is a plague to schoolboys. Now I am admitting, and indeed contending, that in order to discover what is actually in my mind when I judge about Julius Caesar, we must substitute for the proper name a description made up of some of the things I know about him. (A description which will often serve to express my thought is "the man whose name was Julius Caesar." For whatever else I may have forgotten about him, it is plain that when I mention him I have not forgotten that that was his name.) But although I think the theory that judgments consist of ideas may have been suggested in some such way, yet I think the theory itself is fundamentally mistaken. The view seems to be that there is some mental existent which may be called the "idea" of something outside the mind of the person who has the idea, and that, since judgment is a mental event, its constituents must be constituents of the mind of the person judging. But in this view ideas become a veil between us and outside things – we never really, in knowledge, attain to the things we are supposed to be knowing about, but only to the ideas of those things. The relation of mind, idea, and object, on this view, is utterly obscure, and, so far as I can see, nothing discoverable by inspection warrants the intrusion of the idea between the mind and the object. I suspect that the view is fostered by the dislike of relations, and that it is felt the mind could not know objects unless there were something "in" the mind which could be called the state of knowing the object. Such a view, however, leads at once to a vicious endless regress, since the relation of idea to object will have to be explained by supposing that the idea itself has an idea of the object, and so on *ad infinitum*. I therefore see no reason to believe that, when we are acquainted with an object, there is in us something which can be called the "idea" of the object. On the contrary, I hold that acquaintance is wholly a relation, not demanding any such constituent of the mind as is supposed by advocates of "ideas." This is, of course a large question, and one which would take us far from our subject if it were adequately discussed. I therefore content myself with the above indications, and with the corollary that, in judging, the actual objects concerning which we judge, rather than any supposed purely mental entities, are constituents of the complex which is the judgment.

When, therefore, I say that we must substitute for "Julius Caesar" some description of Julius Caesar, in order to discover the meaning of a judgment nominally about him, I am not saying that we must substitute an idea. Suppose our description is "the man whose name was *Julius Caesar*." Let our judgment be "Julius Cesar was assassinated." Then it becomes "the man whose name was *Julius Caesar* was assassinated." Here *Julius Caesar* is a noise or shape with which we are acquainted, and all the other constituents of the judgment (neglecting

Early Analytic Philosophy

the tense in "was") are *concepts* with which we are acquainted. Thus our judgment is wholly reduced to constituents with which we are acquainted, but Julius Caesar himself has ceased to be a constituent of our judgment. This, however, requires a proviso, to be further explained shortly, namely, that "the man whose name was *Julius Caesar*" must not, as a whole, be a constituent of our judgment, that is to say, this phrase must not, as a whole, have a meaning which enters into the judgment. Any right analysis of the judgment, therefore, must break up this phrase, and not treat it as a subordinate complex which is part of the judgment. The judgment "the man whose name was *Julius Caesar* was assassinated" may be interpreted as meaning "One and only one man was called *Julius Caesar*, and that one was assassinated." Here it is plain that there is no constituent corresponding to the phrase "the man whose name was *Julius Caesar*." Thus there is no reason to regard this phrase as expressing a constituent of the judgment, and we have seen that this phrase must be broken up if we are to be acquainted with all the constituents of the judgement. This conclusion, which we have reached from considerations concerned with the theory of knowledge, is also forced upon us by logical considerations, which must now be briefly reviewed.

It is common to distinguish two aspects, *meaning* and *denotation*, in such phrases as "the author of Waverley." The meaning will be a certain complex, consisting (at least) of authorship and Waverley with some relation; the denotation will be Scott. Similarly "featherless bipeds" will have a complex meaning, containing as constituents the presence of two feet and the absence of feathers, while its denotation will be the class of men. Thus when we say "Scott is the author of Waverley" or "men are the same as featherless bipeds," we are asserting an identity of denotation, and this assertion is worth making because of the diversity of meaning. I believe that the duality of meaning and denotation, though capable of a true interpretation, is misleading if taken as fundamental. The denotation, I believe, is not a constituent of the proposition, except in the case of proper names, *i.e.* of words which do not assign a property to an object, but merely and solely name it. And I should hold further that, in this sense, there are only two words which are strictly proper names of particulars, namely, "I" and " this."

One reason for not believing the denotation to be a constituent of the proposition is that we may know the proposition even when we are not acquainted with the denotation. The proposition "the author of Waverley is a novelist" was known to people who did not know that "the author of Waverley" denoted Scott. This reason has been already sufficiently emphasised.

A second reason is that propositions concerning "the so-and-so" are possible even when "the so-and-so " has no denotation. Take, *e.g.*, "the golden mountain does not exist" or "the round square is self-contradictory." If we are to preserve

Bertrand Russell on Relations, Descriptions, and Knowledge

[footnote removed] the duality of meaning and denotation, we have to say, with Meinong, that there are such objects as the golden mountain; and the round square, although these objects do not have being. We even have to admit that the existent round square is existent, but does not exist. Meinong does not regard this as a contradiction, but I fail to see that it is not one. Indeed, it seems to me evident that the judgment "there is no such object as the round square" does not presuppose that there is such an object. If this is admitted, however, we are led to the conclusion that, by parity of form, no judgment concerning "the so-and-so" actually involves the so-and-so as a constituent.

Miss Jones contends that there is no difficulty in admitting contradictory predicates concerning such an object as "the present King of France," on the ground that this object is in itself contradictory. Now it might, of course, be argued that this object, unlike the round square, is not self-contradictory, but merely non-existent. This, however, would not go to the root of the matter. The real objection to such an argument is that the law of contradiction ought not to be stated in the traditional form "A is not both B and not B," but in the form "no proposition is both true and false." The traditional form only applies to certain propositions, namely, to those which attribute a predicate to a subject. When the law is stated of propositions, instead of being stated concerning subjects and predicates, it is at once evident that propositions about the present King of France or the round square can form no exception, but are just as incapable of being both true and false as other propositions.

Miss Jones [footnote removed] argues that "Scott is the author of Waverley" asserts identity of denotation between *Scott* and *the author of Waverley*. But there is some difficulty in choosing among alternative meanings of this contention. In the first place, it should be observed that *the author of Waverley* is not a *mere* name, like *Scott*. *Scott* is merely a noise or shape conventionally used to designate a certain person; it gives us no information about that person, and has nothing that can be called meaning as opposed to denotation. (I neglect the fact, considered above, that even proper names, as a rule, really stand for descriptions.) But *the author of Waverley* is not merely conventionally a name for Scott; the element of mere convention belongs here to the separate words, *the* and *author* and *of* and *Waverley*. Given what these words stand for, *the author of Waverley* is no longer arbitrary. When it is said that Scott is the author of Waverley, we are not stating that these are two *names* for one man, as we should be if we said "Scott is Sir Walter." A man's name is what he is called, but however much Scott had been called the author of Waverley, that would not have made him be the author; it was necessary for him actually to write Waverley, which was a fact having nothing to do with names.

Early Analytic Philosophy

If, then, we are asserting identity of denotation, we must not mean by *denotation* the mere relation of a name to the thing named. In fact, it would be nearer to the truth to say that the *meaning* of "Scott" is the *denotation* of "the author of Waverley." The relation of "Scott" to Scott is that "Scott" means Scott, just as the relation of "author" to the concept which is so called is that "author" means this concept. Thus if we distinguish meaning and denotation in "the author of Waverley," we shall have to say that "Scott" has meaning, but not denotation. Also when we say "Scott is the author of Waverley," the *meaning* of "the author of Waverley" is relevant to our assertion. For if the denotation alone were relevant, any other phrase with the same denotation would give the same proposition. Thus "Scott is the author of Marmion" would be the same proposition as "Scott is the author of Waverley." But this is plainly not the case, since from the first we learn that Scott wrote Marmion and from the second we learn that he wrote Waverley, but the first tells us nothing about Waverley and the second nothing about Marmion. Hence the meaning of "the author of Waverley," as opposed to the denotation, is certainly relevant to "Scott is the author of Waverley."

We have thus agreed that "the author of Waverley" is not a mere name, and. that its meaning is relevant in propositions in which it occurs. Thus if we are to say, as Miss Jones does, that "Scott is the author of Waverley" asserts an identity of denotation, we must regard the denotation of "the author of Waverley" as the denotation of what is *meant* by "the author of Waverley." Let us call the meaning of "the author of Waverley" M. Thus M is what "the author of Waverley" means. Then we are to suppose that "Scott is the author of Waverley " means "Scott is the denotation of M." But here we are explaining our proposition by another of the same form, and thus we have made no progress towards a real explanation. "The denotation of M," like "the author of Waverley," has both meaning and denotation, on the theory we are examining. If we call its meaning, M', our proposition becomes "Scott is the denotation of M'." But this leads at. once to an endless regress. Thus the attempt to regard our proposition as asserting identity of denotation breaks down, and it becomes imperative to find some other analysis. When this analysis has been completed, we shall be able to reinterpret the phrase "identity of denotation," which remains obscure so long as it is taken as fundamental

The first point to observe is that, in any proposition about "the author of Waverley," provided Scott is not explicitly mentioned, the denotation itself, *i.e.* Scott, does not occur, but only the concept of denotation, which will be represented by a variable. Suppose we say "the author of Waverley was the author of Marmion," we are certainly not saying that both were Scott – we may

Bertrand Russell on Relations, Descriptions, and Knowledge   275

have forgotten that there was such a person as Scott. We are saying that there is some man who was the author of Waverley and the author of Marmion. That is to say, there is some one who wrote Waverley and Marmion, and no one else wrote them. Thus the identity is that of a variable, *i.e.*, of an indefinite subject, "some one." This is why we can understand propositions about "the author of Waverley," without knowing who he was. When we say "the author of Waverley was a poet" we mean "one and only one man wrote Waverley, and he was a poet"; when we say "the author of Waverley was Scott" we mean "one and only one man wrote Waverley, and he was Scott." Here the identity is between a variable, *i.e.* an indeterminate subject ("he"), and Scott; "the author of Waverley" has been analysed away, and no longer appears as a constituent of the proposition.

The reason why it is imperative to analyse away the phrase "the author of Waverley" may be stated as follows. It is plain that when we say "the author of Waverley is the author of Marmion," the *is* expresses identity. We have seen also that the common *denotation*, namely Scott, is not a constituent of this proposition, while the *meanings* (if any) of "the author of Waverley" and "the author of Marinion" are not identical. We have seen also that, in any sense in which the meaning of a word is a constituent of a proposition in whose verbal expression the word occurs, "Scott" means the actual man Scott, in the same sense in which "author" means a certain universal. Thus, if "the author of Waverley" were a subordinate complex in the above proposition, its *meaning* would have to be what was said to be identical with the *meaning* of "the author of Marmion." This is plainly not the case; and the only escape is to say that "the author of Waverley" does not, by itself, have a meaning, though phrases of which it is part do have a meaning. That is, in a right analysis of the above proposition, "the author of Waverley" must disappear. This is effected when the above proposition is analysed as meaning: "Some one wrote Waverley and no one, else did, and that some one also wrote Marmion and no one else did." This may be more simply expressed by saying that the propositional function "x wrote Waverley and Marmion, and no one else did" is capable of truth, *i.e.* some value of x makes it true. Thus the true subject of our judgment is a propositional function, *i.e.* a complex containing an undetermined constituent, and becoming a proposition as soon as this constituent is determined.

We may now define the denotation of a phrase. If we know that the proposition "a is the so-and-so" is true, *i.e.* that a is so-and-so and nothing else is, we call a the denotation of the phrase "the so-and-so." A very great many of the propositions we naturally make about "the so-and-so" will remain true or remain false if we substitute a for "the so-and-so," where a is the denotation of

Early Analytic Philosophy

"the so-and-so." Such propositions will also remain true or remain false if we substitute for "the so-and-so" any other phrase having the same denotation. Hence, as practical men, we become interested in the denotation more than in the description, since the denotation decides as to the truth or falsehood of so many statements in which the description occurs. Moreover, as we saw earlier in considering the relations of description and acquaintance, we often wish to reach the denotation, and and are only hindered by lack of acquaintance: in such cases the description is merely the means we employ to get as near as possible to the denotation. Hence it naturally comes to be supposed that the denotation is part of the proposition in which the description occurs. But we have seen, both on logical and on epistemological grounds, that this is an error. The actual object (if any) which is the denotation is not (unless it is explicitly mentioned) a constituent of propositions in which descriptions occur; and this is the reason why, in order to understand such propositions, we need acquaintance with the constituents of the description, but do not need acquaintance with its denotation. The first result of analysis, when applied to propositions whose grammatical subject is "the so-and-so," is to substitute a variable as subject: *i.e.* we obtain a proposition of the form: "There is *something* which alone is so-and-so, and that *something* is such-and-such." The further analysis of propositions concerning "the so-and-so" is thus merged in the problem of the nature of the variable, *i.e.* of the meanings of *some, any,* and *all.* This is a difficult problem, concerning which I do not intend to say anything at present.

To sum up our whole discussion: We began by distinguishing two sorts of knowledge of objects, namely, knowledge by *acquaintance* and knowledge by *description.* Of these it is only the former that brings the object itself before the mind. We have acquaintance with sense-data, with many universals, and possibly with ourselves, but not with physical objects or other minds. We have descriptive knowledge of an object when we know that it is the object having some property or properties with which we are acquainted; that is to say, when we know that the property or properties in question belong to one object and no more, we are said to have knowledge of that one object by description, whether or not we are acquainted with the object. Our knowledge of physical objects and of other minds is only knowledge by description, the descriptions involved being usually such as involve sense-data. All propositions intelligible to us, whether or not they primarily concern things only known to us by description, are composed wholly of constituents with which we are acquainted, for a constituent with which we are not acquainted is unintelligible to us. A judgment, we found, is not composed of mental constituents called "ideas," but consists of a complex whose constituents are a mind and certain objects, particulars or universals. (One at least must be a universal.) When a judgment is rightly analysed, the objects which are constituents of it must all be objects with which the mind which is a constituent of it is acquainted. This conclusion forces us to analyse descriptive phrases occurring in propositions, and to say that the objects denoted by such phrases are not constituents of judgments in which such phrases occur (unless these objects are explicitly mentioned). This leads us to the view (recommended also on purely logical grounds) that when we say "the author of Marmion was the author of Waverley," Scott himself is not a constituent of our judgment, and that the judgment cannot be explained by saying that it affirms identity of denotation with diversity of connotation. It also, plainly, does not assert identity of meaning. Such judgments, therefore, can only be analysed by breaking up the descriptive phrases, introducing a variable, and making propositional functions the ultimate subjects. In fact, "the so-and-so is such-and-such" will mean that "x is so-and-so and nothing else is, and x is such-and-such" is capable of truth. The analysis of such judgments involves many fresh problems, but the discussion of these problems is not undertaken in the present paper.

6

E. E. Constance Jones on Language and Logic

Chapter Outline

Background and commentary

Background	279
Developments in logic	280
Jones and Russell: The 1910–11 debate	284
Concluding remarks	289
Further reading	290

Readings

"Mr. Russell's Objections to Frege's Analysis of Propositions"	291
"A New Law of Thought"	300

Background and commentary

Background

Who was Emily Elizabeth (E. E.) Constance Jones (1848–1922)? Even if you are a student or even a seasoned scholar of philosophy, there is a good chance that you have never heard this name before, or studied Jones's work. As a logician and ethicist, however, Jones's accomplishments were numerous. She was the author of five books—including *Elements of Logic as a Science of Propositions* (1890), *An Introduction to General Logic* (1892), and *A New Law of Thought and Its Logical Bearings* (1911)—and many articles and conference proceedings. As Mistress of Girton College, Cambridge, she presided over one of the few women's colleges at Cambridge, and among her other achievements, she was the first woman to present a paper to the prestigious Cambridge Moral Sciences Club.[1]

Jones did not have an academic career in mind as a student. But soon after she finished her undergraduate studies at Cambridge, her teachers, Henry Sidgwick (1838–1900) and James Ward (1843–1925), asked her to finish the project of translating an important work of the German idealist Hermann Lotze (1817–81), *Mikrokosmus: Ideen zur Naturgeschichte und Geschichte der Menschheit* (1856; translated as *Microcosmus: An Essay Concerning Man and His Relation to the World*). Jones spent three years on this project, which she described as providing "delightful occupation for all my leisure hours," "interesting," and "congenial" (1922: 56). Some years later, however, she attended a lecture by the distinguished politician Lord Haldane (1856–1928), who quoted from Lotze, and who mentioned to her later during a chat that his quotations were from a translation of *Mikrokosmus* by "another lady – I forget her name" (1922: 58). Unfortunately, as we will see below, this would not be the last time that Jones's work would be slighted.

In 1884, Girton College invited Jones to return to tutor students in logic for their Cambridge entrance exams, and she remained there for the next thirty-two years. She proceeded up the academic and administrative ladder from Lecturer, to Librarian, to Vice-Mistress and then to Mistress, the highest rank at the college. One of her achievements at Girton was ridding the college of the considerable debt it had incurred as it expanded to meet the increasing number of women students.[2]

Developments in logic

As we noted in Chapter 4, Aristotle's logic had held sway for millennia until the groundbreaking work of Frege and others. Aside from its emphasis on so-called "categorical" statements or propositions, traditional logic also posited three kinds of propositions as so-called "laws of thought." These were the law of identity (*A is A*); the law of non-contradiction *not* (*A and*

---

[1]Girton was founded in 1869 and went co-ed in 1971. The Moral Sciences Club, a Cambridge society devoted to discussion of philosophical topics, exists to this day.

[2]For this and further biographical information, see Jones 1922, Ostertag 2020, and Waithe 1995.

not-A); and the law of excluded middle (*either A or not-A*). But the law of identity puzzled some nineteenth-century metaphysicians, like Lotze, who explicated the perplexity as follows. *A is A* is true, and trivially true at that. But suppose *B* is the same thing as *A*. What kind of identity could be expressed by *A is B*? This proposition is not the same as *A is A*, clearly. Moreover, either something is *A* or it is not *A* (by the law of excluded middle). If it is not *A* (like, say, *B*) then there cannot be an identity between *A* and *B*. So our options with respect to identity statements appear to be either the trivial truth that *A is A* or the contradiction that *A is not-A*. But *A is not-A* is prohibited by the law of non-contradiction.

As we saw in Chapter 4, Frege begins "On Sinn and Bedeutung" with a focus on the problem of making sense of identity statements without falling into these traps. Russell had also found himself requiring the formulation of a similar distinction in his own early work on the foundations of mathematics. Thus in *The Principles of Mathematics*, Russell writes: "The word *is* is terribly ambiguous, and great care is necessary in order not to confound its various meanings. We have (1) the sense in which it asserts Being, as in "*A is*"; (2) the sense of identity; (3) the sense of predication, in "*A is human*" ..." (1903: 64). In this context, Russell also argued that a "worthwhile" (not trivial) identity can be genuinely affirmed, by way of his "theory of denoting" (1903: 64).

Jones had been working on similarly connected issues. Jones described her work on statements or propositions as follows: "what is asserted when you make a statement, and what is the proper form of a statement – had deeply interested me from the time when I was a student ... the question is keenly contested among such logicians as are interested in this part of the subject" (1922: 71). The metaphysical and logical issues that arise with respect to identity statements were not only "keenly" debated in all corners but were at the heart of the transition from nineteenth-century idealism to the new methodology of analytic philosophy at Cambridge at the turn of the twentieth century. Jones's work was, to be sure, squarely in the Aristotelian tradition, and she did not take the new logic on board in her developing ideas. But from her very earliest efforts, she hit upon an insight that appears closely related to Frege's view in "On Sinn and Bedeutung." Jones's work on this was not unknown or even entirely disregarded within her Cambridge professional circle, but her contribution has been ignored in traditional accounts of the history of analytic philosophy. This raises more than a few questions about the role and influence of women in academic life, in the history of philosophy in general, and in the history of analytic

282 Early Analytic Philosophy

philosophy in particular. Many of these questions go beyond the scope of this volume, but we can take the opportunity to look at some of them a little more closely.

We can begin with Jones's insight itself. In her *Elements of Logic as a Science of Propositions*, she introduced her view about the nature of logic as "the science of the import and relations of propositions" and sought to address the way in which *S is P* can genuinely assert anything, in the face of apparent contradictions. *S is P* is an affirmative assertion, consisting of a subject, a predicate, and a copula. Nineteenth-century metaphysicians like Lotze took the logical form of assertion to be either an identity or a negation, which led to the puzzles above: how can we logically formulate informative (not trivial) identities like *S is P* when the laws of thought do not appear to permit it? What Jones did was to argue that the law of identity was inadequate for understanding the logical form of assertions, which are certainly not for the most part trivial identities like *A is A*. Jones formulated the solution to this puzzle as what she called a "significant" assertion: the view that both the predicate and the subject apply to the same thing, but the way that the predicate does so—the attributes it confers—is different from the way the subject does so. The upshot of Jones's view is that the law of identity was to be understood as the law of significant assertion (significant as opposed to trivial), in that it asserts that there can be genuine identity, even in apparent diversity. The identity occurs at the level of extension (what is picked out by "S" and by "P"); the diversity occurs at the level of the ways in which "S" and "P" pick out their extensions. Jones revisited and refined her initial insight throughout her career. A few years after she first discussed it, in *An Introduction to General Logic*, she formulated it as the Law of Identity in Diversity, and referred to it as no less than a "new" law of thought (1892: 20).

Any account of the evolution or development of a particular discipline will uncover scholarly puzzles. These sometimes concern the priority of discovery, or concern the often complex question of influence. The history of early analytic philosophy is no different. Scholars have critically examined (among others) the discovery of quantification in the work of Frege and Russell, as well as C. S. Peirce (1839–1914)[3]; the influence of German and Austrian logicians on British philosophy; and the mutual influence of

---

[3]Unfortunately, Peirce's work remained mostly unknown during his lifetime.

Moore's and Russell's new ideas at the turn of the twentieth century. To these we can add the role of Jones's work in the development of analytic philosophy. There is no doubt that Jones was a member of an academic philosophical *milieu* who presented her views in academic journals and in conference talks, and who was reviewed and referred to by other academics. Jones herself was unaware of Frege's work until, as she put it:

> I have recently had my attention drawn to the fact that Professor Frege's analysis of Categoricals (published in 1892) was apparently the same as my own, and that a similar view was adopted by Mr. B. Russell (1903) in his *Principles of Mathematics*, where Frege's theory of the import of propositions is expounded with sympathetic approbation. (1911: 12)

Jones does not say who was responsible for drawing her attention to Frege's view; some have speculated that it could have been Philip Jourdain (1879–1919), a philosopher and mathematician who had attended Russell's mathematical and logical lectures in 1900–1 and who went on to publish a large number of commentaries and analyses on the new developments in logic, philosophy of logic, history of mathematics, and formal methods.[4] Jourdain wrote to Russell in 1909 to ask him about the development of the ideas that led to *The Principles of Mathematics*. Although the letter is lost, Jourdain seems to have noted that the important issue of the logical form of identity statements had not only been discussed by Frege in 1892, but by Jones in 1890, because Russell replied apparently dismissively that this kind of distinction is "a commonplace of logic, and everything turns on the form given to the distinction," and goes on to say that he doesn't have Jones's work nearby to be able to check the point himself (Grattan-Guinness 1977: 119). While there is no indisputable evidence to show that Russell knew of Jones's work, appropriated it, and failed to credit it, there is evidence of something like contempt for Jones in a letter that Russell wrote to his lover, Ottoline Morrell (1873–1938). Russell had to miss a Moral Sciences Club meeting at which Jones was speaking, and wrote to Ottoline that "poor Miss Jones, Principal of Girton, inventor of a new law of thought, motherly, prissy, and utterly stupid, is reading" (Russell 1992: 410). It is difficult to know exactly what to make of this, but the condescension is palpable and the swipe at her work is at best distasteful.

---

[4]See Waithe and Cicero 1995.

Jones and Russell: The 1910–11 debate

The readings we have chosen to illustrate Jones's work in logic are part of a debate that she entered into with Russell in 1910–11. This particular debate circles around the details of what counts as a logical name or singular term; what counts as the meaning and the reference of a name, and the meaning and reference of expressions in general; what kinds of linguistic expressions are, or are not, names; the role of names and singular terms in propositions; the nature of a proposition; the semantic and logical puzzles that arise with respect to these questions; and the complexities that arise in the formulation of answers to these puzzles. The debate between Russell and Jones thus highlights both the development of some of the most important ideas in the history of analytic philosophy, and how the transition between the traditional logic and the new formal models was not always so smooth.

The chronology is as follows. Jones's paper "Mr. Russell's Objections to Frege's Analysis of Propositions" was published in July 1910. Jones herself may not have been aware that Russell's own work in *The Principles of Mathematics* and "On Denoting" had included a discussion of identity statements until after she had been discussing the issue, but having been made aware of it (see above), she began to press her claim a bit more firmly. She immediately cites three of her own works at the very start of the paper, and sprinkles references to her formulation of Frege's sense/reference (Sinn/ Bedeutung) distinction throughout. Russell then delivered a paper to the Aristotelian Society in March 1911, which was subsequently published in its Proceedings volume for 1910–11. The paper was "Knowledge by Acquaintance and Knowledge by Description," and in it he refers to the criticisms Jones had made of "On Denoting" in her July 1910 paper (but not to her other work). Jones did not let the matter rest there and delivered a paper of her own, "A New Law of Thought," to the Aristotelian Society, which takes on Russell's remarks in "Knowledge by Acquaintance and Knowledge by Description," published in the same volume of the Proceedings, and presented below.

The context of their dispute began a decade and more before 1910–11 and concerned Frege's and Russell's earliest and most well-known efforts to adapt their discoveries of the new post-Aristotelian understanding of logic to a variety of problems in their quest to formulate the logical basis of mathematics. These efforts—the distinction between sense and reference, as well as the theory of descriptions—are the cornerstones of philosophical logic and the rise of analytic philosophy. Jones did not have the same

E. E. Constance Jones on Language and Logic   285

motivation for her analysis of statements or propositions as Frege and Russell did. For Jones, as above, the problem concerned what Lotze had called a paradox of predication—namely that there is no way to claim that there are informative identity statements without violating the laws of thought. For Frege and Russell, the stakes were far broader—no less than the foundations of mathematics—and they made use of innovations in logic that Jones did not adopt, or, it seems, recognize.

In "Mr. Russell's Objections to Frege's Analysis of Propositions" Jones tackles Russell's resistance to Frege's understanding of sense. We know (though Jones did not seem to) that Russell and Frege were at odds concerning the nature of a proposition (or what Frege called a thought). As we saw in Chapter 4, Frege took propositions or thoughts to be mind-and-language independent entities that consisted of other mind-and-language independent entities. Russell did not disagree in broad outline; but he took Frege's analysis in terms of "Sinn" or sense to be too psychological.[5] As we have seen, for Frege, a linguistic expression has sense even if there is no actual referent, something that Russell was loathe to accept at this stage of his thinking. In addition, Frege never did give an incontestable account of "Sinn" or sense, though as we saw in Chapter 4 it can at least roughly be understood as a set of descriptions, associated with the expression, that provide the criteria for identifying the referent of the expression. Jones herself seems to uncritically assume this in her writing. Finally, in addition to the distinction between sense and reference, Frege also drew attention to the logical understanding of a name: the logical notion of what a name is goes beyond a grammatical proper name or a grammatical general name.[6]

All of these issues are complex, and require detailed attention to the notions of meaning, reference, propositions, descriptions, compositionality, names, singular terms, predicates, relations, and functions, among others. Russell, as we know, was also critically examining Frege's formulation of "name" from the point of view of his new discoveries in logic, as well as the semantic and referential properties of propositions and the role of their constituents. Russell's attention to these issues resulted in one of the more momentous steps in the history of early analytic philosophy: the theory of

---

[5] See Frege 1980. Russell also was leery of Frege's use of "thought."
[6] Russell called issues of this kind "philosophical grammar" in *The Principles of Mathematics* (43). As we noted in Chapter 4, Frege took whole sentences to be names of truth-values as objects: they named truth-values, determined by the compositional result of their constituents.

descriptions, discussed in Chapter 5. A name might be short for a description, but a description itself is not a singular term; thus its role in a proposition in which it is a constituent must be accounted for. Both Russell and Frege analyzed what traditional logic (and Jones) called the "import" of a proposition as a compositional entity: the constituents of a proposition contribute to its overall import (meaning and truth-value) on the model of a mathematical function; what are input as values of a function determine the import of the function. The theory of descriptions could be credited among other things with bringing these disparate notions together. The theory of descriptions reveals that the logical form of an expression that looks grammatically like a name or singular term is not what it seems. The new logic of quantification is what is used both to bear this out and to defend a new view of the "import" of a proposition.

Jones waded into this fray with "Mr. Russell's Objections . . ." and although she was apparently unaware of Frege's and Russell's logical innovations, she nevertheless held her own on a number of points. She introduced the issue by summarizing Russell's approach in "On Denoting": Frege's distinction, according to Russell, won't solve three puzzles. These are: (i) the problem of substitutivity of co-referential expressions in so-called "propositional attitude contexts" like "George IV wished to know that S"; (ii) the problem of negating propositions with constituents that don't refer, like "The present King of France is bald" (how do we say he's not, since there isn't one?); and (iii) how to meaningfully say that something does not exist, since we have to refer to it to say it doesn't exist. What Jones does is to press hard on what she lays claim to: her distinction between intension and denotation (she concedes it to Frege as well).

What Russell did not like about the sense/reference (Sinn/ Bedeutung) distinction with respect to his puzzles as above is that, as he put it in "On Denoting," "we cannot succeed in both preserving the connexion of meaning and denotation *and* preventing them from being one and the same" (486). Jones argued that Russell has somewhat missed the point of Frege's distinction. On her view, Russell doesn't really give a clear definition or criterion of meaning, so that in his criticisms he elides the distinction that Frege meant to defend. Russell argued that we end up in logical difficulties when we try to formulate the meaning of a denoting phrase along Frege's view. The meaning of a denoting phrase, for Russell, is just the thing it denotes. If we interject another level of meaning—that of Frege's "Sinn" or sense—into the relation between an expression and its denotation, we (according to Russell) won't properly or logically refer at all. Instead we end up with a notion of a meaning of the expression that, if anything, takes us farther away from the thing we are meant to be talking about. This is because, on Russell's view, Frege's view about the meaning of an expression redirects us to its sense, not what the expression is meant to be referring to. The way Russell puts it is that a phrase C is meant to have both meaning and denotation, on Frege's view. But if we ask for the meaning of C, what we get is the denotation. So what is the role of sense?

Jones takes Russell to task on this, as well as on his puzzles about non-existence, by wondering in her paper what exactly Russell means by "meaning," and what he means by "is." Her own formulation is as follows. "Whatever we can think of ... must be thought of as something," and every term which is used as S or P in a proposition must have both denotation and intension (1910: 381). Whenever we ask if there is a difference between A and B we are asking for information, and the question itself assumes the "possibility of thinkability" of this difference—even if A and B are "devoid of real Existence." The difference in question is not that in some cases there is both a denotation and a connotation or intension, while in other cases there is not, but that the things denoted and the things connoted "belong to different spheres, regions, contexts, or Universes of Discourse" (1910: 382). Jones's solution is thus: we must understand the "meaning" or "import" of the elements of a proposition according to Frege's formulation of sense, and claim that every term used as a subject or as a predicate in a proposition has both denotation and intension. The details are that "what the term *qua* denotative denotes is the thing to which the term applies" and "what the term *qua* connotative denotes is the attributes of the thing denoted" (1910: 383). This latter is what is "meant" by the term, and what would be given in a "definition of description" of the term. In short, she argues, denotational identity does not imply intensional identity, which gives us a way to make identity statements that have significant and not trivial import. On Jones's view, we do not "detach the meaning of a proposition from the denotation of its terms" at all. Where Russell goes wrong, she argues, stems from his using the word "meaning" as equivalent sometimes to connotation and sometimes not, which leads, she says, to "some want of clearness" (1910: 386).

This point is repeated in the second paper included below, "A New Law of Thought." This paper is a reply to the criticisms that Russell had made of Jones's 1910 "Mr. Russell's Objections ..." paper in his "Knowledge by Acquaintance and Knowledge by Description." What we see now, perhaps

288   Early Analytic Philosophy

inevitably, are the limitations of Jones's criticisms, given how thoroughly Russell's innovations have by then dominated any debate on the logical form of a proposition and of an identity statement. Jones has not absorbed these, nor does she appreciate the way "Knowledge by Acquaintance and Knowledge by Description" is an effort by Russell to adapt his innovations, particularly with respect to the analysis of descriptions, in a new epistemological direction. And there is, moreover, a feature of Russell's theory of descriptions that arises in the context of Jones's paper here that she appears not to appreciate. We will draw our chapter on Jones to a close by taking a look at this.

The issue concerns Russell's (and Frege's) understanding of the logical form of a statement or proposition as compositional. Roughly speaking, a proposition is a whole, and its constituents play a role in the meaning, and the reference, of this whole. Thus one of Russell's explicit contributions to this debate is the insight that certain kinds of expressions do not have meaning in isolation, a point that serves to emphasize the new understanding of the logical form of a proposition. In her paper, Jones begins by reminding her audience that she has been defending a version of an intension/denotation "in season and out of season." She also brusquely remarks that Russell's criticism that her analysis of propositions of the form *S is P* won't hold of categorical propositions that are *not* of the form *S is P* is (i) irrelevant and (ii) based on a disputable point about such categoricals. What we know, but what eluded Jones, is that Russell's work had precisely eclipsed the role of those traditional categorical propositions in logic. Thus her only defense is to argue that she takes "proposition" to be defined "in the sense it is currently used in logic books," or, as she puts it, "an assertion expressed in words," which at this point in the historical development of these views just won't do.

In her discussion of the identity statement "Scott is the author of *Waverley*" she counters Russell by arguing that her theory of identity in diversity removes the problem of what "the author of *Waverley*" might mean. If, as Russell has previously argued, it cannot but mean Scott, then, she argues, Russell is again operating with a double use of the word "meaning," which in this case he is using to indicate that "the author of *Waverley*" denotes Scott. She agrees that "Scott" and "the author of *Waverley*" do not have the same intension, but she takes it as perverse to claim—as she thinks Russell is claiming—that things themselves, and not names of things, are either meanings or denotations. She further takes Russell on with respect to the analysis of a description. As she sees it, "one and only one man wrote *Waverley*" asserts an identity of denotation between "one and only one man" and "writer of *Waverley.*" But what she does not see is that Russell has argued that "one and only one man wrote *Waverley*" is a statement of existential quantification, not a name for an entity. Thus it does not denote the way a (logical) name would; it has no meaning, as Russell argues, in isolation. As we now recognize, the theory of descriptions in effect removes the description as a logical subject expression from a proposition and reconfigures the proposition as an existentially quantified sentence.

Concluding remarks

We will end this chapter with a question. Why, exactly, was Jones not in a position to have absorbed the new logic? As we have noted, she occupied a traditional academic role in a university of great renown. She published her work regularly, she was referred to by other philosophers, and she played a visible role in a number of academic discussions not only in logic but in ethics. For all that, however, she seems to have been stuck on the periphery of the progress in her own subject. About this we might say the following: there were few philosophers of this period that could keep up with the new logic defended by Russell. A contemporary philosopher looking back at this period must be wary of interjecting their own understanding of the progress and of the contemporary role of the views we have been discussing. During this period there were only a handful of mathematicians and logicians who might have been in a position to grasp the general nature of Russell's innovations; even Cambridge University Press struggled to find a way to print the formulae of *Principia Mathematica*, notoriously charging Russell and Whitehead for the privilege of preparing their work for press. Moreover, as we know, the logicist project that is the backdrop to the work we have been discussing here ultimately failed, so perhaps it is not so surprising that Jones would have been nonplussed with respect to Russell's arguments.

In Jones's debate with Russell, we can appreciate the progress of philosophical logic from the traditional to the contemporary, and also appreciate the way that Russell's and Frege's innovations were so up-ending to traditional logical discussions. And it is furthermore to Jones's credit how intrepidly she defended her own contributions as having a legitimate seat at the table.

Further reading

Primary sources

Jones, E. E. C. (1892), *An Introduction to General Logic*, London: Longmans, Green and Co.

Jones, E. E. C. (1894), Rational Hedonism, *International Journal of Ethics* 5: 79–97.

Jones, E. E. C. (1911), *A New Law of Thought and Its Logical Bearings*, Cambridge: Cambridge University Press.

Jones, E. E. C. (1922), *As I Remember: An Autobiographical Ramble*, London: A & C Black.

Secondary sources

Ostertag, G. (2020), "Emily Elizabeth Constance Jones", *Stanford Encyclopedia of Philosophy*. Available online: https://plato.stanford.edu/entries/emily-elizabeth-constance-jones/

Waithe, M. E. and Cicero, S. (1995), "E. E. Constance Jones", in M. E. Waithe, *A History of Women Philosophers*, Vol. 4, Dordrecht: Kluwer.

Readings

Jones, E. E. C. "Mr. Russell's Objections to Frege's Analysis of Propositions".[1]
Reprinted from Jones, E. E. C. (1910), "Mr. Russell's Objections to Frege's Analysis of Propositions", *Mind* 19: 379–86.

According to Frege[2] what a Categorical Affirmative Proposition asserts is: Identity of denotation (or Application – *Bedeutung*) with difference of intension (or connotation or 'meaning ' – *Sinn*). – Hence we may say *a is b*, which means *a is identical with b* (identical in denotation that is, for it is clearly *not* identical in connotation or intension). But we cannot say *a is a* because here difference of connotation (*Sinn*) has vanished. And we cannot say *a is not-a* because here identity of denotation is impossible. Mr. Russell objects (p. 485) to this theory of Frege's that it will not solve the following three puzzles.

"(1) If *a* is identical with *b*, whatever is true of the one is true of the other, and either may be substituted for the other in any proposition without altering the truth or falsehood of that proposition. Now George IV. wished to know whether Scott was the author of *Waverley*; and in fact Scott was the author of *Waverley*. Hence we may substitute *Scott* for *the author of 'Waverley*,' and thereby prove that George IV. wished to know whether Scott was Scott. Yet an interest in the law of identity can hardly be attributed to the first gentleman of Europe."

When George IV. asked whether Scott was the author of *Waverley*, what he wanted to know was, whether the intension ('meaning,' connotation) of *Author of "Waverley"* could be assigned to Scott – *i.e.*, whether identity of denotation could be asserted between *Scott* and *Author of "Waverley"*. The "first gentleman of Europe" did not want to know whether Scott was Scott – this would have been perhaps more in the style of "Farmer George," with his, "What, what, Young, Young, dead, dead," and his sense of the inexplicability of the fact of the apple being inside the dough in an apple dumpling.

No doubt "if *a* is identical [in denotation that is] with *b*," whatever is true of the thing denoted by *a* is true of the same thing when denoted by *b*[3] – with the

---

[1] *Mind* 1905, pp. 483, 485, etc. [Editor's note: as marked in the Preface, references and footnotes in the original texts have been retained unaltered.]

[2] See also my *Elements of Logic*, §VI. p. 46, etc., and §XV. (T. & T. Clark, Edinburgh, 1890), my *General Logic*, Part I. §III., etc. (March, 1892), and MIND, 1893, p. 441, etc.

[3] I am not quite sure what is meant by "whatever is true of the one is true of the other". Do *the one* and *the other* mean *the one thing* and *the other thing* (as Jevons has it)? Or do *one* and *other* refer to the symbols *a* and *b*? Neither alternative is satisfactory.

Early Analytic Philosophy

obvious reservation that *a is a* does not convey the information that *a* has the intension (or connotation) *b*. If we admit *a is a* at all, we must either (1) regard the copula as having a different force in this case from what it has in *a is b*, and must point out what this is, or (2) we must hold that in *a is a* it is only *denotational* identity of *a* with itself which is asserted – and it seems hard to understand why any one who 'asserts' *a is a* with this intent, should ever want, or indeed be able, to assert anything else.

On these lines we reach the entirely hopeless view that any

$$S \text{ is } P = \begin{cases} S \text{ is } S \\ P \text{ is } P \\ S \text{ is not } P \end{cases}$$

as Lotze does – *i.e.*, we divest the Categorical Affirmative of the form *S is P* of coherence and of meaning. It is, I think, of the essence of Frege's theory (and mine) that *S is S* (*a is a*) is valueless as a 'Law' of Thought or of Logic. That it is so is perhaps sufficiently shown in the ill-success of Lotze's determined, elaborate, protracted, yet absolutely futile effort to exhibit it as a fundamental logical principle of the Logic which uses propositions of the form S is P.

"(2) By the law of excluded middle, either 'A is B' or 'A is not B' must be true. Hence either 'the present King of France is bald' or 'the present King of France is not bald' must be true. Yet if we enumerated the existing things that are bald and then the existing things that are not bald, we should not find the present King of France in either list [*i.e.*, The present King of France is not an existing thing that is bald nor an existing thing that is not bald, we cannot 'identify' the 'present King of France' with any 'existing' thing whether bald or not bald]. Hegelians, who love a synthesis, will probably conclude that he wears a wig."

Certainly nothing of which Existence is predicated can without contradiction be denotationally identified with anything of which Existence (in the same sense) is denied. But if the *A* in *A is B* is *the present* (A.D. 1909) *King of France*, then *that A* is *A not-A*, and having admitted it, there can be no further difficulty in the way of asserting of *it* contradictory attributes – since the complex denoting term *A not-A* itself has 'contradictory' connotation, and includes elements which together exhaust the universe.

If *the present King of France* is not (1) a self-contradictory term, then (2) it is assigned to some sphere of predication ("universe of discourse") in which it occurs – which means that the kind of 'being' or 'existence,'[4] is fixed by the

---

[4]I use *Existence* and *Being* as equivalent.

E. E. Constance Jones on Language and Logic   **293**

context, by certain further determinations of the subject-term; and if this is sufficiently done with reference to any accepted 'universe' – *e.g.*, of past time, or of supposition, fiction, or prophecy – there need be no difficulty in choosing between any B and not-B.

"(3) Consider the proposition 'A differs from B'. If this is true, there is a difference between A and B, which fact may be expressed in the form 'the difference between A and B subsists'. But if it is false that A differs from B, then there is no difference between A and B, which fact may be expressed in the form 'the difference between A and B does not subsist'. But how can a non-entity be the subject of the proposition? 'I think, therefore I am' is no more evident than 'I am the subject of a proposition, therefore I am,' provided 'I am' is taken to assert subsistence or being[5], not existence. Hence, it would appear, it must always be self-contradictory to deny the being of anything; but we have seen, in connexion with Meinong, that to admit being also sometimes leads to contradictions. Thus if A and B do not differ, to suppose either that there *is*,[6] or that there is not such an object as 'the difference between A and B ' seems equally impossible."

Considerations similar to those applied in (2) seem to apply in the case of the difficulties raised in (3) – it does no doubt appear self-contradictory to deny *all* 'being' of anything of which we think and speak – we must at least *suppose* a thing or object (with certain attributes), in order to be able to talk about it – even to deny it 'existence' or occurrence in some particular sphere – that is, to deny its possession of certain other attributes. A non-entity for thought, is simply that which is not thought about.

We can think of nothing, speak of nothing, without postulating or assuming both application (or denotation) and intension (*Bedeutung* and *Sinn*) in Frege's sense – without these two elements, significant assertion is always and for ever impossible. Whatever we think of or speak of must be thought of as something and as some sort of something – and every term which is used as Subject or Predicate in a Proposition must have both denotation and intension (as Frege, I believe, holds).

If A and B do not differ, "the difference between A and B" of which we think and speak, is still an object with *Sinn* and *Bedeutung*, with 'being' or 'existence,' and attributes, assumed hypothetically – otherwise how could we deny it? And of course we may quite reasonably decide that A and B do not differ, when A and B have just as little Real Existence (however that may be ascertained) as the 'non-existent' difference between them.

---

[5]I use these as synonyms [Mr. Russell's footnote.]
[6]What does Mr. Russell mean by *is*, and what is his distinction between Being (or Subsistence) and Existence?

294   **Early Analytic Philosophy**

"Is there a difference between A and B? " I ask – *e.g.*, between Fair Trade and Free Trade, between Usefulness and Truth, between those two colour-patterns, between this material and that, between my faith and yours? – I ask for information. – The question: Is *there a difference between A and B?* assumes the possibility or thinkability of such a difference, even though A and B be devoid of Real Existence, and has applicability and intension just as truly as *the shining of the sun* (when it *is* shining), *the convenience of the house I am planning to build next summer, the best measure of social reform of the next Parliament.* The difference between these is not that in some cases there is denotation and connotation (or intension) and not in others, but that the things denoted and connoted belong to different spheres, regions, contexts, or 'Universes of Discourse'. A great deal of our keenest and most absorbing interest is about 'things' of the 'existence' and (sometimes) of the character of which we are doubtful – but in which we could take no interest at all unless they had *Sinn* and *Bedeutung*, what-ness and that-ness, in some region, and as much Reality as that implies. Dr. Cook's finding of the North Pole does not differ from Sir Ernest Shackleton's approximation to the South Pole in *not* having 'denotation' and intension while Shackleton's achievement has both. Dr. Cook's 'discovery' has them just as much, otherwise we could not have thought and talked about it as we have.

I pass to the difficulties which Mr. Russell finds in the relation between 'Meaning' (Frege's *Sinn*, my intension or connotation) and Denotation (Frege's *Bedeutung*, my denotation or application or applicability), pp. 485, etc.

The difficulties are set forth as follows: "When we wish to speak about the *meaning* of a denoting phrase, as opposed to its *denotation*, the natural mode of doing so is by inverted commas. Thus we say: –

The centre of mass of the Solar System is a point, not a denoting complex;
'The centre of mass of the Solar System' is a denoting complex, not a point.

Or again: –

The first line of Gray's 'Elegy' states a proposition.
'The first line of Gray's "Elegy' " does not state a proposition.

Thus taking any denoting phrase, say C, we wish to consider "the relation between C and 'C,' where the difference of the two is of the kind exemplified in the above two instances."

"We say, to begin with, that when C occurs it is the *denotation* that we are speaking about; but when 'C' occurs, it is the *meaning*. Now the relation of meaning and denotation is not merely linguistic through the phrase: there must be a logical relation involved, which we express by saying that the meaning denotes the denotation. But the difficulty which confronts us is that we cannot succeed in *both* preserving the connexion of meaning and denotation and preventing them from being one and the same[7]; also that the meaning cannot be got at except by means of denoting phrases. This happens as follows: –

"The one phrase C was to have both meaning and denotation. But if we speak of 'the meaning of C' that gives us the meaning (if any) of the denotation."

Now using Denotation as equivalent to Application (Frege's *Bedeutung*) and Intension or Connotation (Frege's *Sinn*) as equivalent to 'Meaning,' it seems to me that the difficulty here may be quite simply explained.

First, every term used as Subject or Predicate of a proposition has both Denotation and Intension. And what the term *qua* denotative denotes, is the thing to which it (the Term) applies. And what the Term *qua* connotative connotes, is those attributes of the thing denoted, which are 'meant' by the Term, and which would be given in a Definition of the Term (or description of the thing).

No categorical assertion of the form *S is P* is possible unless S and P have Denotation and Connotation (or Intension) – identity of Denotation and diversity of Connotation. And if S is isolated from its Predicate (which has identical denotation with S) or P from its Subject, S (or P) still has both Denotation and Connotation (*Bedeutuing* and *Sinn*). That "the meaning [Connotation] cannot be got, at except by means of denoting phrases" is no doubt true, but this does not involve any difficulty, for every 'phrase' (word or words) that can be used as a term in a proposition *must* have Denotation (Application, *Bedeutung*).

But to talk of "the meaning denoting the denotation" seems to me a very awkward way of expressing the obvious fact that it is often by means of the connotation (or intension) of a term that we are enabled to see where it should be applied – to find its denotation (I think this must be Mr. Russell's meaning) – and it is surely not the case that "we cannot succeed in *both* preserving the connection of meaning and denotation, *and* preventing them from being one and the same [= ?]" nor that "if we speak of the 'meaning [connotation] of C' that gives us the meaning (if any) of the denotation." If C is a Term, it has Connotation (or Intension) and Denotation, and the connotation of C is the connotation (not of the denotation of C but) of the Term which *qua* denotative, denotes the thing to which C applies – the thing of which C is the name; the Connotation of C implies those attributes of *the thing called C* on account of the possession of which it is called C.

---

[7]What precisely is the meaning of 'one and the same'?

Thus: –

(1) The first line of Gray's Elegy (S) is identical in denotation with the line which runs: The curfew tolls etc. (P).
This line (S) is identical in denotation with a proposition (P).

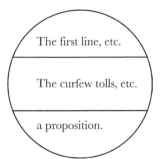

(2) The words: *The first line of Gray's Elegy* connotes a line occurring in a certain position in a well-known poem.

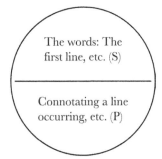

(3) The words: *The first line of Gray's Elegy* are: –

$\begin{cases} \text{identical in denotation with a Term.} \\ \text{not identical in denotation with a proposition.} \end{cases}$

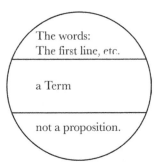

E. E. Constance Jones on Language and Logic 297

(1) The centre of mass of the Solar System is a point (*is* = *denotes*, or *is identical in denotation with*).

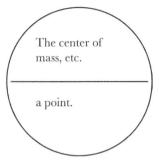

(2) The words: *The centre of mass of the Solar System* connotes the place in the system which etc.

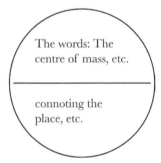

(3) The words: *The centre of mass of the Solar System* are a denoting complex (= Complex-denoting term)

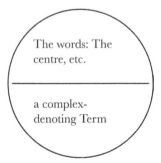

These examples thus examined seem to me to bring out the strength and inevitability of Frege's analysis – in every case we have denotational identity of Subject and Predicate, in intensional (connotational) diversity, though the things identified are not the same in every case. We are concerned with different Subjects and different Predicates.

Early Analytic Philosophy

In (1) the propositions are taken in their ordinary natural sense.

In (2) the Subject-Term is isolated from its original, intensionally-diverse, Predicate, for the purpose of determining, by a definitional Predicate, the Subject-term's connotation, intension, or description.

In (3) the Predicate states the logical character of the words composing the Subject-Term.

Compare: (1) the first book on the shelf is (= denotes) Aristotle's *Ethics*;

(2) "The first book on the shelf " connotes *the book which occupies the definite position described.*

(3) "The first book on the shelf " is a complex denoting Term.

It conduces to clearness when in any of the above cases we prefix "The words" to the phrase in quotation marks. The quotation marks simply indicate that the words which they include have to be taken as a name of which the *connotation* (or description, grammatical character, etc.) is predicated, and are an elliptical device.

And all the time (as has been pointed out) our Subject-Term, whatever it is, has both Denotation and Connotation – and so has our Predicate-Term, whatever it is; and our *connotes* is resolvable into *is connoting* – and so on. Whatever conundrums are stated or solved, it is impossible to state them or their solutions in any other way.

The denoting-complex (complex-denoting term) "the first line of Gray's Elegy" denotes the line which consists of the words "The curfew tolls the knell of parting day" – and this denoting-complex denotes the line by means of the connotation of the complex, which indicates a certain place of occurrence. It is this connotation of the phrase: *The first line of Gray's Elegy* which is given when we say: "The first line of Gray's Elegy" connotes ('means') the line which occurs at the beginning of a certain poem known under the title given.

The *meaning* (propositional force) of the line (which is a proposition) is, the assigning to that which is denoted by *curfew* of the connotation of the predicate: *tolling the knell of parting day* (denotation of Subject and Predicate identical).

Or take the third case: The first book on the shelf is Aristotle's *Ethics*. – The 'denoting-complex' *the first book on the shelf* denotes the volume which has the given title – it denotes (or applies to) the book in virtue of its (the denoting complex's) connotation, which connotation indicates the position occupied by the book. The connotation of this 'denoting complex' is given by saying: 'The first book on the shelf' connotes the book which occupies the position described. Until I know what the phrase 'the first book on the shelf' connotes ('means '), I cannot use that phrase as *denoting* the book referred to.

And 'the first book on the shelf' denotes Aristotle's *Ethics*: – and the connotation of Aristotle's *Ethics* is given by an explanation of Aristotle and of *Ethics*.

There is one thing or object denoted (a copy of Aristotle's *Ethics*): it is referred to by two different phrases, both of which denote that one volume, but denote it by means of different connotations: –

(1) The first book on the shelf.

(2) Aristotle's *Ethics*.

Both (1) and (2) are complex denoting terms. – When "The first book on the shelf " is called a "denoting complex" it is not the connotation of the Term "The first book, etc." (*i.e.* those attributes of the object denoted by the term on account of which the term is applied to it) which is given, but a description of the logical character of the *Term itself*.

It may be noted that in Mr. Russell's use of *Denoting* (or *Denotation*), the term is confined to words or phrases which include some general name – some name having (in Mill's use of the terms) both Denotation and Connotation; and it seems to him to involve difficulty that connotations should be denoted. But in Frege's view as I understand it (and in mine) whatever can be talked about must be denoted – and we are here expressly talking about connotations. As Mr. Russell says: "Frege distinguishes the *two* elements of meaning (connotation or intension), and denotation *everywhere*" (italics mine).

The use of the word *meaning* as equivalent sometimes to *connotation* and sometimes to the *force or significance of a proposition* naturally leads to some want of clearness as between (1) Connotation (or intension) of a term or phrase and (2) Propositional force of an Assertion. It is impossible to detach the 'meaning' of a proposition from the denotation of its terms.

Further, according to Mr. Russell, we do not know whether the denoting phrases which we obtain from propositions denote entities or not, until we know whether the propositions are true (p. 490).

This surely is a very awkward position, for how are we to know (on Mr. Russell's principles see p. 485) whether a proposition is true until we know whether its terms denote actual 'entities' or not? Is it not indispensable to have some analysis of propositions of the form *S is P* which can be applied to *all* propositions of that form, and some theory of denotation which can be applied to *all* denotative terms, at whatever stage of investigation or certainty? I think Frege's theory does this, furnishing an analysis of propositions which seems to meet all legitimate requirements, elucidating Eduction and Deduction as well as Assertion. Does Mr. Russell hold that no analysis of propositions or theory of

Early Analytic Philosophy

predication is acceptable or applicable unless it provides a Criterion of Truth and of 'Real Existence'? Or must the truth of all true propositions have been established before any theory of import of propositions can be arrived at?

Jones, E. E. C., "A New Law of Thought".
Reprinted from Jones, E. E. C. (1910–11), "A New Law of Thought", *Proceedings of the Aristotelian Society* 11: 166–86.

I have for a long time been trying, in season and out of season, to advocate a certain general analysis of Categorical Propositions according to which what is asserted in *S is P* is identity of denotation of S and P with diversity of intension. I have been exceedingly anxious to find that other people agreed with me, and in a little book (published in 1890) and an article on Logical Judgment in *Mind* for 1893 I tried to support this aspiration by extracts from well-known writers who, I thought, came near to doing so. In fact, I made every effort to persuade myself and others that what I had to say about import was what most people had said or thought already – and up to a certain point perhaps this is so. Nearly everyone, for instance, seems to have come in sight of the absolutely obvious circumstance that in *S is P* it is one thing that is referred to by the two terms.

I still feel that there is much similarity between what I try to say and what other writers have said – if this were not so I could hardly have any hope of being on the right track. But I now see that it is the *exact* points of difference that are all-important, and, as far as my knowledge and apprehension go, my analysis of *S is P* has fundamental differences from every other perfectly general analysis that any previous writer on the subject had formulated.

And even if this should not be so, I might still claim that no one else has attempted to make a systematic application of the view involved to the principal topics and problems of Formal Logic. But of course what concerns me chiefly is, that this view should be, and should be recognised as being, true. And it would not have occurred to me to draw attention to anything I had to say as "new" if I had not been really startled a few months ago by a sudden perception that the identity-of-denotation-in-diversity-of-intension analysis can be formulated as a Law of Significant Assertion which is logically prior to those laws of relations of Assertion which are known as the Laws of Contradiction and Excluded Middle, and supplies the explicit recognition and justification of propositions of the form S is P, which Logic has hitherto needed but not had.

E. E. Constance Jones on Language and Logic 301

If it had not been for this *aperçu*, and for the fact that I had recently become aware that Professor Frege's Analysis of Categoricals seemed to be really the same as mine, and had been approved by Mr. Bertrand Russell in his *Principles of Mathematics*, I should not at this time have returned to the attack. In the circumstances, I am particularly grateful for this chance of bringing the matter before the Aristotelian Society in a more complete form than hitherto, and am the. more glad because of the opportunity thus afforded me of saying something in answer to Mr. Russell's criticisms of my account of Import in the paper which he read before this Society in March.

On starting to give now a brief summary of my view, I wish to emphasise two things: –

(1) I set out from, and throughout depend upon, a steady distinction between *denotational one-ness* (identity) and *intensional one-ness* (qualitative same-ness), and I hold that *every* name used in assertion has both denotation and intension – that it is the name of *something*, and implies some qualities or attributes of that something. If there were any name that was not the name of *something* it would be incapable of application to anything; if there were any name that had no qualitative implication whatever, such a name could not be more appropriate to any one occasion than to any other. (*Intension*, in my use, has a wider meaning than *Connotation*.) Identity of *the person accused of a crime*, and *the person who committed it*, is what the prosecutor in any criminal action is called upon to prove, and may be taken as an instance of denotational one-ness.

Such identity-in-diversity is the category of affirmative assertion.

Intensional one-ness, qualitative same-ness (with denotational difference, otherness), is the category not of assertion but of classing. This envelope is qualitatively the same as any other out of the same packet. This animal is called a Quadruped because, as far as four-footed-ness goes, it has qualitative same-ness with other Quadrupeds.

The distinction between the two kinds of one-ness is, I understand, disputed by some logicians.

(2) The second thing which I wish at this point to emphasise is, that what I am attempting in my analysis of categoricals is an *absolutely general* analysis, an analysis of that symbolic and most abstract form of assertion S *is* P which corresponds to $a = b$ as the symbolic form of equations – a mere skeleton analysis, primary and universal, admitting of further determinations, not assuming psychological or philosophical theories, but equally applicable to all theories. The possibility and necessity of such an absolutely general analysis must be admitted by any one who countenances the use of the symbolic form

Early Analytic Philosophy

S is P, and various logicians have attempted to furnish such an analysis, *e.g.*, Hobbes, Jevons, Lotze, and (perhaps) Mill.

It seems to me undeniable that in every proposition of form *S is P*, S and P denote the one thing (SP), the *is* therefore signifies identity of denotation – extensionally or denotationally *S is P*. The attempt to interpret *S is P* in extension only, would reduce us to *S is S*, since difference of intension of the terms is necessary for significant assertion. And we cannot "identify" the extension or denotation of the one term with the intension of the other.

And in intension *S* is not *P*. Taken in intension, we can only say with Lotze that *S is P* is impossible and must be resolved into S is S, P is P, S is not P. It is, however, clearly not *S is P* but this forced conceptualist interpretation of it in the interests of the Law of Identity, *A is A*, that is impossible.

S is not P asserts difference (or otherness) of denotation in intensional diversity, *i.e.*, it denies what *S is P* affirms. *A is related to B* is of the form *A is not B* – (A) (B).

It is not until *S is P*, *S is not P*, have been admitted and justified that we are entitled to formulate the Law of Contradiction and the Law of Excluded Middle and to say that

$$\left.\begin{array}{l} \text{S is P} \\ \text{S is not P} \end{array}\right\} \begin{array}{l} \text{cannot both be true (Law of Contradiction).} \\ \text{``} \qquad \text{'' false (Law of Excluded Middle).} \end{array}$$

The above analysis of *S is P* justifies the assertion that: Any Subject of *affirmative* predication is an identity of denotation in diversity of intension. And taking the Law of Contradiction and the Law of Excluded Middle, together with this analysis of *S is P* into an assertion of *identity of denotation in diversity of intension*, we can say that of any Subject (S) P must be affirmed or denied, i.e., that of any Subject (S), P or not-P (but not both) may be predicated – (SP) or (S not-P). Thus we obtain as a perfectly general Law of Significant Assertion the following formula: –

Any Subject of Predication is an identity of denotation in diversity of intension.

If *S is P* (SP) is analysed as above, Conversion and other Immediate Inferences are at once justified. It is obvious, *e.g.*, that when we can say *S is P*, we can equally say *P is S*, if S and P have identical denotations and the thing we are referring to is both S and P.

Similarly in Mediate Inference. As (SP) (1) corresponds to *S is P* when two diverse intensions are assigned to one denotation, so (S, M, P) (2) corresponds to *S is M* and *M is P* in which three diverse intensions are assigned to one denotation. The speaker or teacher starts in the one case from the whole (SP), in the other from the whole (SMP). The hearer or learner on the other hand puts together in the one case S and P, and in the other S and M and P, and thus constructs the whole from which the speaker started, and (2) justifies the assertion *S is P* as fully as (1) justifies the assertion *P is S*.

No *intensional* one-ness, no similarity or qualitative sameness, can take the place of denotational one-ness (identity) as the unifying element in assertion or in inference. We have explained this fully in the case of assertion, and in the case of Mediate Inference the indispensableness of a Distributed Middle, and the utter inadequacy of any "Substitution of Similars," is evidence in proof, if evidence were wanted.

All Hypothetical propositions are reducible to identities of denotation in (diversity of intension, and are either Immediate Inferences, *e.g.*, If M is P, P is M; or Mediate Inferences, *e.g.*, If M is P and S is M, S is P; if M is P, S is P (because S is M); If A is B, A is E (because B is C and C is D and D is E).

I have tried in the above statement to give an outline of my analysis and its application in Formal Logic, in propositions expressed symbolically. It is easy to show its application in concrete cases: Courage is Valour, The present Prime Minister is Mr. Asquith, convert quite obviously and simply to

Valour is Courage;
Mr. Asquith is the present Prime Minister.

All English Cathedrals are interesting, by the application of Quantification of the Predicate converts to – Some interesting [things] are English Cathedrals.

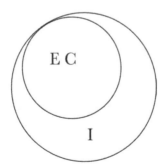

The possibility of quantifying the new Subject-name is indisputable evidence that that name had, as Predicate, a denotational as well as an intensional aspect. The exact use of the actual but un-emphasised denotation-aspect of Predicates and the denotational identity of affirmatives, and when the previous quantification of a term is dropped on its passing from the place of Subject to that of Predicate, this is in accordance with the natural emphasis on the intension-aspect of Predicates.

I borrow here the examination of a few concrete instances of Mediate and Hypothetical Inference from my little book *A New Law of Thought* (pp. 48-53):

"In: All Cavicornia are Ruminants,
All Antelopes are Cavicornia,
All Antelopes are Ruminants,

the relation of Terms may be diagrammatically represented thus:

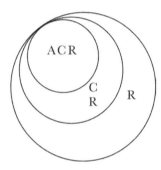

"The true Middle Term is the [*some*] *Cavicornia* of the Minor Premiss; for it is only that part of the denotation of Cavicornia which is common to both Antelopes and Ruminants, that is the bond of connexion between them. The Ruminants that Antelopes are, are the Ruminants whose denotation is identical with that of those Cavicornia that are identical with Antelopes. Of those Ruminants whose denotation does not coincide with that of any Cavicornia, and of those Cavicornia whose denotation does not coincide with that of any Antelopes, it must be said that they are not Antelopes, and that Antelopes are not they. It is the indefiniteness of the *some* by which Ruminants in the Major Premiss, and Cavicornia in the Minor Premiss are implicitly quantified, that makes it necessary to sweep in the whole extension of Cavicornia, so as to make sure that those Cavicornia with which (as being Antelopes) we are concerned are Ruminants.

"Same-ness of Denotation (identity) of Middle Term in Mediate Inference is that which connexion between Major and Minor Terms must depend upon, for it cannot depend on same-ness of intension or exact similarity (*cp.* Jevons' 'Substitution of *Similars*') – *intensional* same-ness, the closest similarity, would not justify substitution – if it would, there would be no reason why the Middle term in a Syllogism should be at distributed – the *intension* M would be all that could be required as a link, and (as in all S is M, all P is M) S might be identified with one part of the Class M, and P with another part, and as a result S identified with P, which is absurd.

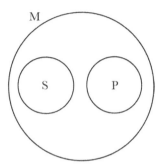

"It is because Class relations as indicated in the A, I, O forms are indeterminate, that in Mediate Inference we cannot make the Terms correspond exactly with the clear and perfectly definite forms of the *S is P, S is not P* type when we are dealing with unquantified class-syllogisms. This may be done, however, in the case of what has been called Traduction, where all the subjects are singular and have identical denotation, *e.g.*,

London is the largest city in the world.
London is the capital of England.
∴ The capital of England is the largest city in the world

"It is done exactly in every Mediate Inference (Traductional or other) in which the denotations of all the Terms are determinate, *e.g.*, –

The Syndics and Night Watch are two of Rembrandt's masterpieces;
The Syndics and Night Watch are two of the pictures in the New Museum at Amsterdam;
Two of the pictures in the New Museum are two of Rembrant's masterpieces.

"An examination of concrete Hypothetical, Disjunctive (Alternative) Propositions shows that here, too, the analysis of Categorical Affirmation as identity of denotation in diversity of intension is applicable. Take the following Conditionals: If any child is spoilt, he is troublesome, asserts the identity of denotation of Spoilt Child with Troublesome Child.

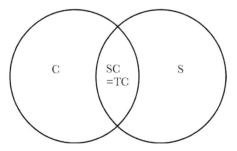

"If any rose is blue, it is a curiosity, asserts denotational identity of Blue Rose with a Curiosity.

"Take the following Hypotheticals, of which (1) is Self-Contained, i.e., the consequent is a necessary consequence of the antecedent taken alone:

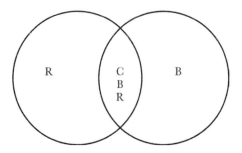

"(1) If all men are fallible and the Pope is a man, the Pope is fallible.

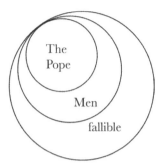

"What is asserted is, that granting the denotation of man is part of the denotation of fallible, and the that the denotation of the Pope is part of the denotation of man, then it follows that the denotation of Pope is part of the denotation of fallible.

"(2) If Charles I had not deserted Strafford he would be deserving of sympathy.

"This asserts that supposing denotation of Charles I to be identical with denotation of one who did not desert Strafford, then (because not to have deserted Strafford would have been to deserve sympathy) the denotation of Charles I would have been the denotation of one deserving of sympathy. In this example it is not from the expressed antecedent alone that the consequence follows, but from that antecedent taken in conjunction with another (unexpressed) proposition."

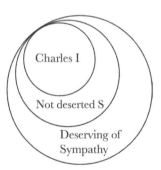

The efficacy of the identity-in-diversity analysis is, I think, nowhere more strikingly seen than in its application to Hypotheticals, especially Hypotheticals of the elliptical and often complicated sort which we so commonly employ.

In the latter part of his paper on "Knowledge by Acquaintance and Knowledge by Description" read before the Aristotelian Society in March, Mr. Russell

Early Analytic Philosophy

criticises my analysis of Categorical Propositions of the form *S is P*, as advocated in *Mind* for January last, and I should now like to say a few words about these criticisms.

I have done my best in the time at my disposal, but do not feel sure that I have always done justice to the criticisms, or have fully grasped the Theory of Knowledge which underlies them. I endeavour to take the criticisms as they are put, but my starting point is *S is P*, and I see identity in diversity wherever that form is applicable.

I must repeat once more here that what I am attempting is to provide an analysis of the *most general* character – one which will apply to any and every proposition which can be put into the forms *S is P, S is not P*. If there are any Categoricals which cannot be put into those forms (which I dispute) I am not concerned with them. Also, I assume the validity of Quantification and Conversion, and hold that neither the relation of Substance and Attribute, nor of percepts to a concept, nor of members of a class to the class or to each other, nor any relations of classes other than identity of denotation, can be expressed by the is of *S is P*. I think that *S is P* gives simply the abstract form of affirmative assertion, and that if there is not a common form of assertion, and a common analysis of such form, ordinary thought and speech is without a Common Measure.

But, as I have insisted, the admission of an absolutely general analysis is no bar to further determination of the various kinds of proposition which are expressible in *S is P, S is not P*, form.

I use *Denotation* and *Intension* in the sense explained in my January article in *Mind* (p. 41), and I think that every Subject and Predicate of a Proposition has both Denotation and Intension. *Proposition* again I understand it is currently used in logic books to mean an assertion expressed in words. In trying to answer Mr. Russell's criticisms, however, I shall, as far as I can, take them as they stand.

Before passing to these criticisms, I will consider for a moment a passage in *Principia Mathematica* to which Mr. Russell refers in his paper. He there propounds the following view: – *Scott is the author of Waverley* expresses an identity. And if we regard *the author of Waverley* as a Proper Name, and put *c* for it, we get *Scott is c*. Since, on this supposition, *Scott* and *c* are both destitute of connotation, *Scott is c* is an identity of *denotation*, and is equivalent to *Scott is Scott*. If *c* is Scott, *i.e.*, if *c* and Scott "stand for the same object," have the same denotation, then *Scott is Scott* is trivial; while if *c* is anyone except Scott, then *Scott is Scott* is false – denotation of Scott is different from denotation of *c*. *The author of Waverley* however (unlike a Proper Name) has "a meaning in use" – but it has no meaning in isolation, for the following reasons (p. 70): "*The author of*

Waverley cannot mean the same as *Scott*, or *Scott is the author of Waverley* would mean the same as *Scott is Scott*, which it plainly does not; nor can *the author of Waverley* mean anything other than *Scott*, or *Scott is the author of Waverley* would be false. Hence *the author of Waverley* means nothing."

Granted that Intension and Denotation are differently defined, this argument seems to depend upon a double use of the word *meaning* – thus: When it is said that *the author of Waverley* cannot *mean* the same as *Scott*, *meaning* signifies intension or connotation; plainly, intension (or connotation) of *the author of Waverley* and of *Scott*, cannot be *the same*. But when it is said that *the author of Waverley* cannot *mean* anything other than *Scott*, or *Scott is the author of Waverley* would be false, "mean anything other than *Scott*" must be understood of denotation; if *Scott* and *the author of Waverley* are two distinct persons, clearly *Scott is the author of Waverley* must be false. (My identity-in-diversity theory removes the difficulty at once.)

Coming to Mr. Russell's article, I may point out that in the paragraph on p. 121 commencing: "It is common to distinguish two aspects, meaning and denotation," instead of saying: The denotation [of *the author of Waverley*] will be Scott, I should prefer to say: The denotation of *the author of Waverley* will be the same as the denotation of *Scott*, *i.e.*, the denotation of Scott is a certain man, and the denotation of *the author of Waverley* is the same man; the thing, the that, which we call *Scott* is the same as the thing which we call *the author of Waverley*.

And I think it is the *names of things* which have denotation and intension, and not *the things themselves* – *name of anything* meaning *any* word or combination of words by which a thing is indicated, which "stand for" the thing.

It is given (p. 121, foot) as a reason "for not believing the denotation to be a constituent of the proposition" that "we may know the proposition even when we are not acquainted with the denotation [= ? thing denoted]. The proposition 'the author of *Waverley* is a novelist' was known to people who did not know that 'the author of *Waverley*' denoted Scott." But I do not see why I might not know that *the author of Waverley* and *Scott* had identical denotation, *without* being "*acquainted*" with Scott – *i.e.* (I suppose) without having direct, present, face-to-face knowledge of the actual object denoted. And I might know that in *The author of Waverley is the author of Marmion*, there is identity of denotation of Subject and Predicate (*i.e.*, that the Subject and Predicate of the Proposition apply to the same object or thing) without knowing that that denotation is identical with the denotation of "Scott," which name I might not have heard.

If I merely know that in any Proposition, Subject and Predicate apply to, "stand for," one thing or object (as they must if the proposition is affirmative) it seems to me that this *is* knowledge of denotation, and inseparable from

310   Early Analytic Philosophy

knowledge or understanding of the proposition. I think that knowledge of denotation may be given by merely descriptive terms, or even by a symbolic statement, *S is P*, and that we can give no meaning to any statement of form *S is P*, unless we regard the diverse intensions of Subject and Predicate as connected or combined in one object – and this is what I mean by saying that the terms have identical denotation.

According to Mr. Russell's own account of *Scott is the author of Waverley* (already referred to) in *Principia Mathematica*, and in relevant passages in his March article, it is admitted: –

(1) That that proposition asserts (or is) an identity;
(2) That the identity cannot be an "identity" of the connotation (meaning, intension) of the Subject with the connotation of the Predicate;
(3) That in, *e.g.*, *Scott is Scott*, the identity is one of denotation, but that this proposition is trivial – and I take it to be involved that the "triviality" is due to the circumstance that there is no difference of intension as between Subject and Predicate.

If *Scott is the author of Waverley* signifies that *Scott* and *the author of Waverley* are one and the same person, the two terms *Scott* and *the author of Waverley* both refer to one identical object, and the assertion may be not trivial and may be worth making because, owing to diversity of intension, it may convey information.

Another reason which Mr. Russell gives (p. 122) for holding that the denotation is not a constituent of the proposition [= ?] is that "propositions concerning the *so-and-so* are possible when the *so-and-so* has no denotation." He considers that in such propositions as:

The golden mountain does not exist, The round-square is contradictory, the Subject of the proposition has *no denotation* – and that in such cases we cannot "preserve the duality of meaning and denotation."

But how are we to explain "The round-square is self-contradictory," if Meaning = Intension, and there is no Denotation in the case? In *intension*, "round-square " cannot be "identified" with "self-contradictory" - *intensionally*, in *meaning, round-square* is *not* the same as *self-contradictory, round- square* and *self-contradictory* must be differently defined.

Of the golden mountain which "exists" in imagination or a fairy tale, we may assert that it does not exist as a physical fact known to us. If we say it *is non-existent*, the identity which is indicated by *is* must be an identity of denotation, it *cannot* be an identity of intensions, because *golden mountain* and *non-existent* are differently defined.

The round-square cannot indeed be "imagined" by any sane and trained mind, but it can be in some sense *supposed* – when we talk of a *round-square* and (quite justifiably) call it self-contradictory, it seems to me that "denotation" is required not only by the proposition which asserts self-contradictoriness, but also by the Subject *round-square* itself – it is only the supposition of roundness and squareness in *one* denotation, as co-existent attributes of an object which is both square and round, that is self-contradictory and gives rise to difficulty.

I think that when we use phrases of the form "*the* so-and-so," there is reference to some understood or supposed case of so-and-so. *E.g.*, "The Golden River" might refer to the Golden River of Ruskin's Fairy Tale, the "round-square" might refer to something so-called in a deliberate geometrical extravaganza by the author of *Flatland*. In other cases we should generally say *a* golden river (or mountain), *a* round-square, and so on. Similarly, I should hardly talk of "the man called Scott" or "the author of *Waverley*" unless I had knowledge somehow attained which transcended the connotations of the connotative words used.

An *existent-round-square* is as much (or as little) existent as it is round and square, and if I deny it to be existent I am asserting *A is not A* just as much as if I deny it to be round or square – that is, unless I use Existent in different senses, meaning, *e.g.*, (1) existent merely in a region of supposition, (2) existent in physical space. *Unless I make the supposition of roundness and squareness being co-existent in one object or thing* (in which case roundness and squareness are supposed to have identical denotation), what is there that is self-contradictory, what is there to deny? Even in the wildest region of supposition, no one has ever affirmed that roundness *is* squareness, that the definition of roundness is the definition of squareness; to suppose that the round thing is also square, that the square thing is also round, is as far as anyone can go.

If we have admitted a Term containing self-contradictory elements, there is no further difficulty in asserting of it contradictory predicates. A round-square is round, and it is also square, *i.e.*, not-round. The predicates are contradictory certainly, but they follow from the Subject; the contradictory statements are analytic.

And if a thing is (by supposition) both round and square, it follows that its angles are all right-angles, and its diameters all equal, though either one of the predicates cannot be true if the other is.

I do not think it is of essential importance (see p. 122, last paragraph) whether the Law of Contradiction is expressed as:

312   **Early Analytic Philosophy**

$$\left.\begin{array}{l} A \text{ is } B \\ A \text{ is not } B \end{array}\right\} \text{ cannot both be true}$$

or as:

No proposition is both true and false,

because I think that *A is B* may stand for any proposition, and to say that *A is B*, and also that *A is not B*, is to assert that the proposition *A is B* is both true and false.

On p. 125 Mr. Russell says: "The first point to observe is that, in any proposition about 'the author of *Waverley*,' provided Scott is not explicitly mentioned, the denotation itself, *i.e.*, Scott, does not occur [I cannot see what particular virtue there can be in the explicit mention of Scott], but only the concept of denotation, which will be represented by a variable. Suppose we say 'the author of *Waverley* was the author of *Marmion*,' we are certainly not saying that both were Scott – we may have forgotten that there was such a person as Scott. We are saying that there is some man who was the author of *Waverley* and the author of *Marmion*. That is to say, there is some one who wrote *Waverley* and *Marmion*, and no one else who wrote them."

It seems to me that in "the author of *Waverley* was the author of *Marmion*," "the author of *Waverley*" is tied down to one person specified as "the author of *Marmion*," and that *the someone and no one else* who wrote a definite specified book ought hardly to be called "a variable" and "an indefinite or indeterminate subject." Mr. Russell goes on to say that in "the author of *Waverley* is the author of *Marmion*," the is expresses *identity*. But that the meanings (*i.e.*, the intensions) of "the author of *Waverley*" and "the author of *Marmion*" are not identical – *i.e.*, I suppose they have not qualitative one-ness, they are dissimilar (to this it might be added that no two *intensions*, intensions which differ qualitatively, which are not synonymous, could possibly have any "identity" except the identity of a common denotation, *i.e.*, of both belonging to one thing, one subject of predication). It remains that the identity expressed by *is* in the sentence under discussion is an identity of denotation. In other words, *the author of Waverley* and *the author of Marmion* have a "common denotation" – that is they both denote one and only one man, who, if we happen to have sufficient information in the case, may be indicated by us as *Scott*.

Mr. Russell does not admit this, and says that the only escape from the difficulty caused by the non-identity of the "meanings" of "the author of Waverley" and "the author of Marmion" is to say that "the author of Waverley" does not *by itself* have a meaning.

But unless it has a meaning, how can we interpret it into "Some one wrote Waverley and no one else did," and how could we say, as Mr. Russell does on p. 125 (foot), that the *meanings* of "the author of *Waverley*" and "the author of *Marmion*" are not identical? How can we know that their meanings are not identical unless (1) they both have meanings, and (2) we know what those meanings are?

On p. 123 Mr. Russell says that "*Scott* is merely a noise or shape conventionally used to designate a certain person; it gives us no information about that person, and has nothing that can be called meaning as opposed to denotation." He goes on to observe that he here "neglects the fact considered above that even proper names as a rule really stand for descriptions," *i.e.* (in my way of speaking), proper names (in use) have some intension. The "above" to which Mr. Russell refers is the statement on p. 121 (foot) that "there are only two words which in this sense are strictly proper names of particulars, namely, 'I' and 'this'" (words which are strictly proper names "in this sense" are " words which do not assign a property to an object, but merely and solely name it").

But if it is a fact that so-called Proper Names (*e.g.*, Scott) are to some extent descriptive, I feel that a refutation of my identity-in-diversity analysis founded on the assumption that *Scott* is merely "a noise or shape" and entirely without intension, cannot, so far, be regarded as very conclusive.

When (p. 125) The author of Waverley was Scott is analysed so as to get rid of *the author of Waverley* and the proposition becomes *One and only one man wrote Waverley, and he was Scott*, it appears to be beyond question (1) that this substitution could not have been made unless the original proposition had been taken as an identity of denotation in diversity of intension, (2) that each of the clauses of the substituted statement is itself an identity of denotation in diversity of connotation.

One and only one man wrote Waverley, asserts identity of denotation between *one and only one man* and *writer of Waverley*.

He (*that one and only one man*) *was Scott*, asserts identity of denotation between *that man* and *Scott* (there is, of course, diversity of intension in both cases). Indeed, in every sentence which is used to get rid of and discredit the identity-in-diversity interpretation, this interpretation seems to me to be unavoidably depended on at every step.

On the other hand, I am unable to feel the force of the objection urged on p. 124 to the identity-in-diversity analysis, to the effect that it involves explaining one proposition by another *of the same form*, and thus prevents any progress towards real explanation and leads to an endless regress.

314   Early Analytic Philosophy

In general, Mr. Russell's objection to allowing that in propositions of form *S is P*, there is identity of denotation in diversity of intension appears to be based upon the following considerations:–

Of the two sorts of knowledge which he recognizes –

(1) Knowledge by acquaintance,
(2) Knowledge by description,

(1) may be explained as: Knowledge that brings the object itself before the mind; it is what has been called Immediate, or Direct, or Intuitive, knowledge, or *knowledge of*. Such knowledge Mr. Russell holds we have of sense-data, of many universals, and (possibly) of ourselves. Sense-data, and universals when objects of immediate knowledge, may (I believe he would say – *cp*. p. 121, foot) be regarded as items of knowledge to which the word *this* is applicable in virtue not of their intrinsic character, but of their presence in consciousness. He does not allow that we have either sort of knowledge by means of *ideas*, but in every case there is directly present to the mind either (1) sense-data, or universals, or self, or (2) concepts of properties (universals) by which, *e.g.*, physical objects and other minds are described. Further, it is said (p. 128) that "All propositions intelligible to us . . . are composed wholly of constituents with which we are acquainted, for a constituent with which we are not acquainted is unintelligible to us."

It follows that since in descriptive phrases the "constituents" directly known are concepts, etc., and *not* the particular physical objects, etc., descriptively or indirectly known by means of those directly known concepts, such particular objects cannot be "constituents of judgments in which such phrases occur" (p. 128).

That is, I suppose, we know by description the *sort* of thing, talked about, but unless it is actually perceived, we do "know" in the sense of *Knowledge* which is necessary for intelligibility, we are not "acquainted with" the thing itself which is described, the elements of the description are not definitely assigned to a definite subject of predication at a definite time and place. If we use a name that is absolutely without intension, that can only be used denotatively, only as a label, it can be used in this way only when the object is there to be pointed at or labelled. Hence its use involves the presence of the thing labelled, the object denoted, and so the object denoted (the "denotation" in Mr. Russell's phrase, I think) actually *is* a constituent of the *proposition*, *i.e.*, I believe, here, in Mr. Russell's terminology, of the state of the case to which the relevant verbal expression corresponds. But I agree with Mr. Russell that even Proper Names

E. E. Constance Jones on Language and Logic 315

really stand for descriptions – *as a rule*, he says – *always*, I think, except when first actually attached as a label. A name would be of no use, and therefore would not continue to be used, even as a label, if it did not carry with it *some* intensional implication.

On p. 124 Mr. Russell explains my meaning to be that the denotation of *the author of Waverley* is the denotation of what is *meant* by *the author of Waverley*. But I do not accept this. Meaning, intension, of *author*, is *authorship*; denotation of *author* is *person of whom authorship is an attribute*. I do not see that from the fact of one proposition being explained by another of the same form (p. 124) it follows that we "have made no progress towards a real explanation." This would seem to involve that one categorical proposition cannot be explained by other categorical propositions.

I am not sure what is meant by the clause in a parenthesis on p. 128 "(unless these objects are explicitly mentioned)" – unless *explicitly mentioned* means mentioned by a name which is entirely undescriptive – as in Mr. Russell's view *I* and *this* are. But Mr. Russell holds that these are "the only two words which are strictly proper names of particulars" (p. 121), and the use of which in a proposition suffices to make their denotation a "constituent" of the proposition.

I believe that so-called Proper Names always *in use* (though not always in isolation) have some measure of intension – in as far as they have not, one name would be as appropriate, on any occasion, as any other. I think, on the other hand, that e.g., *generous, persevering*, always have both intension and denotation, and that abstracts like, *e.g., generosity* or *perseverance*, have intension always, and denotation in use. If not, we could never say, *e.g.,* Generosity is attractive, Perseverance is admirable, since Generosity does not *mean* attractive and Perseverance does not *mean* admirable, their intensions are not the same.

When Mr. Russell says (p. 124) that if in *Scott is the author of Waverley*, "the denotation alone were relevant, any other phrase with the same denotation would give the same proposition," I entirely agree – in fact, I have myself insisted on this, and have pointed out that unless intension as well as denotation is taken account of in both Subject and Predicate of propositions, all affirmative Categoricals reduce to *A is A*.

On p. 128 Mr. Russell observes that "when we say 'the author of *Marmion* was the author of *Waverley*,' Scott himself is not a constituent of our judgment – and that the judgment cannot be explained by saying that it affirms identity of denotation with [in] diversity of connotation" [intension]. No doubt it is true that if I now make the assertion in question, Scott himself is not present to my consciousness, but that does not seem to me to be a reason for saying that in

Early Analytic Philosophy

"the author of *Marmion* was the author of *Waverley*" there is not identity of denotation in diversity of intension, in the sense in which I affirm that there is such identity. "Scott," to me, may be just the author of *Waverley* and *Marmion*, and a man to whom such authorship is attributable – the authorship of one book is not the authorship of the other, but there was one man who (I suppose) wrote the two, and I mean nothing else than this by saying that the denotation of "author of *Waverley*" is identical with denotation of "author of *Marmion*." To borrow De Morgan's phrase, if I touch the author of *Marmion* I touch the author of *Waverley*, if I destroy the one I destroy the other – and, though the man himself is not and never has been present to me, if I refer to him by these phrases and so convey to any hearer the fact of the double authorship, I do not see how the identity indicated in the case of absence differs from that indicated in a case of presence.

The clue to the whole discussion is perhaps to be sought in the nature of "concepts," and their relation to the mind; but, however this may be decided, when I have no concrete object actually present, but only such knowledge of it as is conveyed by description, any *S is P* of which the S and P are descriptive terms, implies and requires a *point de repere* to which the intensions of S and of P are assigned.

My identity-in-diversity analysis leaves it quite open, I think, whether we adopt a Theory of Knowledge which admits the use of *ideas* in judgment, or professes to deal directly with the things themselves which are the objects of knowledge.

Perhaps the difference of opinion between Mr. Russell and myself as to the analysis of propositions might be expressed as due to a difference in the meaning assigned to *Denotation* – I should maintain that, *whatever* has so much presence to the mind as to be made a Subject of Predication, of this it may be said that any term by which it is referred to, has denotation – *Authorship* as well as *Author, An Author* as well as *The Author, One and only one man* as well as *The man*. It is not because the thing referred to is a Subject of Predication that the term referring to it has Denotation, but no term unless it *has* Denotation can indicate a Subject of Predication, or itself be the subject of a proposition. The *Term* has Denotation, *that which is denoted* has as much "Existence" as makes it possible to assign to it some qualification; and there is no significant proposition which does not take account of both Denotation and Intension in both Terms.

7

Ludwig Wittgenstein on Language and Philosophy

Chapter Outline

Background and commentary
Background	317
Language, reality, and philosophy in the *Tractatus*	320
After the *Tractatus*	328
Concluding remarks	330
Further reading	331

Readings
Tractatus Logico-Philosophicus (selections)	332

Background and commentary

Background

Who was Ludwig Wittgenstein (1889–1951)? Unlike the other philosophers encountered in this book (perhaps with the exception of Russell), academics and non-academics alike have been absorbed as much by Wittgenstein's scholarly work as by his personal demeanor and disposition. As G. H. Von Wright (1916–2003) put it in his biographical sketch of Wittgenstein,

> [His] very unusual and forceful personality exerted a great influence over others. No one who came in touch with him could fail to be impressed. Some were repelled. Most were attracted or fascinated. ([1954] 2001: 17)

Early Analytic Philosophy

Norman Malcolm (1911–90), a student of Wittgenstein's at Cambridge in the 1930s, similarly described his personality as "commanding, even imperial" ([1958] 2001: 24). Wittgenstein published only one academic book during his lifetime, *Tractatus Logico-Philosophicus* (1922),[1] along with one academic article, "Some Remarks on Logical Form" (1926). *Philosophical Investigations* ([1953] 2001) was largely completed during Wittgenstein's lifetime, but was published posthumously. Wittgenstein's method was to record his thoughts in notebooks, then cull his thoughts into further notebooks, revising, rearranging, and revisiting themes and problems in successive layers of thought and formulations (what he called "remarks"). In some cases, these amounted to nearly completed philosophical works, and have been published posthumously as, for example, *The Blue and Brown Books* (1958) and *On Certainty* (1969). Indeed, at his death, his executors (Von Wright, along with G. E. M Anscombe (1919–2001) and Rush Rhees (1905–69)) received some 12,000 pages of manuscript and 8,000 pages of typescript. Much of this material has been now published and is electronically available.[2]

Broadly speaking, there are two periods of work in Wittgenstein's life: the "early work" that culminated in the *Tractatus,* and the "later work" that is at least partially represented in the *Philosophical Investigations.* Despite differences in focus, orientation, and content—indeed, in some respects the *Philosophical Investigations* can be read as a critique of the *Tractatus*—throughout his career Wittgenstein made important contributions to the philosophy of logic, the philosophy of language, and the nature of philosophical inquiry.

Wittgenstein was born into one of the wealthiest families in Austria and, indeed, all of Europe. His father was a leading industrialist and the Wittgenstein family was active in the arts and, especially, music. The composer and pianist Johannes Brahms (1833–97) was a notable family friend. Wittgenstein was one of eight children, with four brothers and three sisters. Three of his brothers died of self-inflicted causes and Wittgenstein himself flirted with the idea of suicide throughout his life. He was home educated until he was fourteen, at which point he went to Linz to study for three years. He went on to study engineering in Berlin until 1908 before registering as a research student at Manchester University in England, where he studied aeronautics. He reported being especially unhappy during this time, though he experienced depression, sometimes severe, throughout his life. It was while he was a student at

---

[1]Wittgenstein also published a dictionary for school children, *Wörterbuch für Volksschulen* ("Dictionary for Elementary Schools") while working at elementary schools in the 1920s. Unlike the *Tractatus* (see below), Wittgenstein had no difficulties in publishing this dictionary.
[2]See *Wittgenstein's Nachlass: The Bergen Electronic Edition.*

Ludwig Wittgenstein on Language and Philosophy   319

Manchester that Wittgenstein developed an interest in the foundations of mathematics. After expressing this to one of his professors, he was given a copy of Russell's *The Principles of Mathematics*. This was an important event in Wittgenstein's life: it was from Russell's book that he apparently learned of Frege, whom he would then visit in 1911; Frege would then direct Wittgenstein to visit Russell in Cambridge. Wittgenstein began studying with Russell in 1911 and remained in Cambridge until 1913, forming a close though sometimes tumultuous relationship with Russell. Russell would later write that "getting to know Wittgenstein was one of the most exciting intellectual adventures of my life" (1951: 298). While at Cambridge, Wittgenstein also attended Moore's lectures. It was also during this time that Wittgenstein met David Pinsent (1891–1918), a fellow student, whom Wittgenstein described in a letter to David's mother as "my first and only friend." After vacationing with Pinsent in Norway, Wittgenstein decided to take up residence there, hoping that it would provide him with the solitude needed to further his studies in logic and philosophy. After being visited by Moore in 1914 in Norway, Wittgenstein sought to submit a manuscript that he had been working on for an undergraduate degree at Cambridge. When Moore wrote him a letter telling him that this was not feasible, Wittgenstein wrote Moore a letter telling him (in effect) that he might as well "go to hell" if he didn't think his work was worthy of the degree. Moore was so distressed by this that they were estranged until 1929, when they met on a train. Upon the outbreak of the First World War, Wittgenstein sought active duty for the Austrian military, hoping that it would bring about a profound personal change. He served in several roles in the military and was awarded for his bravery on multiple occasions. Sadly, Pinsent, who enlisted in the British military, died during the war in an airplane accident.

Following the war, Wittgenstein gave away the fortune that he had inherited from his father to his siblings, along with various intellectuals, and took up residence as a schoolteacher in the Austrian countryside until 1926. Despite having some success as a teacher, there was continual friction between Wittgenstein and the local population, and he abruptly resigned from his position when charges were brought against him for repeatedly striking a student. For the next two years, Wittgenstein worked as an architect constructing a house for one of his sisters in Vienna. It was during this time that Wittgenstein met Marguerite Respinger (1904–2000), with whom he became close friends and who was apparently the only woman with whom he ever fell in love. Unfortunately, when Wittgenstein expressed his desire that he and Marguerite get married, she quickly distanced herself from him

320 **Early Analytic Philosophy**

(perhaps due to Wittgenstein's desire that the marriage be Platonic and childless). During this time, Wittgenstein began meeting with Frank Ramsey (1903–30),[3] a gifted mathematics and philosophy student at Cambridge, as well as with Moritz Schlick (1882–1936), who played an important role in the logical empiricist movement that we will discuss in Chapter 8. In part as a result of these meetings, Wittgenstein decided to return to Cambridge in 1929, where he was then awarded a PhD in philosophy for the *Tractatus*, which had been published seven years earlier. He was soon appointed as a fellow and began lecturing at Cambridge. Von Wright described his classes as follows:

> As might be expected, his lectures were highly 'unacademic'. He nearly always held them in his own rooms or in the college rooms of a friend. He had no manuscript or notes. He thought before the class. The impression was of tremendous concentration. The exposition usually led to a question, to which the audience were supposed to suggest an answer. The answers in turn became starting points for new thoughts leading to new questions. ([1954] 2001: 15)

For his part, Malcolm reported that Wittgenstein was a "frightening person at these classes," "very impatient and easily angered," and "always exhausted" by the end ([1958] 2001: 25–6). Wittgenstein lived in Britain for much of the remainder of his life, giving his last lecture in 1947. He was ill from cancer for the last two years of life, though he continued writing in his notebooks during this period. According to his doctor, his last words were "tell them I've had a wonderful life."[4]

Language, reality, and philosophy in the *Tractatus*

Wittgenstein's *Tractatus* was the culmination of his thinking and writing that began when he first arrived at Cambridge in 1911. In his review, Ramsey, who along with C. K. Ogden (1889–1957) was responsible for the first English translation of the *Tractatus* (and the one presented below), described it as being of "extraordinary interest" and deserving "the attention of all philosophers" (1923: 465). Russell similarly described the *Tractatus* as "an important event in the philosophical world" (1922). The Latin title was

---

[3]In one of the more unfortunate episodes in the analytic tradition, Ramsey—considered one of the brightest young thinkers at the time—passed away at twenty-six years of age as a result of complications stemming from liver problems.

[4]For this and further biographical information, see Biletzki and Matar 2020, Malcolm [1958] 2001, Monk 1990, and Von Wright [1954] 2001.

allegedly suggested by Moore as a play on Spinoza's *Tractatus Theologico-Politicus* (1670). While Wittgenstein regarded the *Tractatus* as providing the definitive and last word on the topics that it addresses, he struggled to find a publisher. When it was eventually published, this was mainly the result of Russell's advocacy, and on condition that Russell include a lengthy introduction (which Wittgenstein disliked). While many of the ideas on the philosophy of logic were likely developed by Wittgenstein prior to his service in the Austrian military, several key aspects of the work—including the so-called "picture theory" of language as well as the ethical and mystical remarks developed in the later sections—appear to have been developed during his service.[5] Wittgenstein dedicated the *Tractatus* to the memory of Pinsent.

The *Tractatus* consists of a series of numbered remarks centered on seven core comments, as follows:

1 The world is everything that is the case.
2 What is the case, the fact, is the existence of atomic facts.
3 The logical picture of the facts is the thought.
4 A thought is the significant proposition.
5 Propositions are truth-functions of elementary propositions.
  (An elementary proposition is a truth-function of itself.)
6 The general form of the truth-function is $[p, \xi, N(\xi)]$
  This is the general form of the proposition.
7 Whereof one cannot speak, thereof one must be silent.

Each of these remarks contains further remarks, numbered as decimal expansions. As Wittgenstein explains in a footnote to the first proposition: "The decimal figures as numbers of the separate propositions indicate the logical importance of the propositions, the emphasis laid upon them in my exposition. The propositions n.1, n.2, n.3, etc., are comments on proposition No. n; the propositions n.m1, n.m2, etc., are comments on the proposition No. n.m; and so on."

While the *Tractatus* is subject to difficult interpretative questions, it is generally agreed that a main concern in the book is with the general conditions for representation, the general conditions for a thought or statement to represent the world as being a certain sort of way and so be capable of truth or falsity. As Russell put it in his introduction to the *Tractatus*, one of Wittgenstein's concerns in the book is to answer the question "what

---

[5]For his part, Russell took Wittgenstein's mystical remarks to result, in part, from his having read William James's *The Varities of Religious Experience* ([1902] 1929) (see Misak 2016: 119). This was, moreover, a movement in Wittgenstein's thought for which Russell seemed to have had little respect.

Early Analytic Philosophy

relation must one fact (such as a sentence) have to another in order to be *capable* of being a symbol for that other?" (1922). And one of Wittgenstein's core ideas here is that in order for a thought or statement to be capable of representing the world as being a certain way, there needs to be a kind of isomorphism or structural correspondence between the thought or statement and the world. In respect, Wittgenstein supposes that thought and language models the reality that it represents. Thus he writes:

2.1 We make to ourselves pictures of facts.

2.11 The picture presents the facts in logical space, the existence and nonexistence of atomic facts.

2.12 The picture is a model of reality.

2.13 To the objects correspond in the picture the elements of the picture.

2.131 The elements of the picture stand, in the picture, for the objects.

2.14 The picture consists in the fact that its elements are combined with one another in a definite way.

. . . .

2.16 In order to be a picture a fact must have something in common with what it pictures.

2.161 In the picture and the pictured there must be something identical in order that the one can be a picture of the other at all.

1.17 What the picture must have in common with reality in order to be able to represent it after its manner—rightly or falsely—is its form of representation.

This correspondence between the structure of thought and language on the one hand and the reality represented by thought and language seems to have occurred to Wittgenstein early in his military service. Von Wright describes the episode as follows:

It was in the autumn of 1914, on the Eastern Front. Wittgenstein was reading in a magazine about a lawsuit in Paris concerning an automobile accident. At the trial a miniature model of the accident was presented before the court. The model here served as a proposition . . . a description of a possible state of affairs. It has this function owing to a correspondence between the parts of the model (the miniature houses, cars, people) and the things . . . It now occurred to Wittgenstein that one might reverse the analogy and say that a proposition serves as a model or picture, in virtue of a similar correspondence between its parts and the world. The way in which the parts of the proposition are combined – the structure of the proposition – depicts a possible combination of elements in reality, a possible state of affairs. ([1954] 2001: 8)

In this respect, Wittgenstein held that thoughts and statements are pictures of reality. Wittgenstein develops this idea throughout the beginning sections of the *Tractatus*:

> 2.15   That the elements of the picture are combined with one another in a definite way, represents that the things are so combined with one another.
>
> This connection of the elements of the picture is called its structure, and the possibility of this structure is called the form of representation of the picture.
>
> 2.151   The form of representation is the possibility that the things are combined with one another as are the elements of the picture.
>
> 2.1511   Thus the picture is linked with reality; it reaches up to it.
>
> 2.1512   It is like a scale applied to reality.
>
> . . .
>
> 2.18   What every picture, of whatever form, must have in common with reality in order to be able to represent it at all—rightly or falsely—is the logical form, that is, the form of reality.

Thus, according to Wittgenstein, in any representation, and so any thought or statement that represents the world as being a certain way, there is a sort of correspondence between the relations that obtain between the constituents of the thought or statement and the constituents of the world so represented.

Wittgenstein believed that given this view of the necessary conditions for representation, a certain sort of atomism must be true of both the world on the one hand and language and thought on the other hand. Specifically, he held that the world must consist of simple objects, which combine into simple or "atomic" facts, and that corresponding to such simple objects are simple representational items, names, that stand for such objects, along with simple statements or propositions that are true or false depending on whether the objects so named are combined in the appropriate way. Wittgenstein never provided an example of simple objects or atomic facts, nor did he ever provide an example of a name of such an object or a simple statement or proposition. Further, unlike Russell, epistemological considerations appear to be absent from his project. Nonetheless, he believed that there must be such objects and facts and that there must be a correspondence between such objects and facts on the one hand and representational items (themselves facts of a certain sort) on the other hand. His case for the need for simple objects is given in 2.02 and the comments that follow.

Wittgenstein held that atomic facts are always contingent, in that they could have failed to obtain, and that corresponding to this, simple

Early Analytic Philosophy

representational items (elementary thoughts, statements, propositions) are likewise contingent, in that for any such representational item, even if it is true, it could have been false. Similarly, Wittgenstein held that atomic facts obtain or do not obtain independently of each other, that "Any one can either be the case or not be the case, and everything else remain the same" (1.21) and that "From the existence or nonexistence of an atomic fact we cannot infer the existence or nonexistence of another" (2.062). Corresponding to this, he held that simple representational items (elementary thoughts, statements, propositions) are true or false independently of the truth or falsity of all other simple representational items, that "From an elementary proposition no other can be inferred" (5.134) and that "In no way can an inference be made from the existence of one state of affairs to the existence of another entirely different from it" (5.135).

What about those statements and thoughts that do not consist of names for simple objects—perhaps all of those statements and thoughts that we actually utter and think? According to Wittgenstein, these must be truth-functional compounds of simple statements and thoughts; as he puts it, "All propositions are results of truth-operations on the elementary propositions" (5.3), "All truth-functions are results of the successive application of a finite number of truth-operations to elementary propositions" (5.32). Generally, a statement or proposition S is a truth-functional compound when the truth-value of S is a function of (that is, uniquely and wholly determined by) the truth-values of its components. For example, "Bob is tall and Bob is smart" is a truth-functional compound, since whether it is true or false is a function of the truth-values of "Bob is tall" and "Bob is smart." Similarly, "it's not the case that Bob is tall" is a truth-functional compound, since whether it is true is entirely determined by the truth-value of "Bob is tall." Wittgenstein's idea, then, is that whether any non-elementary statement (aside from tautologies, which are true simply in virtue of the logical form they exhibit, and contradictions, which are false simply in virtue of the form they exhibit) is true or false is entirely determined by the truth-values of simple statements, which in turn consist of names for simple objects. The reader should think about the various passages where Wittgenstein expresses these ideas and should consider the import of the considerations that he puts forward in favor of them.

This is all highly abstract, and Wittgenstein evidently arrives at this kind of position not through examining ordinary and scientific language but rather through reflection on the very conditions for representing the world in thought and language. Nonetheless, Wittgenstein argues that this conception of language and reality has important consequences for what can and cannot be said, consequences for the limits of meaningful discourse. In particular, he contends that it follows from this view of language and reality that most of what passes for philosophy turns out to be nonsense— that philosophers are guilty of trying to say what cannot in fact be said. This is perhaps most explicit in the following remark:

4.003　Most propositions and questions, that have been written about philosophical matters, are not false, but senseless. We cannot, therefore, answer questions of this kind at all, but only state their senselessness. Most questions and propositions of the philosophers result from the fact that we do not understand the logic of our language.

(They are of the same kind as the question whether the Good is more or less identical than the Beautiful.)

And so it is not to be wondered at that the deepest problems are really *no* problems.

He continues:

4.111　Philosophy is not one of the natural sciences.
(The word "philosophy" must mean something which stands above or below, but not beside the natural sciences.)

4.112　The object of philosophy is the logical clarification of thoughts.
Philosophy is not a theory but an activity.
A philosophical work consists essentially of elucidations.
The result of philosophy is not a number of "philosophical propositions," but to make propositions clear.

. . .

4.113　Philosophy limits the disputable sphere of natural science.

4.114　It should limit the thinkable and thereby the unthinkable.
It should limit the unthinkable from within through the thinkable.

He moreover takes this to recommend a positive method for philosophy, which is much different from how philosophers have traditionally proceeded:

6.53　The right method of philosophy would be this: To say nothing except what can be said, i.e. the propositions of natural science, i.e. something that has nothing to do with philosophy: and then always, when someone else wished to say something metaphysical, to demonstrate to him that he had given no meaning to certain signs in his propositions. This method would be unsatisfying to the other—he would not have the feeling that we were teaching him philosophy—but it would be the only strictly correct method.

326 Early Analytic Philosophy

Why does Wittgenstein think that his view of language and reality has these results? While this is a difficult question, one way to think of it is as follows. According to Wittgenstein, there are only three types of meaningful statements. First, there are the atomic statements, which describe atomic facts. These are contingent; they are logically independent, in that the truth of one is consistent with the truth or falsity of the others; and they are empirical and not true *a priori* (see, for example, 2.223–2.225, 3.04, 3.05, 4.05, 4.06, 5.134, 5.135, 5.634, 6.113). Second, there are truth-functions of atomic statements. Third, there are contradictions and tautologies, statements that are true or false not in virtue of the world and its objects but rather in virtue of the form they exhibit (as "Bob is tall or Bob isn't tall" is a tautology, true in virtue of the form it exhibits, while "Bob is tall and Bob isn't tall" is a contradiction, false in virtue of the form it exhibits). The problem is that the apparent statements that one finds in philosophy—especially those found in metaphysics and ethics—do not seem to fall into any of these categories. For instance, the statements (or apparent statements) that one finds in philosophy are often thought to be *a priori* and non-contingent; but in this case, they can be neither atomic facts nor truth-functions of atomic facts. The reader is encouraged to think further about some examples from metaphysics and ethics and why they cannot be easily understood as atomic statements, truth-functional compounds, or contradictions or tautologies.

Wittgenstein further suggests in various places that putative statements in philosophy attempt to describe the world as a whole in a way that, given his conception of language and reality, cannot be done. The following passages are pertinent:

6.41 The sense of the world must lie outside the world. In the world everything is as it is and happens as it does happen. *In* it there is no value—and if there were, it would be of no value.

If there is a value which is of value, it must lie outside all happening and being-so. For all happening and being-so is accidental.

What makes it non-accidental cannot lie *in* the world, for otherwise this would again be accidental.

It must lie outside the world.

6.42 Hence also there can be no ethical propositions.

Propositions cannot express anything higher.

6.421 It is clear that ethics cannot be expressed.

Ethics is transcendental.

(Ethics and aesthetics are one.)

The idea seems to be that ethical and metaphysical discourse attempts to make claims about the world as a whole. However, given Wittgenstein's conception of language and reality, it is only possible to speak of some portion of the world, some object or objects in relation. One attempts, in a sense, to get outside of the world and view it from an external perspective, which is evidently impossible. Attempts at ethical discourse are further frustrated by the fact that objects either do or do not stand in certain relations; there is nothing normative or value-laden about whether they do or do not stand in certain relations.

Despite thinking that much of philosophy is strictly nonsense, Wittgenstein evidently held that there is a difference between what we might regard as valuable as opposed to non-valuable nonsense. Consider, for example, the following remarks:

6.52 We feel that even if *all* possible scientific questions be answered, the problems of life have still not been touched at all. Of course there is then no question left, and just this is the answer.

6.521 The solution of the problem of life is seen in the vanishing of this problem.

(Is not this the reason why men to whom after long doubting the sense of life became clear, could not then say wherein this sense consisted?)

6.522 There is indeed the inexpressible. This shows itself; it is the mystical.

Wittgenstein sometimes puts this as the idea that certain things can only be shown, and not said. How exactly this difference between saying and showing is a matter of dispute. Indeed, Wittgenstein recognizes that given his constraints on meaningful discourse, it turns out that much of the *Tractatus* proves to be nonsense, as it attempts to say what cannot be said. As he puts it:

6.54 My propositions are elucidatory in this way: he who understands me finally recognizes them as senseless, when he has climbed out through them, on them, over them. (He must so to speak throw away the ladder, after he has climbed up on it.)

He must surmount these propositions; then he sees the world rightly.

Perhaps, then, among the valuable sort of nonsense are the apparent statements that make up the *Tractatus*—the apparent statements show something that cannot strictly speaking be said. As Wittgenstein says, perhaps they are like a ladder that, at least as far as saying something about

328   **Early Analytic Philosophy**

the world that can be evaluated as true or false, needs to be discarded once it has been used.[6] Again, however, this is only one interpretative possibility, and one should consider how else these cryptic remarks might be understood.

After the *Tractatus*

Wittgenstein wrote in the Preface to the *Tractatus* that "the *truth* of thoughts that here communicated seems to me unassailable and definitive," that "the problems have in essentials been finally solved" (1922). Of course, not everybody shared this confidence in Wittgenstein's conclusions including, eventually, Wittgenstein himself.

Some of the potential problems were in fact noted by Wittgenstein in the *Tractatus*. One concerns the propositional attitudes, which we encountered previously in the discussion of Frege. Take statements of the form x believes that S, x knows that S, x wishes that S, and so on, where x is some person and S is some statement or proposition. In general, whether some such statement is true is not a function of the truth-value of S. For example, whether a statement x believes that S is not fixed by the truth of value S: given that S is true, a statement x believes that S may be true or false; likewise, given that S is false, a statement x believes that S may be true or false. This suggests, contra Wittgenstein, that not all compound statements are truth-functional compounds of elementary statements or propositions. Wittgenstein addresses this concern in 5.541; however, it is a matter of dispute whether his rather terse response is satisfactory. Another potential problem arises from the apparent incompatibility of color statements—for example, a statement to the effect that some patch is uniformly blue seems to exclude the possibility that the patch is also uniformly red. However, this seems to contravene Wittgenstein's contention that "There is only *logical* necessity" (6.37). Indeed, it could be maintained that such statements are examples of statements representing atomic facts, thus apparently contravening Wittgenstein's claim

---

[6]Wittgenstein's ladder remark at the end of the *Tractatus* is similar to Fritz Mauthner's (1849–1923) remark: "If I want to ascend into the critique of language, which is the most important business of thinking mankind, then I must destroy language behind me and in me, step by step: I must destroy every rung of the ladder while climbing upon it" (quoted in Weiler 1958). Wittgenstein mentions Mauthner at 4.0031, writing that "All philosophy is a 'Critique of Language' (but not all in Mauthner's sense)." Mauthner was a journalist, writer, and playwright, who also published philosophical works, including *Beiträge zu einer Kritik der Sprache* (three volumes: 1901, 1906, 1923; translated as *Contributions to a Critique of Language*). See Weiler 1958 for discussion.

Ludwig Wittgenstein on Language and Philosophy   329

that "From the existence or nonexistence of an atomic fact we cannot infer the existence or nonexistence of another" (2.062). Wittgenstein was aware of problems in this vicinity and attempted to address them in 6.3751; again, however, one may reasonably wonder whether his rather brief response is adequate.

More generally, however, Wittgenstein came to question some of the central presuppositions of the *Tractatus* following his time as a schoolteacher in the Austrian countryside, eventually culminating in his *Philosophical Investigations* (at times, Wittgenstein conceived that the *Investigations* and the *Tractatus* be published together in a single volume so as to fully exhibit the changes in his thinking). Some of the changes were a matter of orientation and focus. Perhaps most prominently, while the *Tractatus* focuses on the use of language to describe and represent the world, Wittgenstein came to be impressed by the wide variety of functions performed by language: we use language to speak about the world, but we also use language to tell jokes, give commands, influence and manipulate moods, and so on. Wittgenstein sometimes referred to these myriad functions of language as different "language games" and he seems to have believed that the representative function of language, the use of language to describe the world, cannot be fruitfully disentangled from the various other uses of language. Another, related change in orientation concerns Wittgenstein's increased emphasis on ordinary language and how we actually use language in our everyday lives: whereas the *Tractatus* is more or less entirely free of actual examples of linguistic behavior, the *Investigations* focuses on the idea of language as a public phenomenon used to facilitate human interaction. It is in part because of this that Wittgenstein's later work (as well as some of Moore's later work) came to influence so-called "ordinary language" philosophy, a sub-movement in the analytic tradition that was centered at Oxford and included thinkers such as Malcolm, as well as Gilbert Ryle (1900–76), J. L. Austin (1911–60), H. P. Grice (1913–88), P. F. Strawson (1919–2006), Alice Ambrose (1906–2001), and John Wisdom (1904–93), among others.

Despite these differences, there are a number of continuities across Wittgenstein's early and later work. The most obvious continuity is a focus on language. Closely related to the focus on language is skepticism about much traditional philosophy, based on his views about language and language use; throughout his career, Wittgenstein was skeptical about constructive, theory-building projects in philosophy, and skeptical as a result of his views about language and meaning. His reasons for this, however, seem to have changed: whereas in the *Tractatus*, Wittgenstein charged much traditional philosophy with trying to say what cannot be said, in the *Investigations* Wittgenstein charged much traditional philosophy with misusing language, in the sense of using words outside of the "language games" for which they are suited. Corresponding to his trenchant criticisms of traditional philosophical inquiry premised on views about language and language use, across his career Wittgenstein proposed an alternative conception of philosophy whereby philosophy consists not in the construction of theories but rather as a kind of activity aimed at pointing out, from a broadly linguistic perspective, just where traditional theory-building philosophy goes wrong. In the *Tractatus*, this involved pointing out and explaining why philosophical discourse frequently involves the attempt to say what cannot be said; in the *Investigations*, this involved, in part, pointing out the regular and effective use of language in ordinary communication and how various putative philosophical puzzles involve taking language out of the contexts for which it is well-suited and an effective tool for interpersonal communication. As he put it, the aim of philosophy is to "show the fly the way out of the fly-bottle" ([1953] 2001: 87), and in this way can be described as a kind of therapy.

Concluding remarks

Wittgenstein published little in his lifetime. His emotional life was tulmultous, as was his relationship with philosophy; indeed, he sometimes seemed to view philosophy as something that one ought to be able to overcome. In one way or another, throughout his career Wittgenstein viewed philosophy as an activity which, rather than function to create grand metaphysical theories, ought to instead focus on clarification of ordinary and scientific discourse and, in doing so, uncover the confusions that give rise to many traditional philosophical problems and puzzles.

While he published little, Wittgenstein's influence on the development of the analytic tradition was immense. He influenced Russell in myriad ways, culminating in Russell's *The Philosophy of Logical Atomism*, which Russell described as "very largely concerned with explaining certain ideas" due to Wittgenstein, despite not knowing, at the time, whether Wittgenstein was alive or dead due to his active service in the military ([1918] 2009: 35). Likewise, as we will see in Chapter 8, Wittgenstein played an important role in the logical empiricist movement in the 1920s and 1930s, providing what they viewed as the philosophical foundations for a properly scientific philosophy. Finally, as marked above, Wittgenstein's later work provided the background out of which the "ordinary language" movement arose at Oxford and elsewhere. It suffices to say that analytic philosophy would not be what it is without Wittgenstein's many important contributions to the study of language and, in turn, to the very nature and purpose of philosophical inquiry.

Further reading

Primary sources

Wittgenstein, L. ([1953] 2001), *Philosophical Investigations*, G. E. M. Anscombe (trans.), Oxford: Oxford University Press.

Secondary sources

Anscombe, G. E. M. (1959), *An Introduction to Wittgenstein's Tractatus*, London: Hutchinson.

Black, M. (1967), *A Companion to Wittgenstein's Tractatus*, Ithaca: Cornell University Press.

Fogelin, R. (1976), *Wittgenstein*, New York: Routledge.

Malcolm, N. ([1958] 2001), *Ludwig Wittgenstein: A Memoir*, Oxford: Oxford University Press.

Monk. R. (1990), *Ludwig Wittgenstein: The Duty of Genius*, New York: Penguin Books.

Ramsey, F. (1923), "Critical Notice of *Tractatus Logico-Philosophicus*", *Mind* 32: 465–78.

Russell, B. (1922), "Introduction to *Tractatus Logico-Philosophicus*", in *Tractatus Logico-Philosophicus*, C. K. Ogden (trans.), London: Kegan Paul, Trench, Trubner & Co.

Sluga, H and Stern, D. (1996), *The Cambridge Companion to Wittgenstein*, Cambridge: Cambridge University Press.

Stern, D. (2004), *Wittgenstein's Philosophical Investigations: An Introduction*, Cambridge: Cambridge University Press.

Von Wright, G. H. ([1954] 2001), "A Biographical Sketch", in N. Malcolm, *Ludwig Wittgenstein: A Memoir*, Oxford: Oxford University Press.

Readings

Wittgenstein, L. *Tractatus Logico-Philosophicus* (selections).
Reprinted from Wittgenstein, L. (1922), *Tractatus Logico-Philosophicus*, C. K. Ogden (trans.), London: Kegan Paul, Trench, Trubner & Co.

Preface

This book will perhaps only be understood by those who have themselves already thought the thoughts which are expressed in it—or similar thoughts. It is therefore not a text-book. Its object would be attained if there were one person who read it with understanding and to whom it afforded pleasure.

The book deals with the problems of philosophy and shows, as I believe, that the method of formulating these problems rests on the misunderstanding of the logic of our language. Its whole meaning could be summed up somewhat as follows: What can be said at all can be said clearly; and whereof one cannot speak thereof one must be silent.

The book will, therefore, draw a limit to thinking, or rather—not to thinking, but to the expression of thoughts; for, in order to draw a limit to thinking we should have to be able to think both sides of this limit (we should therefore have to be able to think what cannot be thought).

The limit can, therefore, only be drawn in language and what lies on the other side of the limit will be simply nonsense.

How far my efforts agree with those of other philosophers I will not decide. Indeed what I have here written makes no claim to novelty in points of detail; and therefore I give no sources, because it is indifferent to me whether what I have thought has already been thought before me by another.

I will only mention that to the great works of Frege and the writings of my friend Bertrand Russell I owe in large measure the stimulation of my thoughts.

If this work has a value it consists in two things. First that in it thoughts are expressed, and this value will be the greater the better the thoughts are expressed. The more the nail has been hit on the head. – Here I am conscious that I have fallen far short of the possible. Simply because my powers are insufficient to cope with the task. May others come and do it better.

On the other hand the *truth* of the thoughts communicated here seems to me unassailable and definitive. I am, therefore, of the opinion that the problems have in essentials been finally solved. And if I am not mistaken in this, then the value of this work secondly consists in the fact that it shows how little has been done when these problems have been solved.

1 The world is everything that is the case.

1.1 The world is the totality of facts, not of things.

1.11 The world is determined by the facts, and by these being *all* the facts.

1.12 For the totality of facts determines both what is the case, and also all that is not the case.

1.13 The facts in logical space are the world.

1.2 The world divides into facts.

1.21 Any one can either be the case or not be the case, and everything else remain the same.

2 What is the case, the fact, is the existence of atomic facts.

2.01 An atomic fact is a combination of objects (entities, things).

2.011 It is essential to a thing that it can be a constituent part of an atomic fact.

2.012 In logic nothing is accidental: if a thing *can* occur in an atomic fact the possibility of that atomic fact must already be prejudged in the thing.

2.0121 It would, so to speak, appear as an accident, when to a thing that could exist alone on its own account, subsequently a state of affairs could be made to fit.

If things can occur in atomic facts, this possibility must already lie in them.

(A logical entity cannot be merely possible. Logic treats of every possibility, and all possibilities are its facts.)

Just as we cannot think of spatial objects at all apart from space, or temporal objects apart from time, so we cannot think of *any* object apart from the possibility of its connection with other things.

If I can think of an object in the context of an atomic fact, I cannot think of it apart from the *possibility* of this context.

2.0122 The thing is independent, in so far as it can occur in all *possible* circumstances, but this form of independence is a form of connection with the atomic fact, a form of dependence. (It is impossible for words to occur in two different ways, alone and in the proposition.)

2.0123 If I know an object, then I also know all the possibilities of its occurrence in atomic facts.

(Every such possibility must lie in the nature of the object.)

A new possibility cannot subsequently be found.

Early Analytic Philosophy

2.01231 In order to know an object, I must know not its external but all its internal qualities.

2.0124 If all objects are given, then thereby are all *possible* atomic facts also given.

2.013 Every thing is, as it were, in a space of possible atomic facts. I can think of this space as empty, but not of the thing without the space.

2.0131 A spatial object must lie in infinite space. (A point in space is an argument place.)

A speck in a visual field need not be red, but it must have a colour; it has, so to speak, a colour space round it. A tone must have *a* pitch, the object of the sense of touch *a* hardness, etc.

2.014 Objects contain the possibility of all states of affairs.

2.0141 The possibility of its occurrence in atomic facts is the form of the object.

2.02 The object is simple.

2.0201 Every statement about complexes can be analysed into a statement about their constituent parts, and into those propositions which completely describe the complexes.

2.021 Objects form the substance of the world. Therefore they cannot be compound.

2.0211 If the world had no substance, then whether a proposition had sense would depend on whether another proposition was true.

2.0212 It would then be impossible to form a picture of the world (true or false).

2.022 It is clear that however different from the real one an imagined world may be, it must have something—a form—in common with the real world.

2.023 This fixed form consists of the objects.

2.0231 The substance of the world *can* only determine a form and not any material properties. For these are first presented by the propositions—first formed by the configuration of the objects.

2.0232 Roughly speaking: objects are colourless.

2.0233 Two objects of the same logical form are—apart from their external properties—only differentiated from one another in that they are different.

2.02331 Either a thing has properties which no other has, and then one can distinguish it straight away from the others by a description and refer to it; or, on the other hand, there are several things which have the

Ludwig Wittgenstein on Language and Philosophy   335

totality of their properties in common, and then it is quite impossible to point to any one of them.

For if a thing is not distinguished by anything, I cannot distinguish it—for otherwise it would be distinguished.

2.024   Substance is what exists independently of what is the case.

2.025   It is form and content.

2.0251   Space, time and colour (colouredness) are forms of objects.

2.026   Only if there are objects can there be a fixed form of the world.

2.027   The fixed, the existent and the object are one.

2.0271   The object is the fixed, the existent; the configuration is the changing, the variable.

2.0272   The configuration of the objects forms the atomic fact.

2.03   In the atomic fact objects hang one in another, like the links of a chain.

2.031   In the atomic fact the objects are combined in a definite way.

2.032   The way in which objects hang together in the atomic fact is the structure of the atomic fact.

2.033   The form is the possibility of the structure.

2.034   The structure of the fact consists of the structures of the atomic facts.

2.04   The totality of existent atomic facts is the world.

2.05   The totality of existent atomic facts also determines which atomic facts do not exist.

2.06   The existence and nonexistence of atomic facts is the reality.

2.061   Atomic facts are independent of one another.

2.062   From the existence or nonexistence of an atomic fact we cannot infer the existence or nonexistence of another.

2.063   The total reality is the world.

2.1   We make to ourselves pictures of facts.

2.11   The picture presents the facts in logical space, the existence and nonexistence of atomic facts.

2.12   The picture is a model of reality.

2.13   To the objects correspond in the picture the elements of the picture.

2.131   The elements of the picture stand, in the picture, for the objects.

2.14   The picture consists in the fact that its elements are combined with one another in a definite way.

2.141   The picture is a fact.

2.15   That the elements of the picture are combined with one another in a definite way, represents that the things are so combined with one another.

336   **Early Analytic Philosophy**

This connection of the elements of the picture is called its structure, and the possibility of this structure is called the form of representation of the picture.

2.151   The form of representation is the possibility that the things are combined with one another as are the elements of the picture.

2.1511   Thus the picture is linked with reality; it reaches up to it.

2.1512   It is like a scale applied to reality.

2.15121   Only the outermost points of the dividing lines touch the object to be measured.

2.1513   According to this view the representing relation which makes it a picture, also belongs to the picture.

2.1514   The representing relation consists of the coordinations of the elements of the picture and the things.

2.1515   These coordinations are as it were the feelers of its elements with which the picture touches reality.

2.16   In order to be a picture a fact must have something in common with what it pictures.

2.161   In the picture and the pictured there must be something identical in order that the one can be a picture of the other at all.

2.17   What the picture must have in common with reality in order to be able to represent it after its manner—rightly or falsely—is its form of representation.

2.171   The picture can represent every reality whose form it has.

The spatial picture, everything spatial, the coloured, everything coloured, etc.

2.172   The picture, however, cannot represent its form of representation; it shows it forth.

2.173   The picture represents its object from without (its standpoint is its form of representation), therefore the picture represents its object rightly or falsely.

2.174   But the picture cannot place itself outside of its form of representation.

2.18   What every picture, of whatever form, must have in common with reality in order to be able to represent it at all—rightly or falsely—is the logical form, that is, the form of reality.

2.181   If the form of representation is the logical form, then the picture is called a logical picture.

2.182   Every picture is *also* a logical picture. (On the other hand, for example, not every picture is spatial.)

2.19   The logical picture can depict the world.

Ludwig Wittgenstein on Language and Philosophy

2.2   The picture has the logical form of representation in common with what it pictures.

2.201   The picture depicts reality by representing a possibility of the existence and nonexistence of atomic facts.

2.202   The picture represents a possible state of affairs in logical space.

2.203   The picture contains the possibility of the state of affairs which it represents.

2.21   The picture agrees with reality or not; it is right or wrong, true or false.

2.22   The picture represents what it represents, independently of its truth or falsehood, through the form of representation.

2.221   What the picture represents is its sense.

2.222   In the agreement or disagreement of its sense with reality, its truth or falsity consists.

2.223   In order to discover whether the picture is true or false we must compare it with reality.

2.224   It cannot be discovered from the picture alone whether it is true or false.

2.225   There is no picture which is *a priori* true.

3   The logical picture of the facts is the thought.

3.001   "An atomic fact is thinkable"—means: we can imagine it.

3.01   The totality of true thoughts is a picture of the world.

3.02   The thought contains the possibility of the state of affairs which it thinks. What is thinkable is also possible.

3.03   We cannot think anything unlogical, for otherwise we should have to think unlogically.

3.031   It used to be said that God could create everything, except what was contrary to the laws of logic. The truth is, we could not *say* of an "unlogical" world how it would look.

3.032   To present in language anything which "contradicts logic" is as impossible as in geometry to present by its coordinates a figure which contradicts the laws of space; or to give the coordinates of a point which does not exist.

3.0321   We could present spatially an atomic fact which contradicted the laws of physics, but not one which contradicted the laws of geometry.

3.04   An *a priori* true thought would be one whose possibility guaranteed its truth.

3.05   Only if we could know *a priori* that a thought is true if its truth was to be recognized from the thought itself (without an object of comparison).

Early Analytic Philosophy

3.1 In the proposition the thought is expressed perceptibly through the senses.

3.11 We use the sensibly perceptible sign (sound or written sign, etc.) of the proposition as a projection of the possible state of affairs.

The method of projection is the thinking of the sense of the proposition.

3.12 The sign through which we express the thought I call the propositional sign. And the proposition is the propositional sign in its projective relation to the world.

3.13 To the proposition belongs everything which belongs to the projection; but not what is projected.

Therefore the possibility of what is projected but not this itself.

In the proposition, therefore, its sense is not yet contained, but the possibility of expressing it.

("The content of the proposition" means the content of the significant proposition.)

In the proposition the form of its sense is contained, but not its content.

3.14 The propositional sign consists in the fact that its elements, the words, are combined in it in a definite way.

The propositional sign is a fact.

3.141 The proposition is not a mixture of words (just as the musical theme is not a mixture of tones).

The proposition is articulate.

3.142 Only facts can express a sense, a class of names cannot.

3.143 That the propositional sign is a fact is concealed by the ordinary form of expression, written or printed.

For in the printed proposition, for example, the sign of a proposition does not appear essentially different from a word.

(Thus it was possible for Frege to call the proposition a compounded name.)

3.1431 The essential nature of the propositional sign becomes very clear when we imagine it made up of spatial objects (such as tables, chairs, books) instead of written signs.

The mutual spatial position of these things then expresses the sense of the proposition.

3.1432 We must not say, "The complex sign 'a R b' says 'a stands in relation R to b'"; but we must say, "*That* 'a' stands in a certain relation to 'b' says *that a R b*".

3.144	States of affairs can be described but not *named*.
	(Names resemble points; propositions resemble arrows, they have sense.)
3.2	In propositions thoughts can be so expressed that to the objects of the thoughts correspond the elements of the propositional sign.
3.201	These elements I call "simple signs" and the proposition "completely analysed."
3.202	The simple signs employed in propositions are called names.
3.203	The name means the object. The object is its meaning. ("*a*" is the same sign as "*a*".)
3.21	To the configuration of the simple signs in the propositional sign corresponds the configuration of the objects in the state of affairs.
3.22	In the proposition the name represents the object.
3.221	Objects I can only *name*. Signs represent them. I can only speak *of* them. I cannot *assert them*. A proposition can only say *how* a thing is, not *what* it is.
3.23	The postulate of the possibility of the simple signs is the postulate of the determinateness of the sense.
3.24	A proposition about a complex stands in internal relation to the proposition about its constituent part.
	A complex can only be given by its description, and this will either be right or wrong. The proposition in which there is mention of a complex, if this does not exist, becomes not nonsense but simply false.
	That a propositional element signifies a complex can be seen from an indeterminateness in the propositions in which it occurs. We *know* that everything is not yet determined by this proposition. (The notation for generality *contains* a prototype.)
	The combination of the symbols of a complex in a simple symbol can be expressed by a definition.
3.25	There is one and only one complete analysis of the proposition.
3.251	The proposition expresses what it expresses in a definite and clearly specifiable way: the proposition is articulate.
3.26	The name cannot be analysed further by any definition. It is a primitive sign.
3.261	Every defined sign signifies via those signs by which it is defined, and the definitions show the way.
	Two signs, one a primitive sign, and one defined by primitive signs, cannot signify in the same way. Names *cannot* be taken to pieces by definition (nor any sign which alone and independently has a meaning).

Early Analytic Philosophy

3.262 What does not get expressed in the sign is shown by its application. What the signs conceal, their application declares.

3.263 The meanings of primitive signs can be explained by elucidations. Elucidations are propositions which contain the primitive signs. They can, therefore, only be understood when the meanings of these signs are already known.

3.3 Only the proposition has sense; only in the context of a proposition has a name meaning.

3.31 Every part of a proposition which characterizes its sense I call an expression (a symbol).

(The proposition itself is an expression.)

Expressions are everything—essential for the sense of the proposition—that propositions can have in common with one another.

An expression characterizes a form and a content.

3.311 An expression presupposes the forms of all propositions in which it can occur. It is the common characteristic mark of a class of propositions.

3.312 It is therefore represented by the general form of the propositions which it characterizes.

And in this form the expression is *constant* and everything else *variable*.

3.313 An expression is thus presented by a variable, whose values are the propositions which contain the expression.

(In the limiting case the variable becomes constant, the expression a proposition.)

I call such a variable a "propositional variable."

3.314 An expression has meaning only in a proposition. Every variable can be conceived as a propositional variable.

(Including the variable name.)

3.315 If we change a constituent part of a proposition into a variable, there is a class of propositions which are all the values of the resulting variable proposition. This class in general still depends on what, by arbitrary agreement, we mean by parts of that proposition. But if we change all those signs, whose meaning was arbitrarily determined, into variables, there always remains such a class. But this is now no longer dependent on any agreement; it depends only on the nature of the proposition. It corresponds to a logical form, to a logical prototype.

3.316 What values the propositional variable can assume is determined.The determination of the values *is* the variable.

| 3.317 | The determination of the values of the propositional variable is done by *indicating the propositions* whose common mark the variable is.

The determination is a description of these propositions.

The determination will therefore deal only with symbols not with their meaning.

And *only* this is essential to the determination, *that it is only a description of symbols and asserts nothing about what is symbolized.*

The way in which we describe the propositions is not essential. |
3.318	I conceive the proposition—like Frege and Russell—as a function of the expressions contained in it.
3.32	The sign is the part of the symbol perceptible by the senses.
3.321	Two different symbols can therefore have the sign (the written sign or the sound sign) in common—they then signify in different ways.
3.322	It can never indicate the common characteristic of two objects that we symbolize them with the same signs but by different *methods of symbolizing.* For the sign is arbitrary. We could therefore equally well choose two different signs and where then would be what was common in the symbolization?
3.323	In the language of everyday life it very often happens that the same word signifies in two different ways—and therefore belongs to two different symbols—or that two words, which signify in different ways, are apparently applied in the same way in the proposition.

Thus the word "is" appears as the copula, as the sign of equality, and as the expression of existence; "to exist" as an intransitive verb like "to go"; "identical" as an adjective; we speak of *something* but also of the fact of *something* happening. |
| 3.324 | Thus there easily arise the most fundamental confusions (of which the whole of philosophy is full). |
| 3.325 | In order to avoid these errors, we must employ a symbolism which excludes them, by not applying the same sign in different symbols and by not applying signs in the same way which signify in different ways. A symbolism, that is to say, which obeys the rules of *logical* grammar— of logical syntax.

(The logical symbolism of Frege and Russell is such a language, which, however, does still not exclude all errors.) |
| 3.326 | In order to recognize the symbol in the sign we must consider the significant use. |
| 3.327 | The sign determines a logical form only together with its logical syntactic application. |

342 Early Analytic Philosophy

3.328   If a sign is *not necessary* then it is meaningless. That is the meaning of Occam's razor.

        (If everything in the symbolism works as though a sign had meaning, then it has meaning.)

3.33   In logical syntax the meaning of a sign ought never to play a role; it must admit of being established without mention being thereby made of the *meaning* of a sign; it ought to presuppose *only* the description of the expressions.

3.331   From this observation we get a further view—into Russell's "Theory of Types." Russell's error is shown by the fact that in drawing up his symbolic rules he has to speak about the things his signs mean.

3.332   No proposition can say anything about itself, because the propositional sign cannot be contained in itself (that is the "whole theory of types").

3.333   A function cannot be its own argument, because the functional sign already contains the prototype of its own argument and it cannot contain itself.

        If, for example, we suppose that the function $F(fx)$ could be its own argument, then there would be a proposition "$F(F(fx))$", and in this the outer function F and the inner function F must have different meanings; for the inner has the form $\varphi(fx)$, the outer the form $\psi(\varphi(fx))$. Common to both functions is only the letter "F", which by itself signifies nothing.

        This is at once clear, if instead of "$F(Fu)$" we write "$(\exists\varphi):F(\varphi u). \varphi u=Fu$".

        Herewith Russell's paradox vanishes.

3.334   The rules of logical syntax must follow of themselves, if we only know how every single sign signifies.

3.34   A proposition possesses essential and accidental features.

        Accidental are the features which are due to a particular way of producing the propositional sign. Essential are those which alone enable the proposition to express its sense.

3.341   The essential in a proposition is therefore that which is common to all propositions which can express the same sense.

        And in the same way in general the essential in a symbol is that which all symbols which can fulfill the same purpose have in common.

3.3411   One could therefore say the real name is that which all symbols, which signify an object, have in common. It would then follow, step by step, that no sort of composition was essential for a name.

3.342   In our notations there is indeed something arbitrary, but *this* is not arbitrary, namely that *if* we have determined anything arbitrarily, then

Ludwig Wittgenstein on Language and Philosophy **343**

something else *must* be the case. (This results from the *essence* of the notation.)

3.3421 A particular method of symbolizing may be unimportant, but it is always important that this is a *possible* method of symbolizing. And this happens as a rule in philosophy: The single thing proves over and over again to be unimportant, but the possibility of every single thing reveals something about the nature of the world.

3.343 Definitions are rules for the translation of one language into another. Every correct symbolism must be translatable into every other according to such rules. It is *this* which all have in common.

3.344 What signifies in the symbol is what is common to all those symbols by which it can be replaced according to the rules of logical syntax.

3.3441 We can, for example, express what is common to all notations for the truth-functions as follows: It is common to them that they all, for example, *can be replaced* by the notations of "~p" ("not p") and "p ∨ q" ("p or q").

(Herewith is indicated the way in which a special possible notation can give us general information.)

3.3442 The sign of the complex is not arbitrarily resolved in the analysis, in such a way that its resolution would be different in every propositional structure.

3.4 The proposition determines a place in logical space: the existence of this logical place is guaranteed by the existence of the constituent parts alone, by the existence of the significant proposition.

3.41 The propositional sign and the logical coordinates: that is the logical place.

3.411 The geometrical and the logical place agree in that each is the possibility of an existence.

3.42 Although a proposition may only determine one place in logical space, the whole logical space must already be given by it.

(Otherwise denial, the logical sum, the logical product, etc., would always introduce new elements—in coordination.)

(The logical scaffolding round the picture determines the logical space. The proposition reaches through the whole logical space.)

3.5 The applied, thought, propositional sign, is the thought.

4 The thought is the significant proposition.

4.001 The totality of propositions is the language.

4.002 Man possesses the capacity of constructing languages, in which every sense can be expressed, without having an idea how and what each

344   **Early Analytic Philosophy**

word means—just as one speaks without knowing how the single sounds are produced.

Colloquial language is a part of the human organism and is not less complicated than it.

From it it is humanly impossible to gather immediately the logic of language.

Language disguises the thought; so that from the external form of the clothes one cannot infer the form of the thought they clothe, because the external form of the clothes is constructed with quite another object than to let the form of the body be recognized.

The silent adjustments to understand colloquial language are enormously complicated.

4.003   Most propositions and questions, that have been written about philosophical matters, are not false, but senseless. We cannot, therefore, answer questions of this kind at all, but only state their senselessness. Most questions and propositions of the philosophers result from the fact that we do not understand the logic of our language.

(They are of the same kind as the question whether the Good is more or less identical than the Beautiful.)

And so it is not to be wondered at that the deepest problems are really *no* problems.

4.0031   All philosophy is "Critique of language" (but not at all in Mauthner's sense). Russell's merit is to have shown that the apparent logical form of the proposition need not be its real form.

4.01   The proposition is a picture of reality.

The proposition is a model of the reality as we think it is.

4.011   At the first glance the proposition—say as it stands printed on paper— does not seem to be a picture of the reality of which it treats. But nor does the musical score appear at first sight to be a picture of a musical piece; nor does our phonetic spelling (letters) seem to be a picture of our spoken language.

And yet these symbolisms prove to be pictures—even in the ordinary sense of the word—of what they represent.

4.012   It is obvious that we perceive a proposition of the form $a \, R \, b$ as a picture. Here the sign is obviously a likeness of the signified.

4.013   And if we penetrate to the essence of this pictorial nature we see that this is not disturbed by *apparent irregularities* (like the use of ♯ and ♭ in the score).

Ludwig Wittgenstein on Language and Philosophy   345

For these irregularities also picture what they are to express; only in another way.

4.014   The gramophone record, the musical thought, the score, the waves of sound, all stand to one another in that pictorial internal relation, which holds between language and the world.

To all of them the logical structure is common.

(Like the two youths, their two horses and their lilies in the story. They are all in a certain sense one.)

4.0141 In the fact that there is a general rule by which the musician is able to read the symphony out of the score, and that there is a rule by which one could reconstruct the symphony from the line on a gramophone record and from this again—by means of the first rule—construct the score, herein lies the internal similarity between these things which at first sight seem to be entirely different. And the rule is the law of projection which projects the symphony into the language of the musical score. It is the rule of translation of this language into the language of the gramophone record.

4.015   The possibility of all similes, of all the images of our language, rests on the logic of representation.

4.016   In order to understand the essence of the proposition, consider hieroglyphic writing, which pictures the facts it describes.

And from it came the alphabet without the essence of the representation being lost.

4.02   This we see from the fact that we understand the sense of the propositional sign, without having had it explained to us.

4.021   The proposition is a picture of reality, for I know the state of affairs presented by it, if I understand the proposition. And I understand the proposition, without its sense having been explained to me.

4.022   The proposition *shows* its sense.

The proposition *shows* how things stand, *if* it is true. And it *says*, that they do so stand.

4.023   The proposition determines reality to this extent, that one only needs to say "Yes" or "No" to it to make it agree with reality.

Reality must therefore be completely described by the proposition.

A proposition is the description of a fact.

As the description of an object describes it by its external properties so propositions describe reality by its internal properties.

The proposition constructs a world with the help of a logical scaffolding, and therefore one can actually see in the proposition all

346   Early Analytic Philosophy

the logical features possessed by reality *if* it is true. One can *draw conclusions* from a false proposition.

4.024   To understand a proposition means to know what is the case, if it is true.

(One can therefore understand it without knowing whether it is true or not.)

One understands it if one understands its constituent parts.

4.025   The translation of one language into another is not a process of translating each proposition of the one into a proposition of the other, but only the constituent parts of propositions are translated.

(And the dictionary does not only translate substantives but also adverbs and conjunctions, etc., and it treats them all alike.)

4.026   The meanings of the simple signs (the words) must be explained to us, if we are to understand them.

By means of propositions we explain ourselves.

4.027   It is essential to propositions, that they can communicate a *new* sense to us.

4.03   A proposition must communicate a new sense with old words.

The proposition communicates to us a state of affairs, therefore it must be *essentially connected* with the state of affairs.

And the connection is, in fact, that it is its logical picture.

The proposition only asserts something, in so far as it is a picture.

4.031   In the proposition a state of affairs is, as it were, put together for the sake of experiment.

One can say, instead of, This proposition has such and such a sense, This proposition represents such and such a state of affairs.

4.0311   One name stands for one thing, and another for another thing, and they are connected together. And so the whole, like a living picture, presents the atomic fact.

4.0312   The possibility of propositions is based upon the principle of the representation of objects by signs.

My fundamental thought is that the "logical constants" do not represent. That the *logic* of the facts cannot be represented.

4.032   The proposition is a picture of its state of affairs, only in so far as it is logically articulated.

(Even the proposition "ambulo" is composite, for its stem gives a different sense with another termination, or its termination with another stem.)

4.04   In the proposition there must be exactly as many things distinguishable as there are in the state of affairs, which it represents.

Ludwig Wittgenstein on Language and Philosophy   347

They must both possess the same logical (mathematical) multiplicity (cf. Hertz's Mechanics, on Dynamic Models).

4.041   This mathematical multiplicity naturally cannot in its turn be represented. One cannot get outside it in the representation.

4.0411   If we tried, for example, to express what is expressed by "(x).fx" by putting an index before fx, like: "Gen. fx", it would not do, we should not know what was generalized. If we tried to show it by an index g, like: "f(x$_g$)" it would not do—we should not know the scope of the generalization.

If we were to try it by introducing a mark in the argument places, like "(G,G). F(G,G)", it would not do—we could not determine the identity of the variables, etc.

All these ways of symbolizing are inadequate because they have not the necessary mathematical multiplicity.

4.0412   For the same reason the idealist explanation of the seeing of spatial relations through "spatial spectacles" does not do, because it cannot explain the multiplicity of these relations.

4.05   Reality is compared with the proposition.

4.06   Propositions can be true or false only by being pictures of the reality.

4.061   If one does not observe that propositions have a sense independent of the facts, one can easily believe that true and false are two relations between signs and things signified with equal rights.

One could, then, for example, say that "p" signifies in the true way what "~p" signifies in the false way, etc.

4.062   Can we not make ourselves understood by means of false propositions as hitherto with true ones, so long as we know that they are meant to be false? No! For a proposition is true, if what we assert by means of it is the case; and if by "p" we mean ~p, and what we mean is the case, then "p" in the new conception is true and not false.

4.0621   That, however, the signs "p" and "~p" can say the same thing is important, for it shows that the sign "~" corresponds to nothing in reality.

That negation occurs in a proposition, is no characteristic of its sense (~~p=p).

The propositions "p" and "~p" have opposite senses, but to them corresponds one and the same reality.

4.063   An illustration to explain the concept of truth. A black spot on white paper; the form of the spot can be described by saying of each point of the plane whether it is white or black. To the fact that a point is black

348   **Early Analytic Philosophy**

corresponds a positive fact; to the fact that a point is white (not black), a negative fact. If I indicate a point of the plane (a truth-value in Frege's terminology), this corresponds to the assumption proposed for judgment, etc. etc.

But to be able to say that a point is black or white, I must first know under what conditions a point is called white or black; in order to be able to say "p" is true (or false) I must have determined under what conditions I call "p" true, and thereby I determine the sense of the proposition.

The point at which the simile breaks down is this: we can indicate a point on the paper, without knowing what white and black are; but to a proposition without a sense corresponds nothing at all, for it signifies no thing (truth-value) whose properties are called "false" or "true"; the verb of the proposition is not "is true" or "is false"—as Frege thought—but that which "is true" must already contain the verb.

4.064   Every proposition must *already* have a sense; assertion cannot give it a sense, for what it asserts is the sense itself. And the same holds of denial, etc.

4.0641   One could say, the denial is already related to the logical place determined by the proposition that is denied.

The denying proposition determines a logical place *other* than does the proposition denied.

The denying proposition determines a logical place, with the help of the logical place of the proposition denied, by saying that it lies outside the latter place.

That one can deny again the denied proposition, shows that what is denied is already a proposition and not merely the preliminary to a proposition.

4.1   A proposition presents the existence and nonexistence of atomic facts.

4.11   The totality of true propositions is the total natural science (or the totality of the natural sciences).

4.111   Philosophy is not one of the natural sciences.

(The word "philosophy" must mean something which stands above or below, but not beside the natural sciences.)

4.112   The object of philosophy is the logical clarification of thoughts.

Philosophy is not a theory but an activity.

A philosophical work consists essentially of elucidations.

The result of philosophy is not a number of "philosophical propositions," but to make propositions clear.

Ludwig Wittgenstein on Language and Philosophy 349

Philosophy should make clear and delimit sharply the thoughts which otherwise are, as it were, opaque and blurred.

4.1121 Psychology is no nearer related to philosophy, than is any other natural science.

The theory of knowledge is the philosophy of psychology.

Does not my study of sign-language correspond to the study of thought processes which philosophers held to be so essential to the philosophy of logic? Only they got entangled for the most part in unessential psychological investigations, and there is an analogous danger for my method.

4.1122 The Darwinian theory has no more to do with philosophy than has any other hypothesis of natural science.

4.113 Philosophy limits the disputable sphere of natural science.

4.114 It should limit the thinkable and thereby the unthinkable.

It should limit the unthinkable from within through the thinkable.

4.115 It will mean the unspeakable by clearly displaying the speakable.

4.116 Everything that can be thought at all can be thought clearly. Everything that can be said can be said clearly.

4.12 Propositions can represent the whole reality, but they cannot represent what they must have in common with reality in order to be able to represent it—the logical form.

To be able to represent the logical form, we should have to be able to put ourselves with the propositions outside logic, that is outside the world.

4.121 Propositions cannot represent the logical form: this mirrors itself in the propositions.

That which mirrors itself in language, language cannot represent.

That which expresses *itself* in language, *we* cannot express by language.

The propositions *show* the logical form of reality.

They exhibit it.

4.1211 Thus a proposition "fa" shows that in its sense the object a occurs, two propositions "fa" and "ga" that they are both about the same object.

If two propositions contradict one another, this is shown by their structure; similarly if one follows from another, etc.

4.1212 What *can* be shown *cannot* be said.

4.1213 Now we understand our feeling that we are in possession of the right logical conception, if only all is right in our symbolism.

[material removed]

350   Early Analytic Philosophy

4.2   The sense of a proposition is its agreement and disagreement with the possibilities of the existence and nonexistence of the atomic facts.

4.21   The simplest proposition, the elementary proposition, asserts the existence of an atomic fact.

4.211   It is a sign of an elementary proposition, that no elementary proposition can contradict it.

4.22   The elementary proposition consists of names. It is a connection, a concatenation, of names.

4.221   It is obvious that in the analysis of propositions we must come to elementary propositions, which consist of names in immediate combination.

The question arises here, how the propositional connection comes to be.

4.2211 Even if the world is infinitely complex, so that every fact consists of an infinite number of atomic facts and every atomic fact is composed of an infinite number of objects, even then there must be objects and atomic facts.

4.23   The name occurs in the proposition only in the context of the elementary proposition.

4.24   The names are the simple symbols, I indicate them by single letters (x, y, z).

The elementary proposition I write as function of the names, in the form "fx", "$\varphi(x,y)$", etc.

Or I indicate it by the letters p, q, r.

4.241   If I use two signs with one and the same meaning, I express this by putting between them the sign "=".

"a=b" means then, that the sign "a" is replaceable by the sign "b".

(If I introduce by an equation a new sign "b", by determining that it shall replace a previously known sign "a", I write the equation—definition—(like Russell) in the form "a=b Def." A definition is a symbolic rule.)

4.242   Expressions of the form "a=b" are therefore only expedients in presentation: They assert nothing about the meaning of the signs "a" and "b".

4.243   Can we understand two names without knowing whether they signify the same thing or two different things? Can we understand a proposition in which two names occur, without knowing if they mean the same or different things?

> If I know the meaning of an English and a synonymous German word, it is impossible for me not to know that they are synonymous, it is impossible for me not to be able to translate them into one another.
>
> Expressions like "a=a", or expressions deduced from these are neither elementary propositions nor otherwise significant signs. (This will be shown later.)

4.25   If the elementary proposition is true, the atomic fact exists; if it is false the atomic fact does not exist.

4.26   The specification of all true elementary propositions describes the world completely. The world is completely described by the specification of all elementary propositions plus the specification, which of them are true and which false.

4.27   With regard to the existence of n atomic facys, there are

$$K_n = \sum_{v=0}^{n} \binom{n}{v}$$

possibilities.

It is possible for all combinations of atomic facts to exist, and the others not to exist.

4.28.   To these combinations correspond the same number of possibilities of the truth—and falsehood—of n elementary propositions.

4.3.   The truth-possibilities of the elementary propositions mean the possibilities of the existence and nonexistence of the atomic facts.

4.31   The truth-possibilities can be presented by schemata of the following kind ("T" means "true," "F" "false." The rows of T's and F's under the row of the elementary propositions mean their truth-possibilities in an easily intelligible symbolism).

p	*q*	*r*
T	T	T
F	T	T
T	F	T
T	T	F
F	F	T
F	T	F
T	F	F
F	F	F

352   Early Analytic Philosophy

p	*q*
T	T
F	T
T	F
F	F

p
T
F

4.4   A proposition is the expression of agreement and disagreement with the truth-possibilities of the elementary propositions.

4.41   The truth-possibilities of the elementary propositions are the conditions of the truth and falsehood of the propositions.

4.411   It seems probable even at first sight that the introduction of the elementary propositions is fundamental for the comprehension of the other kinds of propositions. Indeed the comprehension of the general propositions depends *palpably* on that of the elementary propositions.

4.42.   With regard to the agreement and disagreement of a proposition with the truth-possibilities of *n* elementary propositions there are

$$\sum_{\kappa=0}^{K_n} \binom{K_n}{\kappa} = L_n$$

possibilities.

4.43   Agreement with the truth-possibilities can be expressed by coordinating with them in the schema the mark "T" (true).

Absence of this mark means disagreement.

4.431   The expression of the agreement and disagreement with the truth-possibilities of the elementary propositions expresses the truth-conditions of the proposition.

The proposition is the expression of its truth-conditions.

(Frege has therefore quite rightly put them at the beginning, as explaining the signs of his logical symbolism. Only Frege's explanation of the truth-concept is false: if "the true" and "the false" were real objects and the arguments in ~p, etc., then the sense of ~p would by no means be determined by Frege's determination.)

4.44   The sign which arises from the coordination of that mark "T" with the truth-possibilities is a propositional sign.

Ludwig Wittgenstein on Language and Philosophy 353

4.441 It is clear that to the complex of the signs "F" and "T" no object (or complex of objects) corresponds; any more than to horizontal and vertical lines or to brackets. There are no "logical objects."

Something analogous holds of course for all signs, which express the same as the schemata of "T" and "F".

4.442. Thus, e.g.,:

$$
\begin{array}{lll}
p & q & \\
T & T & T \\
F & T & T \\
T & F & \\
F & F & T
\end{array}
$$

is a propositional sign.

(Frege's assertion sign "⊢" is logically altogether meaningless; in Frege (and Russell) it only shows that these authors hold as true the propositions marked in this way. "⊢" belongs therefore to the propositions no more than does the number of the proposition. A proposition cannot possibly assert of itself that it is true.)

If the sequence of the truth-possibilities in the schema is once for all determined by a rule of combination, then the last column is by itself an expression of the truth-conditions. If we write this column as a row the propositional sign becomes: "(TT—T)(p,q)," or more plainly, "(TTFT)(p,q)".

(The number of places in the left-hand bracket is determined by the number of terms in the right-hand bracket.)

4.45 For n elementary propositions there are Ln possible groups of truth-conditions.

The groups of truth-conditions which belong to the truth-possibilities of a number of elementary propositions can be ordered in a series.

4.46 Among the possible groups of truth-conditions there are two extreme cases.

In the one case the proposition is true for all the truth-possibilities of the elementary propositions. We say that the truth-conditions are *tautological.*

In the second case the proposition is false for all the truth-possibilities. The truth-conditions are *self-contradictory.*

In the first case we call the proposition a tautology, in the second case a contradiction.

354 Early Analytic Philosophy

4.461   The proposition shows what it says, the tautology and the contradiction that they say nothing.

The tautology has no truth-conditions, for it is unconditionally true; and the contradiction is on no condition true.

Tautology and contradiction are without sense.

(Like the point from which two arrows go out in opposite directions.)

(I know, e.g. nothing about the weather, when I know that it rains or does not rain.)

4.4611 Tautology and contradiction are, however, not nonsensical; they are part of the symbolism, in the same way that "0" is part of the symbolism of Arithmetic.

4.462   Tautology and contradiction are not pictures of the reality. They present no possible state of affairs. For the one allows *every* possible state of affairs, the other *none*.

In the tautology the conditions of agreement with the world—the presenting relations—cancel one another, so that it stands in no presenting relation to reality.

4.463   The truth-conditions determine the range, which is left to the facts by the proposition.

(The proposition, the picture, the model, are in a negative sense like a solid body, which restricts the free movement of another: in a positive sense, like the space limited by solid substance, in which a body may be placed.)

Tautology leaves to reality the whole infinite logical space; contradiction fills the whole logical space and leaves no point to reality. Neither of them, therefore, can in any way determine reality.

4.464   The truth of tautology is certain, of propositions possible, of contradiction impossible.

(Certain, possible, impossible: here we have an indication of that gradation which we need in the theory of probability.)

4.465   The logical product of a tautology and a proposition says the same as the proposition. Therefore that product is identical with the proposition. For the essence of the symbol cannot be altered without altering its sense.

4.466   To a definite logical combination of signs corresponds a definite logical combination of their meanings; *every arbitrary* combination only corresponds to the unconnected signs.

Ludwig Wittgenstein on Language and Philosophy 355

That is, propositions which are true for every state of affairs cannot be combinations of signs at all, for otherwise there could only correspond to them definite combinations of objects.

(And to no logical combination corresponds no combination of the objects.)

Tautology and contradiction are the limiting cases of the combination of symbols, namely their dissolution.

4.4661 Of course the signs are also combined with one another in the tautology and contradiction, i.e. they stand in relations to one another, but these relations are meaningless, unessential to the *symbol*.

[material removed]

5.14 If a proposition follows from another, then the latter says more than the former, the former less than the latter.

5.141 If p follows from q and q from p then they are one and the same proposition.

5.142 A tautology follows from all propositions: it says nothing.

5.143 Contradiction is something shared by propositions, which no proposition has in common with another. Tautology is that which is shared by all propositions, which have nothing in common with one another.

Contradiction vanishes so to speak outside, tautology inside all propositions.

Contradiction is the external limit of the propositions, tautology their substanceless centre.

[material removed]

5.3 All propositions are results of truth-operations on the elementary propositions.

The truth-operation is the way in which a truth-function arises from elementary propositions.

According to the nature of truth-operations, in the same way as out of elementary propositions arise their truth-functions, from truth-functions arises a new one. Every truth-operation creates from truth-functions of elementary propositions, another truth-function of elementary propositions i.e. a proposition. The result of every truth-operation on the results of truth-operations on elementary propositions is also the result of *one* truth-operation on elementary propositions.

Every proposition is the result of truth-operations on elementary propositions.

5.31 The schemata No. 4.31 are also significant, if "p", "q", "r", etc. are not elementary propositions.

Early Analytic Philosophy

And it is easy to see that the propositional sign in No. 4.442 expresses one truth-function of elementary propositions even when "p" and "q" are truth-functions of elementary propositions.

5.32   All truth-functions are results of the successive application of a finite number of truth-operations to elementary propositions.

5.4   Here it becomes clear that there are no such things as "logical objects" or "logical constants" (in the sense of Frege and Russell).

5.41   For all those results of truth-operations on truth-functions are identical, which are one and the same truth-function of elementary propositions.

5.42   That ∨, ⊃, etc., are not relations in the sense of right and left, etc., is obvious.

The possibility of crosswise definition of the logical "primitive signs" of Frege and Russell shows by itself that these are not primitive signs and that they signify no relations.

And it is obvious that the "⊃" which we define by means of "~" and "∨" is identical with that by which we define "∨" with the help of "~", and that this "∨" is the same as the first, and so on.

5.43   That from a fact p an infinite number of *others* should follow, namely, ~~p, ~~~~p, etc., is indeed hardly to be believed, and it is no less wonderful that the infinite number of propositions of logic (of mathematics) should follow from half a dozen "primitive propositions."

But the propositions of logic say the same thing. That is, nothing.

[material removed]

5.6   *The limits of my language* mean the limits of my world.

5.61   Logic fills the world: the limits of the world are also its limits.

We cannot therefore say in logic: This and this there is in the world, that there is not.

For that would apparently presuppose that we exclude certain possibilities, and this cannot be the case since otherwise logic must get outside the limits of the world: that is, if it could consider these limits from the other side also.

What we cannot think, that we cannot think: we cannot therefore say what we cannot think.

5.62   This remark provides a key to the question, to what extent solipsism is a truth.

In fact what solipsism *means*, is quite correct, only it cannot be *said*, but it shows itself.

That the world is my world, shows itself in the fact that the limits of the language (*the* language which I understand) mean the limits of *my* world.

5.621 The world and life are one.

5.63 I am my world. (The microcosm.)

5.631 The thinking, presenting subject; there is no such thing.

If I wrote a book "The world as I found it," I should also have therein to report on my body and say which members obey my will and which do not, etc. This then would be a method of isolating the subject or rather of showing that in an important sense there is no subject: that is to say, of it alone in this book mention could not be made.

5.632 The subject does not belong to the world but it is a limit of the world.

5.633 *Where in* the world is a metaphysical subject to be noted?

You say that this case is altogether like that of the eye and the field of sight. But you do not really see the eye.

And from nothing *in the field of sight* can it be concluded that it is seen from an eye.

5.6331 For the field of sight has not a form like this:

5.634 This is connected with the fact that no part of our experience is also *a priori*.

Everything we see could also be otherwise.

Everything we describe at all could also be otherwise.

There is no order of things *a priori*.

5.64 Here we see that solipsism strictly carried out coincides with pure realism. The I in solipsism shrinks to an extensionless point and there remains the reality coordinated with it.

5.641 There is therefore really a sense in which the philosophy we can talk of a non-psychological I.

The I occurs in philosophy through the fact that the "world is my world."

The philosophical I is not the man, not the human body or the human soul of which psychology treats, but the metaphysical subject, the limit—not a part of the world.

[material removed]

6.37 A necessity for one thing to happen because another has happened does not exist. There is only *logical* necessity.

6.371 At the basis of the whole modern view of the world lies the illusion that the so-called laws of nature are the explanations of natural phenomena.

Early Analytic Philosophy

6.372 So people stop short at natural laws as something unassailable, as did the ancients at God and Fate.

And they are both right and wrong. But the ancients were clearer, in so far as they recognized one clear terminus, whereas the modern system makes it appear as though *everything* were explained.

6.373 The world is independent of my will.

6.374 Even if everything we wished were to happen, this would only be, so to speak, a favour of fate, for there is no *logical* connection between will and world, which would guarantee this, and the assumed physical connection itself we could not again will.

6.375 As there is only a *logical* necessity, so there is only a *logical* impossibility.

6.3751 For two colours, e.g. to be at one place in the visual field, is impossible, logically impossible, for it is excluded by the logical structure of colour.

Let us consider how this contradiction presents itself in physics. Somewhat as follows: That a particle cannot at the same time have two velocities, i.e. that at the same time it cannot be in two places, i.e. that particles in different places at the same time cannot be identical.

It is clear that the logical product of two elementary propositions can neither be a tautology nor a contradiction. The assertion that a point in the visual field has two different colours at the same time, is a contradiction.

6.4 All propositions are of equal value.

6.41 The sense of the world must lie outside the world. In the world everything is as it is and happens as it does happen. *In* it there is no value—and if there were, it would be of no value.

If there is a value which is of value, it must lie outside all happening and being-so. For all happening and being-so is accidental.

What makes it non-accidental cannot lie *in* the world, for otherwise this would again be accidental.

It must lie outside the world.

6.42 Hence also there can be no ethical propositions.

Propositions cannot express anything higher.

6.421 It is clear that ethics cannot be expressed.

Ethics is transcendental.

(Ethics and aesthetics are one.)

6.422 The first thought in setting up an ethical law of the form "thou shalt . . ." is: And what if I do not do it? But it is clear that ethics has nothing to do with punishment and reward in the ordinary sense. This question as to the *consequences* of an action must therefore be irrelevant. At least these consequences will not be events. For there must be

Ludwig Wittgenstein on Language and Philosophy **359**

something right in that formulation of the question. There must be some sort of ethical reward and ethical punishment, but this must lie in the action itself.

(And this is clear also that the reward must be something acceptable, and the punishment something unacceptable.)

6.423   Of the will as the subject of the ethical we cannot speak.

And the will as a phenomenon is only of interest to psychology.

6.43   If good or bad willing changes the world, it can only change the limits of the world, not the facts; not the things that can be expressed in language.

In brief, the world must thereby become quite another, it must so to speak wax or wane as a whole.

The world of the happy is quite another than that of the unhappy.

6.431   As in death, too, the world does not change, but ceases.

6.4311   Death is not an event of life. Death is not lived through.

If by eternity is understood not endless temporal duration but timelessness, then he lives eternally who lives in the present.

Our life is endless in the way that our visual field is without limit.

6.4312   The temporal immortality of the human soul, that is to say, its eternal survival also after death, is not only in no way guaranteed, but this assumption in the first place will not do for us what we always tried to make it do. Is a riddle solved by the fact that I survive forever? Is this eternal life not as enigmatic as our present one? The solution of the riddle of life in space and time lies *outside* space and time.

(It is not problems of natural science which have to be solved.)

6.432   *How* the world is, is completely indifferent for what is higher. God does not reveal himself in the world.

6.4321   The facts all belong only to the task and not to its performance.

6.44   Not *how* the world is, is the mystical, but *that* it is.

6.45   The contemplation of the world *sub specie aeterni* is its contemplation as a limited whole.

The feeling that the world is a limited whole is the mystical feeling.

6.5   For an answer which cannot be expressed the question too cannot be expressed.

The riddle does not exist.

If a question can be put at all, then it *can* also be answered.

6.51   Scepticism is *not* irrefutable, but palpably senseless, if it would doubt where a question cannot be asked.

360   Early Analytic Philosophy

> For doubt can only exist where there is a question; a question only where there is an answer, and this only where something *can* be *said*.

6.52   We feel that even if *all* possible scientific questions be answered, the problems of life have still not been touched at all. Of course there is then no question left, and just this is the answer.

6.521   The solution of the problem of life is seen in the vanishing of this problem.

> (Is not this the reason why men to whom after long doubting the sense of life became clear, could not then say wherein this sense consisted?)

6.522   There is indeed the inexpressible. This shows itself; it is the mystical.

6.53   The right method of philosophy would be this: To say nothing except what can be said, i.e. the propositions of natural science, i.e. something that has nothing to do with philosophy: and then always, when someone else wished to say something metaphysical, to demonstrate to him that he had given no meaning to certain signs in his propositions. This method would be unsatisfying to the other—he would not have the feeling that we were teaching him philosophy—but it would be the only strictly correct method.

6.54   My propositions are elucidatory in this way: he who understands me finally recognizes them as senseless, when he has climbed out through them, on them, over them. (He must so to speak throw away the ladder, after he has climbed up on it.)

> He must surmount these propositions; then he sees the world rightly.

7   Whereof one cannot speak, thereof one must be silent.

8

Logical Empiricism: Meaning, Metaphysics, and Mathematics

Chapter Outline

Background and commentary

Background	362
Meaning, verification, and the critique of metaphysics	363
Ethical discourse	371
Philosophy of mathematics and logic	373
Concluding remarks	375
Further reading	376

Readings

Schlick, "Meaning and Verification"	377
Carnap, "The Elimination of Metaphysics Through the Logical Analysis of Language"	402
Ayer, *Language, Truth, and Logic* (selections from Chs 4, 6)	421

Background and commentary

Background

With the exception of Chapter 1, each of the previous chapters focused on a particular thinker and his or her contributions to the development of the analytic tradition. The present chapter, in contrast, focuses on a movement within the analytic tradition and the thinkers involved in that movement. Specifically, it focuses on logical empiricism (sometimes referred to as "logical positivism") as an outlook that developed in the 1920s and 1930s in Europe and which continued in the 1940s and 1950s in the United States (in part because many members of the movement came to the United States upon the outbreak of the turmoil in Europe that would culminate in the Second World War).

As a sustained and self-conscious movement, logical empiricism arose in Europe most centrally around two groups, the Vienna Circle in Austria and the Berlin Society for Empirical Philosophy in Germany. Both groups consisted of scientifically informed philosophers along with philosophically minded physicists, mathematicians, logicians, economists, and so on. The Berlin Society was led by Hans Reichenbach (1891–1953), and included thinkers such as Kurt Grelling (1886–1942), Richard von Mises (1883–1953), Paul Oppenheim (1885–1977), and Carl Hempel (1905–97). For its part, the Vienna Circle held weekly discussions from 1924 through 1936 and was led by Moritz Schlick (1882–1936). Carnap, along with Otto Neurath (1882–1945), Hans Hahn (1879–1934), and Olga Hahn-Neurath (1882–1937) were regular participants; the Circle was also visited by Ayer, Carnap, Gödel, and Quine, along with Alfred Tarski (1901–83) and others. The Circle became comparable to a political party of sorts following the 1929 publication of its manifesto, "The Scientific World Conception: The Vienna Circle" (written by Carnap, Neurath, and Hahn), which characterizes the Circle as continuing an Austrian tradition of scientific philosophy in the work of Ernst Mach (1838–1916) and Ludwig Boltzmann (1844–1906), and which cites Russell, Wittgenstein, and Frege as more recent influences. It was also during 1929 that the Circle held its first conference in conjunction with the Berlin Society, "Epistemology of the Exact Sciences." This was the first of many conferences that the Circle held across continental Europe and the United Kingdom, which helped to further its international reputation and contacts, including British philosophers like Ryle and Wisdom, along with Susan Stebbing (1885–1943) and others. The Circle founded the journal *Erkenntnis* (which, after a brief interruption, has been in publication ever since and continues to be a leading journal in philosophy of science and related fields) and sponsored multiple book series dedicated to its ideas, such as the *Schriften zur Wissenschaftliche Weltauffassung* series (*Writings on the Scientific World Conception*).[1]

While the members of these groups disagreed on many matters of detail, they were committed to scientific methodology as a paradigmatic source of knowledge and sought to provide a role for philosophy consistent with the rejection of speculative metaphysics, a role for philosophy consistent with denying that philosophy provides some kind of supra-empirical insight into the nature of reality. They also viewed science, and a corresponding rejection of speculative metaphysics, as providing a basis for the improvement of society at large, especially given the destruction and upheaval precipitated by the First World War. As for a general philosophical outlook, it can be said that logical empiricism combined elements of the classical empiricism of Berkeley and Hume with the modern logical and analytical techniques due to Frege, Russell, and Whitehead. Following the empiricism of Hume, along with views on language due to Wittgenstein, they viewed traditional metaphysics—and much of traditional philosophy—as misguided and, indeed, meaningless in at least one sense of "meaning."

Meaning, verification, and the critique of metaphysics

Consider the following passage from Russell's *Our Knowledge of the External World*, in which Russell draws a connection between meaning and verification:

> I think it may be laid down quite generally that, in so far as physics or common sense is verifiable, it must be capable of interpretation in terms of actual sense-data alone. The reason for this is simple. Verification consists always in the occurrence of an expected sense-datum. Astronomers tell us there will be an eclipse of the moon. We look at the moon, and find the earth's shadow biting into it, that is to say, we see an appearance quite different from that of the usual full moon. Now if an expected sense datum constitutes a verification, what was asserted must have been about sense-data; or, at any rate, if part of what was asserted was not about sense-data, then only the other part has been verified. (88—9)

---

[1]For this and further historical details regarding logical empiricism, see Ayer 1959a, Creath 2017, and Uebel 2019.

Early Analytic Philosophy

In this passage, Russell suggests that since verification consists in some experience—what he calls a "sense-datum"—to the extent that a statement is verifiable at all, it must be about the sense-datum itself. Generally, the suggestion is that meaning is closely connected to verification, the conditions under which a statement is or is not verified.

For the logical empiricists, meaning consisted in verification. Schlick is explicit about this in "Meaning and Verification," writing:

> Stating the meaning of a sentence amounts to stating the rules according to which the sentence is to be used, and this is the same as stating the way in which it can be verified (or falsified). The meaning of a proposition is the method of its verification. (341)

One might think of it like this. On one approach to meaning, the meaning of a sentence consists of its truth conditions, the conditions under which the sentence is true and the conditions under which the sentence is false. Thus Schlick leads into the passage above by remarking that

> Whenever we ask about a sentence, 'What does it mean?', what we expect is instruction as to the circumstances in which the sentence is to be used; we want a description of the conditions under which the sentence will form a true proposition, and of those which will make it false. (341)

For Schlick and other logical empiricists—and drawing from earlier empiricists like Hume—the connection between meaning and truth conditions is given a distinctively epistemological gloss, whereby truth conditions are equated with conditions for verification, the conditions that we would take to verify some statement.

Before moving on to look at how the empiricists wielded this connection between meaning and verification against traditional metaphysics, there are several points worth marking. First, as Schlick notes, to say that a statement is verifiable does not mean that it is is currently being verified (345); rather, it concerns the possibility of verification, and in this sense having implications for experience (347). This, in turn, raises the question: what does "possibility" mean in this context, or, similarly, what does it mean to say that a statement could be verified? Here, Schlick appeals to a notion of logical possibility and distinguishes it from a narrower notion of empirical or physical possibility, possibility given the laws of nature. The following passage is salient; here Schlick is discussing the meaningfulness of statements that purport to concern the other side of the moon:

Logical Empiricism: Meaning, Metaphysics, and Mathematics   365

> The question whether it be physically possible for a human being – or indeed any other living being – to travel around the moon does not even have to be raised here; it is entirely irrelevant. Even if it could be shown that a journey to another celestial body were absolutely incompatible with the known laws of nature, a proposition about the other side of the moon would still be meaningful. (354)

In effect, in the context of "possibly be verified," "possibly" is understood by Schlick in a broad sense, so as to outrun, say, what is merely consistent with the laws of nature. In this particular example, statements about the far side of the moon are verifiable, even if the laws of nature rule against anyone undertaking some such journey so as to verify such statements. Finally, when it comes to "logical" possibility, similar to the empiricist approach to mathematics discussed below, Schlick seeks to ground this in linguistic conventions, rules governing the use of language.

In the above passage, Russell does not condemn statements as meaningless if they cannot be verified or, likewise, if they lack definite implications for experience. Rather, Russell seemed content to regard any non-verifiable content as outside the bounds of a properly scientific view of the world, given that such content would go beyond what could be verified by way of experience. Nonetheless, this kind of maneuver was not far away; in particular, one might suppose that if meaning indeed consists in conditions for verification, then if some statement cannot, in principle, be verified or, more generally, lacks definite implications for experience, that statement (or apparent statement) should be condemned as meaningless, a kind of verbiage without meaning. This, in effect, is a position that the logical empiricists endorsed. Moreover, as we will see, they used this condition for meaningfulness to raise concerns about much traditional philosophy and, likewise, to support an alternative conception of the proper aims and methods of philosophical inquiry.

In this context, it is worth recalling how Wittgenstein used certain ideas about language, meaning, and reality to argue that much of traditional philosophy attempts to say what cannot be said. On Wittgenstein's view, the problem is not that traditional philosophy says things that are false, or says things that cannot be known to be true or false. Rather, the problem is that traditional philosophy fails to say anything at all. Wittgenstein seemed to hold that ethics and metaphysics could be of some value, but this value could not consist in describing the world. As suggested in Chapter 7, on one way of presenting Wittgenstein's critique of traditional philosophy, the problem is that all meaningful discourse falls into one of three categories—namely, all

Early Analytic Philosophy

meaningful discourse consists of tautologies and contradictions (which say nothing about the world), elementary statements or propositions, and truth-functional compounds of elementary statements or propositions. The problem is that putative philosophical statements cannot fit into any of these categories.

The empiricist critique of metaphysics can be understood in a similar way, though with a distinctively epistemological bent. In particular, the empiricist critique can be understood as building on what is sometimes known as "Hume's fork," which is expressed in the following passage from Hume's *Enquiry Concerning Human Understanding* ([1748] 1975):

> All the objects of human reason or enquiry may naturally be divided into two kinds, to wit, *Relations of Ideas*, and *Matters of Fact*. Of the first kind are the sciences of Geometry, Algebra, and Arithmetic... Propositions of this kind are discoverable by the mere operation of thought, without dependence on what is anywhere in the universe. [...] Matters of fact, which are the second objects of human reason, are not ascertained in this manner; nor is our evidence of their truth, however great, of a like nature with the foregoing. The contrary of every matter of fact is still possible; because it can never imply a contradiction. (25)

Hume seems to be saying that all legitimate areas of inquiry and knowledge fall into one of two categories: first, there are those statements or propositions that can be known "by the mere operation of thought"; second, there are those statements or propositions that must be known through experience, through observation. This raises a problem for metaphysics—and perhaps other areas of philosophical inquiry, such as ethics—given that metaphysical statements fall into neither category: they are neither "analytic," concerning mere "relations of ideas"; nor do they concern "matters of fact," such that they can be known through empirical observation.

Logical empiricists endorsed this kind of picture and moreover used an empiricist view of knowledge to furnish a condition for meaningfulness. First, as we will see below, the empiricists typically held that the truths of mathematics and logic are analytic and record conventions to use symbols in a certain way. Second, they held that in order for a non-analytic sentence to say something that is true or false, it must be verifiable, roughly in that it must have some implications for experience and observation. This is the so-called "verificationist criterion of meaning." The problem, however, is that the sentences of metaphysics fall into neither category: the metaphysician does not intend to be putting forward purely analytic statements that hold in

Logical Empiricism: Meaning, Metaphysics, and Mathematics 367

virtue of linguistic conventions; nor, however, do the sentences of metaphysics seem to have empirical or observational implications. In the latter case, Carnap develops the critique of metaphysics in "The Elimination of Metaphysics..." by distinguishing two ways in which one may generate a "pseudo-statement"—a sentence that appears to say something that can be evaluated as true or false, but in fact fails to do so. First, the sentence may include a word that lacks empirical conditions for application. Carnap suggests that words like "principle" and "God" are often used in such a way, so that there are no definitive empirical, observational conditions for their application. This line of criticism is similar to Hume's critique of words like "cause" and "substance," the putative meanings of which, he argued, cannot be traced back to immediate experience (what Hume called "impressions"). Second, Carnap suggests that a sentence may amount to a "pseudo-statement" not in virtue of containing "metaphysical words," but in virtue of containing meaningful words combined in counter-meaningful ways. For example, Carnap claims that Heidegger was guilty of producing such "pseudo-statements" in his use of sentences containing the expression "nothing" and its cognates.

The notion of a "pseudo-statement" may seem strange: how can a sentence, to all appearances, seem to say something true or false, but in fact fail to do so? Well, we just saw two ways that, according to Carnap, this can happen. More generally, it is useful to recall Russell's theory of descriptions from Chapter 5. Take sentences like "The present King of France is bald" or "Bismarck was a German politician." These seem to have a subject-predicate form; they seem to be ascribing a property to an individual object. According to Russell, this is a mistake, since on his preferred analysis, both of these are in fact quantificational statements, statements about the quantity of things to which one or more predicate applies. It is because of this that Wittgenstein remarked in the *Tractatus* that it was "Russell's merit is to have shown that the apparent logical form of the proposition need not be its real form" (4.0031). Ayer, Carnap, and Wittgenstein took this idea one step further in claiming that a sentence can exhibit all of the superficial signs of being meaningful, being evaluable as true or false, and yet fail to do so. For empiricists like Ayer and Carnap, this was essentially because a sentence can be formed in a grammatically correct way but fail to have empirical consequences and so fail to conform to the verificationist criterion of meaning.

As we saw in Chapter 4 when discussing Frege's distinction between sense and reference, there are various things that one may mean when speaking

Early Analytic Philosophy

about "meaning." In denying that the sentences of metaphysics are meaningful, neither Carnap nor Ayer wishes to maintain that there is no sense of "meaning" under which the pronouncements that one finds, say, in Bradley's *Appearance and Reality* are meaningful. In particular, while they deny that metaphysical sentences (as well as the sentences that figure in ethical discourse) are meaningful in the sense of being evaluable as true or false (which they equate with being verifiable, having implications for experience and observation), they allow that such sentences may be meaningful in the sense that they may stir up emotions and feelings, roughly in the same way as poetic discourse. The problem is that this is not how the metaphysician views his or her work: metaphysicians offer arguments for their positions, and in doing so presuppose that the sentences they utter are meaningful in the sense of being evaluable as true or false. Thus Carnap writes:

> But in the case of metaphysics we find this situation: through the form of its works it pretends to be something that it is not. The form in question is that of a system of statements which are apparently related as premises and conclusions, that is, the form of a theory. In this way the fiction of theoretical content is generated, whereas, as we have seen, there is no such content. [. . .] The harmonious feeling or attitude, which the metaphysician tries to express in a monistic system, is more clearly expressed in the music of Mozart... Metaphysicians are musicians without musical ability. (79–80)

Similarly, in "The Scientific Conception of the World. . .," Hahn, Neurath, and Carnap write that:

> Analysis shows that these statements [namely, those of traditional metaphyiscs] say nothing but merely express a certain mood and spiit. To express such feelings for life can be a significant task. But the proper medium for doing so is art... It is dangerous to choose the linguistic garb of a theory instead: a theoretical content is simulated where none exists.

In other words, the metaphysician attempts to express, in declarative, seemingly truth-evaluable sentences, what could be better expressed through an artistic medium like music, poetry, or painting.

Given the rejection of metaphysics, logical empiricists sought to provide a role for philosophy whereby philosophy could yet somehow constitute a genuine branch of knowledge. On the one hand, they believed that philosophy could not function alongside empirical science as furnishing some further sort of supra-empirical knowledge. As Hahn, Neurath, and Carnap put it, "there is no such thing as philosophy as a basic or universal science alongside or above the various fields of the one empirical science" ([1929] 1973). On the other

Logical Empiricism: Meaning, Metaphysics, and Mathematics   369

hand, however, the empiricists did not intend to dismiss all of philosophy as nonsense. While differing in details, the basic strategy that they employed was to think of philosophy as the analysis of scientific discourse—a project aimed, in part, at clarifying scientific (and ordinary) concepts, showing how the various sciences fit together to provide a coherent picture of the world, along with a clarification and analysis of epistemological concepts related to knowledge and justification. As far as a positive conception of philosophy goes, this—perhaps like Wittgenstein's conception of philosophical inquiry in the *Tractatus*—is apt to leave some disappointed. However, given the rejection of philosophy as affording some kind of supra-empirical knowledge, and a commitment to natural science, and observation more generally, as a paradigmatic source of knowledge, the empiricists maintained that any more robust role for philosophy would inevitably devolve into speculative metaphysics. Rather, they took the view of philosophy as the analysis of scientific discourse to provide a way in which philosophy could be relevant to the progress of science and contribute to a scientific understanding of the world.

The empiricist critique of metaphysics raises a number of questions. One concerns just how much traditional philosophy should indeed condemned as meaningless, given the verificationist condition for a sentence to be evaluable as true or false. But a further issue—and perhaps a more important one—is the status of the verificationist criterion of meaning itself. A basic aim of the empiricists was to formulate such a criterion so that while traditional metaphysics can be condemned as meaningless, scientific discourse comes out as perfectly meaningful. Unfortunately, it proved difficult to lay down a criterion that could meet both of these desiderata.[2] Among the problems that they encountered is that much scientific discourse does not, at least not obviously, concern that which is immediately available in experience and so directly verifiable. For example, scientific laws may take the form of universally quantified statements—statements of the form for all x, if x is F, then x is G— which cannot be conclusively verified on the basis of a finite number of experiences or observations. Similarly, science includes myriad "theoretical entities"—entities like electrons, for example—that cannot be directly observed or experienced. Finally, science includes an array of dispositional concepts—concepts like fragility—that concern, at least in part, what would happen if something else were to happen, which cannot be easily rendered into discourse about what is available to experience and observation. Given

---

[2]For a detailed examination of these issues, see Hempel 1950.

these sorts of issues, any plausible verificationist view of meaning will have to maintain, it seems, that meaningfulness has to do with relevance to experience, with in some sense having empirical implications. The problem is then spelling out this "in some sense" in a way that secures the meaningfulness of scientific discourse, while condemning metaphysics as meaningless. Again, however, it proved difficult to articulate the notion of relevance to experience and observation in a way that could satisfy both desiderata.[3]

A further issue concerns the status of the verificationist theory of meaning itself. As we saw, the empiricists divided all meaningful discourse into two categories: the analytic and contradictory sentences on the one hand, and empirically relevant discourse on the other hand. The problem is that the verificationist theory of meaning and the idea that a sentence is evaluable as true or false only if it is in some sense relevant to experience does not fit neatly into either category: it does not seem analytic; nor, however, does it seem to be the sort of thing that can be verified by way of empirical tests. Given this, it may seem that the verificationist theory of meaning is self-undermining, in that if it is true, it is itself meaningless and so cannot be evaluated as true or false.

One way in which empiricists responded to this challenge was to accept that the criterion of meaning is itself neither true nor false, but to then give an account under which it is nonetheless in better shape than metaphysical sentences. On Carnap's approach, for example, the verificationist criterion of meaning should be regarded as a pragmatic recommendation: it does not concern some mind-independent facts about meaning, but is rather a recommendation about how we should speak about meaning, one that we can have pragmatic reasons to adopt. The reader is encouraged to think about this issue further and whether, for example, regarding the verificationist criterion as a kind of pragmatic recommendation really does justice to controversies in the theory of meaning and the use that empiricists made of the verificationist theory to condemn much traditional philosophy.

---

[3] A related issue is that the empiricists typically supposed that all meaningful discourse could somehow be reduced to statements about what is immediately given in experience (though they had various different views about just what is given in this way). This, in turn, played a role in the empiricist desire for "unified science," that all science might be based on experience and observation. Some have argued, in contrast, that nothing is immediately given in the way that the empiricists seemed to suppose; see, for example, Wilfrid Sellars's (1912–1989) "Empiricism and the Philosophy of Mind" (1956). Likewise, some have argued that individual statements, as opposed to whole scientific theories or outlooks, simply do not have definite implications for experience, immediate or otherwise; see, for example, Quine's "Two Dogmas of Empiricism," presented in Chapter 10.

Ethical discourse

Back in Chapter 3, we considered Moore's critique of "naturalistic" theories of goodness, according to which goodness just means some "natural" property like causing happiness, being what it is desirable to desire, and so on. Upon rejecting all such attempts to define goodness, Moore inferred that goodness must be a simple, non-analyzable property, the presence of which can only be known through a kind of intellectual intuition. This kind of position is antithetical to the empiricism endorsed by Ayer, Carnap, and others. Yet the empiricists generally agreed with Moore's premise concerning the indefinability of goodness and other ethical concepts. Consider, for example, the following passage from Ayer's *Language, Truth, and Logic,* which is reminiscent of Moore's "open question" argument against naturalistic theories of ethics:

> We reject the subjectivist view that to call an action right, or a thing good, is to say that it is generally approved of, because it is not self-contradictory to assert that some actions which are generally approved of are not right, or that some things which are generally approved of are not good. [...] We cannot agree that to call an action right is to say that of all the actions possible in the circumstances it would cause, or be likely cause, the greatest happiness... because we find that it is not self-contradictory to say that it is sometimes wrong to perform the action which would actually or probably cause the greatest happiness. (104–5)

However, unlike Moore, Ayer does not infer that goodness is a simple, unanalyzable property and, moreover, a property that can only be known via some form of intellectual intuition. Rather, Ayer responds to the "absolutist" position associated with Moore:

> We [admit] that the fundamental ethical concepts are unanalyzable... But unlike the absolutists, we are able to give an explanation of this fact about ethical concepts. We say that the reason why they are unanalyzable is that they are mere pseudo-concepts. The presence of an ethical symbol in a proposition adds nothing to its factual content. If I say to someone, "You acted wrongly in stealing that money", I am not stating anything more than if I had simply says, "You stole that money".... I am simply evincing my moral disapproval of it. It is as if I had said, "You stole that money", in a peculiar tone of horror, or written it with the addition of some special exclamation mark... in saying that a certain type of action is right or wrong, I am not making any factual statement, not even a statement about my own state of mind. I am merely expressing certain moral sentiments. (107)

Early Analytic Philosophy

This is sometimes referred to as an "emotivist" theory of ethical discourse. On this kind of position, the function of ethical discourse is not to describe the world, but rather to express feelings of approval and disapproval and, more generally, to express emotions. To say that something is wrong, on this kind of position, is not to describe the action or event, but is rather a matter of expressing approval or disapproval towards that action or event. As Ayer puts it, to say that "You acted wrongly in stealing that money" is like saying that the action or event occurred—like saying "You stole that money"—in a certain tone of voice. A tone of voice may express a negative emotion towards the action or event so described, but does not add further descriptive content that can be evaluated as true or false.

It is again useful to recall Russell's theory of descriptions and the idea that the ordinary grammatical form of a sentence may not mirror its underlying logical form. In the present case, the idea is that while certain sentences seem to ascribe properties to actions or events—namely, sentences that use predicates like "is good" and "is wrong"—such sentences and the predicates they use are in fact doing something different entirely. Rather, according to Ayer and other emotivists, the function of predicates like "is good" and "is wrong" is not to describe but rather to function more like exclamation points and related devices (such as different tones of voice). To the extent that such expressions have "meaning," this is a kind of non-descriptive meaning, comparable to the sense in which an exclamation point or a certain tone of voice may be said to have a "meaning." Given Ayer's agreement with Moore about, in effect, the irreducibility of moral discourse to empirical discourse, this is a natural position for an empiricist to take, as it provides a role for ethical language but without conceding that the function of this language is to describe some non-empirical or non-observable realm of ethical facts.

The emotivist strategy for dealing with ethical language within an empiricist framework raises a number of issues, some of which Ayer recognizes. Among these questions is the extent to which the emotivist framework can account for apparent ethical disagreements, which seem unintelligible if ethical discourse cannot be evaluated as true or false. More generally, a core question is whether an emotivist can do full justice to the fact that ethical discourse and ethical predicates certainly seem to function descriptively, seem to function to describe actions and events in the world. While Ayer addresses some concerns in this vicinity, the reader is encouraged to reflect on these issues and whether, for example, an emotivist view of ethical discourse can indeed account for apparent disagreements over what is right and wrong. We will return to some

Logical Empiricism: Meaning, Metaphysics, and Mathematics

related issues in Chapter 11. We also note, moreover, that Ayer's emotivism, while perhaps a natural route for an empiricist to take, was not uniformly endorsed by those in the logical empiricist movement.[4]

Philosophy of mathematics and logic

Empiricist philosophy maintains, in one form or another, that experience and observation is the central, and perhaps the only, source of genuine knowledge about the world. Given this, empiricist philosophy has often had difficulty accounting for mathematics and logic, which do not seem be epistemically grounded in experience and observation in the way that, say, biology and physics are epistemically grounded in experience and observation. However, given their healthy respect for science and the role of mathematics and logic in science, empiricists have typically not been willing to dismiss mathematics and logic as meaningless or, similarly, unknowable. Now, some empiricists, such as John Stuart Mill (1806–73) sought to show that mathematics and logic are, in fact, epistemically grounded in experience. Unfortunately, following Frege and Russell, the logical empiricists found this kind of position untenable. Here is Russell describing the situation in *The Problems of Philosophy* (1912):

> All pure mathematics is a priori, like logic. This was strenuously denied by the empiricist philosophers... They maintained that the repeated experience of seeing two things and two other things, and finding that together they made four things, were led by induction to the conclusion that two things and two other things would always make four things altogether. If, however, this were the source of our knowledge that two and two are four, we should proceed differently, in persuading ourselves of its truth, from the way in which we do actually proceed. In fact, a certain number of instances are needed to make us think of two abstractly, rather than of two coins or two books or two people... But as soon as we are able to divest our thoughts of irrelevant particularity, we become able to see the general principle that two and two are four; any one instance is seen to be typical, and the examination of other instances becomes unnecessary.

Russell is pointing out that among the problems with trying to explain mathematical knowledge in terms of some finite number of experiences or observations is that it conflicts with actual practice. We do not think, for

---

[4]See, for example, Schlick [1930] 1939.

Early Analytic Philosophy

example, that repeated observations that one thing together with one other thing (say, one apple and another apple) yields two things make us more confident that $1 + 1 = 2$, which it should if $1 + 1 = 2$ is regarded as an empirical generalization over observed instances. Ayer provides related reasons for doubting the Millian attempt to understand mathematics and logic within an empiricist framework, and related critiques were developed earlier by Frege in *The Foundations of Arithmetic*.

Instead, the logical empiricists typically opted for a position more akin to that of Hume. In particular, recall that for Hume, "all the objects of human reason or enquiry may naturally be divided into two kinds, to wit, *Relations of Ideas*, and *Matters of Fact*." Drawing in part from Wittgenstein, the logical empiricists held that mathematics and logic, rather than concerning facts about mathematical objects or properties, concern what Hume regarded as "relations of ideas" or, more specifically, the determination to use symbols in a certain way. For Ayer and others, this kind of approach could simultaneously address a number of concerns facing an empiricist view of mathematics and logic. For instance, it seems to account for the *a priori* character of these areas of inquiry—they are independent of experience precisely because they are not about the world but rather about conventions governing the use of certain symbols. Likewise, Ayer believed that the view of mathematics and logic as consisting of nothing but analytic truths could account for the apparent necessity of mathematical and logical truths. He put this as follows:

> The principles of logic and mathematics are true universally simply because we never allow them to be anything else. And the reason for this is that we cannot abandon them without contradicting ourselves, without sinning against the rules which govern the use of language... the truths of logic and mathematics are analytic propositions or tautologies. (77)

> [Analytic propositions] simply record our determination to use words in a certain fashion. We cannot deny them without infringing on the conventions which are presupposed by our very denial, and so falling into self-contradiction. And this is the sole ground of their necessity. As Wittgenstein puts it, our justification for holding that the world could not conceivably disobey the laws of logic is simply that we could not say of an unlogical world how it would look. (84)

The dialectic here can be described as follows. On one way of construing empiricism, it is a central tenet of an empiricist position that there are no "synthetic *a priori*" truths—truths about the world but that can be known

Logical Empiricism: Meaning, Metaphysics, and Mathematics 375

independently of experience. On the present approach, the statements that figure in mathematics and logic are *a priori*, but they are not synthetic, since they are not about a realm of mathematical and logical objects and properties. Rather, they are analytic, and on the empiricist view of analyticity, analytic truths are themselves grounded in conventions governing the use of symbols.

The empiricist view of mathematics and logic as analytic raises a number of issues. One issue, which is to some extent addressed by Ayer, is whether it can really do justice to mathematical and logical discourse and inquiry, such as the fact that mathematicians and logicians can be genuinely surprised by the results at which they arrive. A further issue is that the present strategy for dealing with mathematics and logic turns on the notion of an analytic truth and the corresponding idea of analytic truths as grounded in conventions. However, as we will see in Chapter 10, the very notion of analytic truth, and the distinction between analytic and synthetic truths, faces important objections.

Concluding remarks

Logical empiricism is sometimes regarded as outdated, a curious but forgettable error in the analytic tradition. Thus in 1967, John Passmore (1914–2004) wrote that "Logical Positivism, then, is dead, or as a dead as a philosophical movement ever becomes" (56). It is true that certain doctrines central to the movement—especially, perhaps, the verificationist criterion of meaning—have been widely rejected. Nonetheless, it should first be marked that some of the most influential critiques of logical empiricist ideas came from within the movement itself and, at least in some cases, were consistent with an overarching empiricist philosophy. Moreover, the themes that occupied the empiricists continue to play a role in much contemporary discussion, especially in the philosophy of science, epistemology, and philosophy of mind.[5] Likewise, the broadly naturalistic approach that characterized the empiricist movement—the idea of science as a paradigm of knowledge, the idea that philosophy ought to be consistent with science and part of the scientific enterprise—continues to provide the background for much work in contemporary analytic philosophy.

---

[5]For discussion of the influence of logical empiricist ideas on contemporary disputes in the philosophy of mind and the metaphysics of physicalism, see Morris 2018.

Further reading

Primary sources

Ayer, A. J. ([1936–7] 1959b), "Verification and Experience", in A. J. Ayer (ed.), *Logical Positivism*, New York: The Free Press.

Carnap, R. ([1928] 1967), *The Logical Structure of the World*, Berkeley: University of California Press.

Carnap, R. (1936–7), "Testability and Meaning", *Philosophy of Science* 3: 419–71 and 4: 1–40.

Hempel, C. (1950), "Problems and Changes in the Empiricist Criterion of Meaning", *Revenue Internationale de Philosophie* 11: 41–63.

Neurath, O. ([1931–2] 1959), "Sociology and Physicalism", in A. J. Ayer (ed.), *Logical Positivism*, New York: The Free Press.

Schlick, M. ([1930] 1939), *Problems of Ethics*, New York: Prentice-Hall.

Schlick, M. ([1934] 1959), "The Foundation of Knowledge", in A. J. Ayer (ed.), *Logical Positivism*, New York: The Free Press.

Secondary sources

Ayer, A. J. (1959a), "Editor's Introduction", in A .J. Ayer (ed.), *Logical Positivism*, New York: The Free Press.

Creath, R. (2017), "Logical Empiricism", *Stanford Encyclopedia of Philosophy*. Available online: https://plato.stanford.edu/entries/logical-empiricism/

Edmonds, D. (2020), *The Murder of Professor Schlick*, Princeton: Princeton University Press.

Rogers, B. (1999), *A. J. Ayer: A Life*, New York: Grove Press.

Sigmund, Karl. (2017), *Exact Thinking in Demented Times*, New York: Basic Books.

Uebel, T. (2019), "Vienna Circle", *Stanford Encyclopedia of Philosophy*. Available online: https://plato.stanford.edu/entries/vienna-circ

Readings

Schlick, M. "Meaning and Verification".
Reprinted from Schlick, M. (1936), "Meaning and Verification", *The Philosophical Review* 45: 339–69.

I

Philosophical questions, as compared with ordinary scientific problems, are always strangely paradoxical. But it seems to be an especially strange paradox that the question concerning the meaning of a proposition should constitute a serious philosophical difficulty. For is it not the very nature and purpose of every proposition to express its own meaning? In fact, when we are confronted with a proposition (in a language familiar to us) we usually know its meaning immediately. If we do not, we can have it explained to us, but the explanation will consist of a new proposition; and if the new one is capable of expressing the meaning, why should not the original one be capable of it? So that a snippy person when asked what he meant by a certain statement might be perfectly justified in saying, 'I meant exactly what I said!'.

It is logically legitimate and actually the normal way in ordinary life and even in science to answer a question concerning the meaning of a proposition by simply repeating it either more distinctly or in slightly different words. Under what circumstances, then, can there be any sense in asking for the meaning of a statement which is well before our eyes or ears?

Evidently the only possibility is that we have not *understood* it. And in this case what is actually before our eyes or ears is nothing but a series of words which we are unable to handle; we do not know how to use it, how to 'apply it to reality'. Such a series of words is for us simply a complex of signs 'without meaning', a mere sequel of sounds or a mere row of marks on paper, and we have no right to call it 'a proposition' at all; we may perhaps speak of it as 'a sentence'.

If we adopt this terminology we can now easily get rid of our paradox by saying that we cannot inquire after the meaning of a proposition, but can ask about the meaning of a sentence, and that this amounts to asking, 'What proposition does the sentence stand for?'. And this question is answered either by a proposition in a language with which we are already perfectly familiar; or by indicating the logical rules which will make a proposition out of the sentence, i.e., will tell us exactly in what circumstances the sentence is to be *used*. These two methods do not actually differ in principle; both of them give meaning to the sentence (transform it into a proposition) by locating it, as it were, within the system of a definite language; the first method making use of a language which is already in our possession, the second one building it up for us. The first method represents the simplest kind of ordinary 'translation'; the second one affords a deeper insight into the nature of meaning, and will have to be used in order to overcome philosophical difficulties connected with the understanding of sentences.

The source of these difficulties is to be found in the fact that very often we do not know how to handle our own words; we speak or write without having first agreed upon a definite logical grammar which will constitute the signification of our terms. We commit the mistake of thinking that we know the meaning of a sentence (i.e., understand it as a proposition) if we are familiar with all the words occurring in it. But this is not sufficient. It will not lead to confusion or error as long as we remain in the domain of everyday life by which our words have been formed and to which they are adapted, but it will become fatal the moment we try to think about abstract problems by means of the same terms without carefully fixing their signification for the new purpose. For every word has a definite signification only within a definite context into which it has been fitted; in any other context it will have no meaning unless we provide new rules for the use of the word in the new case, and this may be done, at least in principle, quite arbitrarily.

Let us consider an example. If a friend should say to me, 'Take me to a country where the sky is three times as blue as in England!' I should not know how to fulfill his wish; his phrase I would appear nonsensical to me, because the word 'blue' is used in a way which is not provided for by the rules of our language. The combination of a numeral and the name of a color does not occur in it; therefore my friend's sentence has no meaning, although its exterior linguistic form is that of a command or a wish. But he can, of course, give it a meaning. If I ask him, 'What do you mean by "three times as blue"?', he can arbitrarily indicate certain definite physical circumstances concerning the serenity of the sky which he wants his phrase to be the description of. And then, perhaps, I shall be able to follow his directions; his wish will have become meaningful for me.

Thus, whenever we ask about a sentence, 'What does it mean?', what we expect is instruction as to the circumstances in which the sentence is to be used; we want a description of the conditions under which the sentence will form a *true* proposition, and of those which will make it *false*. The meaning of a word or a combination of words is, in this way, determined by a set of rules which regulate their use and which, following Wittgenstein, we may call the rules of their grammar, taking this word in its widest sense.

Logical Empiricism: Meaning, Metaphysics, and Mathematics

(If the preceding remarks about meaning are as correct as I am convinced they are, this will, to a large measure, be due to conversations with Wittgenstein which have greatly influenced my own views about these matters. I can hardly exaggerate my indebtedness to this philosopher. I do not wish to impute to him any responsibility for the contents of this article, but I have reason to hope that he will agree with the main substance of it.)

Stating the meaning of a sentence amounts to stating the rules according to which the sentence is to be used, and this is the same as stating the way in which it can be verified (or falsified). The meaning of a proposition is the method of its verification.

The 'grammatical' rules will partly consist of ordinary definitions, i.e., explanations of words by means of other words, partly of what are called 'ostensive' definitions, i.e., explanations by means of a procedure which puts the words to actual use. The simplest form of an ostensive definition is a pointing gesture combined with the pronouncing of the word, as when we teach a child the signification of the sound 'blue' by showing a blue object. But in most cases the ostensive definition is of a more complicated form; we cannot point to an object corresponding to words like 'because', 'immediate', 'chance', 'again', etc. In these cases we require the presence of certain complex situations, and the meaning of the words is defined by the way we use them in these different situations.

It is clear that in order to understand a verbal definition we must know the signification of the explaining words beforehand, and that the only explanation which can work without any previous knowledge is the ostensive definition. We conclude that there is no way of understanding any meaning without ultimate reference to ostensive definitions, and this means, in an obvious sense, reference to 'experience' or 'possibility of verification'.

This is the situation, and nothing seems to me simpler or less questionable. It is this situation and nothing else that we describe when we affirm that the meaning of a proposition can be given only by giving the rules of its verification in experience. (The addition, 'in experience', is really superfluous, as no other kind of verification has been defined.)

This view has been called the "experimental theory of meaning"; but it certainly is no theory at all, for the term 'theory' is used for a set of hypotheses about a certain subject-matter, and there are no hypotheses involved in our view, which proposes to be nothing but a simple statement of the way in which meaning is actually assigned to propositions, both in everyday life and in science. There has never been any other way, and it would be a grave error to suppose that we believe we have discovered a new conception of meaning which is

Early Analytic Philosophy

contrary to common opinion and which we want to introduce into philosophy. On the contrary, our conception is not only entirely in agreement with, but even derived from, common sense and scientific procedure. Although our criterion of meaning has always been employed in practice, it has very rarely been formulated in the past, and this is perhaps the only excuse for the attempts of so many philosophers to deny its feasibility.

The most famous case of an explicit formulation of our criterion is Einstein's answer to the question, What do we mean when we speak of two events at distant places happening simultaneously? This answer consisted in a description of an experimental method by which the simultaneity of such events was actually ascertained. Einstein's philosophical opponents maintained—and some of them still maintain—that they knew the meaning of the above question independently of any method of verification. All I am trying to do is to stick consistently to Einstein's position and to admit no exceptions from it. (Professor Bridgman's book on *The Logic of Modern Physics* is an admirable attempt to carry out this program for all concepts of physics.) I am not writing for those who think that Einstein's philosophical opponents were right.

II

Professor C. I. Lewis, in a remarkable address on "Experience and Meaning" (published in this *Review*, March 1934), has justly stated that the view developed above (he speaks of it as the "empirical-meaning requirement") forms the basis of the whole philosophy of what has been called the "logical positivism of the Viennese Circle". He criticizes this basis as inadequate chiefly on the ground that its acceptance would impose certain limitations upon "significant philosophic discussion" which, at some points, would make such discussion altogether impossible and, at other points, restrict it to an intolerable extent.

Feeling responsible as I do for certain features of the Viennese philosophy (which I should prefer to call Consistent Empiricism), and being of the opinion that it really does not impose any restrictions upon significant philosophizing at all, I shall try to examine Professor Lewis's chief arguments and point out why I think that they do not endanger our position—at least as far as I can answer for it myself. All of my own arguments will be derived from the statements made in section I.

Professor Lewis describes the empirical-meaning requirement as demanding "that any concept put forward or any proposition asserted shall have a definite denotation; that it shall be intelligible not only verbally and logically but in the further sense that one can specify those empirical items which would determine the applicability of the concept or constitute the verification of the proposition" (loc. cit. 125). Here it seems to me that there is no justification for the words "but in the *further* sense . . .", i.e., for the distinction of two (or three?) senses of intelligibility. The remarks in section I. show that, according to our opinion, 'verbal and logical' understanding *consists in* knowing how the proposition in question could be verified. For, unless we mean by 'verbal understanding' that we know how the words are actually used, the term could hardly mean anything but a shadowy feeling of being acquainted with the words, and in a philosophical discussion it does not seem advisable to call such a feeling 'understanding'. Similarly, I should not advise that we speak of a sentence as being 'logically intelligible' when we just feel convinced that its exterior form is that of a proper proposition (if, e.g. it has the form, substantive—copula—adjective, and therefore appears to predicate a property of a thing). For it seems to me that by such a phrase we want to say much *more*, namely, that we are completely aware of the whole grammar of the sentence, i.e., that we know exactly the circumstances to which it is fitted. Thus knowledge of how a proposition is verified is not anything over and above its verbal and logical understanding, but is identical with it. It seems to me, therefore, that when we demand that a proposition be verifiable we are not adding a new requirement but are simply formulating the conditions which have actually always been acknowledged as necessary for meaning and intelligibility.

The mere statement that no sentence has meaning unless we are able to indicate a way of testing its truth or falsity is not very useful if we do not explain very carefully the signification of the phrases 'method of testing' and 'verifiability'. Professor Lewis is quite right when he asks for such an explanation. He himself suggests some ways in which it might be given, and I am glad to say that his suggestions appear to me to be in perfect agreement with my own views and those of my philosophical friends. It will be easy to show that there is no serious divergence between the point of view of the pragmatist as Professor Lewis conceives it and that of the Viennese Empiricist. And if in some special questions they arrive at different conclusions, it may be hoped that a careful examination will bridge the difference.

How do we define verifiability?

In the first place I should like to point out that when we say that "a proposition has meaning only if it is verifiable" we are not saying ". . . if it is verified". This simple remark does away with one of the chief objections; the "here and now predicament", as Professor Lewis calls it, does not exist any more. We fall into the snares of this predicament only if we regard verification itself as the criterion of meaning, instead of 'possibility of verification' (= verifiability); this would

Early Analytic Philosophy

indeed lead to a "reduction to absurdity of meaning". Obviously the predicament arises through some fallacy by which these two notions are confounded. I do not know if Russell's statement, "Empirical knowledge is confined to what we actually observe" (quoted by Professor Lewis loc. cit. 130), must be interpreted as containing this fallacy, but it would certainly be worth while to discover its genesis.

Let us consider the following argument which Professor Lewis discusses (131), but which he does not want to impute to anyone:

> Suppose it maintained that no issue is meaningful unless it can be put to the test of decisive verification. And no verification can take place except in the immediately present experience of the subject. Then nothing can be meant except what is actually present in the experience in which that meaning is entertained.

This argument has the form of a conclusion drawn from two premisses. Let us for the moment assume the second premiss to be meaningful and true. You will observe that even then the conclusion does *not* follow. For the first premiss assures us that the issue has meaning if it *can* be verified; the verification does not have to take place, and therefore it is quite irrelevant whether it can take place in the future or in the present only. Apart from this, the second premiss is, of course, nonsensical; for what fact could possibly be described by the sentence 'verification can take place only in present experience'? Is not verifying an act or process like hearing or feeling bored? Might we not just as well say that I can hear or feel bored only in the present moment? And what could I mean by this? The particular nonsense involved in such phrases will become clearer when we speak of the 'egocentric predicament' later on; at present we are content to know that our empirical-meaning postulate has nothing whatever to do with the now-predicament. 'Verifiable' does not even mean 'verifiable here now'; much less does it mean 'being verified now'.

Perhaps it will be thought that the only way of making sure of the verifiability of a proposition would consist in its actual verification. But we shall soon see that this is not the case.

There seems to be a great temptation to connect meaning and the 'immediately given' in the wrong way; and some of the Viennese positivists may have yielded to this temptation, thereby getting dangerously near to the fallacy we have just been describing. Parts of Carnap's *Logischer Aufbau der Welt*, for instance, might be interpreted as implying that a proposition about future events did not really refer to the future at all but asserted only the present existence of certain expectations (and, similarly, speaking about the past would really mean

Logical Empiricism: Meaning, Metaphysics, and Mathematics   **383**

speaking about present memories). But it is certain that the author of that book does not hold such a view now, and that it cannot be regarded as a teaching of the new positivism. On the contrary, we have pointed out from the beginning that our definition of meaning does not imply such absurd consequences, and when someone asked, "But how can you verify a proposition about a future event?", we replied, "Why, for instance, by waiting for it to happen! 'Waiting' is a perfectly legitimate method of verification."

* * *

Thus I think that everybody—including the Consistent Empiricist—agrees that it would be nonsense to say, 'We can mean nothing but the immediately given'. If in this sentence we replace the word 'mean' by the word 'know' we arrive at a statement similar to Bertrand Russell's mentioned above. The temptation to formulate phrases of this sort arises, I believe, from a certain ambiguity of the verb 'to know' which is the source of many metaphysical troubles and to which, therefore, I have often had to call attention on other occasions (see e.g. *Allgemeine Erkenntnislehre* 2nd ed. 1925, Section 12). In the first place the word may stand simply for 'being aware of a datum', i.e. for the mere presence of a feeling, a color, a sound, etc.; and if the word 'knowledge' is taken in this sense the assertion 'Empirical knowledge is confined to what we actually observe' does not say anything at all, but is a mere tautology. (This case, I think, would correspond to what Professor Lewis calls "identity-theories" of the "knowledge-relation". Such theories, resting on a tautology of this kind, would be empty verbiage without significance.)

In the second place the word 'knowledge' may be used in one of the significant meanings which it has in science and ordinary life; and in this case Russell's assertion would obviously (as Professor Lewis remarked) be false. Russell himself, as is well known, distinguishes between 'knowledge by acquaintance' and 'knowledge by description', but perhaps it should be noted that this distinction does not entirely coincide with the one we have been insisting upon just now.

* * *

III

Verifiability means possibility of verification. Professor Lewis justly remarks that to "omit all examination of the wide range of significance which could attach to 'possible verification', would be to leave the whole conception rather obscure" (loc. cit. 137). For our purpose it suffices to distinguish between two of the

Early Analytic Philosophy

many ways in which the word 'possibility' is used. We shall call them 'empirical possibility' and 'logical possibility'. Professor Lewis describes two meanings of verifiability which correspond exactly to this difference; he is fully aware of it, and there is hardly anything left for me to do but carefully to work out the distinction and show its bearing upon our issue.

I propose to call 'empirically possible' anything that does not contradict the laws of nature. This is, I think, the largest sense in which we may speak of empirical possibility; we do not restrict the term to happenings which are not only in accordance with the laws of nature but also with the actual state of the universe (where 'actual' might refer to the present moment of our own lives, or to the condition of human beings on this planet, and so forth). If we chose the latter definition (which seems to have been in Professor Lewis's mind when he spoke of "possible experience as conditioned by the actual", loc. cit. 141) we should not get the sharp boundaries we need for our present purpose. So 'empirical possibility' is to mean 'compatibility with natural laws'.

Now, since we cannot boast of a complete and sure knowledge of nature's laws, it is evident that we can never assert with certainty the empirical possibility of any fact, and here we may be permitted to speak of *degrees* of possibility. Is it possible for me to lift this book? Surely!—This table? I think so!—This billiard table? I don't think so!—This automobile? Certainly not!—It is clear that in these cases the answer is given by *experience*, as the result of experiments performed in the past. Any judgment about empirical possibility is based on experience and will often be rather uncertain; there will be no sharp boundary between possibility and impossibility.

Is the possibility of verification which we insist upon of this empirical sort? In that case there would be different degrees of verifiability, the question of meaning would be a matter of more or less, not a matter of yes or no. In many disputes concerning our issue it is the empirical possibility of verification which is discussed; the various examples of verifiability given by Professor Lewis, e.g., are instances of different empirical circumstances in which the verification is carried out or prevented from being carried out. Many of those who refuse to accept our criterion of meaning seem to imagine that the procedure of its application in a special case is somewhat like this: A proposition is presented to us ready made, and in order to discover its meaning we have to try various methods of, verifying or falsifying it, and if one of these methods works we have found the meaning of the proposition; but if not, we say it has no meaning. If we really had to proceed in this way, it is clear that the determination of meaning would be entirely a matter of experience, and that in many cases no sharp and ultimate decision could be obtained. How could we ever know that we had tried

Logical Empiricism: Meaning, Metaphysics, and Mathematics 385

long enough, if none of our methods were successful? Might not future efforts disclose a meaning which we were unable to find before?

This whole conception is, of course, entirely erroneous. It speaks of meaning as if it were a kind of entity inherent in a sentence and hidden in it like a nut in its shell, so that the philosopher would have to crack the shell or sentence in order to reveal the nut or meaning. We know from our considerations in section I that a proposition cannot be given 'ready made'; that meaning does not inhere in a sentence where it might be discovered, but that it must be bestowed upon it. And this is done by applying to the sentence the rules of the logical grammar of our language, as explained in section I. These rules are not facts of nature which could be 'discovered', but they are prescriptions stipulated by acts of definition. And these definitions have to be known to those who pronounce the sentence in question and to those who hear or read it. Otherwise they are not confronted with any proposition at all, and there is nothing they could try to verify, because you can't verify or falsify a mere row of words. You cannot even start verifying before you know the meaning, i.e., before you have established the possibility of verification.

In other words, the possibility of verification which is relevant to meaning cannot be of the empirical sort; it cannot be established *post festum*. You have to be sure of it before you can consider the empirical circumstances and investigate whether or no or under what conditions they will permit of verification. The empirical circumstances are all-important when you want to know if a proposition is *true* (which is the concern of the scientist), but they can have no influence on the meaning of the proposition (which is the concern of the philosopher). Professor Lewis has seen and expressed this very clearly (loc. cit. 142, first six lines), and our Vienna positivism, as far as I can answer for it, is in complete agreement with him on this point. It must be emphasized that when we speak of verifiability we mean *logical* possibility of verification, and nothing but this.

* * *

I call a fact or a process 'logically possible' if it can be *described*, i.e., if the sentence which is supposed to describe it obeys the rules of grammar we have stipulated for our language. (I am expressing myself rather incorrectly. A fact which could not be described would, of course, not be any fact at all; any fact is logically possible. But I think my meaning will be understood.) Take some examples. The sentences, 'My friend died the day after tomorrow'; 'The lady wore a dark red dress which was bright green'; 'The campanile is 100 feet and 150 feet high'; 'The child was naked, but wore a long white nightgown', obviously violate the rules which, in ordinary English, govern the use of the words occurring

386   Early Analytic Philosophy

in the sentences. They do not describe any facts at all; they are meaningless, because they represent logical impossibilities.

It is of the greatest importance (not only for our present issue but for philosophical problems in general) to see that whenever we speak of logical impossibility we are referring to a discrepancy between the definitions of our terms and the way in which we use them. We must avoid the severe mistake committed by some of the former Empiricists like Mill and Spencer, who regarded logical principles (e.g. the Law of Contradiction) as laws of nature governing the psychological process of thinking. The nonsensical statements alluded to above do not correspond to thoughts which, by a sort of psychological experiment, we find ourselves unable to think; they do not correspond to any thoughts at all. When we hear the words, 'A tower which is both 100 feet and 150 feet high', the image of two towers of different heights may be in our mind, and we may find it psychologically (empirically) impossible to combine the two pictures into one image, but it is not this fact which is denoted by the words 'logical impossibility'. The height of a tower cannot be 100 feet and 150 feet at the same time; a child cannot be naked and dressed at the same time—not because we are unable to imagine it, but because our definitions of 'height', of the numerals, of the terms 'naked' and 'dressed', are not compatible with the particular combinations of those words in our examples. 'They are not compatible with such combinations' means that the rules of our language have not provided any use for such combinations; they do not describe any fact. We could change these rules, of course, and thereby arrange a meaning for the terms 'both red and green', 'both naked and dressed'; but if we decide to stick to the ordinary definitions (which reveal themselves in the way we actually use our words) we have decided to regard those combined terms as meaningless, i.e., not to use them as the description of *any* fact. Whatever fact we may or may not imagine, if the word 'naked' (or 'red') occurs in its description we have decided that the word 'dressed' (or 'green') cannot be put in its place in the same description. If we do not follow this rule it means that we want to introduce a new definition of the words, or that we don't mind using words without meaning and like to indulge in nonsense. (I am far from condemning this attitude under all circumstances; on certain occasions—as in *Alice in Wonderland*—it may be the only sensible attitude and far more delightful than any treatise on Logic. But in such a treatise we have a right to expect a different attitude.)

The result of our considerations is this: Verifiability, which is the sufficient and necessary condition of meaning, is a possibility of the logical order; it is created by constructing the sentence in accordance with the rules by which its terms are defined. The only case in which verification is (logically) impossible is the

Logical Empiricism: Meaning, Metaphysics, and Mathematics   387

case where you have *made* it impossible by not setting any rules for its verification. Grammatical rules are not found anywhere in nature, but are made by man and are, in principle, arbitrary; so you cannot give meaning to a sentence by discovering a method of verifying it, but only by stipulating how it shall be done. Thus logical possibility or impossibility of verification is always *self-imposed*. If we utter a sentence without meaning it is always *our own fault*.

The tremendous philosophic importance of this last remark will be realized when we consider that what we said about the meaning of *assertions* applies also to the meaning of *questions*. There are, of course, many questions which can never be answered by human beings. But the impossibility of finding the answer may be of two different kinds. If it is merely empirical in the sense defined, if it is due to the chance circumstances to which our human existence is confined, there may be reason to lament our fate and the weakness of our physical and mental powers, but the problem could never be said to be absolutely insoluble, and there would always be some hope, at least for future generations. For the empirical circumstances may alter, human facilities may develop, and even the laws of nature may change (perhaps even suddenly and in such a way that the universe would be thrown open to much more extended investigation). A problem of this kind might be called practically unanswerable or technically unanswerable, and might cause the scientist great trouble, but the philosopher, who is concerned with general principles only, would not feel terribly excited about it.

But what about those questions for which it is *logically* impossible to find an answer? Such problems would remain insoluble under all imaginable circumstances; they would confront us with a definite hopeless *Ignorabimus*; and it is of the greatest importance for the philosopher to know whether there are any such issues. Now it is easy to see from what has been said before that this calamity could happen only if the question itself had no meaning. It would not be a genuine question at all, but a mere row of words with a question-mark at the end. We must say that a question is meaningful, if we can *understand* it, i.e., if we are able to decide for any given proposition whether, if true, it would be an answer to our question. And if this is so, the actual decision could only be prevented by empirical circumstances, which means that it would not be *logically* impossible. Hence no meaningful problem can be insoluble in *principle*. If in any case we find an answer to be logically impossible we know that we really have not been asking anything, that what sounded like a question was actually a nonsensical combination of words. A genuine question is one for which an answer is logically possible. This is one of the most characteristic results of our empiricism. It means that in principle there are no limits to our knowledge. The boundaries which must be acknowledged are of an empirical

Early Analytic Philosophy

nature and, therefore, never ultimate; they can be pushed back further and further; there is no unfathomable mystery in the world.

* * *

The dividing line between logical possibility and impossibility of verification is absolutely sharp and distinct; there is no gradual transition between meaning and nonsense. For either you have given the grammatical rules for verification, or you have not; *tertium non datur.*

Empirical possibility is determined by the laws of nature, but meaning and verifiability are entirely independent of them. Everything that I can describe or define is logically possible—and definitions are in no way bound up with natural laws. The proposition 'Rivers flow uphill' is meaningful, but happens to be false because the fact it describes is *physically* impossible. It will not deprive a proposition of its meaning if the conditions which I stipulate for its verification are incompatible with the laws of nature; I may prescribe conditions, for instance, which could be fulfilled only if the velocity of light were greater than it actually is, or if the Law of Conservation of Energy did not hold, and so forth.

An opponent of our view might find a dangerous paradox or even a contradiction in the preceding explanations, because on the one hand we insisted so strongly on what has been called the "*empirical* meaning requirement", and on the other hand we assert most emphatically that meaning and verifiability do not depend on any empirical conditions whatever, but are determined by purely logical possibilities. The opponent will object: if meaning is a matter of experience, how can it be a matter of definition and logic?

In reality there is no contradiction or difficulty. The word 'experience' is ambiguous. Firstly, it may be a name for any so-called 'immediate data'—which is a comparatively modern use of the word—and secondly we can use it in the sense in which we speak e.g., of an 'experienced traveller', meaning a man who has not only seen a great deal but also knows how to profit from it for his actions. It is in this second sense (by the way, the sense the word has in Hume's and Kant's philosophy) that verifiability must be declared to be independent of experience. The possibility of verification does not rest on any 'experiential truth', on a law of nature or any other true general proposition, but is determined solely by our definitions, by the rules which have been fixed for our language, or which we can fix arbitrarily at any moment. All of these rules ultimately point to ostensive definitions, as we have explained, and through them verifiability is linked to *experience* in the *first* sense of the word. No rule of expression presupposes any law or regularity in the world (which is the condition of 'experience' as Hume and Kant use the word), but it does

Logical Empiricism: Meaning, Metaphysics, and Mathematics 389

presuppose data and situations, to which names can be attached. The rules of language are rules of the application of language; so there must be something to which it can be applied. Expressibility and verifiability are one and the same thing. There is no antagonism between logic and experience. Not only can the logician be an empiricist at the same time; he *must* be one if he wants to understand what he himself is doing.

* * *

IV

Let us glance at some examples in order to illustrate the consequences of our attitude in regard to certain issues of traditional philosophy. Take the famous case of the reality of the other side of the moon (which is also one of Professor Lewis's examples). None of us, I think, would be willing to accept a view according to which it would be nonsense to speak of the averted face of our satellite. 'Can there be the slightest doubt that, according to our explanations, the conditions of meaning are amply satisfied in this case?

I think there can be no doubt. For the question, 'What is the other side of the moon like?', could be answered, for instance, by a description of what would be seen or touched by a person located somewhere behind the moon. The question whether it be physically possible for a human being—or indeed any other living being—to travel around the moon does not even have to be raised here; it is entirely irrelevant. Even if it could be shown that a journey to another celestial body were absolutely incompatible with the known laws of nature, a proposition about the other side of the moon would still be meaningful. Since our sentence speaks of certain places in space as being filled with matter (for that is what the words 'side of the moon' stand for), it will have meaning if we indicate under what circumstances a proposition of the form, 'this place is filled with matter', shall be called true or false. The concept 'physical substance at a certain place' is defined by our language in physics and geometry. Geometry itself is the grammar of our propositions about 'spatial' relations, and it is not very difficult to see how assertions about physical properties and spatial relations are connected with 'sense-data' by ostensive definitions. This connection, by the way, is not such as to entitle us to say that physical substance is 'a mere construction put upon sense-data', or that a physical body is 'a complex of sense-data'—unless we interpret these phrases as rather inadequate abbreviations of the assertion that all propositions containing the term 'physical body' require for their verification the presence of sense-data. And this is certainly an exceedingly trivial statement.

Early Analytic Philosophy

In the case of the moon we might perhaps say that the meaning-requirement is fulfilled if we are able to 'imagine' (picture mentally) situations which would verify our proposition. But if we should say in general that verifiability of an assertion implies possibility of 'imagining' the asserted fact, this would be true only in a restricted sense. It would not be true in so far as the possibility is of the empirical kind, i.e., implying specific human capacities. I do not think, for instance, that we can be accused of talking nonsense if we speak of a universe of ten dimensions, or of beings possessing sense-organs and having perceptions entirely different from ours; and yet it does not seem right to say that we are able to 'imagine' such beings and such perceptions, or a ten-dimensional world. But we *must* be able to say under what *observable* circumstances we should assert the existence of the beings or sense-organs just referred to. It is clear that I can speak meaningfully of the sound of a friend's voice without being able actually to recall it in my imagination.—This is not the place to discuss the logical grammar of the word 'to imagine'; these few remarks may caution us against accepting too readily a *psychological* explanation of verifiability.

We must not identify meaning with any of the psychological data which form the material of a mental sentence (or 'thought') in the same sense in which articulated sounds form the material of a spoken sentence, or black marks on paper the material of a written sentence. When you are doing a calculation in arithmetic it is quite irrelevant whether you have before your mind the images of black numbers or of red numbers, or no visual picture at all. And even if it were empirically impossible for you to do any calculation without imagining black numbers at the same time, the mental pictures of those black marks could, of course, in no way be considered as constituting the meaning, or part of the meaning, of the calculation.

Carnap is right in putting great stress upon the fact (always emphasized by the critics of 'psychologism') that the question of meaning has nothing to do with the psychological question as to the mental processes of which an act of thought may consist. But I am not sure that he has seen with equal clarity that reference to ostensive definitions (which we postulate for meaning) does *not* involve the error of a confusion of the two questions. In order to understand a sentence containing, e.g., the words 'red flag', it is indispensable that I should be able to indicate a situation where I could point to an object which I should call a 'flag', and whose color I could recognize as 'red' as distinguished from other colors. But in order to do this it is not necessary that I should actually call up the image of a red flag. It is of the utmost importance to see that these two things have nothing in common. At this moment I am trying in vain to imagine the shape of a capital G in German print; nevertheless I can speak about it without

Logical Empiricism: Meaning, Metaphysics, and Mathematics

talking nonsense, and I know I should recognize it if I saw the letter. Imagining a red patch is utterly different from referring to an ostensive definition of 'red'. Verifiability has nothing to do with any images that may be associated with the words of the sentence in question.

* * *

No more difficulty than in the case of the other side of the moon will be found in discussing, as another significant example, the question of 'immortality', which Professor Lewis calls, and which is usually called, a *metaphysical* problem. I take it for granted that 'immortality' is not supposed to signify never-ending life (for that might possibly be meaningless on account of infinity being involved), but that we are concerned with the question of survival after 'death'. I think we may agree with Professor Lewis when he says about this hypothesis: "Our understanding of what would verify it has no lack of clarity." In fact, I can easily imagine e.g. witnessing the funeral of my own body and continuing to exist without a body, for nothing is easier than to describe a world which differs from our ordinary world only in the complete absence of all data which I would call parts of my own body.

We must conclude that immortality, in the sense defined, should not be regarded as a 'metaphysical problem', but is an empirical hypothesis, because it possesses logical verifiability. It could be verified by following the prescription: 'Wait until you die!' Professor Lewis seems to hold that this method is not satisfactory from the point of view of science. He says (143):

> The hypothesis of immortality is unverifiable in an obvious sense. . . if it be maintained that only what is scientifically verifiable has meaning, then this conception is a case in point. It could hardly be verified by science; and there is no observation or experiment which science could make, the negative result of which would disprove it.

I fancy that in these sentences the private method of verification is rejected as being unscientific because it would apply only to the individual case of the experiencing person himself, whereas a scientific statement should be capable of a *general* proof, open to any careful observer. But I see no reason why even this should be declared to be impossible. On the contrary, it is easy to describe experiences such that the hypothesis of an invisible existence of human beings after their bodily death would be the most acceptable explanation of the phenomena observed. These phenomena, it is true, would have to be of a much more convincing nature than the ridiculous happenings alleged to have occurred in meetings of the occultists—but I think there cannot be the slightest doubt as

Early Analytic Philosophy

to the possibility (in the logical sense) of phenomena which would form a scientific justification of the hypothesis of survival after death, and would permit an investigation by scientific methods of that form of life. To be sure, the hypothesis could never be established as absolutely true, but it shares this fate with all hypotheses. If it should be urged that the souls of the deceased might inhabit some supercelestial space where they would not be accessible to our perception, and that therefore the truth or falsity of the assertion could never be tested, the reply would be that if, the words 'supercelestial space' are to have any meaning at all, that space must be defined in such a way that the impossibility of reaching it or of perceiving anything in it would be merely empirical, so that some means of overcoming the difficulties could at least be described, although it might be beyond human power to put them into use.

Thus our conclusion stands. The hypothesis of immortality is an empirical statement which owes its meaning to its verifiability, and it has no meaning beyond the possibility of verification. If it must be admitted that science could make no experiment the negative result of which would disprove it, this is true only in the same sense in which it is true for many other hypotheses of similar structure—especially those that have sprung up from other motives than the knowledge of a great many facts of experience

* * *

The question about the 'existence of the external world' will be discussed in the next section.

V

Let us now turn to a point of fundamental importance and the deepest philosophic interest. Professor Lewis refers to it as the "egocentric predicament", and he describes as one of the most characteristic features of logical positivism its attempt to take this predicament seriously. It seems to be formulated in the sentence (128), "Actually given experience is given in the first person", and its importance for the doctrine of logical positivism seems to be evident from the fact that Carnap, in his *Der logische Aufbau der Welt*, states that the method of this book may be called "methodological solipsism". Professor Lewis thinks, rightly, that the egocentric or solipsistic principle is not implied by our general principle of verifiability, and so he regards it as a second principle which, together with that of verifiability, leads, in his opinion, to the main results of the Viennese philosophy.

If I may be permitted to make a few general remarks here I should like to say that one of the greatest advantages and attractions of true positivism seems to

Logical Empiricism: Meaning, Metaphysics, and Mathematics 393

me to be the antisolipsistic attitude which characterizes it from the very beginning. There is as little danger of solipsism in it as in any 'realism', and it seems to me to be the chief point of difference between idealism and positivism that the latter keeps entirely clear of the egocentric predicament. I think it is the greatest misunderstanding of the positivist idea (often even committed by thinkers who called themselves positivists) to see in it a tendency towards solipsism or a kinship to subjective idealism. We may regard Vaihinger's *Philosophy of 'As If'* as a typical example of this mistake (he calls his book a "System of Idealistic Positivism"), and perhaps the philosophy of Mach and Avenarius as one of the most consistent attempts to avoid it. It is rather unfortunate that Carnap has advocated what he calls "methodological solipsism", and that in his construction of all concepts out of elementary data the "eigen-psychische Gegenstainde" (for-me entities) come first and form the basis for the construction of physical objects, which finally lead to the concept of other selves; but if there is any mistake here it is chiefly in the terminology, not in the thought. "Methodological solipsism" is *not* a kind of solipsism, but a *method* of building up concepts. And it must be borne in mind that the order of construction which Carnap recommends—beginning with "for-me entities"—is not asserted to be the only possible one. It would have been better to have chosen a different order, but in principle Carnap was well aware of the fact that original experience is "without a subject" (see Lewis loc. cit. 145).

The strongest emphasis should be laid on the fact that primitive experience is absolutely neutral or, as Wittgenstein has occasionally put it, that immediate data "have no owner". Since the genuine positivist denies (with Mach etc.) that original experience "has that quality or status, characteristic of all given experience, which is indicated by the adjective 'first person'" (loc. cit. 145), he cannot possibly take the 'egocentric predicament' seriously; for him this predicament does not exist. To see that primitive experience is not first-person experience seems to me to be one of the most important steps which philosophy must take towards the clarification of its deepest problems.

The unique position of the 'self' is not a basic property of all experience, but is itself a fact (among other facts) of experience. Idealism (as represented by Berkeley's "*esse = percipi*" or by Schopenhauer's "DieWelt ist meineVorstellung") and other doctrines with egocentric tendencies commit the great error of mistaking the unique position of the ego, which is an empirical fact, for a logical, *a priori* truth, or, rather, substituting the one for the other. It is worth while to investigate this matter and analyse the sentence which seems to express the egocentric predicament. This will not be a digression, for without the clarification of this point it will be impossible to understand the basic position of our empiricism.

Early Analytic Philosophy

How does the idealist or the solipsist arrive at the statement that the world, as far as I know it, is 'my own idea', that ultimately I know nothing but the 'content of my own consciousness'?

Experience teaches that all immediate data depend in some way or other upon those data that constitute what I call 'my body'. All visual data disappear when the eyes of this body are closed; all sounds cease when its ears are stuffed up; and so on. This body is distinguished from the 'bodies of other beings' by the fact that it always appears in a peculiar perspective (its back or its eyes, for instance, never appear except in a looking glass); but this is not nearly so significant as the other fact that the quality of all data is conditioned by the state of the organs of this particular body. Obviously these two facts—and perhaps originally the first one—form the only reason why this body is called 'my' body. The possessive pronoun singles it out from among other bodies; it is an adjective which denotes the uniqueness described.

The fact that all data are dependent upon 'my' body (particularly those parts of it which are called 'sense-organs') induces us to form the concept of 'perception'. We do not find this concept in the language of unsophisticated, primitive people; they do not say, 'I perceive a tree', but simply, 'there is a tree'. 'Perception' implies the distinction between a subject which perceives and an object which is perceived. Originally the perceiver is the sense-organ or the body to which it belongs, but since the body itself—including the nervous system—is also one of the perceived things, the original view is soon 'corrected' by substituting for the perceiver a new subject, which is called 'ego' or 'mind' or 'consciousness'. It is usually thought of as somehow residing in the body, because the sense-organs are on the surface of the body. The mistake of locating consciousness or mind inside the body ('in the head'), which has been called "introjection" by R. Avenarius, is the main source of the difficulties of the so-called 'mind-body problem'. By avoiding the error of introjection we avoid at the same time the idealistic fallacy which leads to solipsism. It is easy to show that introjection is an error. When I see a green meadow the 'green' is declared to be a content of my consciousness, but it certainly is not inside my head. Inside my skull there is nothing but my brain; and if there should happen to be a green spot in my brain, it would obviously not be the green of the meadow, but the green of the brain.

But for our purpose it is not necessary to follow this train of thought; it is sufficient to restate the facts clearly.

It is a fact of experience that all data depend in some way or other upon the state of a certain body which has the peculiarity that its eyes and its back are never seen (except by means of a mirror). It is usually called 'my' body; but here, in order to avoid mistakes, I shall take the liberty of calling it the body 'M'.

Logical Empiricism: Meaning, Metaphysics, and Mathematics   395

A particular case of the dependence just mentioned is expressed by the sentence, 'I do not perceive anything unless the sense-organs of the body M are affected'. Or, taking a still more special case, I may make the following statement:

'I feel pain only when the body M is hurt.' (P)

I shall refer to this statement as 'proposition P'.
Now let us consider another proposition (Q):

'I can feel only my pain.' (Q)

The sentence Q may be interpreted in various ways. *Firstly*, it may be regarded as equivalent to P, so that P and Q would just be two different ways of expressing one and the same empirical fact. The word 'can' occurring in Q would denote what we have called 'empirical possibility', and the words 'I' and 'my' would refer to the body M. It is of the utmost importance to realize that in this first interpretation Q is the description of a fact of experience, i.e., a fact which we could very well imagine to be different.

We could easily imagine (here I am closely following ideas expressed by Mr. Wittgenstein) that I experience a pain every time the body of my friend is hurt, that I am gay when his face bears a joyful expression, that I feel tired after he has taken a long walk, or even that I do not see anything when his eyes are closed, and so forth. Proposition Q (if interpreted as being equivalent to P) denies that these things ever happen; but if they did happen, Q would be falsified. Thus we indicate the meaning of Q (or P) by describing facts which make Q true, and other facts that would make it false. If facts of the latter kind occurred our world would be rather different from the one in which we are actually living; the properties of the 'data' would depend on other human bodies (or perhaps only one of them) as well as upon the body M.

This fictitious world may be empirically impossible, because incompatible with the actual laws of nature—though we cannot at all be sure of this—but it is logically possible, because we were able to give a description of it. Now let us for a moment suppose this fictitious world to be real. How would our language adapt itself to it? It might be done in two different ways which are of interest for our problem.

Proposition P would be false. As regards Q, there would be two possibilities. The first is to maintain that its meaning is still to be the same as that of P. In this case Q would be false and could be replaced by the true proposition,

'I can feel somebody else's pain as well as my own.' (R)

Early Analytic Philosophy

R would state the empirical fact (which for the moment we suppose to be true) that the datum 'pain' occurs not only when M is hurt, but also when some injury is inflicted upon some other body, say, the body 'O'.

If we express the supposed state of affairs by the proposition R, there will evidently be no temptation and no pretext to make any 'solipsistic' statement. *My* body—which in this case could mean nothing but 'body M'—would still be unique in that it would always appear in a particular perspective (with invisible back, etc.), but it would no longer be unique as being the only body upon whose state depended the properties of all other data. And it was only this latter characteristic which gave rise to the ego-centric view. The philosophic doubt concerning the 'reality of the external world' arose from the consideration that I had no knowledge of' that world except by perception, i.e., by means of the sensitive organs of *my* body. If this is no longer true, if the data depend also on other bodies O (which differ from M in certain empirical respects, but not in *principle*), then there will be no more justification in calling the data 'my own'; other individuals O will have the same right to be regarded as owners or proprietors of the data. The sceptic was afraid that other bodies O might be nothing but images owned by the 'mind' belonging to the body M, because everything seemed to depend on the state of the latter; but under the circumstances described there exists perfect symmetry between O and M; the egocentric predicament has disappeared.

You will perhaps call my attention to the fact that the circumstances we have been describing are fictitious, that they do not occur in our real world, so that in this world, unfortunately, the egocentric predicament holds its sway. I answer that I wish to base my argument only on the fact that the difference between the two words is merely empirical, i.e., proposition P just happens to be true in the actual world as far as our experience goes. It does not even seem to be incompatible with the known laws of nature; the probability which these laws give to the falsity of P is not zero.

Now if we still agree that proposition Q is to be regarded as identical with P (which means that 'my' is to be defined as referring to M), the word 'can' in Q will still indicate *empirical* possibility. Consequently, if a philosopher tried to use Q as the basis of a kind of solipsism, he would have to be prepared to see his whole construction falsified by some future experience. But this is exactly what the true solipsist *refuses* to do. He contends that no experience whatever could possibly contradict him, because it would always necessarily have the peculiar for-me character, which may be described by the 'egocentric predicament'. In other words, he is well aware that solipsism cannot be based on Q as long as Q is, by definition, nothing but another way of expressing P. As a matter of fact,

Logical Empiricism: Meaning, Metaphysics, and Mathematics   397

the solipsist who makes the statement Q attaches a different meaning to the same words; he does not wish merely to assert P, but he intends to say something entirely different. The difference lies in the word 'my'. He does not want to define the personal pronoun by reference to the body M, but uses it in a much more general way. What meaning does he give to the sentence Q?

Let us examine this *second* interpretation which may be given to Q.

The idealist or solipsist who says, 'I can feel only my own pain', or, more generally, 'I can be aware only of the data of my own consciousness', believes that he is uttering a necessary, self-evident truth which no possible experience can force him to sacrifice. He will have to admit the possibility of circumstances such as those we described for our fictitious world; but, he will say, even if I feel pain every time when another body O is hurt, I shall never say, 'I feel O's pain', but always, 'My pain is in O's body'.

We cannot declare this statement of the idealist to be *false*; it is just a different way of adapting our language to the imagined new circumstances, and the rules of language are, in principle, arbitrary. But, of course, some uses of our words may recommend themselves as practical and well adapted; others may be condemned as misleading. Let us examine the idealist's attitude from this point of view.

He rejects our proposition R and replaces it by the other one:

'I can feel pain in other bodies as well as in my own.' (S)

He wants to insist that any pain I feel must be called *my* pain, no matter where it is felt, and in order to assert this he says:

'I *can* feel only *my* pain.' (T)

Sentence T is, as far as the words are concerned, the same as Q. I have used slightly different signs by having the words 'can' and 'my' printed in italics, in order to indicate that, when used by the solipsist, these two words have a signification which is different from the signification they had in Q when we interpreted Q as meaning the same as P. In T 'my pain' no longer means 'pain in body M', because, according to the solipsist's explanation, 'my pain' may also be in another body O; so we must ask: what does the pronoun 'my' signify here?

It is easy to see that it does not signify *anything*; it is a superfluous word which may just as well be omitted. 'I feel pain' and 'I feel my pain' are, according to the solipsist's definition, to have identical meaning; the word 'my', therefore, has no function in the sentence. If he says, 'The pain which I feel is my pain', he is uttering a mere tautology, because he has declared that whatever the empirical circumstances may be, he will never allow the pronouns 'your' or 'his'

Early Analytic Philosophy

to be used in connection with 'I feel pain', but always the pronoun 'my'. This stipulation, being independent of empirical facts, is a logical rule, and if it is followed, T becomes a tautology; the word 'can' in T (together with 'only') does not denote empirical impossibility, but *logical* impossibility. In other words it would not be false, it would be *nonsense* (grammatically forbidden) to say 'I can feel somebody else's pain'. A tautology, being the negation of nonsense, is itself devoid of meaning in the sense that it does not assert anything, but merely indicates a rule concerning the use of words.

We infer that T, which is the second interpretation of Q, adopted by the solipsist and forming the basis of his argument, is strictly meaningless. It does not say anything at all, does not express any interpretation of the world or view about the world; it just introduces a strange way of speaking, a clumsy kind of language, which attaches the index 'my' (or 'content of my consciousness') to everything without exception. Solipsism is nonsense, because its starting-point, the egocentric predicament, is meaningless.

The words 'I' and 'my', if we use them according to the solipsist's prescription, are absolutely empty, mere adornments of speech. There would be no difference of meaning between the three expressions, 'I feel my pain'; 'I feel pain'; and 'there is pain'. Lichtenberg, the wonderful eighteenth-century physicist and philosopher, declared that Descartes had no right to start his philosophy with the proposition 'I think', instead of saying 'it thinks'. Just as there would be no sense in speaking of a white horse unless it were logically possible that a horse might *not* be white, so no sentence containing the words 'I' or 'my' would be meaningful unless we could replace them by 'he' or 'his' without speaking nonsense. But such a substitution is impossible in a sentence that would seem to express the egocentric predicament or the solipsistic phlosophy.

R and S are not different explanations or interpretations of a certain state of affairs which we have described, but simply verbally different formulations of this description. It is of fundamental importance to see that R and S are not two propositions, but one and the same proposition in two different languages. The solipsist, by rejecting the language of R and insisting upon the language of S, has adopted a terminology which makes Q tautological, transforms it into T. Thus he has made it impossible to verify or falsify his own statements; he himself has deprived them of meaning. By refusing to avail himself of the opportunities (which we showed him) to make the statement 'I can feel somebody else's pain' meaningful, he has at the same time lost the opportunity of giving meaning to the sentence 'I can feel only my own pain'.

The pronoun 'my' indicates *possession*; we cannot speak of the 'owner' of a pain—or any other datum—except in cases where the word 'my' can be used

Logical Empiricism: Meaning, Metaphysics, and Mathematics

meaningfully, i.e., where by substituting 'his' or 'your' we would get the description of a possible state of affairs. This condition is fulfilled if 'my' is defined as referring to the body M, and it would also be fulfilled if I agree to call 'my body' any body in which I can feel pain. In our actual world these two definitions apply to one and the same body, but that is an empirical fact which might be different. If the two definitions did not coincide and if we adopted the second one we should need a new word to distinguish the body M from other bodies in which I might have sensations; the word 'my' would have meaning in a sentence of the form 'A is one of my bodies, but B is not', but it would be meaningless in the statement 'I can feel pain only in my bodies', for this would be a mere tautology.

The grammar of the word 'owner' is similar to that of the word 'my': it makes sense only where it is logically possible for a thing to *change* its owner, i.e., where the relation between the owner and the owned object is empirical, not logical ('external', not 'internal'). Thus one could say 'Body M is the owner of this pain', or 'that pain is owned by the bodies M and O'. The second proposition can, perhaps, never be truthfully asserted in our actual world (although I cannot see that it would be incompatible with the laws of nature), but both of them would make sense. Their meaning would be to express certain relations of dependence between the pain and the state of certain bodies, and the existence of such a relation could easily be tested.

The solipsist refuses to use the word 'owner' in this sensible way. He knows that many properties of the data do not depend at all upon any states of human bodies, viz., all those regularities of their behavior that can be expressed by 'physical laws'; he knows, therefore, that it would be wrong to say 'my body is the owner of everything', and so he speaks of a 'self', or 'ego', or 'consciousness', and declares this to be the owner of everything. (The idealist, by the way, makes the same mistake when he asserts that we know nothing but 'appearances'.) This is nonsense because the word 'owner', when used in this way, has lost its meaning. The solipsistic assertion cannot be verified or falsified, it will be true by definition, whatever the facts may be; it simply consists in the verbal prescription to add the phrase 'owned by Me' to the names of all objects, etc.

Thus we see that unless we choose to call our body the owner or bearer of the data—which seems to be a rather misleading expression—we have to say that the data have no owner or bearer. This neutrality of experience—as against the subjectivity claimed for it by the idealist—is one of the most fundamental points of true positivism. The sentence 'All experience is first-person experience' will either mean the simple empirical fact that all data are in certain respects dependent on the state of the nervous system of my body M, or it will be meaningless. Before this physiological fact is discovered, experience is not 'my'

Early Analytic Philosophy

experience at all, it is self-sufficient and does not 'belong' to anybody. The proposition 'The ego is the centre of the world' may be regarded as an expression of the same fact, and has meaning only if it refers to the body. The concept of 'ego' is a construction put upon the same fact, and we could easily imagine a world in which this concept would not have been formed, where there would be no idea of an insurmountable barrier between what is inside the Me and what is outside of. it. It would be a world in which occurrences like those corresponding to proposition R and similar ones were the rule, and in which the facts of 'memory' were not so pronounced as they are in our actual world. Under those circumstances we should not be tempted to fall into the 'egocentric predicament', but the sentence which tries to express such a predicament would be meaningless under any circumstances.

* * *

After our last remarks it will be easy to deal with the so-called problem concerning the existence of the external world. If, with Professor Lewis (143), we formulate the 'realistic' hypothesis by asserting, "If all minds should disappear from the universe, the stars would still go on in their courses", we must admit the impossibility of verifying it, but the impossibility is merely empirical. And the empirical circumstances are such that we have every reason to believe the hypothesis to be true. We are as sure of it as of the best founded physical laws that science has discovered.

As a matter of fact, we have already pointed out that there are certain regularities in the world which experience shows to be entirely independent of what happens to human beings on the earth. The laws of motion of the celestial bodies are formulated entirely without reference to any human bodies, and *this is the reason* why we are justified in maintaining that they will go on in their courses after mankind has vanished from the earth. Experience shows no connection between the two kinds of events. We observe that the course of the stars is no more changed by the death of human beings than, say, by the eruption of a volcano, or by a change of government in China. Why should we suppose that there would be any difference if all living beings on our planet, or indeed everywhere in the universe, were extinguished? There can be no doubt that on the strength of empirical evidence the existence of living beings is no necessary condition for the existence of the rest of the world.

The question 'Will the world go on existing after I am dead?' has no meaning unless it is interpreted as asking 'Does the existence of the stars etc. depend upon the life or death of a human being?', and this question is answered in the

Logical Empiricism: Meaning, Metaphysics, and Mathematics   401

negative by experience. The mistake of the solipsist or idealist consists in rejecting this empirical interpretation and looking for some metaphysical issue behind it; but all their efforts to construct a new sense of the question end only in depriving it of its old one.

It will be noticed that I have taken the liberty of substituting the phrase 'if all living beings disappeared from the universe' for the phrase 'if all *minds* disappeared from the universe'. I hope it will not be thought that I have changed the meaning of the issue by this substitution. I have avoided the word 'mind' because I take it to signify the same as the words 'ego' or 'consciousness', which we have found to be so dark and dangerous. By living beings I meant beings capable of perception, and the concept of perception had been defined only by reference to living *bodies*, to physical organs. Thus I was justified in substituting 'death of living beings' for 'disappearance of minds'. But the arguments hold for any empirical definition one may choose to give for 'mind'. I need only point out that, according to experience, the motion of the stars etc. is quite independent of all 'mental' phenomena such as feeling joy or sorrow, meditating, dreaming, etc.; and we may infer that the course of the stars would not be affected if those phenomena should cease to exist.

But is it true that this inference could be verified by experience? Empirically it seems to be impossible, but we know that only logical possibility of verification is required. And verification without a 'mind' is logically possible on account of the 'neutral', impersonal character of experience on which we have insisted. Primitive experience, mere existence of ordered data, does not presuppose a 'subject', or 'ego', or 'Me', or 'mind'; it can take place without any of the facts which lead to the formation of those concepts; it is not an experience of anybody. It is not difficult to imagine a universe without plants and animals and human bodies (including the body M), and without the mental phenomena just referred to: it would certainly be a 'world without minds' (for what else could deserve this name?), but the laws of nature might be exactly the same as in our actual world. We could describe this universe in, terms of our actual experience (we would only have to leave out all terms referring to human bodies and emotions); and that is sufficient to speak of it as a world of possible experience.

The last considerations may serve as an example of one of the main theses of true positivism: that the naive representation of the world, as the man in the street sees it, is perfectly correct; and that the solution of the great philosophical issues consists in returning to this original world-view, after having shown that the troublesome problems arose only from an inadequate description of the world by means of a faulty language.

402　Early Analytic Philosophy

Carnap, R. "The Elimination of Metaphysics Through the Logical Analysis of Language".
Reprinted from Carnap, R. (1959), "The Elimination of Metaphysics Through the Logical Analysis of Language", in A. J. Ayer (ed.), *Logical Positivism*, New York: The Free Press. Originally published as "*Uberwindung der Metaphysik durch Logishe Analyse der Sprache*," *Erkenntnis*, Vol. II (1932).

1. Introduction

There have been many *opponents of metaphysics* from the Greek skeptics to the empiricists of the 19th century. Criticisms of very diverse kinds have been set forth. Many have declared that the doctrine of metaphysics is *false*, since it contradicts our empirical knowledge. Others have believed it to be *uncertain*, on the ground that its problems transcend the limits of human knowledge. Many anti-metaphysicians have declared that occupation with metaphysical questions is *sterile*. Whether or not these questions can be answered, it is at any rate unnecessary to worry about them; let us devote ourselves entirely to the practical tasks which confront active men every day of their lives!

The development of *modern logic* has made it possible to give a new and sharper answer to the question of the validity and justification of metaphysics. The researches of applied logic or the theory of knowledge, which aim at clarifying the cognitive content of scientific statements and thereby the meanings of the terms that occur in the statements, by means of logical analysis, lead to a positive and to a negative result. The positive result is worked out in the domain of empirical science; the various concepts of the various branches of science are clarified; their formal logical and epistemological connections are made explicit. In the domain of *metaphysics*, including all philosophy of value and normative theory, logical analysis yields the negative result *that the alleged statements in this domain are entirely meaningless*. Therewith a radical elimination of metaphysics is attained, which was not yet possible from the earlier antimetaphysical standpoints. It is true that related ideas may be found already in several earlier trains of thought, e.g. those of a nominalistic kind; but it is only now when the development of logic during recent decades provides us with a sufficiently sharp tool that the decisive step can be taken.

In saying that the so-called statements of metaphysics are *meaningless*, we intend this word in its strictest sense. In a loose sense of the word a statement or a question is at times called meaningless if it is entirely sterile to assert or ask it. We might say this for instance about the question "what is the average weight of those inhabitants of Vienna whose telephone number ends with '3'?" or about a statement which is quite obviously false like "in 1910 Vienna had 6 inhabitants" or about a statement which is not just empirically, but logically false, a contradictory statement such as "persons A and B are each a year older than the other." Such sentences are really meaningful, though they are pointless or false; for it is only meaningful sentences that are even divisible into (theoretically) fruitful and sterile, true and false. In the strict sense, however, a sequence of words is *meaningless* if it does not, within a specified language, constitute a statement. It may happen that such a sequence of words looks like a statement at first glance; in that case we call it a *pseudo-statement.* Our thesis, now, is that logical analysis reveals the alleged statements of metaphysics to be pseudo-statements.

A language consists of a vocabulary and a syntax, i.e. a set of words which have meanings and rules of sentence formation. These rules indicate how sentences may be formed out of the various sorts of words. Accordingly, there are two kinds of pseudo-statements: either they contain a word which is erroneously believed to have meaning, or the constituent words are meaningful, yet are put together in a counter-syntactical way, so that they do not yield a meaningful statement. We shall show in terms of examples that pseudo-statements of both kinds occur in metaphysics. Later we shall have to inquire into the reasons that support our contention that metaphysics in its entirety consists of such pseudo-statements.

2. The Significance of a Word

A word which (within a definite language) has a meaning, is usually also said to designate a concept; if it only seems to have a meaning while it really does not, we speak of a "pseudo-concept." How is the origin of a pseudo-concept to be explained? Has not every word been introduced into the language for no other purpose than to express something or other, so that it had a definite meaning from the very beginning of its use? How, then, can a traditional language contain meaningless words? To be sure, originally every word (excepting rare cases which we shall illustrate later) had a meaning. In the course of historical development a word frequently changes its meaning. And it also happens at times that a word loses its old sense without acquiring a new one. It is thus that a pseudo-concept arises.

What, now, is *the meaning of a word*? What stipulations concerning a word must be made in order for it to be significant? (It does not matter for our investigation whether these stipulations are explicitly laid down, as in the case of

Early Analytic Philosophy

some words and symbols of modern science, or whether they have been tacitly agreed upon, as is the case for most words of traditional language.) First, the *syntax* of the word must be fixed, i.e. the mode of its occurrence in the simplest sentence form in which it is capable of occurring; we call this sentence form its *elementary sentence*. The elementary sentence form for the word "stone" e.g. is "x is a stone"; in sentences of this form some designation from the category of things occupies the place of "x," e.g. "this diamond," "this apple." Secondly, for an elementary sentence S containing the word an answer must be given to the following question, which can be formulated in various ways:

(1) What sentences is S *deducible* from, and what sentences are deducible from S?
(2) Under what conditions is S supposed to be true, and under what conditions false?
(3) How is S to be *verified*?
(4) What is the *meaning* of S?

(1) is the correct formulation; formulation (2) accords with the phraseology of logic, (3) with the phraseology of the theory of knowledge, (4) with that of philosophy (phenomenology). Wittgenstein has asserted that (2) expresses what philosophers mean by (4): the meaning of a sentence consists in its truth-condition. ((1) is the "metalogical" formulation; it is planned to give elsewhere a detailed exposition of metalogic as the theory of syntax and meaning, i.e. relations of deducibility.)

In the case of many words, specifically in the case of the overwhelming majority of scientific words, it is possible to specify their meaning by reduction to other words ("constitution," definition). E.g. " 'arthropodes' are animals with segmented bodies and jointed legs." Thereby the above-mentioned question for the elementary sentence form of the word "arthropode," that is for the sentence form "the thing x is an arthropode," is answered: it has been stipulated that a sentence of this form is deducible from premises of the form "x is an animal," "x has a segmented body," "x has jointed legs," and that conversely each of these sentences is deducible from the former sentence. By means of these stipulations about deducibility (in other words: about the truth-condition, about the method of verification, about the meaning) of the elementary sentence about "arthropode" the meaning of the word "arthropode" is fixed. In this way every word of the language is reduced to other words and finally to the words which occur in the so-called "observation sentences" or "protocol sentences." It is through this reduction that the word acquires its meaning.

Logical Empiricism: Meaning, Metaphysics, and Mathematics

For our purposes we may ignore entirely the question concerning the content and form of the primary sentences (protocol sentences) which has not yet been definitely settled. In the theory of knowledge it is customary to say that the primary sentences refer to "the given"; but there is no unanimity on the question what it is that is given. At times the position is taken that sentences about the given speak of the simplest qualities of sense and feeling (e.g. "warm," "blue," "joy" and so forth); others incline to the view that basic sentences refer to total experiences and similarities between them; a still different view has it that even the basic sentences speak of things. Regardless of this diversity of opinion it is certain that a sequence of words has a meaning only if its relations of deducibility to the protocol sentences are fixed, whatever the characteristics of the protocol sentences may be; and similarly, that a word is significant only if the sentences in which it may occur are reducible to protocol sentences.

Since the meaning of a word is determined by its criterion of application (in other words: by the relations of deducibility entered into by its elementary sentence-form, by its truth-conditions, by the method of its verification), the stipulation of the criterion takes away one's freedom to decide what one wishes to "mean" by the word. If the word is to receive an exact meaning, nothing less than the criterion of application must be given; but one cannot, on the other hand, give more than the criterion of application, for the latter is a sufficient determination of meaning. The meaning is implicitly contained in the criterion; all that remains to be done is to make the meaning explicit.

Let us suppose, by way of illustration, that someone invented the new word "teavy" and maintained that there are things which are teavy and things which are not teavy. In order to learn the meaning of this word, we ask him about its criterion of application: how is one to ascertain in a concrete case whether a given thing is teavy or not? Let us suppose to begin with that we get no answer from him: there are no empirical signs of teavyness, he says. In that case we would deny the legitimacy of using this word. If the person who uses the word says that all the same there are things which are teavy and there are things which are not teavy, only it remains for the weak, finite intellect of man an eternal secret which things are teavy and which are not, we shall regard this as empty verbiage. But perhaps he will assure us that he means, after all, something by the word "teavy." But from this we only learn the psychological fact that he associates some kind of images and feelings with the word. The word does not acquire a meaning through such associations. If no criterion of application for the word is stipulated, then nothing is asserted by the sentences in which it occurs, they are but pseudo-statements.

Secondly, take the case when we are given a criterion of application for a new word, say "toovy"; in particular, let the sentence "this thing is toovy" be

Early Analytic Philosophy

true if and only if the thing is quadrangular (It is irrelevant in this context whether the criterion is explicitly stated or whether we derive it by observing the affirmative and the negative uses of the word). Then we will say: the word "toovy" is synonymous with the word "quadrangular." And we will not allow its users to tell us that nevertheless they "intended" something else by it than "quadrangular"; that though every quadrangular thing is also toovy and conversely, this is only because quadrangularity is the visible manifestation of toovyness, but that the latter itself is a hidden, not itself observable property. We would reply that after the criterion of application has been fixed, the synonymy of "toovy" and "quadrangular" is likewise fixed, and that we are no further at liberty to "intend" this or that by the word.

Let us briefly summarize the result of our analysis. Let "a" be any word and "S(a)" the elementary sentence in which it occurs. Then the sufficient and necessary condition for "a" being meaningful may be given by each of the following formulations, which ultimately say the same thing:

1. The *empirical criteria* for a are known.
2. It has been stipulated from what protocol sentences "S(a)" is *deducible*.
3. The *truth-conditions* for "S(a)" are fixed.
4. The method of *verification* of "S(a)" is known.[1]

3. Metaphysical Words Without Meaning

Many words of metaphysics, now, can be shown not to fulfill the above requirement, and therefore to be devoid of meaning.

Let us take as an example the metaphysical term "principle" (in the sense of principle of being, not principle of knowledge or axiom). Various metaphysicians offer an answer to the question which is the (highest) "principle of the world" (or of "things," of "existence," of "being"), e.g. water, number, form, motion, life, the spirit, the idea, the unconscious, activity, the good, and so forth. In order to discover the meaning of the word "principle" in this metaphysical question we must ask the metaphysician under what conditions a statement of the form "x is the principle of y" would be true and under what conditions it would be

---

[1]For the logical and epistemological conception which underlies our exposition, but can only briefly be intimated here, cf. Wittgenstein, *Tractatus Logico-Philosophicus*, 1922, and Carnap, *Der logische Aufbau der Welt*, 1928. [Editor's note: as marked in the Preface, footnotes and references have been left unaltered from the original text from which the readings are pulled.]

Logical Empiricism: Meaning, Metaphysics, and Mathematics   407

false. In other words: we ask for the criteria of application or for the definition of the word "principle." The metaphysician replies approximately as follows: "x is the principle of y" is to mean "y arises out of x," "the being of y rests on the being of x," "y exists by virtue of x" and so forth. But these words are ambiguous and vague. Frequently they have a clear meaning; e.g., we say of a thing or process y that it "arises out of" x when we observe that things or processes of kind x are frequently or invariably followed by things or processes of kind y (causal connection in the sense of a lawful succession). But the metaphysician tells us that he does not mean this empirically observable relationship. For in that case his metaphysical theses would be merely empirical propositions of the same kind as those of physics. The expression "arising from" is not to mean here a relation of temporal and causal sequence, which is what the word ordinarily means. Yet, no criterion is specified for any other meaning. Consequently, the alleged "metaphysical" meaning, which the word is supposed to have here in contrast to the mentioned empirical meaning, does not exist. If we reflect on the original meaning of the word "principium" (and of the corresponding Greek word ἀρχη) we notice the same development. The word is explicitly deprived of its original meaning "beginning"; it is not supposed to mean the temporally prior any more, but the prior in some other, specifically metaphysical, respect. The criteria for this "metaphysical respect," however, are lacking. In both cases, then, the word has been deprived of its earlier meaning without being given a new meaning; there remains the word as an empty shell. From an earlier period of significant use, it is still associatively connected with various mental images; these in turn get associated with new mental images and feelings in the new context of usage. But the word does not thereby become meaningful; and it remains meaningless as long as no method of verification can be described.

Another example is the word "God." Here we must, apart from the variations of its usage within each domain, distinguish the linguistic usage in three different contexts or historical epochs, which however overlap temporally. In its *mythological* use the word has a clear meaning. It, or parallel words in other languages, is sometimes used to denote physical beings which are enthroned on Mount Olympus, in Heaven or in Hades, and which are endowed with power, wisdom, goodness and happiness to a greater or lesser extent. Sometimes the word also refers to spiritual beings which, indeed, do not have manlike bodies, yet manifest themselves nevertheless somehow in the things or processes of the visible world and are therefore empirically verifiable. In its *metaphysical* use, on the other hand, the word "God" refers to something beyond experience. The word is deliberately

Early Analytic Philosophy

divested of its reference to a physical being or to a spiritual being that is immanent in the physical. And as it is not given a new meaning, it becomes meaningless. To be sure, it often looks as though the word "God" had a meaning even in metaphysics. But the definitions which are set up prove on closer inspection to be pseudo-definitions. They lead either to logically illegitimate combinations of words (of which we shall treat later) or to other metaphysical words (e.g. "primordial basis," "the absolute," "the unconditioned," "the autonomous," "the self-dependent" and so forth), but in no case to the truth-conditions of its elementary sentences. In the case of this word not even the first requirement of logic is met, that is the requirement to specify its syntax, i.e. the form of its occurrence in elementary sentences. An elementary sentence would here have to be of the form "x is a God"; yet, the metaphysician either rejects this form entirely without substituting another, or if he accepts it he neglects to indicate the syntactical category of the variable x. (Categories are, for example, material things, properties of things, relations between things, numbers etc.).

The *theological* usage of the word "God" falls between its mythological and its metaphysical usage. There is no distinctive meaning here, but an oscillation from one of the mentioned two uses to the other. Several theologians have a clearly empirical (in our terminology, "mythological") concept of God. In this case there are no pseudo-statements; but the disadvantage for the theologian lies in the circumstance that according to this interpretation the statements of theology are empirical and hence are subject to the judgment of empirical science. The linguistic usage of other theologians is clearly metaphysical. Others again do not speak in any definite way, whether this is because they follow now this, now that linguistic usage, or because they express themselves in terms whose usage is not clearly classifiable since it tends towards both sides.

Just like the examined examples "principle" and "God," most of the other *specifically metaphysical terms are devoid of meaning*, e.g. "the Idea," "the Absolute," "the Unconditioned," "the Infinite," "the being of being," "non-being," "thing in itself," "absolute spirit," "objective spirit," "essence," "being-in-itself," "being-in-and-for-itself," "emanation," "manifestation," "articulation," "the Ego," "the non-Ego," etc. These expressions are in the same boat with "teavy," our previously fabricated example. The metaphysician tells us that empirical truth-conditions cannot be specified; if he adds that nevertheless he "means" something, we know that this is merely an allusion to associated images and feelings which, however, do not bestow a meaning on the word. The alleged statements of metaphysics which contain such words have no sense, assert nothing, are mere pseudo-statements. Into the explanation of their historical origin we shall inquire later.

4. The Significance of a Sentence

So far we have considered only those pseudo-statements which contain a meaningless word. But there is a second kind of pseudo-statement. They consist of meaningful words, but the words are put together in such a way that nevertheless no meaning results. The syntax of a language specifies which combinations of words are admissible and which inadmissible. The grammatical syntax of natural languages, however, does not fulfill the task of elimination of senseless combinations of words in all cases. Let us take as examples the following sequences of words:

1. "Caesar is and"
2. "Caesar is a prime number"

The word sequence (1) is formed countersyntactically; the rules of syntax require that the third position be occupied, not by a conjunction, but by a predicate, hence by a noun (with article) or by an adjective. The word sequence "Caesar is a general," e.g., is formed in accordance with the rules of syntax. It is a meaningful word sequence, a genuine sentence. But, now, word sequence (2) is likewise syntactically correct, for it has the same grammatical form as the sentence just mentioned. Nevertheless (2) is meaningless. "Prime number" is a predicate of numbers; it can be neither affirmed nor denied of a person. Since (2) looks like a statement yet is not a statement, does not assert anything, expresses neither a true nor a false proposition, we call this word sequence a "pseudo-statement." The fact that the rules of grammatical syntax are not violated easily seduces one at first glance into the erroneous opinion that one still has to do with a statement, albeit a false one. But "a is a prime number" is false if and only if a is divisible by a natural number different from a and from 1; evidently it is illicit to put here "Caesar" for "a." This example has been so chosen that the nonsense is easily detectable. Many so-called statements of metaphysics are not so easily recognized to be pseudo-statements. The fact that natural languages allow the formation of meaningless sequences of words without violating the rules of grammar, indicates that grammatical syntax is, from a logical point of view, inadequate. If grammatical syntax corresponded exactly to logical syntax, pseudo-statements could not arise. If grammatical syntax differentiated not only the word-categories of nouns, adjectives, verbs, conjunctions etc., but within each of these categories made the further distinctions that are logically indispensable, then no pseudo-statements could be formed. If, e.g., nouns were grammatically subdivided into several kinds of words, according as they designated properties of physical objects, of

Early Analytic Philosophy

numbers etc., then the words "general" and "prime number" would belong to grammatically different word-categories, and (2) would be just as linguistically incorrect as (1). In a correctly constructed language, therefore, all nonsensical sequences of words would be of the kind of example (1). Considerations of grammar would already eliminate them as it were automatically; i.e. in order to avoid nonsense, it would be unnecessary to pay attention to the meanings of the individual words over and above their syntactical type (their "syntactical category," e.g. thing, property of things, relation between things, number, property of numbers, relation between numbers, and so forth). It follows that if our thesis that the statements of metaphysics are pseudo-statements is justifiable, then metaphysics could not even be expressed in a logically constructed language. This is the great philosophical importance of the task, which at present occupies the logicians, of building a logical syntax.

5. Metaphysical Pseudo-statements

Let us now take a look at some examples of metaphysical pseudo-statements of a kind where the violation of logical syntax is especially obvious, though they accord with historical-grammatical syntax. We select a few sentences from that metaphysical school which at present exerts the strongest influence in Germany.[2]

"What is to be investigated is being only and—nothing else; being alone and further—*nothing*; solely being, and beyond being— *nothing. What about this Nothing? . . . Does the Nothing exist only because the Not, i.e. the Negation, exists? Or is it the other way around? Does Negation and the Not exist only because the Nothing exists? . . .* We assert: *the Nothing is prior to the Not and the Negation. . . .* Where do we seek the Nothing? How do we find the Nothing. . . . We know the Nothing. . . . *Anxiety reveals the Nothing. . . .* That for which and because of which we were anxious, was 'really'—nothing. Indeed: the Nothing itself—as such—was present. . . . *What about this Nothing?—The Nothing itself nothings.*"

In order to show that the possibility of forming pseudo-statements is based on a logical defect of language, we set up the schema below. The sentences under I are grammatically as well as logically impeccable, hence meaningful. The

---

[2]The following quotations (original italics) are taken from M. Heidegger, *Was Ist Metaphysik?* 1929. We could just as well have selected passages from any other of the numerous metaphysicians of the present or of the past; yet the selected passages seem to us to illustrate our thesis especially well.

Logical Empiricism: Meaning, Metaphysics, and Mathematics

sentences under II (excepting B3) are in grammatical respects perfectly analogous to those under I. Sentence form IIA (as question and answer) does not, indeed, satisfy the requirements to be imposed on a logically correct language. But it is nevertheless meaningful, because it is translatable into correct language. This is shown by sentence IIIA, which has the same meaning as IIA. Sentence form IIA then proves to be undesirable because we can be led from it, by means of grammatically faultless operations, to the meaningless sentence forms IIB, which are taken from the above quotation. These forms cannot even be constructed in the correct language of Column III. Nonetheless, their nonsensicality is not obvious at first glance, because one is easily deceived by the analogy with the meaningful sentences IB. The fault of our language identified here lies, therefore, in the circumstance that, in contrast to a logically correct language, it admits of the same grammatical form for meaningful and meaningless word sequences. To each sentence in words we have added a corresponding formula in the notation of symbolic logic; these formulae facilitate recognition of the undesirable analogy between IA and IIA and therewith of the origin of the meaningless constructions IIB.

I. Meaningful Sentences of Ordinary Language	II. Transition from Sense to Nonsense in Ordinary Language	III. Logically Correct Language
A. What is outside? Ou(?)	A. What is outside? Ou(?)	A. There is nothing (does not exist anything) which is outside. $\sim(\exists x).Ou(x)$
Rain is outside Ou(r)	Nothing is outside Ou(no)	
B. What about this rain? (i.e. what does the rain do? or: what else can be said about this rain? ?(r)	B. "What about this Nothing?" ?(no)	B. None of these forms can even be constructed.
1. We know the rain K(r)	1. "We seek the Nothing" "We find the Nothing" "We know the Nothing" K(no)	
2. The rain rains R(r)	2. "The Nothing nothings" No(no)	
	3. "The Nothing exists only because . . ." Ex(no)	

Early Analytic Philosophy

On closer inspection of the pseudo-statements under IIB, we also find some differences. The construction of sentence (1) is simply based on the mistake of employing the word "nothing" as a noun, because it is customary in ordinary language to use it in this form in order to construct a negative existential statement (see IIA). In a correct language, on the other hand, it is not a particular *name*, but a certain *logical form* of the sentence that serves this purpose (see IIIA). Sentence IIB2 adds something new, viz. the fabrication of the meaningless word "to nothing." This sentence, therefore, is senseless for a twofold reason. We pointed out before that the meaningless words of metaphysics usually owe their origin to the fact that a meaningful word is deprived of its meaning through its metaphorical use in metaphysics. But here we confront one of those rare cases where a new word is introduced which never had a meaning to begin with. Likewise sentence IIB3 must be rejected for two reasons. In respect of the error of using the word "nothing" as a noun, it is like the previous sentences. But in addition it involves a contradiction. For even if it were admissible to introduce "nothing" as a name or description of an entity, still the existence of this entity would be denied in its very definition, whereas sentence (3) goes on to affirm its existence. This sentence, therefore, would be contradictory, hence absurd, even if it were not already meaningless.

In view of the gross logical errors which we find in sentences IIB, we might be led to conjecture that perhaps the word "nothing" has in Heidegger's treatise a meaning entirely different from the customary one. And this presumption is further strengthened as we go on to read there that anxiety reveals the Nothing, that the Nothing itself is present as such in anxiety. For here the word "nothing" seems to refer to a certain emotional constitution, possibly of a religious sort, or something or other that underlies such emotions. If such were the case, then the mentioned logical errors in sentences IIB would not be committed. But the first sentence of the quotation at the beginning of this section proves that this interpretation is not possible. The combination of "only" and "nothing else" shows unmistakably that the word "nothing" here has the usual meaning of a logical particle that serves for the formulation of a negative existential statement. This introduction of the word "nothing" is then immediately followed by the leading question of the treatise: "What about this Nothing?".

But our doubts as to a possible misinterpretation get completely dissolved as we note that the author of the treatise is clearly aware of the conflict between his questions and statements, and logic. "*Question and answer* in regard to the Nothing are equally *absurd* in themselves. . . . The fundamental rule of thinking commonly appealed to, the law of prohibited contradiction, general '*logic*,' destroys this question." All the worse for logic! We must abolish its sovereignty:

Logical Empiricism: Meaning, Metaphysics, and Mathematics   413

"If thus the power of the *understanding* in the field of questions concerning Nothing and Being is broken, then the fate of the sovereignty of 'logic' within philosophy is thereby decided as well. The very idea of 'logic' dissolves in the whirl of a more basic questioning." But will sober science condone the whirl of counter-logical questioning? To this question too there is a ready answer: "The alleged sobriety and superiority of science becomes ridiculous if it does not take the Nothing seriously." Thus we find here a good confirmation of our thesis; a metaphysician himself here states that his questions and answers are irreconcilable with logic and the scientific way of thinking.

The difference between our thesis and that of the *earlier anti-metaphysicians* should now be clear. We do not regard metaphysics as "mere speculation" or "fairy tales." The statements of a fairy tale do not conflict with logic, but only with experience; they are perfectly meaningful, although false. Metaphysics is not "*superstition*"; it is possible to believe true and false propositions, but not to believe meaningless sequences of words. Metaphysical statements are not even acceptable as "*working hypotheses*"; for an hypothesis must be capable of entering into relations of deducibility with (true or false) empirical statements, which is just what pseudo-statements cannot do.

With reference to the so-called *limitation of human knowledge* an attempt is sometimes made to save metaphysics by raising the following objection: metaphysical statements are not, indeed, verifiable by man nor by any other finite being; nevertheless they might be construed as conjectures about the answers which a being with higher or even perfect powers of knowledge would make to our questions, and as such conjectures they would, after all, be meaningful. To counter this objection, let us consider the following. If the meaning of a word cannot be specified, or if the sequence of words does not accord with the rules of syntax, then one has not even asked a question. (Just think of the pesudo-questions: "Is this table teavy?", "is the number 7 holy?", "which numbers are darker, the even or the odd ones?"). Where there is no question, not even an omniscient being can give an answer. Now the objector may say: just as one who can see may communicate new knowledge to the blind, so a higher being might perhaps communicate to us metaphysical knowledge, e.g. whether the visible world is the manifestation of a spirit. Here we must reflect on the meaning of "new knowledge." It is, indeed, conceivable that we might encounter animals who tell us about a new sense. If these beings were to prove to us Fermat's theorem or were to invent a new physical instrument or were to establish a hitherto unknown law of nature, then our knowledge would be increased with their help. For this sort of thing we can test, just the way even a blind man can understand and test the whole of physics (and therewith any statement made by those who can see). But if those hypothetical beings tell us something which we cannot verify, then we cannot understand it either; in that case no information has been communicated to us, but mere verbal sounds devoid of meaning though possibly associated with images. It follows that our knowledge can only be quantitatively enlarged by other beings, no matter whether they know more or less or everything, but no knowledge of an essentially different kind can be added. What we do not know for certain, we may come to know with greater certainty through the assistance of other beings; but what is unintelligible, meaningless for us, cannot become meaningful through someone else's assistance, however vast his knowledge might be. Therefore no god and no devil can give us metaphysical knowledge.

6. Meaninglessness of All Metaphysics

The examples of metaphysical statements which we have analyzed were all taken from just one treatise. But our results apply with equal validity, in part even in verbally identical ways, to other metaphysical systems. That treatise is completely in the right in citing approvingly a statement by Hegel ("pure Being and pure Nothing, therefore, are one and the same"). The metaphysics of Hegel has exactly the same logical character as this modern system of metaphysics. And the same holds for the rest of the metaphysical systems, though the kind of phraseology and therewith the kind of logical errors that occur in them deviate more or less from the kind that occurs in the examples we discussed.

It should not be necessary here to adduce further examples of specific metaphysical sentences in diverse systems and submit them to analysis. We confine ourselves to an indication of the most frequent kinds of errors.

Perhaps the majority of the logical mistakes that are committed when pseudo-statements are made, are based on the logical faults infecting the use of the word "to be" in our language (and of the corresponding words in other languages, at least in most European languages). The first fault is the ambiguity of the word "to be." It is sometimes used as copula prefixed to a predicate ("I am hungry"), sometimes to designate existence ("I am"). This mistake is aggravated by the fact that metaphysicians often are not clear about this ambiguity. The second fault lies in the form of the verb in its second meaning, the meaning of *existence*. The verbal form feigns a predicate where there is none. To be sure, it has been known for a long time that existence is not a property (cf. Kant's refutation of the ontological proof of the existence of God). But it was not until the advent of modern logic that full consistency on this point

Logical Empiricism: Meaning, Metaphysics, and Mathematics   415

was reached: the syntactical form in which modern logic introduces the sign for existence is such that it cannot, like a predicate, be applied to signs for objects, but only to predicates (cf. e.g. sentence IIIA in the above table). Most metaphysicians since antiquity have allowed themselves to be seduced into pseudo-statements by the verbal, and therewith the predicative form of the word "to be," e.g. "I am," "God is."

We meet an illustration of this error in Descartes' "cogito, ergo sum." Let us disregard here the material objections that have been raised against the premise – viz. whether the sentence "I think" adequately expresses the intended state of affairs or contains perhaps an hypostasis – and consider the two sentences only from the formal-logical point of view. We notice at once two essential logical mistakes. The first lies in the conclusion "I am." The verb "to be" is undoubtedly meant in the sense of existence here; for a copula cannot be used without predicate; indeed, Descartes' "I am" has always been interpreted in this sense. But in that case this sentence violates the above-mentioned logical rule that existence can be predicated only in conjunction with a predicate, not in conjunction with a name (subject, proper name). An existential statement does not have the form "a exists" (as in "I am," i.e. "I exist"), but "there exists something of such and such a kind." The second error lies in the transition from "I think" to "I exist." If from the statement "P(a)" ("a has the property P") an existential statement is to be deduced, then the latter can assert existence only with respect to the predicate P, not with respect to the subject a of the premise. What follows from "I am a European" is not "I exist," but "a European exists." What follows from "I think" is not "I am" but "there exists something that thinks."

The circumstance that our languages express existence by a verb ("to be" or "to exist") is not in itself a logical fault; it is only inappropriate, dangerous. The verbal form easily misleads us into the misconception that existence is a predicate. One then arrives at such logically incorrect and hence senseless modes of expression as were just examined. Likewise such forms as "Being" or "Not-Being," which from time immemorial have played a great role in metaphysics, have the same origin. In a logically correct language such forms cannot even be constructed. It appears that in the Latin and the German languages the forms "ens" or "das Seiende" were, perhaps under the seductive influence of the Greek example, introduced specifically for use by metaphysicians; in this way the language deteriorated logically whereas the addition was believed to represent an improvement.

Another very frequent violation of logical syntax is the so-called "*type confusion*" of concepts. While the previously mentioned mistake consists in the predicative use of a symbol with non-predicative meaning, in this case a

Early Analytic Philosophy

predicate is, indeed, used as predicate yet as predicate of a different type. We have here a violation of the rules of the so-called theory of types. An artificial example is the sentence we discussed earlier: "Caesar is a prime number." Names of persons and names of numbers belong to different logical types, and so do accordingly predicates of persons (e.g. "general") and predicates of numbers ("prime number"). The error of type confusion is, unlike the previously discussed usage of the verb "to be," not the prerogative of metaphysics but already occurs very often in conversational language also. But here it rarely leads to nonsense. The typical ambiguity of words is here of such a kind that it can be easily removed.

Example: 1. "This table is larger than that." 2. "The height of this table is larger than the height of that table." Here the word "larger" is used in (1) for a relation between objects, in (2) for a relation between numbers, hence for two distinct syntactical categories. The mistake is here unimportant; it could, e.g., be eliminated by writing "larger1" and "larger2"; "larger1" is then defined in terms of "larger2" by declaring statement form (1) to be synonymous with (2) (and others of a similar kind).

Since the confusion of types causes no harm in conversational language, it is usually ignored entirely. This is, indeed, expedient for the ordinary use of language, but has had unfortunate consequences in metaphysics. Here the conditioning by everyday language has led to confusions of types which, unlike those in everyday language, are no longer translatable into logically correct form. Pseudo-statements of this kind are encountered in especially large quantity, e.g., in the writings of Hegel and Heidegger. The latter has adopted many peculiarities of the Hegelian idiom along with their logical faults (e.g. predicates which should be applied to objects of a certain sort are instead applied to predicates of these objects or to "being" or to "existence" or to a relation between these objects).

Having found that many metaphysical statements are meaningless, we confront the question whether there is not perhaps a core of meaningful statements in metaphysics which would remain after elimination of all the meaningless ones.

Indeed, the results we have obtained so far might give rise to the view that there are many dangers of falling into nonsense in metaphysics, and that one must accordingly endeavor to avoid these traps with great care if one wants to do metaphysics. But actually the situation is that meaningful metaphysical statements are impossible. This follows from the task which metaphysics sets itself: to discover and formulate a kind of knowledge which is not accessible to empirical science.

Logical Empiricism: Meaning, Metaphysics, and Mathematics 417

We have seen earlier that the meaning of a statement lies in the method of its verification. A statement asserts only so much as is verifiable with respect to it. Therefore a sentence can be used only to assert an empirical proposition, if indeed it is used to assert anything at all. If something were to lie, in principle, beyond possible experience, it could be neither said nor thought nor asked.

(Meaningful) statements are divided into the following kinds. First there are statements which are true solely by virtue of their form ("tautologies" according to Wittgenstein; they correspond approximately to Kant's "analytic judgments"). They say nothing about reality. The formulae of logic and mathematics are of this kind. They are not themselves factual statements, but serve for the transformation of such statements. Secondly there are the negations of such statements ("*contradictions*"). They are self-contradictory, hence false by virtue of their form. With respect to all other statements the decision about truth or falsehood lies in the protocol sentences. They are therefore (true or false) *empirical statements* and belong to the domain of empirical science. Any statement one desires to construct which does not fall within these categories becomes automatically meaningless. Since metaphysics does not want to assert analytic propositions, nor to fall within the domain of empirical science, it is compelled to employ words for which no criteria of application are specified and which are therefore devoid of sense, or else to combine meaningful words in such a way that neither an analytic (or contradictory) statement nor an empirical statement is produced. In either case pseudo-statements are the inevitable product.

Logical analysis, then, pronounces the verdict of meaninglessness on any alleged knowledge that pretends to reach above or behind experience. This verdict hits, in the first place, any speculative metaphysics, any alleged knowledge by *pure thinking* or by *pure intuition* that pretends to be able to do without experience. But the verdict equally applies to the kind of metaphysics which, starting from experience, wants to acquire knowledge about that which *transcends experience* by means of special *inferences* (e.g. the neo-vitalist thesis of the directive presence of an "entelechy" in organic processes, which supposedly cannot be understood in terms of physics; the question concerning the "essence of causality," transcending the ascertainment of certain regularities of succession; the talk about the "thing in itself"). Further, the same judgment must be passed on all *philosophy of norms*, or *philosophy of value*, on any ethics or esthetics as a normative discipline. For the objective validity of a value or norm is (even on the view of the philosophers of value) not empirically verifiable nor deducible from empirical statements; hence it cannot be asserted (in a meaningful statement) at all. In other words: Either empirical criteria are

418   **Early Analytic Philosophy**

indicated for the use of "good" and "beautiful" and the rest of the predicates that are employed in the normative sciences, or they are not. In the first case, a statement containing such a predicate turns into a factual judgment, but not a value judgment; in the second case, it becomes a pseudo-statement. It is altogether impossible to make a statement that expresses a value judgment.

Finally, the verdict of meaninglessness also hits those metaphysical movements which are usually called, improperly, epistemological movements, that is *realism* (insofar as it claims to say more than the empirical fact that the sequence of events exhibits a certain regularity, which makes the application of the inductive method possible) and its opponents: subjective *idealism*, solipsism, phenomenalism, and *positivism* (in the earlier sense).

But what, then, is left over for *philosophy*, if all statements whatever that assert something are of an empirical nature and belong to factual science? What remains is not statements, nor a theory, nor a system, but only a *method*: the method of logical analysis. The foregoing discussion has illustrated the negative application of this method: in that context it serves to eliminate meaningless words, meaningless pseudo-statements. In its positive use it serves to clarify meaningful concepts and propositions, to lay logical foundations for factual science and for mathematics. The negative application of the method is necessary and important in the present historical situation. But even in its present practice, the positive application is more fertile. We cannot here discuss it in greater detail. It is the indicated task of logical analysis, inquiry into logical foundations, that is meant by "*scientific philosophy*" in contrast to metaphysics.

The question regarding the logical character of the statements which we obtain as the result of a logical analysis, e.g. the statements occurring in this and other logical papers, can here be answered only tentatively: such statements are partly analytic, partly empirical. For these statements about statements and parts of statements belong in part to pure *metalogic* (e.g. "a sequence consisting of the existence-symbol and a noun, is not a sentence"), in part to descriptive metalogic (e.g. "the word sequence at such and such a place in such and such a book is meaningless"). Metalogic will be discussed elsewhere. It will also be shown there that the metalogic which speaks about the sentences of a given language can be formulated in that very language itself.

7. Metaphysics as Expression of an Attitude Toward Life

Our claim that the statements of metaphysics are entirely meaningless, that they do not assert anything, will leave even those who agree intellectually with

Logical Empiricism: Meaning, Metaphysics, and Mathematics   419

our results with a painful feeling of strangeness: how could it be explained that so many men in all ages and nations, among them eminent minds, spent so much energy, nay veritable fervor, on metaphysics if the latter consisted of nothing but mere words, nonsensically juxtaposed? And how could one account for the fact that metaphysical books have exerted such a strong influence on readers up to the present day, if they contained not even errors, but nothing at all? These doubts are justified since metaphysics does indeed have a content; only it is not theoretical content. The (pseudo) statements of metaphysics do not serve for the *description of states of affairs*, neither existing ones (in that case they would be true statements) nor non-existing ones (in that case they would be at least false statements). They serve for the *expression of the general attitude of a person towards life* ("Lebenseinstellung, Lebensgefühl").

Perhaps we may assume that metaphysics originated from *mythology*. The child is angry at the "wicked table" which hurt him. Primitive man endeavors to conciliate the threatening demon of earthquakes, or he worships the deity of the fertile rains in gratitude. Here we confront personifications of natural phenomena, which are the quasi-poetic expression of man's emotional relationship to his environment. The heritage of mythology is bequeathed on the one hand to poetry, which produces and intensifies the effects of mythology on life in a deliberate way; on the other hand, it is handed down to theology, which develops mythology into a system. Which, now, is the historical role of metaphysics? Perhaps we may regard it as a substitute for theology on the level of systematic, conceptual thinking. The (supposedly) transcendent sources of knowledge of theology are here replaced by natural, yet supposedly trans-empirical sources of knowledge. On closer inspection the same content as that of mythology is here still recognizable behind the repeatedly varied dressing: we find that metaphysics also arises from the need to give expression to a man's attitude in life, his emotional and volitional reaction to the environment, to society, to the tasks to which he devotes himself, to the misfortunes that befall him. This attitude manifests itself, unconsciously as a rule, in everything a man does or says. It also impresses itself on his facial features, perhaps even on the character of his gait. Many people, now, feel a desire to create over and above these manifestations a special expression of their attitude, through which it might become visible in a more succinct and penetrating way. If they have artistic talent they are able to express themselves by producing a work of art. Many writers have already clarified the way in which the basic attitude is manifested through the style and manner of a work of art (e.g. Dilthey and his students). [In this connection the term "world view" ("Weltanschauung") is often used; we prefer to avoid it because of its ambiguity, which blurs the difference between attitude and theory, a difference which is of decisive importance for our analysis.] What is here essential for our considerations is only the fact that art is an adequate, metaphysics an inadequate means for the expression of the basic attitude. Of course, there need be no intrinsic objection to one's using any means of expression one likes. But in the case of metaphysics we find this situation: through the form of its works it pretends to be something that it is not. The form in question is that of a system of statements which are apparently related as premises and conclusions, that is, the form of a theory. In this way the fiction of theoretical content is generated, whereas, as we have seen, there is no such content. It is not only the reader, but the metaphysician himself who suffers from the illusion that the metaphysical statements say something, describe states of affairs. The metaphysician believes that he travels in territory in which truth and falsehood are at stake. In reality, however, he has not asserted anything, but only expressed something, like an artist. That the metaphysician is thus deluding himself cannot be inferred from the fact that he selects language as the medium of expression and declarative sentences as the form of expression; for lyrical poets do the same without succumbing to self-delusion. But the metaphysician supports his statements by arguments, he claims assent to their content, he polemicizes against metaphysicians of divergent persuasion by attempting to refute their assertions in his treatise. Lyrical poets, on the other hand, do not try to refute in their poem the statements in a poem by some other lyrical poet; for they know they are in the domain of art and not in the domain of theory.

Perhaps music is the purest means of expression of the basic attitude because it is entirely free from any reference to objects. The harmonious feeling or attitude, which the metaphysician tries to express in a monistic system, is more clearly expressed in the music of Mozart. And when a metaphysician gives verbal expression to his dualistic-heroic attitude towards life in a dualistic system, is it not perhaps because he lacks the ability of a Beethoven to express this attitude in an adequate medium? Metaphysicians are musicians without musical ability. Instead they have a strong inclination to work within the medium of the theoretical, to connect concepts and thoughts. Now, instead of activating, on the one hand, this inclination in the domain of science, and satisfying, on the other hand, the need for expression in art, the metaphysician confuses the two and produces a structure which achieves nothing for knowledge and something inadequate for the expression of attitude.

Our conjecture that metaphysics is a substitute, albeit an inadequate one, for art, seems to be further confirmed by the fact that the metaphysician who perhaps had artistic talent to the highest degree, viz. Nietzsche, almost entirely avoided the error of that confusion. A large part of his work has predominantly

Logical Empiricism: Meaning, Metaphysics, and Mathematics   **421**

empirical content. We find there, for instance, historical analyses of specific artistic phenomena, or an historical-psychological analysis of morals. In the work, however, in which he expresses most strongly that which others express through metaphysics or ethics, in *Thus Spake Zarathustra*, he does not choose the misleading theoretical form, but openly the form of art, of poetry.

Ayer, A. J., *Language, Truth, and Logic* **(Selections from Chs 4, 6). Reprinted from Ayer, A. J. (1952),** *Language, Truth, and Logic.* **New York: Dover. Originally published in 1936.**

Chapter 4: The *A Priori*

The view of philosophy which we have adopted may, I think, fairly be described as a form of empiricism. For it is characteristic of an empiricist to eschew metaphysics, on the ground that every factual proposition must refer to sense-experience. And even if the conception of philosophizing as an activity of analysis is not to be discovered in the traditional theories of empiricists, we have seen that it is implicit in their practice. At the same time, it must be made clear that, in calling ourselves empiricists, we are not avowing a belief in any of the psychological doctrines which are commonly associated with empiricism. For even if these doctrines were valid, their validity would be independent of the validity of any philosophical thesis. It could be established only by observation, and not by the purely logical considerations upon which our empiricism rests.

Having admitted that we are empiricists, we must now deal with the objection that is commonly brought against ill forms of empiricism; the objection, namely, that it is impossible on empiricist principles to account for our knowledge of necessary truths. For, as Hume conclusively showed, no general proposition whose validity is subject to the test of actual experience can ever be logically certain. No matter how often it is verified in practice, there still remains the possibility that it will be confuted on some future occasion. The fact that a law has been substantiated in $n - 1$ cases affords no logical guarantee that it will be substantiated in the nth case also, no matter how large we take n to be. And this means that no general proposition referring to a matter of fact can ever be shown to be necessarily and universally true. It can at best be a probable hypothesis. And this, we shall find, applies not only to general propositions, but to all propositions which have a factual content. They can none of them ever become logically certain. This conclusion, which we shall elaborate later on, is

Early Analytic Philosophy

one which must be accepted by every consistent empiricist. It is often thought to involve him in complete scepticism: but this is not the case. For the fact that the validity of a proposition cannot be logically guaranteed in no way entails that it is irrational for us to believe it. On the contrary, what is irrational is to look for a guarantee where none can be forthcoming: to demand certainty where probability is all that is obtainable. We have already remarked upon this, in referring to the work of Hume. And we shall make the point clearer when we come to treat of probability, in explaining the use which we make of empirical propositions. We shall discover that there is nothing perverse or paradoxical about the view that all the 'truths' of science and common sense are hypotheses; and consequently that the fact that it involves this view constitutes no objection to the empiricist thesis.

Where the empiricist does encounter difficulty is in connexion with the truths of formal logic and mathematics. For whereas a scientific generalization is readily admitted to be fallible, the truths of mathematics and logic appear to everyone to be necessary and certain. But if empiricism is correct no proposition which has a factual content can be necessary or certain. Accordingly the empiricist must deal with the truths of logic and mathematics in one of the two following ways: he must say either that they are not necessary truths, in which case he must account for the universal conviction that they are; or he must say that they have no factual content, and then he must explain how a proposition which is empty of all factual content can be true and useful and surprising.

If neither of these courses proves satisfactory, we shall be obliged to give way to rationalism. We shall be obliged to admit that there are some truths about the world which we can know independently of experience; that there are some properties which we can ascribe to all objects, even though we cannot conceivably observe that all objects have them. And we shall have to accept it as a mysterious inexplicable fact that our thought has this power to reveal to us authoritatively the nature of objects which we have never observed. Or else we must accept the Kantian explanation which, apart from the epistemological difficulties which we have already touched on, only pushes the mystery a stage further back.

It is clear that any such concession to rationalism would upset the main argument of this book. For the admission that there were some facts about the world which could be known independently of experience would be incompatible with our fundamental contention that a sentence says nothing unless it is empirically verifiable. And thus the whole force of our attack on metaphysics would be destroyed. It is vital, therefore, for us to be able to show that one or other of the empiricist accounts of the propositions of logic and mathematics is correct. If we are successful in this, we shall have destroyed the foundations of

Logical Empiricism: Meaning, Metaphysics, and Mathematics   423

rationalism. For the fundamental tenet of rationalism is that thought is an independent source of knowledge, and is moreover a more trustworthy source of knowledge than experience; indeed some rationalists have gone so far as to say that thought is the only source of knowledge. And the ground for this view is simply that the only necessary truths about the world which are known to us are known through thought and not through experience. So that if we can show either that the truths in question are not necessary or that they are not 'truths about the world', we shall be taking away the support on which rationalism rests. We shall be making good the empiricist contention that there are no 'truths of reason' which refer to matters of fact.

The course of maintaining that the truths of logic and mathematics are not necessary or certain was adopted by Mill. He maintained that these propositions were inductive generalizations based on an extremely large number of instances. The fact that the number of supporting instances was so very large accounted, in his view, for our believing these generalizations to be necessarily and universally true. The evidence in their favour was so strong that it seemed incredible to us that a contrary instance should ever arise. Nevertheless it was in principle possible for such generalizations to be confuted. They were highly probable, but, being inductive generalizations, they were not certain. The difference between them and the hypotheses of natural science was a difference in degree and not in kind. Experience gave us very good reason to suppose that a 'truth' of mathematics or logic was true universally; but we were not possessed of a guarantee. For these 'truths' were only empirical hypotheses which had worked particularly well in the past; and. like all empirical hypotheses, they were theoretically fallible.

I do not think that this solution of the empiricist's difficulty with regard to the propositions of logic and mathematics is acceptable. In discussing it, it is necessary to make a distinction which is perhaps already enshrined in Kant's famous dictum that, although there can be no doubt that all our knowledge begins with experience, it does not follow that it all arises out of experience.[1] When we say that the truths of logic are known independently of experience, we are not of course saying that they are innate, in the sense that we are born knowing them. It is obvious that mathematics and logic have to be learned in the same way as chemistry and history have to be learned. Nor are we denying that the first person to discover a given logical or mathematical truth was led to it by an inductive procedure. It is very probable, for example, that the principle of the syllogism was

---

[1]*Critique of Pure Reason*, 2nd ed., Introduction, section i. [Editor's note: as marked in the Preface, footnotes and references have been left unaltered from the original text from which the readings are pulled.]

Early Analytic Philosophy

formulated not before but after the validity of syllogistic reasoning had been observed in a number of particular cases. What we are discussing, however, when we say that logical and mathematical truths are known independently of experience, is not a historical question concerning the way in which these truths were originally discovered, nor a psychological question concerning the way in which each of us comes to learn them, but an epistemological question. The contention of Mill's which we reject is that the propositions of logic and mathematics have the same status as empirical hypotheses; that their validity is determined in the same way. We maintain that they are independent of experience in the sense that they do not owe their validity to empirical verification. We may come to discover them through an inductive process; but once we have apprehended them we see that they are necessarily true, that they hold good for every conceivable instance. And this serves to distinguish them from empirical generalizations. For we know that a proposition whose validity depends upon experience cannot be seen to be necessarily and universally true.

In rejecting Mill's theory, we are obliged to be somewhat dogmatic. We can do no more than state the issue clearly and then trust that his contention will be seen to be discrepant with the relevant logical facts. The following considerations may serve to show that of the two ways of dealing with logic and mathematics which are open to the empiricist, the one which Mill adopted is not the one which is correct.

The best way to substantiate our assertion that the truths of formal logic and pure mathematics are necessarily true is to examine cases in which they might seem to be confuted. It might easily happen, for example, that when I came to count what I had taken to be five pairs of objects, I found that they amounted only to nine. And if I wished to mislead people I might say that on this occasion twice five was not ten. But in that case I should not be using the complex sign '2 x 5 = 10' in the way in which is it ordinarily used. I should be taking it not as the expression of a purely mathematical proposition, but as the expression of an empirical generalization, to the effect that whenever I counted what appeared to me to be five pairs of objects I discovered that they were ten in number. This generalization may very well be false. But if it proved false in a given case, one would not say that the mathematical proposition '2 x 5 = 10' had been confuted. One would say that I was wrong in supposing that there were five pairs of objects to start with, or that one of the objects had been taken away while I was counting, or that two of them had coalesced, or that I had counted wrongly. One would adopt as an explanation whatever empirical hypothesis fitted in best with the accredited facts. The one explanation which would in no circumstances he adopted is that ten is not always the product of two and five.

Logical Empiricism: Meaning, Metaphysics, and Mathematics   **425**

To take another example: if what appears to be a Euclidean triangle is found by measurement not to have angles totalling 180 degrees, we do not say that we have met with an instance which invalidates the mathematical proposition that the sum of the three angles of a Euclidean triangle is 180 degrees. We say that we have measured wrongly, or, more probably, that the triangle we have been measuring is not Euclidean. And this is our procedure in every case in which a mathematical truth might appear to be confuted. We always preserve its validity by adopting some other explanation of the occurrence.

The same thing applies to the principles of formal logic. We may take an example relating to the so-called law of excluded middle, which states that a proposition must be either true or false, or, in other words, that it is impossible that a proposition and its contradictory should neither of them be true. One might suppose that a proposition of the form 'x has stopped doing y' would in certain cases constitute an exception to this law. For instance, if my friend has never yet written to me, it seems fair to say that it is neither true nor false that he has stopped writing to me. But in fact one would refuse to accept such an instance as an invalidation of the law of excluded middle. One would point out that the proposition 'My friend has stopped writing to me' is not a simple proposition, but the conjunction of the two propositions 'My friend wrote to me in the past' and 'My friend does not write to me now': and, furthermore, that the proposition 'My friend has not stopped writing to me' is not, as it appears to be, contradictory to 'My friend has stopped writing to me', but only contrary to it. For it means 'My friend wrote to me in the past, and he still writes to me'. When, therefore, we say that such a proposition as 'My friend has stopped writing to me' is sometimes neither true nor false, we are speaking inaccurately. For we seem to be saying that neither it nor its contradictory is true. Whereas what we mean, or anyhow should mean, is that neither it nor its apparent contradictory is true. And its apparent contradictory is really only its contrary. Thus we preserve the law of excluded middle by showing that the negating of a sentence does not always yield the contradictory of the proposition originally expressed.

There is no need to give further examples. Whatever instance we care to take, we shall always find that the situations in which a logical or mathematical principle might appear to be confuted are accounted for in such a way as to leave the principle unassailed. And this indicates that Mill was wrong in supposing that a situation could arise which would overthrow a mathematical truth. The principles of logic and mathematics are true universally simply because we never allow them to be anything else. And the reason for this is that we cannot abandon them without contradicting ourselves, without sinning against the rules which govern the use of language, and so making our utterances self-

Early Analytic Philosophy

stultifying. In other words, the truths of logic and mathematics are analytic propositions or tautologies. In saying this we are making what will be held to be an extremely controversial statement, and we must now proceed to make its implications clear.

The most familiar definition of an analytic proposition, or judgement, as be called it, is that given by Kant. He said[2] that an analytic judgement was one in which the predicate B belonged to the subject A as something which was covertly contained in the concept of A. He contrasted analytic with synthetic judgements, in which the predicate B lay outside the subject A, although it did stand in connexion with it. Analytic judgements, he explains, 'add nothing through the predicate to the concept of the subject, but merely break it up into those constituent concepts that have all along been thought in it, although confusedly'. Synthetic judgements, on the other hand, 'add to the concept of the subject a predicate which has not been in any wise thought in it, and which no analysis could possibly extract from it'. Kant gives 'all bodies are extended' as an example of an analytic judgement, on the ground that the required predicate can be extracted from the concept of 'body', 'in accordance with the principle of contradiction'; as an example of a synthetic judgement, be gives 'all bodies are heavy'. He refers also to '7+5=12' as a synthetic judgement, on the ground that the concept of twelve is by no means already thought in merely thinking the union of seven and five. And he appears to regard this as tantamount to saying that the judgement does not rest on the principle of contradiction alone. He holds, also, that through analytic judgements our knowledge is not ex-tended as it is through synthetic judgements. For in analytic judgements 'the concept which I already have is merely set forth and made intelligible to me'.

I think that this is a fair summary of Kant's account of the distinction between analytic and synthetic propositions, but I do not think that it succeeds in making the distinction clear. For even if we pass over the difficulties which arise out of the use of the vague term 'concept', and the unwarranted assumption that every judgement, as well as every German or English sentence, can be said to have a subject and a predicate, there remains still this crucial defect: Kant does not give one straightforward criterion for distinguishing between analytic and synthetic propositions; he gives two distinct criteria, which are by no means equivalent. Thus his ground for holding that the proposition '7 + 5 = 12' is synthetic is, as we have seen, that the subjective intension of '7 + 5' does not comprise the subjective intension of '12'; whereas his ground for holding that

---

[2] *Critique of Pure Reason*, 2nd ed., Introduction, sections iv and v.

Logical Empiricism: Meaning, Metaphysics, and Mathematics   427

'all bodies are extended' is an analytic proposition is that it rests on the principle of contradiction alone. That is, he employs a psychological criterion in the first of these examples, and a logical criterion in the second, and takes their equivalence for granted. But, in fact, a proposition which is synthetic according to the former criterion may very well be analytic according to the latter. For, as we have already pointed out, it is possible for symbols to be synonymous without having the same intentional meaning for anyone: and accordingly from the fact that one can think of the sum of seven and five without necessarily thinking of twelve, it by no means follows that the proposition '7 + 5 = 12' can be denied without self-contradiction. From the rest of his argument, it is clear that it is this logical proposition, and not any psychological proposition, that Kant is really anxious to establish. His use of the psychological criterion leads him to think that he has established it, when he has not.

I think that we can preserve the logical import of Kant's distinction between analytic and synthetic propositions, while avoiding the confusions which mar his actual account of it, if we say that a proposition is analytic when its validity depends solely on the definitions of the symbols it contains, and synthetic when its validity is determined by the facts of experience. Thus, the proposition 'There are ants which have established a system of slavery' is a synthetic proposition. For we cannot tell whether it is true or false merely by considering the definitions of the symbols which constitute it. We have to resort to actual observation of the behaviour of ants. On the other hand, the proposition 'Either some ants are parasitic or none are' is an analytic proposition. For one need not resort to observation to discover that there either are or are not ants which are parasitic. If one knows what is the function of the words 'either', 'or', and 'not', then one can see that any proposition of the form 'Either p is true or p is not true' is valid, independently of experience. Accordingly, all such propositions are analytic.

It is to be noticed that the proposition 'Either some ants are parasitic or none are' provides no information whatsoever about the behaviour of ants, or, indeed, about any matter of fact. And this applies to all analytic propositions. They none of them provide any information about any matter of fact. In other words, they are entirely devoid of factual content. And it is for this reason that no experience can confute them.

When we say that analytic propositions are devoid of factual content, and consequently that they say nothing, we are not suggesting that they are senseless in the way that metaphysical utterances are senseless. For, although they give us no information about any empirical situation, they do enlighten us by illustrating the way in which we use certain symbols. Thus if I say, 'Nothing

Early Analytic Philosophy

can be coloured in different ways at the same time with respect to the same part of itself', I am not saying anything about the properties of any actual thing; but I am not talking nonsense. I am expressing an analytic proposition, which records our determination to call a colour expanse which differs in quality from a neighbouring colour expanse a different part of a given thing. In other words, I am simply calling attention to the implications of a certain linguistic usage. Similarly, in saying that if all Bretons are Frenchmen, and all Frenchmen Europeans, then all Bretons are Europeans, I am not describing any matter of fact. But I am showing that in the statement that all Bretons are Frenchmen, and all Frenchmen Europeans, the further statement that all Bretons are Europeans is implicitly contained. And I am thereby indicating the convention which governs our usage of the words 'if' and 'all'.

We see, then, that there is a sense in which analytic propositions do give us new knowledge. They call attention to linguistic usages, of which we might otherwise not be conscious, and they reveal unsuspected implications in our assertions and beliefs. But we can see also that there is a sense in which they may be said to add nothing to our knowledge. For they tell us only what we may be said to know already. Thus, if I know that the existence of May Queens is a relic of tree-worship, and I discover that May Queens still exist in England, I can employ the tautology 'If p implies q, and p is true, q is true' to show that there still exists a relic of tree-worship in England. But in saying that there are still May Queens in England, and that the existence of May Queens is a relic of tree-worship, I have already asserted the existence in England of a relic of tree-worship. The use of the tautology does, indeed, enable me to make this concealed assertion explicit. But it does not provide me with any new knowledge, in the sense in which empirical evidence that the election of May Queens had been forbidden by law would provide me with new knowledge. If one had to set forth all the information one possessed, with regard to matters of fact, one would not write down any analytic propositions. But one would make use of analytic propositions in compiling one's encyclopedia, and would thus come to include propositions which one would otherwise have overlooked. And, besides enabling one to make one's list of information complete, the formulation of analytic propositions would enable one to make sure that the synthetic propositions of which the list was composed formed a self-consistent system. By showing which ways of combining propositions resulted in contradictions, they would prevent one from including incompatible propositions and so making the list self-stultifying. But in so far as we had actually used such words as 'all' and 'or' and 'not' without falling into self-contradiction, we might be said already to know what was revealed in the formulation of analytic propositions illustrating

Logical Empiricism: Meaning, Metaphysics, and Mathematics   **429**

the rules which govern our usage of these logical particles. So that here again we are justified in saying that analytic propositions do not increase our knowledge.

The analytic character of the truths of formal logic was obscured in the traditional logic through its being insufficiently formalized. For in speaking always of judgements, instead of propositions, and introducing irrelevant psychological questions, the traditional logic gave the impression of being concerned in some specially intimate way with the workings of thought. What it was actually concerned with was the formal relationship of classes, as is shown by the fact that all its principles of inference are subsumed in the Boolean class-calculus, which is subsumed in its turn in the propositional calculus of Russell and Whitehead.[3] Their system, expounded in *Principia Mathematica*, makes it clear that with the properties of men's minds, much less with the properties of material objects, but simply with the possibility of combining propositions by means of logical particles into analytic propositions, and with studying the formal relationship of these analytic propositions, in virtue of which one is deducible from another. Their procedure is to exhibit the propositions of formal logic as a deductive system, based on five primitive propositions, subsequently reduced in number to one. Hereby the distinction between logical truths and principles of inference, which was maintained in the Aristotelian logic, very properly disappears. Every principle of inference is put forward as a logical truth and every logical truth can serve as a principle of inference. The three Aristotelian 'Laws of thought', the law of identity, the law of excluded middle, and the law of non-contradiction, are incorporated in the system, but they are not considered more important than the other analytic propositions. They are not reckoned among the premises of the system. And the system of Russell and Whitehead itself is probably only one among many possible logics, each of which is composed of tautologies as interesting to the logician as the arbitrarily selected Aristotelian 'laws of thought'.[4]

A point which is not sufficiently brought out by Russell, if indeed it is recognized by him at all, is that every logical proposition is valid in its own right. Its validity does not depend on its being incorporated in a system, and deduced from certain propositions which are taken as self-evident. The construction of systems of logic is useful as a means of discovering and certifying analytic propositions, but it is not in principle essential even for this purpose. For it is

---

[3] Vide Karl Menger, 'Die Neue Logik', *Krise und Neuaufbau in den Exakten Wissenschaften*, pp 94-6; and Lewis and Langford, *Symbolic Logic*, Chapter v.

[4] Vide Lewis and Langford, *Symbolic Logic*, Chapter vii, for an elaboration of this point.

430   Early Analytic Philosophy

possible to conceive of a symbolism in which every analytic proposition could be seen to be analytic in virtue of its form alone.

The fact that the validity of an analytic proposition in no way depends on its being deducible from other analytic propositions is our justification for disregarding the question whether the propositions of mathematics are reducible to propositions of formal logic, in the way that Russell supposed.[5] For even if it is the case that the definition of a cardinal number as a class of classes similar to a given class is circular, and it is not possible to reduce mathematical notions to purely logical notions, it will still remain true that the propositions of mathematics are analytic propositions. They will form a special class of analytic propositions, containing special terms, but they will be none the less analytic for that. For the criterion of an analytic proposition is that its validity should follow simply from the definition of the terms contained in it. and this condition is fulfilled by the propositions of pure mathematics.

The mathematical propositions which one might most pardonably suppose to be synthetic are the propositions of geometry. For it is natural for us to think, as Kant thought, that geometry is the study of the properties of physical space, and consequently that its propositions have factual content. And if we believe this, and also recognize that the truths of geometry are necessary and certain, then we may be inclined to accept Kant's hypothesis that space is the form of intuition of our outer sense, a form imposed by us on the matter of sensation, as the only possible explanation of our *a priori* knowledge of these synthetic propositions. But while the view that pure geometry is concerned with physical space was plausible enough in Kant's day, when the geometry of Euclid was the only geometry known, the subsequent invention of non-Euclidean geometries has shown it to be mistaken. We see now that the axioms of a geometry are simply definitions. and that the theorems of a geometry are simply the logical consequences of these definitions.[6] A geometry is not in itself about physical space; in itself it cannot be said to be 'about' anything. But we can use a geometry to reason about physical space. That is to say, once we have given the axioms a physical interpretation, we can proceed to apply the theorems to the objects which satisfy the axioms. Whether a geometry can be applied to the actual physical world or not, is an empirical question which falls outside the scope of the geometry itself. There is no sense, therefore, in asking which of the various geometries known to us are false and which are true. In so far as they are all free from contradiction, they are all true. What one can ask is which of them is the

---

[5]Vide *Introduction to Mathematical Philosophy*, Chapter ii.
[6]cf. H. Poincaré, *La Science et l'Hypothèse*, Part II, Chapter iii.

most useful on any given occasion, which of them can be applied most easily and most fruitfully to an actual empirical situation. But the proposition which states that a certain application of a geometry is possible is not itself a proposition of that geometry. All that the geometry itself tells us is that if anything can be brought under the definitions, it will also satisfy the theorems. It is therefore a purely logical system, and its propositions are purely analytic propositions.

It might be objected that the use made of diagrams in geometrical treatises shows that geometrical reasoning it not purely abstract and logical, but depends on our intuition of the properties of figures. In fact, however, the use of diagrams is not essential to completely rigorous geometry. The diagrams are introduced as an aid to our reason. They provide us with a particular application of the geometry, and so assist us to perceive the more general truth that the axioms of the geometry Involve certain consequences. But the fact that most of us need the help of an example to make us aware of those consequences does not show that the relation between them and the axioms is not a purely logical relation. It shows merely that our intellects are unequal to the task of carrying out very abstract processes of reasoning without the assistance of intuition. In other words, it has no bearing on the nature of geometrical propositions, but is simply an empirical fact about ourselves. Moreover, the appeal to intuition, though generally of psychological value, is also a source of danger to the geometer. He is tempted to make assumptions which are accidentally true of the particular figure he is taking as an illustration, but do not follow from his axioms. It has, indeed, been shown that Euclid himself was guilty of this, and consequently that the presence of the figure is essential to some of his proofs.[7] This shows that his system is not, as he presents it, completely rigorous, although of course it can be made so. It does not show that the presence of the figure is essential to a truly rigorous geometrical proof. To suppose that it did would be to take as a necessary feature of all geometries what is really only an incidental defect in one particular geometrical system.

We conclude, then, that the propositions of pure geometry are analytic. And this leads us to reject Kant's hypothesis that geometry deals with the form of intuition of our outer sense. For the ground for this hypothesis was that it alone explained how the propositions of geometry could be both true *a priori* and synthetic: and we have seen that they are not synthetic. Similarly our view that the propositions of arithmetic are not synthetic but analytic leads us to reject the Kantian hypothesis[8] that arithmetic is concerned with our pure intuition of

---

[7] cf. M. Black, *The Nature of Mathematics*, p.154.
[8] This hypothesis is not mentioned in the *Critique of Pure Reason* but was maintained by Kant at an earlier date.

Early Analytic Philosophy

time, the form of our inner sense. And thus we are able to dismiss Kant's transcendental aesthetic without having to bring forward the epistemological difficulties which it is commonly said to involve. For the only argument which can be brought in favour of Kant's theory is that it alone explains certain 'facts'. And now we have found that the 'facts' which it purports to explain are not facts at all. For while it is true that we have *a priori* knowledge of necessary propositions, it is not true, as Kant supposed, that any of these necessary propositions are synthetic. They are without exception analytic propositions, or, in other words, tautologies.

We have already explained how it is that these analytic propositions are necessary and certain. We saw that the reason why they cannot be confuted in experience is that they do not make any assertion about the empirical world. They simply record our determination to use words in a certain fashion. We cannot deny them without infringing the conventions which are presupposed by our very denial, and so falling into self-contradiction. And this is the sole ground of their necessity. As Wittgenstein puts it, our justification for holding that the world could not conceivably disobey the laws of logic is simply that we could not say of an unlogical world how it would look.[9] And just as the validity of an analytic proposition is independent of the nature of the external world, so is it independent of the nature of our minds. It is perfectly conceivable that we should have employed different linguistic conventions from those which we actually do employ. But what-ever these conventions might be, the tautologies in which we recorded them would always be necessary. For any denial of them would be self-stultifying.

We see, then, that there is nothing mysterious about the apodeictic certainty of logic and mathematics. Our knowledge that no observation can ever confute the proposition '7 + 5 = 12' depends simply on the fact that the symbolic expression '7 + 5' is synonymous with '12', just as our knowledge that every occulist is an eye-doctor depends on the fact that the symbol 'eye-doctor' is synonymous with 'oculist'. And the same explanation holds good for every other *a priori* truth.

What is mysterious at first sight is that these tautologies should on occasion be so surprising, that there should be in mathematics and logic the possibility of invention and discovery. As Poincaré says: 'If all the assertions which mathematics puts forward can be derived from one another by formal logic, mathematics cannot amount to anything more than an immense tautology.

---

[9] *Tractatus Logico-Philosophicus*, 3.031.

Logical Empiricism: Meaning, Metaphysics, and Mathematics   **433**

Logical inference can teach us nothing essentially new, and if everything is to proceed from the principle of identity, everything must be reducible to it. But can we really allow that these theorems which fill so many books serve no other purpose than to say in a roundabout fashion 'A=A'[10]?' Poincaré finds this incredible. His own theory is that the sense of invention and discovery in mathematics belongs to it in virtue of mathematical induction, the principle that what is true for the number 1, and true for $n+1$ when it is true for n[11] is true for all numbers. And he claims that this is a synthetic *a priori* principle. It is, in fact, *a priori*, but it is not synthetic. It is a defining principle of the natural numbers. serving to distinguish them from such numbers as the infinite cardinal numbers, to which it cannot be applied.[12] Moreover, we must remember that discoveries can be made, not only in arithmetic, but also in geometry and formal logic, where no use is made of mathematical induction. So that even if Poincaré were right about mathematical induction, he would not have provided a satisfactory explanation of the paradox that a mere body of tautologies can be so interesting and so surprising.

The true explanation is very simple. The power of logic and mathematics to surprise us depends, like their usefulness, on the limitations of our reason. A being whose intellect was infinitely powerful would take no interest in logic and mathematics.[13] For he would be able to see at a glance everything that his definitions implied, and, accordingly, could never learn anything from logical inference which he was not fully conscious of already. But our intellects are not of this order. It is only a minute proportion of the consequences of our definitions that we are able to detect at a glance. Even so simple a tautology as '91 x 79 = 7189' is beyond the scope of our immediate apprehension. To assure ourselves that '7189' is synonymous with '91 x 79' we have to resort to calculation, which is simply a process of tautological transformation—that is, a process by which we change the form of expressions without altering their significance. The multiplication tables are rules for carrying out this process in arithmetic, just as the laws of logic are rules for the tautological transformation of sentences expressed in logical symbolism or in ordinary language. As the process of calculation is carried out more or less mechanically, it is easy for us to make a slip and so unwittingly contradict ourselves. And this accounts for the existence

---

[10]*La Science et l'Hypothèse*, Part I, Chapter i.

[11]This was wrongly stated in previous editions as 'true for n when it is true for $n+1$'.

[12]cf. B. Russell's *Introduction to Mathematical Philosophy*, Chapter iii, p. 27.

[13]cf. Hans Hahn, 'Logik. Mathematik und Naturerkennen', *Einheitswissenschaft*. Heft II, p. 18. 'Ein allwissendes Wesen braucht keine Logik und keine Mathematik.'

of logical and mathematical 'falsehoods', which otherwise might appear paradoxical. Clearly the risk of error in logical reasoning is proportionate to the length and the complexity of the process of calculation. And in the same way, the more complex an analytic proposition is, the more chance it has of interesting and surprising us.

It is easy to see that the danger of error in logical reasoning can be minimized by the introduction of symbolic devices, which enable us to express highly complex tautologies in a conveniently simple form. And this gives us an opportunity for the exercise of invention in the pursuit of logical inquiries. For a well-chosen definition will call our attention to analytic truths, which would otherwise have escaped us. And the framing of definitions which are useful and fruitful may well be regarded as a creative act.

Having thus shown that there is no inexplicable paradox involved in the view that the truths of logic and mathematics are all of them analytic, we may safely adopt it as the only satisfactory explanation of their *a priori* necessity. And in adopting it we vindicate the empiricist claim that there can be no *a priori* knowledge of reality. For we show that the truths of pure reason, the propositions which we know to be valid independently of all experience. are so only in virtue of their lack of factual content. To say that a proposition is true *a priori* is to say that it is a tautology. And tautologies, though they may serve to guide us in our empirical search for knowledge, do not in themselves contain any information about any matter of fact

Chapter 6: Critique of Ethics and Theology

There is still one objection to be met before we can claim to have justified our view that all synthetic propositions are empirical hypotheses. This objection is based on the common supposition that our speculative knowledge is of two distinct kinds - that which relates to questions of empirical fact, and that which relates to questions of value. It will be said that 'statements of value' are genuine synthetic propositions, but that they cannot with any show of justice be represented as hypotheses, which are used to predict the course of our sensations; and, accordingly, that the existence of ethics and aesthetics as branches of speculative knowledge presents an insuperable objection to our radical empiricist thesis.

In face of this objection, it is our business to give an account of 'judgements of value' which is both satisfactory in itself and consistent with our general empiricist principles. We shall set ourselves to show that in so far as statements of value are significant, they are ordinary 'scientific' statements; and that in so far as they are not scientific, they are not in the literal sense significant, but are simply expressions of emotion which can be neither true nor false. In maintaining this view, we may confine ourselves for the present to the case of ethical statements. What is said about them will be found to apply, *mutatis mutandis*, to the case of aesthetic statements also.[1]

The ordinary system of ethics, as elaborated in the works of ethical philosophers, is very far from being a homogeneous whole. Not only is it apt to contain pieces of metaphysics, and analyses of non-ethical concepts: its actual ethical contents are themselves of very different kinds. We may divide them, indeed, into four main classes. There are, first of all, propositions which express definitions of ethical terms, or judgements about the legitimacy or possibility of certain definitions. Secondly, there are propositions describing the phenomena of moral experience, and their causes. Thirdly, there are exhortations to moral virtue. And, lastly, there are actual ethical judgements. It is unfortunately the case that the distinction between these four classes, plain as it is, is commonly ignored by ethical philosophers; with the result that it is often very difficult to tell from their works what it is that they are seeking to discover or prove.

In fact, it is easy to see that only the first of our four classes, namely that which comprises the propositions relating to the definitions of ethical terms, can be said to constitute ethical philosophy. The propositions which describe the phenomena of moral experience, and their causes, must be assigned to the science of psychology, or sociology. The exhortations to moral virtue are not propositions at all, but ejaculations or commands which are designed to provoke the reader to action of a certain sort. Accordingly, they do not belong to any branch of philosophy or science. As for the expressions of ethical judgements. we have not yet determined how they should be classified. But inasmuch as they are certainly neither definitions nor comments upon definitions, nor quotations, we may say decisively that they do not belong to ethical philosophy. A strictly philosophical treatise on ethics should therefore make no ethical pronouncements. But it should, by giving an analysis of ethical terms, show what is the category to which all such pronouncements belong. And this is what we are now about to do.

A question which is often discussed by ethical philosophers is whether it is possible to find definitions which would reduce all ethical terms to one or two fundamental terms. But this question, though it undeniably belongs to ethical philosophy, is not relevant to our present inquiry. We are not now concerned to

---

[1]The argument that follows should be read in conjunction with the Introduction, pp. 25-8.

Early Analytic Philosophy

discover which term, within the sphere of ethical terms, is to be taken as fundamental; whether, for example, 'good' can be defined in terms of 'right' or 'right' in terms of 'good', or both in terms of 'value'. What we are interested in is the possibility of reducing the whole sphere of ethical terms to non-ethical terms. We are inquiring whether statements of ethical value can be translated into statements of empirical fact.

That they can be so translated is the contention of those ethical philosophers who are commonly called subjectivists, and of those who are known as utilitarians. For the utilitarian defines the rightness of actions, and the goodness of ends, in terms of the pleasure, or happiness, or satisfaction, to which they give rise; the subjectivist, in terms of the feelings of approval which a certain person, or group of people, has towards them. Each of these types of definition makes moral judgements into a sub-class of psychological or sociological judgements; and for this reason they are very attractive to us. For, if either was correct, it would follow that ethical assertions were not genetically different from the factual assertions which are ordinarily contrasted with them; and the account which we have already given of empirical hypotheses would apply to them also.

Nevertheless we shall not adopt either a subjectivist or a utilitarian analysis of ethical terms. We reject the subjectivist view that to call an action right, or a thing good, is to say that it is generally approved of. because it is not self-contradictory to assert that some actions which are generally approved of are not right, or that some things which are generally approved of are not good. And we reject the alternative subjectivist view that a man who asserts that a certain action is right, or that a certain thing is good, is saying that he himself approves of it, on the ground that a man who confessed that he sometimes approved of what was bad or wrong would not be contradicting himself. And a similar argument is fatal to utilitarianism. We cannot agree that to call an action right is to say that of all the actions possible in the circumstances it would cause, or be likely to cause, the greatest happiness, or the greatest balance of pleasure over pain, or the greatest balance of satisfied over unsatisfied desire, because we find that it is not self-contradictory to say that it is sometimes wrong to perform the action which would actually or probably cause the greatest happiness, or the greatest balance of pleasure over pain, or of satisfied over unsatisfied desire. And since it is not self-contradictory to say that some pleasant things are not good, or that some bad things are desired, it cannot be the case that the sentence 'x is good' is equivalent to 'x is pleasant', or to 'x is desired'. And to every other variant of utilitarianism with which I am acquainted the same objection can be made. And therefore we should. I think, conclude that the

Logical Empiricism: Meaning, Metaphysics, and Mathematics

validity of ethical judgements is not determined by the felicific tendencies of actions, any more than by the nature of people's feelings; but that it must be regarded as 'absolute' or 'intrinsic', and not empirically calculable.

If we say this, we are not, of course, denying that it is possible to invent a language in which all ethical symbols are definable in non-ethical terms, or even that it is desirable to invent such a language and adopt it in place of our own; what we are denying is that the suggested reduction of ethical to non-ethical statements is consistent with the conventions of our actual language. That is, we reject utilitarianism and subjectivism, not as proposals to replace our existing ethical notions by new ones, but as analyses of our existing ethical notions. Our contention is simply that, in our language, sentences which contain normative ethical symbols are not equivalent to sentences which express psychological propositions, or indeed empirical propositions of any kind.

It is advisable here to make it plain that it is only normative ethical symbols, and not descriptive ethical symbols, that are held by us to be indefinable in factual terms. There is a danger of confusing these two types of symbols, because they are commonly constituted by signs of the same sensible form. Thus a complex sign of the form 'x is wrong' may constitute a sentence which expresses a moral judgement concerning a certain type of conduct, or it may constitute a sentence which states that a certain type of conduct is repugnant to the moral sense of a particular society. In the latter case, the symbol 'wrong' is a descriptive ethical symbol, and the sentence in which it occurs expresses an ordinary sociological proposition; in the former case, the symbol 'wrong' is a normative ethical symbol, and the sentence in which it occurs does not, we maintain, express an empirical proposition at all. It is only with normative ethics that we are at present concerned; so that whenever ethical symbols are used in the course of this argument without qualification, they are always to be interpreted as symbols of the normative type.

In admitting that normative ethical concepts are irreducible to empirical concepts, we seem to be leaving the way clear for the 'absolutist' view of ethics – that is, the view that statements of value are not controlled by observation, as ordinary empirical propositions are, but only by a mysterious 'intellectual intuition'. A feature of this theory, which is seldom recognized by its advocates, is that it makes statements of value unverifiable. For it is notorious that what seems intuitively certain to one person may seem doubtful, or even false, to another. So that unless it is possible to provide some criterion by which one may decide between conflicting intuitions, a mere appeal to intuition is worthless as a test of a proposition's validity. But in the case of moral judgements no such criterion can be given. Some moralists claim to settle the matter by saying that

Early Analytic Philosophy

they 'know' that their own moral judgements are correct. But such an assertion is of purely psychological interest, and has not the slightest tendency to prove the validity of any moral judgement. For dissentient moralists may equally well 'know' that their ethical views are correct. And. as far as subjective certainty goes, there will be nothing to choose between them. When such differences of opinion arise in connexion with an ordinary empirical proposition, one may attempt to resolve them by referring to, or actually carrying out, some relevant empirical test. But with regard to ethical statements, there is, on the 'absolutist' or 'intuitionist' theory, no relevant empirical test. We are therefore justified in saying that on this theory ethical statements are held to be unverifiable. They are, of course, also held to be genuine synthetic proportions.

Considering the use which we have made of the principle that a synthetic proposition is significant only if it is empirically verifiable, it is clear that the acceptance of an 'absolutist' theory of ethics would undermine the whole of our main argument. And as we have already rejected the 'naturalistic' theories which are commonly supposed to provide the only alternative to 'absolutism' in ethics, we seem to have reached a difficult position. We shall meet the difficulty by showing that the correct treatment of ethical statements is afforded by a third theory, which is wholly compatible with our radical empiricism.

We begin by admitting that the fundamental ethical concepts are unanalysable, inasmuch as there is no criterion by which one can test the validity of the judgements in which they occur. So far we are in agreement with the absolutists. But, unlike the absolutists, we are able to give an explanation of this fact about ethical concepts. We say that the reason why they are unanalysable is that they are mere pseudo-concepts. The presence of an ethical symbol in a proposition adds nothing to its factual content. Thus if I say to someone, 'You acted wrongly in stealing that money,' I am not stating anything more than if I had simply said, 'You stole that money.' In adding that this action is wrong I am not making any further statement about it. I am simply evincing my moral disapproval of it. It is as if I had said, 'You stole that money,' in a peculiar tone of horror, or written it with the addition of some special exclamation marks. The tone, or the exclamation marks, adds nothing to the literal meaning of the sentence. It merely serves to show that the expression of it is attended by certain feelings in the speaker.

If now I generalize my previous statement and say, 'Stealing money is wrong,' I produce a sentence which has no factual meaning – that is, expresses no proposition which can be either true or false. It is as if I had written 'Stealing money!!' – where the shape and thickness of the exclamation marks show, by a suitable convention, that a special sort of moral disapproval is the feeling

Logical Empiricism: Meaning, Metaphysics, and Mathematics 439

which is being expressed. It is clear that there is nothing said here which can be true or false. Another man may disagree with me about the wrongness of stealing, in the sense that he may not have the same feelings about stealing as I have, and he may quarrel with me on account of my moral sentiments. But he cannot, strictly speaking, contradict me. For in saying that a certain type of action is right or wrong, I am not making any factual statement, not even a statement about my own state of mind. I am merely expressing certain moral sentiments. And the man who is ostensibly contradicting me is merely expressing his moral sentiments. So that there is plainly no sense in asking which of us is in the right. For neither of us is asserting a genuine proposition.

What we have just been saying about the symbol 'wrong' applies to all normative ethical symbols. Sometimes they occur in sentences which record ordinary empirical facts besides expressing ethical feeling about those facts: sometimes they occur in sentences which simply express ethical feeling about a certain type of action, or situation, without making any statement of fact. But in every case in which one would commonly be said to be making an ethical judgement, the function of the relevant ethical word is purely 'emotive'. It is used to express feeling about certain objects, but not to make any assertion about them.

It is worth mentioning that ethical terms do not serve only to express feeling. They are calculated also to arouse feeling, and so to stimulate action. Indeed some of them are used in such a way as to give the sentences in which they occur the effect of commands. Thus the sentence 'It is your duty to tell the truth' may be regarded both as the expression of a certain sort of ethical feeling about truthfulness and as the expression of the command 'Tell the truth.' The sentence 'You ought to tell the truth' also involves the command 'Tell the truth', but here the tone of the command is less emphatic. In the sentence 'It is good to tell the truth' the command has become little more than a suggestion. And thus the 'meaning" of the word 'good', in its ethical usage, is differentiated from that of the word 'duty' or the word 'ought'. In fact we may define the meaning of the various ethical words in terms both of the different feelings they are ordinarily taken to express, and also the different responses which they are calculated to provoke.

We can now see why it is impossible to find a criterion for determining the validity of ethical judgements. It is not because they have an 'absolute' validity which is mysteriously independent of ordinary sense-experience, but because they have no objective validity whatsoever. If a sentence makes no statement at all, there is obviously no sense in asking whether what it says is true or false. And we have seen that sentences which simply express moral judgements do not say anything. They are pure expressions of feeling and as such do not come

Early Analytic Philosophy

under the category of truth and falsehood. They are unverifiable for the same reason as a cry of pain or a word of command is unverifiable – because they do not express genuine propositions.

Thus, although our theory of ethics might fairly be said to be radically subjectivist, it differs in a very important respect from the orthodox subjectivist theory. For the orthodox subjectivist does not deny, as we do, that the sentences of a moralizer express genuine propositions. All he denies is that they express propositions of a unique nonempirical character. His own view is that they express propositions about the speaker's feelings. If this were so, ethical judgements clearly would be capable of being true or false. They would be true if the speaker had the relevant feelings, and false if he had not. And this is a matter which is, in principle, empirically verifiable. Furthermore they could be significantly contradicted. For if I say, 'Tolerance is a virtue,' and someone answers, 'You don't approve of it,' he would, on the ordinary subjectivist theory, be contradicting me. On our theory, he would not be contradicting me, because, in saying that tolerance was a virtue, I should not be making any statement about my own feelings or about anything else. I should simply be evincing my feelings, which is not at all the same thing as saying that I have them.

The distinction between the expression of feeling and the assertion of feeling is complicated by the fact that the assertion that one has a certain feeling often accompanies the expression of that feeling, and is then, indeed, a factor in the expression of that feeling. Thus I may simultaneously express boredom and say that I am bored, and in that case my utterance of the words 'I am bored' is one of the circumstances which make it true to say that I am expressing or evincing boredom. But I can express boredom without actually saying that I am bored. I can express it by my tone and gestures, while making a statement about something wholly unconnected with it, or by an ejaculation, or without uttering any words at all. So that even if the assertion that one has a certain feeling always involves the expression of that feeling, the expression of a feeling assuredly does not always involve the assertion that one has it. And this is the important point to grasp in considering the distinction between our theory and the ordinary subjectivist theory. For whereas the subjectivist holds that ethical statements actually assert the existence of certain feelings, we hold that ethical statements are expressions and excitants of feeling which do not necessarily involve any assertions.

We have already remarked that the main objection to the ordinary subjectivist theory is that the validity of ethical judgements is not determined by the nature of their author's feelings. And this is an objection which our theory escapes. For it does not imply that the existence of any feelings is a necessary and sufficient

Logical Empiricism: Meaning, Metaphysics, and Mathematics 441

condition of the validity of an ethical judgement. It implies, on the contrary, that ethical judgements have no validity.

There is, however, a celebrated argument against subjectivist theories which our theory does not escape. It has been pointed out by Moore that if ethical statements were simply statements about the speaker's feelings, it would be impossible to argue about questions of value.[2] To take a typical example: if a man said that thrift was a virtue, and another replied that it was a vice, they would not, on this theory, be disputing with one another. One would be saying that he approved of thrift, and the other that *he* didn't; and there is no reason why both these statements should not be true. Now Moore held it to be obvious that we do dispute about questions of value, and accordingly concluded that the particular form of subjectivism which he was discussing was false.

It is plain that the conclusion that it is impossible to dispute about questions of value follows from our theory also. For as we hold that such sentences as 'Thrift is a virtue' and 'Thrift is a vice' do not express propositions at all, we clearly cannot hold that they express incompatible propositions. We must therefore admit that if Moore's argument really refutes the ordinary subjectivist theory, it also refutes ours. But, in fact, we deny that it does refute even the ordinary subjectivist theory. For we hold that one really never does dispute about questions of value.

This may seem, at first sight, to be a very paradoxical assertion. For we certainly do engage in disputes which are ordinarily regarded as disputes about questions of value. But, in all such cases, we find, if we consider the matter closely, that the dispute is not really about a question of value, but about a question of fact. When someone disagrees with us about the moral value of a certain action or type of action, we do admittedly resort to argument in order to win him over to our way of thinking. But we do not attempt to show by our arguments that he has the 'wrong' ethical feeling towards a situation whose nature he has correctly apprehended. What we attempt to show is that he is mistaken about the facts of the case. We argue that he has misconceived the agent's motive: or that he has misjudged the effects of the action, or its probable effects in view of the agent's knowledge; or that he has failed to take into account the special circumstances in which the agent was placed. Or else we employ more general arguments about the effects which actions of a certain type tend to produce, or the qualities which are usually manifested in their performance. We do this in the hope that we have only to get our opponent to

---

[2] cf. *Philosophical Studies*, 'The Nature of Moral Philosophy'.

Early Analytic Philosophy

agree with us about the nature of the empirical facts for him to adopt the same moral attitude towards them as we do. And as the people with whom we argue have generally received the same moral education as ourselves, and live in the same social order, our expectation is usually justified. But if our opponent happens to have undergone a different process of moral 'conditioning' from ourselves, so that, even when he acknowledges all the facts, he still disagrees with us about the moral value of the actions under discussion, then we abandon the attempt to convince him by argument. We say that it is impossible to argue with him because he has a distorted or undeveloped moral sense; which signifies merely that he employs a different set of values from our own. We feel that our own system of values is superior, and therefore speak in such derogatory terms of his. But we cannot bring forward any arguments to show that our system is superior. For our judgement that it is so is itself a judgement of value, and accordingly outside the scope of argument. It is because argument fails us when we come to deal with pure questions of value, as distinct from questions of fact, that we finally resort to mere abuse.

In short, we find that argument is possible on moral questions only if some system of values is presupposed. If our opponent concurs with us in expressing moral disapproval of all actions of a given type t, then we may get him to condemn a particular action A, by bringing forward arguments to show that A is of type t. For the question whether A does or does not belong to that type is a plain question of fact. Given that a man has certain moral principles, we argue that he must, in order to be consistent, react morally to certain things in a certain way. What we do not and cannot argue about is the validity of these moral principles. We merely praise or condemn them in the light of our own feelings.

If anyone doubts the accuracy of this account of moral disputes, let him try to construct even an imaginary argument on a question of value which does not reduce itself to an argument about a question of logic or about an empirical matter of fact. I am confident that he will not succeed in producing a single example. And if that is the case, we must allow that its involving the impossibility of purely ethical arguments is not, as Moore thought, a ground of objection to our theory, but rather a point in favour of it.

Having upheld our theory against the only criticism which appeared to threaten it, we may now use it to define the nature of all ethical inquiries. We find that ethical philosophy consists simply in saying that ethical concepts are pseudo-concepts and therefore unanalysable. The further task of describing the different feelings that the different ethical terms are used to express, and the different reactions that they customarily provoke, is a task for the psychologist. There cannot be such a thing as ethical science, if by ethical science one means

Logical Empiricism: Meaning, Metaphysics, and Mathematics **443**

the elaboration of a 'true' system of morals. For we have seen that, as ethical judgements are mere expressions of feeling, there can be no way of determining the validity of any ethical system, and, indeed, no sense in asking whether any such system is true. All that one may legitimately inquire in this connexion is, What are the moral habits of a given person or group of people, and what causes them to have precisely those habits and feelings? And this inquiry falls wholly within the scope of the existing social sciences.

It appears, then, that ethics, as a branch of knowledge, is nothing more than a department of psychology and sociology. And in case anyone thinks that we are overlooking the existence of casuistry, we may remark that casuistry is not a science, but is a purely analytical investigation of the structure of a given moral system. In other words, it is an exercise in formal logic.

When one comes to pursue the psychological inquiries which constitute ethical science, one is immediately enabled to account for the Kantian and hedonistic theories of morals. For one finds that one of the chief causes of moral behaviour is fear, both conscious and unconscious, of a god's displeasure, and fear of the enmity of society. And this, indeed, is the reason why moral precepts present themselves to some people as 'categorical' commands. And one finds, also, that the moral code of a society is partly determined by the beliefs of that society concerning the conditions of its own happiness – or, in other words, that a society tends to encourage or discourage a given type of conduct by the use of moral sanctions according as it appears to promote or detract from the contentment of the society as a whole. And this is the reason why altruism is recommended in most moral codes and egotism condemned. It is from the observation of this connexion between morality and happiness that hedonistic or eudaemonistic theories of morals ultimately spring, just as the moral theory of Kant is based on the fact, previously explained, that moral precepts have for some people the force of inexorable commands. As each of these theories ignores the fact which lies at the root of the other, both may be criticized as being one-sided; but this is not the main objection to either of them. Their essential defect is that they treat propositions which refer to the causes and attributes of our ethical feelings as if they were definitions of ethical concepts. And thus they fail to recognize that ethical concepts are pseudo-concepts and consequently indefinable.

As we have already said, our conclusions about the nature of ethics apply to aesthetics also. Aesthetic terms are used in exactly the same way as ethical terms. Such aesthetic words as 'beautiful' and 'hideous' are employed, as ethical words are employed, not to make statements of fact, but simply to express certain feelings and evoke a certain response. It follows, as in ethics,

Early Analytic Philosophy

that there is no sense in attributing objective validity to aesthetic judgements, and no possibility of arguing about questions of value in aesthetics, but only about questions of fact. A scientific treatment of aesthetics would show us what in general were the causes of aesthetic feeling, why various societies produced and admired the works of art they did, why taste varies as it does within a given society, and so forth. And these are ordinary psychological or sociological questions. They have, of course, little or nothing to do with aesthetic criticism as we understand it. But that is because the purpose of aesthetic criticism is not so much to give knowledge as to communicate emotion. The critic, by calling attention to certain features of the work under review, and expressing his own feelings about them, endeavours to make us share his attitude towards the work as a whole. The only relevant propositions that he formulates are propositions describing the nature of the work. And these are plain records of fact. We conclude, therefore, that there is nothing in aesthetics, any more than there is in ethics, to justify the view that it embodies a unique type of knowledge.

It should now be clear that the only information which we can legitimately derive from the study of our aesthetic and moral experiences is information about our own mental and physical make-up. We take note of these experiences as providing data for our psychological and sociological generalizations. And this is the only way in which they serve to increase our knowledge. It follows that any attempt to make our use of ethical and aesthetic concepts the basis of a metaphysical theory concerning the existence of a world of values, as distinct from the world of facts, involves a false analysis of these concepts. Our own analysis has shown that the phenomena of moral experience cannot fairly be used to support any rationalist or metaphysical doctrine whatsoever. In particular, they cannot, as Kant hoped, be used to established the existence of a transcendent god.

This mention of God brings us to the question of the possibility of religious knowledge. We shall see that this possibility has already been ruled out by our treatment of metaphysics. But. as this is a point of considerable interest, we may be permitted to discuss it at some length.

It is now generally admitted, at any rate by philosophers, that the existence of a being having the attributes which define the god of any non-animistic religion cannot be demonstratively proved. To see that this is so, we have only to ask ourselves what are the premises from which the existence of such a god could be deduced. If the conclusion that a god exists is to be demonstratively certain, then these premises must be certain; for, as the conclusion of a deductive argument is already contained in the premises, any uncertainty there

Logical Empiricism: Meaning, Metaphysics, and Mathematics   445

may be about the truth of the premises is necessarily shared by it. But we know that no empirical proposition can ever be anything more than probable. It is only *a priori* propositions that are logically certain. But we cannot deduce the existence of a god from an *a priori* proposition. For we know that the reason why *a priori* propositions are certain is that they are tautologies. And from a set of tautologies nothing but a further tautology can be validly deduced. It follows that there is no possibility of demonstrating the existence of a god.

What is not so generally recognized is that there can be no way of proving that the existence of a god. such as the God of Christianity, is even probable. Yet this also is easily shown. For if the existence of such a god were probable, then the proposition that he existed would be an empirical hypothesis. And in that case it would be possible to deduce from it, and other empirical hypotheses, certain experiential propositions which were not deducible from those other hypotheses alone. But in fact this is not possible. It is sometimes claimed, indeed, that the existence of a certain sort of regularity in nature constitutes sufficient evidence for the existence of a god. But if the sentence 'God exists' entails no more than that certain types of phenomena occur in certain sequences, then to assert the existence of a god will be simply equivalent to asserting that there is the requisite regularity in nature; and no religious man would admit that this was all he intended to assert in asserting the existence of a god. He would say that in talking about God he was talking about a transcendent being who might be known through certain empirical manifestations, but certainly could not be defined in terms of those manifestations. But in that case the term 'god' is a metaphysical term. And if 'god' is a metaphysical term, then it cannot be even probable that a god exists. For to say that 'God exists' is to make a metaphysical utterance which cannot be either true or false. And by the same criterion, no sentence which purports to describe the nature of a transcendent god can possess any literal significance.

It is important not to confuse this view of religious assertions with the view that is adopted by atheists, or agnostics.[3] For it is characteristic of an agnostic to hold that the existence of a god is a possibility in which there is no good reason either to believe or disbelieve; and it is characteristic of an atheist to hold that it is at least probable that no god exists. And our view that all utterances about the nature of God are nonsensical, so far from being identical with, or even lending any support to, either of these familiar contentions, is actually incompatible with them. For if the assertion that there is a god is nonsensical, then the atheist's

---

[3]This point was suggested to me by Professor H. H. Price.

Early Analytic Philosophy

assertion that there is no god is equally nonsensical, since it is only a significant proposition that can be significantly contradicted. As for the agnostic, although he refrains from saying either that there is or that there is not a god. he does not deny that the question whether a transcendent god exists is a genuine question. He does not deny that the two sentences 'There is a transcendent god' and 'There is no transcendent god' express propositions one of which is actually true and the other false. All he says is that we have no means of telling which of them is true, and therefore ought not to commit ourselves to either. But we have seen that the sentences in question do not express propositions at all. And this means that agnosticism also is ruled out.

Thus we offer the theist the same comfort as we gave to the moralist. His assertions cannot possibly be valid, but they cannot be invalid either. As he says nothing at all about the world, he cannot justly be accused of saying anything false, or anything for which he has insufficient grounds. It is only when the theist claims that in asserting the existence of a transcendent god he is expressing a genuine proposition that we are entitled to disagree with him.

It is to be remarked that in cases where deities are identified with natural objects, assertions concerning them may be allowed to be significant. If, for example, a man tells me that the occurrence of thunder is alone both necessary and sufficient to establish the truth of the proposition that Jehovah is angry, I may conclude that, in his usage of words, the sentence 'Jehovah is angry' is equivalent to 'It is thundering.' But in sophisticated religions, though they may be to some extent based on men's awe of natural processes which they cannot sufficiently understand, the 'person' who is supposed to control the empirical world is not himself located in it; he is held to be superior to the empirical world, and so outside it; and he is endowed with super-empirical attributes. But the notion of a person whose essential attributes are non-empirical is not an intelligible notion at all. We may have a word which is used as if it named this 'person', but, unless the sentences in which it occurs express propositions which are empirically verifiable, it cannot be said to symbolize anything. And this is the case with regard to the word 'god', in the usage in which it is intended to refer to a transcendent object. The mere existence of the noun is enough to foster the illusion that there is a real, or at any rate a possible entity corresponding to it. It is only when we inquire what God's attributes are that we discover that 'God', in this usage, is not a genuine name.

It is common to find belief in a transcendent god conjoined with belief in an after-life. But, in the form which it usually takes, the content of this belief is not a genuine hypothesis. To say that men do not ever die, or that the state of death is merely a state of prolonged insensibility, is indeed to express a significant

Logical Empiricism: Meaning, Metaphysics, and Mathematics **447**

proposition, though all the available evidence goes to show that it is false. But to say that there is something imperceptible inside a man, which is his soul or his real self, and that it goes on living after he is dead, is to make a metaphysical assertion which has no more factual content than the assertion that there is a transcendent god.

It is worth mentioning that, according to the account which we have given of religious assertions, there is no logical ground for antagonism between religion and natural science. As far as the question of truth or falsehood is concerned, there is no opposition between the natural scientist and the theist who believes in a transcendent god. For since the religious utterances of the theist are not genuine propositions at all, they cannot stand in any logical relation to the propositions of science. Such antagonism as there is between religion and science appears to consist in the fact that science takes away one of the motives which make men religious. For it is acknowledged that one of the ultimate sources of religious feeling lies in the inability of men to determine their own destiny; and science tends to destroy the feeling of awe with which men regard an alien world, by making them believe that they can understand and anticipate the course of natural phenomena, and even to some extent control it. The fact that it has recently become fashionable for physicists themselves to be sympathetic towards religion is a point in favour of this hypothesis. For this sympathy towards religion marks the physicists' own lack of confidence in the validity of their hypotheses, which is a reaction on their part from the anti-religious dogmatism of nineteenth century scientists, and a natural outcome of the crisis through which physics has just passed.

It is not within the scope of this inquiry to enter more deeply into the causes of religious feeling, or to discuss the probability of the continuance of religious belief. We are concerned only to answer those questions which arise out of our discussion of the possibility of religious knowledge. The point which we wish to establish is that there cannot be any transcendent truths of religion. For the sentences which the theist uses to express such 'truths' are not literally significant.

An interesting feature of this conclusion is that it accords with what many theists are accustomed to say themselves. For we are often told that the nature of God is a mystery which transcends the human understanding. But to say that something transcends the human understanding is to say that it is unintelligible. And what is unintelligible cannot significantly be described. Again, we are told that God is not an object of reason but an object of faith. This may be nothing more than an admission that the existence of God must be taken on trust, since it cannot be proved. But it may also be an assertion that God is the object of a purely mystical intuition, and cannot therefore be defined in terms which are

Early Analytic Philosophy

intelligible to the reason. And I think there are many theists who would assert this. But if one allows that it is impossible to define God in intelligible terms, then one is allowing that it is impossible for a sentence both to be significant and to be about God. If a mystic admits that the object of his vision is something which cannot be described, then he must also admit that he is bound to talk nonsense when he describes it.

For his part, the mystic may protest that his intuition does reveal truths to him, even though he cannot explain to others what these truths are; and that we who do not possess this faculty of intuition can have no ground for denying that it is a cognitive faculty. For we can hardly maintain *a priori* that there are no ways of discovering true propositions except those which we ourselves employ. The answer is that we set no limit to the number of ways in which one may come to formulate a true proposition. We do not in any way deny that a synthetic truth may be discovered by purely intuitive methods as well as by the rational method of induction. But we do say that every synthetic proposition, however it may have been arrived at, must be subject to the test of actual experience. We do not deny *a priori* that the mystic is able to discover truths by his own special methods. We wait to hear what are the propositions which embody his discoveries, in order to see whether they are verified or confuted by our empirical observations. But the mystic so far from producing propositions which are empirically verified, is unable to produce any intelligible propositions at all. And therefore we say that his intuition has not revealed to him any facts. It is no use his saying that he has apprehended facts but is unable to express them. For we know that if he really had acquired any information, he would be able to express it. He would be able to indicate in some way or other how the genuineness of his discovery might be empirically determined. The fact that he cannot reveal what he 'knows', or even himself devise an empirical test to validate his 'knowledge', shows that his state of mystical intuition is not a genuinely cognitive state. So that in describing his vision the mystic does not give us any information about the external world; he merely gives us indirect information about the condition of his own mind.

These considerations dispose of the argument from religious experience, which many philosophers still regard as a valid argument in favour of the existence of a god. They say that it is logically possible for men to be immediately acquainted with God, as they are immediately acquainted with a sense-content, and that there is no reason why one should be prepared to believe a man when he says that be is seeing a yellow patch, and refuse to believe him he says that he is seeing God. The answer to this is that if the man who asserts that he is seeing God is merely asserting that he is experiencing a peculiar kind of sense-

Logical Empiricism: Meaning, Metaphysics, and Mathematics

content, then we do not for a moment deny that his assertion may be true. But, ordinarily, the man who says that he is seeing God is saying not merely that he is experiencing a religious emotion, but also that there exists a transcendent being who is the object of this emotion; just as the man who says that he sees a yellow patch is ordinarily saying not merely that his visual sense-field contains a yellow sense-content, but also that there exists a yellow object to which the sense-content belongs. And it is not irrational to be prepared to believe a man when he asserts the existence of a yellow object, and to refuse to believe him when he asserts the existence of a transcendent god. For whereas the sentence 'There exists here a yellow-coloured material thing' expresses a genuine synthetic proposition which could be empirically verified, the sentence 'There exists a transcendent god' has, as we have seen, no literal significance.

We conclude, therefore, that the argument from religious experience is altogether fallacious. The fact that people have religious experiences is interesting from the psychological point of view, but it does not in any way imply that there is such a thing as religious knowledge, any more than our having moral experiences implies that there is such a thing as moral knowledge. The theist, like the moralist, may believe that his experiences are cognitive experiences, but, unless he can formulate his 'knowledge' in propositions that are empirically verifiable, we may be sure that he is deceiving himself. It follows that those philosophers who fill their books with assertions that they intuitively 'know' this or that moral or religious 'truth' are merely providing material for the psychoanalyst. For no act of intuition can be said to reveal a truth about any matter of fact unless it issues in verifiable propositions. And all such propositions are to be incorporated in the system of empirical propositions which constitutes science.

9

Susan Stebbing on Logic, Language, and Analysis

Chapter Outline

Background and commentary
    Background   452
    Logic and language   454
    Language and science   456
    Empiricism and analysis   459
    Concluding remarks   460
    Further reading   460
Readings
    A Modern Introduction to Logic (selections from
        Chs. 1, 24)   462
    Philosophy and the Physicists (selections from Ch. 3)   481
    "Logical Positivism and Analysis"   495

Background and commentary

Background

Who was Lizzie Susan Stebbing[1] (1885–1943)? While she was an accomplished and widely respected philosopher during what could be called the second wave of early analytic philosophy in the 1930s, her work has mostly passed into obscurity since her death. She was sympathetic to the rejection of the Bradleyan conception of logic and metaphysics that characterized Russell's and Moore's development of early analytic philosophy and was a skillful interpreter of the formal methods that christened the new direction in philosophy. Stebbing published several monographs during her lifetime, including *A Modern Introduction to Logic* (1930), *Philosophy and the Physicists* (1937), and *Thinking to Some Purpose* (1939), along with many academic articles. Her work can be seen as a pivot point between approaches to language, logic, and method in the early work of Russell, Moore, and Wittgenstein, the critique of metaphysics that characterized the development of logical empiricism in the 1920s and 1930s, and the expansion of philosophical inquiry into ordinary language in the 1940s and 1950s. It is the more regrettable that her work has mostly passed into obscurity, as she was one of few philosophers who labored to formulate, elucidate, and dissolve the many misconceptions about the nature of analytic philosophy and its relation to language and logic that took hold in the twentieth century.

Stebbing's philosophical work was primarily focused on language, in several different ways. Her earliest work emphasized formal methods and issues surrounding the logical form of language. From there, she began to turn her attention to the connection between logical form and the actual process of thinking. Her later work emphasized the ways in which natural language is full of semantic and logical pitfalls, how to account for those, and how to sort them out. When the Second World War broke out, her attention turned more explicitly practical, specifically to the use and misuse of language in political expression and other contexts. Thus her later books illustrate the methods of logical analysis (as she understood it) to emphasize the importance of clarifying the meanings and inferential relations of expressions and concepts as they appear in day-to-day life. In this sense, her work could also be seen as a precursor of the ordinary language movement that was centered

---

[1]Stebbing couldn't stand her given name "Lizzie" and was professionally known as "Susan Stebbing."

at Oxford in the 1940s and 1950s. Indeed, while many histories of twentieth-century analytic philosophy have emphasized the rise of ordinary language philosophy as a reaction to the role of logical analysis in the philosophy of language, Stebbing's work shows that there are more overlapping branches in the twentieth-century emphasis in philosophy on logic, language, and analysis than may have seemed to be the case. In retrospect, it may be possible to say that her work was among the first in twentieth-century philosophy to address the philosophy of language in the fullest and widest sense.

Stebbing studied history at Cambridge in 1907 and 1908, during which she read Bradley's *Appearance and Reality*. The exposure to Bradley sparked enough interest in philosophy for her to study moral sciences at Cambridge. At that time women could not earn degrees at Cambridge, and since her ambition was to work as a professional philosopher, she decided to complete her studies at King's College London, earning an MA in philosophy in 1912. She did not find proper full-time work as a philosopher until 1920, though she did pursue philosophical work through part-time visiting posts at several colleges in Cambridge (Girton, Newnham, and Homerton), as well as at King's College and Westfield College. Stebbing suffered from a variety of illnesses that would incapacitate her consistently throughout her life, but in spite of her less than optimal physical health, her career included teaching and lecturing in philosophy; reading philosophical work in three languages; giving lectures and writing papers for philosophical societies and conferences; traveling abroad to lecture in philosophy (she was Visiting Professor at Columbia University in 1931–2); running the philosophy department at Bedford College as professor and chair; and establishing and assisting with the running of the Kingsley Lodge School for Girls (with her sister and two close friends). Stebbing was held in enough esteem by her colleagues that she was elected as president of the eminent Aristotelian Society in 1933 and of the Mind Association in 1934. She was also founding editor of *Analysis*, which continues to be a central journal in the field, and of the first academic journal of British Marxism, *The Modern Quarterly*. She was the first woman to hold a professorship in philosophy in England (at Bedford College), an achievement notable enough to make headlines outside of academia.

Like Russell before her, Stebbing credited Moore with a high degree of influence on her philosophical development. In her contribution to a volume of papers on Moore's work and legacy, she recounted an audience member's objections to a paper she delivered at the Aristotelian Society in 1917, objections characterized by "a vehement insistence" that she clarify her assertions. She did not know that the objector was Moore, and what she

Early Analytic Philosophy

described as "his patience in pursuing the question to its end" was something that made her "forget not to be a philosopher" and influenced her approach to analysis as a philosophical method thereafter (Schilpp 1942: 530). When Moore was retiring as professor at Cambridge in 1939, she considered applying for the job. However, the Oxford philosopher Gilbert Ryle (1900-1976) told her that "of course everyone thinks you are the right person to succeed Moore, except that you are a woman," while the Cambridge philosopher Richard Braithwaite (1900–90) perhaps added insult to injury by remarking that "your being a woman would of course prevent you from applying" (Mac Cumhaill and Wiseman 2022: 208). Indeed, women were not permitted full membership in the university until 1948, five years after Stebbing's death. Ryle and Braithwaite were probably supposing that under those restrictions it would not even have been possible to offer her the position of professor—though clearly neither thought it was on the cards to encourage her to apply as a way to push Cambridge into a more modern and equitable direction.

Stebbing also wrote about many of the key issues concerning the relation between logical empiricism and the so-called "Cambridge School of Analysis" (centered around the work of Russell, Moore, and Wittgenstein), particularly on the status of metaphysics and the nature of analysis, logic, and language. Histories of this period of thought have generally credited Ayer's *Language, Truth and Logic* as the first introduction of logical empiricism into British philosophy, but it was Stebbing who invited Carnap—a main figure in this philosophical development—to give a series of papers on philosophy and logical syntax at Bedford College in 1934. Moreover it was Stebbing who delivered a lecture to the British Academy in 1933, "Logical Positivism and Analysis," which contains a meticulous criticism of the empiricist understanding of analysis, and which features in the readings below.[2]

Logic and language

Stebbing's *A Modern Introduction to Logic* was considered the first textbook in analytic philosophy. It explained the formal methods of logic developed by Russell and Whitehead in *Principia Mathematica*, explicated the distinction between the new modern logic and traditional logic, made the new logic accessible, and set it into context with commentary and critique. Stebbing's aim in the book was to show how "logic will benefit by being brought more

---

[2]For this and further biographical information, see Beaney 2016, Beaney and Chapman 2017, Janssen-Lauret 2017.

into touch with practical life," and she spent a significant portion of the book discussing the nature of logic over the preceding centuries (1930: 33). Although intended as a resource for students, the book succeeded in giving a fresh assessment of the nature of logic itself. *A Modern Introduction to Logic* includes discussion of nearly every element relevant to the nature of rational thought and its application: in the course of twenty-five chapters, Stebbing gives an account of the nature of inference, the nature of system and order, causality, hypothesis, the principles of causal determination, the nature of scientific theories, induction, quantitative analysis and statistical methods, definition, abstraction, and generalization, and the development of logic. Nonetheless, again, perhaps the most unique feature of the book is that Stebbing is concerned to present the new logic due to Frege, Russell, and Whitehead, as well as logic in general, as foundational to "principles exemplified in everyday reflective thinking no less than in mathematical deductions" (1930: xii). The excerpts presented below are characteristic of this approach.

In Chapter I, "Reflective Thinking in Ordinary Life," Stebbing begins with the variety of ways we use the word "thought," to distinguish between what she calls "unreflective" and "reflective" thinking. In reflective thinking, according to Stebbing, mental states take on a purpose. Instead of a complex but passive set of mental events happening in us, genuine thinking is something we must consciously direct. One of her examples is of a person in danger of being caught in a high tide. In being focused to finding an escape, it becomes clear, according to Stebbing, that his thinking becomes a tool to solve a problem, and the elements of this thinking—perception, awareness, planning, intention—become meaningful in that particular way. The contexts in which we apply our thinking as a problem-solving tool will vary. Sometimes they will be very practical (how do I avoid drowning in a high tide?) and sometimes they will be the process of discovering an answer for its own sake to a question that arises. The element of problem solving, characteristic of reflective thinking, is inference—the process of seeing connections between the elements of thought. It also requires the element of relevance. Stebbing cites "the importance of abstraction" with respect to this property of thinking: "without abstraction there can be no recognition of similarity; without recognition of similarity there can be no advance in knowledge" (1930: 6). Thus "reflective thinking is... relevant thinking," because "what is relevant in a given situation depends upon its connections" (1930: 7). Reflective thinking is shaped by the conditions of the problem to be solved and has a "natural end"; the stages of such thinking are related to this natural end ("conclusion") as "the grounds upon which it is based" (1930: 9). Thus for Stebbing, reflective thinking exhibits what students, in part, learn to do in a logic class: determining the inferences that can be drawn from a set of premises.

Chapter XXIV, "The Characteristics of Logical Thinking," builds on the claims that Stebbing introduced in Chapter I. In this chapter she examines in a perhaps surprisingly contemporary way the nature of belief, truth-value and assent, justification, and knowledge. She meticulously describes five modes of belief acquisition and the logical pitfalls that can arise in each. She then turns to the principles that undergird all logical thinking: the law of identity (everything is what it is); the law of contradiction (A is not both B and not B); and the law of excluded middle (A either is or is not B) (1930: 469). Stebbing points out that these conditions aren't sufficient as the "foundation of all reasoning" and that there are too many to discuss, but they can be categorized as principles of implication and of deduction (1930: 472). Perhaps her most useful discussion in this chapter comes in the final section, "The Normative Aspect of Logic." Students who were (or are!) tempted to wonder whether logic is subjective—captured in the idea that since thinking is subjective, then logic is too—might find this a usefully clear explanation of the normative and objective aspect of logic. It is true, Stebbing points out, that a logician takes note of the processes of psychology and of mind, but the point of the logician's work is "analytical and critical." Logic, she argues, is a pure science of form; it differs from the empirical sciences, which are concerned with specific facts in the actual world. Logic instead is concerned not with the actual but with the possible. Scientists do their work via inference just as much as logicians and mathematicians, but the true importance of the nature of logical thought is not merely to understand logical form but to practice it. An example of this would be learning a sport. You can read books about ice hockey and watch YouTube videos on skating and puck control. But you will never learn how to play hockey that way. You must apply the principles of skating and stick handling in action to learn how to play hockey. Similarly, to think logically, you need to understand the standards and principles of reasoning that govern good reasoning, and then practice their application.

Language and science

Stebbing developed her discussion of logic and reflective thinking in everyday life throughout her career. In *Philosophy and the Physicists*, she applies her position and formulation of clarity and analysis to the work of two physicists of her day, Arthur Eddington (1882–1944) and James Jeans (1877–1946).

Both had written books—for example, Eddington's *The Nature of the Physical World* (1928) and Jeans's *The Mysterious Universe* (1930)—that were intended to popularize some of the new developments in physics, and books of this kind had a wide public influence during this period. But the new developments in physics and allied sciences had philosophical implications. Stebbing's motivation in her criticisms of the work of these physicists was to clarify the logical and philosophical implications of technical subjects that have real-world effects, like physics, but more than that as well: it was also to show the downright negligence in the failure to be clear.

Stebbing does not pull her punches with respect to Eddington: "Eddington has set forth for the benefit of the common reader an interpretation of recent developments in physics...His interpretation, however, suffers from very serious omissions and from an altogether misleading emphasis" (1937: xi). As for Jeans: "...we as common readers surely have the right to expect that a scientist setting out to discuss for our benefit philosophical problems arising from his special studies will do so in scientific spirit...to be under a special obligation to avoid cheap emotionalism and specious appeals...Of this obligation Sir James Jeans seems to be totally unaware..." (1937: 6).

Lack of clarity in popular scientific writing had other hazards that Stebbing was anxious to thwart as well, such as the possibility that scientific results could be "forced into an interpretation which will yield the special philosophical views upon which their political philosophy is professedly based." During this period a debate had reignited between philosophical materialists and philosophical idealists, because of "the belief that the 'new physics' is favorable to some form of philosophical idealism" (1937: xi). Stebbing, whose main intention in this book was to clear up instances of logical incoherence, warns that in this debate she remains relatively neutral: "If I have succeeded in showing that the present state of physical theories does not warrant any form of idealism, it must not thereby be concluded that I suppose it to warrant any form of materialism" (1937: xii).

In Chapter III, presented below, Stebbing takes on Eddington on the subject of "The Furniture of the Earth," in order to demonstrate that "nothing but confusion can result if, in one and the same sentence, we mix up language used appropriately for the furniture of the earth and our daily dealings with it with language used for the purpose of philosophical and scientific discussion" (1937: 47). This chapter is a representative example of Stebbing's firm commitment to not only philosophical clarity but common sense—the two, in her view, were not in opposition. When, as in this chapter, she takes on Eddington's discussion of the nature of the physical world, she is

458   Early Analytic Philosophy

concerned to attack what she calls "his use of language...as gravely misleading," which "reveals serious confusions in [Eddington's] own thinking" (1937: 48). The passage in question is Eddington's "picturesque" description of entering a room. He states, among other things, that entering a room is a "complicated business," which will involve resisting atmospheric pressure of 14 pounds of force on one's body; doing this while "hanging from a round planet head outward into space"; and carefully timing one's landing on a piece of the floor that is traveling at 20 miles per second around the sun. Moreover, the piece of the floor one is stepping on "has no solidity of substance" and is like a "swarm of flies," each one of which is preventing one's slipping through it (1937: 49). Stebbing acknowledges that she may sound as if she is taking too seriously a passage meant to be lyrical rather than literal. But her main concern is that Eddington draws at least two philosophical conclusions from this that do not follow.

First: in denying that a floorboard plank has solidity, he is contravening the conditions of understanding: we cannot understand what a denial of solidity comes to unless we already understand the concept of solidity. The common usage of language enables us to attribute a meaning to the phrase "a solid plank," but "there is no common usage of language that provides a meaning for the word 'solid' that would make sense to say that the plank on which I stand is not *solid*" (1937: 52). Second: according to Stebbing, Eddington appears to defend, on the basis of his use of language, not only the questionable metaphysical conclusion that there are two tables, but also the questionable metaphysical and epistemological conclusions that problems of perception arise "only because we have allowed the physicists to speak of a 'real world' that does not contain any of the qualities relevant to perception" (1937: 64). This common philosophical problem is familiar to anyone who has been in an introductory philosophy class. Asking the question "is that chair green when we are not perceiving it?" will result in at least one answer defending a materialist view of the concept of color: that color just is a wave-length of light absorbed or not absorbed by a physical object. What this answer neglects to account for is the content of color experience in human vision. While wave-lengths and light reflection/absorption can be measured in material terms, the conscious experience of color appears to evade explanation of that kind: when we experience the green chair, our experience is not that of a wave-length, but of what we call a color. It is worth reflecting on how Eddington might respond to Stebbing's critiques; for instance, that he misuses the very concept of solidity in his discussions.

Empiricism and analysis

As above, Stebbing played an influential role in the transition from the work of the early Russell, Moore, and Wittgenstein in the development of analytic philosophy to the influx of logical positivism. Stebbing's central contribution here is her paper "Logical Positivism and Analysis" (1933), presented below. In this paper, Stebbing gives a detailed account of the concepts at the very foundation of the philosophical upheavals that characterized the first half of the twentieth century: the concept of analysis; the nature of language and logic; and their metaphysical implications. Philosophers like Russell and Moore did not take themselves to be denying or rejecting metaphysics by shifting their attention to an analysis of language and form. If anything, they were attempting to clarify the precise meaning and reference of expressions via the analysis of the form of expressions. For example, Russell held that his theory of descriptions—his analysis of expressions like "the present King of France" and the sentences in which such expressions occur—could resolve longstanding metaphysical and ontological disputes. Similarly, Moore held that a proper analysis of discourse involving "good" and cognate expressions revealed that goodness is unanalyzable, and thus a kind of simple quality of objects, actions, or events.

The logical postivists, by contrast, were concerned to eradicate metaphysics altogether. Stebbing characterizes this as the idea that for these thinkers, analysis was not a means to uncover the basic facts, those that make certain sentences or propositions true. Stebbing makes several objections to this approach in her paper. Her most trenchant point is that the logical positivists not only fail to adequately distinguish among varieties of analysis, they also fail to admit a role for an analysis of facts. For one thing, their conception of facts is linguistic, which limits their conception of analysis to principles of symbolism. This, according to Stebbing, consists of a formulation of a boundary of delimitation on what it is strictly speaking meaningful to express, which she rejects. In the course of this paper, she gives a formulation of the relationship between philosophy and language that is unusual for this period in giving a detailed and meticulously thorough bird's-eye view of the possible approaches that were under debate; it not only explains and formulates the concept of analysis, but is an example of analysis, as she understands it, in itself. Throughout these discussions, and in her earlier paper, "The Method of Analysis in Metaphysics" (1932–3), Stebbing appeals to Moore's distinction (in "A Defence of Common Sense," (Moore, 1925) for instance) between understanding an expression or sentence and knowing the analysis of an expression or sentence, and a corresponding distinction between knowing a sentence or proposition to be true and knowing the analysis of that sentence or proposition. Given this, Stebbing contends that the point of analysis is not to provide justification for our taking certain sentences to be true, nor is it needed to demonstrate that we indeed understand certain expressions or sentences. Part of the problem with empiricism, Stebbing contends, is that empiricists neglect this distinction, and in doing so fail to fully appreciate the point and purpose of analysis. The reader is encouraged to think about Stebbing's myriad criticisms of logical empiricism and how empiricists like Ayer, Carnap, and others might respond.

Concluding remarks

During her lifetime, Stebbing was a well-known and prolific member of the academic philosophical community. However, unlike some of the other authors we have discussed, she was interested not only in purely academic work, but also in applying ideas about logic and language to real-world issues and bringing these ideas to a wider audience, and her writing, as we see in the selections below, was replete with real-world examples and applications. In both her academic and more popular writings, Stebbing used techniques of modern logic and linguistic analysis to tackle difficult philosophical issues and resolve potential points of confusion, but made these accessible and clear by her attention to and analysis of language and linguistic usage. Stebbing also played an important role in introducing the ideas of logical empiricism to Britain and the English-speaking world more generally. Her discussions of the nature and influence of logical empiricism are important contributions to mid-century analytic philosophy, but she has rarely received the credit she deserves for her historical role in bringing this work to prominence in the development of analytic philosophy.

Further reading

Primary sources
Stebbing, S. (1932), "The Method of Analysis in Metaphysics", *Proceedings of the Aristotelian Society* 33: 65–94.
Stebbing, S. (1939), *Thinking to Some Purpose*, Hammondsworth: Penguin.

Secondary sources

Beaney, M. (2003), "Susan Stebbing on Cambridge and Vienna Analysis", in F. Stadler (ed.), *The Vienna Circle and Logical Empiricism*, Netherlands: Springer.

Beaney, M. (2016), "Susan Stebbing and the Early Reception of Logical Empiricism in Britain", in C. Dambock (ed.), *Influences on the Aufbau*, Switzerland: Springer.

Beaney, M. and Chapman, S. (2017), "Susan Stebbing", *Stanford Encyclopedia of Philosophy*. Available online at: https://plato.stanford.edu/entries/stebbing/

Chapman, S. (2013), *Susan Stebbing and the Language of Common Sense*, Basingstoke: Palgrave.

Mac Cumhaill, C. and Wiseman, R. (2022), *Metaphysical Animals: How Four Women Brought Philosophy Back to Life*, London and New York: Knopf/Doubleday.

Moore, G. E. (1925), "A Defence of Common Sense," in *Contemporary British Philosophy* (2nd series), ed. J. Muirhead. George Allen and Unwin: 191–224.

Readings

Stebbing, S. *A Modern Introduction to Logic* (selections from Chs 1, 24).
Reprinted from Stebbing, S. (1930), *A Modern Introduction to Logic*, London: Methuen.

Chapter 1: Reflective Thinking in Ordinary Life

Logic, in the most usual and widest sense of the word, is concerned with reflective thinking. We all constantly use the words 'thinking' and 'thought'. So long as we are not asked to define them we feel confident that we know what these words mean. But we do not always use the word 'thinking' in the same sense. Sometimes we contrast "I think of" with "I am now seeing." In this sense we are using "think" to denote our awareness of something not directly presented to sense. Thus anything that 'passes through our heads' is called a thought. For example, lying on the sea-shore on a hot sunny day, in an idle mood, we may have a train of thoughts, a set of more or less disconnected ideas passing through our minds. These thoughts may be intimately bound up with our present sense-impressions—the heat of the stones, the sound of the waves, the call of the sea-gulls. In such a mood we do not connect one thought with another; we are at the mercy of any sense-impression that may break in upon us. Suppose now that the idler on the rocks is aroused by such loud, insistent shouting that he recognizes 'in a flash', as we say, that this shouting has some peculiar significance for him. His reverie ended, he jumps up and looks around. Let us suppose that he now sees the water breaking on the rocks just below. He turns round to find that the rock on which he is standing is completely cut off from the shore in front. Behind is a steep, overhanging cliff, which he could not scale. The tide will soon completely cover the place where he has been lying. He cannot swim. What is he to do? He supposes that the people on the cliff, who shouted to him, have probably realized his situation. He wonders whether they can help him. Looking up he sees that some one is pointing to the face of the cliff. Does that mean that there are footholes? He looks, but can find none. Then he observes above his head a narrow projection of cliff. If he could clamber on to that perhaps he would be out of reach of the incoming tide. Would that be so? Again he looks, and sees that just below the ledge there is the dark brown discolouring of the rocks that is the mark of high tide. That ledge, then, will be safe, if he can reach it.

Susan Stebbing on Logic, Language, and Analysis   463

In the above situation we have a concrete illustration of the contrast between unreflective and reflective thinking as the latter occurs in ordinary experience. At first the man was not attending to his sense-impressions; nor was his thinking consciously controlled. But as soon as he was conscious that the situation was one of danger he was confronted with a problem to be solved. Consequently, he was forced to think about the situation so as to alter it in accordance with his practical needs. He becomes aware of the sea as menacing; he not only sees the water near his feet, he sees it as a sign of danger because he interprets it as signifying 'retreat to shore cut off'. Similarly, he not only hears people shouting; he interprets their shouts as having special meaning for him. He not only sees the various shades of brown on the face of the cliff, he interprets them as signs of high tide level. Suppose now that he asks himself the question whether the tide is likely to rise above the normal level to-day. He considers that last night the moon was in its first quarter; therefore, it will be a neap tide; hence, if he can reach the ledge he will be safe. In this last stage of his reflective thinking he is obviously relying upon previous knowledge of facts relevant to the situation. He remembers that the moon was at its first quarter the night before; he knows that a neap tide is connected with the moon in that position, he infers that the tide will not rise high to-day. In this process of thinking directed to a practical end it is unlikely that the thinker will consciously use words. He may have merely a visual image of the appearance of the moon as he saw it yesterday, and pass directly to the reflection – 'a neap tide', and thence, to the conclusion: "So that's all right." The remembered appearance of last night's moon is thus directly interpreted as signifying what he wanted to know.

Suppose that, once he is perched on the ledge, the man looks about him to distract his thoughts. He sees on the other side of the cove, some way up in the side of a rocky headland that juts into the sea, a wide opening, not previously noticed, or taken to be a natural cleft in the rock. Now that his attention is directed to it, he sees that the opening is not the entrance to a cave, for he can discern bricks cemented together. Taken in itself there is nothing startling in a brick wall, but in this situation its discovery suggests the question how a brick wall came to be there. It can't be the remains of a house, for it is about half-way up in the side of a steep cliff below which the tide never goes out. The headland is seen to be connected with the mainland by a narrow ledge of rock more than a hundred feet high. He knows that on the top of the headland are the ruins of a castle which is supposed to have been King Arthur's. Perhaps the brick wall was once right inside the rock, the face of which has now fallen away. That is a reasonable supposition, for it is a stormy coast and rocks that have evidently fallen are piled below. In that case, however, the bricked chamber would have

Early Analytic Philosophy

had no outlet to the light. Perhaps it is a secret chamber, or a dungeon. In that case it is probable that there will be some connexion with the mainland – perhaps a secret underground passage. At this point of his reflection, he must perforce cease his questioning. In his present position he has no means of testing his suppositions. Next day he may proceed to test the correctness of his theory with regard to the brick wall. On investigation of the headland he finds a disused shaft which he calculates to be in the right position to connect with the chamber. He discovers a not unsimilar shaft on the main cliff, near the church. He reflects that a passage running from the one shaft to the other would pass beside the brick wall, and connect the underground chamber with the church. At this point he will feel that he has accounted for the brick wall in the cliff.

Simple as these two illustrations are, they suffice to show how thinking essentially consists in solving a problem. The first was a practical problem, namely, how to reach a place of safety. The second was a problem arising out of the perception of something unexpected in a familiar situation. In this case the solution of the problem was sought merely for its own sake, in order to answer the question, "Why is so-and-so such-and-such?" – a question asked only when the such-and-such has features that would not be expected to occur in the given situation. The occurrence of these unexpected features is felt to be explained as soon as they are related to a situation in which their occurrence would not be unexpected. The explanation consists in finding intermediate links that connect the brick wall and the cliff. It is reached as a process of reflective thinking in which each link, brick wall, disused shaft, castle, church, is attended to not for its own sake but as being a sign of something else. Such a process of reflective thinking is known as inferring. In this case there was a passage from something sensibly presented to something not presented but inferred, which may, or may not, be the case. To determine whether it is the case, or not, the inference must be further tested. Such testing may be carried out in two widely different ways. The inferred conclusion may admit of direct inspection. In this case, the test would consist in verifying the conclusion by direct observation of something presented to sense. Clearly it is not always possible to perform such a test as, for example, in our illustration, which was concerned with a question about a state of affairs in the past. In such cases the conclusion is tested by its power to connect together various observable items which, apart from the supposed connexions, would remain disconnected.

We have spoken of 'directly observing something'. But what we directly observe, see with our eyes, for instance, is a very small part of what we observe when we say that we are perceiving so-and-so. Thus, for example, in looking at a puzzle picture where a man's head is suggested by the lines drawn to indicate the leaves of a tree, we suddenly discover the head. Knowing what we are in search of we attend to some only of the lines drawn and actively connect them with others, finally making out of the set of lines attended to the representation of a man's head. No hard and fast line can be drawn between what is actually seen and what is suggested by what is seen. We see what we have a mind to see. In the situations of everyday life our senses are being constantly stimulated by a variety of sense-impressions amongst which we have learnt to pay attention to some as being specially significant, that is as being signs of something else in which we are interested. When one thing signifies another, there is between them that connexion which enables us to pass in thought from the one to the other. The sun setting in a bank of clouds may be noticed merely for its shape and colour, and appreciated for its beauty. But it may also be apprehended as signifying wet day to-morrow. Again, waving a flag may be a sign of high spirits, or of a certain state of mind called patriotism.

Thinking, we have seen, essentially consists in solving a problem. The ability to think depends upon the power of seeing connexions. Reflective thinking consists in pondering upon a given set of facts so as to elicit their connexions. "I didn't think" often means "I failed to connect", that is, "I didn't recognize that given that, I must have this." There are various kinds of connexion from the bare juxtaposition of this and that to the essential connexion of an X with a Y which must be if X is.[1] The mere addition of one fact to another would be of little value for reflective thinking. It is unlikely that we ever have mere additions, even in the idle reverie of day-dreaming. In day-dreams one idea follows another with no apparent connexion; they are said to occur 'at random'. Yet modern psychologists say that there are 'reasons' why this idea follows that. Freud, for instance, has attempted to explain these occurrences, i.e. to set out the conditions upon which the succession of ideas is consequent although the day-dreamer himself may not be aware of any connexions. When, however, we contrast daydreaming, taken as it occurs, with directed thought, even of such a simple type as in our two illustrations, we seem to be moving on a different plane. Directed thought is thought directed to the solution of a problem; it originates in a felt difficulty and is controlled throughout by the initial apprehension of the conditions of the problem.

---

[1]Compare, for instance, the connexion implies in

'A rainbow and a cuckoo's song
May never come together again'

with the connexion implied in 'All equilateral triangles are equiangular'.

Early Analytic Philosophy

Without some degree of direction there is nothing in our mental processes which merits the name "thinking." Day-dreaming must, therefore, be excluded since, in so far as it is directed, it is directed by factors which lie outside the course of the reverie itself. In the widest sense of the word "thinking" every one thinks. In the strictest sense, in which "to think" means "to think logically", some people never think, and no one is always thinking even when be appears to be doing so. It may be doubted, for instance, whether Mrs. Nickleby ever thought. Consider the following extract:

'I think there must be something in the place', said Mrs. Nickleby, who had been listening in silence; 'for, soon after I was married, I went to Stratford with my poor dear Nickleby, in a post-chaise from Birmingham—was it a post-chaise though!' said Mrs. Nickleby, considering; 'Yes, it must have been a post-chaise, because I recollect remarking at the time that the driver had a green shade over his left eye;—in a post-chaise from Birmingham, and after we had seen Shakespeare's tomb and birthplace, we went back to the inn there, where we slept that night, and I recollect that all night long I dreamed of nothing but a black gentleman, at full length, in plaster-of-Paris, with a lay-down collar tied with two tassels, leaning against a post and thinking; and when I woke in the morning and described him to Mr. Nickleby, he said it was Shakespeare just as he had been when he was alive, which was very curious indeed. Stratford—Stratford', continued Mrs. Nickleby, considering. 'Yes, I am positive about that, because I recollect that I was in the family way with my son Nicholas at the time, and I had been very much frightened by an Italian image boy that morning. In fact, it was quite a mercy, ma'am', added Mrs. Nickleby, in a whisper to Mrs. Wititterly, 'that my son didn't turn out to be a Shakespeare, and what a dreadful thing that would have been!'

An examination of Mrs. Nickleby's mental processes, as revealed in this passage, shows no sign of direction to an end. Clearly Mrs. Nickleby could observe, and she was able to recollect what she had observed. But her recollections were at the mercy of random associations; there is a connexion but it is the connexion of temporal contiguity. What happened is remembered and recorded as it happened. There is no selection, no omission under the influence of an explicit relevant interest. What she observes does not signify anything beyond itself; hence, its suggestive power is confined to what happened next, and then to what happened after that, and so on. There is no thinking here, for there is no direction to a conclusion. Presumably Mrs. Nickleby would stop for lack of breath or of listeners. There is no train of thought that, having worked itself out to a conclusion, comes to a natural end.

Contrast now Boswell's report of a conversation with Samuel Johnson:

'Mr. Langton told us that he was about to establish a school upon his estate, but it had been suggested to him that it might have a tendency to make the people less industrious. JOHNSON: "No, Sir. While learning to read and write is a distinction, the few who have that distinction may be the less inclined to work; but when everybody learns to read and write, it is no longer a distinction. A man who has a laced waistcoat is too fine a man to work; but if everybody had laced waistcoats, we should have people working in laced waistcoats. There are no people more industrious, none who work more than our manufacturers; yet they have all learnt to read and write. Sir, you must not neglect doing a thing immediately good, from fear of remote evil;—from fear of its being abused. A man who has candles may sit up too late, which he would not do if he had not candles; but nobody will deny that the art of making candles, by which light is continued to us beyond the time that the sun gives us light, is a valuable art, and ought to be preserved." BOSWELL: "But, Sir, would it not be better to follow nature; and go to bed and rise just as nature gives us light or withholds it?" JOHNSON: "No, Sir; for then we should have no kind of equality in the partition of our time between sleeping and waking. It would be very different in different seasons and in different places. In some of the northern parts of Scotland how little light is there in the depth of winter."'

In this conversation each statement is connected relevantly with the next and the whole is directed by the initial suggestion. Although Johnson passes from the consideration of the advisability of educating the people to a reflection with regard to the length of a winter night in northern Scotland there is no abrupt break. The transition is effected for the purpose of adducing relevant examples. In each example there is the selection of a characteristic that bears upon the conclusion, whilst those that are irrelevant are ignored. Reflective thinking is essentially selective, and thus involves abstraction. The characteristic that is abstracted from a total situation may be by no means obvious.

Consider, for instance, the following passage:

'A rope suggests other ropes and cords, if we look to the appearance; but looking to the use, it may suggest an iron cable, a wooden prop, an iron girding, a leather band or bevelled gear. In spite of the diversity of appearance, the suggestion turns on what answers a common end. . . . We become oblivious of the difference between a horse, a steam-engine, and a waterfall, when our minds are engrossed with the one circumstance of moving power.

Early Analytic Philosophy

The diversity in these had, no doubt, for a long time the effect of keeping back their first identification; and to obtuse intellects, this identification might have been for ever impossible. A strong concentration of mind upon the single peculiarity of mechanical force, and a degree of indifference to the general aspect of the things themselves, must conspire with the intellectual energy of resuscitation by similars, in order to summon together in the view, three structures so different. We can see by an instance like this, how new adaptations of existing machinery might arise in the mind of a mechanical inventor.'[2]

This example affords a good illustration of the way in which an unobvious characteristic may be abstracted by the thinker in order to further a relevant interest. The similarity between objects having many differences that would be important in other connexions may be noted because it is relevant in this connexion. Hence the importance of abstraction. Without abstraction there can be no recognition of similarity; without the recognition of similarity there can be no advance in knowledge. Every human being is capable of some degree of abstractness in thinking, that is, of imaginatively selecting some one character out of a complex situation so that it may be attended to in isolation. There is an effort of abstraction required in the case of the puzzle picture mentioned above. So long as the observer sees the line as constituting part of the foliage of the tree, he will fail to see it as part of the face he is trying to discover. In a way strictly analogous to this, the scientific genius selects from a mass of facts characteristics that are ignored by the ordinary man. In the practical affairs of everyday life we normally attend only to stimuli that are insistent and striking. Familiarity with a complex situation enables us, we say, to 'take it in at a glance'. But this rapid glance may fail to reveal features that are of significance in certain connexions. Moreover, our reactions to situations rapidly become habitual and are not modified in response to small variations in the situation itself. Undoubtedly rapidity of habitual response is necessary in order that life may be preserved and its ordinary business successfully carried out. But the success of habitual response checks the impulse to wonder and is thus inimical to the development of reflective thinking. A situation that seems perfectly familiar fails to arouse inquiry; it is accepted at its face value. Accordingly, it does not become the occasion of investigations designed to lead to the acquirement of fresh knowledge. The familiar use of language which enables us to refer, sometimes

---

[2]Bain, *The Senses and the Intellect*, p. 521. [Editor's note: as marked in the Preface, footnotes and references have bee left unaltered from the original texts from which the readings are pulled.]

Susan Stebbing on Logic, Language, and Analysis   469

by a single word, to a complex situation, may hinder us from noting unexpected features that are nevertheless present. For instance, if a doctor observing a set of symptoms were to label the disease from which the patient was suffering as "influenza", and were then content to treat the diagnosis as complete, he might be led into serious error. It might be necessary for him to look for some symptom not commonly associated with the other set, which would lead him to make a fresh diagnosis. What seemed to be influenza may turn out to be typhoid. We shall see later how the advance of knowledge is dependent upon the ability to attend to what is unusual and to observe its connexions with what is already familiar.

Reflective thinking is, then, relevant thinking. What is relevant in a given situation depends upon its connexions. The detection of relevant factors presupposes a large fund of knowledge bearing upon the situation, which may not all be consciously present in the process of reflection. In ordinary life we often possess a considerable amount of knowledge relevant to the situations within which we are called upon to act. We take for granted a number of generalizations that can be directly applied to a given case. We say, "It will rain to-morrow, because the sun has set in a bank of clouds", "Don't wear that dress at the seaside, for it will fade." If we were asked, "Why will it fade?" our reply might be, "Oh! that is the shade of blue that always does fade in sea air." This latter statement is an empirical generalization, that is, an assertion that a certain set of characters have in our past experience been found to be conjoined on an indefinite number of occasions, with the implication that they will continue to be so conjoined. If, however, the reply were: "Because that blue colour is due to a dye that is chemically unstable, so that it becomes unfixed under the influence of strong sea air", a beginning would have been made in analysing the factors contained in the total situation blue dress and sea air, and thus in connecting one relevant factor with another. This process of analysis and subsequent synthesis plays an important part in the process of discovering true generalizations with regard to what happens in the world. This process is sometimes known as induction, with which we shall be later concerned. At present, it is sufficient to notice that we constantly make generalizations going beyond what has been observed, which we proceed to apply to particular cases. Thus a certain character m comes to be recognized as a sign of another character p; whereupon, we conclude that, since *this S* has *m*, it has *p*.

Were it not the case that we find in experience that characters are constantly conjoined in such a way that one may be taken as the sign of another, reasoning would be impossible. Thus, whenever we reason we recognize that a certain state of affairs is the case because it is signified by some other state of affairs.

The latter is said to be the ground upon which our belief in the former is based. This belief is the conclusion of the reasoning. The conclusion is a reasoned conclusion because it is based upon evidence; something is taken as the sign of something else. A mistake may be made on both counts. What is may not be what we have taken it to be; or it may be that, and yet may not be connected in the way we have supposed. Even in such a case, however, the conclusion would be a reasoned, though a faulty, conclusion.

To sum up. We have distinguished between reflective thinking and idle reverie. We have further distinguished between directed thinking, which alone merits the name of thinking, and reminiscent thinking of the kind indulged in by Mrs. Nickleby. We have seen that reflective thinking originates in a problem to be solved and is throughout controlled by the conditions of the problem and is directed to its solution. Hence, reflective thinking has a natural end, the conclusion of the reflection. The various stages in this process are related to the conclusion as the grounds upon which it is based. These grounds may be called premisses. Relatively to the conclusion the premisses are taken for granted. The premisses may be obtained by means of direct observation or as the result of a previous process of reasoning. In either case the apprehension of the premisses depends upon a considerable amount of relevant knowledge which does not enter explicitly into the reflective thinking. There are various relations that may hold between premiss and conclusion; these will have to be distinguished. They are, however, all various modes of signifying. Wherever a relation such as that of signifying holds, there is a basis for reasoning.

Chapter 24: The Characteristics of Logical Thinking

'If a man can play the true logician, and have as well judgement as invention, he may do great matters' – Francis Bacon

§1. Persuasion and Conviction

The purpose of logical thinking is to reach conclusions. The process of reaching conclusions is reasoning. Ordinarily we reason from something we know to something which, prior to our reasoning, we did not know, but which we now know as the result of our reasoning. Strictly speaking we cannot be said to *know* anything unless it is the case. Thus, in order that a proposition should be *known* it is necessary both that the proposition should be believed and that it should be true. Although *to believe* a proposition and *to believe it to be true* are

Susan Stebbing on Logic, Language, and Analysis 471

one and the same thing, yet we believe many propositions which are in fact false. Sometimes we discover their falsity by reasoning from the propositions we believe to conclusions which we recognize to be false. When we reason we desire to ascertain what is true, or what must be true if something else is true. We can *know* our conclusions to be true only when we know both that the premisses are true and that these premisses imply the conclusion. Sometimes we can recognize that we *believe* a proposition, and therefore believe it to be *true*, although we recognize that we do not yet *know* it to be true. Often, however, we fail to distinguish between our *beliefs* and our *knowledge*. When our belief is challenged then we may come to recognize that, after all, we did not *know* but only *believed* that so-and-so was the case. Doubting is a mental state clearly distinguishable from belief. We doubt a proposition when with regard to it we *know* that we do not know whether it is true or whether it is false. The state of doubting is usually unpleasant; hence, we desire to resolve a doubt. Reasoning from true premisses, or from premisses believed to be true, is a method of resolving doubt. But we may be persuaded to believe by other methods than reasoning. Also many of our beliefs are due neither to persuasion nor to reasoning. Were this not the case we could have but few beliefs, since neither our mental power nor our length of days permit us to inquire into the foundation of all that we believe. Thus many of our beliefs are not *well-founded* beliefs even though what we believe may happen to be true.

There are at least five different ways in which belief may be attained. First, we may believe a proposition because we always have believed it. How we first came to believe it we need not here inquire. We are concerned only to notice that we believe some propositions only because we have never seen fit to doubt with regard to them. Such beliefs are usually pleasant, that is to say, the truth of the propositions thus believed seems to us to be conducive to our interests; were this not the case we should be tempted to doubt, since unpleasantness is a stimulus to activity. The fact that some people, of a melancholy cast of mind, may believe a proposition that something unpleasant is the case, for no other reason than its unpleasantness, does not contradict this contention. For it is just this unpleasantness that satisfies their melancholy, hence, their *belief* that something unpleasant is the case is not *itself* unpleasant. This way of attaining belief may be called, by a perhaps permissible metaphor, *the way of the limpet*. The thinker sticks to his belief as the limpet to its rock, without taking note of its connexion with anything else in the neighbourhood. Thus, for instance, the ardent hunter may believe that foxes enjoy being hunted; the wealthy old lady, tender-hearted but unimaginative and conservative, may believe that the unemployed are "the

Early Analytic Philosophy

won't-works".[1] The chief advantage of this way of belief is its comfortableness. Its disadvantage is due to the fact that beliefs thus attained may be upset by the pressure of facts, and that this upset may have disastrous consequences.

The second way of attaining belief may be described as the way of authority. Two different types of authority may be distinguished. To accept a proposition on authority is to accept it on the ground that some one whose opinion we respect has asserted it to be true. Our respect may be due to the office occupied by this person or to our recognition that he is an expert with regard to the subject-matter of our belief. The first case is exemplified in the acceptance of the authority of a church, or of a parent, or of a teacher whom we have not learnt to doubt.[2] The disadvantage of acquiring beliefs in this way is that the acceptance of authority stifles inquiry. Moreover, authorities may be mistaken. The advantages resemble the advantages of the way of the limpet. The second case is exemplified in the acceptance of expert testimony. When a man has made a careful study of a subject, and has come to conclusions for which he is prepared to offer evidence that seems to him conclusive, then it is not unreasonable to believe that his opinion has more weight than that of one who has made no such study. When there is a consensus of expert opinion with regard to a given proposition it is reasonable to accept the opinion of these experts if we have not ourselves examined the evidence upon which the proposition is asserted to be based. Thus it is reasonable for the layman to accept the authority of the expert. With regard to the greater part of our beliefs we are all in the position of laymen. It follows that to believe a proposition on authority is often the wisest course to pursue. The danger of this way of belief is that we are liable to confuse one kind of authority with another and to be confident that experts cannot err. But even a consensus of experts is not infallible.

Thirdly, we may attain belief by the way of self-evidence. We cannot disbelieve what is self-evident, for to say that a proposition is self-evident is to say that its truth is obvious. But what is obvious may nevertheless not be the case. If there are propositions which no one can doubt, then they are in fact indubitable. But propositions that have been accepted by many careful thinkers as self-evident

---

[1] There is a difficulty in giving examples of this way of belief, since the writer is bound to give examples which appear to her to be baseless beliefs, whereas, with regard to any example chosen, the reader may have sources of knowledge, unknown to the writer, which would justify these beliefs. In that case, the reader will have no difficulty in finding examples, supplied by other peoples' beliefs, which seem to him baseless. To recognize that a belief is after all only a prejudice is to recognize that it was attained by the way of the limpet.

[2] It is not unreasonable to suppose that a teacher (in the educational sense) whose pronouncements are never doubted is a bad teacher.

Susan Stebbing on Logic, Language, and Analysis **473**

have finally been found not to be indubitable. Thus we must distinguish between the assertion that a given proposition is psychologically self-evident, in the sense that no one doubts it, and the assertion that it is self-evident in some *other* sense, strictly relevant to logic. Whether there are any propositions self-evident in the latter sense is a matter for investigation.[3] To recognize that self-evident propositions may require investigation is already to have abandoned the way of self-evidence. The danger of this way of belief is that it checks inquiry and may encourage erroneous beliefs. To avoid this danger it is well to form the habit of suspending judgement, and hence of being prepared to doubt whatever can be doubted.

The fourth and fifth ways of attaining belief are to be distinguished from the first three in that they involve a process of inquiry the purpose of which is to resolve a state of doubt. This process may be terminated either by persuasion or by conviction. Here "persuasion" is used in opposition to "conviction", although no doubt they are sometimes used as synonyms. The way of persuasion is to be distinguished from the way of conviction by the nature of the process whereby doubt is resolved. Even if rationality is the distinguishing characteristic of human nature, it must be admitted that few of our beliefs are based upon rational grounds. Moreover, not only do we tend to believe what we wish to believe but, further, this wish to believe often operates in making us suppose that what we believe is a logical consequence of something else that may be taken for granted. Rhetoric is a means of persuasion. The aim of the orator is to induce belief, not to demonstrate a conclusion; his art consists in persuading others to accept a conclusion for which there is no adequate evidence. Since our beliefs are determined to such a small extent by logical considerations the orator employs various devices to persuade us. If his hearers were clear thinkers, free from the bias of special interest, and if his conclusions were susceptible of demonstration, then he would need no other method of producing belief than the method of logical argument. Seldom, however, is either of these conditions satisfied. Consequently, the orator substitutes persuasion for conviction, appealing to emotion rather than to reason. The speech of a great orator is a work of art; as such, it has nothing to do with logic, and, as such it can be admired by those whom it does not persuade. But the way of persuasion is not confined to great orators; it is employed with considerable success by advertising experts, whose insight into practical psychology makes them adepts in persuading those who do not think to buy goods which are either useless or

---

[3]See Chap. X, pp. 175–7.

harmful. Possibly in this case there is action without belief so that this topic lies outside the scope of our discussion.

The way of conviction is by reasoning. This is the method of science and the proper business of the logician. It might be supposed that as logicians we have no concern with any other way of attaining belief. In a sense this is so, but it is often difficult to determine *how* a belief has been attained although the ways of attainment are distinct. Not all thinking is logical thinking, nor all reasoning good. We may more easily apprehend the characteristics of good reasoning when we have recognized the various ways in which we attain our beliefs. A well-constructed argument the purpose of which is to produce conviction exhibits the characteristics of clearness, connectedness or relevance, freedom from contradiction or consistency, demonstrativeness or cogency. Throughout our discussion of logical method we have laid stress upon relevance as an essential characteristic of logical thinking. To know what is relevant to a situation is to apprehend connexions. The discovery of relevance requires judgement, for not all relevance is logical. But in connected thinking certain logical principles are implicit, upon which the cogency of the argument depends. These principles will be considered in the next section.

§2. Logical Principles and the Traditional "Laws of Thought"

All logical thinking exemplifies certain abstract principles in accordance with which such thinking takes place. It is extremely difficult to determine what these principles are, and which, if any, are independent of the rest. Three of these principles have been singled out by the traditional Logicians and described as "Laws of Thought." This description is unfortunate, since it suggests a reference to uniformities of thinking, i.e. to psychological laws, which was probably not intended.[4] But the chief objection to the traditional treatment lies not in the description but in the conception of what it was that was thus described. For "*the* laws" must mean *all* the laws; but it is absurd to suppose that there are only three. There has been considerable difference of opinion as to how these "laws" should be stated. The starting-point of the traditional theory of logic is to be found in the Aristotelian category of substance-attribute. Assertions with regard to the attributes of a substance can be most naturally expressed in singular propositions of the subject-predicate form, viz. *This S is P.* Accordingly the "laws" have often been expressed in a manner appropriate only

---

[4]See Sir William Hamilton, *Lectures on Logic* (Sect. V).

Susan Stebbing on Logic, Language, and Analysis   475

to propositions of this form. An affirmation with regard to *This S* was held both by Plato and Aristotle to be an affirmation with regard to a definite thing, or individual, having a determinate nature. From this point of view the Laws may be stated as follows:

(1) *The Law of Identity.* Everything is what it is; or, A is A.
(2) *The Law of Contradiction.* A thing cannot both be and not be so and so; or, A is not both B and not B.
(3) *The Law of Excluded Middle.* A thing either is or is not so and so; or, A either is or is not B.

The formulation of (1) as "A is A" may be regarded as expressing an important principle of symbolism, but it is not usually so regarded. From the point of view of a principle concerned with the use of symbols, the principle of identity can be formulated as follows: *Sameness of symbol indicates sameness of referend.* Clearly symbols which refer to different referends are different symbols. Hence, it must always be non-significant to write 'A = A'. It is true that it is convenient in practice to say that a name is identical with a given description (e.g. 'Scott is identical with the author of *Waverley*'), or that two descriptions are identical (e.g. 'The author of *Waverley* is identical with the author of *Marmion*'). But in these cases analysis reveals that what is meant by "is identical with" involves the notion of *applying to.* But neither the traditional Law of Identity nor any principle of identity concerning the use of symbols has ever been interpreted in terms of *applying to.* Consequently, these expressions cannot be regarded as exemplifications of the law of identity. The traditional interpretation of this law is metaphysical. If "A" be regarded as symbolizing a subject of attributes, then the formula may be interpreted as expressing the permanence of substance, or as the persisting of something through change. Such an interpretation is clearly metaphysical; it expresses a theory with regard to the nature of persistent individuality. This could not properly be regarded as a fundamental principle of logical thinking, so that this interpretation need not be discussed here. Aristotle did not himself formulate any "law of identity", but such a law might be extracted from his assertion, 'Everything that is true must in every respect agree with itself.'[5]

It is worth while to consider briefly how Aristotle was led to formulate the law of contradiction. He was in search of an indemonstrable principle which could be regarded as the basis of all demonstration. For, as he points out, 'it is

---

[5]*Anal. Priora*, 47a9. See Sigwart, *Logic*, I, pp. 83–9, for a discussion of the principle of identity.

Early Analytic Philosophy

impossible that there should be demonstration of absolutely everything; for there would be an infinite regress, so that there would still be no demonstration'.[6] Now, he argues, 'the most certain principle of all is that regarding which it is impossible to be mistaken'. Such a principle is 'that the same attribute cannot at the same time belong, and not belong to the same subject in the same respect. . . . This, then, is the most certain of all principles, since it answers to the definition given above. For it is impossible for any one to believe the same thing to be and not to be, as some think Heraclitus says'.[7] This statement suggests the formulations given of (2) above. But Aristotle was aware that contradiction is a relation that holds between two propositions which are such that one must be true one false. In discussing the relations between propositions he formulated both the laws of contradiction and excluded middle as follows:

> 'If it is true to say that a thing is white, it must necessarily be white; if the reverse proposition is true, it will of necessity not be white. Again, if it is white, the proposition stating that it was white was true; if it is not white, the proposition to the opposite effect was true. And if it is not white, the man who states that it is is making a false statement; and if the man who states that it is white is making a false statement, it follows that it is not white. It may therefore be argued that it is necessary that affirmations or denials must be either true or false'.[8]

It is not difficult to extract from this passage the formulations: (i) This S is p and This S is not p cannot both be true; (ii) Either *This S is p is* true or *This S is not p* is true. These are respectively the laws (2) and (3). This passage also brings out clearly that *both* these laws, or principles, are required in order to define the *relation of contradiction* between propositions, since contradictory propositions cannot *both* be true and one must be true.

With regard to these three Laws there has been considerable discussion as to whether they are laws of *thought* or of *things*. They are clearly not laws of thought in the sense that they express ways in which we always do think, since we sometimes fall into contradiction. If it be maintained that on such occasions we are *not thinking*, then "thinking" must be taken as equivalent to "logical thinking." In that case these "laws" cannot be regarded as uniformities, or generalizations derived from experience.[9] Probably few, if any, logicians to-day

---

[6]*Metaphysica*, 1006a, 7.
[7]Ibid, 1005b, 17. Cf. Socrates' attempt to express this principle in *Republic*.
[8]*De Interpretatione*, 18b, 1–5.
[9]The view that these laws are generalizations from experience was held by Mill.

would take this view. Mr. Joseph says: 'Now though these are called laws of thought, and in fact we cannot think except in accordance with them, yet they are really statements which we cannot but hold true about things. We *cannot think* contradictory propositions, because we see that *a thing cannot have* at once and not have the same character; and the so-called necessity of thought is really the apprehension of a necessity in the being of things'.[10] This passage suggests that Mr. Joseph holds both that these laws are laws of *thought* and that they are laws of *things*. There seems nothing to be said in favour of this view. We have already seen reason to reject the view that these "laws" are laws of *thought*. It is also misleading to describe them as laws of *things* since such an expression suggests that they in some way determine what is actual, or given. They are, however, purely *formal* principles which are independent of what is given; they are negative determinations of what is *possible*. Only in the sense that what is *actual* must also be *possible* could these principles be regarded as determining what is *actual*; they do not determine what is actual *in so far as* it is actual; they in no sense limit the *actual* to be *so-and-so*.

Dr. J. N. Keynes says: 'The so-called fundamental laws of thought . . . are to be regarded as the foundation of all reasoning in the sense that consecutive thought and coherent argument are impossible unless they are taken for granted'.[11] It is certainly true that 'consecutive thought and coherent argument' must exemplify these principles, but it would be incorrect to suppose that they are *sufficient* to constitute 'the foundation of all reasoning'. We cannot here attempt to state all the principles that would together be sufficient; we shall select those which are most obviously exemplified in ordinary reasoning.[12] We may first restate the 'three laws' in the form of principles exemplified in the relations between propositions. We shall, as usual, employ p, q, to stand for any propositions.

(1) *Principle of Identity*. If *p*, then *p*.
(2) *Principle of Contradiction*. *p* cannot be both true and false.
(3) *Principle of Excluded Middle*. Either *p* is true or *p* is false.

This formulation brings out the essential relation of the three principles. They cannot, however, be reduced to a single principle, since the deduction of, for instance, (3) *Either p is true or p is false* from (1) If *p*, then *p*, or from (2) Not both

---

[10]*Introd.*, p. 13. It is clear that Mr. Joseph supposes that all *thinking* is *logical* thinking
[11]*F.L.*, p. 450. Appendix B to the *Formal Logic* contains a long discussion of the traditional laws.
[12]See Chapter X, §5, for a fuller statement of these principles.

478   Early Analytic Philosophy

p true and *p* false, requires the independent notion of *falsity*, or of *negation*, which cannot be defined without using the principles themselves.[13]

We require principles of implication and of deduction. These may be stated as follows :

(4) *Principle of Syllogism.* If *p* implies *q*, and *q* implies *r*, then *p* implies *r*.

(5) *Principle of Deduction.* If *p* implies *q*, and *p* is true, then *q* is true.

This principle is required in order that conclusions should be drawn: the principle permits the omission of an implicans provided that the implicans is *true*.

There is further required a principle permitting the substitution of any *given* member of a class in an assertion about every member of the class. This might be expressed as follows:

(6) Whatever can be asserted about *any instance* however chosen, can be asserted about *any given instance*.

This principle may be described as the "principle of substitution" since it is in virtue of this principle that we can substitute constant values for the variables in a functional expression. Mr. Johnson calls this the 'Applicative Principle' and says that it 'may be said to formulate what is involved in the intelligent use of "every'."[14] This principle together with the principle of deduction is exemplified in all chains of reasoning.

There are three principles relating to the conjunctive use of *and* which are important.[15] These are:

(7) *Principle of Tautology. p and p* is equivalent to *p*. This principle asserts that the reiteration of a proposition adds nothing to the original assertion.

(8) *Principle of Commutation. p and q* is equivalent to *q and p*. This principle asserts that the order in which propositions are asserted is indifferent. This principle follows from the fact that and is a symmetrical relation.

(9) *Principle of Association. p and q and also r* is equivalent to *p and also q and r*. This principle asserts that the order in which propositions are grouped is indifferent. These principles also relate to the alternative or. They can be restated by substituting *or* for *and* in each case.

---

[13]See p. 191 above.
[14]W. E. J., II, p. 9.
[15]W. E. J. I., pp. 29–30.

(10) There is a *Principle of Distribution* relating to the combination of propositions connected by *and* and by *or*. This may be stated in the form: *p or q, and also r* is equivalent to *p and r, or q and r*.

It is not likely to be denied that these principles are all psychologically self-evident. Within a given deductive system these principles may be deduced from logically more primitive principles. But these primitive principles will not be self-evident in any sense in which the derived principles are not also self-evident; they will be *primitive*, or *underived*, only because they are taken for granted, and thus form the basis of the given system. Fundamental logical principles cannot be proved in any absolute sense, for all proof must presuppose them. To think logically some principles must be assumed, since logical thinking is thinking in accordance with logical principles. The notion of proof is relative to something unproved; what is taken as unproved determines what can be proved. The principles can be used so that they can be proved by themselves. Such proof is circular. This circularity is a test of self-consistency. Those principles which appear in every deductive development from given principles, *either* as unproved principles *or* as deductions from these principles, may be regarded as fundamental logical principles. The three principles selected by the traditional Logicians have this characteristic only in a more obvious manner than the other principles we have stated.

§ 3. The Normative Aspect of Logic

Logicians have been wont to raise the question whether logic is a science or an art. Presumably, a science is a systematic study, whilst an art is a set of rules the learning of which may fit some one to do something. If this be so, there seems little doubt that logic is not an art, but a science. There may be an art of thinking. Not a few public men have recently written books professing to deal with such an art. But the art of thinking must not be confused with logic. No doubt the man who sets out to instruct us how to think must be conversant with the logical principles of reasoning as well as with the ordinary workings of the human mind. The logician also may have to take note of psychological processes, but his interest in these processes is analytical and critical. We shall see in the next chapter that the study of logic originated in an attempt to determine the nature and conditions of valid thinking by criticizing types of argumentative discussion. This criticism resulted in the discovery that the validity of reasoning depends only upon its form. Once this is realized it becomes clear that logic is a pure science.

The position of logic amongst the sciences has certain peculiarities. The natural, or empirical, sciences are concerned with given regions of fact. Their

Early Analytic Philosophy

field of investigation is the actual world. Logic, on the contrary, is concerned not with what is actual but with what is possible. Yet the relation between logic and the other sciences is very close. Were this not the case our discussion of scientific method would have been a sheer irrelevance. The scientist aims at discovering true propositions with regard to the field of his inquiry. Consequently, he infers, and he desires that his inferences should be valid. In so far as scientific thinking is methodical, or orderly, it will exhibit logical form. Accordingly, the logician is interested in the analysis and criticism of the methods employed by those who are attempting to introduce order into a set of facts.

It is sometimes said that logic is to be distinguished from the other sciences in virtue of the fact that it is normative. A normative science, as the name suggests, is concerned with norms, or standards. In so far as logic is concerned with the criticism of modes of thinking it has a normative aspect. From this point of view logic may be regarded as a regulative science. But this normative aspect is, as it were, a by-product. We do not study logic in order to establish norms by reference to which the validity of reasoning may be tested. The discovery of norms of thinking – when, indeed, they are discovered – results from the fact that valid thinking is formal and that logic is the science of possible forms. It is a mistake to regard the normative aspect of logic as constituting its distinguishing characteristic. Nevertheless, this is the aspect that is important from the point of view of reflective thinking, and which makes the study of logic useful even for journalists and politicians. The utility of logic has often been based upon the claim that in studying the principles of reasoning we learn to be good reasoners. Certainly we are less likely to be misled by erroneous reasoning if we have clear ideas with regard to the nature of proof and the forms of our arguments. Mill, whose interests were mainly practical, stressed this aspect of logic and hoped to promote clear thinking by making evident the nature of logical method. 'Logic', he says, 'is the common judge and arbiter of all particular investigations. It does not undertake to find evidence, but to determine whether it has been found. Logic neither observes, nor invents, nor discovers; but judges.'[16] Such a conception of logic suggests that, though it be a science, yet it is primarily to be studied as an art. To take this view is to misconceive the nature of logic. Rather is it the case that the attempt to study the art of reasoning may lead to the apprehension of logical form. Knowledge of logical form, on the other hand, no more suffices to make men good reasoners than knowledge of prosodical form suffices to make them good poets. No one really understands the form of his reasoning, or is able

---

[16]*Logic, Introd.*, §5.

to estimate its validity, unless he can recognize this form when it is exhibited in different subject-matters. As Locke has rightly insisted: 'Nobody is made any thing by hearing of rules, or laying them up in his memory; practice must settle the habit of doing, without reflecting on the rule: and you may as well hope to make a good painter or musician, extempore, by a lecture and instruction in the arts of music and painting, as a coherent thinker, or strict reasoner, by a set of rules, showing him wherein right reasoning consists'.[17] But this 'reflecting on the rule' – to use Locke's expression – is just precisely the concern of the logician. The study of examples, the criticism of thought in the light of normative principles, these are but means to enable him to abstract. The analysis of particular examples is an aid to the beginner; it puts him in a favourable position for the apprehension of form. In a similar way the beginner in Latin learns to apprehend the structure of a latin sentence, i.e. its syntactical form, only by studying particular examples of latin sentences. So it is also with geometry. Just because form is abstract it is not easily apprehended. Small wonder, then, that logic was first conceived as limited to the study of modes of reasoning as they are exemplified in the special sciences or in argumentative discussion. To this limitation is due the emphasis upon the normative aspect of logic. When the norms of thinking are seen to be norms only because they are pure forms, the exemplification of these forms can be recognized to be irrelevant to the science of logic.

Stebbing, S. *Philosophy and the Physicists* (selections from Ch. 3).
Reprinted from Stebbing, S. (1937), *Philosophy and the Physicists*, London: Methuen.

Chapter 3: 'Furniture of the Earth'

'Roused by the shock he started from his trance—
The cold white light of morning, the blue moon
Low in the west, the clear and garish hills,
The distant valley and the vacant woods,
Spread round him where he stood. Whither have fled
The hues of heaven that canopied his bower
Of yesternight? The sounds that soothed his sleep,

---

[17]*The Conduct of the Understanding*, §4.

482   **Early Analytic Philosophy**

> The mystery and the majesty of Earth,
> The joy, the exultation?'

Wordsworth

I enter my study and see the blue curtains fluttering in the breeze, for the windows are open. I notice a bowl of roses on the table; it was not there when I went out. Clumsily I stumble against the table, bruising my leg against its hard edge; it is a heavy table and scarcely moves under the impact of my weight. I take a rose from the bowl, press it to my face, feel the softness of the petals, and smell its characteristic scent. I rejoice in the beauty of the graded shading of the crimson petals. In short – I am in a familiar room, seeing, touching, smelling familiar things, thinking familiar thoughts, experiencing familiar emotions.

In some such way might any common reader describe his experiences in the familiar world that he inhabits. With his eyes shut he may recognize a rose from its perfume, stumble against a solid obstacle and recognize it to be a table, and feel the pain from its contact with his comparatively yielding flesh. You, who are reading this chapter, may pause and look around you. Perhaps you are in your study, perhaps seated on the seashore, or in a cornfield, or on board ship. Wherever you may be, you will see objects distinguishable one from another, differing in colour and in shape; probably you are hearing various sounds. You can see the printed marks on this page, and notice that they are black marks on a whitish background. That you are perceiving something coloured and shaped you will not deny; that your body presses against something solid you are convinced; that, if you wish, you can stop reading this book, you know quite well. It may be assumed that you have some interest in philosophy; otherwise you would not be reading *this*. Perhaps you have allowed yourself to be persuaded that the page is not 'really coloured', that the seat upon which you are sitting is not 'really solid'; that you hear only 'illusory sounds'. If so, it is for such as you that this chapter is written.

Imagine the following scene. You are handed a dish containing some apples – rosy-cheeked, green apples. You take the one nearest to you, and realize that you have been 'had'. The 'apple' is too hard and not heavy enough to be really an apple; as you tap it with your finger-nail it gives out a sound such as never came from tapping a 'real' apple. You admire the neatness of the imitation. To sight the illusion is perfect. It is quite sensible to contrast this ingenious fake with a 'real' apple, for a 'real' apple just is an object that *really* is an apple, and not only *seems* to be one. This fake is an object that looks to your eyes to be an apple, but neither feels nor tastes as an apple does. As soon as you pick it up you know that it is not an apple; there is no need to taste it. We should be speaking in

Susan Stebbing on Logic, Language, and Analysis 483

conformity with the rules of good English if we were to say that the dish contained real apples and imitation apples. But this mode of speaking does not lead us to suppose that there are two varieties of *apples,* namely real and imitation apples, as there are Bramley Seedlings and Blenheim pippins. Again, a shadow may be thrown on a wall, or an image may be thrown through a lantern on to a screen. We distinguish the shadow from the object of which it is the shadow, the image from that of which it is the image. Shadow and image are apprehensible only by sight; they really are visual, i.e. *seeable,* entities. I can see a man, and I can see his shadow; but there is not both a *real* man and a *shadow* man; there is just the shadow of the man.

This point may seem to have been unduly laboured. It is, however, of great importance. The words "real" and "really" are familiar words; they are variously used in every-day speech, and are not, as a rule, used ambiguously. The opposition between a *real* object and an *imitation* of a real object is clear. So, too, is the opposition between 'really seeing a man' and having an illusion.[1] We can speak sensibly of the distinction between 'the real size' and 'the apparent size' of the moon, but we know that both these expressions are extremely elliptical. The significance of the words "real" and "really" can be determined only by reference to the context in which they are used. Nothing but confusion can result if, in one and the same sentence, we mix up language used appropriately for the furniture of earth and our daily dealings with it with language used for the purpose of philosophical and scientific discussion.

A peculiarly gross example of such a linguistic mixture is provided by one of Eddington's most picturesque passages:

I am standing on a threshold about to enter a room. It is a complicated business. In the first place I must shove against an atmosphere pressing with a force of fourteen pounds on every square inch of my body. I must make sure of landing on a plank travelling at twenty miles a second round the sun – a fraction of a second too early or too late, the plank would be miles away. I must do this whilst hanging from a round planet head outward into space, and with a wind of aether blowing at no one knows how many miles a second through every interstice of my body. The plank has no solidity of substance. To step on it is like stepping on a swarm of flies. Shall I not slip through? No, if I make the venture one of the flies hits me and gives me a boost up again; I fall again and am knocked upwards by another fly; and so

---

[1] Cf. 'How easy is that bush supposed a bear!'

on. I may hope that the net result will be that I remain steady; but if unfortunately I should slip through the floor or be boosted too violently up to the ceiling the occurrence would be, not a violation of the laws of Nature, but a rare coincidence. (*N.Ph.W.* 342.)

Whatever we may think of Eddington's chances of slipping through the floor, we must regard his usage of language in this statement as gravely misleading to the common reader. I cannot doubt that it reveals serious confusion in Eddington's own thinking about 'the nature of the physical world'. Stepping on a plank is not in the least like 'stepping on a swarm of flies'. This language is drawn from, and is appropriate to, our daily intercourse with the familiar furniture of earth. We understand well what it is like to step on to a solid plank; we can also imagine what it would be like to step on to a swarm of flies. We know that two such experiences would be quite different. The plank is solid. If it be securely fixed, it will support our weight. What, then, are we to make of the comparison of stepping on to a plank with stepping on to a swarm of flies? What can be meant by saying that 'the plank has no solidity of substance'?

Again, we are familiar with the experience of shoving against an obstacle, and with the experience of struggling against a strong head-wind. We know that we do not have 'to shove against an atmosphere' as we cross the threshold of a room. We can imagine what it would be like to jump on to a moving plank. We may have seen in a circus an equestrian acrobat jump from the back of a swiftly moving horse on to the back of another horse moving with approximately the same speed. We know that no such acrobatic feat is required to cross the threshold of a room.[2]

I may seem too heavy-handed in my treatment of a picturesque passage, and thus to fall under the condemnation of the man who cannot see a joke and needs to be 'in contact with merry-minded companions'[3] in order that he may develop a sense of humour. But the picturesqueness is deceptive; the passage needs serious criticism since Eddington draws from it a conclusion that is important. 'Verily' he says, 'it is easier for a camel to pass through the eye of a needle than for a scientific man to pass through a door. And whether the door be barn door or church door it might be wiser that he should consent to be an ordinary man and walk in rather than wait until all the difficulties involved in a really scientific ingress are resolved.' It is, then, suggested that an ordinary man

---

[2]Eddington's words suggest that he is standing on a stationary plank and has to land on to another plank that is moving, relatively to himself, with a speed of twenty miles a second. It would be charitable to regard this as a slip, were it not that its rectification would spoil this part of his picture. There is an equally gross absurdity in the statement that he is 'hanging head outward into space'.
[3]See *N.Ph.W.* 336.

Susan Stebbing on Logic, Language, and Analysis 485

has no difficulty in crossing the threshold of a room but that 'a really scientific ingress' presents difficulties.[4] The suggested contrast is as absurd as the use of the adjective 'scientific' prefixed to 'ingress' in this context, is perverse. Whatever difficulties a scientist, by reason of his scientific knowledge, may encounter in becoming a member of a spiritual church, these difficulties bear no comparison with the difficulties of the imagined acrobatic feat. Consequently, they are not solved by the consideration that Eddington, no less than the ordinary man, need not hesitate to cross the threshold of his room. The false emotionalism of the picture is reminiscent of Jeans's picture of human beings standing on 'a microscopic fragment of a grain of sand'. It is open to a similar criticism.[5]

If Eddington had drawn this picture for purely expository purposes, it might be unobjectionable. The scientist who sets out to give a popular exposition of a difficult and highly technical subject must use what means he can devise to convey to his readers what it is all about. At the same time, if he wishes to avoid being misunderstood, he must surely warn his readers that, in the present stage of physics, very little can be conveyed to a reader who lacks the mathematical equipment required to understand the methods by which results are obtained and the language in which these results can alone find adequate expression. Eddington's picture seems to me to be open to the objection that the image of a swarm of flies used to explain the electronic structure of matter is more appropriate to the old-fashioned classical conceptions that found expression in a model than to the conceptions he is trying to explain. Consequently, the reader may be misled unless he is warned that nothing resembling the spatial relations of flies in a swarm can be found in the collection of electrons. No concepts drawn from the level of common-sense thinking are appropriate to sub-atomic, i.e. microphysical, phenomena. Consequently, the language of common sense is not appropriate to the description of such phenomena. Since, however, the

---

[4] In the article 'The Domain of Physical Science' (*Science, Religion and Reality*) a similar passage begins as follows:

'The learned physicist and the man in the street were standing together on the threshold about to enter a room.

The man in the street moved forward without trouble, planted his foot on a solid unyielding plank at rest before him, and entered.

The physicist was faced with an intricate problem.' (There follows much the same account of the difficulties as in the passage quoted.)

Eddington here goes on to suggest that the physicist may be 'content to follow *the same crude conception* of his task that presented itself to the mind of his unscientific colleague' (my italics).

[5] See p. 11 above.

486   Early Analytic Philosophy

man in the street tends to think in pictures and may desire to know something about the latest developments of physics, it is no doubt useful to provide him with some rough picture.[6] The danger arises when the scientist uses the picture for the purpose of making explicit denials, and expresses these denials in common-sense language used in such a way as to be devoid of sense. This, unfortunately, is exactly what Eddington has done in the passage we are considering, and indeed, in many other passages as well.

It is worth while to examine with some care what exactly it is that Eddington is denying when he asserts that 'the plank has no solidity of substance'. What are we to understand by "solidity"? Unless we do understand it we cannot understand what the denial of solidity to the plank amounts to. But we can understand "solidity" only if we can truly say that the plank is solid. For "solid" just is the word we use to describe a certain respect in which a plank of wood resembles a block of marble, a piece of paper, and a cricket ball, and in which each of these differs from a sponge, from the interior of a soap-bubble, and from the holes in a net. We use the word "solid" sometimes as the opposite of "empty", sometimes as the opposite of "hollow", sometimes as the opposite of "porous." We may also, in a very slightly technical usage, contrast "solid" with "liquid" or with "gaseous." There is, no doubt, considerable variation in the precise significance of the word "solid" in various contexts. Further, as is the case with all words, "solid" may be misused, and may also be used figuratively. But there could not be a *misuse,* nor a *figurative* use, unless there were some correct and literal usages. The point is that the common usage of language enables us to attribute a meaning to the phrase "a solid plank"; but there is no common usage of language that provides a meaning for the word "solid" that would make sense to say that the plank on which I stand is not *solid.* We oppose the solidity of the walls of a house to the emptiness of its unfurnished rooms; we oppose the solidity of a piece of pumice-stone to the porous loofah sponge. We do not deny that the pumice-stone is to some degree porous, that the bricks of the wall have chinks and crevices. But we do not know how to use a word that has no sensible opposite. If the plank is non-solid, then what does "solid" *mean*? In the companion passage to the one quoted above, and to which reference was made in a preceding footnote, Eddington depicts the physicist, about to enter a room, as reflecting that 'the plank is not what it appears to be – a continuous support for his weight'. This remark is absurd. The plank appears

---

[6]Jeans has a happy gift of using such pictures in his purely expository works. See, for example, his image of the postage-stamp, the penny, and Cleopatra's needle, used to illustrate certain proportions of the history of the world – *The Universe Around Us*, p. 342.

to be capable of supporting his weight, and, as his subsequent entry into the room showed, it *was* capable of supporting his weight. If it be objected that the plank is 'a support for his weight' but not 'a *continuous* support', I would reply that the word "continuous" is here used without any assigned meaning. The plank appears *solid* in that sense of the word "solid" in which the plank is, in fact, solid. It is of the utmost importance to press the question: If the plank appears to be *solid,* but is really *nonsolid,* what does "solid" mean? If "solid" has no assignable meaning, then "non-solid" is also without sense. If the plank is non-solid, then where can we find an example to show us what "solid" means? The pairs of words, "solid" − "empty", "solid" − "hollow", "solid" − "porous", belong to the vocabulary of common-sense language; in the case of each pair, if one of the two is without sense, so is the other.

This nonsensical denial of solidity is very common in popular expositions of the physicist's conception of material objects. The author of a recently published book says: 'A table, a piece of paper, no longer possess that solid reality which they appear to possess; they are both of them porous, and consist of very small electrically charged particles, which are arranged in a peculiar way'.[7] How are we to understand the statement that the table *no longer* possesses 'the solid reality' which it appears to possess? The context of the statement must be taken into account. The sentence quoted occurs in a summary of the view of the physical world according to classical physics. It immediately follows the statement: 'This picture formed by the physicists has one great drawback as compared with the picture formed by the non-scientific man in the street. It is much more abstract.' In a later chapter we shall find reason to consider carefully what is meant by 'more abstract'. Here we are concerned only with the suggestion that the non-scientific man forms one 'picture' of the material world and the scientist another. There are, then, two pictures. Of what, we must ask, are they pictures? Where are we to find application for the words "solid reality", which we may not use with reference to the table? Again we must ask: If the table is non-solid, what does "solid" mean?

No doubt the author had in mind the nineteenth-century view of the ultra-microscopic world as consisting of solid, absolutely hard, indivisible billiard-ball-like atoms, which were assumed to be solid and hard in a perfectly straightforward sense of the words "solid" and "hard." If so, it would be more appropriate to say that the modern physicist no longer believes that the table *consists* of solid

---

[7]Ernst Zimmer: *The Revolution of Physics,* trans, by H. Stafford Hatfield, 1936, p. 51. I have not been able to consult the German original, so I am unable to determine whether 'solid reality ' is a good rendering of Zimmer's meaning. Certainly the juxtaposition of the two words is unfortunate, but is evidently judged to be appropriate at least by his translator.

488 **Early Analytic Philosophy**

atomic balls, than to say that 'the table no longer possesses solid reality'. There is, indeed, a danger in talking about *the table* at all, for the physicist is not, in fact, concerned with tables. The recent habit of talking as though he were is responsible for much confusion of thought. It leads Eddington into the preposterous nonsense of the 'two tables'. This view will be familiar to every one who is interested in the philosophy of the physicists. Nevertheless, it is desirable to quote a considerable part of Eddington's statement, since it is important to examine his view in some detail.

> I have settled down to the task of writing these lectures and have drawn up my chairs to my two tables. Two tables! Yes; there are duplicates of every object about me – two tables, two chairs, two pens. . . One of them has been familiar to me from earliest years. It is a commonplace object of that environment which I call the world. How shall I describe it? It has extension; it is comparatively permanent; it is coloured; above all, it is *substantial*. . . Table No. 2 is my scientific table. It is a more recent acquaintance and I do not feel so familiar with it. . .My scientific table is mostly emptiness. Sparsely scattered in that emptiness are numerous electric charges rushing about with great speed; but their combined bulk amounts to less than a billionth of the bulk of the table itself. Notwithstanding its strange construction it turns out to be an entirely efficient table. It supports my writing paper as satisfactorily as table No. 1; for when I lay the paper on it the little electric particles with their headlong speed keep on hitting the underside, so that the paper is maintained in shuttlecock fashion at a nearly steady level. If I lean upon this table I shall not go through; or, to be strictly accurate, the chance of my scientific elbow going through my scientific table is so excessively small that it can be neglected in practical life. . .There is nothing *substantial* about my second table. It is nearly all empty space – space pervaded it is true by fields of force, but these are assigned to the categories of 'influences', not of 'things'.[8]

There is so much to criticize in this passage that it is difficult to know where to begin. Probably Eddington's defence against any criticism would be that this is one of the passages in which he 'was leading the reader on'[9] (presumably – to put it vulgarly – 'up the garden path'), and that consequently it must not be taken as giving 'explicit statements' of his philosophical ideas. But he has nowhere

---

[8]*N.Ph.W.* xi, xii, xiii. I assume the reader's familiarity with the rest of the chapter in which this passage occurs.

[9]*N.P.Sc.* 291, and see p. 98 below.

Susan Stebbing on Logic, Language, and Analysis   **489**

expounded his philosophical ideas in non-popular language. Moreover, the mistakes are so frequently repeated in his writings and seem to be so inextricably bound up with his philosophical conclusions, that it is inevitable that these mistakes should be submitted to detailed criticism.

Perhaps the first comment that should be made is that Eddington takes quite seriously the view that there are *two tables*; one belongs to 'the external world of physics', the other to 'a world of familiar acquaintance in human consciousness'. Eddington's philosophy may be regarded as the outcome of a sustained attempt to answer the question: How are the two tables related to one another? It never seems to occur to him that the form of the question is absurd. In answering the question he is hampered from the start by his initial assumption that the tables are *duplicates* of each other, i.e. that it really isn't nonsensical to speak of two *tables*. I hazard the conjecture that Eddington is an inveterate visualizer,[10] and that once he has committed himself to the language of 'two tables' he cannot avoid thinking of one as the shadow and of the other as the substance. (In this sentence, I have used the word "substance" simply as the correlative of "shadow." This usage has undoubtedly influenced Eddington's thinking on this topic.) It is evident that the scientific table is to be regarded as the shadow. There are statements that conflict with this interpretation, but Eddington does not leave us in doubt that, whenever he is using the language of *shadowing*, it is the scientific table that is a shadow of the familiar table. It is true that he says, 'I need not tell you that modern physics has by delicate test and remorseless logic assured me that my second scientific table is the only one which is really there – wherever "there" may be'. Elsewhere he says, 'Our conception of the familiar table was an illusion' *(N.Ph.W.* 323). These discrepancies result from the deep-seated confusions out of which his philosophy springs; they will be examined in the following chapters. At present we are concerned with the view – in conflict with the statements just quoted – that the scientific table is a shadow. 'In the world of physics', he says, 'we watch a shadowgraph performance of the drama of familiar life. The shadow of my elbow rests on the shadow table as the shadow ink flows over the shadow paper. It is all symbolic, and as a

---

[10]The following passage is significant: 'When I think of an electron there rises to my mind a hard, red, tiny ball; the proton similarly is neutral grey. Of course the colour is absurd – perhaps not more absurd than the rest of the conception – but I am incorrigible' *(N.Ph. W.* xviii).

Cf. also, 'I am liable to visualize a Test-Match in Australia as being played upside down' *(N.P.Sc.* 314). Perhaps this habit is responsible for the queer statement (quoted above, p. 48) that the feat of entering his study has to be accomplished whilst he is 'hanging from a round planet head outward into space'. Only, in that case, he has forgotten that his study would be hanging outward the same way. What is more important is that he has created a difficulty out of a mode of speech.

490 **Early Analytic Philosophy**

symbol the physicist leaves it' (xvi). Elsewhere he suggests that physicists would generally say that 'the matter of this familiar table is *really* a curvature of space', but that is a view difficult to reconcile with either of the statements we are considering now.

Certainly there is much in the passage about the two tables that seems to conflict with the view of the scientific table as a shadow. It is said to be 'mostly emptiness', but scattered in the emptiness are numerous electric charges whose 'combined bulk' is compared in amount with 'the bulk of the table itself'. Is 'the table itself' the familiar table? I think it must be. But the comparison of the *two* bulks is surely nonsensical. Moreover, a shadow can hardly be said to have *bulk*. Yet Eddington insists that the two tables are 'parallel' – an odd synonym, no doubt, for a 'shadow'. He contrasts the scientific *table*, which has a familiar *table* parallel to it, with the scientific electron, quantum, or potential, which have no familiars that are parallel. Of the latter he says that the physicist is scrupulously careful to guard them 'from contamination by conceptions borrowed from the other [i.e. the familiar] world'. But if electrons, belonging to world No. 2, are to be scrupulously guarded from contamination by world No. 1, how can it make sense to say that they 'keep on hitting the underside' of a sheet of paper that, indubitably, is part of the familiar furniture of earth? It is Eddington who reintroduces contamination when he talks in this fashion, and he does so because he supposes that there is a scientific table parallel to the familiar table. I venture to suggest that it is as absurd to say that there is a scientific table as to say that there is a familiar electron or a familiar quantum, or a familiar potential. Eddington insists upon the lack of familiar parallels in the latter cases; surely he is justified in doing so. What is puzzling is his view that there are parallel *tables.* It suggests a return to the days when physicists demanded a model; 'the physicist', says Eddington, 'used to borrow the raw material of his world from the familiar world, but he does so no longer' (xv). But if the 'scientific table' is to be regarded as the product of the 'raw material of the scientific world', how can it be regarded as parallel to the familiar table? Eddington seems unable to free himself from the conviction that the physicist is concerned with things of the same nature as the things of the familiar world; hence, *tables* are to be found in both world No. 1 and world No. 2. There is a statement in his exposition of 'The Downfall of Classical Physics' that shows how deep-rooted this conviction is. 'The atom,' he says, 'is as porous as the solar system. If we eliminated all the unfilled space in a man's body and collected his protons and electrons into one mass, the man would be reduced to a speck just visible with a magnifying glass' *(N.Ph.W.* 1-2). The comparison is useful enough; the absurdity comes from speaking of the speck as a *man.* If this statement stood alone, it might well be

Susan Stebbing on Logic, Language, and Analysis   **491**

regarded as an expository device. But the constant cropping up of the parallel tables shows that Eddington does not regard it as absurd to think of the reduction as still leaving a *man*. When, later in the book, he is expounding the conception of space required by relativity theory, he points out that our difficulty in conceiving it is due to the fact that we are 'using a conception of space which must have originated many millions of years ago and has become rather firmly embedded in human thought' (81). He adds: 'But the space of physics ought not to be dominated by this creation of the dawning mind of an enterprising ape.' It seems to me that in allowing himself to speak of the speck as a man, Eddington is allowing himself to be thus dominated. It is true that, in the statement just quoted, Eddington was speaking of relativity physics, but I do not think that 'the creation of the dawning mind of an enterprising ape' is any more appropriate to the conception of space in atomic physics. To this point we must return later.[11] It must suffice at the moment to insist that a *man* is an object belonging to the familiar world, and has no duplicate in 'the scientific world'.

Perhaps we may be convinced of the absurdity of the notion that there are 'duplicates of every object' in the familiar world, if we return to the consideration of the description of a familiar scene with which this chapter opened. I spoke there of 'blue curtains', of a crimson and scented rose, of a bruised leg. Neglecting at present the consideration of the bruised leg, which – judging by Eddington's account of the adventures of an elephant[12] – is beneath the notice of a scientist, we may ask what duplicate of *blue* is to be found in the scientific world. The answer is that there is no duplicate. True that it has a 'counterpart' but that is a very different matter. The counterpart of colour is 'its scientific equivalent electromagnetic wavelength' (88). 'The wave', says Eddington, 'is the reality – or the nearest we can get to a description of reality; the colour is mere mind-spinning. The beautiful hues which flood our consciousness under stimulation of the waves have no relevance to the objective reality.' It is obvious that here Eddington is regarding the scientific world as 'the objective reality'; the familiar world is subjective. This does not square with the view that the scientific world is the shadow of the familiar world, but it is hopeless to attempt to extract from Eddington any consistent view of their relation. With this difficulty, however, we are not at the moment concerned. The point is that Eddington firmly extrudes *colour* from the scientific world, and rightly so. But the *rose* is coloured, the *table* is coloured, the *curtains* are coloured. How, then, can that which is not

---

[11]See below, p. 201.
[12]See below, p. 92–3.

Early Analytic Philosophy

coloured duplicate the rose, the curtains, the table? To say that an electromagnetic wave-length is coloured would be as nonsensical as to say that symmetry is coloured. Eddington does not say so. But he has failed to realize that a coloured object could be *duplicated* only by something with regard to which it would not be meaningless to say that it was coloured.

It seems to me that in his theory of the duplicate worlds Eddington has fallen into the error of which Berkeley accused the Newtonians. Berkeley was strongly convinced that the sensible world[13] was pre-eminently a *seeable* world. No doubt he over-stressed the sense of sight at the expense of the other senses, but in the climate of opinion in which he was living this over-emphasis served a useful purpose. Consider the following passage:

> How vivid and radiant is the lustre of the fixed stars! how magnificent and rich that negligent profusion, with which they appear to be scattered throughout the whole azure vault! Yet if you take the telescope, it brings into your sight a new host of stars that escape the naked eye. . . Is not the whole system immense, beautiful, glorious beyond expression and beyond thought? What treatment then do those philosophers deserve, who would deprive these noble and delightful scenes of all reality? How should those principles be entertained, that lead us to think all the visible beauty of the creation a false imaginary glare?[14]

It seemed to Berkeley that the metaphysics of Descartes and Newton resulted in the description of a 'real world' that had all the properties of the sensible world except the vital property of being seeable. 'Ask a Cartesian,' he said,[15] 'whether he is wont to imagine his globules without colour. Pellucidness is a colour. The colour of ordinary light of the sun is white. Newton in the right in assigning colour to the rays of light.[16] A man born blind would not imagine Space as we do. We give it always some dilute, or duskish, or dark colour – in short, we imagine it as visible, or intromitted by the eye, which he would not do'. *Black* also is, in the sense required, a *colour*; a 'dark world' is no less a world apprehensible only by sight than a 'bright world' is. But the pure mathematician cannot take note of colour. Hence, under the influence of the *Mathematical Principles of Natural Philosophy* and of the rapidly developing science of optics,

---

[13]I use the phrase "sensible world" here with the same denotative reference as Eddington's phrase "familiar world".

[14]*Three Dialogues between Hylas and Philonous* (Second Dialogue).

[15]*Commonplace Book*, ed. by G. A. Johnston, p. 50.

[16]But see below, p. 63.

Susan Stebbing on Logic, Language, and Analysis 493

Berkeley's contemporaries looked to the principles of optics to account for the *seeability* of things. It is Berkeley's merit to have realized that the Cartesian-Newtonian philosophers, seeking to account for a *seeable* world, succeeded only in substituting a world that could in no sense be *seen*. He realized that they had substituted a theory of optics for a theory of visual perception. The outcome of this mistake is a duplication of worlds – the Image-World, sensibly perceived by men, the Real-World apprehended only by God. Newton is quite explicit on this point:

> Was the Eye contrived without Skill in Opticks, and the Ear without Knowledge of Sounds?. . . Is not the sensory of Animals that place to which the sensitive Substance is present, and into which the sensible Species of Things are carried through the Nerves and Brain, that there they may be perceived by their immediate presence to that Substance? And these things being rightly dispatch'd, does it not appear from Phaenomena that there is a Being incorporeal, living, intelligent, omnipresent, who in infinite Space, as it were in his Sensory, sees the things themselves intimately, and thoroughly perceives them, and comprehends them wholly by their immediate presence to himself: Of which things the Images only carried through the Organs of Sense into our little Sensoriums, are there seen and beheld by that which in us perceives and thinks.[17]

Berkeley saw the absurdity of this duplication; he failed to realize that it was rendered necessary only by the confusion of the theory of optics with the theory of vision. He saw that the question – How is perception possible? – is devoid of sense; he saw that it is no less absurd to look to physics for an answer to the question. Unfortunately he accepted the account of objects of sight that was provided by the Optical Theory, and thus abolished the duplication of worlds only by locating (however indirectly) 'the things by me perceived' in the Mind of the Infinite Spirit. Newton had transferred colours from *things seen* into 'our little Sensoriums'; he conceived them as optical Images; accordingly, there were still required the things in them- selves *of which* they were Images. These things must be found in the Sensory of God. Berkeley abolished the Images but only by carrying to a conclusion the absurdities initiated by the use of the language of Optics.

The achievement of Newton in the theory of Optics was that by his discovery of differently refrangible rays he discovered *measurable correlates of colour*; he

---

[17]*Opticks*, Query 28. (Edition reprinted 1931, p. 370.)

494 Early Analytic Philosophy

thereby made the use of quantitative methods possible in a domain which would otherwise be excluded from the scope of physics. His extremely confused metaphysics is the result of his refusal to admit that there is anything in the perceived world except the measurable correlates, which ought, accordingly, to be regarded as the correlates of nothing. Newton saved himself from this manifest contradiction by having resort to a transmissive theory of Nature, and thus to a causal theory of perception. Allowing for the difference of phraseology we may surely see in the following quotation from Newton an anticipation of Eddington's theory of the sensible world.

> The homogeneal Light and Rays which appear red, or rather make Objects appear so, I call Rubrifick or Red-making; those which make Objects appear yellow, green, blue, and violet, I call Yellowmaking, Green-making, Blue-making, Violet-making, and so of the rest. And if at any time I speak of Light and Rays as coloured or endued with Colours, I would be understood to speak not philosophically and properly, but grossly, and accordingly to such Conceptions as vulgar People in seeing all these experiments would be apt to frame. For the Rays to speak properly are not coloured. In them there is nothing else than a certain Power and Disposition to stir up a Sensation of this or that Colour. For as Sound in a Bell or musical String, or other sounding Body, is nothing but a trembling Motion, and in the Air nothing but that motion propagated from the Object, and in the Sensorium 'tis a Sense of that Motion under the Form of Sound; so Colours in the Object are nothing but a Disposition to reflect this or that sort of Rays more copiously than the Rest ; in the Rays they are nothing but their Dispositions to propagate this or that Motion into the Sensorium, and in the Sensorium they are Sensations of those Motions under the Forms of Colours.[18]

This wholly fallacious argument has been strangely persuasive to physicists. Sensible qualities have no place in the world; they are *nothing but* 'dispositions to propagate this or that motion into the Sensorium'. There they undergo a transformation, not in the mathematical sense of that word, but a strange transformation indeed – a metamorphosis of 'the external world of physics' into 'a world of familiar acquaintance in human consciousness'.[19] The transformation remains inexplicable. Small wonder that Mr. Joad, reflecting upon the philosophical consequences of 'modern physics', exclaimed in perplexity, 'But,

---

[18]*Opticks*, Bk. I, Pt. II (1931 ed., pp. 124-5).
[19]See *N.Ph. W.* xiv.

if I never know directly events in the external world, but only their alleged effects on my brain, and if I never know my brain except in terms of its alleged effects on my brain, I can only reiterate in bewilderment my original questions: "What sort of thing is it that I know?" and "Where is it?'"[20] Such perplexity can be resolved only by reconsidering the assumptions that led to the asking of these unanswerable questions. We shall find that the problem of perception, in this form, arose only because we have allowed the physicists to speak of a 'real world' that does not contain any of the qualities relevant to perception. To adopt the striking phrase of Professor E. A. Burtt, we have allowed the physicists 'to make a metaphysic out of a method', In so doing they have forgotten, and philosophers do not seem to remember, that their method has been designed to facilitate investigations originating from a study of 'the furniture of the earth'.

Stebbing, S. "Logical Positivism and Analysis". Reprinted from Stebbing, S. (1933), "Logical Positivism and Analysis", *Proceedings of the British Academy*: 53–87.

'Philosophy', said Mr. Wisdom in a provocative footnote in *Mind*,[1] 'is concerned with the analysis of facts – a doctrine which Wittgenstein has lately preached and Moore long practised.' Although Mr. Wisdom's antithesis between 'preaching' and 'practice' is not very pleasantly phrased, yet it has some appropriateness. Wittgenstein has said much about the nature of philosophy, but he appears to have left to others the task of working out the consequences of this conception. Moore, on the other hand, can scarcely be said to have stated explicitly his conception of philosophy, but he has shown in the clearest possible manner what he conceives to be the nature of those problems with which a philosopher is concerned. This he has done by stating clearly, in the case of each problem with which he has dealt, *what* exactly the problem is, and *how* exactly he proposes to deal with it. This, it must be admitted, is a virtue rare among philosophers.[2]

I must make clear at the outset that in speaking of Moore's philosophical work I am referring to his published writings. It is not possible for me to determine whether – and, if so, to what extent – he has of late changed his views. Nor can

---

[20]*Aristotelian Society*: Supp. Vol. IX, p. 137.

[1]April 1931, p. 195 n.

[2]Many of us who know something about Prof Moore's work may, indeed, be said to have been shown by him *how* philosophical problems should be tackled, however little we may be able to follow his example.

496   Early Analytic Philosophy

I be sure that I have always rightly interpreted his statements, although I should like to believe that I have not gravely misrepresented his views. For my knowledge of Wittgenstein's doctrine I am forced to rely mainly upon the writings of the group of philosophers, sometimes referred to as 'der Wiener Kreis', who appear to have devoted themselves to working out the consequences of his view concerning the nature of philosophy. Wittgenstein's one published work, the *Tractatus Logico-Philosophicus*, is excessively condensed and, no doubt deliberately, oracular. Few who have no other knowledge of his views are likely to understand the cryptic statements in the *Tractatus*. It seems, however, that in lectures and conversations Wittgenstein has made a less cryptic statement of his views. These views have been reported by various members of the Vienna group; I refer especially to Moritz Schlick, Rudolf Carnap, Friedrich Waismann, and Otto Neurath. Notwithstanding divergences in detail, these philosophers hold in common a theory which has come to be described as 'Logical Positivism'.[3] So far as I know this description was not chosen by members of the group. Schlick prefers the description 'konsequenter Empiricismus'.[4] Nevertheless, the former description is not inept, since the Logical Positivists combine the repudiation of metaphysics – in the sense in which Auguste Comte[5] used the word – with a thoroughgoing acceptance of the logical theory of Frege, Peano, Whitehead, and Russell, as developed by Wittgenstein. This 'new logic', as Carnap calls it,[6] enables them to avoid the difficulties encountered by the empiricism of Comte, J. S. Mill, and Mach, who strove to treat logic and mathematics as empirical, inductive studies. I shall point out later that this new logic has a still more important part to play as a formative influence upon the theory of the Logical Positivists. Certainly Logical Positivism may be regarded as in no small measure due to the inspiration of Wittgenstein. It is this theory which I shall mainly consider in relation to the philosophical practice of Moore.

It would not, I think, be surprising if Wittgenstein's theory were in accord with the practice of Moore. There can be no doubt that Wittgenstein has been profoundly influenced by Bertrand Russell, whilst the interaction between

---

[3]It is also described as 'Logistischer Positivismus'. See a book with this title by Ake Petzall. He quotes the following interesting statement, from a manifesto published by 'the circle' in 1929: 'Dieser Kreis hat keine feste Organisation, er besteht aus Menschen gleicher wissenschaftlicher Grundeinstellung, der Einzelne bemuht sich urn Eingliederung, jeder schiebt das Verbindende in den Vordergrund, keiner will durch Besonderheit den Zusammenhang storen, In vielem kann der eine den anderen vertreten, die Arbeit des einen kann durch den anderen weitergefuhrt werden' (loc. cit., p. 5).
[4]*Erkenntnis*, Band III, Heft I, 'Positivismus und Realismus', p. 30.
[5]Carnap definitely claims Comte as the Founder of the movement (see Band II, Heft 5-6, p. 461).
[6]Erkenntnis, Band I, Heft I.

the views of Moore and Russell must be evident to anyone who studies their writings in chronological order. Such a study would be well worth while for the light it would throw. upon the present position of what has, somewhat unfortunately, come to be called 'the Cambridge school of philosophy'. This study obviously lies outside the scope of this lecture. It is, however, important to bear in mind the various strands which have contributed to the development of Logical Positivism. Moore and the Logical Positivists, including Wittgenstein, agree in rejecting certain traditional, and still not uncommon views, concerning the nature of philosophy.[7] This point of agreement is, in my opinion, of considerable importance and full of hope for the future development of philosophy. I think, however, that it is misleadingly described as agreement in the view that 'philosophy is concerned with the analysis of facts'. Even if Moore and Wittgenstein both accepted this statement it would not follow that they agreed with regard to what is meant by 'analysis' nor with what is meant by 'fact'. Accordingly, there seems to me room for doubt whether the doctrine 'lately preached' by Wittgenstein is the same as the doctrine 'long practised' by Moore. My purpose in this lecture is to inquire to what extent there is a divergence between these and to ask how fundamental this divergence is. First, I shall inquire in what sense exactly Moore may be said to hold, or to have held, that philosophy is concerned with the analysis of facts. Secondly, I shall consider the theory of Logical Positivism, and shall ask what use it makes of analysis. I shall suggest that this use departs, in certain respects, from the practice of Moore. Thirdly, I shall attempt to indicate that this departure reveals a certain weakness in the theory of Logical Positivism. I shall conclude with a brief statement of what seems to me to be the nature and importance of analysis in philosophical inquiry.

A certain attitude to philosophical problems and a certain method of dealing with them are characteristic of Moore's philosophical practice. This attitude he has consistently maintained notwithstanding important changes in his views with regard to various questions. In my opinion one of Moore's great contributions to philosophy is his insistence that philosophers must begin by accepting as *true* certain commonsense statements which we should all – when we are not supposed to be engaged in philosophy – *unhesitatingly* admit to be true. In other words, Moore has insisted that it is not the business of the philosopher to deny

---

[7]With this rejection I also agree. The views rejected are those which hold that philosophy is concerned with 'the ultimate nature of reality'. But in this phrase "ultimate" stands for nothing. I have considered elsewhere the grounds on which this view must be rejected, and have pointed out that the consequence of this rejection involves the denial of the possibility of deductive metaphysics. (See *Proc. Arist. Soc.*, N.S., xxxiii, pp. 65-70.)

498 Early Analytic Philosophy

the truth of a commonsense statement, which would 'ordinarily' be said to be 'true', on the ground that there is some *not* ordinary sense in which it is not true, or on the ground that its truth has not been established. On the contrary, the business of the philosopher is to *analyse* these true statements. Moore has consistently maintained three important positions. First, he holds that 'at different moments in our lives we know a great many different empirical facts'.[8] To say this is equivalent to saying that at various moments in our lives we are in a position to assert with regard to a certain proposition that we *know* this proposition to be *true*. For example, at the present moment I *know* that *I am now speaking* is true; you each of you know a fact which you could each of you express by saying 'I know that *I am now sitting on a chair* is true'.[9] Secondly, Moore holds that with regard to many such propositions there are expressions in ordinary usage which unambiguously express these propositions which we know to be true. A proposition is unambiguously expressed when what is said is *understood*.[10] Thirdly, Moore holds that *to understand an expression* is not equivalent to being able *to give a correct analysis* of its meaning.[11] He has pointed out that the failure to see that these are *not* equivalent has been responsible for a good many mistakes with regard to the nature of philosophical problems and with regard to their possible solution. Moore has vigorously protested against the view that the answer to such a question as 'Do you believe that the earth has existed for many years past?' cannot be a plain 'Yes' or 'No', but must depend upon what is meant by the words "the earth" and "exists" and "years". The passage in which this answer occurs will be familiar to every one. It was published in 1925. Twenty years previously Moore had begun to see how important it is to distinguish the question whether we *know* that a given proposition is true from the question whether we are able *correctly to analyse it,* although he did not then make the distinction as clear as he has subsequently. Nevertheless, his earlier statement brings out clearly enough what I have called 'one of Moore's greatest contributions to philosophy'; it also indicates the method which, I believe, he has consistently followed. I shall accordingly quote the passage in full.

Taking as an example the proposition *Hens lay eggs,* Moore said: 'I am willing to allow the possibility that, as some Idealists would say, the proposition "Hens

---

[8]*Aristotelian Society: Supplementary Volume,* ix, p. 22.
[9]It will be remembered that this lecture was spoken to an audience of people, who were sitting on chairs.
[10]See *Contemporary British Philosophy,* Series II, p. 198.
[11]An *unambiguous expression* is not equivalent to a *perfectly clear expression,* since we may understand more or less clearly. It is important not to confuse *ambiguity, vagueness, unclearness*; these three are quite different, and mutually independent.

lay eggs" is false, unless we mean by it: A certain kind of collection of spirits or monads sometimes has a certain intelligible relation to another kind of collection of spirits or monads. I am willing to allow the possibility that, as Reid and some scientists would say, the proposition "Hens lay eggs" is false, if we mean by it anything more than that: Certain configurations of invisible material particles sometimes have a certain spatio-temporal relation to another kind of configuration of invisible material particles. Or again, I am willing to allow, with certain other philosophers, that we must, if it is to be true, interpret this proposition as meaning that certain kinds of sensations have to other kinds a relation which may be expressed by saying that the one kind of sensations "lay" the other kind. Or again, as other philosophers say, the proposition "Hens lay eggs" may possibly mean: Certain sensations of mine *would,* under certain conditions, have to certain other sensations of mine a relation which may be expressed by saying that the one set would "lay" the other set. But whatever the proposition "Hens eggs are generally laid by hens" may *mean,* most philosophers would, I think, allow that, in some sense or other, this proposition was true.'[12]

Were Moore to rewrite this passage to-day he would not phrase it differently. Yet, as it stands, it brings out with sufficient clearness the point I wish to stress, namely, that we may know with regard to a certain proposition that it is *true* although we do not know its analysis. This contention is important. It suggests that it is futile for philosophers to dispute the truth of commonsense statements merely on the ground that the analysis of these statements cannot be given, or on the ground that if an analysis were given, it would be shocking to common sense. Moore, in the passage I have quoted, admits the possibility of four different views with regard to the analysis of "Hens lay eggs", whilst insisting that the question which, if any, of them is correct is entirely independent of the question whether we can *know* that hens do lay eggs.

I prefer to use somewhat different language from that used by Moore in either of the papers to which I have referred. Where he, in his later and clearer statement, speaks of 'understanding *the meaning of a proposition*' I prefer to speak of 'understanding a *sentence*'. Where he speaks of 'knowing what a proposition *means,* in the sense of being able *to give a correct analysis* of its meaning' I prefer to speak of 'knowing *the analysis of a sentence*'. I wish to avoid the word "meaning" on account of its ambiguity. I wish to avoid, as far as possible, using the word "proposition", because I believe that what we analyse are *expressions,* of which sentences are one kind; and that when we analyse a

---

[12]*Proc. Arist. Soc.,* 1905-6: 'The Nature and Reality of Objects of Perception.' Republished in *Philosophical Studies,* see pp. 64-5.

Early Analytic Philosophy

sentence expressing a proposition what we obtain is not *another proposition* but *another expression.* Using the language which seems to me clearer I can now restate what I believe to be Moore's contribution to the problem concerning the nature of philosophy. He has shown that the chief task of philosophy is to discover the correct analysis of expressions which everyone would agree are sometimes used to say what is true. This problem may be expressed in the form: *What is it I am knowing (or judging) when I know (or judge) so-and-so to he such-and-such?* Since the 'so-and-so' and the 'such-and-such' in this formulation can be replaced by anything which makes sense, it will be seen that there are no significant statements which are insusceptible of philosophical treatment. If it be correct to describe the problem, formulated above, as the problem of the analysis of facts, then I think it is true to say that Moore's philosophical practice is concerned with the analysis of facts. Certainly he would repudiate the view that philosophy is concerned to justify our commonsense beliefs. Either they cannot be justified, I should contend, or their justification falls within the scope of commonsense knowledge or of one or other of the special sciences. Some of our beliefs, indeed, stand in no need of justification; for example, my belief that I am now speaking. It does not require justification since I *know* it to be true. What the philosopher has to do is not to justify our beliefs, but to make them *clear.*

My last remark will probably have reminded those familiar with the work of Wittgenstein of one of his most famous statements. It is so important in this connexion that I shall quote it in full. He says: 'The object of philosophy is the logical clarification of thought. Philosophy is not a theory but an activity. A philosophical work consists essentially of elucidations. The result of philosophy is not a number of "philosophical propositions", but to make propositions clear. Philosophy should make clear and delimit sharply the thoughts which otherwise are, as it were, opaque and blurred.'[13] There is undoubtedly some agreement between this statement and the practice of Moore. But it is important to ask what Wittgenstein means by 'the clarification of thought', how this clarification is to be achieved, and in what sense philosophy is said to be an *activity.* Wittgenstein has himself to some extent answered the first two of these questions. The question in what sense philosophy is an *activity* has been explicitly answered by Schlick. I shall for the moment postpone its consideration.

If I do not misunderstand Wittgenstein, he maintains that to clarify our thought we must understand the logic of our language. This understanding is

---

[13]*Tractatus Logico-Philosophicus,* 4.112.

achieved when we have discerned the principles of symbolism, and can thus answer the question *how* it is that sentences *mean*. He states that the purpose of his book is to 'draw a limit to thinking, or rather – not to thinking, but to the expression of thoughts'. This limit can, he says, 'only be drawn in language and what lies on the other side of the limit will be simply nonsense'.[14] He is thus concerned to lay down certain principles in accordance with which language can be so used as to construct significant propositions. I have not time to give a detailed statement of the way in which Wittgenstein attempts to achieve this aim. I am more concerned to consider the consequences – drawn by the Logical Positivists – from one of his principles, which I shall call the *principle of verifiability,* which is, at most, only hinted at in his book. Accordingly the following brief statement of Wittgenstein's more important doctrines must suffice.

Wittgenstein seems to distinguish three kinds of sentences: (1) meaningless, or nonsensical, sentences; (2) tautologies and contradictions; (3) significant sentences. The word "sentence" is here used in the widest possible sense to cover all arrangements of objects which, in accordance with some convention, can be so used as to convey information about arrangements of other objects. What I am calling a sentence Wittgenstein calls a *Satzzeichen* (propositional sign).[15] His usage of the words "proposition" and "propositional sign" is far from consistent, but it is at least clear that the propositional sign is *the fact* that the words have a certain syntactical form.[16] I think that Wittgenstein wishes to maintain that, for a set of words to constitute a sentence, these words, thus arranged, must be *used* to express a thought. What is thus expressed is a proposition. Propositions assert that a certain state of affairs *(Sachlage)* is the case, although it might quite well not have been the case. Indeed, some propositions *are false*. Significant propositions *say something* about the world, they exclude some possible states of affairs, whilst allowing some other state of affairs. For example, 'There is a table in this room', or 'Franklin Roosevelt is President of the United States now'.[17] Tautologies and contradictions, however,

---

[14]Ibid. *Preface.*

[15]See ibid., 3.12.

[16]Ibid. 3.14. The difference between a *propositional sign,* a *proposition,* and a *significant proposition,* is indicated in 3.13. So far as I can discover *the proposition* is *the propositional sign as used by a thinker* to express his thoughts (cf. 3.22). *The significant proposition* is the *proposition as used to refer to a definite state of affairs.* The *proposition* must be distinguished from a *sentence* used to express it, since the same proposition can be expressed in different languages; it must also be distinguished from *the fact* to which a true proposition is sometimes said to correspond, since we can think about a proposition independently of its truth or falsity.

[17]Such significant propositions as these Wittgenstein would now, I understand, call 'hypotheses'.

Early Analytic Philosophy

are not significant because they *say nothing* about the world. For tautologies agree with all the possibilities, whilst contradictions agree with none of them. Obviously, if I say 'There is a table here or there is not a table here', I have said nothing about what is here; I have given no information. Likewise, if I say 'There is a table here and there is not a table here' I have told you nothing; I have excluded no possible state of affairs. No one, I think, would be likely to deny this contention. What is important about Wittgenstein's treatment of tautologies is his claim that all the propositions of logic and mathematics are tautological, so that whenever the propositions p and q are mutually deducible they say same, and are thus not two different propositions.[18] It must be granted that tautologies and contradictions are to be sharply distinguished from significant propositions, but it is misleading to say that they are nonsensical. A nonsensical sentence may, from the point of view of logic, be regarded as not a sentence at all but as a mere juxtaposition of words; it may, however, be regarded as a sentence in the grammatical sense provided that it does not violate the rules of grammatical syntax. Perhaps

> 'Twas brillig, and the slithy toves
> Did gyre and gimble in the wabe;
> All mimsy were the borogroves,
> And the mome raths outgrabe,

may be taken as an example, in spite of Humpty Dumpty's explanation. We should all probably agree that 'Is blue more identical than music?' does not ask a question at all, although the words are so combined as to look like an interrogative sentence to anyone who happened not to understand the word 'blue', say, or the word 'more', but did understand the other words. Now, Wittgenstein maintains that 'most propositions and questions, that have been written about philosophical matters, are not false but senseless'.[19] This point has been emphasized and illustrated by Schlick, from whom my nonsensical interrogative sentence was taken. He says, 'a careful analysis shows that this is the case with most so-called philosophical problems. They look like questions, and it is very difficult to recognize them as nonsensical, but logical analysis proves them to be merely some kind of confusion of words.'[20] In my opinion Wittgenstein has rendered a great service to philosophy in explicitly calling

---

[18]Herein, according to Wittgenstein, lies the nature of logical necessity.
[19]Op. cit., 4.003.
[20]*College of the Pacific, Publications in Philosophy*, vol. I, p. 59.

attention to the ease with which we mistake a nonsensical set of words for the formulation of a profound philosophical problem. Here, again, his theory is in accordance with the practice of Moore, who some years ago enlightened philosophers with regard to the senselessness of the conception of *Reality,* and showed how Bradley, for instance, by using the word 'real' had been led into talking nonsense.[21] It is assuredly the first qualification of a philosopher to be able to distinguish grammatical sentences which are nonsensical from those which are not. Nor is it so easy to make this distinction as plain men and lecturers in philosophy are apt to suppose. In my opinion, however, we also stand in need of some kind of classification of different *sorts* of nonsense. Wittgenstein, I gather,[22] distinguishes between important and unimportant nonsense, but how precisely he would draw the distinction I do not know. It might not be difficult to hazard a guess, but to do so would take me longer than time permits. I must proceed to consider how Wittgenstein proposes to discover whether what *seems* to be a proposition or a question has sense, or not. In the *Tractatus* he merely asserts that the senseless 'questions and propositions of the philosophers result from the fact that we do not understand the logic of our language'.[23] But in his lectures he appears to have answered more fully the question under what conditions a proposition has sense. This answer I shall take from the writings of the Logical Positivists.

In an important article on *Logische Analyse des Wahrscheinlichkeitsbegrijfs,* Waismann says: 'Eine Aussage beschreibt einen Sachverhalt. Der Sachverhalt besteht oder er besteht nicht. Ein Mittelding gibt es nicht, und daher gibt es auch keinen Uebergang zwischen wahr und falsch. Kann auf keine Weise angegeben werden, wann ein Satz wahr ist, so hat der Satz uberhaupt keinen Sinn; denn der Sinn des Satzes ist die Methode seiner Verifikation. In der Tat, wer einen Satz ausspricht, der muss wissen, unter welch en Bedingungen er den Satz wahr oder falsch nennt; vermag er das nicht anzugeben, so weiss er auch nicht, was er gesagt hat. Eine Aussage, die nicht endgultig verifiziert werden kann, ist tiberhaupt nicht verifizierbar; sie entbehrt eben jeden Sinn.'[24] In this statement Waismann supplies also the answer to the problem whether a question has sense, i.e. is properly a question and not merely a grammatical

---

[21]See *Philosophical Studies,* pp. 218–19.
[22]For this point I am indebted to Mr. R. B. Braithwaite, who has kindly let me read, in proof, an account of Wittgenstein's views, which he has given in an article shortly to be published. See *Cambridge University Studies.*
[23]Loc. cit., 4.003.
[24]*Erkenntnis,* Band IX, Heft 2–4, p. 229.

Early Analytic Philosophy

arrangement of words. A question has sense when it is *in principle* answerable. A question which is unanswerable in principle is not properly a question at all; it is a pseudo-question, i.e. a meaningless interrogative sentence. A distinction must be drawn between those questions which are *in principle (grundsätzlich)* unanswerable, and those which only happen to be unanswerable owing to our technical limitations or to lack of determinate information. For example, the question: 'Are there mountains on the other side of the moon?' is not in fact answerable because we happen not to be able to observe the other side of the moon. Similarly, I cannot answer the question: 'What is King George V doing *now?*' because I happen not to know. But I could imagine the *sort* of answer which might be given, and which would be true, or false. A question is, then, *unanswerable in principle* if we could not understand any proposition offered as an answer to it. A question is *answerable in principle* if the proposition offered in answer can be understood. A proposition is understood only if it is verifiable; it is verifiable if, and only if, we know the conditions under which the proposition would be true, and the conditions under which it would be false.

This notion of verifiability is of the greatest importance for the understanding of the distinctive tenets of Logical Positivism. I shall, therefore, quote another statement of Wittgenstein's principle of verifiability. Schlick has reported Wittgenstein as follows: 'In order to understand a proposition we must be able exactly to indicate those particular circumstances that would make it true and those other particular circumstances that would make it false. "Circumstances" means facts of experience; and so experience decides about the truth or falsity of propositions, experience "verifies" propositions, and therefore the criterion of the solubility of a problem is its reducibility to possible experience.'[25] As thus stated by Schlick and by Waismann, the principle of verifiability seems innocuous enough. So much the Logical Positivists might have learnt from Moore, or even from Hume. But their interpretation of *verifiability* depends upon another important strand in their theory, namely, the 'new logic' of Russell and Wittgenstein. This theory of logic has turned their attention to symbolism, i.e. to problems of the structure of language and to the possibility of constructing deductive systems. Both these points are important. I shall consider first the problem of language, returning later to the consideration of the use made by the Logical Positivists, especially Carnap, of constructed deductive systems.

---

[25]*College of the Pacific, Publications*, vol. i, p. 114. Cf. also Carnap, *Der logische Aufbau der Welt*, § 180; *Scheinprobleme in der Philosophic*, p.27; Schlick, 'Positivismus und Realismus', p. 29 (*Erkenntnis*, 1932).

Language is to be understood as any means of communication; it is not directly presentative or pictorial, for language does not *present* what it is used to say, but *communicates* it. Knowledge consists in communicability. The Logical Positivists insist upon the importance of the distinction between *Erkenntnis* (knowledge proper) and *Erlebnis* (direct experience) – which they take to be equivalent to Russell's distinction between 'knowledge by description' and 'acquaintance'.[26] Knowledge, i.e. the communicable, is concerned with structure: acquaintance, i.e. direct experience, is concerned with content *(Inhalt)*. Content cannot be communicated; it is directly given; it can at best only be pointed to. For example. Here is a piece of green blotting paper. You can *see* the shade of green presented to you. But I could not *communicate* its shade to you. I might make efforts to *describe* this shade by recalling to you some other green patch which you have seen. But this description could only give what the Logical Positivists call 'structure'; it could only communicate the place of this shade within a comprehensive system of shades of colour, and finally, its place in the spectrum. If you were blind you would not know what is this shade of green which I seek to communicate to you by description, Since you are *not* blind, you now see the content *green*. Suppose we met to-morrow and I wished to remind you of this *green*. I might try to do so in either of two ways. I might produce this same piece of blotting paper. Even then I should not have *expressed*, i.e. *communicated*, content. This, for two reasons. First, I should *present* content, not communicate it; secondly, the shade might have changed. That it had not done so would be an assumption. Or, again, I might ask you to recall the shade. But, then, I should clearly only be describing this shade by reminding you of its relation to something else. Hence, *content* cannot be communicated. As Schlick put it – in a lecture given to the University of London, last November – 'The inexpressibility of content is not an accidental feature that we discover it to possess; it belongs to its very nature. We must regard it as the defining characteristic of content.'[27] According to Schlick, it is a blunder to say we *know* content, and dangerous to say we *intuit* content, since the phrase 'intuition of content' suggests that content is an object grasped by the mind. But it is nonsense to say 'I perceive content', and equally nonsense to say 'I do not perceive content', for *content* cannot in any way be brought within the context

---

[26]I am somewhat doubtful whether the Logical Positivists, in adopting Russell's terminology, are nevertheless in agreement with his view of this distinction. This, however, is a minor point. What is important are the consequences they draw from the distinction thus expressed.

[27]This quotation is taken from a verbatim report of Prof. Schlick's Lectures, which I owe to the kindness of Miss Margaret MacDonald.

Early Analytic Philosophy

of language. It is a mistake, Schlick urges, to suppose that 'by means of a gesture our words can be linked to content'. Hence, in my opinion, we ought not even to say, as some Logical Positivists do, that we can *point* to content. You will observe that on this view most of my remarks since I began to speak about this blotting paper have been nonsensical. It is the sort of nonsense, no doubt, which it is very difficult to avoid.

From the point of view of knowledge (i.e. *Erkenntnis* as distinguished from *Erlebnis)* what the word "green" expresses is not content, but a unique set of relations to what may be called 'other qualities'. I have dwelt on this point because it seems to me to involve at least three important consequences. (1) All knowledge is recognition; if I say I know X, then I must be able to say *as what I recognize* X. (2) All knowledge is communication of structure. The word "green" – when it occurs in a sentence expressing a fact – can say nothing about *the shade;* it can only express the place of the colour in the world. Accordingly, in physics, colour is *replaced* by wave length. (3) To communicate is to use language. Hence, as I have pointed out, for Logical Positivisim, the problem of knowledge resolves itself into the problem *how* language *can* be used to communicate. This is just the question: *How* do sentences *mean?* To which, from this point of view, the reply must be that sentences *mean* by conveying structure.

At this point it is important to bear in mind the other contention of the Logical Positivists, namely, that a sentence is meaningless *(Sinnlos)* unless it is known under what circumstances the sentence could be used to say what is true and under what circumstances it could be used to say what is false. This is Wittgenstein's principle of verifiability: *the meaning of a proposition is the method of its verification.*[28] How could a proposition be verified if what is communicated is never content *(Inhalt)* but only structure? Clearly, verification depends upon the presence of content. Accordingly, every significant proposition which I assert says what could be verified only by my own direct experience, either present or future. Thus, though you and I use the same words[29] if I say 'This is a table', and you say 'This is a table', *what* we are referring to is not the same. That the same form of words used by two different people may not refer to the same is obviously sometimes the case. For example, if *I* say 'I have toothache', or 'I am thirsty', and *you* say 'I have toothache', or 'I am thirsty', then

---

[28]See the quotation from Waismann, p. 64 above. It seems to me that Wittgenstein may have been suggesting this principle when he wrote one of his cryptic statements in the *Tractatus*, viz: 'Irn Satz wird gleichsam eine Sachlage probeweise zusammengestellt' (4.031).

[29]A full discussion of this point would require a full discussion of what we take to be 'the same words'. This is not possible now. But I do not think that type-token ambiguities raise any difficulties here.

Susan Stebbing on Logic, Language, and Analysis **507**

clearly, not only does the word 'I' have a different reference in the case of *my* saying from its reference in the case of *your* saying, but also my experienced toothache (or thirst) is *one* direct experience, your experienced toothache (or thirst) is *another* direct experience. Not only could these never be the same, but *I* cannot refer directly to *your* toothache (or your thirst) nor *you* to *mine*. Hence "having toothache" does not mean the same in "I have toothache" as in *"You* have toothache". It is characteristic of the Logical Positivists' view that cases where personal pronouns enter are not fundamentally different from such cases as my saying 'There are people here' or 'This is a table'. The meaning *(Sinn)* of the proposition I express by saying 'This is a table' *is* just how it would be verified, i.e, how it would be found true and how it would be found false. This verification must lie within my own experience.

It is to Carnap that – so far as I know – the fullest development of this view is due. What I have now to say is based mainly upon an important article of his[30] in which he seeks to maintain the thesis of the unity of science, i.e. that all the sciences are parts of one science, namely, physics. More precisely, he maintains that every scientific proposition can be expressed in the language of physics. This contention is to be established by the following considerations. Whenever I am using what would commonly be said to be an ordinary language – such as I am using in this lecture – what I am saying is either senseless or it can be transformed into a language which directly reports my own direct experience. Such a language Carnap calls 'Protokollsprache'.[31] Knowledge possessed by the scientist is based upon propositions expressed in protocol-language. Thus Carnap says: 'Wir stellen uns hierbei das Verfahren so schematisiert vor, als wiirden alle unsere Erlebnisse, Wahrnehmungen, aber auch Gefiihle, Gedanken usw. sowohl in der Wissenschaft als auch im gewohnlichen Leben zunachst schriftlich protokolliert, so dass die weitere Verarbeitung immer an ein Protokoll als Ausgangspunkt ankniipft. Mit dem "urspriinglichen" Protokoll ist dasjenige gemeint, das wir erhalten wiirden, wenn wir Protokollaufnahme und Verarbeitung der Protokollsatze im wissenschaftlichen Verfahren scharf voneinander trennen wiirden, also in das Protokoll keine indirect gewonnenen Satze aufnehmen wurden.'[32] This basic protocol would, Carnap says, be very clumsy. As an approximation Carnap gives the example: 'Versuchsanordnung: an den und den

---

[30]'Die physikalische Sprache als Universalsprache der Wissenschaft', *Erkenntnis*, Band II, Heft 5-6. The quotations which follow are all taken from this article.

[31]I shall not try to translate this term, but I suppose it may be regarded as equivalent to 'direct-record-language'.

[32]p. 437.

Early Analytic Philosophy

Stellen sind Korper von der und der Beschaffenheit (z. B., "Kupferdraht"; vielleicht diirfte statt dessen nur gesagt werden: "ein dunner, langer, brauner Korper", wah rend die Bestimmung "Kupfer" durch Verarbeitung fruherer Protokolle, in denen derselbe Korper auftritt, gewonnen wird); jetzt hier Zeiger auf 5, zugleich dort Funke und Knall, dann Ozongeruch.' Simpler examples would be: 'boredom now', 'here-now blue', 'there red'.

At this point it is important to notice that, according to Carnap, protocol-language can be looked at from two different points of view – or, perhaps, it would be more accurate to say that any language using ordinary words can be regarded as one or other of two different modes of speech, which Carnap calls respectively the formal mode and the content *(inhaltliche)* mode. The formal mode speaks of *words* and refers only to linguistic forms. The content mode speaks of 'objects', 'states of affairs' *(Sachverhalten),* 'sense' *(Sinn),* 'content', 'meaning' *(Bedeutung).* Carnap maintains that the use of the content mode leads to pseudoproblems. For, as he points out, it was not strictly correct to speak *of the* basic protocol. On the contrary, each subject, or experient, has his *own* protocol. Thus there are as many protocol-languages as there are experients. This, it seems to me, follows directly from Wittgenstein's interpretation of the principle of verifiability. If we attempt to interpret a protocol as referring to, or indicating, content, we shall be led into insuperable difficulties. Suppose, for instance, that an experient, A, says a definite proposition in his own protocol, e.g. A says, 'I am thirsty', or better, 'Thirst-now'. If this be interpreted in the content mode the problem arises: Can this state of affairs, expressed by A in his protocol-language, be expressed in the protocol-language of another experient, B? If so, then B, using his own protocol, speaks of *the experience of A as experienced by B.* But the experience of B cannot be the experience of A. On the content view, then, what A says refers to a different state of affairs from what B says. *No* proposition in B's protocol can express the thirst of A; B *can* refer only to what is directly given to himself. It is true that we say that B can *recognize* the thirst of A, but what B actually recognizes is only the material circumstances of A's body. This is all that B can *verify;* hence, on this view, this is all that B can *say.* If we try to make B's expression "the thirst of A" refer to *A's experience of thirst,* then we are saying something that is in principle unverifiable. Accordingly, on the content view "A is thirsty" is, *for B,* a meaningless set of words; they have no *sense.* Thus, Carnap holds, if we insist that protocol propositions must refer to content, then each protocol-language can be used only *monadically.* There would be no intersubjective protocol-language. But we do manage to communicate. You do manage to understand me when I say 'I am thirsty', or when I say, 'This is a table'. How, then, is this possible, since your direct experience and my direct experience do not overlap, have nothing in common? How *can* we communicate?

Carnap maintains that such difficulties disappear if we interpret protocol-language in the formal mode, i.e. as expressing structure, not as expressing content, as *containing words,* not as *describing states of affairs.* We then discover, he urges, that a protocol-language is a part of physical language, a sub-language of the language of physics. This language is inter-subjective and inter-sensory. It may be called 'the physicalistic language'.[33] On the formal interpretation a protocol proposition *consists* of words arranged in syntactical form. Carnap maintains for these words to be understood, i.e. have sense (*Sinn*), it is not necessary that the meaning (*Bedeutung*) should be given. For the meaning of a word can be given either by translation or by definition, i.e. by rules for transforming one word into another word, or set of words. Translation is a rule for transforming a word into one language into a word of another language. For example, 'mensa' is translated by 'table'. Definition is a rule of transformation within the same language. Now, it is Carnap's contention that propositions in my protocol-language can be translated into the physicalistic language; so can propositions in each of your private, protocol-languages. Conversely, physical propositions, expressed in the physicalistic language, can be translated into my protocol-language, and into each of your protocol-languages. What *cannot* happen is that my protocol proposition could be translated into your protocol-languages, nor conversely. You understand me – when you do – only because your protocols and my protocol are *all* sub-languages (*Teilsprache*) of the universal, physicalistic language, although these various sub-languages contain nothing in common. It is difficult to see how out of a number of private languages, which do not overlap, it is possible to derive a public, i.e. inter-subjective, universal language. Yet, as Carnap admits, verification in physics is based upon protocol propositions. He attempts to get over the difficulty of making physics private by asserting that scientific verification depends not upon a singular, determinate proposition – such as 'Red here-now' – but upon a sub-system of such propositions. He says: 'wenn eine hinreichende Menge physikalischer Satze gegeben ist, ein Satz der Protokollsprache abgeleitet werden kann'.[34] For example, a protocol proposition '*Brown now*' *seen by me* could be deduced by you from a sufficiently definite description of my body. Carnap maintains that such a deduction always takes place when in ordinary life

---

[33]Carnap uses the term 'physicalistic' in order to distinguish this language from what may be called 'the language of contemporary physics'.

[34]p. 457.

Early Analytic Philosophy

people understand each other. Thus my protocol-language, which never overlaps with your protocol-languages, can nevertheless be understood by you, since my protocol can be transformed into the language of physics. It is true that a proposition *p*, in my protocol, which only *I* can understand, will not seem the same to me as the proposition *p'* into which it is transformed in the physicalistic language. This is because *p* is associated by me with my own protocol, and *p'* with the physicalistic language. Nevertheless, if *p* and *p'* are mutually deducible, they express the same, and what they express is structure. According to the Logical Positivists, if *p* and *p'* are mutually deducible, *p* and *p'* are the *same* proposition; the difference is only in the language, i.e. in the propositional-sign. To establish the possibility that *p* and *p'* are mutually deducible, we *must* adopt the formal mode of interpreting language. So long as we persist in attempting to use the content mode, *no* proposition in my protocol could be deduced from the propositions of physics, nor conversely. Nor can you understand what I am saying now unless you interpret what I say as communicating structure. But this, according to the Logical Positivists, you *must* do. Thus, from a somewhat different point of view, Carnap enforces Wittgenstein's interpretation of the principle of verifiability.

In my opinion Carnap's discussion throws light upon one of Wittgenstein's cryptic statements in the *Tractatus*. He there says: 'What solipsism *means* (*meint*) is quite correct, only it cannot be *said*, but it shows itself. That the world is *my* world shows itself in that the limits of the language (the language which only I understand) mean the limits of *my* world' (5.62). From this statement it follows that it is nonsense to *say* 'I am a solipsist' and equally nonsense to *say* 'I am not a solipsist'. But, I gather,[35] to say 'I am a solipsist' is to say important nonsense, the kind of nonsense which Wittgenstein allows himself to talk. But, even if it be nonsense to *say* 'I am a solipsist', still – according to this statement of Wittgenstein's – what I thus *intend* to say (if I do say it) is true, only, in this case, I *cannot* say what I intend.

Any philosophical view which leads to the conclusion that what solipsism *means*, or *intends*, to say is quite correct is, in my opinion, obviously false. It should, however, be noticed that Wittgenstein's solipsistic conclusion (if I may be allowed to talk what Wittgenstein would call nonsense) is not based upon the usual grounds – namely, the difficulty, or the supposed difficulty, of finding

---

[35]See article by Braithwaite, referred to above. I think, however, that it is important to take into account Wittgenstein's further statement: 'The subject does not belong to the world but it is a limit of the world' (5.632. Cf, also, 5.6331 and 5.64).

reasons for my belief in the existence of anything except myself. It is derived entirely from a theory with regard to the way in which language may become a significant symbolism, a theory leading to what I have called Wittgenstein's interpretation of the principle of verifiability. Carnap attempts to evade the solipsistic conclusion by prefixing 'methodological' and turning the theory into the doctrine of 'physicalism'.[36] This theory permits you and me to communicate by using the physicalistic language in the formal mode. Carnap stresses the point that methodological solipsism allows no assertion that other minds *exist*, or that an external world *exists*. On the contrary, propositions *about* other minds, or *about*, an external object, will be propositions conveying structure, not propositions asserting that there are other *existents*. Such propositions would have to attempt to refer to *content;* hence, they could have no equivalent in the universal, physicalistic language. The doctrines of both Carnap and Wittgenstein seem to me to suggest that Wittgenstein's statement – 'What solipsism *means* is quite correct, only it cannot be *said*' – is just the reverse of what they require. For, in my opinion, methodological solipsism ought to assert: 'What solipsism *means* is NOT correct, but only solipsism *can be said*'. I do not, however, suppose for a moment that either Carnap or Wittgenstein would regard my suggestion as other than absurd.

Although the intentional solipsism of Wittgenstein and the methodological solipsism of Carnap are not reached along traditional lines, they both seem to me to be open to serious criticism. I think the point of my criticism can be made clearer if I first consider Carnap's attempt to construct the world on the basis of direct experience. This attempt is contained in his important book *Der logische Aufbau der Welt*. In the brief time at my disposal I cannot give even the barest summary of his argument. I must confine attention to two points relating especially to my present discussion. First, the world is to be *logically* constructed. Secondly, Carnap takes as his motto Russell's reformulation of Occam's Razor, namely, 'The supreme maxim in scientific philosophizing is this: Whenever possible, logical constructions are to be substituted for inferred entities'. These two points are, of course, closely connected. Carnap seems to follow Russell in supposing that if I could truly say that I *know* that this is a table, my knowledge of the table would be inferential knowledge. But such inferential *knowledge* is impossible. Moreover, it is nonsense to talk of *this table* as an 'inferred entity'; hence, they conclude, it must be a logical construct of the given. In accordance with Russell's principle, Carnap attempts to show that *all* the concepts of the empirical sciences can be *constructed* by purely logical operations upon a *single*

---

[36]See op. cit., p. 462.

512   **Early Analytic Philosophy**

fundamental relation and the fundamental elements between which it holds. This fundamental relation is taken to be directly *given;* everything else is to be defined in terms of it. Carnap selects for the fundamental relation 'remembrance of similarity' (*Aehnlichkeitserinnerung*). The elements between which the relation holds are momentary direct experiences. On this basis, Carnap believes, it is possible to translate any empirical scientific proposition into a set of propositions involving reference only to the relational structure of the given, i.e. to the fundamental elements and the fundamental relation holding between them.

Now, it is not necessary to my point to deny that such a construction could be achieved; hence, it is not to my purpose to inquire whether Carnap has been successful in his attempt. My criticism bears upon a quite different consideration. It is that such logically constructed systems remain essentially *abstract*. No doubt it is both interesting and important to see just *what* can be achieved by selecting the fewest possible assumptions and the fewest possible undefined terms. This is exactly what Carnap attempts in his logical construction of the world, and it is very like what Eddington has attempted in his game of world-building. Doubtless it would be possible, by a judicious selection of the fundamental relation and by a judicious choice of applicational definitions (*Zuordnungsdefinitionen*) to construct a deductive system which would be susceptible of being interpreted as the system of the world. *If we knew enough,* that is, which we can hardly be said to know at present. We do not even know that the world is a system. Certainly it does not present the appearance of one. The world of the physicist may be a system. Physicists hope it is. They like to speak of a *Weltbild;* they regard this 'world-picture' as having the coherence of a work of art. But physics could present a system only because its world-picture is essentially abstract. Thus physics ignores what does not fit in. Carnap's construction of the world ought not to be abstract. I think that the Logical Positivists fail to see the defect of their attempts at construction because they have adopted the point of view of methodological solipsism. It is by no means impossible to suppose that a theoretical, abstract system may be adequate to describe what *I* suppose to be happening to *other* minds, or to bodies. Hence, there is a temptation – to which logicians are peculiarly prone – to suppose that such a construction is adequate even in the case of my *own* experience. If nothing is *given* except direct experience, and if direct experience is *my own experience now,* then we are indeed forced to solipsism-of-the-present moment, and I may well try to order my own experience in a system *based* upon this directly given experience, and *constructed* by means of logical operations. This procedure would accord with views expressed by Eddington and by Russell.

Susan Stebbing on Logic, Language, and Analysis   513

You will have noticed how frequently I have in the course of this lecture tacitly denied solipsism. For instance, I just now said that (under certain conditions) 'we are forced to solipsism'. This was not a slip; it was intentional. I have the best of grounds for denying solipsism, namely, that I *know* it to be false. You, who are listening to me, and enable me to speak in the plural, *also* know it to be false.[37] I suggest that there is something wrong with a theory which, as a consequence of its fundamental principles, involves solipsism in any form. I think Carnap's methodological solipsism results from his accepting Wittgenstein's criterion of verifiability, which leads to the consequence that *tables* and *other minds* must either be inferred entities – which, I agree, is nonsense – or be logical constructs of the directly given, namely, the subject's own experience.

Wittgenstein simply takes it for granted that *the given* is, and could be, nothing but *my own direct experience*.[38] From this assumption, combined with his interpretation of the principle of verifiability, it follows that every genuine proposition says, and can say, only something about my present or my future experience. From this two queer consequences follow. (1) Every proposition which *apparently* asserts a fact with regard to the past, e.g. *Queen Anne died in 1714*, asserts a number of hypothetical facts with regard to my own future experience, e.g. that *if* I consult such and such records I shall find that certain statements have been made to the effect that a certain event happened at a certain date.[39] (2) Every proposition about a material object, e.g, *this table,* likewise asserts a number of hypothetical facts with regard to my future experience, e.g. that *if* I lean against this table, the table will not rise into the air, and so on. This view closely resembles Mill's theory of material things as permanent possibilities of sensation. With regard to both theories, it seems to me that an objection – once urged by Moore against Mill – is conclusive. Owing to lack of time, I must state the objection briefly, in my own words.[40] Although when I do know that I perceive this table I *also* know certain hypothetical facts of the form, *If such conditions were fulfilled I should have such and such experiences,* yet, in knowing what these conditions are I am knowing that if this, or that, *material thing* were in such and such positions, then so and so would be the case. Thus the material thing has not been reduced to my own direct experience.

---

[37]Cf. G. E. Moore, *Coni. British Philos.*, Series II, p. 203.

[38]I suppose he would say that the phrase "My own experience" is nonsensical. But there is no other way of saying shortly what must be said. I do not wish to suggest that I own experience as I own a coat.

[39]From lack of time I cannot make this statement with sufficient precision, but the required improvements are easily made.

[40]Op. cit., p. 222.

514 Early Analytic Philosophy

In my opinion Wittgenstein's conception of *verifiability* depends upon a serious equivocation with regard to *the given,* and hence upon a muddle with regard to the notion of *direct experience* and *content,* as these are understood by the Logical Positivists. *This table* is not *an experience* of mine. Hence, in saying 'I perceive this table', I am *not* saying 'I perceive an experience of mine'. Perceiving, I should contend, is neither direct nor inferential. To suppose that these alternatives are exhaustive is a prime mistake of Logical Positivism. Perceiving is certainly *indirect;* but it is a non-inferential, indirect *knowing.*[41] Hence, in the case when I do perceive this table, *this table* is indirectly *given.* Accordingly, I see no reason for supposing that Wittgenstein is correct in supposing that every genuine proposition is a proposition about my own experience. Thus there would seem to be no justification for his view that every such proposition can only refer either to the present or to the future.

Wittgenstein's mistakes with regard to verifiability arise, I think, from an erroneous conception of the way in which the philosopher is concerned with questions of symbolism, and hence, from an unduly restricted view of the possible *kinds* of analysis and of the different *kinds* of facts which it is the business of philosophy to analyse.

There are various kinds of analysis. For my present purpose it is sufficient to refer to four different kinds, and two of these I have time barely to mention. These four kinds are: (1) analytic definition of a symbolic expression; (2) analytic clarification of a concept; (3) postulational analysis; (4) directional analysis.

(1) Under the analytic definition of symbolic expressions I have time to consider only the analysis of complete *sentences.* Let E and E' be two different complete sentences. Then "E' is an analysis of E" is to be defined as follows: "(i) E' says what E says; (ii) if '*a*' is a symbol occurring in E, then what '*a*' refers to is not less distinctly referred to in E', and there is some symbol '*b*' occurring in E' but not occurring in E".[42] Russell's analysis of "The author of *Waverley* is Scotch" would be an example of this kind of analysis; so would the analysis of a relative product into its constituent factors. It must be observed that the symbols occurring in "E'", the definiens, are being *used* but are not being *talked about;* whereas the symbols occurring in "E", the definiendum, *are being talked about,*

---

[41]This statement is excessively dogmatic, owing to the need for brevity. I have touched on this point in a paper published in *Aristotelian Society: Supplementary Volume,* ix, p. 154 seq.

[42]This definition could also be expressed as follows: "E and E' have the same reference, and there are more symbols in E' than in E, and these symbols more distinctly refer to what E also refers". To complete this statement it is necessary to define "more distinctly referring to". This is impossible here. (See my *A Modern Introduction to Logic,* ch. xxii, §§ 1, 4, and *Proc. Arist. Soc.,* N.S. xxxiii, pp. 83-4.)

Susan Stebbing on Logic, Language, and Analysis 515

and what is being said about the symbols constituting the definiendum is that they *mean* the definiens. Such an analysis may involve a clarification of our thoughts, because in using "E'" we may understand more clearly what we were saying when we used "E". Russell has effected such a clarification of thought in his theory of descriptions, which Ramsey calls 'that paradigm of philosophy'.

(2) The analytic clarification of a concept differs considerably from the other three kinds of analysis I have mentioned. It consists in the elimination of elements supposed to be referred to whenever we use a symbol "S", but which are not such that these elements *must* be referred to whenever we so use a sentence containing "S" that the sentence says what is true. Examples of concepts which have been thus clarified are *mass, force, simultaneity.* The need for such analytic clarification is due to the fact that we often manage to say something which is true although in so saying we believe ourselves to be referring to what is not in fact the case, and are thus also saying something false. This happens when we understand to some extent what we are saying but do not understand clearly *exactly* what we are saying; hence, we suppose something to be essential to the truth of what we say which is, however, not essential. Certainly Newton did not clearly understand what he was referring to when he spoke of "force", but he often said what was nevertheless true when he used sentences containing "force". A striking example is provided by the concept of *simultaneity.* Before Einstein had asked the question how we determine whether two events are simultaneous, we thought we knew quite well what was meant by saying 'happening at the same time in London and New York'. Einstein has made us see that we did not know quite well what we meant; we now understand that what we thought to be essential is not so. This analytic clarification of a concept cannot be made quite tidy. It involves a change in the significance of all statements in which the concept occurs. I have not time to deal fully with this kind of analysis, but it is important for my purpose to refer to it.

(3) Postulational analysis is the kind of analysis used in the construction of a deductive system.[43] I take this kind of analysis to be familiar. It is sufficient here to remind you that postulational analysis may very well be circular, and must be systematic. Analytic definition of a symbolic expression must not be circular; analytic clarification of a concept *could* not be circular and *cannot* be systematic. The purpose of every kind of analysis is to enable us to understand something

---

[43]In a' paper on 'The Method of Analysis in Metaphysics' (*Proc. Arist. Soc.,* N.S. xxxiii) I used the phrase 'symbolic analysis' instead of 'postulational analysis', but it seems to me that the former phrase is misleading.

516   Early Analytic Philosophy

more clearly. It is important in this connexion to remember, as Ramsey has pointed out, that 'we must realize the vagueness of our whole idea of understanding, the reference it involves to a multitude of performances any of which may fail and require to be restored'.[44] Wittgenstein seems to me to forget this. Otherwise he could not have said, 'That logic is a priori consists in the fact that we *cannot* think illogically' (5.4731). In my opinion Ramsey is right in insisting that our chief danger 'apart from laziness and woolliness, is *scholasticism,* the essence of which is treating what is vague as if it were precise and trying to fit it into an exact logical category'. I want to urge that it is a grave mistake to suppose that the alternatives are *understanding,* on the one hand, and *simply not understanding,* on the other. We understand more or less clearly. In the endeavor to understand more clearly we *use* words and sentences, and then reflect upon *how* we are using them, and whether we are so using them as to say what is true, or what might have been true although it happens to be false. Such reflection is required in the case of directional analysis.[45]

(4) A directional analysis of a sentence "S" consists of a set of steps such that (i) each step results in a sentence (to be called 'a resultant') which is such that this sentence reveals more clearly the multiplicity of the fact (expressed both by "S" and by the resultant) so that the resultant shows more clearly the structure of the fact expressed; and (ii) if the analysis were completed, *the final* resultant would have the *same* multiplicity as the fact expressed by "S" and by the resultant at each step. Thus the final resultant would reveal the form, the elements, and the mode of their combination.

It seems to me that Moore's philosophical practice has often been concerned with problems of directional analysis. At least, I believe that it is from him that I have learnt what directional analysis is, and why it is important. The set of simple facts terminating a directional analysis I call *basic facts.* In my opinion the fact expressed by "This is a table" is based upon a set of basic facts, each of which is an absolutely, specific fact. If I judge truly that *this is a table,* then *this is a table* entails the set of basic facts upon which *this is a table* is based. But it is not true, conversely, that the set of basic facts entails *this is a table.* Hence, the conjunction of the set of absolutely simple sentences, each indicating a basic fact, which constitute the final resultant does not yield a complete analysis of

---

[44]*Foundations of Mathematics,* p. 264. I am very much indebted to Ramsey's 'Last Papers', published in this volume. But I know that I have not always understood what he has said.

[45]In the paper already referred to, on 'The Method of Analysis in Metaphysics', I dealt with the nature of directional analysis. My treatment in that paper is very unclear, but I cannot, within the limits of this lecture, attempt to state the position more clearly.

Susan Stebbing on Logic, Language, and Analysis **517**

the expression "This is a table", for an analysis must both entail and be entailed by the analysed expression. Accordingly, to complete the analysis we have to consider not only the symbols but also *how* they are *being used* in a given case. Thus we require further a theory of generality.[46]

In my opinion Logical Positivism fails in its treatment of analysis. Wittgenstein and the other Logical Positivists talk much about analysis, but they do not consider the various kinds of analysis, nor do they show in what sense philosophy is the analysis of facts. They make use of analytic definition of a symbolic expression, and of the analytic clarification of a concept, but they do not distinguish between them. They also employ postulational analysis. But they do not seem to understand directional analysis, and, accordingly, they fail to apprehend the need for it. In this way they depart, in my opinion, from the practice of Moore. Not only is their conception of analysis defective, but, further, their conception of the *kinds* of facts to be analysed is inadequate. They treat all facts as *linguistic facts*. Hence, they suppose that the first problem of philosophy. is to determine the principles of symbolism, and *from these principles* to draw limits with regard to what we *can* think. This assumption has two important consequences. First, it leads to the view that philosophy is 'the activity of finding meaning', to quote Schlick's statement.[47] The second consequence is that they are apt to place too much reliance upon the construction of postulational systems. A few words must be said about each of these consequences.

Schlick's answer to the question in what sense Wittgenstein holds that philosophy is an activity is given in the statement I have just quoted. I do not know how far Wittgenstein would accept Schlick's development of his views, so that I confine my criticism to Schlick's treatment. He says, 'before the sciences can discover the truth or falsity of a proposition they have to get at the meaning first. And sometimes in the course of their work they are surprised to find, by the contradictory results at which they arrive, that they have been using words without a perfectly clear meaning, and then they will have to turn to the philosophical activity of clarification, and they cannot go on with the pursuit of truth before the pursuit of meaning has been successful.' I hope I am not misinterpreting what Schlick has said, but this statement suggests to me that he supposes that 'the pursuit of meaning' precedes the determination of the truth or falsity of a proposition. This is, I think, quite precisely wrong. In my opinion our

---

[46]It is not only lack of time but also incompetence which prevents me from. completing the treatment of directional analysis by providing a theory of generality. I think some help in this problem may be afforded by Ramsey's treatment of variable hypotheticals (see op. cit., pp. 237-54).

[47]Op. cit., p. 58.

Early Analytic Philosophy

procedure must be as follows. Understanding more or less unclearly what we say, we nevertheless may know that what we say is true. We then inquire what must be the case if what we have said is true. In this way we may come to see more clearly what it is we were knowing. It is correct to assert that scientific concepts must be clarified, but it is a muddle to suppose that this clarification is a pursuit of meaning. The word 'meaning' is too ambiguous, unclear, and vague, to be helpful in this connexion. I think that Schlick's example of the clarification of the concept of simultaneity shows that he has fallen into some confusion. This point would repay detailed consideration but I have not time to spare for it now.

The second point relates to the use of postulational analysis. The Logical Positivists have, in my opinion, been misled, first, by accepting Wittgenstein's equivocal conception of *the given;* secondly by relying exclusively upon Russell's supreme principle of scientific philosophizing. Consequently, they regard *tables,* for instance, as *constructs of the given.* But a *table* is not a *construct.* It is true that we speak correctly when we say that 'tables are logical constructions', but in so saying we are saying something about the way in which the word "table" may be used in ordinary sentences; we are *not* saying that what the word "table" refers to is itself a *construct.*[48] *Points* and *electrons* may be constructs; *tables* certainly are not.

Earlier in this lecture I said that Wittgenstein's principle of verifiability 'seemed innocuous enough'. It is true that we do not understand a proposition unless we know *what is the case* if the proposition is true. But the expression "what is the case" is not a *clear* expression; it is, indeed, excessively unclear. It is their interpretation of this expression which has led the Logical Positivists towards solipsism. This interpretation needs to be questioned. Wittgenstein says: 'Die Welt ist alles, was der Fall ist. Die Welt ist die Gesamtheit der Tatsachen . . . die Gesamtheit der Tatsachen bestimmt was der Fall ist und auch, was alles nicht der Fall ist . . . Was der Fall ist, die Tatsache, ist das Bestehen von Sachverhalten.'[49] Thus it seems that Wittgenstein holds that a 'fact' is 'what is the case', and that what is the case is a definite state of affairs. Thus interpreted, Wittgenstein is in agreement with the ordinary usage of the word "fact". Now, it is usual to say that *a fact* is what *makes a proposition true or false.* Thus Russell explicitly states, 'If I say "It is raining", what I say is true in a certain condition of weather and is false in other conditions of weather. The condition of weather that makes my

---

[48]See my *A Modern Introduction to Logic,* and J. Wisdom, 'Logical Constructions', in *Mind,* 1931–3.
[49]*Tractatus Logico-Philosophicus,* 1, 1.1, 1.12, 2. I have quoted from the German instead of from the English translation because it seems to me that in some respects the English translation may misrepresent Wittgenstein's views.

Susan Stebbing on Logic, Language, and Analysis **519**

statement true (or false as the case may be) is what I should call "a fact".[50] At first sight there does not appear to be a divergence between Russell's statement of what *a fact* is and Wittgenstein's conception of *a fact*. But to suppose that they are in agreement would be to fall into a serious mistake. On Russell's view a fact is what *makes* a proposition true, or false; on Wittgenstein's view a fact is what *verifies* a proposition, and what verifies a proposition is an experience of mine. Hence, to take Russell's example of 'the condition of weather', we cannot say, according to Wittgenstein, that the proposition 'It is raining' is made true by, or corresponds to, a certain determinate fact, which could be described by 'the rainy-condition of weather'. On the contrary, 'It is raining' *means* a set of *hypothetical* facts concerning my own experience, present or future; those hypothetical facts *verify* the proposition.

I have already pointed out that Moore's objection to Mill's theory of material things seems to me to hold also against Wittgenstein's interpretation of verifiability. I want now to suggest that an important point of difference between Moore's practice and Wittgenstein's theory seems to arise with regard to their conception of the relation of propositions to facts. The point at issue could be formulated in the question whether there are *final* facts. Can we say that there are facts which make propositions true, or can we only say that propositions are verifiable by reference to my own experience? In my opinion there are final facts, and these final facts are the facts which make propositions true (or false).

In conclusion I wish to state very briefly how, in my opinion, philosophy is concerned with language. What we ordinarily say, we say unclearly. We speak unclearly because we think unclearly. It is the task of philosophy to render our thoughts clear. Hence, it is not incorrect to say that the 'object of philosophy is the logical clarification of thoughts'. But, though not incorrect, this statement is not itself a *clear* statement. We cannot clarify our thoughts by thinking about thinking, nor by thinking about logic. We have to think *about* what we *were* thinking about. The philosopher considers a *given expression,* and analyses it in order to find *another expression* which says *more* clearly what the original expression said *less* clearly. This investigation is not linguistic. We must first *know* what facts are the case before we can fruitfully employ analysis for the purpose of clarifying our thoughts about the world. Accordingly, Logical Positivism fails, I think, in so far as it attempts to start from *a priori* assumptions with regard to the nature of language and the principles of symbolism, and, by means of these, to draw limits with regard to what we *can* think. Their mistake is that they

---

[50] *The Monist*, vol. xxviii (1918), pp. 500–1.

520　Early Analytic Philosophy

seek to make *everything* clear at once. But it is not in this way that philosophy can develop. We must proceed step by step, beginning with propositions which we *know* to be true, not ruling out initially what does not fit in. Wittgenstein's statement, 'What can be said at all can be said clearly', is gravely misleading. If it be interpreted as asserting that philosophy is not concerned with what is *inexpressible,* then the statement is true. Certainly, about the inexpressible, *nothing* can be said. If, however, it be interpreted as asserting that what is said is either clear or is nonsense, then it is false. But I believe that Wittgenstein does intend his assertion to be given this second interpretation. In that case, his fundamental principle should, in my opinion, be rejected. For, as Ramsey has well said, 'we can make several things clearer, but we cannot make anything clear'.

10

W. V. O. Quine on Analyticity and Ontology

Chapter Outline

Background and commentary

Background	521
Analyticity rejected	523
Ontological commitment	527
Concluding remarks	531
Further reading	532

Readings

"On What There Is"	533
"Two Dogmas of Empiricism"	547

Background and commentary

Background

Who was W. V. O. Quine (1908–2000)? If you have taken a course in contemporary analytic philosophy, it is likely that you have heard this name before opening this book, as Quine's ideas continue to be widely discussed and debated. Quine began his career as a logician; his PhD dissertation focused on Russell and Whitehead's *Principia Mathematica* and was later published as *A System of Logistic* (1934). Quine published in logic and set theory throughout his life. Nonetheless, he is probably best known for his

Early Analytic Philosophy

work in the philosophy of language and the philosophy of science. Aside from the two papers presented below, "On What There Is" (1948) and "Two Dogmas of Empiricism" (1951), Quine published a number of monographs and collections of essays over his career, including *From a Logical Point of View* (1953), *Word and Object* (1960), *Theories and Things* (1981), and *From Stimulus to Science* (1995). On the one hand, as we will see below, Quine developed substantive and important critiques of ideas at the heart of logical empiricism. On the other hand, however, Quine himself was deeply influenced by empiricist ideas—especially the ideas of Carnap—and spent time visiting the Vienna Circle, along with other centers of broadly empiricist thinking in Europe, during 1932 and 1933, which he would later describe as "the intellectually most rewarding months I have known" (1986: 12). Indeed, despite Quine's criticisms of certain empiricist ideas, Hilary Putnam (1926–2016), one of Quine's colleagues at Harvard, went so far as to describe him as "the last and greatest logical positivist" (1988: 269). For these reasons, Quine's criticisms of logical empiricism are best viewed as "internal critiques"; they are best understood as critiquing certain empiricist ideas, but nonetheless from within a broadly empiricist point of view. Quine's commitment to naturalism and the idea that philosophy is in some manner continuous with science continues to influence much contemporary thinking.

Quine was born in Akron, Ohio into a comfortable middle-class family. According to Quine, his first philosophical concerns came to him when he was around nine years and "began to worry about the absurdity of heaven and eternal life" (1985: 14). Quine was fascinated by geography and maps through his youth and into adulthood. He reported in his autobiography, *The Time of My Life*, that schoolwork seldom aroused his interest, and that "sitting in school, I would long for a trapdoor under my desk through which I could slip into the cool basement and out to freedom" (1985: 13). He attended Oberlin College in Ohio and was drawn to Russell's work on the foundations of mathematics at the suggestion of a fellow student. He received a degree in mathematics in 1930 with honors reading in mathematical philosophy. Only two years later, he received his PhD from Harvard under the direction of Whitehead. After returning from his trip to Europe in 1932-33, Quine received a fellowship at Harvard; he would later be appointed as an instructor (1936), associate professor (1941), professor (1948), and Edgar Pierce professor (1956), all at Harvard. While Quine was associated with Harvard for the entirety of his philosophical career, he enjoyed frequent lectureships and appointments around the globe, which suited his liking for travel. He served in the United States Navy during the Second World War.

Quine married his first wife, Naomi Clayton (1907–97), soon after his graduation from Oberlin. They would divorce in 1947 after two years of separation and after having two children together. He married his second wife, Marjorie Boynton (1918–98), in 1948, with whom he would also have two children. While Quine retired in 1978, he remained a fixture in the philosophy department at Harvard for many more years.[1]

Analyticity rejected

As we saw in Chapter 8, logical empiricists such as Ayer appealed to the notion of analytic truth, and a corresponding distinction between the analytic and the synthetic, to give an empiricist account of seemingly *a priori* disciplines like logic and mathematics. In particular, setting aside matters of detail, they typically maintained that mathematical and logical truths are analytic and record our determination to use symbols in a certain way. They moreover utilized the distinction between analytic truths on the one hand and empirically verifiable, synthetic truths on the other hand, in part to condemn metaphysical sentences as "pseudo-statements," given that such sentences are neither analytic nor empirically verifiable.

Quine's "Two Dogmas of Empiricism" takes issue with two ideas central to the empiricist program, as follows:

> One is a belief in some fundamental cleavage between truths which are *analytic*, or grounded in meanings independently of matters of fact, and truth which are *synthetic*, or grounded in fact. The other dogma is *reductionism*: the belief that each meaningful statement is equivalent to some logical construct upon terms which refer to immediate experience. (20)

As we will see below, Quine argues that there are connections between the empiricist commitment to analytic truth and the dogma of "reductionism." Given its rejection of these ideas, "Two Dogmas" is often presented as representing the decisive case against logical empiricism. But it should be noted that by the time "Two Dogmas" appeared in 1951, logical empiricism had already been subjected to a number of important criticisms, often from empiricists themselves. For example, as we discussed in Chapter 8, empiricists themselves were never able to settle on a criterion of meaningfulness that could vindicate scientific discourse while condemning metaphysics. Further, Quine himself had raised important concerns about the idea of logical truth

---

[1] For this and further biographical information, see Quine 1985 and Quine 1986.

Early Analytic Philosophy

as grounded in linguistic conventions fifteen years earlier in "Truth by Convention" (1936). At least for these reasons, the relationship between Quine's "Two Dogmas" and the downfall of logical empiricism is not as straightforward as some discussions suggest.

Quine argues in "Two Dogmas" that there is no empiricist-friendly way to articulate the notion of analytic truth, and as a consequence no empiricist-friendly way to develop a sharp, philosophically important distinction between the analytic and the synthetic. Quine's main strategy is essentially to consider an array of proposals and to argue that none of them succeed. Thus in the first parts of the paper, Quine considers a variety of notions—notions like analyticity, synonymy, definition, and necessity—that might be used to define what it is for a statement to be analytic. In each case, he concedes that such notions can be articulated and understood, if one or more of the other notions is taken for granted. The problem, Quine urges, is that none of these notions can be taken for granted by an empiricist. This is perhaps clearest when it comes to the connection between analyticity and necessity. Here, Quine concedes that if the notion of necessity is taken for granted, one can use that notion to articulate a notion of analytic truth. But an empiricist cannot take the notion of necessity for granted—especially because they typically understood necessity itself in terms of analyticity! In the second part of the paper, Quine considers some further proposals for understanding analyticity within an empiricist framework. For example, he proposes that if "reductionism" can be sustained, according to which each statement is associated with a unique range of experiences that would confirm that statement, one might define an analytic truth as one that is confirmed no matter what. The problem now, however, is that "reductionism," the second dogma of empiricism, should also be rejected, since according to Quine, it is false that any individual statement, taken apart from other statements, is associated with a unique set of confirmatory and discomfirmatory experiences. We will return to Quine's rejection of "reductionism" below.

Quine's case against analyticity, and the distinction between the analytic and the synthetic, raises a number of issues. One might, for example, take issue with his overall strategy and contend that even if the notion of analytic truth does not admit of a precise, uncontested definition, it does not follow that there is no such notion or that there is no worthwhile distinction between the analytic and the synthetic. Thus in "In Defense of a Dogma" (1956), Grice and Strawson note that the use of "analytic" seems principled: it has a "more or less established philosophical *use*" and "this agreement extends not only to cases which they [philosophers] have been *taught* to so characterize, but to new cases" (143). But, they argue, "if a pair of expressions are habitually and generally used in application to the same cases, where these cases do not form a closed list, this is a sufficient condition for saying that there are kinds of cases to which the expressions apply; and nothing more is needed for them to mark a distinction" (143). In other words, Grice and Strawson suggest that the lack of a precise definition of "analytic" does not show that "analytic" does not mark off a well-defined class of truths along with a philosophically salient distinction between one class of truths, the analytic ones, and another class of truths, the synthetic ones.

More generally, in assessing Quine's rejection of analytic truth, it should be marked that Quine does not deny that there are ways in which one may make sense of analytic truth. He claims, however, that the proposals are either too vague, and themselves in need of articulation, or fit uncomfortably with an empiricist framework. In this sense, they represent "dogmas" or "metaphysical articles of faith" (34). Indeed, Quine can be read as proposing what he views as an empiricist-friendly reconceptualization of analyticity; for Quine, the so-called "analytic truths" are those near the center of our "web of belief," those that we would not ordinarily revise in light of empirical findings. However, while this may be a notion of analytic truth, Quine thinks that it cannot do the heavy lifting demanded by the empiricist use of analyticity; nor, likewise, does it support the idea that there is a "fundamental cleavage" between the analytic and the synthetic. That there is such a cleavage is, he argues, a dogma—an idea that, while perhaps acceptable within certain philosophical frameworks, cannot be given a sound basis in empiricist philosophy.

Aside from the failure of particular attempts to define analyticity and to distinguish the analytic from the synthetic, Quine's critique of "reductionism" provides a picture of confirmation, and the relationship between experience and the empirical content of a statement, that suggests quite generally that one cannot divide up the analytic from the synthetic in the way that empiricists seemed to suppose. As above, according to the second dogma, for each synthetic statement "there is associated a unique range of possible sensory events" that may confirm or disconfirm that statement; given this, each "meaningful statement is equivalent to some logical construct upon terms which refer to immediate experience," namely those experiences that would confirm or disconfirm that statement (20). Quine's idea is that to the extent that meaning is tied to confirmation and disconfirmation conditions, the second dogma involves a mistaken conception of confirmation. Specifically, it supposes that it makes good sense to speak of the empirical meaning of a statement apart from all other statements and that because of

526   Early Analytic Philosophy

this, each meaningful statement is translatable into a statement about immediate experience. On Quine's alternative, holistic conception of confirmation (adapted from the views of the French physicist and philosopher Pierre Duhem (1881–1916)), an individual statement only has empirical consequences in conjunction with other statements. On this holistic conception of confirmation, when an empirical consequence of some set of statements fails to be borne out, no single one of the statements in the set needs to be rejected on the basis of the "recalcitrant experience." Rather, on this kind of view, the "unit of empirical significance" is not a single word, or even a single statement, but rather something broader, like a whole theoretical outlook. Thus Quine writes:

> The totality of our so-called knowledge or beliefs, from the most casual matters of geography and history to the profoundest laws of atomic physics or even pure mathematics and logic, is a man-made fabric which impinges on experience only along the edges...A conflict with experience at the periphery occasions readjustments in the interior of the field. Truth values have to be redistributed over some of our statements... No particular experiences are linked with any particular statements in the interior of the field, except indirectly through considerations of equilibrium. (39)

> If this view is right, it is misleading to speak of the empirical content of an individual statement... Any statement can be held true come what may, if we make drastic enough changes elsewhere in the system. Even a statement very close to the periphery can be held true in the face of recalcitrant experience... Conversely, by the same token, no statement is immune to revision. (40)

Consider the statement "There is a chair in the hallway." What is the empirical content of this statement? What sort of experiences would confirm or disconfirm this statement? One might imagine, not incorrectly, that the confirmatory experiences include (among other things) certain visual experiences that one would have, were one to enter the hallway. However, according to Quine, the statement only has these empirical implications together with a variety of other statements and theoretical commitments, including those relating to basic mathematical and logical truths. Given this, suppose that one enters the hallway, but does not have the visual experiences that one expected—in short, one does not see a chair in the hallway. Given this, one could, and typically should, reject the statement that there is a chair in the hallway. However, according to Quine, there is nothing necessary about this. One could, for example, instead reject certain presuppositions and theoretical commitments concerning perceptual experience. On Quine's

W. V. O. Quine on Analyticity and Ontology   527

view, we do not typically reject mathematical and logical truths on the basis of such "recalcitrant experience," given that they play such a central role in our dealing with the world. Yet Quine holds that it is at least in principle possible that we might revise even basic mathematical and logical commitments on the basis of certain experiences and observations. The empirical difference between those commitments at the center of our "web of belief" and those near the periphery is a matter of degree and not the kind of deep, philosophically important difference that the logical empiricists supposed in distinguishing the analytic from the synthetic. The reader is encouraged to think about whether this picture of confirmation does full justice to mathematical and logical discourse and practice, and also to consider what sort of "recalcitrant experiences" could possibly undermine basic mathematical and logical truths.

Ontological commitment

Ontology, the study of what exists, has traditionally been a central part of metaphysics. In "On What There Is," Quine argues, in effect, that there is an empiricist-friendly way of going about doing ontology and that ontological questions, questions about what exists, are on a par with questions of natural science. This, in turn, involves two claims: first, a claim about how we should conceptualize and represent existence claims; second, a claim about how existence claims so understood can be adjudicated.

Regarding the conceptualization or representation of existence claims, Quine essentially follows Russell's lead from "On Denoting." As we saw in Chapter 5, Russell provides an account under which, while sentences in which definite descriptions and ordinary names occur can be evaluated as true or false, the meaning of such expressions does not consist in an object named. Thus for Russell, a sentence like "The present King of France exists" says that there is one and only one present King of France and could be represented in modern symbolic logic as the quantificational sentence "$(\exists x)(Kx \land (\forall y)(Ky \rightarrow x = y))$" ("there is some x such that x is presently King of France and for any y, if y is presently King of France, then y is the same as x"). In this way, existence claims are understood as quantificational claims, claims to the effect that there is something that falls under one or more predicates. On this view, to then deny that such a thing exists simply involves the negation of the quantificational claim. That is, to say that the present King of France does not exist is just to say that it's not the case that something (and only one thing) is presently King of France, which could be written

Early Analytic Philosophy

formally as "~(∃x)(Kx ∧ (∀y)(Ky → x = y)" ("it's not the case that there is some x such that x is presently King of France and for any y, if y is presently King of France, then y is the same as x"). Like Russell, Quine supposes that a central benefit of this analysis is that it makes sense of how a negative existential, a statement that denies that something exists, can be both true and meaningful, as it does not suppose that the meaning of a definite description or an ordinary name consists in some object named, and so avoids puzzles about negative existentials that apparently otherwise arise. As Quine puts it, "We need no longer labor under the delusion that the meaningfulness of a statement containing a singular term presupposes an entity named by the term" and that, in contrast, a "singular term need not name to be significant" (28). This is important for Quine, given his taste for what he calls "desert landscapes" (23), his preference for sparse ontological pictures and his desire to deny that certain things exist. Quine expresses this manner of representing existential claims in quantificational terms as supposing that "to be... is to be the value of a bound variable" (32), writing:

> We can very easily involve ourselves in ontological commitments by saying, e.g., that there is something which red houses and sunsets have in common; or that there is something which is a prime number between 1000 and 1010. But this is, essentially, the only way we can involve ourselves in ontological commitments: by our use of bound variables... To be is, purely and simply, to be the value of a variable... The variables of quantification, 'something', 'nothing', 'everything' range over our whole ontology, whatever it may be; and we are convicted of a particular ontological presupposition if, and only if, the alleged presupositum has to be reckoned among the entities over which our variables range in order to render one of our affirmations true. (32)

In other words, we are "ontologically committed" to some entity just in case that entity is needed in order to make true sentences of the form "There is an x such that Fx" true, where "F" is some predicate expression. More generally, on this approach to ontology there is an especially intimate relationship between what exists, our use of the word "exists," and quantificational claims, claims involving the quantificational expression "some" and related locutions.[2]

Given this manner of conceptualizing existential claims and the formulation of what it takes to be ontologically committed to some entity, it

---

[2]While this connection between existence claims and quantificational was refined and developed most thoroughly by Quine, it dates back at least to the Austrian philosopher Franz Brentano (1838–1917) in his *Pyschologie vom Empirischen Standpunkt* (1874; translated as *Psychology from an Empirical Standpoint*).

is not difficult to see how this could be developed into an empiricist-friendly account of ontological inquiry. In particular, given that "to be is to be the value of a bound variable," what we need to do, on Quine's view, is look to what we regard as the best overall account of the world—especially, our best sciences—and determine what entities are needed in order to make sentences of the form "There is an x such that Fx" true. For Quine, this involves "regimenting" our scientific theories into modern predicate logic and, upon doing so, determining what objects are needed to make true the relevant quantificational claims. This is an empiricist-friendly view of ontological inquiry, as it takes ontological inquiry to require essential reference to science and, indeed, as part of scientific inquiry broadly construed. In this way, Quine seeks to provide an account of ontology under which ontological disputes may be settled not by appealing to *a priori* insight or intuition, but rather by appealing to what we take to be our best scientific picture of the world.

In "Two Dogmas," Quine suggests that his holistic picture of confirmation blurs the boundary between speculative metaphysics and natural science. Quine's idea is that metaphysical theories contribute to our overall understanding of the world in basically the same way as scientific theories and so can at least in principle be judged on similar merits. While perhaps more remote from experience, metaphysical theories nonetheless in some manner contribute to "predicting future experience in the light of past experience" and, in general, contribute to our attempt to make sense of the world around us. On this kind of picture, metaphysics is continuous with science, and metaphysical theories can at least in principle be evaluated on the basis to which they contribute to a plausible, overarching picture of the world. Generally, they can be evaluated in the same way that we evaluate scientific theories—on the basis of explanatory power, simplicity, and related considerations. Ontology is part of this endeavor, as it concerns what entities must be accepted in order for the existential claims of what we take to be our best overall picture of the world to be true.

Many philosophers cite "Two Dogmas" and "On What There Is" as providing an impetus for the revival of metaphysics in the analytic tradition. One needs to be careful here, however. It is true that if Quine's conclusions are taken on board, certain empiricist strategies for rejecting metaphysics cannot be sustained. For example (as we saw in Chapter 8), one way of understanding the empiricist rejection of metaphysics is essentially a version of "Hume's fork," according to which all meaningful discourse consists of either analyticities and contradictions on the one hand or synthetic, empirically verifiable statements on the other hand. Metaphysical statements,

Early Analytic Philosophy

seemingly, are neither. This kind of strategy for rejecting metaphysics cannot be maintained if, as Quine argues, there is no substantive, philosophically rich distinction between the analytic and the synthetic. Similarly, as above, Quine provides what can be viewed as a scientifically respectable method for ontology, according to which one looks to the best science for an account of what must exist in order for the quantificational claims of that science to be true, and in so doing, determine one's ontological commitments. Nonetheless, it would be a mistake to think, for instance, that Quine's discussions in these papers, or anywhere else, support the kind of speculative metaphysics that we found in Bradley. Similarly, consider remarks like the following from near the end of "Two Dogmas":

> As an empiricist I continue to think of the conceptual scheme of science as a tool, ultimately, for predicting future experience in the light of past experience. Physical objects are conceptually imported into the situation as convenient intermediaries – not by definition in terms of experience, but simply as irreducible posits comparable, epistemologically, to the gods of Homer... in point of epistemological footing the physical objects and the gods differ only in degree. (41)

> Consider the question of whether to countenance classes as entities. This, as I have argued elsewhere is the question whether to quantify with respect to variables which take classes as values. Now Carnap has maintained that this is a question not of matters of fact, but of choosing a convenient language form, a convenient conceptual scheme or framework for science. With this I agree, but only on the proviso that the same be conceded regarding scientific hypotheses generally. (43)

> Carnap, Lewis, and others take a pragmatic stand on the question of choosing language forms, scientific frameworks; but their pragmatism leaves off at the imagined boundary between the analytic and the synthetic. In repudiating such a boundary I espouse a more thorough pragmatism. Each man is given a scientific heritage plus a continuing barrage of sensory stimulation; and the considerations which guide him in warping his scientific heritage to fit his continuing sensory promptings are, where rational, pragmatic. (43)

Quine's "more thorough pragmatism" in passages like these would certainly sit uneasily with many of those philosophers who have traditionally been engaged in metaphysics. Moreover, many traditional metaphysicians would scoff at the idea that the epistemological status of physical objects is akin to that of the Homeric gods. Quine's contention, however, is that in either case, we should believe in the relevant entities only because of considerations relating to explanatory power and the role that they play in what we take to be our best overall account of the world. Similarly, consider the following passages from "On What There Is":

> Our acceptance of an ontology... is similar in principle to our acceptance of a scientific theory, say a system of physics: we adopt, at least insofar as we are reasonable, the simplest conceptual scheme into which the disordered fragments of raw experience can be fitted and arranged.... To whatever extent the adoption of any system of scientific theory may be said to be a matter of language, the same – but no more – may be said of the adoption of an ontology. (36)

> But simplicity, as a guiding principle in constructing conceptual schemes, is not a clear and unambiguous idea; and it is quite capable of presenting a double or multiple standard. [Consider] two competing conceptual schemes, a phenomenalistic one and a physicalistic one. Which should prevail? Each has its advantages; each has its special simplicity in its own way. Each, I suggest, deserves to be developed. Each may be said, indeed, to be more fundamental, though in different senses: the one is epistemically, the other physically, fundamental. (36)

In these and related passages, Quine considers the choice of an ontology consisting of physical objects on the one hand as opposed to an ontology consisting of "sense data"—a "phenomenalistic" ontology—on the other hand. For Quine, the question of which ontology to adopt is to be settled on the same kind of grounds as scientific questions generally—on the basis of considerations relating to explanatory power, overall simplicity, and fit with the best scientific picture of the world. One might think that there must be some further fact of the matter about whether the world consists of physical objects on the one hand or experiences on the other hand beyond explanatory power, overall simplicity, and fit with the best scientific picture of the world. Quine would likely reply that his pragmatic, scientific metaphysics is the only metaphysics worth having, but the reader should nonetheless consider the extent to which Quine's discussions legitimize (or delegitimize!) the study of metaphysics and ontology.

Concluding remarks

Despite providing the background for an array of contemporary discussions in philosophy of language, philosophy of science, and epistemology, few philosophers still endorse the details of logical empiricism. Quine, in part, is responsible for this. Moreover, in challenging some of the basic commitments of logical empiricism, Quine paved the way for a conception of philosophy under which philosophical inquiry can be viewed as continuous with science, as part of our overall attempt as human beings to make sense of the world around us.

This concludes our survey of early analytic philosophy. While we end with Quine, it would be a mistake to think that Quine's views have gone unchallenged. Analytic philosophy has continued to develop and change since the middle of the twentieth century. Some of these developments and changes will be sketched in the following chapter.

Further reading

Primary sources

Quine, W. V. O. ([1936] 1976), "Truth by Convention", in *The Ways of Paradox* (2nd edition). Cambridge, MA: Harvard University Press.

Quine, W. V. O. (1960), *Word and Object*, Cambridge, MA: The MIT Press.

Quine, W. V. O. (1985), *The Time of My Life: An Autobiography*, Cambridge, MA: The MIT Press.

Secondary sources

Alston, W. (1958), "Ontological Commitments", *Philosophical Studies* 9: 8–17.

Boghossian, P. (1997), "Analyticity", in B. Hale and C. Wright (eds), *A Companion to the Philosophy of Language*, Oxford: Blackwell.

Carnap, R. (1950), "Empiricism, Semantics, and Ontology", *Revue Internationale de Philosophie* 4: 20–40.

Fodor, J. and Lepore, E. (1992), *Holism: A Shopper's Guide*, Oxford: Blackwell.

Hylton, P. (2007), *Quine*, New York: Routledge.

Hylton, P. and Kemp, G. (2020), "Willard Van Orman Quine", *Stanford Encyclopedia of Philosophy*. Available online: https://plato.stanford.edu/entries/quine/

Kemp, G. (2006), *Quine: A Guide for the Perplexed*, New York: Continuum.

Putnam, H. (1962), "The Analytic and the Synthetic", in H. Feigl and G. Maxwell (eds), *Minnesota Studies in the Philosophy of Science,* Vol. III. Minneapolis: University of Minnesota Press.

Readings

Quine, W. V. O. "On What There Is".
Reprinted from Quine, W. V. O. (1948), "On What There Is",
The Review of Metaphysics 2: 21–38.

A curious thing about the ontological problem is its simplicity. It can be put in three Anglo-Saxon monosyllables: "What is there?" It can be answered, moreover, in a word – "Everything" – and everyone will accept this answer as true. However, this is merely to say that there is what there is. There remains room for disagreement over cases; and so the issue has stayed alive down the centuries.

Suppose now that two philosophers, McX and I, differ over ontology. Suppose McX maintains there is something which I maintain there is not. McX can, quite consistently with his own point of view, describe our difference of opinion by saying that I refuse to recognize certain entities. I should protest of course that he is wrong in his formulation of our disagreement, for I maintain that there are no entities, of the kind which he alleges, for me to recognize; but my finding him wrong in his formulation of our disagreement is unimportant, for I am committed to considering him wrong in his ontology anyway.

When I try to formulate our difference of opinion, on the other hand, I seem to be in a predicament. I cannot admit that there are some things which McX countenances and I do not, for in admitting that there are such things I should be contradicting my own rejection of them.

It would appear, if this reasoning were sound, that in any ontological dispute the proponent of the negative side suffers the disadvantage of not being able to admit that his opponent disagrees with him.

This is the old Platonic riddle of non-being. Non-being must in some sense be, otherwise what is it that there is not? This tangled doctrine might be nicknamed *Plato's beard*; historically it has proved tough, frequently dulling the edge of Occam's razor.

It is some such line of thought that leads philosophers like McX to impute being where they might otherwise be quite content to recognize that there is nothing. Thus, take Pegasus. If Pegasus *were* not, McX argues, we should not be talking about anything when we use the word; therefore it would be nonsense to say even that Pegasus is not. Thinking to show thus that the denial of Pegasus cannot be coherently maintained, he concludes that Pegasus is.

McX cannot, indeed, quite persuade himself that any region of space-time, near or remote, contains a flying horse of flesh and blood. Pressed for further details on Pegasus, then, he says that Pegasus is an idea in men's minds. Here,

Early Analytic Philosophy

however, a confusion begins to be apparent. We may for the sake of argument concede that there is an entity, and even a unique entity (though this is rather implausible), which is the mental Pegasus-idea; but this mental entity is not what people are talking about when they deny Pegasus.

McX never confuses the Parthenon with the Parthenon idea. The Parthenon is physical; the Parthenon-idea is mental (according any way to McX's version of ideas, and I have no better to offer). The Parthenon is visible; the Parthenon-idea is invisible. We cannot easily imagine two things more unlike, and less liable to confusion, than the Parthenon and the Parthenon-idea. But when we shift from the Parthenon to Pegasus, the confusion sets in – for no other reason than that McX would sooner be deceived by the crudest and most flagrant counterfeit than grant the non-being of Pegasus.

The notion that Pegasus must be, because it would otherwise be nonsense to say even that Pegasus is not, has been seen to lead McX into an elementary confusion. Subtler minds, taking the same precept as their starting point, come out with theories of Pegasus which are less patently misguided than McX's, and correspondingly more difficult to eradicate. One of these subtler minds is named, let us say, Wyman. Pegasus, Wyman maintains, has his being as an unactualized possible. When we say of Pegasus that there is no such thing, we are saying, more precisely, that Pegasus does not have the special attribute of actuality. Saying that Pegasus is not actual is on a par, logically, with saying that the Parthenon is not red; in either case we are saying something about an entity whose being is unquestioned.

Wyman, by the way, is one of those philosophers who have united in ruining the good old word 'exist'. Despite his espousal of unactualized possibles, he limits the word 'existence' to actuality – thus preserving an illusion of ontological agreement between himself and us who repudiate the rest of his bloated universe. We have all been prone to say, in our common-sense usage of 'exist', that Pegasus does not exist, meaning simply that there is no such entity at all. If Pegasus existed he would indeed be in space and time, but only because the word 'Pegasus' has spatio-temporal connotations, and not because 'exists' has spatio-temporal connotations. If spatio-temporal reference is lacking when we affirm the existence of the cube root of 27, this is simply because a cube root is not a spatio-temporal kind of thing, and not because we are being ambiguous in our use of 'exist'. However, Wyman, in an ill-conceived effort to appear agreeable, genially grants us the non-existence of Pegasus and then, contrary to what *we* meant by non-existence of Pegasus, insists that Pegasus *is*. Existence is one thing, he says, and subsistence is another. The only way I know of coping with this obfuscation of issues is to give Wyman the word 'exist'. I'll try not to use it again; I still have 'is'. So much for lexicography; let's get back to Wyman's ontology.

Wyman's overpopulated universe is in many ways unlovely. It offends the aesthetic sense of us who have a taste for desert landscapes, but this is not the worst of it. Wyman's slum of possibles is a breeding ground for disorderly elements. Take, for instance, the possible fat man in that doorway; and, again, the possible bald man it that doorway. Are they the same possible man, or two possible men? How do we decide? How many possible men are there in that doorway? Are there more possible thin ones than fat ones? How many of them are alike? Or would their being alike make them one? Are no *two* possible things alike? Is this the same as saying that it is impossible for two things to be alike? Or, finally, is the concept, of identity simply inapplicable to unactualized possibles? But what sense can be found in talking of entities which cannot meaningfully be said to be identical with themselves and distinct from one another? These elements are well high incorrigible. By a Fregean therapy of individual concepts, some effort might be made at rehabilitation; but I feel we'd do better simply to clear Wyman's slum and be done with it.

Possibility, along with the other modalities of necessity and impossibility and contingency, raises problems upon which I do not mean to imply that we should turn our backs. But we can at least limit modalities to whole statements. We may impose the adverb 'possibly' upon a statement as a whole, and we may well worry about the semantical analysis of such usage; but little real advance in such analysis is to be hoped for in expanding our universe to include so-called *possible entities*. I suspect that the main motive for this expansion is simply the old notion that Pegasus, e.g., must be because it would otherwise be nonsense to say even that he is not.

Still, all the rank luxuriance of Wyman's universe of possibles would seem to come to naught when we make a slight change in the example and speak not of Pegasus but of the round square cupola on Berkeley College. If, unless Pegasus were, it would be nonsense to say that he is not, then by the same token, unless the round square cupola on Berkeley College were, it would be nonsense to say that it is not. But, unlike Pegasus, the round square cupola on Berkeley College cannot be admitted even as an unactualized *possible*. Can we drive Wyman now to admitting also a realm of unactualizable impossibles? If so, a good many embarrassing questions could be asked about them. We might hope even to trap Wyman in contradictions, by getting him to admit that certain of these entities are at once round and square. But the wily Wyman chooses the other horn of the dilemna and concedes that it is nonsense to say that the round

Early Analytic Philosophy

square cupola on Berkeley College is not. He says that the phrase 'round square cupola' is meaningless.

Wyman was not the first to embrace this alternative. The doctrine of the meaninglessness of contradictions runs away back. The tradition survives, moreover, in writers such as Wittgenstein who seem to share none of Wyman's motivations. Still I wonder whether the first temptation to such a doctrine may not have been substantially the motivation which we have observed in Wyman. Certainly the doctrine has no intrinsic appeal; and it has led its devotees to such quixotic extremes as that of challenging the method of proof by *reductio ad absurdum* – a challenge in which I seem to detect a quite striking *reductio ad absurdum eius ipsius*.

Moreover, the doctrine of meaninglessness of contradictions has the severe methodological drawback that it makes it impossible, in principle, ever to devise an effective test of what is meaningful and what is not. It would be forever impossible for us to devise systematic ways of deciding whether a string of signs made sense – even to us individually, let alone other people – or not. For, it follows from a discovery in mathematical logic, due to Church, that there can be no generally applicable test of contradictoriness.

I have spoken disparagingly of Plato's beard, and hinted that it is tangled. I have dwelt at length on the inconveniences of putting up with it. It is time to think about taking steps.

Russell, in his theory of so-called singular descriptions, showed clearly how we might meaningfully use seeming names without supposing that the entities allegedly named be. The names to which Russell's theory directly applies are complex descriptive names such as 'the author of *Waverly*', 'the present King of France', 'the round square cupola on Berkeley College'. Russell analyzes such phrases systematically as fragments of the whole sentences in which they occur. The sentence 'The author of *Waverly* was a poet', e.g., is explained as a whole as meaning 'Someone (better: something) wrote *Waverly* and was a poet, and nothing else wrote *Waverly*. (The point of this added clause is to affirm the uniqueness which is implicit in the word 'the', in 'the author of *Waverly*'.) The sentence 'The round square cupola on Berkeley College is pink' is explained as 'Something is round and square and is a cupola on Berkeley College and is pink, and nothing else is round and square and a cupola on Berkeley College'.

The virtue of this analysis is that the seeming name, a descriptive phrase, is paraphrased *in context* as a so-called incomplete symbol. No unified expression is offered as an analysis of the descriptive phrase, but the statement as a whole which was the context of that phrase still gets its full quota of meaning – whether true or false.

W. V. O. Quine on Analyticity and Ontology 537

The unanalyzed statement 'The author of *Waverly* was a poet' contains a part, 'the author of *Waverly*', which is wrongly supposed by McX and Wyman to demand objective reference in order to be meaningful at all. But in Russell's translation, 'Something wrote *Waverly* and was a poet and nothing else wrote *Waverly*', the burden of objective reference which had been put upon the descriptive phrase is now taken over by words of the kind that logicians call bound variables, variables of quantification: namely, words like 'something', 'nothing', 'everything'. These words, far from purporting to be names specifically of the author of *Waverly*, do not purport to be names at all; they refer to entities generally, with a kind of studied ambiguity peculiar to themselves. These quantificational words or bound variables are of course a basic part of language, and their meaningfulness, at least in context, is not to be challenged. But their meaningfulness in no way presupposes there being either the author of *Waverly* or the round square cupola on Berkeley College or any other specifically preassigned objects.

Where descriptions are concerned, there is no longer any difficulty in affirming or denying being. 'There is the author of *Waverly*' is explained by Russell as meaning 'Someone (or, more strictly, something) wrote *Waverly* and nothing else wrote *Waverly*'. 'The author of *Waverly* is not' is explained, correspondingly, as the alternation 'Either each thing failed to write *Waverly* or two or more things wrote *Waverly*.' This alternation is false, but meaningful; and it contains no expression purporting to designate the author of *Waverly*. The statement 'The round square cupola on Berkeley College is not' is analyzed in similar fashion. So the old notion that statements of non-being defeat themselves goes by the board. When a statement of being or non-being is analyzed by Russell's theory of descriptions, it ceases to contain any expression which even purports to name the alleged entity whose being is in question, so that the meaningfulness of the statement no longer can be thought to presuppose that there be such an entity.

Now what of 'Pegasus'? This being a word rather than a descriptive phrase, Russell's argument does not immediately apply to it However, it can easily be made to apply. We have only to rephrase 'Pegasus' as a description, in any way that seems adequately to single out our idea: say 'the winged horse that was captured by Bellerophon'. Substituting such a phrase for 'Pegasus', we can then proceed to analyze the statement 'Pegasus is', or 'Pegasus is not', precisely on the analogy of Russell's analysis of 'The author of *Waverly* is' and 'The author of *Waverly* is not'.

In order thus to subsume a one-word name or alleged name such as 'Pegasus' under Russell's theory of description, we must of course be able first to translate

Early Analytic Philosophy

the word into a description. But this is no real restriction. If the notion of Pegasus had been so obscure or so basic a one that no pat translation into a descriptive phrase had offered itself along familiar lines, we could still have availed ourselves of the following artificial and trivial-seeming device: we could have appealed to the *ex hypothesi* unanalyzable, irreducible attribute of *being Pegasus*, adopting, for its expression, the verb 'is-Pegasus', or 'pegasizes'. The noun 'Pegasus' itself could then be treated as derivative, and identified after all with a description: 'the thing that is Pegasus', 'the thing that pegasizes'.

If the importing of such a predicate as 'pegasizes' seems to commit us to recognizing that there is a corresponding attribute, pegasizing, in Plato's heaven or in the mind of men, well and good. Neither we nor Wyman nor McX have been contending, thus far, about the being or non-being of universals, but rather about that of Pegasus. If in terms of pegasizing we can interpret the noun 'Pegasus' as a description subject to Russell's theory of descriptions, then we have disposed of the old notion that Pegasus cannot be said not to be without pre supposing that in some sense Pegasus is.

Our argument is now quite general. McX and Wyman supposed that we could not meaningfully affirm a statement of the form 'So-and-so is not', with a simple or descriptive singular noun in place of 'so-and-so', unless so-and-so be. This supposition is now seen to be quite generally groundless, since the singular noun in question can always be expanded into a singular description, trivially or otherwise, and then analyzed out a la Russell.

We cannot conclude, however, that man is henceforth free of all ontological commitments. We commit ourselves outright to an ontology containing numbers when we say there are prime numbers between 1000 and 1010; we commit ourselves to an ontology containing centaurs when we say there are centaurs; and we commit ourselves to an ontology containing Pegasus when we say Pegasus is. But we do not commit ourselves to an ontology containing Pegasus or the author of *Waverly* or the round square cupola on Berkeley College when we say that Pegasus or the author of *Waverly* or the cupola in question is not. We need no longer labor under the delusion that the meaningfulness of a statement containing a singular term presupposes an entity named by the term. A singular term need not name to be significant.

An inkling of this might have dawned on Wyman and McX even without benefit of Russell if they had only noticed – as so few of us do – that there is a gulf between *meaning* and *naming* even in the case of a singular term which is genuinely a name of an object. Frege's example will serve: the phrase 'Evening Star' names a certain large physical object of spherical form, which is hurtling through space some scores of millions of miles from here. The phrase 'Morning

Star' names the same thing, as was probably first established by some observant Babylonian. But the two phrases cannot be regarded as having the same meaning; otherwise that Babylonian could have dispensed with his observations and contented himself with reflecting on the meanings of his words. The meanings, then, being different from one another, must be other than the named object, which is one and the same in both cases. Confusion of meaning with naming not only made McX think he could not meaningfully repudiate Pegasus; a continuing confusion of meaning with naming no doubt helped engender his absurd notion that Pegasus is an idea, a mental entity. The structure of his confusion is as follows. He confused the alleged *named object* Pegasus with the *meaning* of the word 'Pegasus', therefore concluding that Pegasus must be in order that the word have meaning. But what sorts of things are meanings? This is a moot point; however, one might quite plausibly explain meanings as ideas in the mind, supposing we can make clear sense in turn of the idea of ideas in the mind. Therefore Pegasus, initially confused with a meaning, ends up as an idea in the mind. It is the more remarkable that Wyman, subject to the same initial motivation as McX, should have avoided this particular blunder and wound up with unactualized possibles instead.

Now let us turn to the ontological problem of universals: the question whether there are such entities as attributes, relations, classes, numbers, functions. McX, characteristically enough, thinks there are. Speaking of attributes, he says: "There are red houses, red roses, red sunsets; this much is prephilosophical common-sense in which we must all agree. These houses, roses, and sunsets, then, have something in common; and this which they have in common is all I mean by the attribute of redness." For McX, thus, there being attributes is even more obvious and trivial than the obvious and trivial fact of there being red houses, roses, and sunsets. This, I think, is characteristic of metaphysics, or at least of that part of metaphysics called ontology: one who regards a statement on this subject as true at all must regard it as trivially true. One's ontology is basic to the conceptual scheme by which he interprets all experiences, even the most commonplace ones. Judged within some particular conceptual scheme – and how else is judgment possible? – an ontological statement goes without saying, standing in need of no separate justification at all. Ontological statements follow immediately from all manner of casual statements of commonplace fact, just as – from the point of view, anyway, of McX's conceptual scheme – 'There is an attribute' follows from 'There are red houses, red roses, red sunsets.'

Judged in another conceptual scheme, an ontological statement which is axiomatic to McX's mind may, with equal immediacy and triviality, be adjudged false. One may admit that there are red houses, roses, and sunsets, but deny,

Early Analytic Philosophy

except as a popular and misleading manner of speaking, that they have anything in common. The words 'houses', 'roses', and 'sunsets' denote each of sundry individual entities which are houses and roses and sunsets, and the word 'red' or 'red object' denotes each of sundry individual entities which are red houses, red roses, red sunsets; but there is not, in addition, any entity whatever, individual or otherwise, which is named by the word 'redness', nor, for that matter, by the word 'househood', 'rosehood', 'sunsethood'. That the houses and roses and sunsets are all of them red may be taken as ultimate and irreducible, and it may be held that McX is no better off, in point of real explanatory power, for all the occult entities which he posits under such names as 'redness'.

One means by which McX might naturally have tried to impose his ontology of universals on us was already removed before we turned to the problem of universals. McX cannot argue that predicates such as 'red' or 'is-red', which we all concur in using, must be regarded as names each of a single universal entity in order that they be meaningful at all. For, we have seen that being a name of something is a much more special feature than being meaningful. He cannot even charge us – at least not by *that* argument – with having posited an attribute of pegasizing by our adoption of the predicate 'pegasizes'.

However, McX hits upon a different stratagem. "Let us grant," he says, "this distinction between meaning and naming of which you make so much. Let us even grant that 'is red', 'pegasizes', etc., are not names of attributes Still, you admit they have meanings. But these *meanings*, whether they are *named* or not, are still universals, and I venture to say that some of them might even be the very things that I call attributes, or something to much the same purpose in the end."

For McX, this is an unusually penetrating speech; and the only way I know to counter it is by refusing to admit meanings. However, I feel no reluctance toward refusing to admit meanings, for I do not thereby deny that words and statements are meaningful. McX and I may agree to the letter in our classification of linguistic forms into the meaningful and the meaningless, even though McX construes meaningfulness as the *having* (in some sense of 'having') of some abstract entity which he calls a meaning, whereas I do not. I remain free to maintain that the fact that a given linguistic utterance is meaningful (or *significant*, as I prefer to say so as not to invite hypostasis of meanings as entities) is an ultimate and irreducible matter of fact; or, I may undertake to analyze it in terms directly of what people do in the presence of the linguistic utterance in question and other utterances similar to it.

The useful ways in which people ordinarily talk or seem to talk about meanings boil down to two: the *having* of meanings, which is significance, and

W. V. O. Quine on Analyticity and Ontology 541

sameness of meaning, or synonymy. What is called *giving* the meaning of an utterance is simply the uttering of a synonym, couched, ordinarily, in clearer language than the original. If we are allergic to meanings as such, we can speak directly of utterances as significant or insignificant, and as synonymous or heteronymous one with another. The problem of explaining these adjectives 'significant' and 'synonymous' with some degree of clarity and rigor – preferably, as I see it, in terms of behavior – is as difficult as it is important. But the explanatory value of special and irreducible intermediary entities called meanings is surely illusory.

Up to now I have argued that we can use singular terms significantly in sentences without presupposing that there be the entities which those terms purport to name. I have argued further that we can use general terms, e.g., predicates, without conceding them to be names of abstract entities. I have argued further that we can view utterances as significant, and as synonymous or heteronymous with one another, without countenancing a realm of entities called meanings. At this point McX begins to wonder whether there is any limit at all to our ontological immunity. Does nothing we may say commit us to the assumption of universals or other entities which we may find unwelcome?

I have already suggested a negative answer to this question, in speaking of bound variables, or variables of quantification, in connection with Russell's theory of descriptions. We can very easily involve ourselves in ontological commitments, by saying, e.g., that *there is something* (bound variable) which red houses and sunsets have in common; or that *there is something* which is a prime number between 1000 and 1010. But this is, essentially, the *only* way we can involve ourselves in ontological commitments: by our use of bound variables. The use of alleged names is no criterion, for we can repudiate their namehood at the drop of a hat unless the assumption of a corresponding entity can be spotted in the things we affirm in terms of bound variables. Names are in fact altogether immaterial to the ontological issue, for I have shown, in connection with 'Pegasus' and 'pegasize', that names can be converted to descriptions, and Russell has shown that descriptions can be eliminated. Whatever we say with help of names can be said in a language which shuns names altogether. To be is, purely and simply, to be the value of a variable. In terms of the categories of traditional grammar, this amounts roughly to saying that to be is to be in the range of reference of a pronoun. Pronouns are the basic media of reference; nouns might better have been named pro-pronouns. The variables of quantification, 'something', 'nothing', 'everything', range over our whole ontology, whatever it may be; and we are convicted of a particular ontological presupposition if, and only if, the alleged presuppositum has to be reckoned

Early Analytic Philosophy

among the entities over which our variables range in order to render one of our affirmations true.

We may say, e.g., that some dogs are white, and not thereby commit ourselves to recognizing either doghood or whiteness as entities. 'Some dogs are white' says that some things that are dogs are white; and, in order that this statement be true, the things over which the bound variable 'something' ranges must include some white dogs, but need not include doghood or whiteness. On the other hand, when we say that some zoological species are cross-fertile, we are committing ourselves to recognizing as entities the several species themselves, abstract though they be. We remain so committed at least until we devise some way of so paraphrasing the statement as to show that the seeming reference to species on the part of our bound variable was an avoidable manner of speaking.

If I have been seeming to minimize the degree to which in our philosophical and unphilosophical discourse we involve ourselves in ontological commitments, let me then emphasize that classical mathematics, as the example of primes between 1000 and 1010 clearly illustrates, is up to its neck in commitments to an ontology of abstract entities. Thus it is that the great mediaeval controversy over universals has flared up anew in the modern philosophy of mathematics. The issue is clearer now than of old, because we now have a more explicit standard whereby to decide what ontology a given theory or form of discourse is committed to; a theory is committed to those and only those entities to which the bound variables of the theory must be capable of referring in order that the affirmations made in the theory be true.

Because this standard of ontological presupposition did not emerge clearly in the philosophical tradition, the modern philosophical mathematicians have not on the whole recognized that they were debating the same old problem of universals in a newly clarified form. But the fundamental cleavages among modern points of view on foundations of mathematics do come down pretty explicitly to disagreements as to the range of entities to which the bound variables should be permitted to refer.

The three main mediaeval points of view regarding universals are designated by historians as *realism*, *conceptualism*, and *nominalism*. Essentially these same three doctrines reappear in twentieth-century surveys of the philosophy of mathematics under the new names *logicism*, *intuitionism*, and *formalism*.

Realism, as the word is used in connection with the mediaeval controversy over universals, is the Platonic doctrine that universals or abstract entities have being independently of the mind; the mind may discover them but cannot create them. *Logicism*, represented by such latter-day Platonists as Frege, Russell,

W. V. O. Quine on Analyticity and Ontology   543

Whitehead, Church, and Carnap, condones the use of bound variables to refer to abstract entities known and unknown, specifiable and unspecifiable, indiscriminately.

Conceptualism holds that there are universals but they are mind-made. *Intuitionism*, espoused in modern times in one form or another by Poincare, Brouwer, Weyl, and others, countenances the use of bound variables to refer to abstract entities only when those entities are capable of being cooked up individually from ingredients specified in advance. As Fraenkel has put it, logicism holds that classes are discovered while intuitionism holds that they are invented – a fair statement indeed of the old opposition between realism and conceptualism. This opposition is no mere quibble; it makes an essential difference in the amount of classical mathematics to one is willing to subscribe. Logicists, or realists, are able on their assumptions to get Cantor's ascending orders of infinity; intuitionists are compelled to stop with the lowest order of infinity, and, as an indirect consequence, to abandon even some of the classical laws of real numbers. The modern controversy between logicism and intuitionism arose, in fact, from disagreements over infinity.

Formalism, associated with the name of Hilbert, echoes intuitionism in deploring the logicist's unbridled recourse to universals. But formalism also finds intuitionism unsatisfactory. This could happen for either of two opposite reasons. The formalist might, like the logicist, object to the crippling of classical mathematics; or he might, like the *nominalists* of old, object to admitting abstract entities at all, even in the restrained sense of mind-made entities. The upshot is the same: the formalist keeps classical mathematics as a play of insignificant notations. This play of notations can still be of utility – whatever utility it has already shown itself to have as a crutch for physicists and technologists. But utility need not imply significance, in any literal linguistic sense. Nor need the marked success of mathematicians in spinning out theorems, and in finding objective bases for agreement with one another's results, imply significance. For, an adequate basis for agreement among mathematicians can be found simply in the rules which govern the manipulation of the notations – these syntactical rules being, unlike the notations themselves, quite significant and intelligible.[1]

I have argued that the sort of ontology we adopt can be consequential – notably in connection with mathematics, although this is only an example. Now how are we to adjudicate among rival ontologies? Certainly the answer is not

---

[1] See Goodman and Quine, "Steps toward a constructive nominalism," *Journal of Symbolic Logic*, vol. 12 (1947), pp. 97–122.

Early Analytic Philosophy

provided by the semantical formula "To be is to be the value of a variable"; this formula serves rather, conversely, in testing the conformity of a given remark or doctrine to a prior ontological standard. We look to bound variables in connection with ontology not in order to know what there is, but in order to know what a given remark or doctrine, ours or someone else's, says there is; and this much is quite properly a problem involving language. But what there is is another question.

In debating over what there is, there are still reasons for operating on a semantical plane. One reason is to escape from the predicament noted at the beginning of the paper: the predicament of my not being able to admit that there are things which McX countenances and I do not. So long as I adhere to my ontology, as opposed to McX's, I cannot allow my bound variables to refer to entities which belong to McX's ontology and not to mine. I can, however, consistently describe our disagreement by characterizing the statements which McX affirms. Provided merely that my ontology countenances linguistic forms, or at least concrete inscriptions and utterances, I can talk about McX's sentences.

Another reason for withdrawing to a semantical plane is to find common ground on which to argue. Disagreement in ontology involves basic disagreement in conceptual schemes; yet McX and I, despite these basic disagreements, find that our conceptual schemes converge sufficiently in their intermediate and upper ramifications to enable us to communicate successfully on such topics as politics, weather, and, in particular, language. In so far as our basic controversy over ontology can be translated upward into a semantical controversy about words and what to do with them, the collapse of the controversy into question-begging may be delayed.

It is no wonder, then, that ontological controversy should tend into controversy over language. But we must not jump to the conclusion that what there is depends on words. Translatability of a question into semantical terms is no indication that the question is linguistic. To see Naples is to bear a name which, when prefixed to the words 'sees Naples', yields a true sentence; still there is nothing linguistic about seeing Naples.

Our acceptance of an ontology is, I think, similar in principle to our acceptance of a scientific theory, say a system of physics; we adopt, at least insofar as we are reasonable, the simplest conceptual scheme into which the disordered fragments of raw experience can be fitted and arranged. Our ontology is determined once we have fixed upon the over-all conceptual scheme which is to accommodate science in the broadest sense; and the considerations which determine a reasonable construction of any part of that conceptual scheme, e.g. the biological or the physical part, are not different in kind from the considerations which determine a reasonable construction of the whole. To whatever extent the adoption of any system of scientific theory may be said to be a matter of language, the same – but no more – may be said of the adoption of an ontology.

But simplicity, as a guiding principle in constructing conceptual schemes, is not a clear and unambiguous idea; and it is quite capable of presenting a double or multiple standard. Imagine, e.g., that we have devised the most economical set of concepts adequate to the play-by-play reporting of immediate experience. The entities under this scheme – the values of bound variables – are, let us suppose, individual subjective events of sensation or reflection. We should still find, no doubt, that a physicalistic conceptual scheme, purporting to talk about external objects, offers great advantages in simplifying our over-all reports. By bringing together scattered sense events and treating them as perceptions of one object, we reduce the complexity of our stream of experience to a manageable conceptual simplicity. The rule of simplicity is indeed our guiding maxim in assigning sense data to objects; we associate an earlier and a later round sensum with the same so-called penny, or with two different so-called pennies, in obedience to the demands of maximum simplicity in our total world-picture.

Here we have two competing conceptual schemes, a phenomenalistic one and a physicalistic one. Which should prevail? Each has its advantages; each has its special simplicity in its own way. Each, I suggest, deserves to be developed. Each may be said, indeed, to be the more fundamental, though in different senses; the one is epistemologically, the other physically, fundamental.

The physical conceptual scheme simplifies our account of experience because of the way myriad scattered sense events come to be associated with single so-called objects; still there is no likelihood that each sentence about physical objects can actually be translated, however deviously and complexly, into the phenomenalistic language. Physical objects are postulated entities which round out and simplify our account of the flux of experience, just as the introduction of irrational numbers simplifies laws of arithmetic. From the point of view of the conceptual scheme of the elementary arithmetic of rational numbers alone, the broader arithmetic of rational and irrational numbers would have the status of a convenient myth, simpler than the literal truth (namely the arithmetic of rationals) and yet containing that literal truth as a scattered part. Similarly, from a phenomenalistic point of view, the conceptual scheme of physical objects is a convenient myth, simpler than the literal truth and yet containing that literal truth as a scattered part.

Now what of classes or attributes of physical objects, in turn? A platonistic ontology of this sort is, from the point of view of a strictly physicalistic conceptual

Early Analytic Philosophy

scheme, as much of a myth as that physicalistic conceptual scheme itself was for phenomenalism. This higher myth is a good and useful one, in turn, in so far as it simplifies our account of physics. Since mathematics is an integral part of this higher myth, the utility of this myth for physical science is evident enough. In speaking of it nevertheless as a myth, I echo that philosophy of mathematics to which I alluded earlier under the name of formalism. But my present suggestion is that an attitude of formalism may with equal justice be adopted toward the physical conceptual scheme, in turn, by the pure aesthete or phenomenalist.

The analogy between the myth of mathematics and the myth of physics is, in some additional and perhaps fortuitous ways, strikingly close. Consider, for example, the crisis which was precipitated in the foundations of mathematics, at the turn of the century, by the discovery of Russell's paradox and other antinomies of set theory. These contradictions had to be obviated by unintuitive, *ad hoc* devices; our mathematical myth-making became deliberate and evident to all. But what of physics? An antinomy arose between the undular and the corpuscular accounts of light; and if this was not as out-and-out a contradiction as Russell's paradox, I suspect that the reason is merely that physics is not as out-and-out as mathematics. Again, the second great modern crisis in the foundations of mathematics – precipitated in 1931 by Gödel's proof that there are bound to be undecidable statements in arithmetic – has its companion-piece in physics in Heisenberg's indeterminacy principle.

In earlier pages I undertook to show that some common arguments in favor of certain ontologies are fallacious. Further, I advanced an explicit standard whereby to decide what the ontological commitments of a theory are. But the question what ontology actually to adopt still stands open, and the obvious counsel is tolerance and an experimental spirit. Let us by all means see how much of the physicalistic conceptual scheme can be reduced to a phenomenalistic one; still physics also naturally demands pursuing, irreducible *in toto* though it be. Let us see how, or to what degree, natural science may be rendered independent of platonistic mathematics; but let us also pursue mathematics and delve into its platonistic foundations.

From among the various conceptual schemes best suited to these various pursuits, one – the phenomenalistic – claims epistemological priority. Viewed from within the phenomenalistic conceptual scheme, the ontologies of physical objects and mathematical objects are myths. The quality of myth, however, is relative; relative, in this case, to the epistemological point of view. This point of view is one among various, corresponding to one among our various interests and purposes.

Quine, W. V. O., "Two Dogmas of Empiricism".[1]
Reprinted from Quine, W. V. O. (1951), "Two Dogmas of Empiricism", *The Philosophical Review* **60: 20–43.**

Modern empiricism has been conditioned in large part by two dogmas. One is a belief in some fundamental cleavage between truths which are *analytic*, or grounded in meanings independently of matters of fact, and truth which are *synthetic*, or grounded in fact. The other dogma is *reductionism*: the belief that each meaningful statement is equivalent to some logical construct upon terms which refer to immediate experience. Both dogmas, I shall argue, are ill founded. One effect of abandoning them is, as we shall see, a blurring of the supposed boundary between speculative metaphysics and natural science. Another effect is a shift toward pragmatism.

I. Background for Analyticity

Kant's cleavage between analytic and synthetic truths was foreshadowed in Hume's distinction between relations of ideas and matters of fact, and in Leibniz's distinction between truths of reason and truths of fact. Leibniz spoke of the truths of reason as true in all possible worlds. Picturesqueness aside, this is to say that the truths of reason are those which could not possibly be false. In the same vein we hear analytic statements defined as statements whose denials are self-contradictory. But this definition has, small explanatory value; for the notion of self-contradictoriness, in the quite broad sense needed for this definition of analyticity, stands in exactly the same need of clarification as does the notion of analyticity itself.[2] The two notions are the two sides of a single dubious coin.

Kant conceived of an analytic statement as one that attributes to its subject no more than is already conceptually contained in the subject. This formulation has two shortcomings: it limits itself to statements of subject-predicate form, and it appeals to a notion of containment which is left at a metaphorical level. But Kant's intent, evident more from the use he makes of the notion of analyticity

---

[1]Much of this paper is devoted to a critique of analyticity which I have been urging orally and in correspondence for years past. My debt to the other participants in those discussions, notably Carnap, Church, Goodman, Tarski, and White, is large and indeterminate. White's excellent essay "The Analytic and the Synthetic: An Untenable Dualism," in *John Dewey: Philosopher of Science and Freedom* (New York, 1950), says much of what needed to be said on the topic; but in the present paper I touch on some further aspects of the problem. I am grateful to Dr. Donald L. Davidson for valuable criticism of the first draft.

[2]See White, *op. cit.*, p. 324. [Editor's note: as marked in the Preface, footnotes and references have been left unaltered from the original texts from which the readings have been pulled.]

Early Analytic Philosophy

than from his definition of it, can be restated thus: a statement is analytic when it is true by virtue of meanings and independently of fact. Pursuing this line, let us examine the concept of meaning which is presupposed.

We must observe to begin with that meaning is not to be identified with naming, or reference. Consider Frege's example of 'Evening Star' and 'Morning Star'. Understood not merely as a recurrent evening apparition but as a body, the Evening Star is the planet Venus, and the Morning Star is the same. The two singular terms name the same thing. But the meanings must be treated as distinct, since the identity 'Evening Star = Morning Star' is a statement of fact established by astronomical observation. If 'Evening Star' and 'Morning Star' were alike in meaning, the identity 'Evening Star = Morning Star' would be analytic.

Again there is Russell's example of 'Scott' and 'the author of *Waverley*'. Analysis of the meanings of words was by no means sufficient to reveal to George IV that the person named by these two singular terms was one and the same.

The distinction between meaning and naming is no less important at the level of abstract terms. The terms '9' and 'the number of planets' name one and the same abstract entity but presumably must be regarded as unlike in meaning; for astronomical observation was needed, and not mere reflection on meanings, to determine the sameness of the entity in question.

Thus far we have been considering singular terms. With general terms, or predicates, the situation is somewhat different but parallel. Whereas a singular term purports to name an entity, abstract or concrete, a general term does not; but a general term is *true of* an entity, or of each of many, or of none. The class of all entities of which a general term is true is called the *extension* of the term. Now paralleling the contrast between the meaning of a singular term and the entity named, we must distinguish equally between the meaning of a general term and its extension. The general terms 'creature with a heart' and 'creature with a kidney', e.g., are perhaps alike in extension but unlike in meaning.

Confusion of meaning with extension, in the case of general terms, is less common than confusion of meaning with naming in the case of singular terms. It is indeed a commonplace in philosophy to oppose intension (or meaning) to extension, or, in a variant vocabulary, connotation to denotation.

The Aristotelian notion of essence was the forerunner, no doubt, of the modern notion of intension or meaning. For Aristotle it was essential in men to be rational, accidental to be two-legged. But there is an important difference between this attitude and the doctrine of meaning. From the latter point of view it may indeed be conceded (if only for the sake of argument) that rationality is

W. V. O. Quine on Analyticity and Ontology   549

involved in the meaning of the word 'man' while two-leggedness is not; but two-leggedness may at the same time be viewed as involved in the meaning of 'biped' while rationality is not. Thus from the point of view of the doctrine of meaning it makes no sense to say of the actual individual, who is at once a man and a biped, that his rationality is essential and his two-leggedness accidental or vice versa. Things had essences, for Aristotle, but only linguistic forms have meanings. Meaning is what essence becomes when it is divorced from the object of reference and wedded to the word.

For the theory of meaning the most conspicuous question is as to the nature of its objects: what sort of things are meanings? They are evidently intended to be ideas, somehow – mental ideas for some semanticists, Platonic ideas for others. Objects of either sort are so elusive, not to say debatable, that there seems little hope of erecting a fruitful science about them. It is not even clear, granted meanings, when we have two and when we have one; it is not clear when linguistic forms should be regarded as *synonymous*, or alike in meaning, and when they should not. If a standard of synonymy should be arrived at, we may reasonably expect that the appeal to meanings as entities will not have played a very useful part in the enterprise.

A felt need for meant entities may derive from an earlier failure to appreciate that meaning and reference are distinct. Once the theory of meaning is sharply separated from the theory of reference, it is a short step to recognizing as the business of the theory of meaning simply the synonymy of linguistic forms and the analyticity of statements; meanings themselves, as obscure intermediary entities, may well be abandoned.

The description of analyticity as truth by virtue of meanings started us off in pursuit of a concept of meaning. But now we have abandoned the thought of any special realm of entities called meanings. So the problem of analyticity confronts us anew.

Statements which are analytic by general philosophical acclaim are not, indeed, far to seek. They fall into two classes. Those of the first class, which may be called *logically true*, are typified by:

(1) No unmarried man is married.

The relevant feature of this example is that it is not merely true as it stands, but remains true under any and all reinterpretations of 'man' and 'married'. If we suppose a prior inventory of *logical* particles, comprising 'no', 'un-', 'not', 'if', 'then', 'and', etc., then in general a logical truth is a statement which is true and remains true under all reinterpretations of its components other than the logical particles.

Early Analytic Philosophy

But there is also a second class of analytic statements, typified by:

(2) No bachelor is married.

The characteristic of such a statement is that it can be turned into logical truth by putting synonyms for synonyms; thus (2) can be turned into (1) by putting 'unmarried man' for its synonym 'bachelor'. We still lack a proper characterization of this second class of analytic statements, and therewith of analyticity generally, inasmuch as we have had in the above description to lean on a notion of "synonymy" which is no less in need of clarification than analyticity itself.

In recent years Carnap has tended to explain analyticity by appeal to what he calls state-descriptions.[3] A state-description is any exhaustive assignment of truth values to the atomic, or noncompound, statements of the language. All other statements of the language are, Carnap assumes, built up of their component clauses by means of the familiar logical devices, in such a way that the truth value of any complex statement is fixed for each state-description by specifiable logical laws. A statement is then explained as analytic when it come out true under every state-description. This account is an adaptation of Leibniz's "true in all possible worlds." But note that this version of analyticity serves its purpose only if the atomic statements of the language are, unlike 'John is a bachelor' and 'John is married', mutually independent. Otherwise there would be a state-description which assigned truth to 'John is a bachelor' and falsity to 'John is married', and consequently 'All bachelors are married' would turn out synthetic rather than analytic under the proposed criterion. Thus the criterion of analyticity in terms of state-descriptions serves only for languages devoid of extralogical synonym-pairs, such as 'bachelor' and 'unmarried man': synonym-pairs of the type which give rise to the "second class" of analytic statements. The criterion in terms of state-descriptions is a reconstruction at best of logical truth.

I do not mean to suggest that Carnap is under any illusions on this point. His simplified model language with its state-descriptions is aimed primarily not at the general problem of analyticity but at another purpose, the clarification of probability and induction. Our problem, however, is analyticity; and here the major difficulty lies not in the first class of analytic statements, the logical truths, but rather in the second class, which depends on the notion of synonymy.

---

[3] R. Carnap, *Meaning and Necessity* (Chicago, 1947), pp. 9ff.; *Logical Foundations of Probability* (Chicago, 1950), pp. 70ff.

II. Definition

There are those who find it soothing to say that the analytic statements of the second class reduce to those of the first class, the logical truths, by *definition*; 'bachelor', e.g., is *defined* as 'unmarried man'. But how do we find that 'bachelor' is defined as 'unmarried man'? Who defined it thus, and when? Are we to appeal to the nearest dictionary, and accept the lexicographer's formulation as law? Clearly this would be to put the cart before the horse. The lexicographer is an empirical scientist, whose business is the recording of antecedent facts; and if he glosses 'bachelor' as 'unmarried man' it is because of his belief that there is a relation of synonymy between these forms, implicit in general or preferred usage prior to his own work. The notion of synonymy presupposed here has still to be clarified, presumably in terms relating to linguistic behavior. Certainly the "definition" which is the lexicographer's report of an observed synonymy cannot be taken as the ground of the synonymy.

Definition is not, indeed, an activity exclusively of philologists. Philosophers and scientists frequently have occasion to "define" a recondite term by paraphrasing it into terms of a more familiar vocabulary. But ordinarily such a definition, like the philologist's, is pure lexicography, affirming a relationship of synonymy antecedent to the exposition in hand.

Just what it means to affirm synonymy, just what the interconnections may be which are necessary and sufficient in order that two linguistic forms be properly describable as synonymous, is far from clear; but, whatever these interconnections may be, ordinarily they are grounded in usage. Definitions reporting selected instances of synonymy come then as reports upon usage.

There is also, however, a variant type of definitional activity which does not limit itself to the reporting of pre-existing synonymies. I have in mind what Carnap calls *explication* – an activity to which philosophers are given, and scientists also in their more philosophical moments. In explication the purpose is not merely to paraphrase the definiendum into an outright synonym, but actually to improve upon the definiendum by refining or supplementing its meaning. But even explication, though not merely reporting a pre-existing synonymy between definiendum and definiens, does rest nevertheless on other pre-existing synonymies. The matter may be viewed as follows. Any word worth explicating has some contexts which, as wholes, are clear and precise enough to be useful; and the purpose of explication is to preserve the usage of these favored contexts while sharpening the usage of other contexts. In order that a given definition be suitable for purposes of explication, therefore, what is required is not that the definiendum in its antecedent usage be synonymous with the definiens, but just that each of these favored contexts of the definiendum, taken as a whole in its antecedent usage, be synonymous with the corresponding context of the definiens.

Two alternative definientia may be equally appropriate for the purposes of a given task of explication and yet not be synonymous with each other; for they may serve interchangeably within the favored contexts but diverge elsewhere. By cleaving to one of these definientia rather than the other, a definition of explicative kind generates, by fiat, a relationship of synonymy between definiendum and definiens which did not hold before. But such a definition still owes its explicative function, as seen, to pre-existing synonymies.

There does, however, remain still an extreme sort of definition which does not hark back to prior synonymies at all; viz., the explicitly conventional introduction of novel notations for purposes of sheer abbreviation. Here the definiendum becomes synonymous with the definiens simply because it has been created expressly for the purpose of being synonymous with the definiens. Here we have a really transparent case of synonymy created by definition; would that all species of synonymy were as intelligible. For the rest, definition rests on synonymy rather than explaining it.

The word 'definition' has come to have a dangerously reassuring sound, due no doubt to its frequent occurrence in logical and mathematical writings. We shall do well to digress now into a brief appraisal of the role of definition in formal work.

In logical and mathematical systems either of two mutually antagonistic types of economy may be striven for, and each has its peculiar practical utility. On the one hand we may seek economy of practical expression: ease and brevity in the statement of multifarious relationships. This sort of economy calls usually for distinctive concise notations for a wealth of concepts. Second, however, and oppositely, we may seek economy in grammar and vocabulary; we may try to find a minimum of basic concepts such that, once a distinctive notation has been appropriated to each of them, it becomes possible to express any desired further concept by mere combination and iteration of our basic notations. This second sort of economy is impractical in one way, since a poverty in basic idioms tends to a necessary lengthening of discourse. But it is practical in another way: it greatly simplifies theoretical discourse *about* the language, through minimizing the terms and the forms of construction wherein the language consists.

Both sorts of economy, though prima facie incompatible, are valuable in their separate ways. The custom has consequently arisen of combining both sorts of economy by forging in effect two languages, the one a part of the other. The inclusive language, though redundant in grammar and vocabulary, is economical in message lengths, while the part, called *primitive notation*, is economical in grammar and vocabulary. Whole and part are correlated by rules of translation where-by each idiom not in primitive notation is equated to some complex built up of primitive notation. These rules of translation are the so-called *definitions* which appear in formalized systems. They are best viewed not as adjuncts to one language but as correlations between two languages, the one a part of the other.

But these correlations are not arbitrary. They are supposed to show how the primitive notations can accomplish all purposes, save brevity and convenience, of the redundant language. Hence the definiendum and its definiens may be expected, in each case, to be related in one or another of the three ways lately noted. The definiens may be a faithful paraphrase of the definiendum into the narrower notation, preserving a direct synonymy as of antecedent usage; or the definiens may, in the spirit of explication, improve upon the antecedent usage of the definiendum; or finally, the definiendum may be a newly created notation, newly endowed with meaning here and now.

In formal and informal work alike, thus, we find that definition – except in the extreme case of the explicitly conventional introduction of new notations – hinges on prior relationships of synonymy. Recognizing then that the notion of definition does not hold the key to synonymy and analyticity, let us look further into synonymy and say no more of definition.

III. Interchangeability

A natural suggestion, deserving close examination, is that the synonymy of two linguistic forms consists simply in their interchangeability in all contexts without change of truth value; interchangeability, in Leibniz's phrase, *salva veritate*. Note that synonyms so conceived need not even be free from vagueness, as long as the vaguenesses match.

But it is not quite true that the synonyms 'bachelor' and 'unmarried many are everywhere interchangeable *salva veritate*. Truths which become false under substitution of 'unmarried man' for 'bachelor' are easily constructed with help of 'bachelor of arts' or 'bachelor's buttons'. Also with help of quotation, thus:

'Bachelor' has less than ten letters.

Such counterinstances can, however, perhaps be set aside by treating the phrases 'bachelor of arts' and 'bachelor's buttons' and the quotation ''bachelor'' each as a single indivisible word and then stipulating that the interchangeability *salva veritate* which is to be the touchstone of synonymy is not supposed to

Early Analytic Philosophy

apply to fragmentary occurrences inside of a word. This account of synonymy, supposing it acceptable on other counts, has indeed the drawback of appealing to a prior conception of "word" which can be counted on to present difficulties of formulation in its turn. Nevertheless some progress might be claimed in having reduced the problem of synonymy to a problem of wordhood. Let us pursue this line a bit, taking "word" for granted.

The question remains whether interchangeability *salva veritate* (apart from occurrences within words) is a strong enough condition for synonymy, or whether, on the contrary, some nonsynonymous expressions might be thus interchangeable. Now let us be clear that we are not concerned here with synonymy in the sense of complete identity in psychological associations or poetic quality; indeed no two expressions are synonymous in such a sense. We are concerned only with what may be called *cognitive synonymy*. Just what this is cannot be said without successfully finishing the present study; but we know something about it from the need which arose for it in connection with analyticity in Section I. The sort of synonymy needed there was merely such that any analytic statement could be turned into a logical truth by putting synonyms for synonyms. Turning the tables and assuming analyticity, indeed, we could explain cognitive synonymy of terms as follows (keeping to the familiar example): to say that 'bachelor' and 'unmarried man' are cognitively synonymous is to say no more nor less than that the statement:

(3) All and only bachelors are unmarried men

is analytic.[4]

What we need is an account of cognitive synonymy not presupposing analyticity – if we are to explain analyticity conversely with help of cognitive synonymy as undertaken in Section I. And indeed such an independent account of cognitive synonymy is at present up for consideration, viz., interchangeability *salva veritate* everywhere except within words. The question before us, to resume the thread at last, is whether such interchangeability is a sufficient condition for cognitive synonymy. We can quickly assure ourselves that it is, by examples of the following sort. The statement:

(4) Necessarily all and only bachelors are bachelors

---

[4]This is cognitive synonymy in a primary, broad sense. Carnap (*Meaning and Necessity*, pp. 56ff.) and Lewis (*Analysis of Knowledge and Valuation* [La Salle, Ill., 1946], pp. 83ff.) have suggested how, once this notion is at hand, a narrower sense of cognitive synonymy which is preferable for some purposes can in turn be derived. But this special ramification of concept-building lies aside from the present purposes and must not be confused with the broad sort of cognitive synonymy here concerned.

W. V. O. Quine on Analyticity and Ontology   555

is evidently true, even supposing 'necessarily' so narrowly construed as to be truly applicable only to analytic statements. Then, *if* 'bachelor' and 'unmarried man' are interchangeable *salva veritate*, the result

(5) Necessarily, all and only bachelors are unmarried men

of putting 'unmarried man' for an occurrence of 'bachelor' in (4) must, like (4), be true. But to say that (5) is true is to say that (3) is analytic, and hence that 'bachelor' and 'unmarried men' are cognitively synonymous.

Let us see what there is about the above argument that gives it its air of hocus-pocus. The condition of interchangeability *salva veritate* varies in its force with variations in the richness of the language at hand. The above argument supposes we are working with a language rich enough to contain the adverb 'necessarily', this adverb being so construed as to yield truth when and only when applied to an analytic statement. But can we condone a language which contains such an adverb? Does the adverb really make sense? To suppose that it does is to suppose that we have already made satisfactory sense of 'analytic'. Then what are we so hard at work on right now?

Our argument is not flatly circular, but something like it. It has the form, figuratively speaking, of a closed curve in space.

Interchangeability *salva veritate* is meaningless until relativized to a language whose extent is specified in relevant respects. Suppose now we consider a language containing just the following materials. There is an indefinitely large stock of one- and many-place predicates, mostly having to do with extralogical subject matter. The rest of the language is logical. The atomic sentences consist each of a predicate followed by one or more variables; and the complex sentences are built up of atomic ones by truth functions and quantification. In effect such a language enjoys the benefits also of descriptions and class names and indeed singular terms generally, these being contextually definable in known ways.[5] Such a language can be adequate to classical mathematics and indeed to scientific discourse generally, except in so far as the latter involves debatable devices such as modal adverbs and contrary-to-fact conditionals. Now a language of this type is *extensional*, in this sense: any two predicates which *agree extensionally* (i.e., are true of the same objects) are interchangeable *salva yeritate*.

In an extensional language, therefore, interchangeability *salva veritate* is no assurance of cognitive synonymy of the desired type. That 'bachelor' and

---

[5]See, e.g., my *Mathematical Logic* (New York, 1940; Cambridge, Mass., 1947), sec. 24, 26, 27; or *Methods of Logic* (New York, 1950), sec. 37ff.

Early Analytic Philosophy

'unmarried man' are interchangeable *salva veritate* in an extensional language assures us of no more than that (3) is true. There is no assurance here that the extensional agreement of 'bachelor' and 'unmarried man' rests on meaning rather than merely on accidental matters of fact, as does extensional agreement of 'creature with a heart' and 'creature with a kidney'.

For most purposes extensional agreement is the nearest approximation to synonymy we need care about. But the fact remains that extensional agreement falls far short of cognitive synonymy of the type required for explaining analyticity in the manner of Section I. The type of cognitive synonymy required there is such as to equate the synonymy of 'bachelor' and 'unmarried man' with the analyticity of (3), not merely with the truth of (3).

So we must recognize that interchangeability *salva veritate*, if construed in relation to an extensional language, is not a sufficient condition of cognitive synonymy in the sense needed for deriving analyticity in the manner of Section I. If a language contains an intentional adverb 'necessarily' in the sense lately noted, or other particles to the same effect, then interchangeability *salva veritate* in such a language does afford a sufficient condition of cognitive synonymy; but such a language is intelligible only if the notion of analyticity is already clearly understood in advance.

The effort to explain cognitive synonymy first, for the sake of deriving analyticity from it afterward as in Section I, is perhaps the wrong approach. Instead we might try explaining analyticity somehow without appeal to cognitive synonymy. Afterward we could doubtless derive cognitive synonymy from analyticity satisfactorily enough if desired. We have seen that cognitive synonymy of 'bachelor' and 'un-married man' can be explained as analyticity of (3). The same explanation works for any pair of one-place predicates, of course, and it can be extended in obvious fashion to many-place predicates. Other syntactical categories can also be accommodated in fairly parallel fashion. Singular terms may be said to be cognitively synonymous when the statement of identity formed by putting '=' between them is analytic. Statements may be said simply to be cognitively synonymous when their biconditional (the result of joining them by 'if and only if') is analytic.[6] If we care to lump all categories into a single formulation, at the expense of assuming again the notion of "word" which was appealed to early in this section, we can describe any two linguistic forms as cognitively synonymous when the two forms are interchangeable (apart from occurrences within "words") *salva* (no longer *veritate* but)

---

[6]The 'if and only if' itself is intended in the truth functional sense. See Carnap, *Meaning and Necessity*, p. 14.

analyticitate. Certain technical questions arise, indeed, over cases of ambiguity or homonymy; let us not pause for them, however, for we are already digressing. Let us rather turn our backs on the problem of synonymy and address ourselves anew to that of analyticity.

IV. Semantical Rules

Analyticity at first seemed most naturally definable by appeal to a realm of meanings. On refinement, the appeal to meanings gave way to an appeal to synonymy or definition. But definition turned out to be a will-o'-the-wisp, and synonymy turned out to be best understood only by dint of a prior appeal to analyticity itself. So we are back at the problem of analyticity.

I do not know whether the statement 'Everything green is extended' is analytic. Now does my indecision over this example really betray an incomplete understanding, an incomplete grasp of the "meanings", of 'green' and 'extended'? I think not. The trouble is not with 'green' or 'extended', but with 'analytic'.

It is often hinted that the difficulty in separating analytic statements from synthetic ones in ordinary language is due to the vagueness of ordinary language and that the distinction is clear when we have a precise artificial language with explicit "semantical rules." This, however, as I shall now attempt to show, is a confusion.

The notion of analyticity about which we are worrying is a purported relation between statements and languages: a statement S is said to be *analytic for* a language L, and the problem is to make sense of this relation generally, i.e., for variable 'S' and 'L'. The point that I want to make is that the gravity of this problem is not perceptibly less for artificial languages than for natural ones. The problem of making sense of the idiom 'S is analytic for L', with variable 'S' and 'L', retains its stubbornness even if we limit the range of the variable 'L' to artificial languages. Let me now try to make this point evident.

For artificial languages and semantical rules we look naturally to the writings of Carnap. His semantical rules take various forms, and to make my point I shall have to distinguish certain of the forms. Let us suppose, to begin with, an artificial language L_0. whose semantical rules have the form explicitly of a specification, by recursion or otherwise, of all the analytic statements of L_0. The rules tell us that such and such statements, and only those, are the analytic statements of L_0. Now here the difficulty is simply that the rules contain the word 'analytic', which we do not understand! We understand what expressions the rules attribute analyticity to, but we do not understand what the rules attribute to those expressions. In short, before we can understand a rule which

558   Early Analytic Philosophy

begins "A statement S is analytic for language L_o if and only if. . . ," we must understand the general relative term 'analytic for'; we must understand 'S is analytic for L' where 'S' and 'L' are variables.

Alternatively we may, indeed, view the so-called rule as a conventional definition of a new simple symbol 'analytic-for- L_o', which might better be written untendentiously as 'K' so as not to seem to throw light on the interesting word 'analytic'. Obviously any number of classes K, M, N, etc. of statements of L_o can be specified for various purposes or for no purpose; what does it mean to say that K, as against M, N, etc., is the class of the "analytic" statements of L_o?

By saying what statements are analytic for L_o we explain 'analytic-for- L_o,' but not 'analytic', not 'analytic for'. We do not begin to explain the idiom 'S is analytic for L' with variable 'S' and 'L', even though we be content to limit the range of 'L' to the realm of artificial languages.

Actually we do know enough about the intended significance of 'analytic' to know that analytic statements are supposed to be true. Let us then turn to a second form of semantical rule, which says not that such and such statements are analytic but simply that such and such statements are included among the truths. Such a rule is not subject to the criticism of containing the un-understood word 'analytic'; and we may grant for the sake of argument that there is no difficulty over the broader term 'true'. A semantical rule of this second type, a rule of truth, is not supposed to specify all the truths of the language; it merely stipulates, recursively or otherwise, a certain multitude of statements which, along with others unspecified, are to count as true. Such a rule may be conceded to be quite clear. Derivatively, afterward, analyticity can be demarcated thus: a statement is analytic if it is (not merely true but) true according to the semantical rule.

Still there is really no progress. Instead of appealing to an unexplained word 'analytic', we are now appealing to an unexplained phrase 'semantical rule'. Not every true statement which says that the statements of some class are true can count as a semantical rule - otherwise all truths would be "analytic" in the sense of being true according to semantical rules. Semantical rules are distinguishable, apparently, only by the fact of appearing on a page under the heading 'Semantical Rules'; and this heading is itself then meaningless.

We can say indeed that a statement is analytic-for- L_o if and only if it is true according to such and such specifically appended "semantical rules," but then we find ourselves back at essentially the same case which was originally discussed: "S is analytic-for- L_o if and only if . . . . " Once we seek to explain 'S is analytic for L' generally for variable 'L' (even allowing limitation of 'L' to artificial languages), the explanation 'true according to the semantical rules of

W. V. O. Quine on Analyticity and Ontology 559

L' is unavailing; for the relative term 'semantical rule of' is as much in need of clarification, at least, as 'analytic for'.

It might conceivably be protested that an artificial language L (unlike a natural one) is a language in the ordinary sense plus a set of explicit semantical rules – the whole constituting, let us say, an ordered pair; and that the semantical rules of L then are specifiable simply as the second component of the pair L. But, by the same token and more simply, we might construe an artificial language L outright as an ordered pair whose second component is the class of its analytic statements; and then the analytic statements of L become specifiable simply as the statements in the second component of L. Or better still, we might just stop tugging at our bootstraps altogether.

Not all the explanations of analyticity known to Carnap and his readers have been covered explicitly in the above considerations, but the extension to other forms is not hard to see. Just one additional factor should be mentioned which sometimes enters: sometimes the semantical rules are in effect rules of translation into ordinary language, in which case the analytic statements of the artificial language are in effect recognized as such from the analyticity of their specified translations in ordinary language. Here certainly there can be no thought of an illumination of the problem of analyticity from the side of the artificial language.

From the point of view of the problem of analyticity the notion of an artificial language with semantical rules is a *feu follet par excellence*. Semantical rules determining the analytic statements of an artificial language are of interest only in so far as we already understand the notion of analyticity; they are of no help in gaining this understanding.

Appeal to hypothetical languages of an artificially simple kind could conceivably be useful in clarifying analyticity, if the mental or behavioral or cultural factors relevant to analyticity – whatever they may be – were somehow sketched into the simplified model. But a model which takes analyticity merely as in irreducible character is unlikely to throw light on the problem of explicating analyticity.

It is obvious that truth in general depends on both language and extralinguistic fact. The statement 'Brutus killed Caesar' would be false if the world had been different in certain ways, but it would also be false if the word 'killed' happened rather to have the sense of 'begat'. Hence the temptation to suppose in general that the truth of a statement is somehow analyzable into a linguistic component and a factual component. Given this supposition, it next seems reasonable that in some statements the factual component should be null; and these are the analytic statements. But, for all its a priori reasonableness, a boundary between analytic and synthetic statements simply has not been drawn. That there is such a distinction to be drawn at all is an un-empirical dogma of empiricists, a metaphysical article of faith.

V. The Verification Theory and Reductionism

In the course of these somber reflections we have taken a dim view first of the notion of meaning, then of the notion of cognitive synonymy, and finally of the notion of analyticity. But what, it may be asked, of the verification theory of meaning? This phrase has established itself so firmly as a catchword of empiricism that we should be very unscientific indeed not to look beneath it for a possible key to the problem of meaning and the associated problems.

The verification theory of meaning, which has been conspicuous in the literature from Peirce onward, is that the meaning of a statement is the method of empirically confirming or infirming it. An analytic statement is that limiting case which is confirmed no matter what.

As urged in Section I, we can as well pass over the question of meanings as entities and move straight to sameness of meaning, or synonymy. Then what the verification theory says is that statements are synonymous if and only if they are alike in point of method of empirical confirmation or infirmation.

This is an account of cognitive synonymy not of linguistic forms generally, but of statements.[7] However, from the concept of synonymy of statements we could derive the concept of synonymy for other linguistic forms, by considerations somewhat similar to those at the end of Section III. Assuming the notion of "word," indeed, we could explain any two forms as synonymous when the putting of the one form for an occurrence of the other in any statement (apart from occurrences within "words") yields a synonymous statement. Finally, given the concept of synonymy thus for linguistic forms generally, we could define analyticity in terms of synonymy and logical truth as in Section I. For that matter, we could define analyticity more simply in terms of just synonymy of statements together with logical truth; it is not necessary to appeal to synonymy of linguistic forms other than statements. For a statement may be described as analytic simply when it is synonymous with a logically true statement.

---

[7]The doctrine can indeed be formulated with terms rather than statements as the units. Thus C. I. Lewis describes the meaning of a term as "*a criterion in mind*, by reference to which one is able to apply or refuse to apply the expression in question in the case of presented, or imagined, things or situations" (*op. cit.*, p. 133).

So, if the verification theory can be accepted as an adequate account of statement synonymy, the notion of analyticity is saved after all. However, let us reflect. Statement synonymy is said to be likeness of method of empirical confirmation or infirmation. Just what are these methods which are to be compared for likeness? What, in other words, is the nature of the relationship between a statement and the experiences which contribute to or detract from its confirmation?

The most naive view of the relationship is that it is one of direct report. This is *radical reductionism*. Every meaningful held to be translatable into a statement (true or false) about immediate experience. Radical reductionism, in one form or another, well antedates the verification theory of meaning explicitly so-called. Thus Locke and Hume held that every idea must either originate directly in sense experience or else be compounded of ideas thus originating; and taking a hint from Tooke[8] we might rephrase this doctrine in semantical jargon by saying that a term, to be significant at all, must be either a name of a sense datum or a compound of such names or an abbreviation of such a compound. So stated, the doctrine remains ambiguous as between sense data as sensory events and sense data as sensory qualities; and it remains vague as to the admissible compounding. Moreover, the doctrine is unnecessarily restrictive in the term-by-term critique which it imposes. More reasonably, and without yet exceeding the limits of what radical reductionism, we may take full statements as units – thus demanding that our statements as wholes be translatable into sense-datum language, but not that they be translatable term by term.

This emendation would unquestionably have been welcome to Locke and Hume and Tooke, but historically it had to await two intermediate developments. One of these developments was the increasing emphasis on verification or confirmation, which came with the explicitly so-called verification theory of meaning. The objects of verification or confirmation being statements, this emphasis gave the statement an ascendency over the word or term as unit of significant discourse. The other development, consequent upon the first, was Russell's discovery of the concept of incomplete symbols defined in use.

Radical reductionism, conceived now with statements as units, sets itself the task of specifying a sense-datum language and showing how to translate the rest of significant discourse, statement by statement, into it. Carnap embarked on this project in the *Aufbau*.[9]

---

[8]John Horne Tooke, *The Diversions of Purley* (London, 1766; Boston, 1806), I, ch. ii.
[9]R. Carnap, *Der logische Aufbau der Welt* (Berlin, 1928).

Early Analytic Philosophy

The language which Carnap adopted as his starting point was not a sense-datum language in the narrowest conceivable sense, for it included also the notations of logic, up through higher set theory. In effect it included the whole language of pure mathematics. The ontology implicit in it (i.e., the range of values of its variables) embraced not only sensory events but classes, classes of classes, and so on. Empiricists there are who would boggle at such prodigality. Carnap's starting point is very parsimonious, however, in its extralogical or sensory part. In a series of constructions in which he exploits the resources of modern logic with much ingenuity, he succeeds in defining a wide array of important additional sensory concepts which, but for his constructions, one would not have dreamed were definable on so slender a basis. Carnap was the first empiricist who, not content with asserting the reducibility of science to terms of immediate experience, took serious steps toward carrying out the reduction.

Even supposing Carnap's starting point satisfactory, his constructions were, as he himself stressed, only a fragment of the full program. The construction of even the simplest statements about the physical world was left in a sketchy state. Carnap's suggestions on this subject were, despite their sketchiness, very suggestive. He explained spatio-temporal point-instants as quadruples of real numbers and envisaged assignment of sense qualities to point-instants according to certain canons. Roughly summarized, the plan was that qualities should be assigned to point-instants in such a way as to achieve the laziest world compatible with our experience. The principle of least action was to be our guide in constructing a world from experience.

Carnap did not seem to recognize, however, that his treatment of physical objects fell short of reduction not merely through sketchiness, but in principle. Statements of the form 'Quality q is at point-instant x; y; z; t' were, according to his canons, to be apportioned truth values in such a way as to maximize and minimize certain over-all features, and with growth of experience the truth values were to be progressively revised in the same spirit. I think this is a good schematization (deliberately oversimplified, to be sure) of what science really does; but it provides no indication, not even the sketchiest, of how a statement of the form 'Quality q is at x; y; z; t' could ever be translated into Carnap's initial language of sense data and logic. The connective 'is at' remains an added undefined connective; the canons counsel us in its use but not in its elimination.

Carnap seems to have appreciated this point afterward; for in his later writings he abandoned all notion of the translatability of statements about the physical world into statements about immediate experience. Reductionism in its radical form has long since ceased to figure in Carnap's philosophy.

W. V. O. Quine on Analyticity and Ontology   563

But the dogma of reductionism has, in a subtler and more tenuous form, continued to influence the thought of empiricists. The notion lingers that to each statement, or each synthetic statement, there is associated a unique range of possible sensory events such that the occurrence of any of them would add to the likelihood of truth of the statement, and that there is associated also another unique range of possible sensory events whose occurrence would detract from that likelihood. This notion is of course implicit in the verification theory of meaning.

The dogma of reductionism survives in the supposition that each statement, taken in isolation from its fellows, can admit of confirmation or infirmation at all. My countersuggestion, issuing essentially from Carnap's doctrine of the physical world in the *Aufbau*, is that our statements about the external world face the tribunal of sense experience not individually but only as a corporate body.

The dogma of reductionism, even in its attenuated form, is intimately connected with the other dogma: that there is a cleavage between the analytic and the synthetic. We have found ourselves led, indeed, from the latter problem to the former through the verification theory of meaning. More directly, the one dogma clearly supports the other in this way: as long as it is taken to be significant in general to speak of the confirmation and infirmation of a statement, it seems significant to speak also of a limiting kind of statement which is vacuously confirmed, *ipso facto*, come what may; and such a statement is analytic.

The two dogmas are, indeed, at root identical. We lately reflected that in general the truth of statements does obviously depend both upon language and upon extralinguistic fact; and we noted that this obvious circumstance carries in its train, not logically but all too naturally, a feeling that the truth of a statement is somehow analyzable into a linguistic component and a factual component. The factual component must, if we are empiricists, boil down to a range of confirmatory experiences. In the extreme case where the linguistic component is all that matters, a true statement is analytic. But I hope we are now impressed with how stubbornly the distinction between analytic and synthetic has resisted any straightforward drawing. I am impressed also, apart from prefabricated examples of black and white balls in an urn, with how baffling the problem has always been of arriving at any explicit theory of the empirical confirmation of a synthetic statement. My present suggestion is that it is nonsense, and the root of much nonsense, to speak of a linguistic component and a factual component in the truth of any individual statement. Taken collectively, science has its double dependence upon language and experience; but this duality is not significantly traceable into the statements of science taken one by one.

Early Analytic Philosophy

Russell's concept of definition in use was, as remarked, an advance over the impossible term-by-term empiricism of Locke and Hume. The statement, rather than the term, came with Russell to be recognized as the unit accountable to an empiricist critique. But what I am now urging is that even in taking the statement as unit we have drawn our grid too finely. The unit of empirical significance is the whole of science.

VI. Empiricism Without the Dogmas

The totality of our so-called knowledge or beliefs, from the most casual matters of geography and history to the profoundest laws of atomic physics or even of pure mathematics and logic, is a man-made fabric which impinges on experience only along the edges. Or, to change the figure, total science is like a field of force whose boundary conditions are experience. A conflict with experience at the periphery occasions readjustments in the interior of the field. Truth values have to be redistributed over some of our statements. Re-evaluation of some statements entails re-evaluation of others, because of their logical interconnections – the logical laws being in turn simply certain further statements of the system, certain further elements of the field. Having re-evaluated one statement we must re-evaluate some others, whether they be statements logically connected with the first or whether they be the statements of logical connections themselves. But the total field is so undetermined by its boundary conditions, experience, that there is much latitude of choice as to what statements to re-evaluate in the light of any single contrary experience. No particular experiences are linked with any particular statements in the interior of the field, except indirectly through considerations of equilibrium affecting the field as a whole.

If this view is right, it is misleading to speak of the empirical content of an individual statement – especially if it be a statement at all remote from the experiential periphery of the field. Furthermore it becomes folly to seek a boundary between synthetic statements, which hold contingently on experience, and analytic statements which hold come what may. Any statement can be held true come what may, if we make drastic enough adjustments elsewhere in the system. Even a statement very close to the periphery can be held true in the face of recalcitrant experience by pleading hallucination or by amending certain statements of the kind called logical laws. Conversely, by the same token, no statement is immune to revision. Revision even of the logical law of the excluded middle has been proposed as a means of simplifying quantum mechanics; and what difference is there in principle between such a shift and the shift whereby Kepler superseded Ptolemy, or Einstein Newton, or Darwin Aristotle?

W. V. O. Quine on Analyticity and Ontology   565

For vividness I have been speaking in terms of varying distances from a sensory periphery. Let me try now to clarify this notion without metaphor. Certain statements, though *about* physical objects and not sense experience, seem peculiarly germane to sense experience – and in a selective way: some statements to some experiences, others to others. Such statements, especially germane to particular experiences, I picture as near the periphery. But in this relation of "germaneness" I envisage nothing more than a loose association reflecting the relative likelihood, in practice, of our choosing one statement rather than another for revision in the event of recalcitrant experience. For example, we can imagine recalcitrant experiences to which we would surely be inclined to accommodate our system by re-evaluating just the statement that there are brick houses on Elm Street, together with related statements on the same topic. We can imagine other recalcitrant experiences to which we would be inclined to accommodate our system by re-evaluating just the statement that there are no centaurs, along with kindred statements. A recalcitrant experience can, I have already urged, be accommodated by any of various alternative re-evaluations in various alternative quarters of the total system; but, in the cases which we are now imagining, our natural tendency to disturb the total system as little as possible would lead us to focus our revisions upon these specific statements concerning brick houses or centaurs. These statements are felt, therefore, to have a sharper empirical reference than highly theoretical statements of physics or logic or ontology. The latter statements may be thought of as relatively centrally located within the total network, meaning merely that little preferential connection with any particular sense data obtrudes itself.

As an empiricist I continue to think of the conceptual scheme of science as a tool, ultimately, for predicting future experience in the light of past experience. Physical objects are conceptually imported into the situation as convenient intermediaries – not by definition in terms of experience, but simply as irreducible posits comparable, epistemologically, to the gods of Homer. Let me interject that for my part I do, qua lay physicist, believe in physical objects and not in Homer's gods; and I consider it a scientific error to believe otherwise. But in point of epistemological footing the physical objects and the gods differ only in degree and not in kind. Both sorts of entities enter our conception only as cultural posits. The myth of physical objects is epistemologically superior to most in that it has proved more efficacious than other myths as a device for working a manageable structure into the flux of experience.

Imagine, for the sake of analogy, that we are given the rational numbers. We develop an algebraic theory for reasoning about them, but we find it inconveniently complex, because certain functions such as square root lack

Early Analytic Philosophy

values for some arguments. Then it is discovered that the rules of our algebra can be much simplified by conceptually augmenting our ontology with some mythical entities, to be called irrational numbers. All we continue to be really interested in, first and last, are rational numbers; but we find that we can commonly get from one law about rational numbers to another much more quickly and simply by pretending that the irrational numbers are there too.

I think this a fair account of the introduction of irrational numbers and other extensions of the number system. The fact that the mythical status of irrational numbers eventually gave way to the Dedekind-Russell version of them as certain infinite classes of ratios is irrelevant to my analogy. That version is impossible anyway as long as reality is limited to the rational numbers and not extended to classes of them.

Now I suggest that experience is analogous to the rational numbers and that the physical objects, in analogy to the irrational numbers, are posits which serve merely to simplify our treatment of experience. The physical objects are no more reducible to experience than the irrational numbers to rational numbers, but their incorporation into the theory enables us to get more easily from one statement about experience to another.

The salient differences between the positing of physical objects and the positing of irrational numbers are, I think, just two. First, the factor of simplification is more overwhelming in the case of physical objects than in the numerical case. Second, the positing of physical objects is far more archaic, being indeed coeval, I expect, with language itself. For language is social and so depends for its development upon intersubjective reference.

Positing does not stop with macroscopic physical objects. Objects at the atomic level and beyond are posited to make the laws of macroscopic objects, and ultimately the laws of experience, simpler and more manageable; and we need not expect or demand full definition of atomic and subatomic entities in terms of macroscopic ones, any more than definition of macroscopic things in terms of sense data. Science is a continuation of common sense, and it continues the common-sense expedient of swelling ontology to simplify theory.

Physical objects, small and large, are not the only posits. Forces are another example; and indeed we are told nowadays that the boundary between energy and matter is obsolete. Moreover, the abstract entities which are the substance of mathematics – ultimately classes and classes of classes and so on up – are another posit in the same spirit. Epistemologically these are myths on the same footing with physical objects and gods, neither better nor worse except for differences in the degree to which they expedite our dealings with sense experiences.

The over-all algebra of rational and irrational numbers is under-determined by the algebra of rational numbers, but is smoother and more convenient; and it includes the algebra of rational numbers as a jagged or gerrymandered part. Total science, mathematical and natural and human, is similarly but more extremely underdetermined by experience. The edge of the system must be kept squared with experience; the rest, with all its elaborate myths or fictions, has as its objective the simplicity of laws.

Ontological questions, under this view, are on a par with questions of natural science. Consider the question whether to countenance classes as entities. This, as I have argued 'elsewhere,[10] is the question whether to quantify with respect to variables which take classes as values. Now Carnap has maintained[11] that this is a question not of matters of fact but of choosing a convenient language form, a convenient conceptual scheme or framework for science. With this I agree, but only on the proviso that the same be conceded regarding scientific hypotheses generally. Carnap has recognized[12] that he is able to preserve a double standard for ontological questions and scientific hypotheses only by assuming an absolute distinction between the analytic and the synthetic; and I need not say again that this is a distinction which I reject.

Some issues do, I grant, seem more a question of convenient conceptual scheme and others more a question of brute fact. The issue over there being classes seems more a question of convenient conceptual scheme; the issue over there being centaurs, or brick houses on Elm Street, seems more a question of fact. But I have been urging that this difference is only one of degree, and that it turns upon our vaguely pragmatic inclination to adjust one strand of the fabric of science rather than another in accommodating some particular recalcitrant experience. Conservatism figures in such choices, and so does the quest for simplicity.

Carnap, Lewis, and others take a pragmatic stand on the question of choosing between language forms, scientific frameworks; but their pragmatism leaves off at the imagined boundary between the analytic and the synthetic. In repudiating such a boundary I espouse a more thorough pragmatism. Each man is given a scientific heritage plus a continuing barrage of sensory stimulation; and the considerations which guide him in warping his scientific heritage to fit his continuing sensory promptings are, where rational, pragmatic.

---

[10]E.g., in "Notes on Existence and Necessity," *Journal of Philosophy*, XL (1943), 113-127.
[11]Carnap, "Empiricism, Semantics, and Ontology," *Revue internationale philosophie*, IV (1950), 20-40.
[12]*Op. cit.*, p. 32, footnote.

11

Analytic Philosophy Since 1950

We have now looked at and examined the work of some of the main figures in early analytic philosophy. Our survey of early analytic philosophy ended with Quine on analytic truth and ontology, so we may ask: what has happened in analytic philosophy since around 1950? Analytic philosophy has not gone away. Indeed, as we remarked back in Chapter 1, so far as we can discern, most philosophers in most English-speaking philosophy departments identify as part of the analytic tradition, and the reach of analytic philosophy now extends, for example, well into the German-speaking world and, indeed, may be regarded as something of a global phenomenon. In short, analytic philosophy is thriving.

As we noted in Chapter 1, there is no common doctrine or theory that unites all and only analytic philosophers, and the discussions in the subsequent chapters have exhibited the diversity of doctrines and theories in the analytic tradition. Indeed, while early analytic philosophers like Moore and Russell saw themselves as revolting against monism and idealism, opposition to these doctrines is not uniformly accepted among analytic philosophers, and in recent years there have been analytic defenses of both monist and idealist metaphysics.[1] In this chapter, we will look at some developments in analytic philosophy since around 1950, though our survey here is not at all intended to be exhaustive. We will also note various important works for further reading.[2]

---

[1]See, for example, Schaffer 2010 and Foster 1982.
[2]Unlike previous chapters, the books and articles mentioned in the present chapter are not included in the list of references at the end of the book (this, in part, is due to the sheer volume of books and articles mentioned in this chapter). We believe that the information here provided—book and article titles, along with author and publication date—is sufficient for any interested student to track down the relevant material.

570 Early Analytic Philosophy

Metaphysics: Aside from Quine's attempt to show that metaphysics and ontology can be fit into a broadly empiricist framework, an increasing number of analytic philosophers have been convinced, contra the logical empiricists, that central notions of metaphysics—notions like cause, necessity, essence, existence—are legitimate and can figure in genuine intellectual inquiry. Some of the more important work here is due to Saul Kripke (b. 1940), both in the form of his technical work in modal logic (the logic of necessity and possibility) as well as his non-technical but rigorous discussions in *Naming and Necessity* (1972).[3] This in turn has spurred much work on the notions of necessity and possibility including, for example, David Lewis's (1941–2001) *The Plurality of Worlds* (1986). There has also been a renewed interest in the traditional mind–body problem—the question of how consciousness and thought is related to physical reality. While this issue began to really take hold in contemporary analytic thinking with the publication of J. J. C. Smart's (1920–2012) "Sensations and Brain Processes" (1959) and Thomas Nagel's (b. 1937) "What is it Like to be a Bat?" (1974), among the more important works here is David Chalmers's (b. 1966) *The Conscious Mind* (1996), which argues against attempts to understand consciousness as a purely physical phenomenon. There has similarly been a renewed interest in the metaphysical problem of mental causation, the question of how experiences and thoughts can cause physical behavior. Important works on this topic include Donald Davidson's (1917–2003) "Mental Events" (1970) and Jaegwon Kim's (1934–2019) *Mind in a Physical World* (1998).

Ethics and value theory: Many philosophers have also been convinced, again contra the logical empiricists, that ethics, and what can be referred to as "value theory" more broadly, is a legitimate area of philosophical inquiry. With some exceptions, many analytic philosophers have come to believe that the "emotivist" view of ethical discourse due to Ayer and others cannot be sustained, and that ethical discourse indeed functions to describe the world, to attribute ethical properties to individuals, actions, and events. Aside from purely philosophical critiques, at least some of the motivation for moving towards more "realist" conceptions of ethics was likely in response to the atrocities committed by the Nazi regime during the Second World War.[4] This

---

[3] There is debate concerning the origins of some of Kripke's ideas, as at least some of them were anticipated by Ruth Barcan Marcus's (1921–2012) insights in "Modalities and Intensional Languages" (1961) and elsewhere.

[4] As suggested in Lipscomb 2021 in the context of discussing the significance of Anscomb's work, as well as that of Philippa Foot (1920–2010), Mary Midgley (1919–2018), and Iris Murdoch (1919–99) for the trajectory of contemporary ethical theory.

Analytic Philosophy Since 1950 **571**

has led to a strong interest in various traditional ethical theories, including utilitarianism, Kantian deontology, and virtue-based accounts of ethics of the sort discernable in some of Aristotle's works. Important works here include Anscombe's "Modern Moral Philosophy" (1958), as well as Christine Korsgaard's (b. 1952) *The Sources of Normativity* (1996) and Peter Singer's (b. 1946) *Practical Ethics* (1979). From a different perspective, some have argued that while the function of moral discourse is to describe the world, there are no genuine moral properties and that because of this moral discourse— discourse that aims to attribute to moral properties—is uniformly false; see J. L. Mackie's (1917–81) *Inventing Right and Wrong* (1977). There have also been various attempts to show, contra Moore, that goodness and other normative properties can be understood as part of the natural, physical world; see, for example, Frank Jackson's (b. 1943) *From Metaphysics to Ethics* (1998) and Peter Railton's (b. 1950) "Moral Realism" (1986). There has also been a renewed interest in political philosophy, philosophical inquiry into the nature and aims of political society. Important works here include John Rawls's (1921–2002) *A Theory of Justice* (1971) and Robert Nozick's (1938–2002) *Anarchy, State, and Utopia* (1974). Finally, there has been a surge of interest in applied ethics, which focuses on ethical issues in science, medicine, and technology.

Philosophy of science: Influenced in part by logical empiricism, which conceived of philosophy as, in part, the logical analysis of scientific discourse, philosophy of science has continued to thrive in the analytic tradition. Some of this literature, particularly around the middle of the twentieth century, is best conceived as working out details from within a broadly empiricist point of view. Thus Carl Hempel's (1905–97) *Aspects of Scientific Explanation* (1965) and Ernest Nagel's (1901–85) *The Structure of Science* (1961) focus on the logical structure of scientific theories and, especially, the nature and purpose of explanations within scientific discourse; likewise, Karl Popper's (1902–94) *The Logic of Scientific Discovery* (1959) challenges some central empiricist ideas about confirmation and falsification in scientific practice, while Thomas Kuhn's (1922–96) *The Structure of Scientific Revolutions* (1962), offers a novel picture of scientific practice and the development of new scientific theories from previous ones.

More recently, while differing in matters of detail, a prominent trend in philosophy of science has been to focus more on the details of actual scientific practice. In focusing on the details of actual scientific practice, philosophers of science have come to very different conclusions than the empiricists regarding the nature and structure of scientific theories. Important works

Early Analytic Philosophy

here include John Dupré's (b. 1952) *The Disorder of Things* (1993), Nancy Cartwright's (b. 1944) *How the Laws of Physics Lie* (1983), and Patricia Churchland's (b. 1943) *Neurophilosophy* (1986). Moreover, when looking at actual scientific practice and theories, philosophers of science have been impressed by the prevalence of so-called "mechanistic explanations"— roughly, explanations that account for the behavior of some system in terms of the components of that system and the relations between them. Important works here include William Bechtel (b. 1951) and Robert Richardson's *Discovering Complexity* (1993) along with Carl Craver's (b. 1967) *Explaining the Brain* (2007). Finally, there has been a considerable work at the intersection of philosophy of mind on the one hand and empirical psychology, cognitive science, and neuroscience on the other hand, with philosophers like Putnam, as well as Jerry Fodor (1935–2017), Daniel Dennett (b. 1942), and Paul Churchland (b. 1942) playing an important role in shaping how the results of these sciences have been interpreted and understood.

Philosophy of language: Following the pioneering work of Frege and Russell, philosophers in the analytic tradition have continued to engage in issues concerning reference, description, and meaning. While some of the work here has concerned the details of Frege's and Russell's doctrines—see, for example, Strawson's "On Referring" (1950)—much of the contemporary work on these topics can be viewed as reacting, in one way or another, to Kripke's *Naming and Necessity* and Putnam's "The Meaning of 'Meaning'" (1975), which challenged certain ideas about reference and descriptions due to Frege and Russell. Specifically, Kripke and Putnam noted that despite differing in details, Frege and Russell apparently held that both ordinary proper names and general terms like "water" and "gold" have robust descriptive content and that the reference of such expressions is fixed or determined by this descriptive content. Against this, Kripke and Putnam argued that in an important sense, both ordinary proper names and general terms like "water" and "gold" function more like labels and lack substantive descriptive content, and that the reference of such expressions is not fixed or determined by whatever descriptive content they might happen to have. Attempts to respond to Kripke and Putnam on these points are provided in Jackson's *From Metaphysics to Ethics* and Chalmers's "Two Dimensional Semantics" (2006), while Kripke's and Putnam's linguistic and semantic insights have been forcefully defended, for instance, in Scott Soames's (b. 1945) *Reference and Description* (2005).

Epistemology: As we saw in the discussions of Moore, Russell, and the logical empiricists, epistemological concerns—concerns about what we can know and how we can know it—played an important role in early analytic philosophy. In several different ways, analytic philosophers have continued to engage with these kinds of issues. From one direction, some analytic philosophers have sought to show—roughly in the manner suggested in Quine's "Epistemological Naturalized" (1969)—that central epistemological notions like knowledge and justification can be understood as referring to natural, and broadly physical, phenomena (for instance, in terms of causal relations between a knower and the external world). Important works here include Alvin Goldman's (b. 1938) "A Causal Theory of Knowing" (1967) and Hilary Kornblith's *Knowledge and Its Place in Nature* (2002). From a different direction, some analytic epistemologists have focused specifically on the concept of knowledge and how this concept can be analyzed. Following Edmund Getter's (1927–2021) discussions in "Is Knowledge Justified True Belief?" (1963), many analytic philosophers have come to believe, contra much traditional epistemology, that knowledge cannot be analyzed or defined in terms of justified belief—that to know that something is the case is not simply a matter of having a justified true belief that something is the case since, according to Gettier, there are scenarios in which one can have a justified true belief but lack the relevant piece of knowledge. Given this, they have sought to understand how, if at all, knowledge can be analyzed. Important works here include Ernest Sosa's "How to Defeat Opposition to Moore" (1999) and Timothy Williamson's (b. 1955) *Knowledge and Its Limits* (2000). Finally, those in the analytic tradition have continued to grapple with traditional skeptical problems concerning how, if at all, we can know about the world beyond our own minds; see, for example, James Pryor's (b. 1968) "The Skeptic and the Dogmatist" (2000) and Barry Stroud's (1935–2019) *The Significance of Philosophical Skepticism* (1984).

In presenting these recent trends and movements in the analytic tradition, the reader will have noticed that we have broken this down into subject matter: the movements in epistemology, ethics, metaphysics, and so on. Two remarks here are pertinent. First, this sort of approach would have been less appropriate in the context of early analytic philosophy, in which most thinkers could not be easily classified as, say, epistemologists or ethicists. Rather, when reflecting on the work, say, of Moore and Russell, they were engaged in various intellectual projects in various areas of philosophy and such thinkers typically sought to develop a broad, systematic view of how issues in various areas of philosophy fit together. With some exceptions to be sure, this is not currently the case in analytic philosophy. Rather, many of those currently working in the analytic tradition are best described as "specialists"—as working, say, specifically in epistemology or ethics. While we will not speculate on the causes of this move towards specialization, and will similarly not comment on its merits, in our view this tendency is one that will not soon go away. Nonetheless, this is a tendency that new analytic philosophers may wish to push back against. Bradley had a systematic picture of reality and our knowledge of reality, but so did Moore, Russell, and Wittgenstein. And while Russell often preached specialization, he certainly did not practice it.

Second, as we saw in several of the previous chapters—especially, perhaps, the respective chapters on Russell, Wittgenstein, and logical empiricism—early analytic philosophers were often interested in what we might refer to as "metaphilosophy," questions concerning the proper aims and methods for philosophical inquiry. This is a focus that does not fit neatly into any of the categories of philosophical reflection previously sketched in this chapter, though perhaps such "metaphilosophical" concerns often, though not always, have epistemological motivations. In any case, this is also an area of inquiry that has continued to be of interest for those in the analytic tradition; analytic philosophers have continued to self-consciously reflect on the very nature of philosophical inquiry, the sort of knowledge (if any!) that such inquiry can be expected to produce, along with various related issues. From a broadly epistemological point of view, this has resulted in various reflections on philosophical method, including the role of "intuitions" in philosophical inquiry and practice. Among the important works here are George Bealer's "Modal Epistemology and the Rationalist Renaissance" (2002) as well as Williamson's *The Philosophy of Philosophy* (2007). This, in turn, has in some cases motivated an interest in so-called "experimental philosophy," which involves, among other things, comparing intuitions on philosophically important topics across diverse cultures and populations; see, for example, Stephen Stich's (b. 1943) "Reflective Equilibrium, Analytic Epistemology and the Problem of Cognitive Diversity" (1998). From a more metaphysical point of view, metaphilosophical concerns have sometimes motivated a renewed interest in the kind of issues that occupied the empiricists concerning whether ontological and metaphysical questions have genuine content and admit of genuine answers; see, for example, Chalmers's "Verbal Disputes" (2011) along with Amie Thomasson's (b. 1968) *Ontology Made Easy* (2015).

This concludes our survey of analytic philosophy since around 1950. As we marked above, this brief survey is not intended to be exhaustive. Nonetheless, we hope that the material here will be sufficient for the interested student to engage with more recent trends in analytic philosophy and to make informed choices about future readings. We also hope that instructors not entirely satisfied with the references here provided will in turn offer alternative readings in more recent analytic philosophy! Analytic philosophy is thriving, and we believe that the readings suggested in this chapter, as well as those provided and suggested in previous chapters, will provide an excellent starting point for students—or anyone, for that matter—with a genuine interest in foundational issues concerning knowledge, reality, and value.

References

Primary sources

Bradley, F. H. ([1876] 1927), *Ethical Studies*, Oxford: Clarendon Press.

Bradley, F. H. ([1883] 2011), *The Principles of Logic*, Cambridge: Cambridge University Press.

Bradley, F. H. ([1893] 1969), *Appearance and Reality*, Oxford: Oxford University Press.

Bradley, F. H. (1935), "Relations", in H. H. Joachim (ed.), *Collected Essays*, Oxford: Clarendon Press.

Carnap, R. ([1932] 1959), "The Elimination of Metaphysics Through the Logical Analysis of Language", in A. J. Ayer (ed.), *Logical Positivism*, New York: The Free Press.

Collingwood, R. G. ([1933] 1950), *An Essay on Philosophical Method*, Oxford: Clarendon Press.

Frege, G. ([1879] 1967), *Concept-Script*, In J. van Heijenoort (ed.), *From Frege to Gödel: A Source Book in Mathematical Logic, 1879–1931*, Cambridge, MA: Harvard University Press.

Frege. G. ([1884] 1980), *The Foundations of Arithmetic*, Chicago: Northwestern University Press.

Frege, G. ([1891] 1997), "On Function and Concept", in M. Beaney (ed.), *The Frege Reader*, Oxford: Blackwell Publishing.

Frege, G. ([1892] 1997), "On Concept and Object", in M. Beaney (ed.), *The Frege Reader*, Oxford: Blackwell Publishing.

Frege, G. ([1892] 1970), "On Sense and Reference", in P. Geach and M. Black (eds), *Translations from the Philosophical Writings of Gottlob Frege*, Oxford: Basil Blackwell.

Frege, G. ([1892, 1903] 2013), *Basic Laws of Arithmetic*, Vol. 1 and 2, Oxford: Oxford University Press.

Frege, G. ([1918] 1997), "Negation", in M. Beaney (ed.), *The Frege Reader*, Oxford: Blackwell Publishing.

Frege, G. ([1918–19] 1956), "The Thought: A Logical Inquiry", *Mind* 65: 289–311.

Frege, G. ([1923] 1963), "Compound Thoughts", *Mind* 72: 1–17.

Frege, G. (1979), *Posthumous Writings*, Oxford: Blackwell Publishing.

578 References

Frege, G. (1980), *Philosophical and Mathematical Correspondence*, Chicago: University of Chicago Press.

Hahn, H., Neurath, O. and Carnap, R. ([1929] 1973), "The Scientific Conception of the World: The Vienna Circle", in M. Neurath and R.S. Cohen (eds), *Empiricism and Sociology*, Dordrecht: Springer.

Hempel, C. (1950), "Problems and Changes in the Empiricist Criterion of Meaning", *Revenue Internationale de Philosophie* 11: 41–63.

Jones, E. E. C. (1890), *Elements of Logic as a Science of Propositions*, Edinburgh: T & T Clark.

Jones, E. E. C. (1892), *An Introduction to General Logic*, Longmans, Green, & Co.

Jones, E. E. C. (1910), "Mr. Russell's Objections to Frege's Analysis of Propositions", *Mind* 19: 379–86.

Jones, E. E. C. (1910–11), "A New Law of Thought", *Proceedings of the Aristotelian Society* 11: 166–86.

Jones, E. E. C. (1911), *A New Law of Thought and Its Logical Bearings*, Cambridge: Cambridge University Press.

Jones, E. E. C. (1922), *As I Remember: An Autobiographical Ramble*, London: A & C Black.

Moore, G. E. ([1897] 2011), "The Metaphysical Basis of Ethics", in T. Baldwin and C. Preti (eds), *G. E. Moore: Early Philosophical Writings*, Cambridge: Cambridge University Press.

Moore, G. E. (1899), "The Nature of Judgement", *Mind* 8: 176–93.

Moore, G. E. ([1903a] 1993), "The Refutation of Idealism", in T. Baldwin (ed.), *G. E. Moore: Selected Writings*, New York: Routledge.

Moore, G. E. ([1903b] 1993), *Principia Ethica*, T. Baldwin (ed.), Cambridge: Cambridge University Press.

Moore, G. E. (1919), "External and Internal Relations", *Proceedings of the Aristotelian Society* 20: 40–62.

Moore, G. E. ([1925] 1993), "A Defence of Common Sense", in T. Baldwin (ed.), *G. E. Moore: Selected Writings*, New York: Routledge.

Moore, G. E. ([1939] 1993), "Proof of an External World", in T. Baldwin (ed.), *G. E. Moore: Selected Writings*. London: Routledge.

Moore, G. E. (1942a), "Autobiography", in P. A. Schlipp (ed.), *The Philosophy of G. E. Moore*, Illinois: Open Court.

Moore, G. E. (1942b), "Reply to My Critics", in P. A. Schlipp (ed.), *The Philosophy of G. E. Moore*, Illinois: Open Court.

Russell, B. (1897), *An Essay on the Foundations of Geometry*, Cambridge: Cambridge University Press.

Russell, B. (1903), *The Principles of Mathematics*, Cambridge: Cambridge University Press.

Russell, B. (1905), "On Denoting", *Mind* 14: 479–93.

Russell, B. (1910), "Knowledge by Acquaintance and Knowledge by Description", *Proceedings of the Aristotelian Society* 11: 108–28.

Russell, B. (1912), *The Problems of Philosophy*, London: Williams & Norgate.

Russell, B. ([1914] 2009), *Our Knowledge of the External World*, New York: Routledge.

Russell, B. (1917), *Political Ideals*, New York: The Century Co.

Russell, B. ([1918] 2009), *The Philosophy of Logical Atomism*, New York: Routledge.

Russell, B. (1919), *Introduction to Mathematical Philosophy*, London: George Allen and Unwin.

Russell, B. (1921), *The Analysis of Mind*, London: George Allen and Unwin.

Russell, B. ([1924] 1993), "Logical Atomism", in D. Pears (ed.), *The Philosophy of Logical Atomism*, Illinois: Open Court.

Russell, B. (1927a), *Why I Am Not a Christian*, London: Watts.

Russell, B. (1927b), *The Analysis of Matter*, London: Keegan Paul, Trench, and Trubner.

Russell, B. (1929), *Marriage and Morals*, London: George Allen and Unwin.

Russell, B. ([1951] 1967), *The Autobiography of Bertrand Russell: 1872 – 1914*, London: George Allen and Unwin.

Russell, B. (1959), *My Philosophical Development*, London: George Allen and Unwin.

Russell, B. (1992), *The Collected Papers of Bertrand Russell*, Vol. 6, New York: Routledge.

Russell, B. and Whitehead, A. N. (1910, 1912, 1913), *Principia Mathematica*, Vol. 1, 2 and 3, Cambridge: Cambridge University Press.

Quine, W. V. O. (1934), *A System of Logistic*, Cambridge, MA: Harvard University Press.

Quine, W. V. O. (1936), "Truth by Convention", in *Philosophical Essays for Alfred North Whitehead*, New York: Longmans, Green, & Co.

Quine, W. V. O. (1948), "On What There Is", *The Review of Metaphysics* 2: 21–38.

Quine, W. V. O. (1951), "Two Dogmas of Empiricism", *The Philosophical Review* 60: 20–43.

Quine, W. V. O. (1953), *From a Logical Point of* View, Cambridge, MA: Harvard University Press.

Quine, W. V. O. (1960), *Word and Object*, Cambridge, MA: The MIT Press.

Quine, W. V. O. (1981), *Theories and Things*, Cambridge, MA: Harvard University Press.

Quine, W. V. O. (1985), *The Time of My Life: An Autobiography*, Cambridge, MA: The MIT Press.

Quine, W. V. O. (1986), "Autobiography", in L. Hahn and P. A. Schilpp (eds), *The Philosophy of W. V. Quine*, Illinois: Open Court.

Quine, W. V. O. (1995), *From Stimulus to Science*, Cambridge, MA: Harvard University Press.

Schlick, M. (1936), "Meaning and Verification", *The Philosophical Review* 45: 339–69.

Schlick, M. ([1930] 1939), *Problems of Ethics*, New York: Prentice-Hall.

Stebbing, L. S. (1930), *A Modern Introduction to Logic*, London: Methuen.

Stebbing, L. S. (1932–33), "The Method of Analysis in Metaphysics", *Proceedings of the Aristotelian Society* 33: 65–94.

Stebbing, L. S. (1933), "Logical Positivism and Analysis", *Proceedings of the British Academy*: 53–87.

Stebbing, L. S. (1937), *Philosophy and the Physicists*, London: Methuen.

Stebbing, S. (1939), *Thinking to Some Purpose*, Hammondsworth: Penguin.

Wittgenstein, L. (1922), *Tractatus Logico-Philosophicus*, C. K. Ogden (trans.), London: Kegan Paul, Trench, Trubner & Co.

Wittgenstein, L. (1926), "Some Remarks on Logical Form", *Proceedings of the Aristotelian Society* 9: 162–71.

Wittgenstein, L. ([1953] 2001), *Philosophical Investigations*, G. E. M. Anscombe (trans.), Oxford: Blackwell.

Wittgenstein, L. (1958), *The Blue and Brown Books*, New York: Harper & Row.

Wittgenstein, L. (1969), *On Certainty*, New York: Harper & Row.

Wittgenstein, L. *Wittgenstein's Nachlass: The Bergen Electronic Edition*, Oxford: Oxford University Press.

Secondary sources

Ayer, A. J. (1959), "Editors Introduction", in A. J. Ayer (ed.), *Logical Positivism*. New York: The Free Press.

Ayer, A. J. (1972), *Bertrand Russell*, New York: The Viking Press.

Baldwin, T. (1990), *G.E. Moore*, New York: Routledge.

Baldwin, T. and Preti, C. (2011), "Editor's Introduction", in T. Baldwin and C. Preti (eds), *G. E. Moore: Early Philosophical Writings*, Cambridge: Cambridge University Press.

Barcan Marcus, R. (1961), "Modalities and Intensional Languages", *Synthese* 13: 303–22.

Beaney, M. (1997), "Introduction", in M. Beaney (ed.), *The Frege Reader*, Oxford: Blackwell Publishing.

Beaney, M. (2016), "Susan Stebbing and the Early Reception of Logical Empiricism in Britain", in C. Dambock (ed.), *Influences on the Aufbau*. Switzerland: Springer.

Beaney, M. (2017), *Analytic Philosophy: A Very Short Introduction*, Oxford: Oxford University Press.

References   581

Beaney, M. and Chapman, S. (2017), "Susan Stebbing", *Stanford Encyclopedia of Philosophy*. Available online: https://plato.stanford.edu/archives/sum2017/entries/stebbing/

Biletzki, A. and Matar, A. (2020), "Ludwig Wittgenstein", *Stanford Encyclopedia of Philosophy*. Available online: https://plato.stanford.edu/entries/wittgenstein/

Blanshard, B. (1925), "Francis Herbert Bradley", *The Journal of Philosophy* 22: 5–15.

Blanshard, B. (1952), "The Philosophy of Analysis", *Proceedings of the British Academy*: 39–69.

Brentano, F. ([1874] 2014), *Psychology from an Empirical Standpoint*, New York: Routledge.

Candlish, S. (2007), *The Russell/Bradley Dispute and its Significance for Twentieth-Century Philosophy*, Basingstoke: Palgrave Macmillan.

Candlish, S. and Basile, P. (2017), "Francis Hebert Bradley", *Stanford Encyclopedia of Philosophy*. Available online: https://plato.stanford.edu/entries/bradley/

Carnap, R. (1963), "Intellectual Autobiography", in P. A. Schilpp (ed.), *The Philosophy of Rudolf Carnap*. Illinois: Open Court.

Coliva, A. (2004), "'Proof of an External World': Transmission-Failure, Begging the Question or Dialectical Ineffectiveness? Moore, Wright, and Pryor", in A. Coliva and E. Picardi (eds), *Wittgenstein Today*. Padova: Il Poligrafo.

Collingwood, R. G. ([1939] 1982), *An Autobiography*, Oxford: Oxford University Press.

Creath, R. (2017), "Logical Empiricism", *Stanford Encyclopedia of Philosophy*. Available online: https://plato.stanford.edu/entries/logical-empiricism/

Della Rocca, M. (2020), *The Parmenidean Ascent*, Oxford: Oxford University Press.

Dummett, M. (1973), *Frege: Philosophy of Language*, Cambridge, MA: Harvard University Press.

Eddington, A. (1928), *The Nature of the Physical World*, Cambridge: Cambridge University Press.

Ewing, A. C. ([1934] 2013), *Idealism: A Critical Survey*, New York: Routledge.

Foster, J. (1982), *The Case for Idealism*, New York: Routledge.

Friedman, M. (2000), *A Parting of the Ways*, Illinois: Open Court.

Glock, H. (2008), *What is Analytic Philosophy?* Cambridge: Cambridge University Press.

Grattan-Guinness, I. (1977), *Dear Russell, Dear Jourdain: A Commentary on Russell's Logic*, New York: Columbia University Press.

Griffin, N. (1991), *Russell's Idealist Apprenticeship*, Oxford: Clarendon Press.

Grice, H. P. and Strawson, P. F. (1956), "In Defense of a Dogma", *The Philosophical Review* 65: 141–58.

582   **References**

Heil, J. (2015), *The Universe as We Find It*, Oxford: Oxford University Press.

Horgan, T. and Timmons, M. (eds) (2006), *Metaethics After Moore*, Oxford: Oxford University Press.

Hume, D. ([1748] 1975), *An Enquiry Concerning Human Understanding*, Oxford: Clarendon Press.

Irvine, A. (2019), "Bertrand Russell", *Stanford Encyclopedia of Philosophy*. Available online: https://plato.stanford.edu/entries/russell/

Irvine, A. and Deutsch, H. (2016), "Russell's Paradox", *Stanford Encyclopedia of Philosophy*. Available online: https://plato.stanford.edu/entries/russell-paradox/

Jacquette, D. (2019), *Frege: A Philosophical Biography*, Cambridge: Cambridge University Press.

Jeans, J. (1930), *The Mysterious Universe*, Cambridge: Cambridge University Press.

James, W. ([1902] 1929), *The Varieties of Religious Experience*, New York: Random House.

James, W. ([1909] 1977), *A Pluralistic Universe*, Cambridge, MA: Harvard University Press.

Janssen-Lauret, F. (2017), "Susan Stebbing, Incomplete Symbols, and Foundherentist Meta-Ontology", *Journal for the History of Analytical Philosophy* 5: 7–17.

Lipscomb, B. (2021), *The Women are Up to Something*, Oxford: Oxford University Press.

Lycan, W. (2001), "Moore Against the New Skeptics", *Philosophical Studies* 103: 35–53.

Mac Cumhaill, C. and Wiseman, R. (2022), *Metaphysical Animals: How Four Women Brought Philosophy Back to Life*, London and New York: Knopf/Doubleday.

Malcolm, N. ([1958] 2001), *Ludwig Wittgenstein: A Memoir*, Oxford: Oxford University Press.

Mauthner, F. (1901, 1906, 1923), *Contributions to a Critique of Language*, Vol. 1, 2, and 3. Leipzig: Meiner.

Meinong, A. ([1904] 1960), "The Theory of Objects", in R. Chisholm (ed.), *Realism and the Background of Phenomenology*. Illinois: The Free Press.

Mendelson, R. (1996), "Diary: Written by professor Dr Gottlob Frege in the time from 10 March to 9 April 1924", *Inquiry* 39: 303–42.

Miller, A. (2007), *Philosophy of Language*, New York: Routledge.

Misak, C. (2016), *Cambridge Pragmatism*, Oxford: Oxford University Press.

Monk. R. (1990), *Ludwig Wittgenstein: The Duty of Genius*, New York: Penguin Books.

Monk, R. (1996), *The Spirit of Solitude: Bertrand Russell, 1872–1921*, New York: The Free Press.

Monk, R. (2001), *The Ghost of Madness: Bertrand Russell, 1921–1970,* New York: The Free Press.

Morris, K. (2018), *Physicalism Deconstructed*, Cambridge: Cambridge University Press.

Morris, K. and Preti, C. (2015), "How to Read Moore's 'Proof of an External World'", *Journal for the History of Analytical Philosophy* 4: 1–16.

Nuccetelli, S. and Seay, G. (eds) (2007), *Themes From G. E. Moore: New Essays in Epistemology and Ethics*, Oxford: Oxford University Press.

Ostertag, G. (2020), "Emily Elizabeth Constance Jones", *Stanford Encyclopedia of Philosophy*. Available online: https://plato.stanford.edu/entries/emily-elizabeth-constance-jones/

Passmore, J. (1967), "Logical Positivism", in P. Edwards (ed.), *The Encyclopedia of Philosophy*, New York: Macmillan.

Preti, C. (2019), "What Russell Meant When He Called Moore a Logician", in S. LaPointe (ed.), *Logic from Kant to Russell: Laying the Foundations for Analytic Philosophy*, New York: Routledge.

Preti, C. (Forthcoming), "Yours Fraternally: Russell and Moore", in K. Klement (ed.), *The Oxford Handbook of Bertrand Russell*, Oxford: Oxford University Press.

Preti, C. (2022), *The Metaphysical Basis of Ethics: G. E. Moore and the Origins of Analytic Philosophy*, Basingstoke: Palgrave Macmillan.

Proops, I. (2014), "Russellian Acquaintance Revisited", *Journal of the History of Philosophy* 52: 779–811.

Pryor, J. (2000), "The Skeptic and the Dogmatist", *Noûs* 34: 517–49.

Pryor, J. (2004), "What's Wrong With Moore's Argument?" *Philosophical Issues* 14: 349–78.

Putnam, H. ([1988] 1990), "The Greatest Logical Positivist", in *Realism with Human Face*, Cambridge, MA: Harvard University Press.

Ramsey, F. (1923), "Critical Notice of *Tractatus Logico-Philosophicus*", *Mind* 32: 465–78.

Russell, B. (1922), "Introduction to *Tractatus Logico-Philosophicus*", in *Tractatus Logico-Philosophicus*, C.K. Ogden (trans.), London: Kegan Paul, Trench, Trubner & Co.

Russell, B. (1944), "My Mental Development", in P.A. Schilpp (ed.), *The Philosophy of Bertrand Russell*, Chicago: Northwestern University Press.

Russell, B. (1951), "Obituary: Ludwig Wittgenstein", *Mind* 60: 297–8.

Russell, B. (1992), "Letter to van Heijenoort", in N. Griffin (ed.), *The Selected Letters of Bertrand Russell: The Private Years, 1884–1914*, New York: Routledge.

Schaffer, J. (2010), "Monism: The Priority of the Whole", *Philosophical Review* 119: 31–76,

References

Sellars, W. (1956), "Empiricism and the Philosophy of Mind", in H. Feigl and M. Scriven (eds), *Minnesota Studies in the Philosophy of Science*, Minnesota: University of Minnesota Press.

Sluga, H. (1980), *Gottlob Frege*, New York: Routledge.

Uebel, T. (2019), "Vienna Circle", *Stanford Encyclopedia of Philosophy*. Available online: https://plato.stanford.edu/entries/vienna-circle/

Von Wright, G. H. ([1954] 2001), "A Biographical Sketch", in N. Malcolm, *Ludwig Wittgenstein: A Memoir*, Oxford: Oxford University Press.

Waithe, M. E. and Cicero, S. (1995), "E. E. Constance Jones", in M. E. Waithe, *A History of Women Philosophers*, Vol. 4, Dordrecht: Kluwer.

Weiler, G. (1958), "On Fritz Mauthner's Critique of Language", *Mind* 67: 80–7.

Wright, C. (2002), "(Anti-)Sceptics Simple and Subtle: G. E. Moore and John McDowell", *Philosophy and Phenomenological Research* 65: 330–48.

Zalta, E. (2019), "Gottlob Frege", *Stanford Encyclopedia of Philosophy*. Available online: https://plato.stanford.edu/entries/frege/

Index

Abbe, E. 152

Absolute, the 15–18, 43, 45, 46, 47, 239, 241, 408

abstraction 11, 18, 23, 24, 30, 32, 36, 37, 41, 42, 44, 53, 70, 105, 210

acquaintance 217–20, 251, 262, 263–78 *passim*, 314, 383, 494, 505

Ambrose, A. 329

analysis 4, 153, 154, 163, 173, 177, 288, 289, 368, 369, 421, 426, 435, 436, 444, 528, 535, 536, 537, 548, 571

  analytic philosophy and 5, 6

  different senses of 5, 495–520 *passim*

  Jones and 300–3, 306, 307, 308, 313, 316

  Jones on Frege's analysis of propositions 283, 285, 291–9 *passim*, 301

  Moore and 59, 60, 74–9, 87, 91, 92, 98, 99, 112, 121, 122, 125, 126, 127, 129, 130

  Russell and 3, 214–18, 222, 223, 224, 234, 236, 237, 252, 255, 266, 269, 272, 274–7, 367, 372, 527, 536, 537

  Stebbing on xi, 452–6, 459, 460, 469, 475, 480, 481, 495–520 *passim*

  Wittgenstein and 339, 343, 350

analytic philosophy

  analysis and 5, 6

  continental philosophy and 6, 7

  linguistic philosophy and 4, 5

  pragmatism and xii

  since 1950 569–76

  themes and ideas 1–7

analytic truth/analyticity 69, 159, 165, 374, 375, 434, 523–7, 547–67 *passim*

Anscombe, G. E. M. 318, 571

appearance 4, 12, 16–18, 20–4, 28, 33–9, 41, 42, 45, 46, 129, 133, 219, 241, 248, 268, 363, 399, 463, 467

a priori 159, 165, 240–3, 326, 337, 357, 373, 374, 375, 393, 429–34, 445, 448, 516, 519, 523, 529

Arendt, H. 6, 7

Aristotle 82, 153, 167 n.5, 280, 298, 299, 475, 476, 548, 549, 564, 571

Aquinas, T. 244

Austin, J. L. 329

Ayer, A. J. xi, 157 n.3, 209 n.2, 219, 362, 363 n.1, 367, 368, 371–5, 421–50 *passim*, 454, 460, 523, 570

Bacon, F. 470

Bain, A. 468 n.2

Baldwin, T. 51 n.2, 56 n.4

Barcan Marcus, R. 570 n.3

Basile, P. 10 n.1

Bealer, G. 574

Beaney, M. 5 n.2, 153 n.2, 454 n.2

Bechtel, W. 572

Bedeutung, *see* reference, Frege on

Bentham, J. 92, 93, 94

Bergson, H. 240

Berkeley, G. 11, 73, 79, 123, 124, 363, 393, 492, 493

Biletzki, A. 320 n.4

Black, D. 209

Black, M. 431 n.7

Blanshard, B. 10

Bloomsbury group 50

Boltzman, L. 362

Boynton, M. 523

586 **Index**

Bradley, F. H. 4, 9-48 *passim*, 50, 51, 53,
    60, 75, 151, 208 n.1, 209–13, 220,
    230, 235, 237, 241, 252 n.5, 368,
    452, 453, 503, 530, 574
  biographical information about 9, 10
  idealism and 11, 17
  influence 9
  our knowledge of reality, on 38–47
  primary and secondary qualities, on
    20–4
  relations and 11–16, 28–34
  Russell's criticisms of 211, 212, 238,
    239, 241, 242
  substantive and adjective, on 24–8
  things in themselves, on 34–8
Brahms, J. 318
Braithwaite, R. 454, 503 n.22, 510 n.35
Brentano, F. 528 n.2
Bridgman, P. C. 380
Burtt, E. A. 495

Caird, W. 11
Cambridge Apostles 50
Cambridge University 6, 50, 51, 152, 209,
    280, 281, 318, 319, 320, 453, 454, 497
Candlish, S. 10 n.1, 14 n.3, 14 n.4, 15 n.5,
    213 n.5
Cantor, G. 543
Carnap, R. 152, 219, 362, 367, 368, 370,
    371, 382, 390, 392, 393, 402–20
    passim, 454, 460, 496, 496 n.6, 504,
    504 n.25, 507–9, 509 n.34, 510–13,
    522, 530, 543, 547 n.1, 550, 550 n.3,
    551, 554 n.4, 556 n.6, 557, 559, 561,
    561 n.9, 562, 563, 567, 567 n.12
Cartwright, N. 572
categorical statements/propositions 153,
    288, 300, 308, 315
certainty 39, 57, 77, 108, 109, 113, 117,
    125, 130, 201, 240, 384, 414, 422,
    432, 438
Chalmers, D. 570, 572, 574
Chapman, S. 454 n.2
Churchland, P. M. 572

Churchland, P. S. 572
Cicero, S. 283 n.4
Clayton, N. 523
Coliva, A. 59
Collingwood, R. G. 10
common sense 380, 422, 534, 539, 566
  analytic philosophy and 4
  Moore and 56–60, 107–30 *passim*
  Russell and 213, 219, 220, 243, 246,
    363
  Stebbing and 457, 485, 486, 487, 499
Comte, A. 496, 496 n.5
connotation 277, 287, 291–300 *passim*,
    301, 308, 309, 310, 313, 315, 548
consciousness 17, 18, 54, 62, 66, 71–8,
    101, 162, 163, 169, 194–202, 314,
    315, 394, 397, 398, 399, 401, 491,
    494, 570
continental philosophy
  analytic philosophy and 6, 7
  philosophers in the tradition 6
contradiction 15, 26, 27, 33, 36, 37, 39, 40,
    41, 44, 67, 69, 70, 105, 106, 144,
    155, 156, 157, 210, 224, 228, 231,
    236, 236 n.10, 237, 241, 243, 253–6,
    262, 273, 280, 281, 282, 292, 293,
    300, 302, 311, 324, 326, 353, 354,
    355, 358, 366, 374, 386, 388, 412,
    417, 426–30, 432, 456, 474–7, 494,
    501, 502, 529, 535, 536, 546
copula 66, 68, 213–14, 282, 292, 341, 381,
    414, 415
Craver, C. 572

Davidson, D. 547 n.1, 570
de Beauvoir, S. 6
Deleuze, G. 6
Derrida, J. 6
DeMorgan, A. 233 n.6, 231 n.4
Dennett, D. 572
denote/denotation
  Jones on 284–9, 291–300 *passim*,
    300–16 *passim*
  Russell on 213–17, 250–63 *passim*

Descartes, R. 132, 149, 217, 219, 241, 398, 415, 492, 493
descriptions 214–17, 266, 509, 527, 528, 250–63 *passim*, 263–78 *passim*
Dilthey, W. 419
Duhem, P. 526
Dummett, M. 152
Dupre, J. 572

Eddington, A. 456, 457, 458, 483, 484, 484 n.2, 485, 485 n.4, 486, 488, 489–92, 492 n.13, 494, 512
Einstein, A. 380, 515, 564
Ely, D. 51
equality 165, 232, 239, 247, 248, 341
    see also identity
esse is *percipi* 62–80 *passim*
ethics 3, 5, 6, 9, 185, 289, 570, 571, 573, 574
    emotivism and 56, 434–44 *passim*
    intuition and 56
    logical empiricism and xi, 365, 366, 371, 372, 373, 417, 421, 434–44 *passim*
    Moore on 2, 50, 51, 55, 56, 60, 80–107 *passim*
    naturalistic fallacy and 55, 56
    Wittgenstein on 326, 358
Euclid. 209, 425, 430, 431
Ewing, A. C. 14 n.4
extension 21, 23, 24
external world, the
    Moore's proof of 58–60, 131–50 *passim*

facts 28, 37, 43, 45, 70, 202, 249, 250, 321–4, 326, 328, 333, 334, 335, 337, 338, 345–8, 350, 351, 354, 359, 372, 374, 385, 386, 395, 398, 422, 424, 432, 439, 442, 444, 459, 495, 497, 500, 513, 514, 516, 517, 519
    mental 65, 73, 74, 76, 119–24, 130
    physical 119, 123, 124, 310
Finch, E. 209
Fodor, J. 572
Foot, P. 570 n.4

Forster, E. M. 50
Foster, J. 569 n.1
Frege, A. 153
Frege, G. ix, xi, 2, 6, 151–205 *passim*, 208, 215, 217, 251, 251 n.1, 254, 254 n.9, 255, 280–5, 285 n.5, 285 n.6, 286–9, 291–5, 297, 299, 301, 319, 328, 332, 338, 341, 348, 352, 353, 356, 362, 363, 367, 373, 374, 455, 496, 535, 538, 542, 548, 572
    biographical information about 151–3
    identity statements 159, 165–7, 185
    logic and logicism 153–8
    philosophy of language 158–63, 165–85 *passim*, 185–205 *passim*
    sense and reference 158–62, 165–85 *passim*
    thoughts 162–3, 195–205 *passim*
    truth 170–4, 185–91

geometry 209, 240, 242, 337, 366, 389, 430, 431, 433, 481
Gettier, E. 573
Glock, H. J. 1
God 124, 125, 337, 358, 359, 367, 407, 408, 414, 444–9, 493
Goldman, A. 573
good
    emotivism and 371–3, 434–44
    Moore on 55–6, 80–107 *passim*
Goodman, N. xi, 543 n.1, 547 n.1
Godel, K. 155, 362
Grice, H. P. 329, 524, 525
Griffin, N. 209 n.2, 210 n.3
Green, T. H. 11
Grelling, K. 362

Hahn, H. 362, 368, 433 n.13
Hahn-Neurath, O. 362
Hamilton, W. 474 n.4
Harvard University 522, 523
Hedonism 93
Hegel, G. F. 11, 51, 71, 102, 105, 209, 210, 246, 256, 292, 414, 416

588 Index

Heidegger, M. 6, 367, 410 n.2, 412, 416
Hempel, C. 362, 369 n.2, 571
Hilbert, D. 543
Hobbes, T. 302
Hume, D. 11, 363, 364, 366, 367, 374, 388,
    421, 422, 504, 529, 547, 561, 564
Husserl, E. 6, 7, 152

idealism 170, 210, 220, 243, 264, 281, 393,
    418, 457, 569
  Bradley and 11, 17, 43, 44, 45
  Moore's critique of 50–5, 57–60,
    62–80 *passim*, 112–16, 119–24
    passim
identity 26, 27, 29, 73, 75, 225 n.1, 347,
    429, 433, 456, 475, 475 n.5, 477,
    548, 556
  Evening Star/Morning Star example
    159, 166, 170, 538, 548
  Frege on 158, 159, 165, 166, 167, 185
  "is" and 213, 214, 287
  Jones on 280–5, 287, 288, 291, 292,
    295, 297, 300–4, 306–10, 312–16
  Russell on 213, 214, 226, 227, 228, 232,
    233, 237, 239, 247, 254, 256, 262,
    272–5, 277
inner world, the
  Frege on 194, 197, 198, 201. 203, 204,
    205
Irigaray, L. 6
Irvine, A. 157 n.3, 209 n.2

James, W. xii n.1, 10, 10 n.2, 208, 208 n.1,
    217 n.8, 244, 321 n.5
Janssen-Lauret, F. 454 n.2
Jeans, J. 456, 457, 485, 486 n.6
Jevons, W. S. 291 n.3, 302, 304
Joachim, H. 11
Joad, C. E. M. 494
Jackson, F. 571, 572
Johnson, S. 467
Johnson, W. E. 478
Jones, E. E. C. xi, 217, 273, 274, 279–316
    passim

biographical information 279, 280
dispute with Russell 284–9
Frege and 281–5, 285 n.5, 285 n.6,
    286–9, 291–5, 297, 299, 301
identity statements on 280–5, 287,
    288, 291, 292, 295, 297, 300–4,
    306–10, 312–16
Joseph, H. W. 477

Kant, I. 11, 16, 51, 58, 69, 79, 131–4, 138,
    140, 141, 146, 148, 150, 165, 236
    n.10, 388, 414, 417, 422, 423, 426,
    427, 430, 431, 432, 443, 444, 447,
    471
Keynes, J. M. 50
Keynes, J. N. 477
Kim, J. 570
Kripke, S. 570, 570 n.3, 572
Koorsgaard, C. 571
Kornblith, H. 573
Kuhn, T. 571

Langford C. H. 429 n.3, 429 n.4
Leibniz, G. 173, 173 n.12, 235, 237, 238,
    547, 550, 553
Lewis, C. I. 380–5, 389, 391, 392, 393, 400,
    429 n.3, 429 n.4, 530, 554 n.4, 560
    n.7, 567
Lewis, D. 570
Lichtenberg, G. 398
Lipscomb, B. 570 n.4
Locke, J. 481, 561, 564
logic 2, 9, 51, 52, 152, 162, 163, 178, 185,
    186, 188 n.1, 202, 208, 211, 213–16,
    225, 231, 239–50, 252, 255, 260,
    262, 263, 269, 318, 319, 321, 325,
    332, 333, 337, 344, 345, 346, 349,
    356, 366, 373–5, 386, 388, 389, 402,
    404, 408, 411, 412, 413, 414, 415,
    417, 422–6, 429, 430, 432, 433, 434,
    442, 443, 521, 523, 526, 527, 529,
    536, 562, 564, 565, 570
  analytic philosophy and 2, 3
  Aristotelean 153, 154, 280–3

form and 153, 244, 245, 249, 250, 282, 283, 286, 288, 323, 324, 334, 336, 337, 340, 341, 344, 349, 367, 372, 412, 452, 456, 480
Frege and 152–8
Jones on 279–89, 291–316 *passim*
logicism and 153–8
Stebbing on 452–6, 459, 460, 462–81 *passim*, 496, 500, 502, 503, 504, 516, 519
logical empiricism
Berlin Society and 362
ethics and 371–3, 434–44 *passim*
mathematics, the *a priori*, and 373–5, 421–34 *passim*
metaphysics and 363–71, 402–20 *passim*
Vienna Circle and 362
logical truth 374, 429, 523, 526, 527, 549, 550, 551, 554, 560
Lotze, H. 235, 280, 281, 282, 285, 292, 302
Lycan, W. 59

Malcolm, N. 318, 320, 320 n.4, 329
MacColl, H. 261
Mac Cumhaill, C. 454
MacDonald, M. 505 n.27
McGuinness, B. xi
Mach, E. 362, 393, 496
Mackie, J. L. 571
McTaggart, J. M. E. 50, 56 n.4, 209
Matar, A. 320 n.4
materialism 11, 22, 23, 24, 264, 457
see also physicalism
mathematics
logical empiricism and 373–5, 417, 418, 421–34 *passim*
logicism and 153–8
Mauthner, F. 328 n.6, 344
Meinong, A. 215, 251, 254, 254 n.7, 255, 256, 261, 273, 293
Menger, K. 429 n.3
mental facts 65, 73, 74, 76, 119–24, 130
mental science 51

metaphysics xi, 3, 5, 6, 10, 11, 18, 24, 34, 51, 52, 60, 155, 210, 220, 242, 246, 269, 326, 363–70, 402, 403, 406, 408, 409, 410, 412–21, 422, 435, 444, 452, 454, 459, 492, 494, 496, 523, 527, 529, 530, 531, 539, 547, 569, 570, 573
Midgley, M. 570 n.4
Mill, J. S. 73, 93, 129, 299, 302, 373, 374, 386, 423, 424, 425, 476 n.9, 480, 496, 513, 519
Misak, C. 12 n.1, 208 n.1, 217 n.8, 321 n.5
mode of presentation, *see* sense, Frege on
Monism
Bradley on 11–16, 28–34
organic unities and 53, 105–7
Russell's critique of 222–50 *passim*
Moore, G. E. ix, xi, 2, 4, 5, 6, 10, 14 n.4, 18, 49–150 *passim*, 151, 158, 161, 163, 209, 210, 213, 221, 225 n.1, 283, 319, 321, 329, 371, 372, 441, 442, 452, 453, 454, 459, 495, 495 n.2, 496–500, 503, 504, 513, 513 n.37, 516, 517, 519, 569, 571, 572, 573, 574
biographical information 50–1
common sense, defense of 56–60, 107–30 *passim*
external world, proof of 58–60, 131–50 *passim*
idealism, critique of 51–4, 62–80 *passim*
monism, critique of 51–4
naturalistic fallacy 55–6, 87, 93, 94
organic unity 53, 100–7
Monk, R. 209 n.2, 320 n.4
Morrell, O. 283
Morris, K. 60 n.7, 375 n.5
Murdoch, I. 570 n.4

Nagel, E. 571
Nagel, T. 570
names 66, 389, 399, 416, 527, 536–42, 565, 561, 572
Frege on 158–63, 165–85 *passim*

590　Index

Jones on 284–9, 291–300 *passim*
Russell on 213–17 250–63 *passim*,
　263–78 *passim*
Wittgenstein on 323, 324, 338, 339, 350
naturalistic fallacy 55–6, 87, 93, 94
necessary truth 68, 69, 70, 79, 100, 328,
　357, 358, 374, 421, 422, 423, 432,
　434, 524, 535
Neurath, O. 362, 368, 496
Newton, I. 515, 564, 492, 493, 494
Nietzsche, F. 6, 7, 244, 420
nonsense 37, 39, 44, 255, 325, 327, 332,
　339, 369, 383, 386, 388–91, 398,
　399, 409, 410, 411, 416, 428, 448,
　501, 503, 505, 506, 510, 511, 513,
　520, 533, 534, 535, 563
Nozick, R. 571

Occam's razor 219, 220, 342, 511, 533
Ogden, C. K. xi, 320
Oppenheim, P. 362
ordinary language philosophy xi, xii, 329,
　331, 452, 453
organic unity
　different notions of 100–7
　Moore's critique of 53, 70, 105–7
organic whole, *see* organic unity
Ostertag, G. 280 n.2
Oxford University xi, 10, 329, 331, 453, 454

parts/ parthood 23, 30, 53, 54, 65, 66, 67,
　70, 72, 74–8, 100, 101, 102, 104,
　105, 106, 108, 109, 126–30, 137,
　161, 168, 171–4, 176, 177, 178, 181,
　182, 184, 185, 191, 192, 198, 200,
　212, 224, 230, 231, 239, 243, 248,
　272, 276, 304, 305, 307, 333, 339,
　340, 341, 357, 428, 464, 468, 537,
　553, 562
Passmore, J. 375
Pears, D. xi
Pearsall Smith, A. 209
perceive/perception 20, 21, 28, 30, 44, 45,
　51, 54, 59, 78, 79, 85, 87, 127, 145,

　194, 198, 203, 251, 390, 392, 394,
　395, 396, 401, 458, 493, 494, 495,
　505, 513, 514, 545
physical fact 119, 123, 124, 310
physical object 133, 134, 135, 142, 145,
　162, 218, 219, 264, 266, 268, 276,
　314, 393, 409, 458, 530, 531, 538,
　545, 546, 562, 565, 566
physicalism 11, 375 n.5, 511
　see also materialism
Pinsent, D. 319
Plato 4, 167 n.5, 223, 246, 475, 533, 536,
　538, 542, 545, 546, 549
Poincare, H. 430 n.6, 432, 433, 543
Popper, K. xi, 571
pragmatism 530, 547, 567
　analytic philosophy and xii
Preti, C. 51 n.2, 52 n.3, 56 n.4, 60 n.7, 210
　n.3
Price, H. H. 445 n.3
propositions xiv, 3, 52, 57, 58, 62, 63, 67,
　70, 71, 77, 84, 86, 92, 106, 108–18
　passim, 123, 125, 126, 130, 149, 153,
　158, 211, 212. 214, 215, 218, 219,
　222, 224–7, 230, 232–39 *passim*,
　244–7, 250, 252-3, 255, 258–63
　passim, 266-7, 269, 272–7 *passim*,
　279–303 *passim*, 306, 310, 314-16,
　321, 323–6 *passim*, 328, 334,
　339–58 *passim*, 360, 374, 379, 398,
　407, 413, 417, 418, 421–49 *passim*,
　459, 471–80 *passim*, 498, 500,
　501–4, 507–12 *passim*, 520, 578
pseudo-concept 371, 402–21 *passim*, 438,
　442, 443
pseudo-statement 367, 402–21 *passim*, 523
Pryor, J. 59, 573
psychologism 51–4, 154, 158, 163, 390
Putnam, H. xi, 522, 572

qualities 13, 14, 20–34 *passim*, 36, 74, 85,
　87, 128, 188, 241, 245, 249, 250,
　301, 334, 405, 458, 494, 495, 506,
　561, 562

Index   591

primary vs. secondary 13, 20–4
Quine, W. V. O. xii, 7, 216, 362, 370 n.3,
    521–68 *passim*, 569, 570, 573
    analyticity 523–7, 547–68 *passim*
    biographical information 521–3
    ontology 527–31, 533–47 *passim*

Railton, P. 571
Ramsey, F. xi, 320, 320 n.3, 515, 516, 516
    n.44, 520
Rawls, J. 571
realism 58, 60, 162, 210, 357, 393, 418,
    542, 543
reality 3, 4, 11–18, 20, 21–9, 33–45, 53, 58,
    62–5, 67, 79, 109, 113, 131, 132,
    163, 187, 205, 210, 211, 212, 230,
    240, 241, 243, 247, 248, 249, 294,
    322–7, 335, 336, 337, 344–7, 349,
    354, 357, 363, 365, 377, 389, 396,
    417, 434, 491, 497 n.7, 503, 574,
    575
Reichenbach, H. 362
reference
    indirect 161, 168, 173–6, 182–5
    Frege on 158–63, 165–85 *passim*
    Jones on 284–9, 291–300 *passim*,
        300–15 *passim*
    Russell on 213–17, 250–63 *passim*
relations
    asymmetrical 211–12, 231–40
    Bradley on 11–16, 24–34
    internal vs. external 14 n.4, 32
    Russell on 210–13, 222–50 *passim*
Respinger, M. 319
Rhees, R. 318
Richardson, R. 572
Royce, J. 249
Russell, B. ix, x, xi, 2, 3, 5, 6, 10, 11, 14 n.4,
    18, 50, 52, 152, 154, 155–8, 157 n.3,
    163, 207–78, 281–5, 285 n.5, 285
    n.6, 286–9, 291, 293 n.6, 293 n.7,
    294, 295, 299, 301, 307–10, 312–16,
    317, 319, 321, 321 n.5, 323, 330,
    332, 341, 342, 344, 350, 353, 356,

    362–5, 367, 372, 373, 382, 383, 429,
    430, 433 n.12, 452–5, 459, 496, 497,
    504, 505, 505 n.27, 511, 512, 514,
    515, 518, 519, 521, 522, 527, 528,
    536, 537, 538, 541, 542, 546, 548,
    561, 564, 566, 569, 572, 573, 574
    biographical information 208–10
    critique of monism 210–13, 222–50
        passim
    descriptions and names 213–17
    knowledge by acquaintance 263–78
        passim
    knowledge by description 263–78
        passim
    reality of relations and 222–50 *passim*
Russell's paradox, *see* logic, logicism and
Ryle, G. 329, 362, 454

Santayana, G. 246
Sartre, J. P. 6, 7
Schaffer, J. 469 n.1
Schlick, M. 320, 362, 364, 365, 373 n.4,
        377–401 *passim*, 496, 500, 502, 504,
        504 n.25, 505, 505 n.27, 506, 507,
        517, 518
Sellars, W. xi, 370 n.3
Schopenhauer, A. 393
sensation 21, 23, 24, 45, 54, 55, 65, 66,
        69–80, 89, 129, 134, 136, 169, 194,
        199, 218, 399, 430, 434, 494, 499,
        513, 545
    see also consciousness
sense
    indirect 161, 168, 173–6
    Frege on 158–63, 165–85 *passim*
    Jones on 284–9, 291–300 *passim*,
        300–16 *passim*
sense data 126, 128, 129, 130, 217–20,
        264, 265, 266, 268, 276, 314, 363,
        389, 531, 545, 561, 562, 565, 566
sentience 11, 17, 18, 43, 44, 45, 66
    see also consciousness
Sidgwick, H. 51, 56 n.4, 92, 93, 94, 280
Sinn, *see* sense, Frege on.

skepticism 57–60, 40, 170, 573
Sluga, H. 152
Smart, J. J. C 570
Singer, P. 571
solipsism 79, 197, 198, 264, 356, 357, 392, 393, 394, 396–9, 401, 418, 510–13
Sosa, E. 573
Spence, H. 209
Spencer, H. 90, 386
Spinoza, B. 11, 235, 246, 321
Stebbing, S. xi, 5 n.2, 362, 451–520 *passim*
  analysis and 459–60, 495–520
  biographical information 452–4
  logic and 454–6, 462–81 *passim*
  logical empiricism, on 452–4, 459–60
  scientific language and 456–9, 481–95 *passim*
Strawson, P. F. 329, 524, 525, 572
Stroud, B. 573
subject-predicate proposition 153, 211, 212, 214, 215, 216, 222, 225, 227, 235–9, 247, 367, 474, 547
subjective idea 159, 161, 162, 168, 169, 170, 194–8, 201–5
synthetic truth 68, 69, 84, 374, 375, 426, 427, 428, 430–4, 438, 448, 449, 523, 524, 525, 527, 529, 530, 547, 550, 557, 560, 563, 564, 567

Tarski, A. 362, 547 n.1
tautology 68, 324, 326, 353, 354, 355, 358, 366, 374, 383, 397, 398, 399, 417, 426, 428, 429, 432, 433, 434, 445, 478, 501, 502
Taylor, A. E. 66
things in themselves 34–8
Thomasson, A. 574
Tooke, J. H. 561, 561 n.8

unity 15, 17, 18, 25, 27, 32, 34, 41, 42, 43, 45, 46, 53, 70, 102, 103, 212, 223, 224, 225, 227, 238, 243
utilitarianism 94, 436, 437, 571

value, intrinsic 92, 96, 98–102, 104, 106
verification/verificationism 219, 363–71, 375, 377–401 *passim*, 404–7, 417, 424, 506, 507, 509, 560, 561, 563
Von Mises, R. 362
Von Wright, G. H. 317, 318, 320, 320 n.4, 322

Waithe, M. E. 280 n.2, 283 n.4
Waismann, F. 496, 503, 504, 506 n.28
Ward, J. 280
White, M. G. 547 n.1
Whitehead, A. N. 2, 154, 208, 209, 289, 363, 429, 454, 455, 496, 521, 522, 543
whole 11, 15–18, 26, 27, 42, 43, 44, 45, 46, 53, 55, 67, 70, 72, 74, 75, 86, 87, 91, 100–7, 126, 171, 173, 174, 176, 180, 181–5, 196, 197, 198, 200, 210–13, 235, 238–41, 243, 248, 259, 260, 272, 288, 302, 303, 304, 326, 327, 343, 346, 349, 354, 359, 535, 536, 552, 552, 559, 564
Williamson, T. 573, 574
Wisdom, J. 329, 362, 495, 518 n.48
Wiseman, R. 454
Wittgenstein, L. xi, xii, 3, 6, 7, 152, 208, 317–60 *passim*, 362, 363, 365, 367, 369, 374, 378, 379, 393, 395, 404, 406 n.1, 417, 432, 452, 454, 459, 495, 496, 497, 500, 501, 501 n.17, 502, 503 n.18, 503, 503 n.22, 504, 506, 506 n.28, 508, 510, 510 n.35, 511, 513, 514, 516, 517, 518, 518 n.49, 519, 520, 536, 574
  biographical information 317–20
  ethics and 325–8, 358, 365
  metaphysics and 325–8, 365
  propositions and reality 320–8
Wordsworth, W. 482
Woolf, V. 50
Wright, C. 59

Zimmer, E. 487 n.7